Android™ Wireless Application Development

Second Edition

Barnes & Noble Special Edition

Android™ Wireless Application Development

Second Edition
Barnes & Noble Special Edition

Shane Conder
Lauren Darcey

✦✦Addison-Wesley

Upper Saddle River, NJ • Boston • Indianapolis • San Francisco
New York • Toronto • Montreal • London • Munich • Paris • Madrid
Cape Town • Sydney • Tokyo • Singapore • Mexico City

Many of the designations used by manufacturers and sellers to distinguish their products are claimed as trademarks. Where those designations appear in this book, and the publisher was aware of a trademark claim, the designations have been printed with initial capital letters or in all capitals.

The authors and publisher have taken care in the preparation of this book, but make no expressed or implied warranty of any kind and assume no responsibility for errors or omissions. No liability is assumed for incidental or consequential damages in connection with or arising out of the use of the information or programs contained herein.

The publisher offers excellent discounts on this book when ordered in quantity for bulk purchases or special sales, which may include electronic versions and/or custom covers and content particular to your business, training goals, marketing focus, and branding interests. For more information, please contact:

U.S. Corporate and Government Sales
(800) 382-3419
corpsales@pearsontechgroup.com

For sales outside the United States please contact:

International Sales
international@pearson.com

Visit us on the Web: informit.com/aw

Library of Congress Cataloging-in-Publication Data:

Conder, Shane, 1975-

Android wireless application development / Shane Conder, Lauren Darcey. — 1st ed.

   p. cm.

   ISBN 978-0-321-74301-5 (pbk. : alk. paper) 1. Application software—Development. 2. Android (Electronic resource) 3. Mobile computing. I. Darcey, Lauren, 1977- II. Title.

   QA76.76.A65C6637 2011

   005.1—dc22

                          2010046618

ISBN-13: 978-0-321-74967-3
ISBN-10: 0-321-74967-7

Text printed in the United States on recycled paper at Edwards Brothers, Ann Arbor, Michigan

First printing December 2010

Editor-in-Chief
Mark Taub

Acquisitions Editor
Trina MacDonald

Development Editor
Songlin Qiu

Managing Editor
Sandra Schroeder

Senior Project Editor
Tonya Simpson

Copy Editor
Charlotte Kughen

Indexer
Heather McNeill

Proofreader
Water Crest Publishing

Technical Reviewers
Charles Stearns

Douglas Jones

Publishing Coordinator
Olivia Basegio

Book Designer
Gary Adair

Compositor
Mark Shirar

Table of Contents

III: Android User Interface Design Essentials

7 Exploring User Interface Screen Elements   133

VI: Deploying Your Android Application to the World

Acknowledgments

This book would never have been written without the guidance and encouragement we received from a number of supportive individuals, including our editorial team, coworkers, friends, and family. We'd like to thank the Android developer community, Google, and the Open Handset Alliance for their vision and expertise. Throughout this project, our editorial team at Pearson Education (Addison-Wesley) always had the right mix of professionalism and encouragement. Thanks especially to Trina MacDonald, Olivia Basegio, Songlin Qiu, and our crack team of technical reviewers: Doug Jones and Charles Stearns (as well as Dan Galpin, Tony Hillerson, and Ronan Schwarz, who reviewed the first edition). Dan Galpin also graciously provided the clever Android graphics used for Tips, Notes, and Warnings. We'd also like to thank Ray Rischpater for his longtime encouragement and advice on technical writing. Amy Badger must be commended for her wonderful waterfall illustration, and we also thank Hans Bodlaender for letting us use the nifty chess font he developed as a hobby project.

About the Authors

Lauren Darcey is responsible for the technical leadership and direction of a small software company specializing in mobile technologies, including Android, iPhone, Blackberry, Palm Pre, BREW, and J2ME and consulting services. With more than two decades of experience in professional software production, Lauren is a recognized authority in application architecture and the development of commercial-grade mobile applications. Lauren received a B.S. in Computer Science from the University of California, Santa Cruz.

She spends her copious free time traveling the world with her geeky mobile-minded husband and is an avid nature photographer. Her work has been published in books and newspapers around the world. In South Africa, she dove with 4-meter-long great white sharks and got stuck between a herd of rampaging hippopotami and an irritated bull elephant. She's been attacked by monkeys in Japan, gotten stuck in a ravine with two hungry lions in Kenya, gotten thirsty in Egypt, narrowly avoided a coup d'état in Thailand, geocached her way through the Swiss Alps, drank her way through the beer halls of Germany, slept in the crumbling castles of Europe, and gotten her tongue stuck to an iceberg in Iceland (while being watched by a herd of suspicious wild reindeer).

Shane Conder has extensive development experience and has focused his attention on mobile and embedded development for the past decade. He has designed and developed many commercial applications for Android, iPhone, BREW, Blackberry, J2ME, Palm, and Windows Mobile—some of which have been installed on millions of phones worldwide. Shane has written extensively about the mobile industry and evaluated mobile development platforms on his tech blogs and is well known within the blogosphere. Shane received a B.S. in Computer Science from the University of California.

A self-admitted gadget freak, Shane always has the latest phone, laptop, or other mobile device. He can often be found fiddling with the latest technologies, such as cloud services and mobile platforms, and other exciting, state-of-the-art technologies that activate the creative part of his brain. He also enjoys traveling the world with his geeky wife, even if she did make him dive with 4-meter-long great white sharks and almost get eaten by a lion in Kenya. He admits that he has to take at least two phones with him when backpacking—even though there is no coverage—that he snickered and whipped out his Android phone to take a picture when Laurie got her tongue stuck to that iceberg in Iceland, and that he is catching on that he should be writing his own bio.

Preface

Thank you for picking up this special edition of *Android Wireless Application Development*, Second Edition. We hope the special features in this version of the book help you master Android quickly and thoroughly with a minimum of fuss and frustration. Whether you're just getting started or are a mobile development veteran, there's something here for you.

Features of the Special Edition

The features of this special edition include

1. **A companion CD with all source code:** This book comes with dozens of completely functional code examples, packaged in Android project files. These projects are organized by chapter. Simply load them up in Eclipse and run them to illustrate concepts discussed in each chapter. Note: You can also download the latest version of the source code from the book website: http://informit.com/ 9780321749673.

2. **Appendix F, "The Android Quick-Start Guide for Beginners":** Accelerate your learning curve with a crash course in Android development, including notes on how to set up your development environment, an overview of the most commonly used development tools, a handy glossary of Android terminology, and Ten Steps to Successful Android Applications.

3. **Appendix G, "A Brief Walkthrough of an Android Application from Start to Finish":** Learn by example with this walkthrough of a completely functional Android application called Peak Bagger. Although most of the code provided in this book is "cookbook" style—short and to the point—this appendix and its accompanying source code provide a "fully baked" sample application that combines many Android concepts to solve real problems developers face every day. There's a little of everything in this app: lifecycle management, user interface design, XML parsing, threading, networking, location-based services, camera support, animation, App Widget support, and more. If you're just getting started, this appendix might be a bit overwhelming, so you may want to simply skim this at first and return after you have mastered some of the basic skills covered in this book.

Introduction

Pioneered by the Open Handset Alliance and Google, Android is a hot, young, free, open source mobile platform making waves in the wireless world. This book provides comprehensive guidance for software development teams on designing, developing, testing, debugging, and distributing professional Android applications. If you're a veteran mobile developer, you can find tips and tricks to streamline the development process and take advantage of Android's unique features. If you're new to mobile development, this book provides everything you need to make a smooth transition from traditional software development to mobile development—specifically, its most promising new platform: Android.

Who Should Read This Book

This book includes tips for successful mobile development based on our years in the mobile industry and covers everything you need to run a successful Android project from concept to completion. We cover how the mobile software process differs from traditional software development, including tricks to save valuable time and pitfalls to avoid. Regardless of the size of your project, this book can work for you.

This book was written for several audiences:

- **Software developers who want to learn to develop professional Android applications.** The bulk of this book is primarily targeted at software developers with Java experience but not necessarily mobile development experience. More seasoned developers of mobile applications can learn how to take advantage of Android and how it differs from the other technologies of the mobile development market today.

- **Quality assurance personnel tasked with testing Android applications.** Whether they are black box or white box testing, quality assurance engineers can find this book invaluable. We devote several chapters to mobile QA concerns, including topics such as developing solid test plans and defect tracking systems for mobile applications, how to manage handsets, and how to test applications thoroughly using all the Android tools available.

- **Project managers planning and managing Android development teams.** Managers can use this book to help plan, hire, and execute Android projects from start to finish. We cover project risk management and how to keep Android projects running smoothly.

- **Other audiences.** This book is useful not only to a software developer, but also for the corporation looking at potential vertical market applications, the entrepreneur thinking about a cool phone application, and hobbyists looking for some fun with their new phone. Businesses seeking to evaluate Android for their specific needs (including feasibility analysis) can also find the information provided valuable. Anyone with an Android handset and a good idea for a mobile application can put this book to use for fun and profit.

Key Questions Answered in This Book

This book answers the following questions:

1. What is Android? How do the SDK versions differ?

2. How is Android different from other mobile technologies, and how can developers take advantage of these differences?

3. How do developers use the Eclipse Development Environment for Java to develop and debug Android applications on the emulator and handsets?

4. How are Android applications structured?

5. How do developers design robust user interfaces for mobile—specifically, for Android?

6. What capabilities does the Android SDK have and how can developers use them?

7. How does the mobile development process differ from traditional desktop development?

8. What development strategies work best for Android development?

9. What do managers, developers, and testers need to look for when planning, developing, and testing a mobile development application?

10. How do mobile teams design bulletproof Android applications for publication?

11. How do mobile teams package Android applications for deployment?

12. How do mobile teams make money from Android applications?

13. And, finally, what is new in the second edition of the book?

How This Book Is Structured

This book is divided into seven parts. The first five parts are primarily of interest to developers; Parts VI and VII provide lots of helpful information for project managers and quality assurance personnel as well as developers.

Here is an overview of the various parts in this book:

- **Part I: An Overview of Android**

  Part I provides an introduction to Android, explaining how it differs from other mobile platforms. You become familiar with the Android SDK and tools, install the development tools, and write and run your first Android application—on the emulator and on a handset.

- **Part II: Android Application Design Essentials**

  Part II introduces the design principles necessary to write Android applications. You learn how Android applications are structured and how to include resources, such as strings, graphics, and user interface components in your projects.

- **Part III: Android User Interface Design Essentials**

  Part III dives deeper into how user interfaces are designed in Android. You learn about the core user interface element in Android: the `view`. You also learn about the basic drawing and animation abilities provided in the Android SDK.

- **Part IV: Using Common Android APIs**

  Part IV is a series of chapters, each devoted to a deeper understanding of the most important APIs within the Android SDK, such as the data and storage APIs (including file and database usage as well as content providers), networking, telephony, Location-Based Services (LBS), multimedia and 3D graphics APIs, and the optional hardware APIs available.

- **Part V: More Android Application Design Principles**

  Part V covers more advanced Android application design principles, such as notifications and services.

- **Part VI: Deploying Your Android Application to the World**

  Part VI covers the software development process for mobile, from start to finish, with tips and tricks for project management, software developers, and quality assurance personnel.

- **Part VII: Appendixes**

  Part VII includes several helpful quick-start guides for the Android development tools: the emulator, ADB and DDMS, Eclipse tips and tricks, and a SQLite tutorial.

An Overview of Changes in This Edition

When we began writing the first edition of this book, there were no Android devices on the market. One Android device became available shortly after we started, and it was available only in the United States. Today there are dozens of devices shipping all over the world. The Android platform has gone through extensive changes since the first edition of this book was published. The Android SDK has many new features, and the development tools have received many much-needed upgrades. Android, as a technology, is now on solid footing within the mobile marketplace.

Within this new edition, we took the opportunity to do a serious overhaul on book content—but don't worry, it's still the book readers loved the first time, just bigger, better, and more comprehensive. In addition to adding newly available content, we've retested and upgraded all existing content (text and sample code) for use with the newest Android SDKs. Here are some of the highlights of the additions and enhancements we've made to this edition:

- Coverage of the latest and greatest Android tools and utilities
- Updates to all existing chapters, often with some entirely new sections
- Complete overhaul of sample code and applications—many more of them, too—organized by topic
- Nine new chapters, which cover new SDK features, including web APIs, the Android NDK, extending application reach, managing users, data synchronization, backups, advanced user input, and compatibility
- Topics such as Android Manifest files, content providers, designing apps, and testing each now have their own chapter
- Updated 3D graphics programming, including OpenGL ES 2.0
- Coverage of hot topics such as Bluetooth, gestures, voice recognition, App Widgets, Live Folders, Live Wallpapers, and global search
- Even more tips and tricks from the trenches to help you design, develop, and test applications for different device targets, including an all-new chapter on tackling compatibility issues
- A new appendix full of Eclipse tips and tricks

As you can see, we cover many of the hottest and most exciting features that Android has to offer. We didn't take this review lightly; we touched every existing chapter, updated content, and added many new chapters as well. Finally, we included many additions, clarifications, and, yes, even a few fixes based upon the feedback from our fantastic (and meticulous) readers. Thank you!

Development Environment Used in This Book

The Android code in this book was written using the following development environments:

- Windows 7 and Mac OS X 10.6.4
- Eclipse Java IDE Version 3.5 (Galileo)
- Eclipse JDT plug-in and Web Tools Platform (WTP)
- Java SE Development Kit (JDK) 6 Update 20

- Android SDK Version 2.2, API Level 8 (FroYo)
    1. ADT Plug-in for Eclipse 0.9.9
    2. NDK Tools Revision 4b
    3. SDK Tools Revision 7
- Android Handsets: T-Mobile G1, HTC Nexus One, HTC Evo 4G, Motorola Droid, ARCHOS 5 internet tablet

Supplementary Materials Available

The source code that accompanies this book for download on the publisher website: http://www.informit.com/title/9780321627094.

We also run a blog at http://androidbook.blogspot.com, which covers a variety of Android topics and presents reader feedback, questions, and further information. You can also find links to our various technical articles.

Where to Find More Information

There is a vibrant, helpful Android developer community on the Web. Here are a number of useful websites for Android developers and followers of the wireless industry:

- **Android Developer Website:** The Android SDK and developer reference site:

    http://developer.android.com/

- **Stack Overflow:** The Android website with great technical information (complete with tags) and an official support forum for developers:

    http://stackoverflow.com/questions/tagged/android

- **Open Handset Alliance:** Android manufacturers, operators, and developers:

    http://www.openhandsetalliance.com/

- **Android Market:** Buy and sell Android applications:

    http://www.android.com/market/

- **Mobiletuts+:** Mobile development tutorials, including Android:

    http://mobile.tutsplus.com/category/tutorials/android/

- **anddev.org:** An Android developer forum:

    http://www.anddev.org

- **Google Team Android Apps:** Open source Android applications:

    http://apps-for-android.googlecode.com/

- **FierceDeveloper:**A weekly newsletter for wireless developers:
  http://www.fiercedeveloper.com/

- **Wireless Developer Network:**Daily news on the wireless industry:
  http://www.wirelessdevnet.com/

- **Developer.com:**A developer-oriented site with mobile articles:
  http://www.developer.com/

Conventions Used in This Book

This book uses the following conventions:

- ➡ is used to signify to readers that the authors meant for the continued code to appear on the same line. No indenting should be done on the continued line.

- Code or programming terms are set in `monospace` text.

This book also presents information in the following sidebars:

Tip
Tips provide useful information or hints related to the current text.

Note
Notes provide additional information that might be interesting or relevant.

Warning
Warnings provide hints or tips about pitfalls that you might encounter and how to avoid them.

Contacting the Authors

We welcome your comments, questions, and feedback. We invite you to visit our blog at
http://androidbook.blogspot.com
or email us at
androidwirelessdev+awad2e@gmail.com

## 1

Introducing Android

The mobile development community is at a tipping point. Mobile users demand more choice, more opportunities to customize their phones, and more functionality. Mobile operators want to provide value-added content to their subscribers in a manageable and lucrative way. Mobile developers want the freedom to develop the powerful mobile applications users demand with minimal roadblocks to success. Finally, handset manufacturers want a stable, secure, and affordable platform to power their devices. Up until now a single mobile platform has adequately addressed the needs of all the parties.

Enter Android, which is a potential game-changer for the mobile development community. An innovative and open platform, Android is well positioned to address the growing needs of the mobile marketplace.

This chapter explains what Android is, how and why it was developed, and where the platform fits in to the established mobile marketplace.

A Brief History of Mobile Software Development

To understand what makes Android so compelling, we must examine how mobile development has evolved and how Android differs from competing platforms.

Way Back When

Remember way back when a phone was just a phone? When we relied on fixed land-lines? When we ran for the phone instead of pulling it out of our pocket? When we lost our friends at a crowded ballgame and waited around for hours hoping to reunite? When we forgot the grocery list (see Figure 1.1) and had to find a payphone or drive back home again?

Those days are long gone. Today, commonplace problems such as these are easily solved with a one-button speed dial or a simple text message like "WRU?" or "20?" or "Milk and?"

Our mobile phones keep us safe and connected. Now we roam around freely, relying on our phones not only to keep in touch with friends, family, and coworkers, but also to tell us where to go, what to do, and how to do it. Even the most domestic of events seem to revolve around my mobile phone.

Figure 1.1   Mobile phones have become a
crucial shopping accessory.

Consider the following true story, which has been slightly enhanced for effect:

Once upon a time, on a warm summer evening, I was happily minding my own business cooking dinner in my new house in rural New Hampshire when a bat swooped over my head, scaring me to death.

The first thing I did—while ducking—was to pull out my cell phone and send a text message to my husband, who was across the country at the time. I typed, "There's a bat in the house!"

My husband did not immediately respond (a divorce-worthy incident, I thought at the time), so I called my dad and asked him for suggestions on how to get rid of the bat.

He just laughed.

Annoyed, I snapped a picture of the bat with my phone and sent it to my husband and my blog, simultaneously guilt-tripping him and informing the world of my treacherous domestic wildlife encounter.

Finally, I googled "get rid of a bat" and then I followed the helpful do-it-yourself instructions provided on the Web for people in my situation. I also learned that late August is when baby bats often leave the roost for the first time and learn to fly. Newly aware that I had a baby bat on my hands, I calmly got a broom and managed to herd the bat out of the house.

Problem solved—and I did it all with the help of my trusty cell phone, the old LG VX9800.

My point here? Mobile phones can solve just about *anything*—and we rely on them for *everything* these days.

You notice that I used half a dozen different mobile applications over the course of this story. Each application was developed by a different company and had a different user interface. Some were well designed; others not so much. I paid for some of the applications, and others came on my phone.

As a user, I found the experience functional, but not terribly inspiring. As a mobile developer, I wished for an opportunity to create a more seamless and powerful application that could handle all I'd done and more. I wanted to build a better bat trap, if you will.

Before Android, mobile developers faced many roadblocks when it came to writing applications. Building the better application, the unique application, the competing application, the hybrid application, and incorporating many common tasks such as messaging and calling in a familiar way were often unrealistic goals.

To understand why, let's take a brief look at the history of mobile software development.

"The Brick"

The Motorola DynaTAC 8000X was the first commercially available cell phone. First marketed in 1983, it was $13 \times 1.75 \times 3.5$ inches in dimension, weighed about 2.5 pounds, and allowed you to talk for a little more than half an hour. It retailed for $3,995, plus hefty monthly service fees and per-minute charges.

We called it "The Brick," and the nickname stuck for many of those early mobile phones we alternatively loved and hated. About the size of a brick, with a battery power just long enough for half a conversation, these early mobile handsets were mostly seen in the hands of traveling business execs, security personnel, and the wealthy. First-generation mobile phones were just too expensive. The service charges alone would bankrupt the average person, especially when roaming.

Early mobile phones were not particularly full featured. (Although, even the Motorola DynaTAC, shown in Figure 1.2, had many of the buttons we've come to know well, such as the SEND, END, and CLR buttons.) These early phones did little more than make and receive calls and, if you were lucky, there was a simple contacts application that wasn't impossible to use.

Figure 1.2   The first commercially available
mobile phone: the Motorola DynaTAC.

The first-generation mobile phones were designed and developed by the handset manufacturers. Competition was fierce and trade secrets were closely guarded. Manufacturers didn't want to expose the internal workings of their handsets, so they usually developed the phone software in-house. As a developer, if you weren't part of this inner circle, you had no opportunity to write applications for the phones.

It was during this period that we saw the first "time-waster" games begin to appear. Nokia was famous for putting the 1970s video game Snake on some of its earliest monochrome phones. Other manufacturers followed suit, adding games such as Pong, Tetris, and Tic-Tac-Toe.

These early phones were flawed, but they did something important—they changed the way people thought about communication. As mobile phone prices dropped, batteries improved, and reception areas grew, more and more people began carrying these handy devices. Soon mobile phones were more than just a novelty.

Customers began pushing for more features and more games. But there was a problem. The handset manufacturers didn't have the motivation or the resources to build every application users wanted. They needed some way to provide a portal for entertainment and information services without allowing direct access to the handset.

What better way to provide these services than the Internet?

Wireless Application Protocol (WAP)

As it turned out, allowing direct phone access to the Internet didn't scale well for mobile.

By this time, professional websites were full color and chock full of text, images, and other sorts of media. These sites relied on JavaScript, Flash, and other technologies to enhance the user experience, and they were often designed with a target resolution of 800x600 pixels and higher.

When the first clamshell phone, the Motorola StarTAC, was released in 1996, it merely had an LCD 10-digit segmented display. (Later models would add a dot-matrix type display.) Meanwhile, Nokia released one of the first slider phones, the 8110—fondly referred to as "The Matrix Phone" because the phone was heavily used in films. The 8110 could display four lines of text with 13 characters per line. Figure 1.3 shows some of the common phone form factors.

Figure 1.3   Various mobile phone form factors: the candy bar, the slider, and the clamshell.

With their postage stamp-sized low-resolution screens and limited storage and processing power, these phones couldn't handle the data-intensive operations required by traditional web browsers. The bandwidth requirements for data transmission were also costly to the user.

The Wireless Application Protocol (WAP) standard emerged to address these concerns. Simply put, WAP was a stripped-down version of HTTP, which is the backbone protocol of the Internet. Unlike traditional web browsers, WAP browsers were designed to run within the memory and bandwidth constraints of the phone. Third-party WAP sites served up pages written in a markup language called Wireless Markup Language (WML). These pages were then displayed on the phone's WAP browser. Users navigated as they would on the Web, but the pages were much simpler in design.

The WAP solution was great for handset manufacturers. The pressure was off—they could write one WAP browser to ship with the handset and rely on developers to come up with the content users wanted.

The WAP solution was great for mobile operators. They could provide a custom WAP portal, directing their subscribers to the content they wanted to provide, and rake in the data charges associated with browsing, which were often high.

Developers and content providers didn't deliver. For the first time, developers had a chance to develop content for phone users, and some did so, with limited success.

Most of the early WAP sites were extensions of popular branded websites, such as CNN.com and ESPN.com, which were looking for new ways to extend their readership. Suddenly phone users accessed the news, stock market quotes, and sports scores on their phones.

Commercializing WAP applications was difficult, and there was no built-in billing mechanism. Some of the most popular commercial WAP applications that emerged during this time were simple wallpaper and ringtone catalogues that enabled users to personalize their phones for the first time. For example, a user browsed a WAP site and requested a specific item. He filled out a simple order form with his phone number and his handset model. It was up to the content provider to deliver an image or audio file compatible with the given phone. Payment and verification were handled through various premium-priced delivery mechanisms such as Short Message Service (SMS), Enhanced Messaging Service (EMS), Multimedia Messaging Service (MMS), and WAP Push.

WAP browsers, especially in the early days, were slow and frustrating. Typing long URLs with the numeric keypad was onerous. WAP pages were often difficult to navigate. Most WAP sites were written one time for all phones and did not account for individual phone specifications. It didn't matter if the end user's phone had a big color screen or a postage stamp-sized monochrome screen; the developer couldn't tailor the user's experience. The result was a mediocre and not very compelling experience for everyone involved.

Content providers often didn't bother with a WAP site and instead just advertised SMS short codes on TV and in magazines. In this case, the user sent a premium SMS message with a request for a specific wallpaper or ringtone, and the content provider sent it back. Mobile operators generally liked these delivery mechanisms because they received a large portion of each messaging fee.

WAP fell short of commercial expectations. In some markets, such as Japan, it flourished, whereas in others, such as the United States, it failed to take off. Handset screens were too small for surfing. Reading a sentence fragment at a time, and then waiting seconds for the next segment to download, ruined the user experience, especially because every second of downloading was often charged to the user. Critics began to call WAP "Wait and Pay."

Finally, the mobile operators who provided the WAP portal (the default home page loaded when you started your WAP browser) often restricted which WAP sites were accessible. The portal enabled the operator to restrict the number of sites users could browse and to funnel subscribers to the operator's preferred content providers and exclude competing sites. This kind of walled garden approach further discouraged third-party developers, who already faced difficulties in monetizing applications, from writing applications.

Proprietary Mobile Platforms

It came as no surprise that users wanted more—they will always want more.

Writing robust applications with WAP, such as graphic-intensive video games, was nearly impossible. The 18-year-old to 25-year-old sweet-spot demographic—the kids with the disposable income most likely to personalize their phones with wallpapers and ringtones—looked at their portable gaming systems and asked for a device that was both a phone and a gaming device or a phone and a music player. They argued that if devices such as Nintendo's Game Boy could provide hours of entertainment with only five buttons, why not just add phone capabilities? Others looked to their digital cameras, Palms, BlackBerries, iPods, and even their laptops and asked the same question. The market seemed to be teetering on the edge of device convergence.

Memory was getting cheaper, batteries were getting better, and PDAs and other embedded devices were beginning to run compact versions of common operating systems such as Linux and Windows. The traditional desktop application developer was suddenly a player in the embedded device market, especially with smartphone technologies such as Windows Mobile, which they found familiar.

Handset manufacturers realized that if they wanted to continue to sell traditional handsets, they needed to change their protectionist policies pertaining to handset design and expose their internal frameworks to some extent.

A variety of different proprietary platforms emerged—and developers are still actively creating applications for them. Some smartphone devices ran Palm OS (now Garnet OS) and RIM BlackBerry OS. Sun Microsystems took its popular Java platform and J2ME emerged (now known as Java Micro Edition [Java ME]). Chipset maker Qualcomm developed and licensed its Binary Runtime Environment for Wireless (BREW). Other platforms, such as Symbian OS, were developed by handset manufacturers such as Nokia, Sony Ericsson, Motorola, and Samsung. The Apple iPhone OS (OS X iPhone) joined the ranks in 2008. Figure 1.4 shows several different phones, all of which have different development platforms.

Many of these platforms have associated developer programs. These programs keep the developer communities small, vetted, and under contractual agreements on what they can and cannot do. These programs are often required and developers must pay for them.

Each platform has benefits and drawbacks. Of course, developers love to debate about which platform is "the best." (Hint: It's usually the platform we're currently developing for.)

The truth is that no one platform has emerged victorious. Some platforms are best suited for commercializing games and making millions—if your company has brand backing. Other platforms are more open and suitable for the hobbyist or vertical market applications. No mobile platform is best suited for all possible applications. As a result, the mobile phone has become increasingly fragmented, with all platforms sharing part of the pie.

Figure 1.4   Phones from various mobile device platforms.

For manufacturers and mobile operators, handset product lines quickly became complicated. Platform market penetration varies greatly by region and user demographic. Instead of choosing just one platform, manufacturers and operators have been forced to sell phones for all the different platforms to compete in the market. We've even seen some handsets supporting multiple platforms. (For instance, Symbian phones often also support J2ME.)

The mobile developer community has become as fragmented as the market. It's nearly impossible to keep track of all the changes in the market. Developer specialty niches have formed. The platform development requirements vary greatly. Mobile software developers work with distinctly different programming environments, different tools, and different programming languages. Porting among the platforms is often costly and not straightforward. Keeping track of handset configurations and testing requirements, signing and certification programs, carrier relationships, and application marketplaces have become complex spin-off businesses of their own.

It's a nightmare for the ACME Company that wants a mobile application. Should it develop a J2ME application? BREW? iPhone? Windows Mobile? Everyone has a different kind of phone. ACME is forced to choose one or, worse, all of the platforms. Some platforms allow for free applications, whereas others do not. Vertical market application opportunities are limited and expensive.

As a result, many wonderful applications have not reached their desired users, and many other great ideas have not been developed at all.

The Open Handset Alliance

Enter search advertising giant Google. Now a household name, Google has shown an interest in spreading its vision, its brand, its search and ad-revenue-based platform, and its suite of tools to the wireless marketplace. The company's business model has been amazingly successful on the Internet and, technically speaking, wireless isn't that different.

Google Goes Wireless

The company's initial forays into mobile were beset with all the problems you would expect. The freedoms Internet users enjoyed were not shared by mobile phone subscribers. Internet users can choose from the wide variety of computer brands, operating systems, Internet service providers, and web browser applications.

Nearly all Google services are free and ad driven. Many applications in the Google Labs suite directly compete with the applications available on mobile phones. The applications range from simple calendars and calculators to navigation with Google Maps and the latest tailored news from News Alerts—not to mention corporate acquisitions such as Blogger and YouTube.

When this approach didn't yield the intended results, Google decided to a different approach—to revamp the entire system upon which wireless application development was based, hoping to provide a more open environment for users and developers: the Internet model. The Internet model allows users to choose between freeware, shareware, and paid software. This enables free market competition among services.

Forming the Open Handset Alliance

With its user-centric, democratic design philosophies, Google has led a movement to turn the existing closely guarded wireless market into one where phone users can move between carriers easily and have unfettered access to applications and services. With its vast resources, Google has taken a broad approach, examining the wireless infrastructure from the FCC wireless spectrum policies to the handset manufacturers' requirements, application developer needs, and mobile operator desires.

Next, Google joined with other like-minded members in the wireless community and posed the following question: What would it take to build a better mobile phone?

The Open Handset Alliance (OHA) was formed in November 2007 to answer that very question. The OHA is a business alliance comprised of many of the largest and most successful mobile companies on the planet. Its members include chip makers, handset manufacturers, software developers, and service providers. The entire mobile supply chain is well represented.

Andy Rubin has been credited as the father of the Android platform. His company, Android Inc., was acquired by Google in 2005. Working together, OHA members, including Google, began developing a nonproprietary open standard platform based upon technology developed at Android Inc. that would aim to alleviate the aforementioned problems hindering the mobile community. The result is the Android project. To this day, most Android platform development is completed by Rubin's team at Google, where he acts as VP of Engineering and manages the Android platform roadmap.

Google's involvement in the Android project has been so extensive that the line between who takes responsibility for the Android platform (the OHA or Google) has blurred. Google hosts the Android open source project and provides online Android documentation, tools, forums, and the Software Development Kit (SDK) for developers. All major Android news originates at Google. The company has also hosted a number of events at conferences and the Android Developer Challenge (ADC), a contest to encourage developers to write killer Android applications—for $10 million dollars in prizes to spur development on the platform. The winners and their apps are listed on the Android website.

Manufacturers: Designing the Android Handsets

More than half the members of the OHA are handset manufacturers, such as Samsung, Motorola, HTC, and LG, and semiconductor companies, such as Intel, Texas Instruments, NVIDIA, and Qualcomm. These companies are helping design the first generation of Android handsets.

The first shipping Android handset—the T-Mobile G1—was developed by handset manufacturer HTC with service provided by T-Mobile. It was released in October 2008. Many other Android handsets were slated for 2009 and early 2010. The platform gained momentum relatively quickly. Each new Android device was more powerful and exciting than the last. Over the following 18 months, 60 different Android handsets (made by 21 different manufacturers) debuted across 59 carriers in 48 countries around the world. By June 2010, at an announcement of a new, highly anticipated Android handset, Google announced more than 160,000 Android devices were being activated each day (for a rate of nearly 60 million devices annually). The advantages of widespread manufacturer and carrier support appear to be really paying off at this point.

The Android platform is now considered a success. It has shaken the mobile marketplace, gaining ground steadily against competitive platforms such as the Apple iPhone, RIM BlackBerry, and Windows Mobile. The latest numbers (as of Summer 2010) show BlackBerry in the lead with a declining 31% of the smartphone market. Trailing close behind is Apple's iPhone at 28%. Android, however, is trailing with 19%, though it's gaining ground rapidly and, according to some sources, is the fastest-selling smartphone platform. Microsoft Windows Mobile has been declining and now trails Android by several percentage points.

Mobile Operators: Delivering the Android Experience

After you have the phones, you have to get them out to the users. Mobile operators from North, South, and Central America; Europe, Asia, India, Australia, Africa, and the Middle East have joined the OHA, ensuring a worldwide market for the Android movement. With almost half a billion subscribers alone, telephony giant China Mobile is a founding member of the alliance.

Much of Android's success is also due to the fact that many Android handsets don't come with the traditional "smartphone price tag"—quite a few are offered free with activation by carriers. Competitors such as the Apple iPhone have no such offering as of yet. For the first time, the average Jane or Joe can afford a feature-full phone. I've lost count of the number of times I've had a waitress, hotel night manager, or grocery store checkout person tell me that they just got an Android phone and it has changed their life. This phenomenon has only added to the Android's rising underdog status.

In the United States, the Android platform was given a healthy dose of help from carriers such as Verizon, who launched a $100 million dollar campaign for the first Droid handset. Many other Droid-style phones have followed from other carriers. Sprint recently launched the Evo 4G (America's first 4G phone) to much fanfare and record one-day sales (http://j.mp/cNhb4b).

Content Providers: Developing Android Applications

When users have Android handsets, they need those killer apps, right?

Google has led the pack, developing Android applications, many of which, such as the email client and web browser, are core features of the platform. OHA members are also working on Android application integration. eBay, for example, is working on integration with its online auctions.

The first ADC received 1,788 submissions, with the second ADC being voted upon by 26,000 Android users to pick a final 200 applications that would be judged professionally—all newly developed Android games, productivity helpers, and a slew of location-based services (LBS) applications. We also saw humanitarian, social networking, and mash-up apps. Many of these applications have debuted with users through the Android Market—Google's software distribution mechanism for Android. For now, these challenges are over. The results, though, are still impressive.

For those working on the Android platform from the beginning, handsets couldn't come fast enough. The T-Mobile G1 was the first commercial Android device on the market, but it had the air of a developer pre-release handset. Subsequent Android handsets have had much more impressive hardware, allowing developers to dive in and design awesome new applications.

As of October 2010, there are more than 80,000 applications available in the Android Market, which is growing rapidly. This takes into account only applications published through this one marketplace—not the many other applications sold individually or on other markets. This also does not take into account that, as of Android 2.2, Flash applications can run on Android handsets. This opens up even more application choices for Android users and more opportunities for Android developers.

There are now more than 180,000 Android developers writing interesting and exciting applications. By the time you finish reading this book, you will be adding your expertise to this number.

Taking Advantage of All Android Has to Offer

Android's open platform has been embraced by much of the mobile development community—extending far beyond the members of the OHA.

As Android phones and applications have become more readily available, many other mobile operators and handset manufacturers have jumped at the chance to sell Android phones to their subscribers, especially given the cost benefits compared to proprietary platforms. The open standard of the Android platform has resulted in reduced operator costs in licensing and royalties, and we are now seeing a migration to open handsets from proprietary platforms such as RIM, Windows Mobile, and the Apple iPhone. The market has cracked wide open; new types of users are able to consider smartphones for the first time. Android is well suited to fill this demand.

Android Platform Differences

Android is hailed as "the first complete, open, and free mobile platform":

- **Complete:** The designers took a comprehensive approach when they developed the Android platform. They began with a secure operating system and built a robust software framework on top that allows for rich application development opportunities.

- **Open:** The Android platform is provided through open source licensing. Developers have unprecedented access to the handset features when developing applications.

- **Free:** Android applications are free to develop. There are no licensing or royalty fees to develop on the platform. No required membership fees. No required testing fees. No required signing or certification fees. Android applications can be distributed and commercialized in a variety of ways.

Android: A Next-Generation Platform

Although Android has many innovative features not available in existing mobile platforms, its designers also leveraged many tried-and-true approaches proven to work in the wireless world. It's true that many of these features appear in existing proprietary platforms, but Android combines them in a free and open fashion while simultaneously addressing many of the flaws on these competing platforms.

The Android mascot is a little green robot, shown in Figure 1.5. This little guy (girl?) is often used to depict Android-related materials.

Android is the first in a new generation of mobile platforms, giving its platform developers a distinct edge on the competition. Android's designers examined the benefits and drawbacks of existing platforms and then incorporated their most successful features. At the same time, Android's designers avoided the mistakes others suffered in the past.

Since the Android 1.0 SDK was released, Android platform development has continued at a fast and furious pace. For quite some time, there was a new Android SDK out every couple of months! In typical tech-sector jargon, each Android SDK has had a project name. In Android's case, the SDKs are named alphabetically after sweets (see Figure 1.6).

The latest version of Android is codenamed Gingerbread.

Figure 1.5   The Android mascot and logo.

Cupcake   **Donut**   **Eclair**   **Froyo**
Android 1.5   Android 1.6   Android 2.0/2.1   Android 2.2

Figure 1.6   Some Android SDKs and their codenames.

Free and Open Source

Android is an open source platform. Neither developers nor handset manufacturers pay royalties or license fees to develop for the platform.

The underlying operating system of Android is licensed under GNU General Public License Version 2 (GPLv2), a strong "copyleft" license where any third-party improvements must continue to fall under the open source licensing agreement terms. The Android framework is distributed under the Apache Software License (ASL/Apache2), which allows for the distribution of both open- and closed-source derivations of the source code. Commercial developers (handset manufacturers especially) can choose to enhance the platform without having to provide their improvements to the open source community. Instead, developers can profit from enhancements such as handset-specific improvements and redistribute their work under whatever licensing they want.

Android application developers have the ability to distribute their applications under whatever licensing scheme they prefer. Developers can write open source freeware or traditional licensed applications for profit and everything in between.

Familiar and Inexpensive Development Tools

Unlike some proprietary platforms that require developer registration fees, vetting, and expensive compilers, there are no upfront costs to developing Android applications.

Freely Available Software Development Kit

The Android SDK and tools are freely available. Developers can download the Android SDK from the Android website after agreeing to the terms of the Android Software Development Kit License Agreement.

Familiar Language, Familiar Development Environments

Developers have several choices when it comes to integrated development environments (IDEs). Many developers choose the popular and freely available Eclipse IDE to design and develop Android applications. Eclipse is the most popular IDE for Android development, and there is an Android plug-in available for facilitating Android development. Android applications can be developed on the following operating systems:

- Windows XP (32-bit) or Vista (32-bit or 64-bit)
- Mac OS X 10.5.8 or later (x86 only)
- Linux (tested on Linux Ubuntu 8.04 LTS, Hardy Heron)

Reasonable Learning Curve for Developers

Android applications are written in a well-respected programming language: Java.

The Android application framework includes traditional programming constructs, such as threads and processes and specially designed data structures to encapsulate objects commonly used in mobile applications. Developers can rely on familiar class libraries, such as `java.net` and `java.text`. Specialty libraries for tasks such as graphics and database management are implemented using well-defined open standards such as OpenGL Embedded Systems (OpenGL ES) or SQLite.

Enabling Development of Powerful Applications

In the past, handset manufacturers often established special relationships with trusted third-party software developers (OEM/ODM relationships). This elite group of software developers wrote native applications, such as messaging and web browsers, which shipped on the handset as part of the phone's core feature set. To design these applications, the manufacturer would grant the developer privileged inside access and knowledge of a handset's internal software framework and firmware.

On the Android platform, there is no distinction between native and third-party applications, enabling healthy competition among application developers. All Android applications use the same libraries. Android applications have unprecedented access to the underlying hardware, allowing developers to write much more powerful applications. Applications can be extended or replaced altogether. For example, Android developers are now free to design email clients tailored to specific email servers, such as Microsoft Exchange or Lotus Notes.

Rich, Secure Application Integration

Recall from the bat story I previously shared that I accessed a variety of phone applications in the course of a few moments: text messaging, phone dialer, camera, email, picture messaging, and the browser. Each was a separate application running on the phone—some built-in and some purchased. Each had its own unique user interface. None were truly integrated.

Not so with Android. One of the Android platform's most compelling and innovative features is well-designed application integration. Android provides all the tools necessary to build a better "bat trap," if you will, by allowing developers to write applications that seamlessly leverage core functionality such as web browsing, mapping, contact management, and messaging. Applications can also become content providers and share their data among each other in a secure fashion.

Platforms such as Symbian have suffered from setbacks due to malware. Android's vigorous application security model helps protect the user and the system from malicious software.

No Costly Obstacles to Publication

Android applications have none of the costly and time-intensive testing and certification programs required by other platforms such as BREW and Symbian.

A "Free Market" for Applications

Android developers are free to choose any kind of revenue model they want. They can develop freeware, shareware, or trial-ware applications, ad-driven, and paid applications. Android was designed to fundamentally change the rules about what kind of wireless applications could be developed. In the past, developers faced many restrictions that had little to do with the application functionality or features:

- Store limitations on the number of competing applications of a given type
- Store limitations on pricing, revenue models, and royalties
- Operator unwillingness to provide applications for smaller demographics

With Android, developers can write and successfully publish any kind of application they want. Developers can tailor applications to small demographics, instead of just large-scale money-making ones often insisted upon by mobile operators. Vertical market applications can be deployed to specific, targeted users.

Because developers have a variety of application distribution mechanisms to choose from, they can pick the methods that work for them instead of being forced to play by others' rules. Android developers can distribute their applications to users in a variety of ways:

- Google developed the Android Market (see Figure 1.7), a generic Android application store with a revenue-sharing model.

Figure 1.7   The Android market.

- Handango.com added Android applications to its existing catalogue using their billing models and revenue-sharing model.
- Developers can come up with their own delivery and payment mechanisms.

Mobile operators are still free to develop their own application stores and enforce their own rules, but it will no longer be the only opportunity developers have to distribute their applications.

A New and Growing Platform

Android might be the next generation in mobile platforms, but the technology is still in its early stages. Early Android developers have had to deal with the typical roadblocks associated with a new platform: frequently revised SDKs, lack of good documentation, and market uncertainties.

On the other hand, developers diving into Android development now benefit from the first-to-market competitive advantages we've seen on other platforms such as BREW and Symbian. Early developers who give feedback are more likely to have an impact on the long-term design of the Android platform and what features will come in the next version of the SDK. Finally, the Android forum community is lively and friendly. Incentive programs, such as the ADC, have encouraged many new developers to dig into the platform.

Each new version of the Android SDK has provided a number of substantial improvements to the platform. In recent revisions, the Android platform has received some much-needed UI "polish," both in terms of visual appeal and performance. Although most of these upgrades and improvements were welcome and necessary, new SDK versions often cause some upheaval within the Android developer community. A number of published applications have required retesting and resubmission to the Android Marketplace to conform to new SDK requirements, which are quickly rolled out to all Android phones in the field as a firmware upgrade, rendering older applications obsolete.

Some older Android handsets are not capable of running the latest versions of the platform. This means that Android developers often need to target several different SDK versions to reach all users. Luckily, the Android development tools make this easier than ever.

The Android Platform

Android is an operating system and a software platform upon which applications are developed. A core set of applications for everyday tasks, such as web browsing and email, are included on Android handsets.

As a product of the OHA's vision for a robust and open source development environment for wireless, Android is an emerging mobile development platform. The platform was designed for the sole purpose of encouraging a free and open market that all mobile applications phone users might want to have and software developers might want to develop.

Android's Underlying Architecture

The Android platform is designed to be more fault-tolerant than many of its predecessors. The handset runs a Linux operating system upon which Android applications are executed in a secure fashion. Each Android application runs in its own virtual machine (see Figure 1.8). Android applications are managed code; therefore, they are much less likely to cause the phone to crash, leading to fewer instances of device corruption (also called "bricking" the phone, or rendering it useless).

The Linux Operating System

The Linux 2.6 kernel handles core system services and acts as a hardware abstraction layer (HAL) between the physical hardware of the handset and the Android software stack.

Some of the core functions the kernel handles include

- Enforcement of application permissions and security
- Low-level memory management

- Process management and threading
- The network stack
- Display, keypad input, camera, Wi-Fi, Flash memory, audio, and binder (IPC) driver access

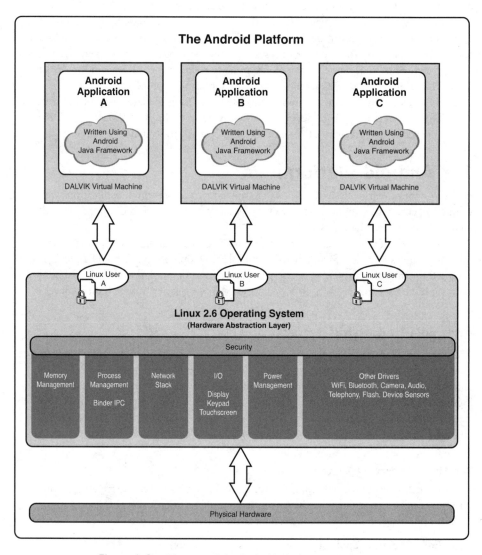

Figure 1.8   Diagram of the Android platform architecture.

Android Application Runtime Environment

Each Android application runs in a separate process, with its own instance of the Dalvik virtual machine (VM). Based on the Java VM, the Dalvik design has been optimized for mobile devices. The Dalvik VM has a small memory footprint, and multiple instances of the Dalvik VM can run concurrently on the handset.

Security and Permissions

The integrity of the Android platform is maintained through a variety of security measures. These measures help ensure that the user's data is secure and that the device is not subjected to malware.

Applications as Operating System Users

When an application is installed, the operating system creates a new user profile associated with the application. Each application runs as a different user, with its own private files on the file system, a user ID, and a secure operating environment.

The application executes in its own process with its own instance of the Dalvik VM and under its own user ID on the operating system.

Explicitly Defined Application Permissions

To access shared resources on the system, Android applications register for the specific privileges they require. Some of these privileges enable the application to use phone functionality to make calls, access the network, and control the camera and other hardware sensors. Applications also require permission to access shared data containing private and personal information, such as user preferences, user's location, and contact information.

Applications might also enforce their own permissions by declaring them for other applications to use. The application can declare any number of different permission types, such as read-only or read-write permissions, for finer control over the application.

Limited Ad-Hoc Permissions

Applications that act as content providers might want to provide some on-the-fly permissions to other applications for specific information they want to share openly. This is done using ad-hoc granting and revoking of access to specific resources using Uniform Resource Identifiers (URIs).

URIs index specific data assets on the system, such as images and text. Here is an example of a URI that provides the phone numbers of all contacts:

```
content://contacts/phones
```

To understand how this permission process works, let's look at an example.

Let's say we have an application that keeps track of the user's public and private birthday wish lists. If this application wanted to share its data with other applications, it could grant URI permissions for the public wish list, allowing another application permission to access this list without explicitly having to ask for it.

Application Signing for Trust Relationships

All Android applications packages are signed with a certificate, so users know that the application is authentic. The private key for the certificate is held by the developer. This helps establish a trust relationship between the developer and the user. It also enables the developer to control which applications can grant access to one another on the system. No certificate authority is necessary; self-signed certificates are acceptable.

Marketplace Developer Registration

To publish applications on the popular Android Market, developers must create a developer account. The Android Market is managed closely and no malware is tolerated.

Developing Android Applications

The Android SDK provides an extensive set of application programming interfaces (APIs) that is both modern and robust. Android handset core system services are exposed and accessible to all applications. When granted the appropriate permissions, Android applications can share data among one another and access shared resources on the system securely.

Android Programming Language Choices

Android applications are written in Java (see Figure 1.9). For now, the Java language is the developer's only choice on the Android platform.

Figure 1.9   Duke, the Java mascot.

There has been some speculation that other programming languages, such as C++, might be added in future versions of Android. If your application must rely on native code in another language such as C or C++, you might want to consider integrating it using the Android Native Development Kit (NDK). We talk more about this in Chapter 18, "Using the Android NDK."

No Distinctions Made Between Native and Third-Party Applications

Unlike other mobile development platforms, there is no distinction between native applications and developer-created applications on the Android platform. Provided the application is granted the appropriate permissions, all applications have the same access to core libraries and the underlying hardware interfaces.

Android handsets ship with a set of native applications such as a web browser and contact manager. Third-party applications might integrate with these core applications, extend them to provide a rich user experience, or replace them entirely with alternative applications.

Commonly Used Packages

With Android, mobile developers no longer have to reinvent the wheel. Instead, developers use familiar class libraries exposed through Android's Java packages to perform common tasks such as graphics, database access, network access, secure communications, and utilities (such as XML parsing).

The Android packages include support for

- Common user interface widgets (Buttons, Spin Controls, Text Input)
- User interface layout
- Secure networking and web browsing features (SSL, WebKit)
- Structured storage and relational databases (SQLite)
- Powerful 2D and 3D graphics (including SGL and OpenGL ES)
- Audio and visual media formats (MPEG4, MP3, Still Images)
- Access to optional hardware such as location-based services (LBS), Wi-Fi, Bluetooth, and hardware sensors

Android Application Framework

The Android application framework provides everything necessary to implement your average application. The Android application lifecycle involves the following key components:

- Activities are functions the application performs.
- Groups of views define the application's layout.
- Intents inform the system about an application's plans.
- Services allow for background processing without user interaction.
- Notifications alert the user when something interesting happens.

Android applications can interact with the operating system and underlying hardware using a collection of managers. Each manager is responsible for keeping the state of some underlying system service. For example, there is a `LocationManager` that facilitates interaction with the location-based services available on the handset. The `ViewManager` and `WindowManager` manage user interface fundamentals.

Applications can interact with one another by using or acting as a `ContentProvider`. Built-in applications such as the Contact manager are content providers, allowing third-party applications to access contact data and use it in an infinite number of ways. The sky is the limit.

Summary

Mobile software development has evolved over time. Android has emerged as a new mobile development platform, building on past successes and avoiding past failures of other platforms. Android was designed to empower the developer to write innovative applications. The platform is open source, with no up-front fees, and developers enjoy many benefits over other competing platforms. Now it's time to dive deeper and start writing Android code, so you can evaluate what Android can do for you.

References and More Information

Android Development:
    http://developer.android.com
Open Handset Alliance:
    http://www.openhandsetalliance.com

## 2

Setting Up Your Android Development Environment

Android developers write and test applications on their computers and then deploy those applications onto the actual device hardware for further testing.

In this chapter, you become familiar with all the tools you need master in order to develop Android applications. You also explore the Android Software Development Kit (SDK) installation and all it has to offer.

Configuring Your Development Environment

To write Android applications, you must configure your programming environment for Java development. The software is available online for download at no cost. Android applications can be developed on Windows, Macintosh, or Linux systems.

To develop Android applications, you need to have the following software installed on your computer:

- The **Java Development Kit** (JDK) Version 5 or 6, available for download at http://java.sun.com/javase/downloads/index.jsp.
- A compatible **Java IDE such as Eclipse** along with its JDT plug-in, available for download at http://www.eclipse.org/downloads/.
- The **Android SDK**, tools and documentation, available for download at http://developer.android.com/sdk/index.html.
- The **Android Development Tools** (ADT) plug-in for Eclipse, available for download through the Eclipse software update mechanism. For instructions on how to install this plug-in, see http://developer.android.com/sdk/eclipse-adt.html. Although this tool is optional for development, we highly recommend it and will use its features frequently throughout this book.

A complete list of Android development system requirements is available at http://developer.android.com/sdk/requirements.html. Installation instructions are at http://developer.android.com/sdk/installing.html.

> **Tip**
>
> Most developers use the popular Eclipse Integrated Development Environment (IDE) for Android development. The Android development team has integrated the Android development tools directly into the Eclipse IDE. However, developers are not constrained to using Eclipse; they can also use other IDEs. For information on using other development environments, begin by reading http://developer.android.com/guide/developing/other-ide.html.

Configuring Your Operating System for Device Debugging

To install and debug Android applications on Android devices, you need to configure your operating system to access the phone via the USB cable (see Figure 2.1). On some operating systems, such as Mac OS, this may just work. However, for Windows installations, you need to install the appropriate USB driver. You can download the Windows USB driver from the following website: http://developer.android.com/sdk/win-usb.html.

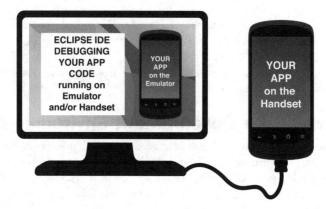

Figure 2.1   Android application debugging using the emulator and an Android handset.

Configuring Your Android Hardware for Debugging

Android devices have debugging disabled by default. Your Android device must be enabled for debugging via a USB connection in order to develop applications and run them on the device.

First, you need to enable your device to install Android applications other than those from the Android Market. This setting is reached by selecting Home, Menu, Settings, Applications. Here you should check (enable) the option called Unknown Sources.

More important development settings are available on the Android device by selecting Home, Menu, Settings, Applications, Development (see Figure 2.2). Here you should enable the following options:

- **USB Debugging:** This setting enables you to debug your applications via the USB connection.

- **Stay Awake:** This convenient setting keeps the phone from sleeping in the middle of your development work, as long as the device is plugged in.
- **Allow Mock Locations:** This setting enables you to send mock location information to the phone for development purposes and is very convenient for applications using location-based services (LBS).

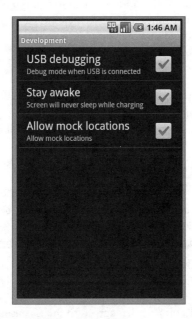

Figure 2.2   Android debug settings.

Upgrading the Android SDK

The Android SDK is upgraded from time to time. You can easily upgrade the Android SDK and tools from within Eclipse using the Android SDK and AVD Manager, which is installed as part of the ADT plug-in for Eclipse.

Changes to the Android SDK might include addition, update, and removal of features; package name changes; and updated tools. With each new version of the SDK, Google provides the following useful documents:

- **An Overview of Changes:** A brief description of major changes to the SDK.
- **An API Diff Report:** A complete list of specific changes to the SDK.
- **Release Notes:** A list of known issues with the SDK.

You can find out more about adding and updating SDK components at http://developer.android.com/sdk/adding-components.html.

Problems with the Android Software Development Kit

Because the Android SDK is constantly under active development, you might come across problems with the SDK. If you think you've found a problem, you can find a list of open issues and their status at the Android project Issue Tracker website. You can also submit new issues for review.

The Issue Tracker website for the Android open source project is http://code.google.com/p/android/issues/list. For more information about logging your own bugs or defects to be considered by the Android platform development team, check out the following website: http://source.android.com/source/report-bugs.html.

Tip

Frustrated with how long it takes for your bug to get fixed? It can be helpful to understand how the Android bug resolution process works. For more information on this process, see the following website: http://source.android.com/source/life-of-a-bug.html.

Exploring the Android SDK

The Android SDK comes with five major components: the Android SDK License Agreement, the Android Documentation, Application Framework, Tools, and Sample Applications.

Understanding the Android SDK License Agreement

Before you can download the Android SDK, you must review and agree to the Android SDK License Agreement. This agreement is a contract between you (the developer) and Google (copyright holder of the Android SDK).

Even if someone at your company has agreed to the Licensing Agreement on your behalf, it is important for you, the developer, to be aware of a few important points:

1. **Rights granted:** Google (as the copyright holder of Android) grants you a limited, worldwide, royalty-free, non-assignable, and non-exclusive license to use the SDK solely to develop applications for the Android platform. Google (and third-party contributors) are granting you license, but they still hold all copyrights and intellectual property rights to the material. Using the Android SDK does not grant you permission to use any Google brands, logos, or trade names. You will not remove any of the copyright notices therein. Third-party applications that your applications interact with (other Android apps) are subject to separate terms and fall outside this agreement.

2. **SDK usage:** You may only develop Android applications. You may not make derivative works from the SDK or distribute the SDK on any device or distribute part of the SDK with other software.

3. **SDK changes and backward compatibility:** Google may change the Android SDK at any time, without notice, without regard to backward compatibility. Although Android API changes were a major issue with prerelease versions of the

SDK, recent releases have been reasonably stable. That said, each SDK update does tend to affect a small number of existing applications in the field, necessitating updates.

4. **Android application developer rights:** You retain all rights to any Android software you develop with the SDK, including intellectual property rights. You also retain all responsibility for your own work.

5. **Android application privacy requirements:** You agree that your applications will protect the privacy and legal rights of its users. If your application uses or accesses personal and private information about the user (usernames, passwords, and so on), then your application will provide an adequate privacy notice and keep that data stored securely. Note that privacy laws and regulations may vary by user location; you as a developer are solely responsible for managing this data appropriately.

6. **Android application malware requirements:** You are responsible for all applications you develop. You agree not to write disruptive applications or malware. You are solely responsible for all data transmitted through your application.

7. **Additional terms for specific Google APIs:** Use of the Android Maps API is subject to further Terms of Service (specifically use of the following packages: `com.google.android.maps` and `com.android.location.Geocoder`). You must agree to these additional terms before using those specific APIs and always include the Google Maps copyright notice provided. Use of Google Data APIs (Google Apps such as Gmail, Blogger, Google Calendar, Google Finance Portfolio Data, Picasa, YouTube, and so on) is limited to access that the user has explicitly granted permission to your application by accepted permissions provided by the developer during installation time.

8. **Develop at your own risk:** Any harm that comes about from developing with the Android SDK is your own fault and not Google's.

Reading the Android SDK Documentation

A local copy of the Android documentation is provided in the /docs subfolder on disk (as shown in Figure 2.3).

The documentation is now divided into seven main sections:

- The **Home** tab is your general starting point within the Android documentation. Here you find developer announcements and important links to the latest hot topics in Android development.

- The **SDK** tab provides information about the different Android SDK versions available, as well as information about the Android Native Development Kit (NDK). You find the Android SDK release notes here as well.

Figure 2.3   The Android SDK documentation.

- The **Dev Guide** tab introduces the Android platform and covers best practices for Android application design and development, as well as information about publishing applications.

- The **Reference** tab provides a drill-down listing of the Android APIs with detailed coverage of specific classes and interfaces.

- The **Resources** tab provides access to Android technical articles and tutorials. Here you also find links to the Android community online (groups, mailing list, and official Twitter feed), as well as the sample applications provided along with the Android SDK.

- The **Videos** tab provides access to online videos pertaining to Android development, including videos about the platform, developer tips, Android development sessions from the annual Google I/O conference, and developer sandbox interviews.

- The **Blog** tab provides access to the online blog published by the Android development team. Here you find announcements about SDK releases, helpful development tips, and notices of upcoming Android events.

The Android documentation is provided in HTML format locally and online at http://developer.android.com. Certain networked features of the Android documentation (such as the Blog and Video tabs) are only available online.

Exploring the Android Application Framework

The Android application framework is provided in the `android.jar` file. The Android SDK is made up of several important packages, as shown in Table 2.1.

Table 2.1   **Important Packages in the Android SDK**

Top-Level Package	Purpose
`android.*`	Android application fundamentals
`dalvik.*`	Dalvik Virtual Machine support classes
`java.*`	Core classes and familiar generic utilities for networking, security, math, and such
`javax.*`	Java extension classes including encryption support, parsers, SQL, and such
`junit.*`	Unit testing support
`org.apache.http.*`	Hypertext Transfer Protocol (HTTP) protocol
`org.json`	JavaScript Object Notation (JSON) support
`org.w3c.dom`	W3C Java bindings for the Document Object Model Core (XML and HTML)
`org.xml.sax.*`	Simple API for XML (SAX) support for XML
`org.xmlpull.*`	High-performance XML parsing

There is also an optional Google APIs Add-On, which is an extension to the Android SDK that helps facilitate development using Google Maps and other Google APIs and services. For example, if you want to include the MapView control in your application, you need to install and use this feature. This Add-On corresponds to the `com.google.*` package (including `com.google.android.maps`) and requires agreement to additional Terms of Service and registration for an API Key. For more information on the Google APIs Add-On, see http://code.google.com/android/add-ons/google-apis/.

Getting to Know the Android Tools

The Android SDK provides many tools to design, develop, debug, and deploy your Android applications. The Eclipse Plug-In incorporates many of these tools seamlessly into your development environment and provides various wizards for creating and debugging Android projects.

Settings for the ADT plug-in are found in Eclipse under Window, Preferences, Android. Here you can set the disk location where you installed the Android SDK and tools, as well as numerous other build and debugging settings.

The ADT plug-in adds a number of useful functions to the default Eclipse IDE. Several new buttons are available on the toolbar, including buttons to

- Launch the Android SDK and AVD Manager
- Create a new project using the Android Project Wizard
- Create a new test project using the Android Project Wizard
- Create a new Android XML resource file

These features are accessible through the Eclipse toolbar buttons shown in Figure 2.4.

Figure 2.4   Android features added to the
Eclipse toolbar.

There is also a special Eclipse perspective for debugging Android applications called DDMS (Dalvik Debug Monitor Server). You can switch to this perspective within Eclipse by choosing Window, Open Perspective, DDMS or by changing to the DDMS perspective in the top-right corner of the screen. We talk more about DDMS later in this chapter. After you have designed an Android application, you can also use the ADT plug-in for Eclipse to launch a wizard to package and sign your Android application for publication. We talk more about this in Chapter 29, "Selling Your Android Application."

Android SDK and AVD Manager

The Android SDK and AVD Manager, shown in Figure 2.5, is a tool integrated into Eclipse. This tool performs two major functions: management of multiple versions of the Android SDK on the development machine and management of the developer's Android Virtual Device (AVD) configurations.

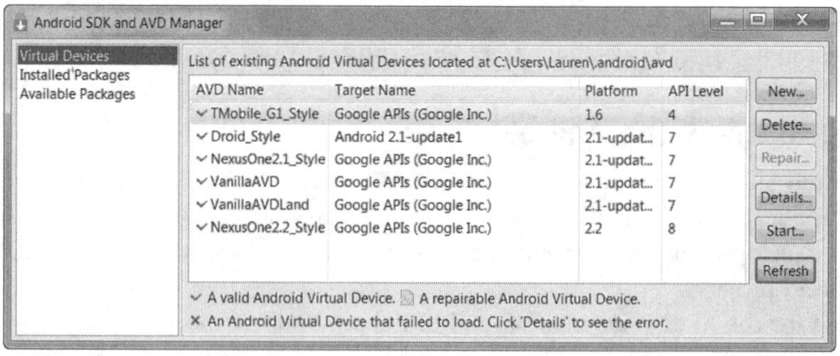

Figure 2.5   The Android SDK and AVD Manager.

Much like desktop computers, different Android devices run different versions of the Android operating system. Developers need to be able to target different Android SDK versions with their applications. Some applications target a specific Android SDK, whereas others try to provide simultaneous support for as many versions as possible.

The Android SDK and AVD Manager facilitate Android development across multiple platform versions simultaneously. When a new Android SDK is released, you can use this tool to download and update your tools while still maintaining backward compatibility and use older versions of the Android SDK.

The tool also manages the AVD configurations. To manage applications in the Android emulator, you must configure an AVD. This AVD profile describes what type of device you want the emulator to simulate, including which Android platform to support. You can specify different screen sizes and orientations, and you can specify whether the emulator has an SD card and, if so, what capacity.

Android Emulator

The Android emulator, shown in Figure 2.6, is one of the most important tools provided with the Android SDK. You will use this tool frequently when designing and developing Android applications. The emulator runs on your computer and behaves much as a mobile device would. You can load Android applications into the emulator, test, and debug them.

Figure 2.6   The Android emulator.

The emulator is a generic device and is not tied to any one specific phone configuration. You describe the hardware and software configuration details that the emulator is to simulate by providing an AVD configuration.

Tip

You should be aware that the Android emulator is a substitute for a real Android device, but it's an imperfect one. The emulator is a valuable tool for testing but cannot fully replace testing on actual target devices.

For more information about the emulator, see Appendix A, "The Android Emulator Quick-Start Guide." You can also find exhaustive information about the Android emulator in the Android SDK Documentation: http://developer.android.com/guide/developing/tools/emulator.html.

Dalvik Debug Monitor Server (DDMS)

The Dalvik Debug Monitor Server (DDMS) is a command-line tool that has also been integrated into Eclipse as a perspective (see Figure 2.7). This tool provides you with direct access to the device—whether it's the emulator virtual device or the physical device. You use DDMS to view and manage processes and threads running on the device, view heap data, attach to processes to debug, and a variety of other tasks.

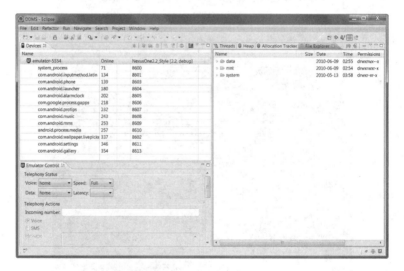

Figure 2.7   Using DDMS integrated into an Eclipse perspective.

For more information about the DDMS, see Appendix B, "The Android DDMS Quick-Start Guide." You can also find exhaustive details about DDMS in the Android SDK Documentation: http://developer.android.com/guide/developing/tools/ddms.html.

Android Debug Bridge (ADB)

The Android Debug Bridge (ADB) is a client-server tool used to enable developers to debug Android code on the emulator and the device using a standard Java IDE such as

Eclipse. The DDMS and the Android Development Plug-In for Eclipse both use the ADB to facilitate interaction between the development environment and the device (or emulator).

Developers can also use ADB to interact with the device file system, install Android applications manually, and issue shell commands. For example, the `sqlite3` shell commands enable you to access device database. The Application Exerciser Monkey commands generate random input and system events to stress test your application. One of the most important aspects of the ADB for the developer is its logging system (`Logcat`).

For more information about the ADB, see Appendix C, "The Android Debug Bridge Quick-Start Guide." For an exhaustive reference, see the Android SDK Documentation at http://developer.android.com/guide/developing/tools/adb.html.

Android Hierarchy Viewer

The Android Hierarchy Viewer (see Figure 2.8), a visual tool that illustrates layout component relationships, helps developers design and debug user interfaces. Developers can use this tool to inspect the `View` properties and develop pixel-perfect layouts. For more information about user interface design and the Hierarchy Viewer, see Chapter 8, "Designing User Interfaces with Layouts."

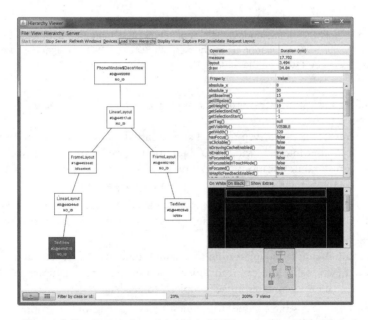

Figure 2.8   Screenshot of the Android Hierarchy Viewer in action.

Other Tools

Android SDK provides a number of other tools provided with the Android SDK. Many of these tools provide the underlying functionality that has been integrated into Eclipse using the Android Development Tools (ADT) plug-in. However, if you are not using Eclipse, these tools may be used on the command-line.

Other tools are special-purpose utilities. For example, the Draw Nine-patch tool enables you to design stretchable PNG images, which is useful for supporting different screen sizes. Likewise, the layoutopt tool helps developers optimize their user interfaces for performance. We discuss a number of these special tools in later chapters as they become relevant.

You can read about all the Android tools in the SDK documentation at http://developer.android.com/guide/developing/tools/index.html.

Exploring the Android Sample Applications

The Android SDK provides many samples and demo applications to help you learn the ropes of Android Development. Many of these demo applications are provided as part of the Android SDK and are located in the /samples subdirectory of the Android SDK. You can find more sample applications on the Android Developer website under the Resources tab.

> **Tip**
>
> On some Android SDK installations, the sample applications must be downloaded separately by updating your SDK installation using the Android SDK and AVD Manager. All sample applications can also be found on the Android Developer website.

Some of the most straightforward demo applications to take a look at are

- **ApiDemos:** A menu-driven utility that demonstrates a wide variety of Android APIs, from user interface widgets to application lifecycle components such as services, alarms, and notifications. You can read a nice write-up about this application at http://developer.android.com/resources/samples/ApiDemos/.
- **Snake:** A simple game that demonstrates bitmap drawing and key events. You can find a nice write-up about this game at http://developer.android.com/resources/samples/Snake/.
- **NotePad:** A simple list application that demonstrates database access and Live Folder functionality. You can read a nice write-up about this application at http://developer.android.com/resources/samples/NotePad/.
- **LunarLander:** A simple game that demonstrates drawing and animation. You can find a nice write-up about this game at http://developer.android.com/resources/samples/LunarLander/.

There are numerous other sample applications, but they demonstrate very specific Android features that are discussed later in this book.

Summary

In this chapter, you installed, configured, and explored all the tools you need to start developing Android applications, including the appropriate JDK, the Eclipse development environment, and the Android SDK. You explored many of the tools provided along with the Android SDK and understand their functions. Finally, you perused the sample applications provided along with the Android SDK. You should now have a reasonable development environment configured to write Android applications.

References and More Information

Google's Android Developer's Guide:
http://developer.android.com/guide/index.html
Android SDK Download Site:
http://developer.android.com/sdk/
Android SDK License Agreement:
http://developer.android.com/sdk/terms.html
The Java Platform, Standard Edition:
http://java.sun.com/javase
The Eclipse Project:
http://www.eclipse.org

## 3

Writing Your First Android Application

You should now have a workable Android development environment set up on your computer. Hopefully, you also have an Android device as well. Now it's time for you to start writing some Android code.

In this chapter, you learn how to add and create Android projects in Eclipse and verify that your Android development environment is set up correctly. You also write and debug your first Android application in the software emulator and on an Android handset.

Testing Your Development Environment

The best way to make sure you configured your development environment correctly is to take an existing Android application and run it. You can do this easily by using one of the sample applications provided as part of the Android SDK in the /samples subdirectory.

Within the Android SDK sample applications, you can find a classic game called Snake. To build and run the Snake application, you must create a new Android project in your Eclipse workspace, create an appropriate Android Virtual Device (AVD) profile, and configure a launch configuration for that project. After you have everything set up correctly, you can build the application and run it on the Android emulator or an Android device.

Adding the Snake Application to a Project in Your Eclipse Workspace

The first thing you need to do is add the Snake project to your Eclipse workspace. To do this, follow these steps:

1. Choose File, New, Project.

2. Choose Android, Android Project Wizard (see Figure 3.1).

Figure 3.1   Creating a new Android project.

Tip

After you use the Android Project wizard once, you can create subsequent projects using File, New, Android Project.

3. Change the Contents to Create Project from Existing Source.

4. Browse to your Android samples directory.

5. Choose the Snake directory. All the project fields should be filled in for you from the Manifest file (see Figure 3.2). You might want to set the Build Target to whatever version of Android your test device is running.

6. Choose Finish. You now see the Snake project files in your workspace (see Figure 3.3).

Warning

Occasionally Eclipse shows the error "Project 'Snake' is missing required source folder: 'gen'" when you're adding an existing project to the workspace. If this happens, simply navigate to the project file called R.java under the /gen directory and delete it. The R.java file is automatically regenerated and the error should disappear.

Creating an Android Virtual Device (AVD) for Your Snake Project

The next step is to create an AVD that describes what type of device you want to emulate when running the Snake application. This AVD profile describes what type of device you want the emulator to simulate, including which Android platform to support. You can specify different screen sizes and orientations, and you can specify whether the emulator has an SD card and, if it does, what capacity the card is.

Figure 3.2   The Snake project details.

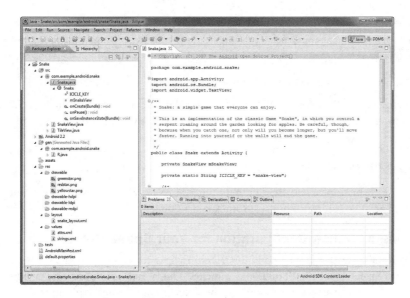

Figure 3.3   The Snake project files.

For the purposes of this example, an AVD for the default installation of Android 2.2 suffices. Here are the steps to create a basic AVD:

1. Launch the Android Virtual Device Manager from within Eclipse by clicking the little Android icon with the downward arrow on the toolbar. If you cannot find the icon, you can also launch the manager through the Window menu of Eclipse.

2. On the Virtual Devices menu, click the New button.

3. Choose a name for your AVD. Because we are going to take all the defaults, give this AVD a name of Android_Vanilla2.2.

4. Choose a build target. We want a basic Android 2.2 device, so choose Android 2.2 from the drop-down menu.

5. Choose an SD card capacity. This can be in kilobytes or megabytes and takes up space on your hard drive. Choose something reasonable, such as 1 gigabyte (1024M). If you're low on drive space or you know you won't need to test external storage to the SD card, you can use a much smaller value, such as 64 megabytes.

6. Choose a skin. This option controls the different resolutions of the emulator. In this case, use the WVGA800 screen. This skin most directly correlates to the popular Android handsets, such as the HTC Nexus One and the Evo 4G, both of which are currently sitting on my desk.

Your project settings will look like Figure 3.4.

Tip

Although we have chosen a higher-resolution skin for this AVD, feel free to choose the most appropriate skin to match the Android handset on which you plan to run the application.

7. Click the Create AVD button, and wait for the operation to complete.

8. Click Finish. Because the AVD manager formats the memory allocated for SD card images, creating AVDs with SD cards could take a few moments.

Tip

You can also create AVDs using the Android command-line tool.

For more information on creating different types of AVDs you can create, check out Appendix A, "The Android Emulator Quick-Start Guide."

Creating a Launch Configuration for Your Snake Project

Next, you must create a launch configuration in Eclipse to configure under what circumstances the Snake application builds and launches. The launch configuration is where you configure the emulator options to use and the entry point for your application.

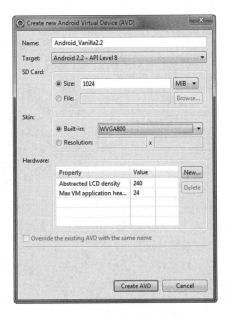

Figure 3.4   Creating a new AVD in Eclipse.

You can create Run Configurations and Debug Configurations separately, each with different options. These configurations are created under the Run menu in Eclipse (Run, Run Configurations and Run, Debug Configurations).

Follow these steps to create a basic Run Configuration for the Snake application:

1. Choose Run, Run Configurations (or right-click the Project and choose Run As).

2. Double-click Android Application.

3. Name your Run Configuration `SnakeRunConfiguration` (see Figure 3.5).

4. Choose the project by clicking the Browse button and choosing the Snake project.

5. Switch to the Target tab and, from the preferred AVD list, choose the Android_Vanilla2.2 AVD created earlier, as shown in Figure 3.5.

You can set other options on the Target and Common tabs, but for now we are leaving the defaults as they are.

Running the Snake Application in the Android Emulator

Now you can run the Snake application using the following steps:

1. Choose the Run As icon drop-down menu on the toolbar (the green circle with the triangle).

2. Pull the drop-down menu and choose the SnakeRunConfiguration you created.

3. The Android emulator starts up; this might take a moment.

Figure 3.5   The Snake project launch configuration,
Target tab with the AVD selected.

Tip

Make sure you don't have your Android device plugged in to your development machine via USB at this time. Automatic is the default selection in the Target tab of the Run Configuration for Device Target Selection mode, so Snake might launch on your device instead of within the emulator if the device is attached.

4. If necessary, swipe the screen from left to right to unlock the emulator, as shown in Figure 3.6.

5. The Snake application now starts, as shown in Figure 3.7.

You can interact with the Snake application through the emulator and play the game. You can also launch the Snake application from the Application drawer at any time by clicking on its application icon.

Building Your First Android Application

Now it's time to write your first Android application. You start with a simple Hello World project and build upon it to explore some of the features of Android.

Tip

Many of the code examples provided in this chapter are taken from the MyFirstAndroidApp application. This source code for the MyFirstAndroidApp application is provided for download on the book's website.

Figure 3.6   The Android emulator launching (locked).

Figure 3.7   The Snake game.

Creating and Configuring a New Android Project

You can create a new Android project in much the same way as when you added the Snake application to your Eclipse workspace.

The first thing you need to do is create a new project in your Eclipse workspace. The Android Project Wizard creates all the required files for an Android application. Follow these steps within Eclipse to create a new project:

1. Choose File, New, Android Project, or choose the Android Project creator icon, which looks like a folder (with the letter *a* and a plus sign), 📁 on the Eclipse toolbar.

2. Choose a Project Name. In this case, name the project `MyFirstAndroidApp`.

3. Choose a Location for the project files. Because this is a new project, select the Create New Project in Workspace radio button. Check the Use Default Location checkbox or change the directory to wherever you want to store the source files.

4. Select a build target for your application. Choose a target that is compatible with the Android handsets you have in your possession. For this example, you might use the Android 2.2 target.

5. Choose an application name. The application name is the "friendly" name of the application and the name shown with the icon on the application launcher. In this case, the Application Name is My First Android App.

6. Choose a package name. Here you should follow standard package namespace conventions for Java. Because all our code examples in this book fall under the com.androidbook.* namespace, we will use the package name `com.androidbook.myfirstandroidapp`, but you are free to choose your own package name.

7. Check the Create Activity checkbox. This instructs the wizard to create a default launch activity for the application. Call this `Activity` class `MyFirstAndroidAppActivity`.

   Your project settings should look like Figure 3.8.

8. Finally, click the Finish button.

Core Files and Directories of the Android Application

Every Android application has a set of core files that are created and are used to define the functionality of the application (see Table 3.1). The following files are created by default with a new Android application.

Figure 3.8   Configuring My First Android App
using the Android Project Wizard.

There are a number of other files saved on disk as part of the Eclipse project in the
workspace. However, the files included in Table 3.1 are the important project files you will
use on a regular basis.

Creating an AVD for Your Project

The next step is to create an AVD that describes what type of device you want to emulate
when running the application. For this example, we can use the AVD we created for the
Snake application. An AVD describes a device, not an application. Therefore, you can use
the same AVD for multiple applications. You can also create similar AVDs with the same
configuration, but different data (such as different applications installed and different SD
card contents).

Note

Again, for more information on creating different types of AVDs and working with the Android
emulator, check out Appendix A, "The Android Emulator Quick-Start Guide."

Table 3.1 **Important Android Project Files and Directories**

Android File	General Description
`AndroidManifest.xml`	Global application description file. It defines your application's capabilities and permissions and how it runs.
`default.properties`	Automatically created project file. It defines your application's build target and other build system options, as required.
`src Folder`	Required folder where all source code for the application resides.
`src/com.androidbook.myfirst-androidapp/MyFirstAndroidApp-Activity.java`	Core source file that defines the entry point of your Android application.
`gen Folder`	Required folder where auto-generated resource files for the application reside.
`gen/com.androidbook.myfirst-androidapp/R.java`	Application resource management source file generated for you; it should not be edited.
`res Folder`	Required folder where all application resources are managed. Application resources include animations, drawable image assets, layout files, XML files, data resources such as strings, and raw files.
`res/drawable-*/icon.png`	Resource folders that store different resolutions of the application icon.
`res/layout/main.xml`	Single screen layout file.
`res/values/strings.xml`	Application string resources.
`assets Folder`	Folder where all application assets are stored. Application assets are pieces of application data (files, directories) that you do not want managed as application resources.

Creating Launch Configurations for Your Project

Next, you must create a Run and Debug launch configuration in Eclipse to configure the circumstances under which the MyFirstAndroidApp application builds and launches. The launch configuration is where you configure the emulator options to use and the entry point for your application.

You can create Run Configurations and Debug Configurations separately, with different options for each. Begin by creating a Run Configuration for the application.

Follow these steps to create a basic Run Configuration for the MyFirstAndroidApp application:

1. Choose Run, Run Configurations (or right-click the Project and Choose Run As).

2. Double-click Android Application.

3. Name your Run Configuration `MyFirstAndroidAppRunConfig`.

4. Choose the project by clicking the Browse button and choosing the MyFirstAndroidApp project.

5. Switch to the Target tab and set the Device Target Selection Mode to Manual.

Tip

If you leave the Device Target Selection mode on Automatic when you choose Run or Debug in Eclipse, your application is automatically installed and run on the device if the device is plugged in. Otherwise, the application starts in the emulator with the specified AVD. By choosing Manual, you are always prompted for whether (a) you want your application to be launched in an existing emulator; (b) you want your application to be launched in a new emulator instance and allowed to specify an AVD; or (c) you want your application to be launched on the device (if it's plugged in). If any emulator is already running, the device is then plugged in, and the mode is set to Automatic, you see this same prompt, too.

Now create a Debug Configuration for the application. This process is similar to creating a Run Configuration. Follow these steps to create a basic Debug Configuration for the MyFirstAndroidApp application:

1. Choose Run, Debug Configurations (or right-click the Project and Choose Debug As).

2. Double-click Android Application.

3. Name your Debug Configuration `MyFirstAndroidAppDebugConfig`.

4. Choose the project by clicking the Browse button and choosing the MyFirstAndroidApp project.

5. Switch to the Target tab and set the Device Target Selection Mode to Manual.

6. Click Apply, and then click Close.

You now have a Debug Configuration for your application.

Running Your Android Application in the Emulator

Now you can run the MyFirstAndroidApp application using the following steps:

1. Choose the Run As icon drop-down menu on the toolbar (the little green circle with the play button and a drop-down arrow).

2. Pull the drop-down menu and choose the Run Configuration you created. (If you do not see it listed, choose the Run Configurations... item and select the appropriate configuration. The Run Configuration shows up on this drop-down list the next time you run the configuration.)

3. Because you chose the Manual Target Selection mode, you are now prompted for your emulator instance. Change the selection to start a new emulator instance, and check the box next to the AVD you created, as shown in Figure 3.9.

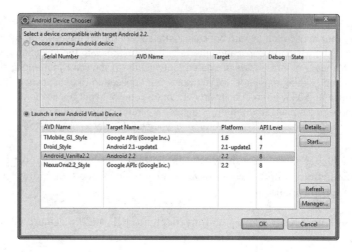

Figure 3.9   Manually choosing a target selection mode.

4. The Android emulator starts up, which might take a moment.

Tip

It can take a long time for the emulator to start up. You might want to leave it around while you work and reattach to it as needed. The tools in Eclipse handle reinstalling the application and re-launching the application, so you can more easily keep the emulator loaded all the time.

5. Press the Menu button to unlock the emulator.

6. The application starts, as shown in Figure 3.10.

7. Click the Home button in the Emulator to end the application.

8. Pull up the Application Drawer to see installed applications. Your screen looks something like Figure 3.11.

9. Click on the My First Android Application icon to launch the application again.

Figure 3.10   My First Android App running in the emulator.

Figure 3.11   My First Android App application icon in the Drawer.

Debugging Your Android Application in the Emulator

Before we go any further, you need to become familiar with debugging in the emulator. To illustrate some useful debugging tools, let's manufacture an error in the My First Android Application.

In your project, edit the file `MyFirstAndroidApp.java` and create a new method called `forceError()` in your class and make a call to this method in your `onCreate()` method. The `forceError()` method forces a new unhandled error in your application.

The `forceError()` method should look something like this:

```
public void forceError() {
    if(true) {
        throw new Error("Whoops");
    }
}
```

Tip

Eclipse has perspectives (each a set of specific panes) for coding and debugging. You can switch between perspectives by choosing the appropriate name in the top-right corner of the Eclipse environment. The Java perspective arranges the appropriate panes for coding and navigating around the project. The Debug perspective enables you to set breakpoints, view LogCat information, and debug. The Dalvik Debug Monitor Service (DDMS) perspective enables you to monitor and manipulate emulator and device status.

It's probably helpful at this point to run the application and watch what happens. Do this using the Run Configuration first. In the emulator, you see that the application has stopped unexpectedly. You are prompted by a dialog that enables you to forcefully close the application, as shown in Figure 3.12.

Shut down the application and the emulator. Now it's time to debug. You can debug the MyFirstAndroidApp application using the following steps:

1. Choose the Debug As icon drop-down menu on the toolbar (the little green bug with the drop-down arrow) ⬚ ⌄ .

2. Pull the drop-down menu and choose the Debug Configuration you created. (If you do not see it listed, choose the Debug Configurations... item and select the appropriate configuration. The Debug Configuration shows up on this drop-down list the next time you run the configuration.)

3. Continue as you did with the Run Configuration and choose the appropriate AVD and launch the emulator again, unlocking it if needed.

It takes a moment for the emulator to start up and for the debugger to attach. If this is the first time you've debugged an Android application, you need to click through some dialog boxes, such as the one shown in Figure 3.13, the first time your application attaches to the debugger.

Figure 3.12   My First Android App crashing gracefully.

Figure 3.13   Switching debug perspectives for Android emulator debugging.

In Eclipse, use the Debug perspective to set breakpoints, step through code, and watch the LogCat logging information about your application. This time, when the application fails, you can determine the cause using the debugger. You might need to click through several dialogs as you set up to debug within Eclipse. If you allow the application to continue after throwing the exception, you can examine the results in the Debug perspective of Eclipse. If you examine the LogCat logging pane, you see that your application was forced to exit due to an unhandled exception (see Figure 3.14).

Figure 3.14   Debugging My First Android App in Eclipse.

Specifically, there's a red `AndroidRuntime` error: `java.lang.Error: Whoops`.

Back in the emulator, click the Force Close button. Now set a breakpoint on the `forceError()` method by right-clicking on the left side of the line of code and choosing Toggle Breakpoint (or Ctrl+Shift+B).

Tip

In Eclipse, you can step through code using Step Into (F5), Step Over (F6), Step Return (F7), and Resume (F8).

On Mac OS X, you might find that the F8 key is mapped globally. If you want to use the keyboard convenience command, you might want to change the keyboard mapping in Eclipse by choosing Eclipse, Preferences, General, Keys and finding the entry for Resume and changing it to something else. Alternatively, you can change the Mac OS X global mapping by going to System Preferences, Keyboard & Mouse, Keyboard Shortcuts and then changing the mapping for F8 to something else.

In the emulator, restart your application and step through your code. You see `MyFirstAndroidApp` has thrown the exception and then the exception shows up in the Variable Browser pane of the Debug Perspective. Expanding the variables contents shows that it is the "Whoops" error.

This is a great time to crash your application repeatedly and get used to the controls. While you're at it, switch over to the DDMS perspective. You note the emulator has a list of processes running on the phone, such as `system_process` and `com.android.phone`. If you launch `MyFirstAndroidApp`, you see `com.androidbook.myfirstandroidapp` show up as a process on the emulator listing. Force the app to close because it crashes, and you note that it disappears from the process list. You can use DDMS to kill processes, inspect threads and the heap, and access the phone file system.

Adding Logging Support to Your Android Application

Before you start diving into the various features of the Android SDK, you should familiarize yourself with logging, a valuable resource for debugging and learning Android. Android logging features are in the `Log` class of the `android.util` package.

Some helpful methods in the `android.util.Log` class are shown in Table 3.2.

Table 3.2   Important **android.util.Log** Methods

Method	Purpose
`Log.e()`	Log errors
`Log.w()`	Log warnings
`Log.i()`	Log informational messages
`Log.d()`	Log Debug messages
`Log.v()`	Log Verbose mesages

To add logging support to `MyFirstAndroidApp`, edit the file `MyFirstAndroidApp.java`. First, you must add the appropriate import statement for the `Log` class:

```
import android.util.Log;
```

Tip

To save time in Eclipse, you can use the imported classes in your code and add the imports needed by hovering over the imported class name and choosing the Add Imported Class option.

You can also use the Organize imports command (Ctrl+Shift+O in Windows or Command+Shift+O on a Mac) to have Eclipse automatically organize your imports. This removes unused imports and adds new ones for packages used but not imported. If a naming conflict arises, as it often does with the Log class, you can choose the package you intended to use.

Next, within the `MyFirstAndroidApp` class, declare a constant string that you use to tag all logging messages from this class. You can use the LogCat utility within Eclipse to filter your logging messages to this debug tag:

```
private static final String DEBUG_TAG= "MyFirstAppLogging";
```

Now, within the `onCreate()` method, you can log something informational:

```
Log.i(DEBUG_TAG, "Info about MyFirstAndroidApp");
```

Warning

While you're here, you must comment out your previous `forceError()` call so that your application doesn't fail.

Now you're ready to run `MyFirstAndroidApp`. Save your work and debug it in the emulator. You notice that your logging messages appear in the LogCat listing, with the Tag field MyFirstAppLogging (see Figure 3.15).

Figure 3.15   A Filtered LogCat log for My First Android App.

Tip

You might want to create a LogCat filter for only messages tagged with your debug tag. To do this, click the green plus sign button in the LogCat pane of Eclipse. Name your filter `Just MyFirstApp`, and fill in the Log Tag with your tag `MyFirstAppLogging`. Now you have a second LogCat tab with only your logging information shown.

Adding Some Media Support to Your Application

Next, let's add some pizzazz to `MyFirstAndroidApp` by having the application play an MP3 music file. Android media player features are found in the `MediaPlayer` class of the `android.media` package.

You can create `MediaPlayer` objects from existing application resources or by specifying a target file using a Uniform Resource Identifier (URI). For simplicity, we begin by accessing an MP3 using the `Uri` class from the `android.net` package.

Some methods in the `android.media.MediaPlayer` and `android.net.Uri` classes are shown in Table 3.3.

Table 3.3   Important MediaPlayer and URI Parsing Methods

Method	Purpose
MediaPlayer.create()	Creates a new Media Player with a given target to play
MediaPlayer.start()	Starts media playback
MediaPlayer.stop()	Stops media playback
MediaPlayer.release()	Releases the resources of the Media Player object
Uri.parse()	Instantiates a Uri object from an appropriately formatted URI address

To add MP3 playback support to `MyFirstAndroidApp`, edit the file
`MyFirstAndroidApp.java`. First, you must add the appropriate import statements for the
`MediaPlayer` class.

```
import android.media.MediaPlayer;
import android.net.Uri;
```

Next, within the `MyFirstAndroidApp` class, declare a member variable for your
`MediaPlayer` object.

```
private MediaPlayer mp;
```

Now, create a new method called `playMusicFromWeb()` in your class and make a call to
this method in your `onCreate()` method. The `playMusicFromWeb()` method creates a
valid `Uri` object, creates a `MediaPlayer` object, and starts the MP3 playing. If the operation should fail for some reason, the method logs a custom error with your logging tag.

The `playMusicFromWeb()` method should look something like this:

```
public void playMusicFromWeb() {
    try {
        Uri file = Uri.parse("http://www.perlgurl.org/podcast/archives"
            + "/podcasts/PerlgurlPromo.mp3");
        mp = MediaPlayer.create(this, file);
        mp.start();
    }
    catch (Exception e) {
        Log.e(DEBUG_TAG, "Player failed", e);
    }
}
```

And finally, you want to cleanly exit when the application shuts down. To do this, you
need to override the `onStop()` method and stop the `MediaPlayer` object and release its
resources.

> **Tip**
>
> In Eclipse, you can right-click within the class and choose Source (or Alt+Shift+S). Choose the option Override/Implement Methods and check the `onStop()` method.

The `onStop()` method should look something like this:

```
protected void onStop() {
    if (mp != null) {
        mp.stop();
        mp.release();
    }
    super.onStop();
}
```

Now, if you run `MyFirstAndroidApp` in the emulator (and you have an Internet connection to grab the data found at the URI location), your application plays the MP3. When you shut down the application, the `MediaPlayer` is stopped and released appropriately.

Adding Location-Based Services to Your Application

Your application knows how to say Hello, but it doesn't know where it's located. Now is a good time to become familiar with some simple location-based calls to get the GPS coordinates.

Creating an AVD with Google APIs

To have some fun with location-based services and maps integration, you should use some of the Google applications often available on Android handsets—most notably, the Google Maps application. Therefore, you must create another AVD. This AVD should have exactly the same settings as the Android_Vanilla2.2 AVD, with one exception: Its Target should be the Google APIs equivalent for that API level (which is 8). You can call this AVD Android_with_GoogleAPIs_2.2.

Configuring the Location of the Emulator

After you have created a new AVD with the Google APIs support, you need to shut down the emulator you've been running. Then debug the My First Android App application again, this time choosing the new AVD.

The emulator does not have location sensors, so the first thing you need to do is seed your emulator with GPS coordinates. To do this, launch your emulator in debug mode with an AVD supporting the Google Maps add-ins and follow these steps:

In the Emulator:

1. Press the Home key to return to the Home screen.

2. Launch the Maps application from the Application drawer.

3. Click the Menu button.

4. Choose the My Location menu item. (It looks like a target.)

In Eclipse:

5. Click the DDMS perspective in the top-right corner of Eclipse.

6. You see an Emulator Control pane on the left side of the screen. Scroll down to the Location Control.

7. Manually enter the longitude and latitude of your location. (Note they are in reverse order.)

8. Click Send.

> **Tip**
>
> To find a specific set of coordinates, you can go to http://maps.google.com. Navigate to the location you want; center the map on the location by right-clicking the map. Choose Link to Map and copy the URL. Take a closer look at the URL and weed out the ll variable, which represents the latitude/longitude of the location. For example, the Yosemite Valley link has the value ll=37.746761, -119.588542, which stands for Latitude: 37.746761 and Longitude: -119.588542.

Back in the emulator, notice that the Google Map now shows the location you seeded. Your screen should now display your location as Yosemite Valley, as shown in Figure 3.16. Your emulator now has a simulated location.

Finding the Last Known Location

To add location support to `MyFirstAndroidApp`, edit the file `MyFirstAndroidApp.java`. First, you must add the appropriate import statements:

```
import android.location.Location;
import android.location.LocationManager;
```

Now, create a new method called `getLocation()` in your class and make a call to this method in your `onCreate()` method. The `getLocation()` method gets the last known location on the phone and logs it as an informational message. If the operation fails for some reason, the method logs an error.

The `getLocation()` method should look something like this:

```
public void getLocation() {
    try {
        LocationManager locMgr = (LocationManager)
            getSystemService(LOCATION_SERVICE);
        Location recentLoc = locMgr.
            getLastKnownLocation(LocationManager.GPS_PROVIDER);
        Log.i(DEBUG_TAG, "loc: " + recentLoc.toString());
    }
```

```
catch (Exception e) {
    Log.e(DEBUG_TAG, "Location failed", e);
}
}
```

Figure 3.16   Setting the location of the emulator
to Yosemite Valley.

Finally, your application requires special permissions to access location-based functionality. You must register this permission in your `AndroidManifest.xml` file. To add location-based service permissions to your application, perform the following steps:

1. Double-click the `AndroidManifest.xml` file.

2. Switch to the Permissions tab.

3. Click the Add button and choose Uses Permission.

4. In the right pane, select `android.permission.ACCESS_FINE_LOCATION`.

5. Save the file.

Now, if you run My First Android App in the emulator, your application logs the GPS
coordinates you provided to the emulator as an informational message, viewable in the
LogCat pane of Eclipse.

Debugging Your Application on the Hardware

You mastered running applications in the emulator. Now let's put the application on real hardware. First, you must register your application as Debuggable in your `AndroidManifest.xml` file. To do this, perform the following steps:

1. Double-click the `AndroidManifest.xml` file.

2. Change to the Application tab.

3. Set the Debuggable Application Attribute to True.

4. Save the file.

You can also modify the `application` element of the `AndroidManifest.xml` file directly with the `android:debuggable` attribute, as shown here:

```
<application ... android:debuggable="true">
```

If you forget to set the `debuggable` attribute to `true`, the handset shows the dialog for waiting for the debugger to connect until you choose Force Close and update the manifest file.

Now, connect an Android device to your computer via USB and re-launch the Run Configuration or Debug Configuration of the application. Because you chose Manual mode for the configuration, you should now see a real Android device listed as an option in the Android Device Chooser (see Figure 3.17).

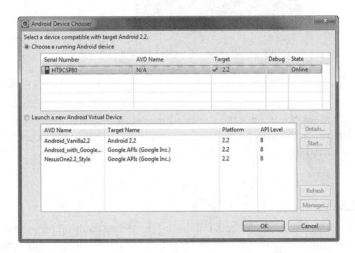

Figure 3.17   Android Device Chooser with USB-connected
Android handset.

Choose the Android Device as your target, and you see that the My First Android App application gets loaded onto the Android handset and launched, just as before. Provided you have enabled the development debugging options on the handset, you can debug the application here as well. You can tell the handset is actively using a USB debugging connection, because there is a little Android bug-like icon in the notification bar.  A screenshot of the application running on a real handset is shown in Figure 3.18.

Figure 3.18   My First Android App running on
Android device hardware.

Debugging on the handset is much the same as debugging on the emulator, but with a couple of exceptions. You cannot use the emulator controls to do things such as send an SMS or configure the location to the device, but you can perform real actions (true SMS, actual location data) instead.

Summary

This chapter showed you how to add, build, run, and debug Android projects using Eclipse. You started by testing your development environment using a sample application from the Android SDK and then you created a new Android application from scratch using Eclipse. You also learned how to make some quick modifications to the application, demonstrating some exciting Android features you learn more about in future chapters.

In the next few chapters, you learn the finer points about defining your Android application using the application manifest file and how the application lifecycle works. You also learn how to organize your application resources, such as images and strings, for use within your application.

References and More Information

USB Drivers for Windows:
  http://developer.android.com/sdk/win-usb.html
Android Dev Guide: "Developing on a Device":
  http://developer.android.com/guide/developing/device.html

4

Understanding the Anatomy of an Android Application

Classical computer science classes often define a program in terms of functionality and data, and Android applications are no different. They perform tasks, display information to the screen, and act upon data from a variety of sources.

Developing Android applications for mobile devices with limited resources requires a thorough understanding of the application lifecycle. Android also uses its own terminology for these application building blocks—terms such as `Context`, `Activity`, and `Intent`. This chapter familiarizes you with the most important components of Android applications.

Mastering Important Android Terminology

This chapter introduces you to the terminology used in Android application development and provides you with a more thorough understanding of how Android applications function and interact with one another. Some of the important terms covered in this chapter are

- **Context:** The context is the central command center for an Android application. All application-specific functionality can be accessed through the context.
- **Activity:** An Android application is a collection of tasks, each of which is called an Activity. Each Activity within an application has a unique task or purpose.
- **Intent:** The Android operating system uses an asynchronous messaging mechanism to match task requests with the appropriate Activity. Each request is packaged as an Intent. You can think of each such request as a message stating an intent to *do* something.
- **Service:** Tasks that do not require user interaction can be encapsulated in a service. A service is most useful when the operations are lengthy (offloading time-consuming processing) or need to be done regularly (such as checking a server for new mail).

Using the Application `Context`

The application `Context` is the central location for all top-level application functionality. The `Context` class can be used to manage application-specific configuration details as well as application-wide operations and data. Use the application `Context` to access settings and resources shared across multiple `Activity` instances.

Retrieving the Application `Context`

You can retrieve the `Context` for the current process using the `getApplicationContext()` method, like this:

```
Context context = getApplicationContext();
```

Using the Application `Context`

After you have retrieved a valid application `Context`, it can be used to access application-wide features and services.

Retrieving Application Resources

You can retrieve application resources using the `getResources()` method of the application `Context`. The most straightforward way to retrieve a resource is by using its resource identifier, a unique number automatically generated within the `R.java` class. The following example retrieves a `String` instance from the application resources by its resource ID:

```
String greeting = getResources().getString(R.string.hello);
```

We talk more about application resources in Chapter 6, "Managing Application Resources."

Accessing Application Preferences

You can retrieve shared application preferences using the `getSharedPreferences()` method of the application `Context`. The `SharedPreferences` class can be used to save simple application data, such as configuration settings.

We talk more about application preferences in Chapter 10, "Using Android Data and Storage APIs."

Accessing Other Application Functionality Using `Context`

The application `Context` provides access to a number of other top-level application features. Here are a few more things you can do with the application `Context`:

- Launch `Activity` instances
- Retrieve assets packaged with the application
- Request a system service (for example, location service)
- Manage private application files, directories, and databases
- Inspect and enforce application permissions

The first item on this list—launching `Activity` instances—is perhaps the most common reason you use the application `Context`.

> **Warning**
>
> Because the `Activity` class is derived from the `Context` class, you can sometimes use this instead of retrieving the application `Context` explicitly. However, don't be tempted to just use your `Activity Context` in all cases because doing so can lead to memory leaks. You can find a great article on this topic at http://android-developers.blogspot.com/2009/01/avoiding-memory-leaks.html.

Performing Application Tasks with Activities

The Android `Activity` class (`android.app.Activity`) is core to any Android application. Much of the time, you define and implement an `Activity` class for each screen in your application. For example, a simple game application might have the following five Activities, as shown in Figure 4.1:

- **A Startup or Splash screen:** This activity serves as the primary entry point to the application. It displays the application name and version information and transitions to the Main menu after a short interval.
- **A Main Menu screen:** This activity acts as a switch to drive the user to the core Activities of the application. Here the users must choose what they want to do within the application.
- **A Game Play screen:** This activity is where the core game play occurs.
- **A High Scores screen:** This activity might display game scores or settings.
- **A Help/About screen:** This activity might display the information the user might need to play the game.

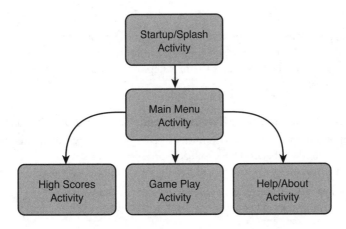

Figure 4.1   A simple game with five activities.

The Lifecycle of an Android `Activity`

Android applications can be multi-process, and the Android operating system allows multiple applications to run concurrently, provided memory and processing power is available. Applications can have background processes, and applications can be interrupted and paused when events such as phone calls occur. There can be only one active application visible to the user at a time—specifically, a single application Activity is in the foreground at any given time.

The Android operating system keeps track of all Activity objects running by placing them on an Activity stack (see Figure 4.2). When a new Activity starts, the Activity on the top of the stack (the current foreground Activity) pauses, and the new Activity pushes onto the top of the stack. When that Activity finishes, that Activity is removed from the activity stack, and the previous Activity in the stack resumes.

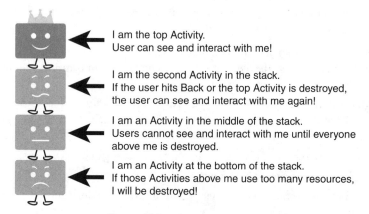

Figure 4.2   The Activity stack.

Android applications are responsible for managing their state and their memory, resources, and data. They must pause and resume seamlessly. Understanding the different states within the `Activity` lifecycle is the first step to designing and developing robust Android applications.

Using `Activity` Callbacks to Manage Application State and Resources

Different important state changes within the Activity lifecycle are punctuated by a series of important method callbacks. These callbacks are shown in Figure 4.3.

Here are the method stubs for the most important callbacks of the `Activity` class:

```
public class MyActivity extends Activity {
    protected void onCreate(Bundle savedInstanceState);
    protected void onStart();
    protected void onRestart();
```

```
protected void onResume();
protected void onPause();
protected void onStop();
protected void onDestroy();
}
```

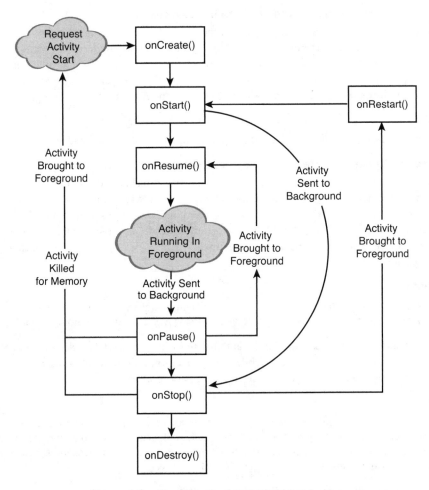

Figure 4.3   The lifecycle of an Android **Activity**.

Now let's look at each of these callback methods, when they are called, and what they are used for.

Initializing Static Activity Data in `onCreate()`

When an `Activity` first starts, the `onCreate()` method is called. The `onCreate()` method has a single parameter, a `Bundle`, which is null if this is a newly started `Activity`. If this

`Activity` was killed for memory reasons and is now restarted, the `Bundle` contains the previous state information for this `Activity` so that it can reinitiate. It is appropriate to perform any setup, such as layout and data binding, in the `onCreate()` method. This includes calls to the `setContentView()` method.

Initializing and Retrieving Activity Data in `onResume()`

When the Activity reaches the top of the activity stack and becomes the foreground process, the `onResume()` method is called. Although the Activity might not be visible yet to the user, this is the most appropriate place to retrieve any instances to resources (exclusive or otherwise) that the Activity needs to run. Often, these resources are the most process-intensive, so we only keep these around while the Activity is in the foreground.

Tip

The `onResume()` method is the appropriate place to start audio, video, and animations.

Stopping, Saving, and Releasing `Activity` Data in `onPause()`

When another `Activity` moves to the top of the activity stack, the current `Activity` is informed that it is being pushed down the activity stack by way of the `onPause()` method.

Here, the `Activity` should stop any audio, video, and animations it started in the `onResume()` method. This is also where you must deactivate resources such as database `Cursor` objects if you have opted to manage them manually, as opposed to having them managed automatically.

Note

Android provides a number of helper utilities for managing queries and Cursor objects. We talk more about these methods in Chapter 10, "Using Android Data and Storage APIs."

The `onPause()` method can also be the last chance for the `Activity` to clean up and release any resources it does not need while in the background. You need to save any uncommitted data here, in case your application does not resume.

Tip

Android applications with data input do not need to follow the typical web form template (data fields plus Submit and Cancel buttons). Instead, data can be saved as the user inputs each field, thus simplifying the user interface and the `onPause()` method. You should provide a button for Cancel, but Save can be implicit.

The `Activity` can also save state information to `Activity`-specific preferences, or application-wide preferences. We talk more about preferences in Chapter 10.

The `Activity` needs to perform anything in the `onPause()` method quickly. The new foreground `Activity` is not started until the `onPause()` method returns.

Warning

Generally speaking, any resources and data retrieved in the `onResume()` method should be released in the `onPause()` method. If they aren't, there is a chance that these resources can't be cleanly released if the process is terminated.

Avoiding Activity Objects Being Killed

Under low-memory conditions, the Android operating system can kill the process for any `Activity` that has been paused, stopped, or destroyed. This essentially means that any `Activity` not in the foreground is subject to a possible shutdown.

If the `Activity` is killed after `onPause()`, the `onStop()` and `onDestroy()` methods might not be called. The more resources released by an `Activity` in the `onPause()` method, the less likely the `Activity` is to be killed while in the background.

The act of killing an `Activity` does not remove it from the activity stack. Instead, the `Activity` state is saved into a `Bundle` object, assuming the `Activity` implements and uses `onSaveInstanceState()` for custom data, though some `View` data is automatically saved. When the user returns to the `Activity` later, the `onCreate()` method is called again, this time with a valid `Bundle` object as the parameter.

Tip

So why does it matter if your application is killed when it is straightforward to resume? Well, it's primarily about responsiveness. The application designer must strike a delicate balance between maintaining data and the resources it needs to resume quickly, without degrading the CPU and system resources while paused in the background.

Saving Activity State into a Bundle with `onSaveInstanceState()`

If an `Activity` is vulnerable to being killed by the Android operating system due to low memory, the `Activity` can save state information to a `Bundle` object using the `onSaveInstanceState()` callback method. This call is not guaranteed under all circumstances, so use the `onPause()` method for essential data commits.

Tip

You might want to use the `onSaveInstanceState()` method to store nonessential information such as uncommitted form field data or any other state information that might make the user's experience with your application less cumbersome.

When this `Activity` is returned to later, this `Bundle` is passed into the `onCreate()` method, allowing the `Activity` to return to the exact state it was in when the `Activity` paused. You can also read `Bundle` information after the `onStart()` callback method using the `onRestoreInstanceState()` callback.

Destroy Static `Activity` Data in `onDestroy()`

When an `Activity` is being destroyed, the `onDestroy()` method is called. The `onDestroy()` method is called for one of two reasons: The `Activity` has completed its lifecycle voluntarily, or the `Activity` is being killed by the Android operating system because it needs the resources.

Tip

The `isFinishing()` method returns false if the `Activity` has been killed by the Android operating system. This method can also be helpful in the `onPause()` method. However, the `Activity` might still be killed in the `onStop()` method at a later time.

Managing Activity Transitions with Intents

In the course of the lifetime of an Android application, the user might transition between a number of different `Activity` instances. At times, there might be multiple `Activity` instances on the activity stack. Developers need to pay attention to the lifecycle of each `Activity` during these transitions.

Some `Activity` instances—such as the application splash/startup screen—are shown and then permanently discarded when the Main menu screen `Activity` takes over. The user cannot return to the splash screen `Activity` without re-launching the application.

Tip

In this case, use the `startActivity()` and appropriate `finish()` methods.

Other `Activity` transitions are temporary, such as a child `Activity` displaying a dialog box, and then returning to the original `Activity` (which was paused on the activity stack and now resumes). In this case, the parent `Activity` launches the child `Activity` and expects a result.

Tip

In this case, use the `startActivityForResult()` and `onActivityResult()` methods.

Transitioning Between Activities with Intents

As previously mentioned, Android applications can have multiple entry points. There is no `main()` function, such as you find in iPhone development. Instead, a specific `Activity` can be designated as the main `Activity` to launch by default within the `AndroidManifest.xml` file; we talk more about this file in Chapter 5, "Defining Your Application Using the Android Manifest File."

Other Activities might be designated to launch under specific circumstances. For example, a music application might designate a generic `Activity` to launch by default from the Application menu, but also define specific alternative entry point Activities for accessing specific music playlists by playlist ID or artists by name.

Launching a New `Activity` by Class Name

You can start activities in several ways. The simplest method is to use the Application `Context` object to call the `startActivity()` method, which takes a single parameter, an `Intent`.

An `Intent` (`android.content.Intent`) is an asynchronous message mechanism used by the Android operating system to match task requests with the appropriate `Activity` or `Service` (launching it, if necessary) and to dispatch broadcast `Intents` events to the system at large.

For now, though, we focus on `Intents` and how they are used with Activities. The following line of code calls the `startActivity()` method with an explicit `Intent`. This `Intent` requests the launch of the target `Activity` named `MyDrawActivity` by its class. This class is implemented elsewhere within the package.

```
startActivity(new Intent(getApplicationContext(),
    MyDrawActivity.class));
```

This line of code might be sufficient for some applications, which simply transition from one `Activity` to the next. However, you can use the `Intent` mechanism in a much more robust manner. For example, you can use the `Intent` structure to pass data between Activities.

Creating Intents with Action and Data

You've seen the simplest case to use an `Intent` to launch a class by name. Intents need not specify the component or class they want to launch explicitly. Instead, you can create an Intent Filter and register it within the Android Manifest file. The Android operating system attempts to resolve the `Intent` requirements and launch the appropriate `Activity` based on the filter criteria.

The guts of the `Intent` object are composed of two main parts: the *action* to be performed and the *data* to be acted upon. You can also specify action/data pairs using `Intent` `Action` types and `Uri` objects. As you saw in Chapter 3, "Writing Your First Android Application," a `Uri` object represents a string that gives the location and name of an object. Therefore, an `Intent` is basically saying "do this" (the action) to "that" (the `Uri` describing what resource to do the action to).

The most common action types are defined in the `Intent` class, including `ACTION_MAIN` (describes the main entry point of an `Activity`) and `ACTION_EDIT` (used in conjunction with a `Uri` to the data edited). You also find `Action` types that generate integration points with Activities in other applications, such as the Browser or Phone Dialer.

Launching an Activity Belonging to Another Application

Initially, your application might be starting only Activities defined within its own package. However, with the appropriate permissions, applications might also launch external Activities within other applications. For example, a Customer Relationship Management (CRM) application might launch the Contacts application to browse the Contact database, choose a specific contact, and return that Contact's unique identifier to the CRM application for use.

Here is an example of how to create a simple `Intent` with a predefined `Action` (`ACTION_DIAL`) to launch the Phone Dialer with a specific phone number to dial in the form of a simple `Uri` object:

```
Uri number = Uri.parse(tel:5555551212);
Intent dial = new Intent(Intent.ACTION_DIAL, number);
startActivity(dial);
```

You can find a list of commonly used Google application Intents at http://developer.android.com/guide/appendix/g-app-intents.html. Also available is the developer managed Registry of Intents protocols at OpenIntents, found at http://www.openintents.org/en/intentstable, which has a growing list of Intents available from third-party applications and those within the Android SDK.

Passing Additional Information Using Intents

You can also include additional data in an `Intent`. The `Extras` property of an `Intent` is stored in a `Bundle` object. The `Intent` class also has a number of helper methods for getting and setting name/value pairs for many common datatypes.

For example, the following `Intent` includes two extra pieces of information—a `string` value and a `boolean`:

```
Intent intent = new Intent(this, MyActivity.class);
intent.putExtra("SomeStringData","Foo");
intent.putExtra("SomeBooleanData",false);
```

Tip

The strings you use to identify your `Intent` object extras can be whatever you want. However, the Android convention for the key name for "extra" data is to include a package prefix—for example, `com.androidbook.Multimedia.SomeStringData`.

Organizing Activities and Intents in Your Application Using Menus

As previously mentioned, your application likely has a number of screens, each with its own `Activity`. There is a close relationship between menus, Activities, and Intents. You often see a menu used in two different ways with Activities and Intents:

- **Main Menu:** Acts as a switch in which each menu item launches a different `Activity` in your application. For instance, menu items for launching the Play Game `Activity`, the High Scores `Activity`, and the Help `Activity`.
- **Drill-Down:** Acts as a directory in which each menu item launches the same `Activity`, but each item passes in different data as part of the `Intent` (for example, a menu of all database records). Choosing a specific item might launch the Edit Record `Activity`, passing in that particular item's unique identifier.

Working with Services

Trying to wrap your head around Activities, Intents, Intent Filters, and the lot when you start with Android development can be daunting. We have tried to distill everything you need to know to start writing Android applications with multiple `Activity` classes, but we'd be remiss if we didn't mention that there's a lot more here, much of which is discussed throughout the book using practical examples. However, we need to give you a "heads up" about some of these topics now because we talk about these concepts very soon when we cover configuring the Android Manifest file for your application in the next chapter.

One application component is the service. An Android `Service` is basically an `Activity` without a user interface. It can run as a background process or act much like a web service does, processing requests from third parties. You can use Intents and Activities to launch services using the `startService()` and `bindService()` methods. Any `Services` exposed by an Android application must be registered in the Android Manifest file.

You can use services for different purposes. Generally, you use a service when no input is required from the user. Here are some circumstances in which you might want to implement or use an Android service:

- A weather, email, or social network app might implement a service to routinely check for updates. (Note: There are other implementations for polling, but this is a common use of services.)

- A photo or media app that keeps its data in sync online might implement a service to package and upload new content in the background when the device is idle.

- A video-editing app might offload heavy processing to a queue on its service in order to avoid affecting overall system performance for non-essential tasks.

- A news application might implement a service to "pre-load" content by downloading news stories in advance of when the user launches the application, to improve performance.

A good rule of thumb is that if the task requires the use of a worker thread and might affect application responsiveness and performance, consider implementing a service to handle the task outside the main application lifecycle.

We talk a lot more about services in Chapter 21, "Working with Services."

Receiving and Broadcasting Intents

Intents serve yet another purpose. You can broadcast an `Intent` object (via a call to `broadcastIntent()`) to the Android system, and any application interested can receive that broadcast (called a `BroadcastReceiver`). Your application might do both sending of and listening for `Intent` objects. These types of `Intent` objects are generally used to inform the greater system that something interesting has happened and use special `Intent` Action types.

For example, the `Intent` action `ACTION_BATTERY_LOW` broadcasts a warning when the battery is low. If your application is a battery-hogging Service of some kind, you might want to listen for this Broadcast and shut down your Service until the battery power is sufficient. You can register to listen for battery/charge level changes by listening for the broadcast `Intent` object with the `Intent` action `ACTION_BATTERY_CHANGED`. There are also broadcast `Intent` objects for other interesting system events, such as SD card state changes, applications being installed or removed, and the wallpaper being changed.

Your application can also share information using the broadcast mechanism. For example, an email application might broadcast an Intent whenever a new email arrives so that other applications (such as spam or anti-virus apps) that might be interested in this type of event can react to it.

Note

We talk more about hardware and the battery in Chapter 19, "Using Android's Optional Hardware APIs," in which you see practical examples of the use of `BroadcastReceiver` objects.

Summary

We tried to strike a balance between providing a thorough reference without overwhelming you with details you won't need to know when developing the average Android application. Instead, we focused on the details you need to know to move forward developing Android applications and to understand every example provided within this book.

`Activity` and `View` classes are the core building blocks of any Android application. Each `Activity` performs a specific task within the application, often with a single user interface screen consisting of `View` widgets. Each `Activity` is responsible for managing its own resources and data through a series of lifecycle callbacks. The transition from one `Activity` to the next is achieved through the `Intent` mechanism. An `Intent` object acts as an asynchronous message that the Android operating system processes and responds to by launching the appropriate `Activity` or `Service`. You can also use `Intent` objects to broadcast system-wide events to any interested `BroadcastReceiver` applications listening.

References and More Information

Android SDK Reference regarding the application Context class:
    http://developer.android.com/reference/android/content/Context.html
Android SDK Reference regarding the Activity class:
    http://developer.android.com/reference/android/app/Activity.html
Android Dev Guide: "Intents and Intent Filters":
    http://developer.android.com/guide/topics/intents/intents-filters.html

## 5

Defining Your Application Using the Android Manifest File

Android projects use a special configuration file called the Android manifest file to determine application settings—settings such as the application name and version, as well as what permissions the application requires to run and what application components it is comprised of. In this chapter, you explore the Android manifest file in detail and learn how different applications use it to define and describe application behavior.

Configuring the Android Manifest File

The Android application manifest file is a specially formatted XML file that must accompany each Android application. This file contains important information about the application's identity. Here you define the application's name and version information and what application components the application relies upon, what permissions the application requires to run, and other application configuration information.

The Android manifest file is named `AndroidManifest.xml` and must be included at the top level of any Android project. The information in this file is used by the Android system to

- Install and upgrade the application package.
- Display the application details such as the application name, description, and icon to users.
- Specify application system requirements, including which Android SDKs are supported, what hardware configurations are required (for example, d-pad navigation), and which platform features the application relies upon (for example, uses multi-touch capabilities).
- Launch application activities.
- Manage application permissions.

- Configure other advanced application configuration details, including acting as a service, broadcast receiver, or content provider.
- Enable application settings such as debugging and configuring instrumentation for application testing.

Tip

When you use Eclipse with the Android Plug-In for Eclipse (ADT), the Android Project Wizard creates the initial `AndroidManifest.xml` file for you. If you are not using Eclipse, then the `android` command-line tool creates the Android manifest file for you as well.

Editing the Android Manifest File

The manifest resides at the top level of your Android project. You can edit the Android manifest file using the Eclipse Manifest File resource editor (a feature of the Android ADT plug-in for Eclipse) or by manually editing the XML.

Editing the Manifest File Using Eclipse

You can use the Eclipse Manifest File resource editor to edit the project manifest file. The Eclipse Manifest File resource editor organizes the manifest information into categories:

- The Manifest tab
- The Application tab
- The Permissions tab
- The Instrumentation tab
- The AndroidManifest.xml tab

Let's take a closer look at a sample Android manifest file. The figures and samples come from the Android application called Multimedia, which you build in Chapter 15, "Using Android Multimedia APIs." We chose this project because it illustrates a number of different characteristics of the Android manifest file, as opposed to the very simple default manifest file you configured for the MyFirstAndroidApp project.

Configuring Package-Wide Settings Using the Manifest Tab

The Manifest tab (see Figure 5.1) contains package-wide settings, including the package name, version information, and supported Android SDK information. You can also set any hardware or feature requirements here.

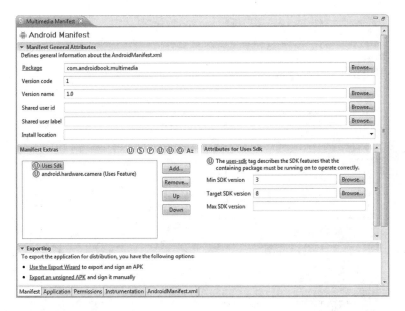

Figure 5.1   The Manifest tab of the Eclipse Manifest File resource editor.

Managing Application and Activity Settings Using the Application Tab

The Application tab (see Figure 5.2) contains application-wide settings, including the application label and icon, as well as information about the application components such as activities, intent filters, and other application components, including configuration for services, intent filters, and content providers.

Enforcing Application Permissions Using the Permissions Tab

The Permissions tab (see Figure 5.3) contains any permission rules required by your application. This tab can also be used to enforce custom permissions created for the application.

Warning

Do not confuse the application Permission field (a drop-down list on the Application tab) with the Permissions tab features. Use the Permissions tab to define the permissions required by the application.

Managing Test Instrumentation Using the Instrumentation Tab

The Instrumentation tab allows the developer to declare any instrumentation classes for monitoring the application. We talk more about instrumentation and testing in Chapter 28, "Testing Android Applications."

Figure 5.2   The Application tab of the Eclipse Manifest
File resource editor.

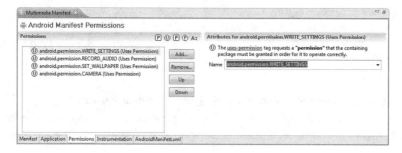

Figure 5.3   The Permissions tab of the Eclipse
Manifest File resource editor.

Editing the Manifest File Manually

The Android manifest file is a specially formatted XML file. You can edit the XML manually by clicking on the AndroidManifest.xml tab.

Android manifest files generally include a single `<manifest>` tag with a single `<application>` tag. The following is a sample `AndroidManifest.xml` file for an application called Multimedia:

```
<?xml version="1.0" encoding="utf-8"?>
<manifest xmlns:android="http://schemas.android.com/apk/res/android"
    package="com.androidbook.multimedia"
    android:versionCode="1"
    android:versionName="1.0">
    <application android:icon="@drawable/icon"
        android:label="@string/app_name"
        android:debuggable="true">
        <activity android:name=".MultimediaMenuActivity"
            android:label="@string/app_name">
            <intent-filter>
                <action
                    android:name="android.intent.action.MAIN" />
                <category
                    android:name="android.intent.category.LAUNCHER" />
            </intent-filter>
        </activity>
        <activity android:name="AudioActivity"></activity>
        <activity android:name="StillImageActivity"></activity>
        <activity android:name="VideoPlayActivity"></activity>
        <activity android:name="VideoRecordActivity"></activity>
    </application>
    <uses-permission
        android:name="android.permission.WRITE_SETTINGS" />
    <uses-permission
        android:name="android.permission.RECORD_AUDIO" />
    <uses-permission
        android:name="android.permission.SET_WALLPAPER" />
    <uses-permission
        android:name="android.permission.CAMERA"></uses-permission>
    <uses-sdk
        android:minSdkVersion="3"
        android:targetSdkVersion="8">
    </uses-sdk>
    <uses-feature
        android:name="android.hardware.camera" />
</manifest>
```

Here's a summary of what this file tells us about the Multimedia application:

- The application uses the package name `com.androidbook.multimedia`.
- The application version name is 1.0.
- The application version code is 1.
- The application name and label are stored in the resource string called `@string/app_name` within the `/res/values/strings.xml` resource file.
- The application is debuggable on an Android device.

- The application icon is the graphic file called `icon` (could be a PNG, JPG, or GIF) stored within the `/res/drawable` directory (there are actually multiple versions for different pixel densities).
- The application has five activities (`MultimediaMenuActivity`, `AudioActivity`, `StillImageActivity`, `VideoPlayActivity`, and `VideoRecordActivity`).
- `MultimediaMenuActivity` is the primary entry point for the application. This is the activity that starts when the application icon is pressed in the application drawer.
- The application requires the following permissions to run: the ability to record audio, the ability to set the wallpaper on the device, the ability to access the built-in camera, and the ability to write settings.
- The application works from any API level from 3 to 8; in other words, Android SDK 1.5 is the lowest supported, and the application was written to target Android 2.2.
- Finally, the application requires a camera to work properly.

Now let's talk about some of these important configurations in detail.

Managing Your Application's Identity

Your application's Android manifest file defines the application properties. The package name must be defined within the Android manifest file within the `<manifest>` tag using the `package` attribute:

```
<manifest
    xmlns:android="http://schemas.android.com/apk/res/android"
    package="com.androidbook.multimedia"
    android:versionCode="1"
    android:versionName="1.0">
```

Versioning Your Application

Versioning your application appropriately is vital to maintaining your application in the field. Intelligent versioning can help reduce confusion and make product support and upgrades simpler. There are two different version attributes defined within the `<manifest>` tag: the version name and the version code.

The version name (`android:versionName`) is a user-friendly, developer-defined version attribute. This information is displayed to users when they manage applications on their devices and when they download the application from marketplaces. Developers use this version information to keep track of their application versions in the field. We discuss appropriate application versioning for mobile applications in detail in Chapter 26, "The Mobile Software Development Process."

Warning

Although you can use an `@string` resource reference for some manifest file settings, such as the `android:versionName`, there are publishing systems that don't support this.

The Android operating system uses the version code (`android:versionCode`) that is a numeric attribute to manage application upgrades. We talk more about publishing and upgrade support in Chapter 29, "Selling Your Android Application."

Setting the Application Name and Icon

Overall application settings are configured with the `<application>` tag of the Android manifest file. Here you set information such as the application icon (`android:icon`) and friendly name (`android:label`). These settings are attributes of the `<application>` tag.

For example, here we set the application icon to a drawable resource provided with the application package and the application label to a string resource:

```
<application android:icon="@drawable/icon"
    android:label="@string/app_name">
```

You can also set optional application settings as attributes in the `<application>` tag, such as the application description (`android:description`) and the setting to enable the application for debugging on the device (`android:debuggable="true"`).

Enforcing Application System Requirements

In addition to configuring your application's identity, the Android manifest file is also used to specify any system requirements necessary for the application to run properly. For example, an augmented reality application might require that the handset have GPS, a compass, and a camera. Similarly, an application that relies upon the Bluetooth APIs available within the Android SDK requires a handset with an SDK version of API Level 5 or higher (Android 2.0). These types of system requirements can be defined and enforced in the Android manifest file. Then, when an application is listed on the Android Market, applications can be filtered by these types of information; the Android platform also checks these requirements when installing the application package on the system and errors out if necessary.

Some of the application system requirements that developers can configure through the Android manifest file include

- The Android SDK versions supported by the application
- The Android platform features used by the application
- The Android hardware configurations required by the application
- The screen sizes and pixel densities supported by the application
- Any external libraries that the application links to

Targeting Specific SDK Versions

Android devices run different versions of the Android platform. Often, you see old, less powerful, or even less expensive devices running older versions of the Android platform, whereas newer, more powerful devices that show up on the market often run the latest Android software.

There are now dozens of different Android devices in users' hands. Developers must decide who their target audience is for a given application. Are they trying to support the largest population of users and therefore want to support as many different versions of the platform as possible? Or are they developing a bleeding-edge game that requires the latest device hardware?

Developers can specify which versions of the Android platform an application supports within its Android manifest file using the <uses-sdk> tag. This tag has three important attributes:

- The **minSdkVersion** attribute: This attribute specifies the lowest API level that the application supports.
- The **targetSdkVersion** attribute: This attribute specifies the optimum API level that the application supports.
- The **maxSdkVersion** attribute: This attribute specifies the highest API level that the application supports.

Tip

The Android Market filters applications available to a given user based upon settings such as the <uses-sdk> tag within an application's manifest file. This is a required tag for applications that want to be published on the Android Market. Neglecting to use this tag results in a warning in the build environment.

Each attribute of the <uses-sdk> tag is an integer that represents the API level associated with a given Android SDK. This value does not directly correspond to the SDK version. Instead, it is the revision of the API level associated with that SDK. The API level is set by the developers of the Android SDK. You need to check the SDK documentation to determine the API level value for each version.

Note

With each new Android SDK version, this API level is incremented. This information is always provided with the SDK release documentation.

Table 5.1 shows the Android SDK versions available for shipping applications.

Table 5.1 **Android SDK Versions and Their API Levels**

Android SDK Version	API Level (Value as Integer)
Android 1.0 SDK	1
Android 1.1 SDK	2
Android 1.5 SDK (Cupcake)	3
Android 1.6 SDK (Donut)	4
Android 2.0 SDK (Éclair)	5
Android 2.0.1 SDK (Éclair)	6
Android 2.1 SDK (Éclair)	7

Table 5.1 **Continued**

Android SDK Version	API Level (Value as Integer)
Android 2.2 SDK (FroYo)	8
Android SDK (Gingerbread)	9

Specifying the Minimum SDK Version

You should always specify the minSdkVersion attribute for your application. This value represents the lowest Android SDK version your application supports.

For example, if your application requires APIs introduced in Android SDK 1.6, you would check that SDK's documentation and find that this release is defined as API Level 4. Therefore, add the following to your Android Manifest file within the `<manifest>` tag block:

```
<uses-sdk android:minSdkVersion="4" />
```

It's that simple. You should use the lowest API level possible if you want your application to be compatible with the largest number of Android handsets. However, you must ensure that your application is tested sufficiently on any non-target platforms (any API level supported below your target SDK, as described in the next section).

Specifying the Target SDK Version

You should always specify the targetSdkVersion attribute for your application. This value represents the Android SDK version your application was built for and tested against.

For example, if your application was built using the APIs that are backward-compatible to Android 1.6 (API Level 4), but targeted and tested using Android 2.2 SDK (API Level 8), then you would want to specify the `targetSdkVersion` attribute as 8. Therefore, add the following to your Android manifest file within the `<manifest>` tag block:

```
<uses-sdk android:minSdkVersion="4" android:targetSdkVersion="8" />
```

Why should you specify the target SDK version you used? Well, the Android platform has built-in functionality for backward-compatibility (to a point). Think of it like this: A specific method of a given API might have been around since API Level 1. However, the internals of that method—its behavior—might have changed slightly from SDK to SDK. By specifying the target SDK version for your application, the Android operating system attempts to match your application with the exact version of the SDK (and the behavior as you tested it within the application), even when running a different (newer) version of the platform. This means that the application should continue to behave in "the old way" despite any new changes or "improvements" to the SDK that might cause unintended consequences in your application.

Specifying the Maximum SDK Version

You will rarely want to specify the maxSdkVersion attribute for your application. This value represents the highest Android SDK version your application supports, in terms of API level. It restricts forward-compatibility of your application.

One reason you might want to set this attribute is if you want to limit who can install the application to exclude devices with the newest SDKs. For example, you might develop a free beta version of your application with plans for a paid version for the newest SDK. By setting the `maxSdkVersion` attribute of the manifest file for your free application, you disallow anyone with the newest SDK to install the free version of the application. The downside of this idea? If your users have phones that receive over-the-air SDK updates, your application would cease to work (and appear) on phones where it had functioned perfectly, which might "upset" your users and result in bad ratings on your market of choice.

The short answer: Use `maxSdkVersion` only when absolutely necessary and when you understand the risks associated with its use.

Enforcing Application Platform Requirements

Android devices have different hardware and software configurations. Some devices have built-in keyboards and others rely upon the software keyboard. Similarly, certain Android devices support the latest 3-D graphics libraries and others provide little or no graphics support. The Android manifest file has several informational tags for flagging the system features and hardware configurations supported or required by an Android application.

Specifying Supported Input Methods

The `<uses-configuration>` tag can be used to specify which input methods the application supports. There are different configuration attributes for five-way navigation, the hardware keyboard and keyboard types; navigation devices such as the directional pad, trackball, and wheel; and touch screen settings.

There is no "OR" support within a given attribute. If an application supports multiple input configurations, there must be multiple `<uses-configuration>` tags—one for each complete configuration supported.

For example, if your application requires a physical keyboard and touch screen input using a finger or a stylus, you need to define two separate `<uses-configuration>` tags in your manifest file, as follows:

```
<uses-configuration android:reqHardKeyboard="true"
    android:reqTouchScreen="finger" />
<uses-configuration android:reqHardKeyboard="true"
    android:reqTouchScreen="stylus" />
```

For more information about the `<uses-configuration>` tag of the Android manifest file, see the Android SDK reference at http://developer.android.com/guide/topics/manifest/uses-configuration-element.html.

Specifying Required Device Features

Not all Android devices support every Android feature. Put another way: There are a number of APIs (and related hardware) that Android devices may optionally include. For example, not all Android devices have multi-touch ability or a camera flash.

The <uses-feature> tag can be used to specify which Android features the application requires to run properly. These settings are for informational purposes only—the Android operating system does not enforce these settings, but publication channels such as the Android Market use this information to filter the applications available to a given user.

If your application requires multiple features, you must create a <uses-feature> tag for each. For example, an application that requires both a light and proximity sensor requires two tags:

```
<uses-feature android:name="android.hardware.sensor.light" />
<uses-feature android:name="android.hardware.sensor.proximity" />
```

One common reason to use the <uses-feature> tag is for specifying the OpenGL ES versions supported by your application. By default, all applications function with OpenGL ES 1.0 (which is a required feature of all Android devices). However, if your application requires features available only in later versions of OpenGL ES, such as 2.0, then you must specify this feature in the Android manifest file. This is done using the android:glEsVersion attribute of the <uses-feature> tag. Specify the lowest version of OpenGL ES that the application requires. If the application works with 1.0 and 2.0, specify the lowest version (so that the Android Market allows more users to install your application).

For more information about the <uses-feature> tag of the Android manifest file, see the Android SDK reference.

Specifying Supported Screen Sizes

Android devices come in many shapes and sizes. Screen sizes and pixel densities vary widely across the range of Android devices available on the market today. The Android platform categorizes screen types in terms of sizes (small, normal, and large) and pixel density (low, medium, and high). These characteristics effectively cover the variety of screen types available within the Android platform.

An application can provide custom resources for specific screen sizes and pixel densities (we cover this in Chapter 6, "Managing Application Resources"). The <supports-screen> tag can be used to specify which Android types of screens the application supports.

For example, if the application supports QVGA screens (small) and HVGA screens (normal) regardless of pixel density, the <supports-screen> tag is configured as follows:

```
<supports-screens android:smallScreens="true"
                android:normalScreens="true"
                android:largeScreens"false"
                android:anyDensity="true"/>
```

For more information about the `<supports-screen>` tag of the Android manifest file, see the Android SDK reference as well as the Android Dev Guide documentation on Screen Support.

Working with External Libraries

You can register any shared libraries your application links to within the Android manifest file. By default, every application is linked to the standard Android packages (such as `android.app`) and is aware of its own package. However, if your application links to additional packages, they must be registered within the `<application>` tag of the Android manifest file using the `<uses-library>` tag. For example

```
<uses-library android:name="com.sharedlibrary.sharedStuff" />
```

This feature is often used for linking to optional Google APIs. For more information about the `<uses-library>` tag of the Android manifest file, see the Android SDK reference.

Registering Activities and Other Application Components

Each Activity within the application must be defined within the Android manifest file with an `<activity>` tag. For example, the following XML excerpt defines an `Activity` class called `AudioActivity`:

```
<activity android:name="AudioActivity" />
```

This `Activity` must be defined as a class within the `com.androidbook.multimedia` package. That is, the package specified in the `<manifest>` element of the Android manifest file. You can also enforce scope of the activity class by using the dot as a prefix in the Activity name:

```
<activity android:name=".AudioActivity" />
```

Or you can specify the complete class name:

```
<activity android:name="com.androidbook.multimedia.AudioActivity" />
```

Warning

You must define the `<activity>` tag for an `Activity` or it will not launch. It is quite common for developers to implement an `Activity` and then try to troubleshoot why it isn't running properly, only to realize they forgot to register it in the Android manifest file. Until they look through the `LogCat` output, the error merely looks like a typical crash, too, further confusing the developer.

Designating a Primary Entry Point Activity for Your Application Using an Intent Filter

An `Activity` class can be designated as the primary entry point by configuring an intent filter using the Android manifest tag `<intent-filter>` in the application's `AndroidManifest.xml` file with the MAIN action type and the LAUNCHER category.

The following tag of XML configures the `Activity` class called
`MultimediaMenuActivity` as the primary launching point of the application:

```
<activity android:name=".MultimediaMenuActivity"
    android:label="@string/app_name">
    <intent-filter>
        <action android:name="android.intent.action.MAIN" />
        <category android:name="android.intent.category.LAUNCHER" />
    </intent-filter>
</activity>
```

Configuring Other Intent Filters

The Android operating system uses Intent filters to resolve implicit intents. That is, Intents
that do not specify the `Activity` or `Component` they want launched. Intent filters can be
applied to `Activities`, `Services`, and `BroadcastReceivers`. The filter declares that this
component is open to receiving any `Intent` sent to the Android operating system that
matches its criteria.

Intent filters are defined using the `<intent-filter>` tag and must contain at least one
`<action>` tag but can also contain other information, such as `<category>` and `<data>`
blocks. Here we have a sample intent filter block, which might be found within an
`<activity>` block:

```
<intent-filter>
    <action android:name="android.intent.action.VIEW" />
        <category android:name="android.intent.category.BROWSABLE" />
        <category android:name="android.intent.category.DEFAULT" />
        <data android:scheme="geoname"/>
</intent-filter>
```

This intent filter definition uses a predefined action called `VIEW`, the action for viewing
particular content. It is also `BROWSABLE` and uses a scheme of geoname so that when a
`Uri` starts with `geoname://`, the activity with this intent filter launches. You can read
more about this particular intent filter in Chapter 14, "Using Location-Based Services
(LBS) APIs."

Tip

You can define custom actions unique to your application. If you do so, be sure to document
these actions if you want them to be used by third parties.

Registering Services and Broadcast Receivers

All application components are defined within the Android manifest file. In addition to
activities, all services and broadcast receivers must be registered within the Android Manifest file.

- Services are registered using the `<service>` tag.
- Broadcast Receivers are registered using the `<receiver>` tag.

Both Services and Broadcast Receivers use intent filters. You learn much more about services, broadcast receivers, and intent filters later in the book.

Registering Content Providers

If your application acts as a content provider, effectively exposing a shared data service for use by other applications, it must declare this capability within the Android manifest file using the `<provider>` tag. Configuring a content provider involves determining what subsets of data are shared and what permissions are required to access them, if any.

> **Note**
>
> We talk more about content providers in Chapter 11, "Sharing Data Between Applications with Content Providers."

Working with Permissions

The Android operating system has been locked down so that applications have limited capability to adversely affect operations outside their process space. Instead, Android applications run within the bubble of their own virtual machine, with their own Linux user account (and related permissions).

Registering Permissions Your Application Requires

Android applications have no permissions by default. Instead, any permissions for shared resources or privileged access—whether it's shared data, such as the Contacts database, or access to underlying hardware, such as the built-in camera—must be explicitly registered within the Android manifest file. These permissions are granted when the application is installed.

> **Tip**
>
> When users install the application, they are informed what permissions the application requires to run and must approve these permissions. Request only the permissions your application requires.

The following XML excerpt for the preceding Android manifest file defines a permission using the `<uses-permission>` tag to gain access to the built-in camera:

```
<uses-permission android:name="android.permission.CAMERA" />
```

A complete list of the permissions can be found in the `android.Manifest.permission` class. Your application manifest should include only the permissions required to run. The user is informed what permissions each Android application requires at install time.

Tip

You might find that, in certain cases, permissions are not enforced (you can operate without the permission). In these cases, it is prudent to request the permission anyway for two reasons. First, the user is informed that the application is performing those sensitive actions, and second, that permission could be enforced in a later SDK version.

Registering Permissions Your Application Grants to Other Applications

Applications can also define their own permissions by using the `<permission>` tag. Permissions must be described and then applied to specific application components, such as Activities, using the `android:permission` attribute.

Tip

Use Java-style scoping for unique naming of application permissions (for example, `com.androidbook.MultiMedia.ViewMatureMaterial`).

Permissions can be enforced at several points:

- When starting an `Activity` or `Service`
- When accessing data provided by a content provider
- At the function call level
- When sending or receiving broadcasts by an `Intent`

Permissions can have three primary protection levels: `normal`, `dangerous`, and `signature`. The `normal` protection level is a good default for fine-grained permission enforcement within the application. The `dangerous` protection level is used for higher-risk Activities, which might adversely affect the device. Finally, the `signature` protection level permits any application signed with the same certificate to use that component for controlled application interoperability. You learn more about application signing in Chapter 29.

Permissions can be broken down into categories, called `permission groups`, which describe or warn why specific Activities require permission. For example, permissions might be applied for Activities that expose sensitive user data such as location and personal information (`android.permission-group.LOCATION` and `android.permission-group.PERSONAL_INFO`), access underlying hardware (`android.permission-group.HARDWARE_CONTROLS`), or perform operations that might incur fees to the user (`android.permission-group.COST_MONEY`). A complete list of permission groups is available within the `Manifest.permission_group` class.

Enforcing Content Provider Permissions at the `Uri` Level

You can also enforce fine-grained permissions at the `Uri` level using the `<grant-uri-permissions>` tag.

For more information about the Android permissions framework, we highly recommend reading the Android Dev Guide documentation on Security and Permissions.

Exploring Other Manifest File Settings

We have now covered the basics of the Android manifest file, but there are many other settings configurable within the Android manifest file using different tag blocks, not to mention attributes within each tag we already discussed.

Some other features you can configure within the Android manifest file include

- Setting application-wide themes as `<application>` tag attributes
- Configuring instrumentation using the `<instrumentation>` tag
- Aliasing activities using the `<activity-alias>` tag
- Creating intent filters using the `<intent-filter>` tag
- Creating broadcast receivers using the `<receiver>` tag

For more detailed descriptions of each tag and attribute available in the Android SDK (and there are many), please review the Android SDK reference.

Summary

Each Android application has a specially formatted XML file called `AndroidManifest.xml`. This file describes the application's identity in great detail. Some information you must define within the Android manifest file includes the application's name and version information, what application components it contains, which device configurations it requires, and what permissions it needs to run. The Android manifest file is used by the Android operating system to install, upgrade, and run the application package. Some details of the Android manifest file are also used by third parties, including the Android Market publication channel.

References and More Information

Android Dev Guide: "The AndroidManifest.xml File":
    http://developer.android.com/guide/topics/manifest/manifest-intro.html
Android Dev Guide: "Android API Levels":
    http://developer.android.com/guide/appendix/api-levels.html
Android Dev Guide: "Supporting Multiple Screens":
    http://developer.android.com/guide/practices/screens_support.html
Android Dev Guide: "Security and Permissions":
    http://developer.android.com/guide/topics/security/security.html

## 6

Managing Application Resources

The well-written application accesses its resources programmatically instead of hard coding them into the source code. This is done for a variety of reasons. Storing application resources in a single place is a more organized approach to development and makes the code more readable and maintainable. Externalizing resources such as strings makes it easier to localize applications for different languages and geographic regions.

In this chapter, you learn how Android applications store and access important resources such as strings, graphics, and other data. You also learn how to organize Android resources within the project files for localization and different device configurations.

What Are Resources?

All Android applications are composed of two things: functionality (code instructions) and data (resources). The functionality is the code that determines how your application behaves. This includes any algorithms that make the application run. Resources include text strings, images and icons, audio files, videos, and other data used by the application.

Tip

Many of the code examples provided in this chapter are taken from the SimpleResource-View, ResourceViewer, ResourceRoundup, and ParisView applications. This source code for these applications is provided for download on the book website.

Storing Application Resources

Android resource files are stored separately from the java class files in the Android project. Most common resource types are stored in XML. You can also store raw data files and graphics as resources.

Understanding the Resource Directory Hierarchy

Resources are organized in a strict directory hierarchy within the Android project. All resources must be stored under the `/res` project directory in specially named subdirectories that must be lowercase.

Different resource types are stored in different directories. The resource sub-directories generated when you create an Android project using the Eclipse plug-in are shown in Table 6.1.

Table 6.1   **Default Android Resource Directories**

Resource Subdirectory	Purpose
/res/drawable-*/	Graphics Resources
/res/layout/	User Interface Resources
/res/values/	Simple Data such as Strings and Color Values, and so on

Each resource type corresponds to a specific resource subdirectory name. For example, all graphics are stored under the /res/drawable directory structure. Resources can be further organized in a variety of ways using even more specially named directory qualifiers. For example, the /res/drawable-hdpi directory stores graphics for high-density screens, the /res/drawable-ldpi directory stores graphics for low-density screens, and the /res/drawable-mdpi directory stores graphics for medium-density screens. If you had a graphic resource that was shared by all screens, you would simply store that resource in the /res/drawable directory. We talk more about resource directory qualifiers later in this chapter.

Using the Android Asset Packaging Tool

If you use the Eclipse with the Android Development Tools Plug-In, you will find that adding resources to your project is simple. The plug-in detects new resources when you add them to the appropriate project resource directory under /res automatically. These resources are compiled, resulting in the generation of the R.java file, which enables you to access your resources programmatically.

If you use a different development environment, you need to use the aapt tool command-line interface to compile your resources and package your application binaries to deploy to the phone or emulator. You can find the aapt tool in the /tools subdirectory of each specific Android SDK version.

> **Tip**
>
> Build scripts can use the aapt for automation purposes and to create archives of assets and compile them efficiently for your application. You can configure the tool using command-line arguments to package only including assets for a specific device configuration or target language, for example. All resources for all targets are included by default.

Resource Value Types

Android applications rely on many different types of resources—such as text strings, graphics, and color schemes—for user interface design.

These resources are stored in the /res directory of your Android project in a strict (but reasonably flexible) set of directories and files. All resources filenames must be lowercase and simple (letters, numbers, and underscores only).

The resource types supported by the Android SDK and how they are stored within the project are shown in Table 6.2.

Table 6.2   **How Important Resource Types Are Stored in Android Project Resource Directories**

Resource Type	Required Directory	Filename	XML Tag
Strings	/res/values/	strings.xml (suggested)	<string>
String Pluralization	/res/values/	strings.xml (suggested)	<plurals>, <item>
Arrays of Strings	/res/values/	strings.xml (suggested)	<string-array>, <item>
Booleans	/res/values/	bools.xml (suggested)	<bool>
Colors	/res/values/	Colors.xml (suggested)	<color>
Color State Lists	/res/color/	Examples include buttonstates.xml indicators.xml	<selector>, <item>
Dimensions	/res/values/	Dimens.xml (suggested)	<dimen>
Integers	/res/values/	integers.xml (suggested)	<integer>
Arrays of Integers	/res/values/	integers.xml (suggested)	<integer-array>, <item>

Table 6.2   **Continued**

Resource Type	Required Directory	Filename	XML Tag
Mixed-Type Arrays	`/res/values/`	`Arrays.xml` (suggested)	`<array>`, `<item>`
Simple Drawables (Paintable)	`/res/values/`	`drawables.xml` (suggested)	`<drawable>`
Graphics	`/res/drawable/`	Examples include `icon.png logo.jpg`	Supported graphics files or drawable definition XML files such as shapes.
Tweened Animations	`/res/anim/`	Examples include `fadesequence.xml spinsequence.xml`	`<set>`, `<alpha>`, `<scale>`, `<translate>`, `<rotate>`
Frame-by-Frame Animations	`/res/drawable/`	Examples include `sequence1.xml sequence2.xml`	`<animation-list>`, `<item>`
Menus	`/res/menu/`	Examples include `mainmenu.xml helpmenu.xml`	`<menu>`
XML Files	`/res/xml/`	Examples include `data.xml data2.xml`	Defined by the developer.
Raw Files	`/res/raw/`	Examples include `jingle.mp3 somevideo.mp4 helptext.txt`	Defined by the developer.
Layouts	`/res/layout/`	Examples include `main.xml help.xml`	Varies. Must be a layout control.
Styles and Themes	`/res/values/`	`styles.xml themes.xml` (suggested)	`<style>`

> **Tip**
>
> Some resource files, such as animation files and graphics, are referenced by variables named from their filename (regardless of file suffix), so name your files appropriately.

Storing Different Resource Value Types

The aapt traverses all properly formatted files in the `/res` directory hierarchy and generates the class file `R.java` in your source code directory `/src` to access all variables.

Later in this chapter, we cover how to store and use each different resource type in detail, but for now, you need to understand that different types of resources are stored in different ways.

Storing Simple Resource Types Such as Strings

Simple resource value types, such as strings, colors, dimensions, and other primitives, are stored under the `/res/values` project directory in XML files. Each resource file under the `/res/values` directory should begin with the following XML header:

```
<?xml version="1.0" encoding="utf-8"?>
```

Next comes the root node `<resources>` followed by the specific resource element types such as `<string>` or `<color>`. Each resource is defined using a different element name.

Although the XML file names are arbitrary, the best practice is to store your resources in separate files to reflect their types, such as `strings.xml`, `colors.xml`, and so on. However, there's nothing stopping the developers from creating multiple resource files for a given type, such as two separate xml files called `bright_colors.xml` and `muted_colors.xml`, if they so choose.

Storing Graphics, Animations, Menus, and Files

In addition to simple resource types stored in the `/res/values` directory, you can also store numerous other types of resources, such as animation sequences, graphics, arbitrary XML files, and raw files. These types of resources are not stored in the `/res/values` directory, but instead stored in specially named directories according to their type. For example, you can include animation sequence definitions in the `/res/anim` directory. Make sure you name resource files appropriately because the resource name is derived from the filename of the specific resource. For example, a file called `flag.png` in the `/res/drawable` directory is given the name `R.drawable.flag`.

Understanding How Resources Are Resolved

Few applications work perfectly, no matter the environment they run in. Most require some tweaking, some special case handling. That's where alternative resources come in. You can organize Android project resources based upon more than a dozen different types of criteria, including language and region, screen characteristics, device modes (night mode, docked, and so on), input methods, and many other device differentiators.

It can be useful to think of the resources stored at the top of the resource hierarchy as *default resources* and the specialized versions of those resources as *alternative resources*. Two common reasons that developers use alternative resources are for internationalization and localization purposes and to design an application that runs smoothly on different device screens and orientations.

The Android platform has a very robust mechanism for loading the appropriate resources at runtime. An example might be helpful here. Let's presume that we have a simple application with its requisite string, graphic, and layout resources. In this application, the resources are stored in the top-level resource directories (for example, */res/values/strings.xml*, */res/drawable/myLogo.png*, and */res/layout/main.xml*). No matter what Android device (huge hi-def screen, postage-stamp-sized screen, English or Chinese language or region, portrait or landscape orientation, and so on), you run this application on, the same resource data is loaded and used.

Back in our simple application example, we could create alternative string resources in Chinese simply by adding a second *strings.xml* file in a resource subdirectory called */res/values-zh/strings.xml* (note the *–zh* qualifier). We could provide different logos for different screen densities by providing three versions of *myLogo.png*:

- `/res/drawable-ldpi/myLogo.png` (low-density screens)
- `/res/drawable-mdpi/myLogo.png` (medium-density screens)
- `/res/drawable-hdpi/myLogo.png` (high-density screens)

Finally, let's say that the application would look much better if the layout was different in portrait versus landscape modes. We could change the layout around, moving controls around, in order to achieve a more pleasant user experience, and provide two layouts:

- `/res/layout-port/main.xml` (layout loaded in portrait mode)
- `/res/layout-land/main.xml` (layout loaded in landscape mode)

With these alternative resources in place, the Android platform behaves as follows:

- If the device language setting is Chinese, the strings in `/res/values-zh/` `strings.xml` are used. In all other cases, the strings in `/res/values/strings.xml` are used.

- If the device screen is a low-density screen, the graphic stored in the `/res/` `drawable-ldpi/myLogo.png` resource directory is used. If it's a medium-density screen, the mdpi drawable is used, and so on.

- If the device is in landscape mode, the layout in the `/res/layout-land/main.xml` is loaded. If it's in portrait mode, the `/res/layout-port/main.xml` layout is loaded.

There are four important rules to remember when creating alternative resources:

1. The Android platform always loads the most specific, most appropriate resource available. If an alternative resource does not exist, the default resource is used. Therefore, know your target devices, design for the defaults, and add alternative resources judiciously.

2. Alternative resources must always be named exactly the same as the default resources. If a string is called `strHelpText` in the `/res/values/strings.xml` file,

then it must be named the same in the `/res/values-fr/strings.xml` (French) and `/res/values-zh/strings.xml` (Chinese) string files. The same goes for all other types of resources, such as graphics or layout files.

3. Good application design dictates that alternative resources should always have a default counterpart so that regardless of the device, some version of the resource always loads. The only time you can get away without a default resource is when you provide every kind of alternative resource (for example, providing `ldpi, mdpi,` and `hdpi` graphics resources cover every eventuality, in theory).

4. Don't go overboard creating alternative resources, as they add to the size of your application package and can have performance implications. Instead, try to design your default resources to be flexible and scalable. For example, a good layout design can often support both landscape and portrait modes seamlessly—if you use the right controls.

Enough about alternative resources; let's spend the rest of this chapter talking about how to create the default resources first. In Chapter 25, "Targeting Different Device Configurations and Languages," we discuss how to use alternative resources to make your Android applications compatible with many different device configurations.

Accessing Resources Programmatically

Developers access specific application resources using the `R.java` class file and its subclasses, which are automatically generated when you add resources to your project (if you use Eclipse). You can refer to any resource identifier in your project by name. For example, the following string resource named `strHello` defined within the resource file called `/res/values/strings.xml` is accessed in the code as

`R.string.strHello`

This variable is not the actual data associated with the string named hello. Instead, you use this resource identifier to retrieve the resource of that type (which happens to be string).

For example, a simple way to retrieve the string text is to call

`String myString = getResources().getString(R.string.strHello);`

First, you retrieve the Resources instance for your application `Context` (`android.content.Context`), which is, in this case, `this` because the `Activity` class extends `Context`. Then you use the `Resources` instance to get the appropriate kind of resource you want. You find that the `Resources` class (`android.content.res.Resources`) has helper methods for handling every kind of resource.

Before we go any further, we find it can be helpful to dig in and create some resources, so let's create a simple example. Don't worry if you don't understand every aspect of the exercise. You can find out more about each different resource type later in this chapter.

Setting Simple Resource Values Using Eclipse

Developers can define resource types by editing resource XML files manually and using the aapt to compile them and generate the `R.java` file or by using Eclipse with the Android plug-in, which includes some very handy resource editors.

To illustrate how to set resources using the Eclipse plug-in, let's look at an example. Create a new Android project and navigate to the `/res/values/strings.xml` file in Eclipse and double-click the file to edit it. Your `strings.xml` resource file opens in the right pane and should look something like Figure 6.1.

Figure 6.1   The string resource file in the Eclipse Resource Editor
(Editor view).

There are two tabs at the bottom of this pane. The Resources tab provides a friendly method to easily insert primitive resource types such as strings, colors, and dimension resources. The `strings.xml` tab shows the raw XML resource file you are creating. Sometimes, editing the XML file manually is much faster, especially if you add a number of new resources. Click the `strings.xml` tab, and your pane should look something like Figure 6.2.

Figure 6.2   The string resource file in the Eclipse Resource Editor
(XML view).

Now add some resources using the Add button on the Resources tab. Specifically, create the following resources:

- A color resource named `prettyTextColor` with a value of #ff0000
- A dimension resource named `textPointSize` with a value of 14pt
- A `drawable` resource named `redDrawable` with a value of #F00

Now you have several resources of various types in your `strings.xml` resource file. If you switch back to the XML view, you see that the Eclipse resource editor has added the appropriate XML elements to your file, which now should look something like this:

```
<?xml version="1.0" encoding="utf-8"?>
<resources>
    <string name="app_name">ResourceRoundup</string>
    <string
        name="hello">Hello World, ResourceRoundupActivity</string>
    <color name="prettyTextColor">#ff0000</color>
    <dimen name="textPointSize">14pt</dimen>
    <drawable name="redDrawable">#F00</drawable>
</resources>
```

Save the `strings.xml` resource file. The Eclipse plug-in automatically generates the `R.java` file in your project, with the appropriate resource IDs, which enable you to programmatically access your resources after they are compiled into the project. If you navigate to your `R.java` file, which is located under the `/src` directory in your package, it looks something like this:

```
package com.androidbook.resourceroundup;
public final class R {
    public static final class attr {
    }
    public static final class color {
        public static final int prettyTextColor=0x7f050000;
    }
    public static final class dimen {
        public static final int textPointSize=0x7f060000;
    }
    public static final class drawable {
        public static final int icon=0x7f020000;
        public static final int redDrawable=0x7f020001;
    }
    public static final class layout {
        public static final int main=0x7f030000;
    }
    public static final class string {
        public static final int app_name=0x7f040000;
        public static final int hello=0x7f040001;
    }
}
```

Now you are free to use these resources in your code. If you navigate to your
ResourceRoundupActivity.java source file, you can add some lines to retrieve your resources and work with them, like this:

```
import android.graphics.drawable.ColorDrawable;
...
String myString = getResources().getString(R.string.hello);
int myColor =
    getResources().getColor(R.color.prettyTextColor);
float myDimen =
    getResources().getDimension(R.dimen.textPointSize);
ColorDrawable myDraw = (ColorDrawable)getResources().
    getDrawable(R.drawable.redDrawable);
```

Some resource types, such as string arrays, are more easily added to resource files by editing the XML by hand. For example, if we go back to the strings.xml file and choose
the strings.xml tab, we can add a string array to our resource listing by adding the following XML element:

```
<?xml version="1.0" encoding="utf-8"?>
<resources>
    <string name="app_name">Use Some Resources</string>
    <string
        name="hello">Hello World, UseSomeResources</string>
    <color name="prettyTextColor">#ff0000</color>
    <dimen name="textPointSize">14pt</dimen>
    <drawable name="redDrawable">#F00</drawable>
    <string-array name="flavors">
        <item>Vanilla</item>
        <item>Chocolate</item>
        <item>Strawberry</item>
    </string-array>
</resources>
```

Save the strings.xml file, and now this string array named "flavors" is available in your
source file R.java, so you can use it programmatically in resourcesroundup.java like
this:

```
String[] aFlavors =
    getResources().getStringArray(R.array.flavors);
```

You now have a general idea how to add simple resources using the Eclipse plug-in, but
there are quite a few different types of data available to add as resources. It is a common
practice to store different types of resources in different files. For example, you might store
the strings in /res/values/strings.xml but store the prettyTextColor color resource
in /res/values/colors.xml and the textPointSize dimension resource in
/res/values/dimens.xml. Reorganizing where you keep your resources in the resource

directory hierarchy does not change the names of the resources, nor the code used earlier to access the resources programmatically.

Now let's have a look at how to add different types of resources to your project.

Working with Resources

In this section, we look at the specific types of resources available for Android applications, how they are defined in the project files, and how you can access this resource data programmatically.

For each type of resource type, you learn what types of values can be stored and in what format. Some resource types (such as `Strings` and `Colors`) are well supported with the Android Plug-in Resource Editor, whereas others (such as `Animation` sequences) are more easily managed by editing the XML files directly.

Working with `String` Resources

`String` resources are among the simplest resource types available to the developer. `String` resources might show text labels on form views and for help text. The application name is also stored as a `string` resource, by default.

`String` resources are defined in XML under the `/res/values` project directory and compiled into the application package at build time. All strings with apostrophes or single straight quotes need to be escaped or wrapped in double straight quotes. Some examples of well-formatted string values are shown in Table 6.3.

Table 6.3   **String Resource Formatting Examples**

String Resource Value	Displays As
Hello, World	Hello, World
"User's Full Name:"	User's Full Name:
User\'s Full Name:	User's Full Name:
She said, \"Hi.\"	She said, "Hi."
She\'s busy but she did say, \"Hi.\"	She's busy but she did say, "Hi."

You can edit the `strings.xml` file using the Resources tab, or you can edit the XML directly by clicking the file and choosing the `strings.xml` tab. After you save the file, the resources are automatically added to your `R.java` class file.

String values are appropriately tagged with the `<string>` tag and represent a name-value pair. The name attribute is how you refer to the specific string programmatically, so name these resources wisely.

Here's an example of the string resource file `/res/values/strings.xml`:

```
<?xml version="1.0" encoding="utf-8"?>
<resources>
    <string name="app_name">Resource Viewer</string>
    <string name="test_string">Testing 1,2,3</string>
    <string name="test_string2">Testing 4,5,6</string>
</resources>
```

Bold, Italic, and Underlined Strings

You can also add three HTML-style attributes to string resources. These are bold, italic, and underlining. You specify the styling using the <b>, <i>, and <u> tags. For example

```
<string
    name="txt"><b>Bold</b>,<i>Italic</i>,<u>Line</u></string>
```

Using String Resources as Format Strings

You can create format strings, but you need to escape all bold, italic, and underlining tags if you do so. For example, this text shows a score and the "win" or "lose" string:

```
<string
    name="winLose">Score: %1$d of %2$d! You %3$s.</string>
```

If you want to include bold, italic, or underlining in this format string, you need to escape the format tags. For example, if want to italicize the "win" or "lose" string at the end, your resource would look like this:

```
<string name="winLoseStyled">
    Score: %1$d of %2$d! You&lt;i&gt;%3$s&lt;/i&gt;.</string>
```

Using String Resources Programmatically

As shown earlier in this chapter, accessing string resources in code is straightforward. There are two primary ways in which you can access this string resource.

The following code accesses your application's string resource named hello, returning only the string. All HTML-style attributes (bold, italic, and underlining) are stripped from the string.

```
String myStrHello =
    getResources().getString(R.string.hello);
```

You can also access the string and preserve the formatting by using this other method:

```
CharSequence myBoldStr =
    getResources().getText(R.string.boldhello);
```

To load a format string, you need to make sure any format variables are properly escaped. One way you can do this is by using the `TextUtils.htmlEncode()` method:

```
import android.text.TextUtils;
...
String mySimpleWinString;
```

```
mySimpleWinString =
    getResources().getString(R.string.winLose);
String escapedWin = TextUtils.htmlEncode("Won");
String resultText =
    String.format(mySimpleWinString, 5, 5, escapedWin);
```

The resulting text in the `resultText` variable is

```
Score: 5 of 5! You Won.
```

Now if you have styling in this format string like the preceding `winLoseStyled` string resource, you need to take a few more steps to handle the escaped italic tags.

```
import android.text.Html;
import android.text.TextUtils;
...
String myStyledWinString;
myStyledWinString =
    getResources().getString(R.string. winLoseStyled);
String escapedWin = TextUtils.htmlEncode("Won");
String resultText =
    String.format(myStyledWinString, 5, 5, escapedWin);
CharSequence styledResults = Html.fromHtml(resultText);
```

The resulting text in the `styledResults` variable is

```
Score: 5 of 5! You <i>won</i>.
```

This variable, `styledResults`, can then be used in user interface controls such as `TextView` objects, where styled text is displayed correctly.

Tip

There is also a special resource type called `<plurals>`, which can be used to define strings that change based upon a singular or plural form. For example, you could define a plural for the related strings: "You caught a goose!" and "You caught %d geese!". Pluralized strings are loaded using the `getQuantityString()` method of the `Resource` class instead of the `getString()` method. For more information, see the Android SDK documentation regarding the plurals element.

Working with String Arrays

You can specify lists of strings in resource files. This can be a good way to store menu options and drop-down list values. `String` arrays are defined in XML under the `/res/values` project directory and compiled into the application package at build time.

`String` arrays are appropriately tagged with the `<string-array>` tag and a number of `<item>` child tags, one for each string in the array. Here's an example of a simple array resource file `/res/values/arrays.xml`:

```
<?xml version="1.0" encoding="utf-8"?>
<resources>
    <string-array name="flavors">
```

```
        <item>Vanilla Bean</item>
        <item>Chocolate Fudge Brownie</item>
        <item>Strawberry Cheesecake</item>
        <item>Coffee, Coffee, Buzz Buzz Buzz</item>
        <item>Americone Dream</item>
    </string-array>
    <string-array name="soups">
        <item>Vegetable minestrone</item>
        <item>New England clam chowder</item>
        <item>Organic chicken noodle</item>
    </string-array>
</resources>
```

As shown earlier in this chapter, accessing string arrays resources is easy. The following code retrieves a string array named `flavors`:

```
String[] aFlavors =
    getResources().getStringArray(R.array.flavors);
```

Working with `Boolean` Resources

Other primitive types are supported by the Android resource hierarchy as well. Boolean resources can be used to store information about application game preferences and default values. Boolean resources are defined in XML under the `/res/values` project directory and compiled into the application package at build time.

Defining Boolean Resources in XML

Boolean values are appropriately tagged with the `<bool>` tag and represent a name-value pair. The name attribute is how you refer to the specific Boolean value programmatically, so name these resources wisely.

Here's an example of the Boolean resource file `/res/values/bools.xml`:

```
<?xml version="1.0" encoding="utf-8"?>
<resources>
    <bool name="bOnePlusOneEqualsTwo">true</bool>
    <bool name="bAdvancedFeaturesEnabled">false</bool>
</resources>
```

Using Boolean Resources Programmatically

To use a Boolean resource, you must load it using the `Resource` class. The following code accesses your application's Boolean resource named `bAdvancedFeaturesEnabled`.

```
boolean bAdvancedMode =
    getResources().getBoolean(R.bool.bAdvancedFeaturesEnabled);
```

Working with `Integer` Resources

In addition to strings and Boolean values, you can also store integers as resources. Integer resources are defined in XML under the `/res/values` project directory and compiled into the application package at build time.

Defining Integer Resources in XML

Integer values are appropriately tagged with the `<integer>` tag and represent a name-value pair. The name attribute is how you refer to the specific integer programmatically, so name these resources wisely.

Here's an example of the integer resource file `/res/values/nums.xml`:

```xml
<?xml version="1.0" encoding="utf-8"?>
<resources>
    <integer name="numTimesToRepeat">25</integer>
    <integer name="startingAgeOfCharacter">3</integer>
</resources>
```

Using Integer Resources Programmatically

To use the integer resource, you must load it using the `Resource` class. The following code accesses your application's integer resource named `numTimesToRepeat`:

```java
int repTimes = getResources().getInteger(R.integer.numTimesToRepeat);
```

> **Tip**
>
> Much like string arrays, you can create integer arrays as resources using the `<integer-array>` tag with child `<item>` tags, defining one for each item in the array. You can then load the integer array using the `getIntArray()` method of the `Resource` class.

Working with Colors

Android applications can store RGB color values, which can then be applied to other screen elements. You can use these values to set the color of text or other elements, such as the screen background. Color resources are defined in XML under the `/res/values` project directory and compiled into the application package at build time.

RGB color values always start with the hash symbol (#). The alpha value can be given for transparency control. The following color formats are supported:

- #RGB (example, #F00 is 12-bit color, red)
- #ARGB (example, #8F00 is 12-bit color, red with alpha 50%)
- #RRGGBB (example, #FF00FF is 24-bit color, magenta)
- #AARRGGBB (example, #80FF00FF is 24-bit color, magenta with alpha 50%)

Color values are appropriately tagged with the `<color>` tag and represent a name-value pair. Here's an example of a simple color resource file `/res/values/colors.xml`:

```xml
<?xml version="1.0" encoding="utf-8"?>
```

```
<resources>
    <color name="background_color">#006400</color>
    <color name="text_color">#FFE4C4</color>
</resources>
```

The example at the beginning of the chapter accessed a color resource. Color resources are simply integers. The following code retrieves a color resource called prettyTextColor:

```
int myResourceColor =
    getResources().getColor(R.color.prettyTextColor);
```

Working with Dimensions

Many user interface layout controls such as text controls and buttons are drawn to specific dimensions. These dimensions can be stored as resources. Dimension values always end with a unit of measurement tag.

Dimension values are appropriately tagged with the <dimen> tag and represent a name-value pair. Dimension resources are defined in XML under the /res/values project directory and compiled into the application package at build time.

The dimension units supported are shown in Table 6.4.

Table 6.4   **Dimension Unit Measurements Supported**

Unit of Measurement	Description	Resource Tag Required	Example
Pixels	Actual screen pixels	px	20px
Inches	Physical measurement	in	1in
Millimeters	Physical measurement	mm	1mm
Points	Common font measurement unit	pt	14pt
Screen density independent pixels	Pixels relative to 160dpi screen (preferable dimension for screen compatibility)	dp	1dp
Scale independent pixels	Best for scalable font display	sp	14sp

Here's an example of a simple dimension resource file /res/values/dimens.xml:

```
<?xml version="1.0" encoding="utf-8"?>
<resources>
    <dimen name="FourteenPt">14pt</dimen>
    <dimen name="OneInch">1in</dimen>
    <dimen name="TenMillimeters">10mm</dimen>
    <dimen name="TenPixels">10px</dimen>
</resources>
```

Dimension resources are simply floating point values. The following code retrieves a dimension resource called textPointSize:

```
float myDimension =
    getResources().getDimension(R.dimen.textPointSize);
```

Warning

Be cautious when choosing dimension units for your applications. If you are planning to target multiple devices, with different screen sizes and resolutions, then you need to rely heavily on the more scalable dimension units, such as dp and sp, as opposed to pixels, points, inches, and millimeters.

Working with Simple Drawables

You can specify simple colored rectangles by using the drawable resource type, which can then be applied to other screen elements. These drawable types are defined in specific paint colors, much like the Color resources are defined.

Simple paintable drawable resources are defined in XML under the /res/values project directory and compiled into the application package at build time. Paintable drawable resources use the <drawable> tag and represent a name-value pair. Here's an example of a simple drawable resource file /res/values/drawables.xml:

```
<?xml version="1.0" encoding="utf-8"?>
<resources>
    <drawable name="red_rect">#F00</drawable>
</resources>
```

Although it might seem a tad confusing, you can also create XML files that describe other `Drawable` subclasses, such as `ShapeDrawable`. `Drawable` XML definition files are stored in the `/res/drawable` directory within your project along with image files. This is not the same as storing `<drawable>` resources, which are paintable drawables. `PaintableDrawable` resources are stored in the `/res/values` directory, as explained in the previous section.

Here's a simple `ShapeDrawable` described in the file `/res/drawable/red_oval.xml`:

```xml
<?xml version="1.0" encoding="utf-8"?>
<shape
    xmlns:android=
        "http://schemas.android.com/apk/res/android"
    android:shape="oval">
    <solid android:color="#f00"/>
</shape>
```

We talk more about graphics and drawing shapes in Chapter 9, "Drawing and Working with Animation."

Drawable resources defined with `<drawable>` are simply rectangles of a given color, which is represented by the Drawable subclass `ColorDrawable`. The following code retrieves a `ColorDrawable` resource called `redDrawable`:

```java
import android.graphics.drawable.ColorDrawable;
...
ColorDrawable myDraw = (ColorDrawable)getResources().
    getDrawable(R.drawable.redDrawable);
```

Tip

There are many additional drawable resource types that can be specified as XML resources. These special drawables correspond to specific drawable classes such as `ClipDrawable` and `LevelListDrawable`. For information on these specialized drawable types, see the Android SDK documentation.

Working with Images

Applications often include visual elements such as icons and graphics. Android supports several image formats that can be directly included as resources for your application. These image formats are shown in Table 6.5.

Table 6.5   **Image Formats Supported in Android**

Supported Image Format	Description	Required Extension
Portable Network Graphics (PNG)	Preferred Format (Lossless)	.png
Nine-Patch Stretchable Images	Preferred Format (Lossless)	.9.png

Table 6.5   **Continued**

Supported Image Format	Description	Required Extension
Joint Photographic Experts Group (JPEG)	Acceptable Format (Lossy)	.jpg, .jpeg
Graphics Interchange Format (GIF)	Discouraged Format	.gif

These image formats are all well supported by popular graphics editors such as Adobe Photoshop, GIMP, and Microsoft Paint. The Nine-Patch Stretchable Graphics can be created from PNG files using the `draw9patch` tool included with the Android SDK under the `/tools` directory.

> **Warning**
>
> All resources filenames must be lowercase and simple (letters, numbers, and underscores only). This rule applies to all files, including graphics.

Adding image resources to your project is easy. Simply drag the image asset into the `/res/drawable` directory, and it is automatically included in the application package at build time.

Working with Nine-Patch Stretchable Graphics

Phone screens come in various dimensions. It can be handy to use stretchable graphics to allow a single graphic that can scale appropriately for different screen sizes and orientations or different lengths of text. This can save you or your designer a lot of time in creating graphics for many different screen sizes.

Android supports Nine-Patch Stretchable Graphics for this purpose. Nine-Patch graphics are simply PNG graphics that have patches, or areas of the image, defined to scale appropriately, instead of scaling the entire image as one unit. Often the center segment is transparent.

Nine-Patch Stretchable Graphics can be created from PNG files using the `draw9patch` tool included with the `Tools` directory of the Android SDK. We talk more about compatibility and using Nine-Patch graphics in Chapter 25.

Using Image Resources Programmatically

Images resources are simply another kind of `Drawable` called a `BitmapDrawable`. Most of the time, you need only the resource ID of the image to set as an attribute on a user interface control.

For example, if I drop the graphics file `flag.png` into the `/res/drawable` directory and add an `ImageView` control to my main layout, we can set the image to be displayed programmatically in the layout this way:

```
import android.widget.ImageView;
...
```

```
ImageView flagImageView =
    (ImageView)findViewById(R.id.ImageView01);
flagImageView.setImageResource(R.drawable.flag);
```

If you want to access the `BitmapDrawable` object directly, you simply request that resource directly, as follows:

```
import android.graphics.drawable.BitmapDrawable;
...
BitmapDrawable bitmapFlag = (BitmapDrawable)
    getResources().getDrawable(R.drawable.flag);
int iBitmapHeightInPixels =
    bitmapFlag.getIntrinsicHeight();
int iBitmapWidthInPixels = bitmapFlag.getIntrinsicWidth();
```

Finally, if you work with Nine-Patch graphics, the call to `getDrawable()` returns a `NinePatchDrawable` instead of a `BitmapDrawable` object.

```
import android.graphics.drawable.NinePatchDrawable;
...
NinePatchDrawable stretchy = (NinePatchDrawable)
    getResources().getDrawable(R.drawable.pyramid);
int iStretchyHeightInPixels =
    stretchy.getIntrinsicHeight();
int iStretchyWidthInPixels = stretchy.getIntrinsicWidth();
```

Tip

There is also a special resource type called `<selector>`, which can be used to define different colors or drawables to be used depending on a control's state. For example, you could define a color state list for a `Button` control: gray when the button is disabled, green when it is enabled, and yellow when it is being pressed. Similarly, you could provide different drawables based on the state of an `ImageButton` control. For more information, see the Android SDK documentation regarding the color and drawable state list resources.

Working with Animation

Android supports frame-by-frame animation and tweening. Frame-by-frame animation involves the display of a sequence of images in rapid succession. Tweened animation involves applying standard graphical transformations such as rotations and fades upon a single image.

The Android SDK provides some helper utilities for loading and using animation resources. These utilities are found in the `android.view.animation.AnimationUtils` class.

We discuss animation in detail in Chapter 9. For now, let's just look at how you define animation data in terms of resources.

Defining and Using Frame-by-Frame Animation Resources

Frame-by-frame animation is often used when the content changes from frame to frame. This type of animation can be used for complex frame transitions—much like a kid's flip-book.

To define frame-by-frame resources, take the following steps:

1. Save each frame graphic as an individual drawable resource. It may help to name your graphics sequentially, in the order in which they are displayed—for example, `frame1.png`, `frame2.png`, and so on.

2. Define the animation set resource in an XML file within `/res/drawable/` resource directory.

3. Load, start, and stop the animation programmatically.

Here's an example of a simple frame-by-frame animation resource file `/res/drawable/juggle.xml` that defines a simple three-frame animation that takes 1.5 seconds:

```
<?xml version="1.0" encoding="utf-8" ?>
<animation-list
    xmlns:android="http://schemas.android.com/apk/res/android"
    android:oneshot="false">
    <item
        android:drawable="@drawable/splash1"
        android:duration="50" />
    <item
        android:drawable="@drawable/splash2"
        android:duration="50" />
    <item
        android:drawable="@drawable/splash3"
        android:duration="50" />
</animation-list>
```

Frame-by-frame animation set resources defined with `<animation-list>` are represented by the Drawable subclass AnimationDrawable. The following code retrieves an Animation-Drawable resource called `juggle`:

```
import android.graphics.drawable.AnimationDrawable;
...
AnimationDrawable jugglerAnimation = (AnimationDrawable)getResources().
    getDrawable(R.drawable.juggle);
```

After you have a valid AnimationDrawable, you can assign it to a View on the screen and use the Animation methods to start and stop animation.

Defining and Using Tweened Animation Resources

Tweened animation features include scaling, fading, rotation, and translation. These actions can be applied simultaneously or sequentially and might use different interpolators.

Tweened animation sequences are not tied to a specific graphic file, so you can write one sequence and then use it for a variety of different graphics. For example, you can make moon, star, and diamond graphics all pulse using a single scaling sequence, or you can make them spin using a rotate sequence.

Graphic animation sequences can be stored as specially formatted XML files in the /res/anim directory and are compiled into the application binary at build time.

Here's an example of a simple animation resource file /res/anim/spin.xml that defines a simple rotate operation—rotating the target graphic counterclockwise four times in place, taking 10 seconds to complete:

```
<?xml version="1.0" encoding="utf-8" ?>
<set xmlns:android
    ="http://schemas.android.com/apk/res/android"
    android:shareInterpolator="false">
    <set>
        <rotate
            android:fromDegrees="0"
            android:toDegrees="-1440"
            android:pivotX="50%"
            android:pivotY="50%"
            android:duration="10000" />
    </set>
</set>
```

If we go back to the example of a BitmapDrawable earlier, we can now add some animation simply by adding the following code to load the animation resource file spin.xml and set the animation in motion:

```
import android.view.animation.Animation;
import android.view.animation.AnimationUtils;
import android.widget.ImageView;
...
ImageView flagImageView =
    (ImageView)findViewById(R.id.ImageView01);
flagImageView.setImageResource(R.drawable.flag);
...
Animation an =
    AnimationUtils.loadAnimation(this, R.anim.spin);
flagImageView.startAnimation(an);
```

Now you have your graphic spinning. Notice that we loaded the animation using the base class object Animation. You can also extract specific animation types using the subclasses that match: RotateAnimation, ScaleAnimation, TranslateAnimation, and AlphaAnimation.

There are a number of different interpolators you can use with your tweened animation sequences.

Working with Menus

You can also include menu resources in your project files. Like animation resources, menu resources are not tied to a specific control but can be reused in any menu control.

Each menu resource (which is a set of individual menu items) is stored as a specially formatted XML files in the `/res/menu` directory and are compiled into the application package at build time.

Here's an example of a simple menu resource file `/res/menu/speed.xml` that defines a short menu with four items in a specific order:

```
<menu xmlns:android
    ="http://schemas.android.com/apk/res/android">
    <item
        android:id="@+id/start"
        android:title="Start!"
        android:orderInCategory="1"></item>
    <item
        android:id="@+id/stop"
        android:title="Stop!"
        android:orderInCategory="4"></item>
    <item
        android:id="@+id/accel"
        android:title="Vroom! Accelerate!"
        android:orderInCategory="2"></item>
    <item
        android:id="@+id/decel"
        android:title="Decelerate!"
        android:orderInCategory="3"></item>
</menu>
```

You can create menus using the Eclipse plug-in, which can access the various configuration attributes for each menu item. In the previous case, we set the title (label) of each menu item and the order in which the items display. Now, you can use string resources for those titles, instead of typing in the strings. For example:

```
<menu xmlns:android=
    "http://schemas.android.com/apk/res/android">
    <item
        android:id="@+id/start"
        android:title="@string/start"
        android:orderInCategory="1"></item>
    <item
        android:id="@+id/stop"
        android:title="@string/stop"
        android:orderInCategory="2"></item>
</menu>
```

To access the preceding menu resource called `/res/menu/speed.xml`, simply override the method `onCreateOptionsMenu()` in your application:

```
public boolean onCreateOptionsMenu(Menu menu) {
    getMenuInflater().inflate(R.menu.speed, menu);
    return true;
}
```

That's it. Now if you run your application and press the menu button, you see the menu. There are a number of other XML attributes that can be assigned to menu items. For a complete list of these attributes, see the Android SDK reference for menu resources at the website http://d.android.com/guide/topics/resources/menu-resource.html. You learn a lot more about menus and menu event handling in Chapter 7, "Exploring User Interface Screen Elements."

Working with XML Files

You can include arbitrary XML resource files to your project. You should store these XML files in the `/res/xml` directory, and they are compiled into the application package at build time.

The Android SDK has a variety of packages and classes available for XML manipulation. You learn more about XML handling in Chapter 10, "Using Android Data and Storage APIs," Chapter 11, "Sharing Data Between Applications with Content Providers," and Chapter 12, "Using Android Networking APIs." For now, we create an XML resource file and access it through code.

First, put a simple XML file in `/res/xml` directory. In this case, the file `my_pets.xml` with the following contents can be created:

```
<?xml version="1.0" encoding="utf-8"?>
<pets>
    <pet name="Bit" type="Bunny" />
    <pet name="Nibble" type="Bunny" />
    <pet name="Stack" type="Bunny" />
    <pet name="Queue" type="Bunny" />
    <pet name="Heap" type="Bunny" />
    <pet name="Null" type="Bunny" />
    <pet name="Nigiri" type="Fish" />
    <pet name="Sashimi II" type="Fish" />
    <pet name="Kiwi" type="Lovebird" />
</pets>
```

Now you can access this XML file as a resource programmatically in the following manner:

```
XmlResourceParser myPets =
    getResources().getXml(R.xml.my_pets);
```

Finally, to prove this is XML, here's one way you might churn through the XML and extract the information:

```
import org.xmlpull.v1.XmlPullParserException;
import android.content.res.XmlResourceParser;
...
int eventType = -1;
while (eventType != XmlResourceParser.END_DOCUMENT) {
    if(eventType == XmlResourceParser.START_DOCUMENT) {
        Log.d(DEBUG_TAG, "Document Start");
    } else if(eventType == XmlResourceParser.START_TAG) {

        String strName = myPets.getName();
        if(strName.equals("pet")) {
            Log.d(DEBUG_TAG, "Found a PET");
            Log.d(DEBUG_TAG,
                "Name: "+myPets.
                getAttributeValue(null, "name"));
            Log.d(DEBUG_TAG,
                "Species: "+myPets.
                getAttributeValue(null, "type"));
        }
    }
    eventType = myPets.next();
}
Log.d(DEBUG_TAG, "Document End");
```

Working with Raw Files

Your application can also include raw files as part of its resources. For example, your application might use raw files such as audio files, video files, and other file formats not supported by the Android Resource packaging tool `aapt`.

All raw resource files are included in the /res/raw directory and are added to your package without further processing.

Warning

All resources filenames must be lowercase and simple (letters, numbers, and underscores only). This also applies to raw file filenames even though the tools do not process these files other than to include them in your application package.

The resource filename must be unique to the directory and should be descriptive because the filename (without the extension) becomes the name by which the resource is accessed.

You can access raw file resources and any resource from the `/res/drawable` directory (bitmap graphics files, anything not using the `<resource>` XML definition method). Here's one way to open a file called `the_help.txt`:

```
import java.io.InputStream;
...
InputStream iFile =
    getResources().openRawResource(R.raw.the_help);
```

References to Resources

You can reference resources instead of duplicating them. For example, your application might want to reference a single string resource in multiple string arrays.

The most common use of resource references is in layout XML files, where layouts can reference any number of resources to specify attributes for layout colors, dimensions, strings, and graphics. Another common use is within style and theme resources.

Resources are referenced using the following format:

```
]resource_type/variable_name
```

Recall that earlier we had a string-array of soup names. If we want to localize the soup listing, a better way to create the array is to create individual string resources for each soup name and then store the references to those string resources in the string-array (instead of the text).

To do this, we define the string resources in the `/res/strings.xml` file like this:

```
<?xml version="1.0" encoding="utf-8"?>
<resources>
    <string name="app_name">Application Name</string>
    <string name="chicken_soup"
        >Organic Chicken Noodle</string>
    <string name="minestrone_soup"
        >Veggie Minestrone</string>
    <string name="chowder_soup"
        >New England Lobster Chowder</string>
</resources>
```

And then we can define a localizable string-array that references the string resources by name in the `/res/arrays.xml` file like this:

```
<?xml version="1.0" encoding="utf-8"?>
<resources>
    <string-array name="soups">
        <item>@string/minestrone_soup</item>
        <item>@string/chowder_soup</item>
        <item>@string/chicken_soup</item>
    </string-array>
</resources>
```

Tip

Save the `strings.xml` file first so that the string resources (which are picked up by the aapt and included in the `R.java` class) are defined prior to trying to save the `arrays.xml` file, which references those particular string resources. Otherwise, you might get the following error:

```
Error: No resource found that matches the given name.
```

You can also use references to make aliases to other resources. For example, you can alias the system resource for the OK string to an application resource name by including the following in your `strings.xml` resource file:

```
<?xml version="1.0" encoding="utf-8"?>
<resources>
    <string id="app_ok">@android:string/ok</string>
</resources>
```

You learn more about all the different system resources available later in this chapter.

Tip

Much like string and integer arrays, you can create arrays of any type of resources using the `<array>` tag with child `<item>` tags, defining one item for each resource in the array. You can then load the array of miscellaneous resources using the `obtainTypedArray()` method of the `Resource` class. The typed array resource is commonly used for grouping and loading a bunch of `Drawable` resources with a single call. For more information, see the Android SDK documentation on typed array resources.

Working with Layouts

Much as web designers use HTML, user interface designers can use XML to define Android application screen elements and layout. A layout XML resource is where many different resources come together to form the definition of an Android application screen. Layout resource files are included in the `/res/layout/` directory and are compiled into the application package at build time. Layout files might include many user interface controls and define the layout for an entire screen or describe custom controls used in other layouts.

Here's a simple example of a layout file (`/res/layout/main.xml`) that sets the screen's background color and displays some text in the middle of the screen (see Figure 6.3).

The `main.xml` layout file that displays this screen references a number of other resources, including colors, strings, and dimension values, all of which were defined in the `strings.xml`, `colors.xml`, and `dimens.xml` resource files. The color resource for the screen background color and resources for a `TextView` control's color, string, and text size follows:

```
<?xml version="1.0" encoding="utf-8"?>
<LinearLayout xmlns:android=
    "http://schemas.android.com/apk/res/android"
    android:orientation="vertical"
```

```
    android:layout_width="fill_parent"
    android:layout_height="fill_parent"
    android:background="@color/background_color">
    <TextView
        android:id="@+id/TextView01"
        android:layout_width="fill_parent"
        android:layout_height="fill_parent"
        android:text="@string/test_string"
        android:textColor="@color/text_color"
        android:gravity="center"
        android:textSize="@dimen/text_size"></TextView>
</LinearLayout>
```

Figure 6.3   How the **main.xml** layout file
displays in the emulator.

The preceding layout describes all the visual elements on a screen. In this example, a LinearLayout control is used as a container for other user interface controls—here, a single TextView that displays a line of text.

Tip

You can encapsulate common layout definitions in their own XML files and then include those layouts within other layout files using the <include> tag. For example, you can use the following <include> tag to include another layout file called /res/layout/mygreenrect.xml within the main.xml layout definition:

```
<include layout="@layout/mygreenrect"/>
```

Designing Layouts in Eclipse

Layouts can be designed and previewed in Eclipse using the Resource editor functionality provided by the Android plug-in (see Figure 6.4). If you click the project file `/res/layout/main.xml` (provided with any new Android project), you see a Layout tab, which shows you the preview of the layout, and a main.xml tab, which shows you the raw XML of the layout file.

Figure 6.4   Designing a layout file using Eclipse.

As with most user interface designers, the Android plug-in works well for your basic layout needs, enables you to create user interface controls such as `TextView` and `Button` controls easily, and enables setting the controls' properties in the Properties pane.

Tip

Moving the Properties pane to the far right of the workspace in Eclipse makes it easier to browse and set control properties when designing layouts.

Now is a great time to get to know the layout resource designer. Try creating a new Android project called ParisView (available as a sample project). Navigate to the `/res/layout/main.xml` layout file and double-click it to open it in the resource editor. It's quite simple by default, only a black (empty) rectangle and string of text.

Below in the Resource pane of the Eclipse perspective, you notice the Outline tab. This outline is the XML hierarchy of this layout file. By default, you see a `LinearLayout`.

If you expand it, you see it contains one `TextView` control. Click on the `TextView` control. You see that the Properties pane of the Eclipse perspective now has all the properties available for that object. If you scroll down to the property called `text`, you see that it's set to a string resource variable `@string/hello`.

> **Tip**
>
> You can also select specific controls by clicking them in the layout designer preview area. The currently selected control is highlighted in red. We prefer to use the Outline view, so we can be sure we are clicking what we expect.

You can use the layout designer to set and preview layout control properties. For example, you can modify the `TextView` property called `text size` by typing 18pt (a dimension). You see the results of your change to the property immediately in the preview area.

Take a moment to switch to the `main.xml` tab. You notice that the properties you set are now in the XML. If you save and run your project in the emulator now, you see similar results to what you see in the designer preview.

Now go back to the Outline pane. You see a green plus and a red minus button. You can use these buttons to add and remove controls to your layout file. For example, select the `LinearLayout` from the Outline view, and click the green button to add a control within that container object.

Choose the `ImageView` object. Now you have a new control in your layout. You can't actually see it yet because it is not fully defined.

Drag two PNG graphics files (or JPG) into your `/res/drawable` project directory, naming them `flag.png` and `background.png`. Now, browse the properties of your `ImageView` control, and set the `src` property by clicking on the resource browser button labeled [...]. You can browse all the `Drawable` resources in your project and select the flag resource you just added. You can also set this property manually by typing `@drawable/flag`.

Now, you see that the graphic shows up in your preview. While we're at it, select the `LinearLayout` object and set its `background` property to the background `Drawable` you added.

If you save the layout file and run the application in the emulator (see Figure 6.5) or on the phone, you see results much like you did in the resource designer preview pane.

Using Layout Resources Programmatically

Layouts, whether they are `Button` or `ImageView` controls, are all derived from the `View` class. Here's how you would retrieve a `TextView` object named `TextView01`:

```
TextView txt = (TextView)findViewById(R.id.TextView01);
```

You can also access the underlying XML of a layout resource much as you would any XML file. The following code retrieves the `main.xml` layout file for XML parsing:

```
XmlResourceParser myMainXml =
    getResources().getLayout(R.layout.main);
```

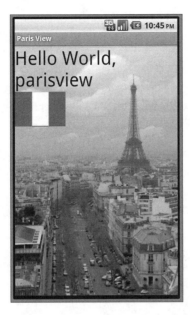

Figure 6.5   A layout with a **LinearLayout**,
TextView, and **ImageView**, shown in the Android
emulator.

Developers can also define custom layouts with unique attributes. We talk much more
about layout files and designing Android user interfaces in Chapter 8, "Designing User Interfaces with Layouts."

> **Warning**
>
> Take care when providing alternative layout resources. Layout resources tend to be compli-
> cated, and the child controls within them are often referred to in code by name. Therefore, if
> you create an alternative layout resource, make sure each important control exists in the lay-
> out and is named the same. For example, if both layouts have a `Button` control, make sure
> its identifier (`android:id`) is the same in both the landscape and portrait mode alternative
> layout resources. You may include different controls in the layouts, but the important ones
> (those referred to and interacted with programmatically) should match in both layouts.

Working with Styles

Android user interface designers can group layout element attributes together in styles.
Layout controls are all derived from the `View` base class, which has many useful attributes.
Individual controls, such as `Checkbox`, `Button`, and `TextView`, have specialized attributes
associated with their behavior.

Styles are tagged with the `<style>` tag and should be stored in the `/res/values/` directory. Style resources are defined in XML and compiled into the application binary at build time.

Tip

Styles cannot be previewed using the Eclipse Resource designer but they are displayed correctly in the emulator and on the device.

Here's an example of a simple style resource file `/res/values/styles.xml` containing two styles: one for mandatory form fields, and one for optional form fields on `TextView` and `EditText` objects:

```
<?xml version="1.0" encoding="utf-8"?>
<resources>
    <style name="mandatory_text_field_style">
        <item name="android:textColor">#000000</item>
        <item name="android:textSize">14pt</item>
        <item name="android:textStyle">bold</item>
    </style>
    <style name="optional_text_field_style">
        <item name="android:textColor">#0F0F0F</item>
        <item name="android:textSize">12pt</item>
        <item name="android:textStyle">italic</item>
    </style>
</resources>
```

Many useful style attributes are colors and dimensions. It would be more appropriate to use references to resources. Here's the `styles.xml` file again; this time, the color and text size fields are available in the other resource files `colors.xml` and `dimens.xml`:

```
<?xml version="1.0" encoding="utf-8"?>
<resources>
    <style name="mandatory_text_field_style">
        <item name="android:textColor"
            >@color/mand_text_color</item>
        <item name="android:textSize"
            >@dimen/important_text</item>
        <item name="android:textStyle">bold</item>
    </style>
    <style name="optional_text_field_style">
        <item name="android:textColor"
            >@color/opt_text_color</item>
        <item name="android:textSize"
            >@dimen/unimportant_text</item>
        <item name="android:textStyle">italic</item>
    </style>
</resources>
```

Now, if you can create a new layout with a couple of TextView and EditText text controls, you can set each control's style attribute by referencing it as such:

```
style="@style/name_of_style"
```

Here we have a form layout called /res/layout/form.xml that does that:

```
<?xml version="1.0" encoding="utf-8"?>
<LinearLayout
    xmlns:android=
        "http://schemas.android.com/apk/res/android"
    android:orientation="vertical"
    android:layout_width="fill_parent"
    android:layout_height="fill_parent"
    android:background="@color/background_color">
    <TextView
        android:id="@+id/TextView01"
        style="@style/mandatory_text_field_style"
        android:layout_height="wrap_content"
        android:text="@string/mand_label"
        android:layout_width="wrap_content" />
    <EditText
        android:id="@+id/EditText01"
        style="@style/mandatory_text_field_style"
        android:layout_height="wrap_content"
        android:text="@string/mand_default"
        android:layout_width="fill_parent"
        android:singleLine="true" />
    <TextView
        android:id="@+id/TextView02"
        style="@style/optional_text_field_style"
        android:layout_width="wrap_content"
        android:layout_height="wrap_content"
        android:text="@string/opt_label" />
    <EditText
        android:id="@+id/EditText02"
        style="@style/optional_text_field_style"
        android:layout_height="wrap_content"
        android:text="@string/opt_default"
        android:singleLine="true"
        android:layout_width="fill_parent" />
    <TextView
        android:id="@+id/TextView03"
        style="@style/optional_text_field_style"
        android:layout_width="wrap_content"
        android:layout_height="wrap_content"
        android:text="@string/opt_label" />
    <EditText
```

```
        android:id="@+id/EditText03"
        style="@style/optional_text_field_style"
        android:layout_height="wrap_content"
        android:text="@string/opt_default"
        android:singleLine="true"
        android:layout_width="fill_parent" />
</LinearLayout>
```

The resulting layout has three fields, each made up of one `TextView` for the label and one `EditText` where the user can input text. The mandatory style is applied to the mandatory label and text entry. The other two fields use the optional style. The resulting layout would look something like Figure 6.6.

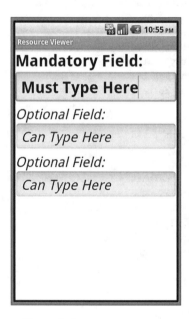

Figure 6.6   A layout using two styles, one for
mandatory fields and another for optional fields.

We talk more about styles in Chapter 7.

Using Style Resources Programmatically

Styles are applied to specific layout controls such as `TextView` and `Button` objects. Usually, you want to supply the style resource `id` when you call the control's constructor. For example, the style named `myAppIsStyling` would be referred to as `R.style.myAppIsStyling`.

Working with Themes

Themes are much like styles, but instead of being applied to one layout element at a time, they are applied to all elements of a given activity (which, generally speaking, means one screen).

Themes are defined in exactly the same way as styles. Themes use the `<style>` tag and should be stored in the `/res/values` directory. The only difference is that instead of applying that named style to a layout element, you define it as the `theme` attribute of an activity in the `AndroidManifest.xml file`.

We talk more about themes in Chapter 7.

Referencing System Resources

You can access system resources in addition to your own resources. The `android` package contains all kinds of resources, which you can browse by looking in the `android.R` subclasses. Here you find system resources for

- Animation sequences for fading in and out
- Arrays of email/phone types (home, work, and such)
- Standard system colors
- Dimensions for application thumbnails and icons
- Many commonly used `drawable` and layout types
- Error strings and standard button text
- System styles and themes

You can reference system resources the same way you use your own; set the package name to `android`. For example, to set the background to the system color for darker gray, you set the appropriate background color attribute to `@android:color/darker_gray`.

You can access system resources much like you access your application's resources. Instead of using your application resources, use the Android package's resources under the `android.R` class.

If we go back to our animation example, we could have used a system animation instead of defining our own. Here is the same animation example again, except it uses a system animation to fade in:

```
import android.view.animation.Animation;
import android.view.animation.AnimationUtils;
import android.widget.ImageView;
...
ImageView flagImageView =
    (ImageView)findViewById(R.id.ImageView01);
flagImageView.setImageResource(R.drawable.flag);
...
Animation an = AnimationUtils.
    loadAnimation(this, android.R.anim.fade_in);
flagImageView.startAnimation(an);
```

Note

The default Android resources are provided as part of the Android SDK under the `/platforms/<platform_version>/data/res` directory on newer SDK installations, and in the `/tools/lib/res/default` directory for older installations. Here you can examine all the drawable resources, full XML layout files, and everything else found in the `android.R.*` package.

Summary

Android applications rely on various types of resources, including strings, string arrays, colors, dimensions, drawable objects, graphics, animation sequences, layouts, styles, and themes. Resources can also be raw files. Many of these resources are defined with XML and organized into specially named project directories. Both default and alternative resources can be defined using this resource hierarchy.

Resources are compiled and accessed using the `R.java` class file, which is automatically generated when the application resources are compiled. Developers access application and system resources programmatically using this special class.

References and More Information

Android Dev Guide: Application Resources:
   http://d.android.com/guide/topics/resources/index.html
Android Dev Guide: Resource Types:
   http://d.android.com/guide/topics/resources/available-resources.html

7

Exploring User Interface Screen Elements

Most Android applications inevitably need some form of user interface. In this chapter, we discuss the user interface elements available within the Android Software Development Kit (SDK). Some of these elements display information to the user, whereas others gather information from the user.

You learn how to use a variety of different components and controls to build a screen and how your application can listen for various actions performed by the user. Finally, you learn how to style controls and apply themes to entire screens.

Introducing Android Views and Layouts

Before we go any further, we need to define a few terms. This gives you a better understanding of certain capabilities provided by the Android SDK before they are fully introduced. First, let's talk about the `View` and what it is to the Android SDK.

Introducing the Android View

The Android SDK has a Java packaged named `android.view`. This package contains a number of interfaces and classes related to drawing on the screen. However, when we refer to the `View` object, we actually refer to only one of the classes within this package: the `android.view.View` class.

The `View` class is the basic user interface building block within Android. It represents a rectangular portion of the screen. The `View` class serves as the base class for nearly all the user interface controls and layouts within the Android SDK.

Introducing the Android Control

The Android SDK contains a Java package named `android.widget`. When we refer to controls, we are typically referring to a class within this package. The Android SDK includes classes to draw most common objects, including `ImageView`, `FrameLayout`,

`EditText`, and `Button` classes. As mentioned previously, all controls are typically derived from the `View` class.

This chapter is primarily about controls that display and collect data from the user. We cover many of these basic controls in detail.

Note

Do not confuse the user interface controls in the `android.widget` package with App Widgets. An `AppWidget` (`android.appwidget`) is an application extension, often displayed on the Android Home screen. We discuss App Widgets in more depth in Chapter 22, "Extending Android Application Reach."

Introducing the Android Layout

One special type of control found within the `android.widget` package is called a layout. A layout control is still a `View` object, but it doesn't actually draw anything specific on the screen. Instead, it is a parent container for organizing other controls (children). Layout controls determine how and where on the screen child controls are drawn. Each type of layout control draws its children using particular rules. For instance, the `LinearLayout` control draws its child controls in a single horizontal row or a single vertical column. Similarly, a `TableLayout` control displays each child control in tabular format (in cells within specific rows and columns).

In Chapter 8, "Designing User Interfaces with Layouts," we organize various controls within layouts and other containers. These special `View` controls, which are derived from the `android.view.ViewGroup` class, are useful only after you understand the various display controls these containers can hold. By necessity, we use some of the layout `View` objects within this chapter to illustrate how to use the controls previously mentioned. However, we don't go into the details of the various layout types available as part of the Android SDK until the next chapter.

Note

Many of the code examples provided in this chapter are taken from the ViewSamples application. This source code for the ViewSamples application is provided for download on the book website.

Displaying Text to Users with `TextView`

One of the most basic user interface elements, or controls, in the Android SDK is the `TextView` control. You use it, quite simply, to draw text on the screen. You primarily use it to display fixed text strings or labels.

Frequently, the `TextView` control is a child control within other screen elements and controls. As with most of the user interface elements, it is derived from `View` and is within the `android.widget` package. Because it is a `View`, all the standard attributes such as width, height, padding, and visibility can be applied to the object. However, as a text-displaying control, you can apply many other `TextView`-specific attributes to control behavior and how the text is viewed in a variety of situations.

First, though, let's see how to put some quick text up on the screen. `<TextView>` is the XML layout file tag used to display text on the screen. You can set the `android:text` property of the `TextView` to be either a raw text string in the layout file or a reference to a string resource.

Here are examples of both methods you can use to set the `android:text` attribute of a `TextView`. The first method sets the text attribute to a raw string; the second method uses a string resource called `sample_text`, which must be defined in the `strings.xml` resource file.

```
<TextView
    android:id="@+id/TextView01"
    android:layout_width="wrap_content"
    android:layout_height="wrap_content"
    android:text="Some sample text here" />
<TextView
    android:id="@+id/TextView02"
    android:layout_width="wrap_content"
    android:layout_height="wrap_content"
    android:text="@string/sample_text" />
```

To display this `TextView` on the screen, all your `Activity` needs to do is call the `setContentView()` method with the layout resource identifier in which you defined the preceding XML shown. You can change the text displayed programmatically by calling the `setText()` method on the `TextView` object. Retrieving the text is done with the `getText()` method.

Now let's talk about some of the more common attributes of `TextView` objects.

Configuring Layout and Sizing

The `TextView` control has some special attributes that dictate how the text is drawn and flows. You can, for instance, set the `TextView` to be a single line high and a fixed width. If, however, you put a long string of text that can't fit, the text truncates abruptly. Luckily, there are some attributes that can handle this problem.

> **Tip**
>
> When looking through the attributes available to `TextView` objects, you should be aware that the `TextView` class contains all the functionality needed by editable controls. This means that many of the attributes apply only to *input* fields, which are used primarily by the subclass `EditText` object. For example, the `autoText` attribute, which helps the user by fixing common spelling mistakes, is most appropriately set on editable text fields (`EditText`). There is no need to use this attribute normally when you are simply displaying text.

The width of a `TextView` can be controlled in terms of the `ems` measurement rather than in pixels. An `em` is a term used in typography that is defined in terms of the point size of a particular font. (For example, the measure of an `em` in a 12-point font is 12 points.) This measurement provides better control over how much text is viewed, regardless of the font size. Through the `ems` attribute, you can set the width of the `TextView`. Additionally, you can use the `maxEms` and `minEms` attributes to set the maximum width and minimum width, respectively, of the `TextView` in terms of `ems`.

The height of a `TextView` can be set in terms of lines of text rather than pixels. Again, this is useful for controlling how much text can be viewed regardless of the font size. The `lines` attribute sets the number of lines that the `TextView` can display. You can also use `maxLines` and `minLines` to control the maximum height and minimum height, respectively, that the `Textview` displays.

Here is an example that combines these two types of sizing attributes. This `TextView` is two lines of text high and 12 `ems` of text wide. The layout width and height are specified to the size of the `TextView` and are required attributes in the XML schema:

```
<TextView
    android:id="@+id/TextView04"
    android:layout_width="wrap_content"
    android:layout_height="wrap_content"
    android:lines="2"
    android:ems="12"
    android:text="@string/autolink_test" />
```

Instead of having the text only truncate at the end, as happens in the preceding example, we can enable the `ellipsize` attribute to replace the last couple characters with an ellipsis (...) so the user knows that not all text is displayed.

Creating Contextual Links in Text

If your text contains references to email addresses, web pages, phone numbers, or even street addresses, you might want to consider using the attribute `autoLink` (see Figure 7.1). The `autoLink` attribute has four values that you can use in combination with each other. When enabled, these `autoLink` attribute values create standard web-style links to the application that can act on that data type. For instance, setting the attribute to `web` automatically finds and links any URLs to web pages.

Your text can contain the following values for the `autoLink` attribute:

- **none**: Disables all linking.
- **web**: Enables linking of URLs to web pages.
- **email**: Enables linking of email addresses to the mail client with the recipient filled.
- **phone**: Enables linking of phone numbers to the dialer application with the phone number filled out, ready to be dialed.
- **map**: Enables linking of street addresses to the map application to show the location.
- **all**: Enables all types of linking.

Turning on the `autoLink` feature relies on the detection of the various types within the Android SDK. In some cases, the linking might not be correct or might be misleading.

Figure 7.1   Three TextViews: Simple, AutoLink All
(not clickable), and AutoLink All (clickable).

Here is an example that links email and web pages, which, in our opinion, are the most reliable and predictable:

```
<TextView
    android:id="@+id/TextView02"
    android:layout_width="wrap_content"
    android:layout_height="wrap_content"
    android:text="@string/autolink_test"
    android:autoLink="web|email" />
```

There are two helper values for this attribute, as well. You can set it to `none` to make sure no type of data is linked. You can also set it to `all` to have all known types linked. Figure 7.2 illustrates what happens when you click on these links. The default for a `TextView` is not to link any types. If you want the user to see the various data types highlighted but you don't want the user to click on them, you can set the `linksClickable` attribute to `false`.

Retrieving Data from Users

The Android SDK provides a number of controls for retrieving data from users. One of the most common types of data that applications often need to collect from users is text. Two frequently used controls to handle this type of job are `EditText` controls and `Spinner` controls.

Figure 7.2   Clickable AutoLinks: URL launches browser, phone number launches dialer, and street address launches Google Maps.

Retrieving Text Input Using `EditText` Controls

The Android SDK provides a convenient control called `EditText` to handle text input from a user. The `EditText` class is derived from `TextView`. In fact, most of its functionality is contained within `TextView` but enabled when created as an `EditText`. The `EditText` object has a number of useful features enabled by default, many of which are shown in Figure 7.3.

First, though, let's see how to define an `EditText` control in an XML layout file:

```
<EditText
    android:id="@+id/EditText01"
    android:layout_height="wrap_content"
    android:hint="type here"
    android:lines="4"
    android:layout_width="fill_parent" />
```

This layout code shows a basic `EditText` element. There are a couple of interesting things to note. First, the `hint` attribute puts some text in the edit box that goes away when the user starts entering text. Essentially, this gives a hint to the user as to what should go there. Next is the `lines` attribute, which defines how many lines tall the input box is. If this is not set, the entry field grows as the user enters text. However, setting a size allows the user to scroll within a fixed sized to edit the text. This also applies to the width of the entry.

By default, the user can perform a long press to bring up a context menu. This provides to the user some basic copy, cut, and paste operations as well as the ability to change the input method and add a word to the user's dictionary of frequently used words (shown in Figure 7.4). You do not need to provide any additional code for this useful behavior to benefit your users. You can also highlight a portion of the text from code, too. A call to `setSelection()` does this, and a call to `selectAll()` highlights the entire text entry field.

Figure 7.3   Various styles of **EditText** controls
and **Spinner** and **Button** controls.

The `EditText` object is essentially an editable `TextView`. This means that you can read text from it in the same way as you did with `TextView`: by using the `getText()` method. You can also set initial text to draw in the text entry area using the `setText()` method. This is useful when a user edits a form that already has data. Finally, you can set the `editable` attribute to `false`, so the user cannot edit the text in the field but can still copy text out of it using a long press.

Helping the User with Auto Completion

In addition to providing a basic text editor with the `EditText` control, the Android SDK also provides a way to help the user with entering commonly used data into forms. This functionality is provided through the auto-complete feature.

There are two forms of auto-complete. One is the more standard style of filling in the entire text entry based on what the user types. If the user begins typing a string that matches a word in a developer-provided list, the user can choose to complete the word with just a tap. This is done through the `AutoCompleteTextView` control (see Figure 7.5, left). The second method allows the user to enter a list of items, each of which has auto-complete functionality (see Figure 7.5, right). These items must be separated in some way by providing a `Tokenizer` to the `MultiAutoCompleteTextView` object that handles this method. A common `Tokenizer` implementation is provided for comma-separated lists and is used by specifying the `MultiAutoCompleteTextView.CommaTokenizer` object. This can be helpful for lists of specifying common tags and the like.

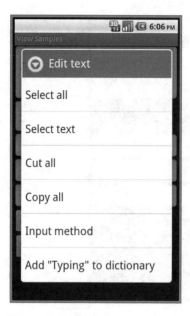

Figure 7.4   A long press on **EditText** controls typically launches a Context menu for Select, Cut, and Paste.

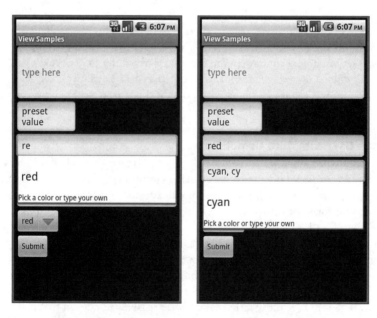

Figure 7.5   Using **AutoCompleteTextView** (left) and **MultiAutoCompleteTextView** (right).

Both of the auto-complete text editors use an adapter to get the list of text that they use to provide completions to the user. This example shows how to provide an `AutoCompleteTextView` for the user that can help them type some of the basic colors from an array in the code:

```
final String[] COLORS = {
    "red", "green", "orange", "blue", "purple",
    "black", "yellow", "cyan", "magenta" };
ArrayAdapter<String> adapter =
    new ArrayAdapter<String>(this,
        android.R.layout.simple_dropdown_item_1line,
        COLORS);
AutoCompleteTextView text = (AutoCompleteTextView)
    findViewById(R.id.AutoCompleteTextView01);
text.setAdapter(adapter);
```

In this example, when the user starts typing in the field, if he starts with one of the letters in the COLORS array, a drop-down list shows all the available completions. Note that this does not limit what the user can enter. The user is still free to enter any text (such as puce). The adapter controls the look of the drop-down list. In this case, we use a built-in layout made for such things. Here is the layout resource definition for this `AutoCompleteTextView` control:

```
<AutoCompleteTextView
    android:id="@+id/AutoCompleteTextView01"
    android:layout_width="fill_parent"
    android:layout_height="wrap_content"
    android:completionHint="Pick a color or type your own"
    android:completionThreshold="1" />
```

There are a couple more things to notice here. First, you can choose when the completion drop-down list shows by filling in a value for the `completionThreshold` attribute. In this case, we set it to a single character, so it displays immediately if there is a match. The default value is two characters of typing before it displays auto-completion options. Second, you can set some text in the `completionHint` attribute. This displays at the bottom of the drop-down list to help users. Finally, the drop-down list for completions is sized to the `TextView`. This means that it should be wide enough to show the completions and the text for the `completionHint` attribute.

The `MultiAutoCompleteTextView` is essentially the same as the regular auto-complete, except that you must assign a `Tokenizer` to it so that the control knows where each auto-completion should begin. The following is an example that uses the same adapter as the previous example but includes a `Tokenizer` for a list of user color responses, each separated by a comma:

```
MultiAutoCompleteTextView mtext =
    (MultiAutoCompleteTextView) findViewById(R.id.MultiAutoCompleteTextView01);
mtext.setAdapter(adapter);
mtext.setTokenizer(new MultiAutoCompleteTextView.CommaTokenizer());
```

As you can see, the only change is setting the `Tokenizer`. Here we use the built-in comma `Tokenizer` provided by the Android SDK. In this case, whenever a user chooses a color from the list, the name of the color is completed, and a comma is automatically added so that the user can immediately start typing in the next color. As before, this does not limit what the user can enter. If the user enters "maroon" and places a comma after it, the auto-completion starts again as the user types another color, regardless of the fact that it didn't help the user type in the color maroon. You can create your own `Tokenizer` by implementing the `MultiAutoCompleteTextView.Tokenizer` interface. You can do this if you'd prefer entries separated by a semicolon or some other more complex separators.

Constraining User Input with Input Filters

There are often times when you don't want the user to type just anything. Validating input after the user has entered something is one way to do this. However, a better way to avoid wasting the user's time is to filter the input. The `EditText` control provides a way to set an `InputFilter` that does only this.

The Android SDK provides some `InputFilter` objects for use. There are `InputFilter` objects that enforce such rules as allowing only uppercase text and limiting the length of the text entered. You can create custom filters by implementing the `InputFilter` interface, which contains the single method called `filter()`. Here is an example of an `EditText` control with two built-in filters that might be appropriate for a two-letter state abbreviation:

```
final EditText text_filtered =
    (EditText) findViewById(R.id.input_filtered);
text_filtered.setFilters(new InputFilter[] {
    new InputFilter.AllCaps(),
    new InputFilter.LengthFilter(2)
});
```

The `setFilters()` method call takes an array of `InputFilter` objects. This is useful for combining multiple filters, as shown. In this case, we convert all input to uppercase. Additionally, we set the maximum length to two characters long. The `EditText` control looks the same as any other, but if you try to type lowercase, the text is converted to uppercase, and the string is limited to two characters. This does not mean that all possible inputs are valid, but it does help users to not concern themselves with making the input too long or bother with the case of the input. This also helps your application by guaranteeing that any text from this input is a length of two. It does not constrain the input to only letters, though. Input filters can also be defined in XML.

Giving Users Input Choices Using `Spinner` Controls

Sometimes you want to limit the choices available for users to type. For instance, if users are going to enter the name of a state, you might as well limit them to only the valid states because this is a known set. Although you could do this by letting them type something and then blocking invalid entries, you can also provide similar functionality with a `Spinner` control. As with the auto-complete method, the possible choices for a spinner can come from an `Adapter`. You can also set the available choices in the layout definition by using the entries attribute with an array resource (specifically a string-array that is referenced as something such as `@array/state-list`). The `Spinner` control isn't actually an `EditText`, although it is frequently used in a similar fashion. Here is an example of the XML layout definition for a `Spinner` control for choosing a color:

```
<Spinner
    android:id="@+id/Spinner01"
    android:layout_width="wrap_content"
    android:layout_height="wrap_content"
    android:entries="@array/colors"
    android:prompt="@string/spin_prompt" />
```

This places a `Spinner` control on the screen (see Figure 7.6). When the user selects it, a pop-up shows the prompt text followed by a list of the possible choices. This list allows only a single item to be selected at a time, and when one is selected, the pop-up goes away.

There are a couple of things to notice here. First, the `entries` attribute is set to the values that shows by assigning it to an array resource, referred to here as `@array/colors`.

Figure 7.6   Filtering choices with a **spinner** control.

Note

See Chapter 6, "Managing Application Resources," for information on how to create an array resource.

Second, the `prompt` attribute is defined to a string resource. Unlike some other string attributes, this one is required to be a string resource. The prompt displays when the pop-up comes up and can be used to tell the user what kinds of values that can be selected from.

Because the `Spinner` control is not a `TextView`, but a list of `TextView` objects, you can't directly request the selected text from it. Instead, you have to retrieve the selected `View` and extract the text directly:

```
final Spinner spin = (Spinner) findViewById(R.id.Spinner01);
TextView text_sel = (TextView)spin. getSelectedView();
String selected_text = text_sel.getText();
```

As it turns out, you can request the currently selected `View` object, which happens to be a `TextView` in this case. This enables us to retrieve the text and use it directly. Alternatively, we could have called the `getSelectedItem()` or `getSelectedItemId()` methods to deal with other forms of selection.

Using Buttons, Check Boxes, and Radio Groups

Another common user interface element is the button. In this section, you learn about different kinds of buttons provided by the Android SDK. These include the basic `Button`, `ToggleButton`, `CheckBox`, and `RadioButton`. You can find examples of each button type in Figure 7.7.

A basic `Button` is often used to perform some sort of action, such as submitting a form or confirming a selection. A basic `Button` control can contain a text or image label.

A `CheckBox` is a button with two states—checked or unchecked. You often use `CheckBox` controls to turn a feature on or off or to pick multiple items from a list.

A `ToggleButton` is similar to a `CheckBox`, but you use it to visually show the state. The default behavior of a toggle is like that of a power on/off button.

A `RadioButton` provides selection of an item. Grouping `RadioButton` controls together in a container called a `RadioGroup` enables the developer to enforce that only one `RadioButton` is selected at a time.

Using Basic Buttons

The `android.widget.Button` class provides a basic button implementation in the Android SDK. Within the XML layout resources, buttons are specified using the `Button` element. The primary attribute for a basic button is the text field. This is the label that appears on the middle of the button's face. You often use basic `Button` controls for buttons with text such as "Ok," "Cancel," or "Submit."

Figure 7.7   Various types of button controls.

Tip

You can find many common application string values in the Android system resource strings, exposed in `android.R.string`. There are strings for common button text such as "yes," "no," "ok," "cancel," and "copy." For more information on system resources, see Chapter 6.

The following XML layout resource file shows a typical `Button` control definition:

```
<Button
    android:id="@+id/basic_button"
    android:layout_width="wrap_content"
    android:layout_height="wrap_content"
    android:text="Basic Button" />
```

A button won't do anything, other than animate, without some code to handle the click event. Here is an example of some code that handles a click for a basic button and displays a `Toast` message on the screen:

```
setContentView(R.layout.buttons);
final Button basic_button = (Button) findViewById(R.id.basic_button);
basic_button.setOnClickListener(new View.OnClickListener() {
    public void onClick(View v) {
```

```
        Toast.makeText(ButtonsActivity.this,
            "Button clicked", Toast.LENGTH_SHORT).show();
    }
});
```

> **Tip**
>
> A `Toast` (`android.widget.Toast`) is a simple dialog-like message that displays for a second or so and then disappears. `Toast` messages are useful for providing the user with non-essential confirmation messages; they are also quite handy for debugging.

To handle the click event for when a button is pressed, we first get a reference to the `Button` by its resource identifier. Next, the `setOnClickListener()` method is called. It requires a valid instance of the class `View.OnClickListener`. A simple way to provide this is to define the instance right in the method call. This requires implementing the `onClick()` method. Within the `onClick()` method, you are free to carry out whatever actions you need. Here, we simply display a message to the users telling them that the button was, in fact, clicked.

A button with its primary label as an image is an `ImageButton`. An `ImageButton` is, for most purposes, almost exactly like a basic button. Click actions are handled in the same way. The primary difference is that you can set its `src` attribute to be an image. Here is an example of an `ImageButton` definition in an XML layout resource file:

```
<ImageButton
    android:layout_width="wrap_content"
    android:layout_height="wrap_content"
    android:id="@+id/image_button"
    android:src="@drawable/droid" />
```

In this case, a small `drawable` resource is referenced. Refer to Figure 7.7 to see what this "Android" button looks like. (It's to the right of the basic button.)

Using Check Boxes and Toggle Buttons

The check box button is often used in lists of items where the user can select multiple items. The Android check box contains a text attribute that appears to the side of the check box. This is used in a similar way to the label of a basic button. In fact, it's basically a `TextView` next to the button.

Here's an XML layout resource definition for a `CheckBox` control:

```
<CheckBox
    android:id="@+id/checkbox"
    android:layout_width="wrap_content"
    android:layout_height="wrap_content"
    android:text="Check me?" />
```

You can see how this `CheckBox` is displayed in Figure 7.7 (center).

The following example shows how to check for the state of the button programmatically and change the text label to reflect the change:

```
final CheckBox check_button = (CheckBox) findViewById(R.id.checkbox);
check_button.setOnClickListener(new View.OnClickListener() {
    public void onClick (View v) {
        TextView tv = (TextView)findViewById(R.id.checkbox);
            tv.setText(check_button.isChecked() ?
                "This option is checked" :
                "This option is not checked");
    }
});
```

This is similar to the basic button. A check box automatically shows the check as enabled or disabled. This enables us to deal with behavior in our application rather than worrying about how the button should behave. The layout shows that the text starts out one way but, after the user presses the button, the text changes to one of two different things depending on the checked state. As the code shows, the `CheckBox` is also a `TextView`.

A `Toggle Button` is similar to a check box in behavior but is usually used to show or alter the on or off state of something. Like the `CheckBox`, it has a state (checked or not). Also like the check box, the act of changing what displays on the button is handled for us. Unlike the `CheckBox`, it does not show text next to it. Instead, it has two text fields. The first attribute is `textOn`, which is the text that displays on the button when its checked state is on. The second attribute is `textOff`, which is the text that displays on the button when its checked state is off. The default text for these is "ON" and "OFF," respectively.

The following layout code shows a definition for a toggle button that shows "Enabled" or "Disabled" based on the state of the button:

```
<ToggleButton
    android:id="@+id/toggle_button"
    android:layout_width="wrap_content"
    android:layout_height="wrap_content"
    android:text="Toggle"
    android:textOff="Disabled"
    android:textOn="Enabled" />
```

This type of button does not actually display the value for the `text` attribute, even though it's a valid attribute to set. Here, the only purpose it serves is to demonstrate that it doesn't display. You can see what this `ToggleButton` looks like in Figure 7.7 (center).

Using `RadioGroups` and `RadioButtons`

You often use radio buttons when a user should be allowed to only select one item from a small group of items. For instance, a question asking for gender can give three options: male, female, and unspecified. Only one of these options should be checked at a time. The `RadioButton` objects are similar to `CheckBox` objects. They have a text label next to them, set via the `text` attribute, and they have a state (checked or unchecked). However, you can group `RadioButton` objects inside a `RadioGroup` that handles enforcing their combined states so that only one `RadioButton` can be checked at a time. If the user selects a `RadioButton` that is already checked, it does not become unchecked. However, you can provide the user with an action to clear the state of the entire `RadioGroup` so that none of the buttons are checked.

Here we have an XML layout resource with a `RadioGroup` containing four `RadioButton` objects (shown in Figure 7.7, toward the bottom of the screen). The `RadioButton` objects have text labels, "Option 1," and so on. The XML layout resource definition is shown here:

```
<RadioGroup
    android:id="@+id/RadioGroup01"
    android:layout_width="wrap_content"
    android:layout_height="wrap_content">
    <RadioButton
        android:id="@+id/RadioButton01"
        android:layout_width="wrap_content"
        android:layout_height="wrap_content"
        android:text="Option 1"></RadioButton>
    <RadioButton
        android:id="@+id/RadioButton02"
        android:layout_width="wrap_content"
        android:layout_height="wrap_content"
        android:text="Option 2"></RadioButton>
    <RadioButton
        android:id="@+id/RadioButton03"
        android:layout_width="wrap_content"
        android:layout_height="wrap_content"
        android:text="Option 3"></RadioButton>
    <RadioButton
        android:id="@+id/RadioButton04"
        android:layout_width="wrap_content"
        android:layout_height="wrap_content"
        android:text="Option 4"></RadioButton>
</RadioGroup>
```

You handle actions on these `RadioButton` objects through the `RadioGroup` object. The following example shows registering for clicks on the `RadioButton` objects within the `RadioGroup`:

```
final RadioGroup group = (RadioGroup)findViewById(R.id.RadioGroup01);
final TextView tv = (TextView)
    findViewById(R.id.TextView01);

group.setOnCheckedChangeListener(new
    RadioGroup.OnCheckedChangeListener() {
        public void onCheckedChanged(
```

```
        RadioGroup group, int checkedId) {
        if (checkedId != -1) {
            RadioButton rb = (RadioButton)
                findViewById(checkedId);
            if (rb != null) {
                tv.setText("You chose: " + rb.getText());
            }
        } else {
            tv.setText("Choose 1");
        }
    }
});
```

As this layout example demonstrates, there is nothing special that you need to do to make the `RadioGroup` and internal `RadioButton` objects work properly. The preceding code illustrates how to register to receive a notification whenever the `RadioButton` selection changes.

The code demonstrates that the notification contains the resource identifier for the specific `RadioButton` that the user chose, as assigned in the layout file. To do something interesting with this, you need to provide a mapping between this resource identifier (or the text label) to the corresponding functionality in your code. In the example, we query for the button that was selected, get its text, and assign its text to another `TextView` control that we have on the screen.

As mentioned, the entire `RadioGroup` can be cleared so that none of the `RadioButton` objects are selected. The following example demonstrates how to do this in response to a button click outside of the `RadioGroup`:

```
final Button clear_choice = (Button) findViewById(R.id.Button01);
clear_choice.setOnClickListener(new View.OnClickListener() {
    public void onClick(View v) {
        RadioGroup group = (RadioGroup)
            findViewById(R.id.RadioGroup01);
        if (group != null) {
            group.clearCheck();
        }
    }
}
```

The action of calling the `clearCheck()` method triggers a call to the `onCheckedChangedListener()` callback method. This is why we have to make sure that the resource identifier we received is valid. Right after a call to the `clearCheck()` method, it is not a valid identifier but instead is set to the value –1 to indicate that no `RadioButton` is currently checked.

Getting Dates and Times from Users

The Android SDK provides a couple controls for getting date and time input from the user. The first is the `DatePicker` control (Figure 7.8, top). It can be used to get a month, day, and year from the user.

Figure 7.8   Date and time controls.

The basic XML layout resource definition for a `DatePicker` follows:

```
<DatePicker
    android:id="@+id/DatePicker01"
    android:layout_width="wrap_content"
    android:layout_height="wrap_content" />
```

As you can see from this example, there aren't any attributes specific to the `DatePicker` control. As with many of the other controls, your code can register to receive a method call when the date changes. You do this by implementing the `onDateChanged()` method. However, this isn't done the usual way.

```
final DatePicker date = (DatePicker)findViewById(R.id.DatePicker01);
date.init(date.getYear(), date.getMonth(), date.getDayOfMonth(),
    new DatePicker.OnDateChangedListener() {
        public void onDateChanged(DatePicker view, int year,
            int monthOfYear, int dayOfMonth) {
                Date dt = new Date(year-1900,
```

```
        monthOfYear, dayOfMonth, time.getCurrentHour(),
        time.getCurrentMinute());
    text.setText(dt.toString());
    }
});
```

The preceding code sets the `DatePicker.OnDateChangedListener` by a call to the `DatePicker.init()` method. A `DatePicker` control is initialized with the current date. A `TextView` is set with the date value that the user entered into the `DatePicker` control. The value of 1900 is subtracted from the year parameter to make it compatible with the `java.util.Date` class.

A `TimePicker` control (also shown in Figure 7.8, bottom) is similar to the `DatePicker` control. It also doesn't have any unique attributes. However, to register for a method call when the values change, you call the more traditional method of `TimePicker.setOnTimeChangedListener()`.

```
time.setOnTimeChangedListener(new TimePicker.OnTimeChangedListener() {
    public void onTimeChanged(TimePicker view,
        int hourOfDay, int minute) {
            Date dt = new Date(date.getYear()-1900, date.getMonth(),
                date.getDayOfMonth(), hourOfDay, minute);
            text.setText(dt.toString());
    }
});
```

As in the previous example, this code also sets a `TextView` to a string displaying the time value that the user entered. When you use the `DatePicker` control and the `TimePicker` control together, the user can set a full date and time.

Using Indicators to Display Data to Users

The Android SDK provides a number of controls that can be used to visually show some form of information to the user. These indicator controls include progress bars, clocks, and other similar controls.

Indicating Progress with `ProgressBar`

Applications commonly perform actions that can take a while. A good practice during this time is to show the user some sort of progress indicator that informs the user that the application is off "doing something." Applications can also show how far a user is through some operation, such as a playing a song or watching a video. The Android SDK provides several types of progress bars.

The standard progress bar is a circular indicator that only animates. It does not show how complete an action is. It can, however, show that something is taking place. This is useful when an action is indeterminate in length. There are three sizes of this type of progress indicator (see Figure 7.9).

Figure 7.9   Various types of progress and rating
indicators.

The second type is a horizontal progress bar that shows the completeness of an action.
(For example, you can see how much of a file is downloading.) This horizontal progress
bar can also have a secondary progress indicator on it. This can be used, for instance, to
show the completion of a downloading media file while that file plays.

This is an XML layout resource definition for a basic indeterminate progress bar:

```
<ProgressBar
    android:id="@+id/progress_bar"
    android:layout_width="wrap_content"
    android:layout_height="wrap_content" />
```

The default style is for a medium-size circular progress indicator; not a "bar" at all. The
other two styles for indeterminate progress bar are `progressBarStyleLarge` and
`progressBarStyleSmall`. This style animates automatically. The next sample shows the
layout definition for a horizontal progress indicator:

```
<ProgressBar
    android:id="@+id/progress_bar"
    style="?android:attr/progressBarStyleHorizontal"
    android:layout_width="fill_parent"
    android:layout_height="wrap_content"
    android:max="100" />
```

We have also set the attribute for `max` in this sample to 100. This can help mimic a percentage progress bar. That is, setting the progress to 75 shows the indicator at 75 percent complete.

We can set the indicator progress status programmatically as follows:

```
mProgress = (ProgressBar) findViewById(R.id.progress_bar);
mProgress.setProgress(75);
```

You can also put these progress bars in your application's title bar (as shown in Figure 7.9). This can save screen real estate. This can also make it easy to turn on and off an indeterminate progress indicator without changing the look of the screen. Indeterminate progress indicators are commonly used to display progress on pages where items need to be loaded before the page can finish drawing. This is often employed on web browser screens. The following code demonstrates how to place this type of indeterminate progress indicator on your `Activity` screen:

```
requestWindowFeature(Window.FEATURE_INDETERMINATE_PROGRESS);
requestWindowFeature(Window.FEATURE_PROGRESS);
setContentView(R.layout.indicators);
setProgressBarIndeterminateVisibility(true);
setProgressBarVisibility(true);
setProgress(5000);
```

To use the indeterminate indicator on your `Activity` objects title bar, you need to request the feature `Window.FEATURE_INDETERMINATE_PROGRESS`, as previously shown. This shows a small circular indicator in the right side of the title bar. For a horizontal progress bar style that shows behind the title, you need to enable the `Window.FEATURE_PROGRESS`. These features must be enabled before your application calls the `setContentView()` method, as shown in the preceding example.

You need to know about a couple of important default behaviors. First, the indicators are visible by default. Calling the visibility methods shown in the preceding example can set their visibility on or off. Second, the horizontal progress bar defaults to a maximum progress value of 10,000. In the preceding example, we set it to 5,000, which is equivalent to 50 percent. When the value reaches the maximum value, the indicators fade away so that they aren't visible. This happens for both indicators.

Adjusting Progress with SeekBar

You have seen how to display progress to the user. What if, however, you want to give the user some ability to move the indicator, for example, to set the current cursor position in a playing media file or to tweak a volume setting? You accomplish this by using the `SeekBar` control provided by the Android SDK. It's like the regular horizontal progress bar, but includes a thumb, or selector, that can be dragged by the user. A default thumb selector is provided, but you can use any `drawable` item as a thumb. In Figure 7.9 (center), we replaced the default thumb with a little Android graphic.

Here we have an example of an XML layout resource definition for a simple `SeekBar`:

```
<SeekBar
    android:id="@+id/seekbar1"
    android:layout_height="wrap_content"
    android:layout_width="240px"
    android:max="500" />
```

With this sample `SeekBar`, the user can drag the thumb to any value between 0 and 500. Although this is shown visually, it might be useful to show the user what exact value the user is selecting. To do this, you can provide an implementation of the `onProgressChanged()` method, as shown here:

```
SeekBar seek = (SeekBar) findViewById(R.id.seekbar1);
seek.setOnSeekBarChangeListener(
    new SeekBar.OnSeekBarChangeListener() {
        public void onProgressChanged(
            SeekBar seekBar, int progress,boolean fromTouch) {
            ((TextView)findViewById(R.id.seek_text))
                .setText("Value: "+progress);
            seekBar.setSecondaryProgress(
                (progress+seekBar.getMax())/2);
        }
});
```

There are two interesting things to notice in this example. The first is that the `fromTouch` parameter tells the code if the change came from the user input or if, instead, it came from a programmatic change as demonstrated with the regular `ProgressBar` controls. The second interesting thing is that the `SeekBar` still enables you to set a secondary progress value. In this example, we set the secondary indicator to be halfway between the user's selected value and the maximum value of the progress bar. You might use this feature to show the progress of a video and the buffer stream.

Displaying Rating Data with `RatingBar`

Although the `SeekBar` is useful for allowing a user to set a value, such as the volume, the `RatingBar` has a more specific purpose: showing ratings or getting a rating from a user. By default, this progress bar uses the star paradigm with five stars by default. A user can drag across this horizontal to set a rating. A program can set the value, as well. However, the secondary indicator cannot be used because it is used internally by this particular control.

Here's an example of an XML layout resource definition for a `RatingBar` with four stars:

```
<RatingBar
    android:id="@+id/ratebar1"
    android:layout_width="wrap_content"
    android:layout_height="wrap_content"
    android:numStars="4"
    android:stepSize="0.25" />
```

This layout definition for a `RatingBar` demonstrates setting both the number of stars and the increment between each rating value. Here, users can choose any rating value between 0 and 4.0, but only in increments of 0.25, the `stepSize` value. For instance, users can set a value of 2.25. This is visualized to the users, by default, with the stars partially filled. Figure 7.9 (center) illustrates how the `RatingBar` behaves.

Although the value is indicated to the user visually, you might still want to show a numeric representation of this value to the user. You can do this by implementing the `onRatingChanged()` method of the `RatingBar.OnRatingBarChangeListener` class.

```
RatingBar rate = (RatingBar) findViewById(R.id.ratebar1);
rate.setOnRatingBarChangeListener(new
    RatingBar.OnRatingBarChangeListener() {
        public void onRatingChanged(RatingBar ratingBar,
            float rating, boolean fromTouch) {
                ((TextView)findViewById(R.id.rating_text))
                    .setText("Rating: "+ rating);
    }
});
```

The preceding example shows how to register the listener. When the user selects a rating using the control, a `TextView` is set to the numeric rating the user entered. One interesting thing to note is that, unlike the `SeekBar`, the implementation of the `onRatingChange()` method is called after the change is complete, usually when the user lifts a finger. That is, while the user is dragging across the stars to make a rating, this method isn't called. It is called when the user stops pressing the control.

Showing Time Passage with the Chronometer

Sometimes you want to show time passing instead of incremental progress. In this case, you can use the `Chronometer` control as a timer (see Figure 7.9, bottom). This might be useful if it's the user who is taking time doing some task or in a game where some action needs to be timed. The `Chronometer` control can be formatted with text, as shown in this XML layout resource definition:

```
<Chronometer
    android:id="@+id/Chronometer01"
    android:layout_width="wrap_content"
    android:layout_height="wrap_content"
    android:format="Timer: %s" />
```

You can use the `Chronometer` object's `format` attribute to put text around the time that displays. A `Chronometer` won't show the passage of time until its `start()` method is called. To stop it, simply call its `stop()` method. Finally, you can change the time from which the timer is counting. That is, you can set it to count from a particular time in the past instead of from the time it's started. You call the `setBase()` method to do this.

Tip

The `Chronometer` uses the `elapsedRealtime()` method's time base. Passing `android.os.SystemClock.elapsedRealtime()` in to the `setBase()` method starts the `Chronometer` control at 0.

In this next example code, the timer is retrieved from the `View` by its resource identifier. We then check its base value and set it to 0. Finally, we start the timer counting up from there.

```
final Chronometer timer =
    (Chronometer)findViewById(R.id.Chronometer01);
long base =  timer.getBase();
Log.d(ViewsMenu.debugTag, "base = "+ base);
timer.setBase(0);
timer.start();
```

Tip

You can listen for changes to the `Chronometer` by implementing the `Chronometer.OnChronometerTickListener` interface.

Displaying the Time

Displaying the time in an application is often not necessary because Android devices have a status bar to display the current time. However, there are two clock controls available to display this information: the `DigitalClock` and `AnalogClock` controls.

Using the `DigitalClock`

The `DigitalClock` control (Figure 7.9, bottom) is a compact text display of the current time in standard numeric format based on the users' settings. It is a `TextView`, so anything you can do with a `TextView` you can do with this control, except change its text. You can change the color and style of the text, for example.

By default, the `DigitalClock` control shows the seconds and automatically updates as each second ticks by. Here is an example of an XML layout resource definition for a `DigitalClock` control:

```
<DigitalClock
    android:id="@+id/DigitalClock01"
    android:layout_width="wrap_content"
    android:layout_height="wrap_content" />
```

Using the `AnalogClock`

The `AnalogClock` control (Figure 7.9, bottom) is a dial-based clock with a basic clock face with two hands, one for the minute and one for the hour. It updates automatically as each minute passes. The image of the clock scales appropriately with the size of its `View`.

Here is an example of an XML layout resource definition for an `AnalogClock` control:

```
<AnalogClock
    android:id="@+id/AnalogClock01"
    android:layout_width="wrap_content"
    android:layout_height="wrap_content" />
```

The `AnalogClock` control's clock face is simple. However you can set its minute and hour hands. You can also set the clock face to specific `drawable` resources, if you want to jazz it up. Neither of these clock controls accepts a different time or a static time to display. They can show only the current time in the current time zone of the device, so they are not particularly useful.

Providing Users with Options and Context Menus

You need to be aware of two special application menus for use within your Android applications: the options menu and the context menu.

Enabling the Options Menu

The Android SDK provides a method for users to bring up a menu by pressing the menu key from within the application (see Figure 7.10). You can use options menus within your application to bring up help, to navigate, to provide additional controls, or to configure options. The `OptionsMenu` control can contain icons, submenus, and keyboard shortcuts.

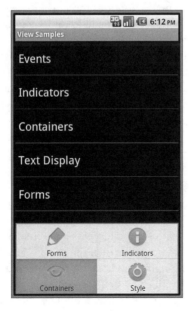

Figure 7.10　An options menu.

For an options menu to show when a user presses the Menu button on their device, you need to override the implementation of onCreateOptionsMenu() in your Activity. Here is a sample implementation that gives the user three menu items to choose from:

```
public boolean onCreateOptionsMenu( android.view.Menu menu) {
    super.onCreateOptionsMenu(menu);
    menu.add("Forms")
        .setIcon(android.R.drawable.ic_menu_edit)
        .setIntent(new Intent(this, FormsActivity.class));
    menu.add("Indicators")
        .setIntent(new Intent(this, IndicatorsActivity.class))
        .setIcon(android.R.drawable.ic_menu_info_details);
    menu.add("Containers")
        .setIcon(android.R.drawable.ic_menu_view)
        .setIntent(new Intent(this, ContainersActivity.class));
    return true;
}
```

For each of the items that are added, we also set a built-in icon resource and assign an Intent to each item. We give the item title with a regular text string, for clarity. You can use a resource identifier, as well. For this example, there is no other handling or code needed. When one of these menu items is selected, the Activity described by the Intent starts.

This type of options menu can be useful for navigating to important parts of an application, such as the help page, from anywhere within your application. Another great use for an options menu is to allow configuration options for a given screen. The user can configure these options in the form of checkable menu items. The initial menu that appears when the user presses the menu button does not support checkable menu items. Instead, you must place these menu items on a SubMenu control, which is a type of Menu that can be configured within a menu. SubMenu objects support checkable items but do not support icons or other SubMenu items. Building on the preceding example, the following is code for programmatically adding a SubMenu control to the previous Menu:

```
SubMenu style_choice = menu.addSubMenu("Style")
    .setIcon(android.R.drawable.ic_menu_preferences);
style_choice.add(style_group, light_id, 1, "Light")
    .setChecked(isLight);
style_choice.add(style_group, dark_id, 2, "Dark")
    .setChecked(!isLight);
style_choice.setGroupCheckable(style_group, true, true);
```

This code would be inserted before the return statement in the implementation of the onCreateOptionsMenu() method. It adds a single menu item with an icon to the previous menu, called "Style." When the "Style" option is clicked, a pop-up menu with the two items of the SubMenu control is displayed. These items are grouped together and the checkable icon, by default, looks like the radio button icon. The checked state is assigned during creation time.

To handle the event when a menu option item is selected, we also implement the `onOptionsItemSelected()` method, as shown here:

```
public boolean onOptionsItemSelected(MenuItem item) {
    if (item.getItemId() == light_id) {
        item.setChecked(true);
        isLight = true;
        return true;
    } else if (item.getItemId() == dark_id) {
        item.setChecked(true);
        isLight = false;
        return true;
    }

    return super.onOptionsItemSelected(item);
}
```

This method must call the super class's `onOptionsItemSelected()` method for basic behavior to work. The actual `MenuItem` object is passed in, and we can use that to retrieve the identifier that we previously assigned to see which one was selected and perform an appropriate action. Here, we switch the values and return. By default, a `Menu` control goes away when any item is selected, including checkable items. This means it's useful for quick settings but not as useful for extensive settings where the user might want to change more than one item at a time.

As you add more menu items to your options menu, you might notice that a "More" item automatically appears. This happens whenever more than six items are visible. If the user selects this, the full menu appears. The full, expanded menu doesn't show menu icons and although checkable items are possible, you should not use them here. Additionally, the full title of an item doesn't display. The initial menu, also known as the icon menu, shows only a portion of the title for each item. You can assign each item a `condensedTitle` attribute, which shows instead of a truncated version of the regular title. For example, instead of the title Instant Message, you can set the `condensedTitle` attribute to "IM."

Enabling the `ContextMenu`

The `ContextMenu` is a subtype of `Menu` that you can configure to display when a long press is performed on a `View`. As the name implies, the `ContextMenu` provides for contextual menus to display to the user for performing additional actions on selected items.

`ContextMenu` objects are slightly more complex than `OptionsMenu` objects. You need to implement the `onCreateContextMenu()` method of your `Activity` for one to display. However, before that is called, you must call the `registerForContextMenu()` method and pass in the `View` for which you want to have a context menu. This means each `View` on your screen can have a different context menu, which is appropriate as the menus are designed to be highly contextual.

Here we have an example of a `Chronometer` timer, which responds to a long click with a context menu:

```
registerForContextMenu(timer);
```

After the call to the `registerForContextMenu()` method has been executed, the user can then long click on the `View` to open the context menu. Each time this happens, your `Activity` gets a call to the `onCreateContextMenu()` method, and your code creates the menu each time the user performs the long click.

The following is an example of a context menu for the `Chronometer` control, as previously used:

```
public void onCreateContextMenu(
    ContextMenu menu, View v, ContextMenuInfo menuInfo) {
    super.onCreateContextMenu(menu, v, menuInfo);

    if (v.getId() == R.id.Chronometer01) {
        getMenuInflater().inflate(R.menu.timer_context, menu);
        menu.setHeaderIcon(android.R.drawable.ic_media_play)
            .setHeaderTitle("Timer controls");
    }
}
```

Recall that any `View` control can register to trigger a call to the `onCreateContextMenu()` method when the user performs a long press. That means we have to check which `View` control it was for which the user tried to get a context menu. Next, we inflate the appropriate menu from a menu resource that we defined with XML. Because we can't define header information in the menu resource file, we set a stock Android SDK resource to it and add a title. Here is the menu resource that is inflated:

```
<menu
    xmlns:android="http://schemas.android.com/apk/res/android">
    <item
        android:id="@+id/start_timer"
        android:title="Start" />
    <item
        android:id="@+id/stop_timer"
        android:title="Stop" />
    <item
        android:id="@+id/reset_timer"
        android:title="Reset" />
</menu>
```

This defines three menu items. If this weren't a context menu, we could have assigned icons. However, context menus do not support icons, submenus, or shortcuts. For more information on setting `Menu` resources in XML, see Chapter 6.

Now we need to handle the `ContextMenu` clicks by implementing the `onContextItemSelected()` method in our `Activity`. Here's an example:

```
public boolean onContextItemSelected(MenuItem item) {
    super.onContextItemSelected(item);
    boolean result = false;
    Chronometer timer = (Chronometer)findViewById(R.id.Chronometer01);
    switch (item.getItemId()){
        case R.id.stop_timer:
            timer.stop();
            result = true;
            break;
        case R.id.start_timer:
            timer.start();
            result = true;
            break;
        case R.id.reset_timer:
            timer.setBase(SystemClock.elapsedRealtime());
            result = true;
            break;
    }
    return result;
}
```

Because we have only one context menu in this example, we find the `Chronometer` view for use in this method. This method is called regardless of which context menu the selected item is on, though, so you should take care to have unique resource identifiers or keep track of which menu is shown. This can be accomplished because the context menu is created each time it's shown.

Handling User Events

You've seen how to do basic event handling in some of the previous control examples. For instance, you know how to handle when a user clicks on a button. There are a number of other events generated by various actions the user might take. This section briefly introduces you to some of these events. First, though, we need to talk about the input states within Android.

Listening for Touch Mode Changes

The Android screen can be in one of two states. The state determines how the focus on `View` controls is handled. When touch mode is on, typically only objects such as `EditText` get focus when selected. Other objects, because they can be selected directly by the user tapping on the screen, won't take focus but instead trigger their action, if any. When not in touch mode, however, the user can change focus between even more object types. These include buttons and other views that normally need only a click to trigger their action. In this case, the user uses the arrow keys, trackball, or wheel to navigate between items and select them with the Enter or select keys.

Knowing what mode the screen is in is useful if you want to handle certain events. If, for instance, your application relies on the focus or lack of focus on a particular control, your application might need to know if the phone is in touch mode because the focus behavior is likely different.

Your application can register to find out when the touch mode changes by using the `addOnTouchModeChangeListener()` method within the `android.view.ViewTreeObserver` class. Your application needs to implement the `ViewTreeObserver.OnTouchModeChangeListener` class to listen for these events. Here is a sample implementation:

```
View all = findViewById(R.id.events_screen);
ViewTreeObserver vto = all.getViewTreeObserver();
vto.addOnTouchModeChangeListener(
    new ViewTreeObserver.OnTouchModeChangeListener() {
        public void onTouchModeChanged(
            boolean isInTouchMode) {
            events.setText("Touch mode: " + isInTouchMode);
        }
});
```

In this example, the top-level `View` in the layout is retrieved. A `ViewTreeObserver` listens to a `View` and all its child `View` objects. Using the top-level `View` of the layout means the `ViewTreeObserver` listens to events within the entire layout. An implementation of the `onTouchModeChanged()` method provides the `ViewTreeObserver` with a method to call when the touch mode changes. It merely passes in which mode the `View` is now in.

In this example, the mode is written to a `TextView` named `events`. We use this same `TextView` in further event handling examples to visually show on the screen which events our application has been told about. The `ViewTreeObserver` can enable applications to listen to a few other events on an entire screen.

By running this sample code, we can demonstrate the touch mode changing to true immediately when the user taps on the touch screen. Conversely, when the user chooses to use any other input method, the application reports that touch mode is false immediately after the input event, such as a key being pressed or the trackball or scroll wheel moving.

Listening for Events on the Entire Screen

You saw in the last section how your application can watch for changes to the touch mode state for the screen using the `ViewTreeObserver` class. The `ViewTreeObserver` also provides three other events that can be watched for on a full screen or an entire `View` and all of its children. These are

- **PreDraw**: Get notified before the `View` and its children are drawn
- **GlobalLayout**: Get notified when the layout of the `View` and its children might change, including visibility changes

- **GlobalFocusChange**: Get notified when the focus within the `View` and its children changes

Your application might want to perform some actions before the screen is drawn. You can do this by calling the method `addOnPreDrawListener()` with an implementation of the `ViewTreeObserver.OnPreDrawListener` class interface.

Similarly, your application can find out when the layout or visibility of a `View` has changed. This might be useful if your application is dynamically changing the display contents of a view and you want to check to see if a `View` still fits on the screen. Your application needs to provide an implementation of the `ViewTreeObserver.OnGlobalLayoutListener` class interface to the `addGlobalLayoutListener()` method of the `ViewTreeObserver` object.

Finally, your application can register to find out when the focus changes between a `View` control and any of its child `View` controls. Your application might want to do this to monitor how a user moves about on the screen. When in touch mode, though, there might be fewer focus changes than when the touch mode is not set. In this case, your application needs to provide an implementation of the `ViewTreeObserver.OnGlobalFocusChangeListener` class interface to the `addGlobalFocusChangeListener()` method. Here is a sample implementation of this:

```
vto.addOnGlobalFocusChangeListener(new
    ViewTreeObserver.OnGlobalFocusChangeListener() {
        public void onGlobalFocusChanged(
            View oldFocus, View newFocus) {
                if (oldFocus != null && newFocus != null) {
                    events.setText("Focus \nfrom: " +
                        oldFocus.toString() + " \nto: " +
                        newFocus.toString());
                }
            }
    });
```

This example uses the same `ViewTreeObserver`, `vto`, and `TextView` events as in the previous example. This shows that both the currently focused `View` and the previously focused `View` pass to the listener. From here, your application can perform needed actions.

If your application merely wants to check values after the user has modified a particular `View`, though, you might need to only register to listen for focus changes of that particular `View`. This is discussed later in this chapter.

Listening for Long Clicks

In a previous section discussing the `ContextMenu` control, you learned that you can add a context menu to a `View` that is activated when the user performs a long click on that view. A long click is typically when a user presses on the touch screen and holds his finger there until an action is performed. However, a long press event can also be triggered if the user navigates there with a non-touch method, such as via a keyboard or trackball, and then holds the Enter or Select key for a while. This action is also often called a press-and-hold action.

Although the context menu is a great typical use case for the long-click event, you can listen for the long-click event and perform any action you want. However, this is the same event that triggers the context menu. If you've already added a context menu to a `View`, you might not want to listen for the long-click event as other actions or side effects might confuse the user or even prevent the context menu from showing. As always with good user interface design, try to be consistent for usability sake.

Tip

Usually a long click is an alternative action to a standard click. If a left-click on a computer is the standard click, a long click can be compared to a right-click.

Your application can listen to the long-click event on any `View`. The following example demonstrates how to listen for a long-click event on a `Button` control:

```
Button long_press = (Button)findViewById(R.id.long_press);
long_press.setOnLongClickListener(new View.OnLongClickListener() {
    public boolean onLongClick(View v) {
        events.setText("Long click: " + v.toString());
        return true;
    }
});
```

First, the `Button` object is requested by providing its identifier. Then the `setOnLongClickListener()` method is called with our implementation of the `View.OnLongClickListener` class interface. The `View` that the user long-clicked on is passed in to the `onLongClick()` event handler. Here again we use the same `TextView` as before to display text saying that a long click occurred.

Listening for Focus Changes

We already discussed focus changes for listening for them on an entire screen. All `View` objects, though, can also trigger a call to listeners when their particular focus state changes. You do this by providing an implementation of the `View.OnFocusChangeListener` class to the `setOnFocusChangeListener()` method. The following is an example of how to listen for focus change events with an `EditText` control:

```
TextView focus = (TextView)findViewById(R.id.text_focus_change);
focus.setOnFocusChangeListener(new View.OnFocusChangeListener() {
    public void onFocusChange(View v, boolean hasFocus) {
        if (hasFocus) {
            if (mSaveText != null) {
                ((TextView)v).setText(mSaveText);
            }
        } else {
            mSaveText = ((TextView)v).getText().toString();
```

```
        ((TextView)v).setText("");
    }
}
```

In this implementation, we also use a private member variable of type `String` for `mSaveText`. After retrieving the `EditText` view as a `TextView`, we do one of two things. If the user moves focus away from the control, we store off the text in `mSaveText` and set the text to empty. If the user changes focus to the control, though, we restore this text. This has the amusing effect of hiding the text the user entered when the control is not active. This can be useful on a form on which a user needs to make multiple, lengthy text entries but you want to provide the user with an easy way to see which one they edit. It is also useful for demonstrating a purpose for the focus listeners on a text entry. Other uses might include validating text a user enters after a user navigates away or prefilling the text entry the first time they navigate to it with something else entered.

Working with Dialogs

An `Activity` can use dialogs to organize information and react to user-driven events. For example, an activity might display a dialog informing the user of a problem or ask the user to confirm an action such as deleting a data record. Using dialogs for simple tasks helps keep the number of application activities manageable.

Tip

Many of the code examples provided in this section are taken from the SimpleDialogs application. This source code for the SimpleDialogs application is provided for download on the book website.

Exploring the Different Types of Dialogs

There are a number of different dialog types available within the Android SDK. Each has a special function that most users should be somewhat familiar with. The dialog types available include

- **Dialog**: The basic class for all `Dialog` types. A basic `Dialog` is shown in the top left of Figure 7.11.
- **AlertDialog**: A `Dialog` with one, two, or three `Button` controls. An `AlertDialog` is shown in the top center of Figure 7.11.
- **CharacterPickerDialog**: A `Dialog` for choosing an accented character associated with a base character. A `CharacterPickerDialog` is shown in the top right of Figure 7.11.
- **DatePickerDialog**: A `Dialog` with a `DatePicker` control. A `DatePickerDialog` is shown in the bottom left of Figure 7.11.
- **ProgressDialog**: A `Dialog` with a determinate or indeterminate `ProgressBar` control. An indeterminate `ProgressDialog` is shown in the bottom center of Figure 7.11.

- **TimePickerDialog**: A `Dialog` with a `TimePicker` control. A `TimePickerDialog` is shown in the bottom right of Figure 7.11.

Figure 7.11   The different dialog types available in Android.

If none of the existing `Dialog` types is adequate, you can also create custom `Dialog` windows, with your specific layout requirements.

Tracing the Lifecycle of a Dialog

Each `Dialog` must be defined within the `Activity` in which it is used. A `Dialog` may be launched once, or used repeatedly. Understanding how an `Activity` manages the `Dialog` lifecycle is important to implementing a `Dialog` correctly. Let's look at the key methods that an `Activity` must use to manage a `Dialog`:

- The `showDialog()` method is used to display a `Dialog`.
- The `dismissDialog()` method is used to stop showing a `Dialog`. The `Dialog` is kept around in the `Activity`'s `Dialog` pool. If the `Dialog` is shown again using `showDialog()`, the cached version is displayed once more.
- The `removeDialog()` method is used to remove a `Dialog` from the `Activity` objects `Dialog` pool. The `Dialog` is no longer kept around for future use. If you call `showDialog()` again, the `Dialog` must be re-created.

Adding the `Dialog` to an `Activity` involves several steps:

1. Define a unique identifier for the `Dialog` within the `Activity`.

2. Implement the `onCreateDialog()` method of the `Activity` to return a `Dialog` of the appropriate type, when supplied the unique identifier.

3. Implement the `onPrepareDialog()` method of the `Activity` to initialize the `Dialog` as appropriate.

4. Launch the `Dialog` using the `showDialog()` method with the unique identifier.

Defining a Dialog

A `Dialog` used by an `Activity` must be defined in advance. Each `Dialog` has a special identifier (an integer). When the `showDialog()` method is called, you pass in this identifier. At this point, the `onCreateDialog()` method is called and must return a `Dialog` of the appropriate type.

It is up to the developer to override the `onCreateDialog()` method of the `Activity` and return the appropriate `Dialog` for a given identifier. If an `Activity` has multiple `Dialog` windows, the `onCreateDialog()` method generally contains a switch statement to return the appropriate `Dialog` based on the incoming parameter—the `Dialog` identifier.

Initializing a Dialog

Because a `Dialog` is often kept around by the `Activity` in its `Dialog` pool, it might be important to re-initialize a `Dialog` each time it is shown, instead of just when it is created the first time. For this purpose, you can override the `onPrepareDialog()` method of the `Activity`.

Although the `onCreateDialog()` method may only be called once for initial `Dialog` creation, the `onPrepareDialog()` method is called each time the `showDialog()` method is called, giving the `Activity` a chance to modify the `Dialog` before it is shown to the user.

Launching a Dialog

You can display any `Dialog` defined within an `Activity` by calling its `showDialog()` method and passing it a valid `Dialog` identifier—one that will be recognized by the `onCreateDialog()` method.

Dismissing a Dialog

Most types of dialogs have automatic dismissal circumstances. However, if you want to force a `Dialog` to be dismissed, simply call the `dismissDialog()` method and pass in the `Dialog` identifier.

Removing a Dialog from Use

Dismissing a `Dialog` does not destroy it. If the `Dialog` is shown again, its cached contents are redisplayed. If you want to force an `Activity` to remove a `Dialog` from its pool and not use it again, you can call the `removeDialog()` method, passing in the valid `Dialog` identifier.

Working with Custom Dialogs

When the dialog types do not suit your purpose exactly, you can create a custom `Dialog`. One easy way to create a custom `Dialog` is to begin with an `AlertDialog` and use an `AlertDialog.Builder` class to override its default layout. In order to create a custom `Dialog` this way, the following steps must be performed:

1. Design a custom layout resource to display in the `AlertDialog`.

2. Define the custom `Dialog` identifier in the `Activity`.

3. Update the `Activity`'s `onCreateDialog()` method to build and return the appropriate custom `AlertDialog`. You should use a `LayoutInflater` to inflate the custom layout resource for the `Dialog`.

4. Launch the `Dialog` using the `showDialog()` method.

Working with Styles

A style is a group of common `View` attribute values. You can apply the style to individual `View` controls. Styles can include such settings as the font to draw with or the color of text. The specific attributes depend on the `View` drawn. In essence, though, each style attribute can change the look and feel of the particular object drawn.

In the previous examples of this chapter, you have seen how XML layout resource files can contain many references to attributes that control the look of `TextView` objects. You can use a style to define your application's standard `TextView` attributes once and then reference to the style either in an XML layout file or programmatically from within Java. In Chapter 6, we see how you can use one style to indicate mandatory form fields and another to indicate optional fields. Styles are typically defined within the resource file `res/values/styles.xml`. The XML file consists of a `resources` tag with any number of `style` tags, which contain an `item` tag for each attribute and its value that is applied with the style.

The following is an example with two different styles:

```
<?xml version="1.0" encoding="utf-8"?>
<resources>
    <style name="padded_small">
        <item name="android:padding">2px</item>
        <item name="android:textSize">8px</item>
    </style>
    <style name="padded_large">
        <item name="android:padding">4px</item>
        <item name="android:textSize">16px</item>
    </style>
</resources>
```

When applied, this style sets the padding to two pixels and the `textSize` to eight pixels. The following is an example of how it is applied to a `TextView` from within a layout resource file:

```
<TextView
    style="@style/padded_small"
    android:layout_width="fill_parent"
    android:layout_height="wrap_content"
    android:text="Small Padded" />
```

Styles support inheritance; therefore, styles can also reference another style as a parent. This way, they pick up the attributes of the parent style. The following is an example of how you might use this:

```
<style name="red_padded">
    <item name="android:textColor">#F00</item>
    <item name="android:padding">3px</item>
</style>

<style name="padded_normal" parent="red_padded">
    <item name="android:textSize">12px</item>
</style>

<style name="padded_italics" parent="red_padded">
    <item name="android:textSize">14px</item>
    <item name="android:textStyle">italic</item>
</style>
```

Here you find two common attributes in a single style and a reference to them from the other two styles that have different attributes. You can reference any style as a parent style; however, you can set only one style as the style attribute of a `View`. Applying the `padded_italics` style that is already defined makes the text 14 pixels in size, italic, red, and padded. The following is an example of applying this style:

```
<TextView
    style="@style/padded_italics"
    android:layout_width="fill_parent"
    android:layout_height="wrap_content"
    android:text="Italic w/parent color" />
```

As you can see from this example, applying a style with a parent is no different than applying a regular style. In fact, a regular style can be used for applying to `Views` and used as a parent in a different style.

```
<style name="padded_xlarge">
    <item name="android:padding">10px</item>
    <item name="android:textSize">100px</item>
</style>
<style name="green_glow" parent="padded_xlarge">
```

```
    <item name="android:shadowColor">#0F0</item>
    <item name="android:shadowDx">0</item>
    <item name="android:shadowDy">0</item>
    <item name="android:shadowRadius">10</item>
</style>
```

Here the `padded_xlarge` style is set as the parent for the `green_glow` style. All six attributes are then applied to any view that this style is set to.

Working with Themes

A theme is a collection of one or more styles (as defined in the resources) but instead of applying the style to a specific control, the style is applied to all `View` objects within a specified `Activity`. Applying a theme to a set of `View` objects all at once simplifies making the user interface look consistent and can be a great way to define color schemes and other common control attribute settings.

An Android theme is essentially a style that is applied to an entire screen. You can specify the theme programmatically by calling the `Activity` method `setTheme()` with the style resource identifier. Each attribute of the style is applied to each `View` within that `Activity`, as applicable. Styles and attributes defined in the layout files explicitly override those in the theme.

For instance, consider the following style:

```
<style name="right">
    <item name="android:gravity">right</item>
</style>
```

You can apply this as a theme to the whole screen, which causes any view displayed within that `Activity` to have its gravity attribute to be right-justified. Applying this theme is as simple as making the method call to the `setTheme()` method from within the `Activity`, as shown here:

```
setTheme(R.style.right);
```

You can also apply themes to specific `Activity` instances by specifying them as an attribute within the `<activity>` element in the `AndroidManifest.xml` file, as follows:

```
<activity android:name=".myactivityname"
    android:label="@string/app_name"
    android:theme="@style/myAppIsStyling">
```

Unlike applying a style in an XML layout file, multiple themes can be applied to a screen. This gives you flexibility in defining style attributes in advance while applying different configurations of the attributes based on what might be displayed on the screen. This is demonstrated in the following code:

```
setTheme(R.style.right);
setTheme(R.style.green_glow);
setContentView(R.layout.style_samples);
```

In this example, both the `right` style and the `green_glow` style are applied as a theme to the entire screen. You can see the results of green glow and right-aligned gravity, applied to a variety of `TextView` controls on a screen, as shown in Figure 7.12. Finally, we set the layout to the `Activity`. You must do this after setting the themes. That is, you must apply all themes before calling the method `setContentView()` or the `inflate()` method so that the themes' attributes can take effect.

Figure 7.12 Packaging styles for glowing text, padding, and alignment into a theme.

A combination of well-designed and thought-out themes and styles can make the look of your application consistent and easy to maintain. Android comes with a number of built-in themes that can be a good starting point. These include such themes as `Theme_Black`, `Theme_Light`, and `Theme_NoTitleBar_Fullscreen`, as defined in the `android.R.style` class. They are all variations on the system theme, `Theme`, which built-in apps use.

Summary

The Android SDK provides many useful user interface components, which developers can use to create compelling and easy-to-use applications. This chapter introduced you to many of the most useful controls, discussed how each behaves, how to style them, and how to handle events from the user.

You learned how controls can be combined to create user entry forms. Important controls for forms include `EditText`, `Button`, `RadioButton`, `CheckBox`, and `Spinner`. You also learned about controls that can indicate progress or the passage of time to users. You mastered a variety of useful user interface constructs Android applications can take advantage of, including context and options menus, as well as various types of dialogs. In addition to drawing controls on the screen, you learned how to detect user actions, such as clicks and focus changes, and how to handle these events. Finally, you learned how to style individual controls and how to apply themes to entire screens (or more specifically, a single `Activity`) so that your application is styled consistently and thoroughly.

We talked about many common user interface controls in this chapter; however, there are many others. In Chapter 9, "Drawing and Working with Animation," and Chapter 15, "Using Android Multimedia APIs," we use graphics controls such as `ImageView` and `VideoView` to display drawable graphics and videos. In the next chapter, you learn how to use various layout and container controls to organize a variety of controls on the screen easily and accurately.

## 8

Designing User Interfaces with Layouts

In this chapter, we discuss how to design user interfaces for Android applications. Here we focus on the various layout controls you can use to organize screen elements in different ways. We also cover some of the more complex `View` objects we call container views. These are `View` objects that can contain other `View` objects and controls.

Creating User Interfaces in Android

Application user interfaces can be simple or complex, involving many different screens or only a few. Layouts and user interface controls can be defined as application resources or created programmatically at runtime.

Creating Layouts Using XML Resources

As discussed in previous chapters, Android provides a simple way to create layout files in XML as resources provided in the `/res/layout` project directory. This is the most common and convenient way to build Android user interfaces and is especially useful for defining static screen elements and control properties that you know in advance, and to set default attributes that you can modify programmatically at runtime.

Warning

The Eclipse layout resource designer can be a helpful tool for designing and previewing layout resources. However, the preview can't replicate exactly how the layout appears to end users. For this, you must test your application on a properly configured emulator and, more importantly, on your target devices.

You can configure almost any `ViewGroup` or `View` (or `View` subclass) attribute using the XML layout resource files. This method greatly simplifies the user interface design process, moving much of the static creation and layout of user interface controls, and basic definition of control attributes, to the XML, instead of littering the code. Developers reserve the ability to alter these layouts programmatically as necessary, but they can set all the defaults in the XML template.

You'll recognize the following as a simple layout file with a `LinearLayout` and a single `TextView` control. This is the default layout file provided with any new Android project in Eclipse, referred to as `/res/layout/main.xml`:

```
<?xml version="1.0" encoding="utf-8"?>
<LinearLayout xmlns:android=
    "http://schemas.android.com/apk/res/android"
    android:orientation="vertical"
    android:layout_width="fill_parent"
    android:layout_height="fill_parent" >
<TextView
    android:layout_width="fill_parent"
    android:layout_height="wrap_content"
    android:text="@string/hello" />
</LinearLayout>
```

This block of XML shows a basic layout with a single `TextView`. The first line, which you might recognize from most XML files, is required. Because it's common across all the files, we do not show it in any other examples.

Next, we have the `LinearLayout` element. `LinearLayout` is a `ViewGroup` that shows each child `View` either in a single column or in a single row. When applied to a full screen, it merely means that each child `View` is drawn under the previous `View` if the orientation is set to vertical or to the right of the previous `View` if orientation is set to horizontal.

Finally, there is a single child `View`—in this case, a `TextView`. A `TextView` is a control, which is also a `View`. A `TextView` draws text on the screen. In this case, it draws the text defined in the "`@string/hello`" string resource.

Creating only an XML file, though, won't actually draw anything on the screen. A particular layout is usually associated with a particular `Activity`. In your default Android project, there is only one activity, which sets the `main.xml` layout by default. To associate the `main.xml` layout with the activity, use the method call `setContentView()` with the identifier of the `main.xml` layout. The ID of the layout matches the XML filename without the extension. In this case, the preceding example came from `main.xml`, so the identifier of this layout is simply `main`:

```
setContentView(R.layout.main);
```

Tip

Although it's a tad confusing, the term *layout* is used for two different (but related) purposes in Android development.

In terms of resources, the /res/layout directory contains XML resource definitions often called layout resource files. These XML files provide a template for how to draw to a screen; layout resource files may contain any number of views. We talk about layout resources in Chapter 6, "Managing Application Resources."

The term *layout* is also used to refer to a set of `ViewGroup` classes such as `LinearLayout`, `FrameLayout`, `TableLayout`, and `RelativeLayout`. These layout classes are used to organize `View` controls. We talk more about these classes later in this chapter.

Therefore, you could have one or more *layouts* (such as a `LinearLayout` with two child controls—a `TextView` and an `ImageView`) defined within a *layout resource file*, such as `/res/layout/myScreen.xml`.

Creating Layouts Programmatically

You can create user interface components such as layouts at runtime programmatically, but for organization and maintainability, it's best that you leave this for the odd case rather than the norm. The main reason is because the creation of layouts programmatically is onerous and difficult to maintain, whereas the XML resource method is visual, more organized, and could be done by a separate designer with no Java skills.

Tip

The code examples provided in this section are taken from the SameLayout application. This source code for the SameLayout application is provided for download on the book website.

The following example shows how to programmatically have an `Activity` instantiate a `LinearLayout` view and place two `TextView` objects within it. No resources whatsoever are used; actions are done at runtime instead.

```
public void onCreate(Bundle savedInstanceState) {
    super.onCreate(savedInstanceState);

    TextView text1 = new TextView(this);
    text1.setText("Hi there!");

    TextView text2 = new TextView(this);
    text2.setText("I'm second. I need to wrap.");
    text2.setTextSize((float) 60);

    LinearLayout ll = new LinearLayout(this);
    ll.setOrientation(LinearLayout.VERTICAL);
    ll.addView(text1);
    ll.addView(text2);

    setContentView(ll);
}
```

The `onCreate()` method is called when the `Activity` is created. The first thing this method does is some normal `Activity` housekeeping by calling the constructor for the base class.

Next, two `TextView` controls are instantiated. The `Text` property of each `TextView` is set using the `setText()` method. All `TextView` attributes, such as `TextSize`, are set by making method calls on the `TextView` object. These actions perform the same function that you have in the past by setting the properties `Text` and `TextSize` using the Eclipse layout resource designer, except these properties are set at runtime instead of defined in the layout files compiled into your application package.

> **Tip**
>
> The XML property name is usually similar to the method calls for getting and setting that same control property programmatically. For instance, `android:visibility` maps to the methods `setVisibility()` and `getVisibility()`. In the preceding example `TextView`, the methods for getting and setting the `TextSize` property are `getTextSize()` and `setTextSize()`.

To display the `TextView` objects appropriately, we need to encapsulate them within a container of some sort (a layout). In this case, we use a `LinearLayout` with the orientation set to `VERTICAL` so that the second `TextView` begins beneath the first, each aligned to the left of the screen. The two `TextView` controls are added to the `LinearLayout` in the order we want them to display.

Finally, we call the `setContentView()` method, part of your `Activity` class, to draw the `LinearLayout` and its contents on the screen.

As you can see, the code can rapidly grow in size as you add more `View` controls and you need more attributes for each `View`. Here is that same layout, now in an XML layout file:

```xml
<?xml version="1.0" encoding="utf-8"?>
<LinearLayout xmlns:android=
    "http://schemas.android.com/apk/res/android"
    android:orientation="vertical"
    android:layout_width="fill_parent"
    android:layout_height="fill_parent"
    >
<TextView
    android:id="@+id/TextView1"
    android:layout_width="fill_parent"
    android:layout_height="wrap_content"
    android:text="Hi There!"
    />
<TextView
    android:id="@+id/TextView2"
    android:layout_width="fill_parent"
    android:layout_height="wrap_content"
    android:textSize="60px"
    android:text="I'm second. I need to wrap."
    />
</LinearLayout>
```

You might notice that this isn't a literal translation of the code example from the previous section, although the output is identical, as shown in Figure 8.1.

Figure 8.1   Two different methods to create a
screen have the same result.

First, in the XML layout files, `layout_width` and `layout_height` are required attributes. Next, you see that each `TextView` object has a unique `id` property assigned so that it can be accessed programmatically at runtime. Finally, the `textSize` property needs to have its units defined. The XML attribute takes a `dimension` type (as described in Chapter 6) instead of a float.

The end result differs only slightly from the programmatic method. However, it's far easier to read and maintain. Now you need only one line of code to display this layout view. Again, if the layout resource is stored in the `/res/layout/ resource_based_layout.xml` file, that is

```
setContentView(R.layout.resource_based_layout);
```

Organizing Your User Interface

In Chapter 7, "Exploring User Interface Screen Elements," we talk about how the class `View` is the building block for user interfaces in Android. All user interface controls, such as `Button`, `Spinner`, and `EditText`, derive from the `View` class.

Now we talk about a special kind of `View` called a `ViewGroup`. The classes derived from `ViewGroup` enable developers to display `View` objects (including all the user interface controls you learn about in Chapter 7) on the screen in an organized fashion.

Understanding `View` versus `ViewGroup`

Like other `View` objects, including the controls from Chapter 7, `ViewGroup` controls represent a rectangle of screen space. What makes `ViewGroup` different from your typical control is that `ViewGroup` objects contain other `View` objects. A `View` that contains other `View` objects is called a *parent view*. The parent `View` contains `View` objects called *child views*, or *children*.

You add child `View` objects to a `ViewGroup` programmatically using the method `addView()`. In XML, you add child objects to a `ViewGroup` by defining the child `View` control as a child node in the XML (within the parent XML element, as we've seen various times using the `LinearLayout ViewGroup`).

`ViewGroup` subclasses are broken down into two categories:

- Layout classes
- View container controls

The Android SDK also provides the Hierarchy Viewer tool to help visualize the layouts you design, as discussed later in this chapter.

Using `ViewGroup` Subclasses for Layout Design

Many important subclasses of `ViewGroup` used for screen design end with the word "Layout;" for example, `LinearLayout`, `RelativeLayout`, `TableLayout`, and `FrameLayout`. You can use each of these layout classes to position groups of `View` objects (controls) on the screen in different ways. For example, we've been using the `LinearLayout` to arrange various `TextView` and `EditText` controls on the screen in a single vertical column. We could have used an `AbsoluteLayout` to specify the exact x/y coordinate locations of each control on the screen instead, but this is not easily portable across many screen resolutions. Users do not generally interact with the `Layout` objects directly. Instead, they interact with the `View` objects they contain.

Using `ViewGroup` Subclasses as View Containers

The second category of `ViewGroup` subclasses is the indirect subclasses. These special `View` objects act as `View` containers like `Layout` objects do, but they also provide some kind of functionality that enables users to interact with them like normal controls. Unfortunately, these classes are not known by any handy names; instead they are named for the kind of functionality they provide.

Some classes that fall into this category include `Gallery`, `GridView`, `ImageSwitcher`, `ScrollView`, `TabHost`, and `ListView`. It can be helpful to consider these objects as different kinds of `View` browsers. A `ListView` displays each `View` as a list item, and the user can browse between the individual `View` objects using vertical scrolling capability. A `Gallery` is a horizontal scrolling list of `View` objects with a center "current" item; the user can browse the View objects in the `Gallery` by scrolling left and right. A `TabHost` is a more complex `View` container, where each Tab can contain a `View`, and the user chooses the tab by name to see the `View` contents.

Using the Hierarchy Viewer Tool

In addition to the Eclipse layout resource designer provided with the Android plug-in, the Android Software Development Kit (SDK) provides a user interface tool called the Hierarchy Viewer. You can find the Hierarchy Viewer in the Android SDK subdirectory called /tools.

The Hierarchy Viewer is a visual tool that enables you to inspect your Android application's View objects and their parent-child relationships. You can drill down on specific View objects and inspect individual View properties at runtime. You can even save screenshots of the current application state on the emulator or the device, although this feature is somewhat unreliable.

Do the following to launch the Hierarchy Viewer with your application in the emulator:

1. Launch your Android application in the emulator.

2. Navigate to the Android SDK /tools directory and launch the Hierarchy Viewer.

3. Choose your emulator instance from the Device listing.

4. Select the application you want to view from the windows available. For example, to load an application from this book, choose one such as the ParisView project from Chapter 6.

5. Click Load View Hierarchy button on the menu bar.

By default, the Hierarchy Viewer loads the Layout View of your application. This includes the parent-child view relationships shown as a Tree View. In addition, a property pane shows the various properties for each View node in the tree when they are selected. A wire-frame model of the View objects on the screen is shown and a red box highlights the currently selected view, which correlates to the same location on the screen.

> **Tip**
>
> You'll have better luck navigating your application View objects with the Hierarchy Viewer tool if you set your View object id properties to friendly names you can remember instead of the auto-generated sequential id tags provided by default. For example, a Button control called SubmitButton is more descriptive than Button01.

Figure 8.2 shows the Hierarchy Viewer loaded with the ParisView project from Chapter 6, which was a one-screen application with a single LinearLayout with a TextView and an ImageView child control within it, all encapsulated within a ScrollView control (for scrolling ability). The bulk of the application is shown in the right sub-tree, starting with LinearLayout with the identifier ParisViewLayout. The other sub-tree is the Application title bar. A simple double-click on each child node opens that View object individually in its own window.

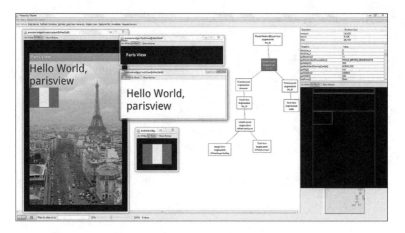

Figure 8.2   The ParisView application, shown in the Hierarchy Viewer tool
(Layout View).

Each `View` can be separately displayed in its own window by selecting the appropriate
`View` in the tree and choosing the Display View button on the menu bar. In Figure 8.2,
you can also see that Display View is enabled on each of the child nodes: the `ImageView`
with the flag, the `TextView` with the text, as well as the `LinearLayout` parent node
(which includes its children), and lastly the application title bar.

You can use the Pixel Perfect view to closely inspect your application using a loupe
(see Figure 8.3). You can also load PNG mockup files to overlay your user interface and
adjust your application's look. You can access the Pixel Perfect view by clicking the button
with the nine pixels on it at the bottom left of the Hierarchy Viewer. Click the button
with the three boxes depicting the Layout view to return.

The Hierarchy Viewer tool is invaluable for debugging drawing issues related to `View`
controls. If you wonder why something isn't drawing or if a `View` is even available, try
launching the Hierarchy Viewer and checking that problem `View` objects' properties.

You can use the Hierarchy Viewer tool to interact and debug your application user interface. Specifically, developers can use the Invalidate and Request Layout buttons on the
menu bar that correspond to `View.invalidate()` and `View.requestLayout()` functions
of the UI thread. These functions initiate `View` objects and draw or redraw them as necessary upon events.

Finally, you can also use the Hierarchy Viewer to deconstruct how other applications
(especially sample applications) have handled their layout and displays. This can be helpful
if you'd like to re-create a layout similar to another application, especially if it uses stock
`View` types. However, you can also run across `View` types not provided in the SDK, and
you need to implement those custom classes for yourself.

Figure 8.3   The ParisView application, shown in the Hierarchy Viewer tool
(Pixel Perfect View).

Using Built-In Layout Classes

We talked a lot about the `LinearLayout` layout, but there are several other types of layouts. Each layout has a different purpose and order in which it displays its child `View` controls on the screen. Layouts are derived from `android.view.ViewGroup`.

The types of layouts built-in to the Android SDK framework include

- `FrameLayout`
- `LinearLayout`
- `RelativeLayout`
- `TableLayout`

Tip

Many of the code examples provided in this section are taken from the SimpleLayout application. This source code for the SimpleLayout application is provided for download on the book website.

All layouts, regardless of their type, have basic layout attributes. Layout attributes apply to any child `View` within that layout. You can set layout attributes at runtime programmatically, but ideally you set them in the XML layout files using the following syntax:

```
android:layout_attribute_name="value"
```

There are several layout attributes that all `ViewGroup` objects share. These include size attributes and margin attributes. You can find basic layout attributes in the

ViewGroup.LayoutParams class. The margin attributes enable each child View within a layout to have padding on each side. Find these attributes in the ViewGroup.MarginLayoutParams classes. There are also a number of ViewGroup attributes for handling child View drawing bounds and animation settings.

Some of the important attributes shared by all ViewGroup subtypes are shown in Table 8.1.

Table 8.1   Important **ViewGroup** Attributes

Attribute Name	Applies To	Description	Value
android: layout_height	Parent view Child view	Height of the view. Required attribute for child view controls in layouts.	Specific dimension value, fill_parent, or wrap_content. The match_parent option is available in API Level 8+.
android: layout_width	Parent view Child view	Width of the view. Required attribute for child view controls in layouts.	Specific dimension value, fill_parent, or wrap_content. The match_parent option is available in API Level 8+.
android: layout_margin	Child view	Extra space on all sides of the view.	Specific dimension value.

Here's an XML layout resource example of a LinearLayout set to the size of the screen, containing one TextView that is set to its full height and the width of the LinearLayout (and therefore the screen):

```
<LinearLayout xmlns:android=
    "http://schemas.android.com/apk/res/android"
    android:layout_width="fill_parent"
    android:layout_height="fill_parent">
    <TextView
        android:id="@+id/TextView01"
        android:layout_height="fill_parent"
        android:layout_width="fill_parent" />
</LinearLayout>
```

Here is an example of a `Button` object with some margins set via XML used in a layout resource file:

```
<Button
    android:id="@+id/Button01"
    android:layout_width="wrap_content"
    android:layout_height="wrap_content"
    android:text="Press Me"
    android:layout_marginRight="20px"
    android:layout_marginTop="60px" />
```

Remember that layout elements can cover any rectangular space on the screen; it doesn't need to be the entire screen. Layouts can be nested within one another. This provides great flexibility when developers need to organize screen elements. It is common to start with a `FrameLayout` or `LinearLayout` (as you've seen in many of the Chapter 7 examples) as the parent layout for the entire screen and then organize individual screen elements inside the parent layout using whichever layout type is most appropriate.

Now let's talk about each of the common layout types individually and how they differ from one another.

Using `FrameLayout`

A `FrameLayout` view is designed to display a stack of child `View` items. You can add multiple views to this layout, but each `View` is drawn from the top-left corner of the layout. You can use this to show multiple images within the same region, as shown in Figure 8.4, and the layout is sized to the largest child `View` in the stack.

You can find the layout attributes available for `FrameLayout` child `View` objects in `android.control.FrameLayout.LayoutParams`. Table 8.2 describes some of the important attributes specific to `FrameLayout` views.

Table 8.2   **Important `FrameLayout` `View` Attributes**

Attribute Name	Applies To	Description	Value
android: foreground	Parent view	Drawable to draw over the content.	Drawable resource.
android: foreground- Gravity	Parent view	Gravity of foreground drawable.	One or more constants separated by "|". The constants available are top, bottom, left, right, center_vertical, fill_vertical, center_horizontal, fill_horizontal, center, and fill.

Table 8.2 **Continued**

Attribute Name	Applies To	Description	Value
android: measureAll- Children	Parent view	Restrict size of layout to all child views or just the child views set to VISIBLE (and not those set to INVISIBLE).	True or false.
android: layout_ gravity	Child view	A gravity constant that describes how to place the child View within the parent.	One or more constants separated by "|". The constants available are top, bottom, left, right, center_vertical, fill_ vertical, center_horizontal, fill_horizontal, center, and fill.

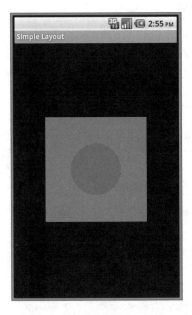

Figure 8.4   An example of **FrameLayout** usage.

Here's an example of an XML layout resource with a FrameLayout and two child View objects, both ImageView objects. The green rectangle is drawn first and the red oval is drawn on top of it. The green rectangle is larger, so it defines the bounds of the FrameLayout:

```
<FrameLayout xmlns:android=
    "http://schemas.android.com/apk/res/android"
```

```
        android:id="@+id/FrameLayout01"
        android:layout_width="wrap_content"
        android:layout_height="wrap_content"
        android:layout_gravity="center">
        <ImageView
            android:id="@+id/ImageView01"
            android:layout_width="wrap_content"
            android:layout_height="wrap_content"
            android:src="@drawable/green_rect"
            android:minHeight="200px"
            android:minWidth="200px" />
        <ImageView
            android:id="@+id/ImageView02"
            android:layout_width="wrap_content"
            android:layout_height="wrap_content"
            android:src="@drawable/red_oval"
            android:minHeight="100px"
            android:minWidth="100px"
            android:layout_gravity="center" />
</FrameLayout>
```

Using `LinearLayout`

A `LinearLayout` view organizes its child `View` objects in a single row, shown in Figure 8.5, or column, depending on whether its orientation attribute is set to horizontal or vertical. This is a very handy layout method for creating forms.

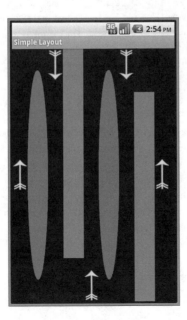

Figure 8.5   An example of **LinearLayout** (horizontal orientation).

You can find the layout attributes available for LinearLayout child View objects in android.control.LinearLayout.LayoutParams. Table 8.3 describes some of the important attributes specific to LinearLayout views.

Table 8.3   Important **LinearLayout** View Attributes

Attribute Name	Applies To	Description	Value
android: orientation	Parent view	Layout is a single row (horizontal) or single column (vertical).	Horizontal or vertical.
android: gravity	Parent view	Gravity of child views within layout.	One or more constants separated by "|". The constants available are top, bottom, left, right, center_ vertical, fill_vertical, center_horizontal, fill_ horizontal, center, and fill.
android: layout_ gravity	Child view	The gravity for a specific child view. Used for positioning of views.	One or more constants separated by "|". The constants available are top, bottom, left, right, center_ vertical, fill_vertical, center_horizontal, fill_ horizontal, center, and fill.
android: layout_ weight	Child view	The weight for a specific child view. Used to provide ratio of screen space used within the parent control.	The sum of values across all child views in a parent view must equal 1. For example, one child control might have a value of .3 and another have a value of .7.

Using **RelativeLayout**

The RelativeLayout view enables you to specify where the child view controls are in relation to each other. For instance, you can set a child View to be positioned "above" or "below" or "to the left of" or "to the right of" another View, referred to by its unique identifier. You can also align child View objects relative to one another or the parent layout edges. Combining RelativeLayout attributes can simplify creating interesting user interfaces without resorting to multiple layout groups to achieve a desired effect. Figure 8.6 shows how each of the button controls is relative to each other.

You can find the layout attributes available for RelativeLayout child View objects in android.control.RelativeLayout.LayoutParams. Table 8.4 describes some of the important attributes specific to RelativeLayout views.

Figure 8.6   An example of **RelativeLayout** usage.

Table 8.4   **Important RelativeLayout View Attributes**

Attribute Name	Applies To	Description	Value
android: gravity	Parent view	Gravity of child views within layout.	One or more constants separated by "|". The constants available are top, bottom, left, right, center_vertical, fill_vertical, center_horizontal, fill_horizontal, center, and fill.
android: layout_ centerInParent	Child view	Centers child view horizontally and vertically within parent view.	True or false.

Table 8.4   **Continued**

Attribute Name	Applies To	Description	Value

`android:`
`layout_`
`centerHorizontal`
	Child view	Centers child view horizontally within parent view.	True or false.

`android:`
`layout_`
`centerVertical`
	Child view	Centers child view vertically within parent view.	True or false.

`android:`
`layout_`
`alignParentTop`
	Child view	Aligns child view with top edge of parent view.	True or false.

`android:`
`layout_`
`alignParentBottom`
	Child view	Aligns child view with bottom edge of parent view.	True or false.

`android:`
`layout_`
`alignParentLeft`
	Child view	Aligns child view with left edge of parent view.	True or false.

`android:`
`layout_`
`alignParentRight`
	Child view	Aligns child view with right edge of parent view.	True or false.

`android:`
`layout_`
`alignRight`
	Child view	Aligns child view with right edge of another child view, specified by ID.	A view ID; for example, `@id/Button1`

`android:`
`layout_`
`alignLeft`
	Child view	Aligns child view with left edge of another child view, specified by ID.	A view ID; for example, `@id/Button1`

`android:`
`layout_`
`alignTop`
	Child view	Aligns child view with top edge of another child view, specified by ID.	A view ID; for example, `@id/Button1`

`android:`
`layout_`
`alignBottom`
	Child view	Aligns child view with bottom edge of another child view, specified by ID.	A view ID; for example, `@id/Button1`

Table 8.4   **Continued**

Attribute Name	Applies To	Description	Value
android: layout_ above	Child view	Positions bottom edge of child view above another child view, specified by ID.	A view ID; for example, @id/Button1
android: layout_ below	Child view	Positions top edge of child view below another child view, specified by ID.	A view ID; for example, @id/Button1
android: layout_ toLeftOf	Child view	Positions right edge of child view to the left of another child view, specified by ID.	A view ID; for example, @id/Button1
android: layout_ toRightOf	Child view	Positions left edge of child view to the right of another child view, specified by ID.	A view ID; for example, @id/Button1

Here's an example of an XML layout resource with a `RelativeLayout` and two child `View` objects, a `Button` object aligned relative to its parent, and an `ImageView` aligned and positioned relative to the `Button` (and the parent):

```
<?xml version="1.0" encoding="utf-8"?>
<RelativeLayout xmlns:android=
    "http://schemas.android.com/apk/res/android"
    android:id="@+id/RelativeLayout01"
    android:layout_height="fill_parent"
    android:layout_width="fill_parent">
    <Button
        android:id="@+id/ButtonCenter"
        android:text="Center"
        android:layout_width="wrap_content"
        android:layout_height="wrap_content"
        android:layout_centerInParent="true" />
    <ImageView
        android:id="@+id/ImageView01"
        android:layout_width="wrap_content"
        android:layout_height="wrap_content"
        android:layout_above="@id/ButtonCenter"
        android:layout_centerHorizontal="true"
        android:src="@drawable/arrow" />
</RelativeLayout>
```

Warning

The `AbsoluteLayout` class has been deprecated. `AbsoluteLayout` uses specific x and y coordinates for child view placement. This layout can be useful when pixel-perfect placement is required. However, it's less flexible because it does not adapt well to other device configurations with different screen sizes and resolutions. Under most circumstances, other popular layout types such as `FrameLayout` and `RelativeLayout` suffice in place of `AbsoluteLayout`, so we encourage you to use these layouts instead when possible.

Using `TableLayout`

A `TableLayout` view organizes children into rows, as shown in Figure 8.7. You add individual `View` objects within each row of the table using a `TableRow` layout `View` (which is basically a horizontally oriented `LinearLayout`) for each row of the table. Each column of the `TableRow` can contain one `View` (or layout with child `View` objects). You place `View` items added to a `TableRow` in columns in the order they are added. You can specify the column number (zero-based) to skip columns as necessary (the bottom row shown in Figure 8.7 demonstrates this); otherwise, the `View` object is put in the next column to the right. Columns scale to the size of the largest `View` of that column. You can also include normal `View` objects instead of `TableRow` elements, if you want the `View` to take up an entire row.

Figure 8.7   An example of **`TableLayout`** usage.

You can find the layout attributes available for `TableLayout` child `View` objects in `android.control.TableLayout.LayoutParams`. You can find the layout attributes available for `TableRow` child `View` objects in `android.control.TableRow.LayoutParams`. Table 8.5 describes some of the important attributes specific to `TableLayout` `View` objects.

Table 8.5   Important **TableLayout** and **TableRow** View Attributes

Attribute Name	Applies To	Description	Value
android: collapseColumns	TableLayout	A comma-delimited list of column indices to collapse (0-based)	String or string resource. For example, "0,1,3,5"
android: shrinkColumns	TableLayout	A comma-delimited list of column indices to shrink (0-based)	String or string resource. Use "*" for all columns. For example, "0,1,3,5"
andriod: stretchColumns	TableLayout	A comma-delimited list of column indices to stretch (0-based)	String or string resource. Use "*" for all columns. For example, "0,1,3,5"
android: layout_column	TableRow child view	Index of column this child view should be displayed in (0-based)	Integer or integer resource. For example, 1
android: layout_span	TableRow child view	Number of columns this child view should span across	Integer or integer resource greater than or equal to 1. For example, 3

Here's an example of an XML layout resource with a `TableLayout` with two rows (two `TableRow` child objects). The `TableLayout` is set to stretch the columns to the size of the screen width. The first `TableRow` has three columns; each cell has a `Button` object. The second `TableRow` puts only one `Button` view into the second column explicitly:

```
<TableLayout xmlns:android=
    "http://schemas.android.com/apk/res/android"
    android:id="@+id/TableLayout01"
    android:layout_width="fill_parent"
    android:layout_height="fill_parent"
    android:stretchColumns="*">
    <TableRow
        android:id="@+id/TableRow01">
        <Button
            android:id="@+id/ButtonLeft"
```

```
            android:text="Left Door" />
        <Button
            android:id="@+id/ButtonMiddle"
            android:text="Middle Door" />
        <Button
            android:id="@+id/ButtonRight"
            android:text="Right Door" />
    </TableRow>
    <TableRow
        android:id="@+id/TableRow02">
        <Button
            android:id="@+id/ButtonBack"
            android:text="Go Back"
            android:layout_column="1" />
    </TableRow>
</TableLayout>
```

Using Multiple Layouts on a Screen

Combining different layout methods on a single screen can create complex layouts. Remember that because a layout contains `View` objects and is, itself, a `View`, it can contain other layouts. Figure 8.8 demonstrates a combination of layout views used in conjunction to create a more complex and interesting screen.

Warning

Keep in mind that individual screens of mobile applications should remain sleek and relatively simple. This is not just because this design results in a more positive user experience; cluttering your screens with complex (and deep) View hierarchies can lead to performance problems. Use the Hierarchy Viewer to inspect your application layouts; you can also use the `layoutopt` command-line tool to help optimize your layouts and identify unnecessary components. This tool often helps identify opportunities to use layout optimization techniques, such as the `<merge>` and `<include>` tags.

Using Built-In `View` Container Classes

Layouts are not the only controls that can contain other `View` objects. Although layouts are useful for positioning other `View` objects on the screen, they aren't interactive. Now let's talk about the other kind of `ViewGroup`: the containers. These `View` objects encapsulate other, simpler `View` types and give the user some interactive ability to browse the child `view` objects in a standard fashion. Much like layouts, these controls each have a special, well-defined purpose.

Figure 8.8   An example of multiple layouts used together.

The types of `ViewGroup` containers built-in to the Android SDK framework include

- Lists, grids, and galleries
- Switchers with `ViewFlipper`, `ImageSwitcher`, and `TextSwitcher`
- Tabs with `TabHost` and `TabControl`
- Scrolling with `ScrollView` and `HorizontalScrollView`
- Hiding and showing content with the `SlidingDrawer`

Tip

Many of the code examples provided in this chapter are taken from the AdvancedLayouts application. This source code for the AdvancedLayouts application is provided for download on the book website.

Using Data-Driven Containers

Some of the `View` container controls are designed for displaying repetitive `View` objects in a particular way. Examples of this type of `View` container control include `ListView`, `GridView`, and `GalleryView`:

- **`ListView`:** Contains a vertically scrolling, horizontally filled list of `View` objects, each of which typically contains a row of data; the user can choose an item to perform some action upon.

- **`GridView`:** Contains a grid of `View` objects, with a specific number of columns; this container is often used with image icons; the user can choose an item to perform some action upon.

- **`GalleryView`:** Contains a horizontally scrolling list of `View` objects, also often used with image icons; the user can select an item to perform some action upon.

These containers are all types of `AdapterView` controls. An `AdapterView` control contains a set of child `View` controls to display data from some data source. An `Adapter` generates these child `View` controls from a data source. As this is an important part of all these container controls, we talk about the `Adapter` objects first.

In this section, you learn how to bind data to `View` objects using `Adapter` objects. In the Android SDK, an `Adapter` reads data from some data source and provides a `View` object based on some rules, depending on the type of `Adapter` used. This `View` is used to populate the `child` `View` objects of a particular `AdapterView`.

The most common Adapter classes are the `CursorAdapter` and the `ArrayAdapter`. The `CursorAdapter` gathers data from a `Cursor`, whereas the `ArrayAdapter` gathers data from an array. A `CursorAdapter` is a good choice to use when using data from a database. The `ArrayAdapter` is a good choice to use when there is only a single column of data or when the data comes from a resource array.

There are some common elements to know about `Adapter` objects. When creating an `Adapter`, you provide a layout identifier. This layout is the template for filling in each row of data. The template you create contains identifiers for particular controls that the `Adapter` assigns data to. A simple layout can contain as little as a single `TextView` control. When making an `Adapter`, refer to both the layout resource and the identifier of the `TextView` control. The Android SDK provides some common layout resources for use in your application.

Using the `ArrayAdapter`

An `ArrayAdapter` binds each element of the array to a single `View` object within the layout resource. Here is an example of creating an `ArrayAdapter`:

```
private String[] items = {
    "Item 1", "Item 2", "Item 3" };
ArrayAdapter adapt =
    new ArrayAdapter<String>
        (this, R.layout.textview, items);
```

In this example, we have a String array called items. This is the array used by the ArrayAdapter as the source data. We also use a layout resource, which is the View that is repeated for each item in the array. This is defined as follows:

```
<TextView xmlns:android=
    "http://schemas.android.com/apk/res/android"
    android:layout_width="fill_parent"
    android:layout_height="wrap_content"
    android:textSize="20px" />
```

This layout resource contains only a single TextView. However, you can use a more complex layout with the constructors that also take the resource identifier of a TextView within the layout. Each child View within the AdapterView that uses this Adapter gets one TextView instance with one of the strings from the String array.

If you have an array resource defined, you can also directly set the entries attribute for an AdapterView to the resource identifier of the array to automatically provide the ArrayAdapter.

Using the CursorAdapter

A CursorAdapter binds one or more columns of data to one or more View objects within the layout resource provided. This is best shown with an example. The following example demonstrates creating a CursorAdapter by querying the Contacts content provider. The CursorAdapter requires the use of a Cursor.

> **Note**
>
> For more information about the Cursor object, see Chapter 10, "Using Android Data and Storage APIs."

```
Cursor names = managedQuery(
    Contacts.Phones.CONTENT_URI, null, null, null, null);
startManagingCursor(names);
ListAdapter adapter = new SimpleCursorAdapter(
    this, R.layout.two_text,
    names, new String[] {
        Contacts.Phones.NAME,
        Contacts.Phones.NUMBER
    }, new int[] {
        R.id.scratch_text1,
        R.id.scratch_text2
    });
```

In this example, we present a couple of new concepts. First, you need to know that the Cursor must contain a field named _id. In this case, we know that the Contacts content provider does have this field. This field is used later when you handle the user selecting a particular item.

Note

Although the Contacts class has been deprecated, it is the only method for accessing Contact information that works on both older and newer editions of Android. We talk more about Contacts and content providers in Chapter 11, "Sharing Data Between Applications with Content Providers."

We make a call to `managedQuery()` to get the `Cursor`. Then, we instantiate a `SimpleCursorAdapter` as a `ListAdapter`. Our layout, `R.layout.two_text`, has two `TextView` objects in it, which are used in the last parameter. `SimpleCursorAdapter` enables us to match up columns in the database with particular controls in our layout. For each row returned from the query, we get one instance of the layout within our `AdapterView`.

Binding Data to the `AdapterView`

Now that you have an `Adapter` object, you can apply this to one of the `AdapterView` controls. Any of them works. Although the `Gallery` technically takes a `SpinnerAdapter`, the instantiation of `SimpleCursorAdapter` also returns a `SpinnerAdapter`. Here is an example of this with a `ListView`, continuing on from the previous sample code:

```
((ListView)findViewById(R.id.list)).setAdapter(adapter);
```

The call to the `setAdapter()` method of the `AdapterView`, a `ListView` in this case, should come after your call to `setContentView()`. This is all that is required to bind data to your `AdapterView`. Figure 8.9 shows the same data in a `ListView`, `Gallery`, and `GridView`.

Figure 8.9   **ListView**, **Gallery**, and **GridView**: same data, same list item, different layout views.

Handling Selection Events

You often use `AdapterView` controls to present data from which the user should select. All three of the discussed controls—`ListView`, `GridView`, and `Gallery`—enable your application to monitor for click events in the same way. You need to call `setOnItemClickListener()` on your `AdapterView` and pass in an implementation of the `AdapterView.OnItemClickListener` class. Here is an example implementation of this class:

```
av.setOnItemClickListener(
    new AdapterView.OnItemClickListener() {
    public void onItemClick(
        AdapterView<?> parent, View view,
        int position, long id) {
        Toast.makeText(Scratch.this, "Clicked _id="+id,
            Toast.LENGTH_SHORT).show();
    }
});
```

In the preceding example, `av` is our `AdapterView`. The implementation of the `onItemClick()` method is where all the interesting work happens. The parent parameter is the `AdapterView` where the item was clicked. This is useful if your screen has more than one `AdapterView` on it. The `View` parameter is the specific `View` within the item that was clicked. The position is the zero-based position within the list of items that the user selects. Finally, the `id` parameter is the value of the `_id` column for the particular item that the user selects. This is useful for querying for further information about that particular row of data that the item represents.

Your application can also listen for long-click events on particular items. Additionally, your application can listen for selected items. Although the parameters are the same, your application receives a call as the highlighted item changes. This can be in response to the user scrolling with the arrow keys and not selecting an item for action.

Using the `ListActivity`

The `ListView` control is commonly used for full-screen menus or lists of items from which a user selects. As such, you might consider using `ListActivity` as the base class for such screens. Using the `ListActivity` can simplify these types of screens.

First, to handle item events, you now need to provide an implementation in your `ListActivity`. For instance, the equivalent of `onListItemClickListener` is to implement the `onListItemClick()` method within your `ListActivity`.

Second, to assign an `Adapter`, you need a call to the `setListAdapter()` method. You do this after the call to the `setContentView()` method. However, this hints at some of the limitations of using `ListActivity`.

To use `ListActivity`, the layout that is set with the `setContentView()` method must contain a `ListView` with the identifier set to `android:list`; this cannot be changed. Second, you can also have a `View` with an identifier set to `android:empty` to have a `View` display when no data is returned from the `Adapter`. Finally, this works only with `ListView` controls, so it has limited use. However, when it does work for your application, it can save on some coding.

Tip

You can create `ListView` headers and footers using `ListView.FixedViewInfo` with the `ListView` methods `addHeaderView()` and `addFooterView()`.

Organizing Screens with Tabs

The Android SDK has a flexible way to provide a tab interface to the user. Much like `ListView` and `ListActivity`, there are two ways to create tabbing on the Android plat-form. You can either use the `TabActivity`, which simplifies a screen with tabs, or you can create your own tabbed screens from scratch. Both methods rely on the `TabHost` control.

Warning

The Eclipse Layout Resource editor does not display `TabHost` controls properly in design mode. In order to design this kind of layout, you should stick to the XML layout mode. You must use the Android emulator or an Android device to view the tabs.

Using `TabActivity`

A screen layout with tabs consists of a `TabActivity` and a `TabHost`. The `TabHost` consists of `TabSpecs`, a nested class of `TabHost`, which contains the tab information including the tab title and the contents of the tab. The contents of the tab can either be a predefined `View`, an `Activity` launched through an `Intent` object, or the `View` can be created with a factory provided by an implementation of `TabContentFactory`.

Tabs aren't as complex as they might sound at first. Each tab is effectively a container for a `View`. That `View` can come from any `View` that is ready to be shown, such as an XML layout file. Alternatively, that `View` can come from launching an `Activity`. The following example demonstrates each of these methods using `View` objects and `Activity` objects created in the previous examples of this chapter:

```
public class TabLayout
    extends TabActivity
    implements android.control.TabHost.TabContentFactory {
    protected void onCreate(Bundle savedInstanceState) {
        super.onCreate(savedInstanceState);
        TabHost tabHost = getTabHost();
        LayoutInflater.from(this).inflate(
            R.layout.example_layout,
            tabHost.getTabContentView(), true);
        tabHost.addTab(tabHost.newTabSpec("tab1")
            .setIndicator("Grid").setContent(
                new Intent(this, GridLayout.class)));
        tabHost.addTab(tabHost.newTabSpec("tab2")
            .setIndicator("List").setContent(
                new Intent(this, List.class)));
        tabHost.addTab(tabHost.newTabSpec("tab3")
```

```
                .setIndicator("Basic").setContent(
                    R.id.two_texts));
        tabHost.addTab(tabHost.newTabSpec("tab4")
            .setIndicator("Factory").setContent(
                this));
    }

    public View createTabContent(String tag) {
        if (tag.compareTo("tab4") == 0) {
            TextView tv = new TextView(this);
            Date now = new Date();
            tv.setText("I'm from a factory. Created: "
                + now.toString());
            tv.setTextSize((float) 24);
            return (tv);
        } else {
            return null;
}}}
```

This example creates a tabbed layout view with four tabs on it, as shown in Figure 8.10.
The first tab is from the recent GridView sample. The second tab is from the ListView
sample before that. The third tab is the basic layout with two TextView objects, fully defined in an XML layout file as previously demonstrated. Finally, the fourth tab is created
with a factory.

Figure 8.10   Four tabs displayed.

The first action is to get the `TabHost` instance. This is the object that enables us to add `Intent` objects and `View` identifiers for drawing the screen. A `TabActivity` provides a method to retrieve the current `TabHost` object.

The next action is only loosely related to tab views. The `LayoutInflater` is used to turn the XML definition of a `View` into the actual `View` objects. This would normally happen when calling `setContentView()`, but we're not doing that. The use of the `LayoutInflater` is required for referencing the `View` objects by identifier, as is done for the third tab.

The code finishes up by adding each of the four tabs to the `TabHost` in the order that they will be presented. This is accomplished by multiple calls to the `addTab()` method of `TabHost`. The first two calls are essentially the same. Each one creates a new `Intent` with the name of an `Activity` that launches within the tab. These are the same `Activity` classes used previously for full-screen display. If the `Activity` isn't designed for full-screen use, this should work seamlessly.

Next, on the third tab, a layout `View` is added using its identifier. In the preceding call to the `LayoutInflater`, the layout file also contains an identifier matching the one used here at the top level of a `LinearLayout` definition. This is the same one used previously to show a basic `LinearLayout` example. Again, there was no need to change anything in this view for it to display correctly in a tab.

Next, a tab referencing the content as the `TabActivity` class is added. This is possible because the class itself also implements `TabHost.TabContentFactory`, which requires implementing the `createTabContent()` method. The view is created the first time the user selects the tab, so no other information is needed here. The tag that creates this tab must be kept track of, though, as that's how the tabs are identified to the `TabHost`.

Finally, the method `createTabContent()` is implemented for use with the fourth tab. The first task here is to check the tag to see if it's the one kept track of for the fourth tab. When that is confirmed, an instance of the `TextView` object is created and a text string assigned to it, which contains the current time. The size of the text is set to 24 pixels. The time stamp used in this string can be used to demonstrate when the view is created and that it's not re-created by simply changing tabs.

The flexibility of tabs that Android provides is great for adding navigation to an application that has a bunch of views already defined. Few changes, if any, need to be made to existing `View` and `Activity` objects for them to work within the context of a `TabHost`.

Implementing Tabbing Without `TabActivity`

It is possible to design tabbed layouts without using the `TabActivity` class. However, this requires a bit of knowledge about the underpinnings of the `TabHost` and `TabWidget` controls. To define a set of tabs within an XML layout file without using `TabActivity`, begin with a `TabHost` (for example, `TabHost1`). Inside the `TabHost`, include a vertically oriented `LinearLayout` that must contain a `TabWidget` (which must have the id `@android:id/tabs`) and a `FrameLayout` (which must have id `@android:id/tabcontent`). The contents of each tab are then defined within the `FrameLayout`.

After you've defined the `TabHost` properly in XML, you must load and initialize it using the `TabHost setup()` method on your activity's `onCreate()` method. First, you need to create a `TabSpec` for each tab, setting the tab indicator using the `setIndicator()` method and the tab content using the `setContent()` method. Next, add each tab using the `addTab()` method of the `TabHost`. Finally, you should set the default tab of the `TabHost`, using a method such as `setCurrentTabByTag()`.

Adding Scrolling Support

One of the easiest ways to provide vertical scrolling for a screen is by using the `ScrollView` (vertical scrolling) and `HorizontalScrollView` (horizontal scrolling) controls. Either control can be used as a wrapper container, causing all child `View` controls to have one continuous scrollbar. The `ScrollView` and `HorizontalScrollView` controls can have only one child, though, so it's customary to have that child be a layout, such as a `LinearLayout`, which then contains all the "real" child controls to be scrolled through. Figure 8.11 shows a screen with and without a `ScrollView` control.

Figure 8.11   A screen with (right) and without (left) a **ScrollView** control.

Tip

Some code examples of scrolling are provided in the SimpleScrolling application. This source code for the SimpleScrolling application is available for download on the book website.

Exploring Other View Containers

Many other user interface controls are available within the Android SDK. Some of these controls are listed here:

- **Switchers:** A `ViewSwitcher` control contains only two child `View` objects and only one of those is shown at a time. It switches between the two, animating as it does so. Primarily, the `ImageSwitcher`, shown in Figure 8.12, and `TextSwitcher` objects are used. Each one provides a way to set a new child `View`, either a `Drawable` resource or a text string, and then animates from what is displayed to the new contents.

Figure 8.12   **ImageSwitcher** while in the middle of switching between two **Drawable** resources.

- **SlidingDrawer:** Another `View` container is the `SlidingDrawer` control. This control includes two parts: a handle and a container view. The user drags the handle open and the internal contents are shown; then the user can drag the handle shut and the content disappears. The `SlidingDrawer` can be used horizontally or vertically and is always used from within a layout representing the larger screen. This makes the `SlidingDrawer` especially useful for application configurations such as game controls. A user can pull out the drawer, pause the game, change some features, and then close the `SlidingDrawer` to resume the game. Figure 8.13 shows how the typical `SlidingDrawer` looks when pulled open.

Figure 8.13   **SlidingDrawer** sliding open to
show contents.

Summary

The Android SDK provides a number of powerful methods for designing usable and great-looking screens. This chapter introduced you to many of these. You first learned about many of the Android layout controls that can control the placement of your controls on the screen. In many cases, these enable you to have a single screen design that works on most screen sizes and aspect ratios.

You then learned about other objects that contain views and how to group or place them on the screen in a particular way. These included such display paradigms as the tab, typically used in a similar way that physical folder tabs are used, in addition to a variety of different controls for placing data on the screen in a readable and browsable way. You now have all the tools you need to develop applications with usable and exciting user interfaces.

## 9

Drawing and Working with Animation

This chapter talks about the drawing and animation features built into Android, including creating custom `View` classes and working with `Canvas` and `Paint` to draw shapes and text. We also talk about animating objects on the screen in a variety of ways.

Drawing on the Screen

In Chapter 7, "Exploring User Interface Screen Elements," and Chapter 8, "Designing User Interfaces with Layouts," we talk about layouts and the various `View` classes available in Android to make screen design simple and efficient. Now we must think at a slightly lower level and talk about drawing objects on the screen. With Android, we can display images such as PNG and JPG graphics, as well as text and primitive shapes to the screen. We can paint these items with various colors, styles, or gradients and modify them using standard image transforms. We can even animate objects to give the illusion of motion.

> **Tip**
>
> Many of the code examples provided in this chapter are taken from the SimpleDrawing application. This source code for the SimpleDrawing application is provided for download on the book website.

Working with Canvases and Paints

To draw to the screen, you need a valid `Canvas` object. Typically we get a valid `Canvas` object by extending the `View` class for our own purposes and implementing the `onDraw()` method.

For example, here's a simple `View` subclass called `ViewWithRedDot`. We override the `onDraw()` method to dictate what the `View` looks like; in this case, it draws a red circle on a black background.

```
private static class ViewWithRedDot extends View {
    public ViewWithRedDot(Context context) {
        super(context);
    }

    @Override
    protected void onDraw(Canvas canvas) {
        canvas.drawColor(Color.BLACK);
        Paint circlePaint = new Paint();
        circlePaint.setColor(Color.RED);
        canvas.drawCircle(canvas.getWidth()/2,
            canvas.getHeight()/2,
            canvas.getWidth()/3, circlePaint);
    }
}
```

We can then use this `View` like any other layout. For example, we might override the `onCreate()` method in our `Activity` with the following:

```
setContentView(new ViewWithRedDot(this));
```

The resulting screen looks something like Figure 9.1.

Figure 9.1   The **ViewWithRedDot** view draws a
red circle on a black canvas background.

Understanding the Canvas

The `Canvas` (`android.graphics.Canvas`) object holds the draw calls, in order, for a rectangle of space. There are methods available for drawing images, text, shapes, and support for clipping regions.

The dimensions of the `Canvas` are bound by the container view. You can retrieve the size of the `Canvas` using the `getHeight()` and `getWidth()` methods.

Understanding the Paint

In Android, the `Paint` (`android.graphics.Paint`) object stores far more than a color. The `Paint` class encapsulates the style and complex color and rendering information, which can be applied to a drawable like a graphic, shape, or piece of text in a given `Typeface`.

Working with Paint Color

You can set the color of the `Paint` using the `setColor()` method. Standard colors are predefined within the `android.graphics.Color` class. For example, the following code sets the paint color to red:

```
Paint redPaint = new Paint();
redPaint.setColor(Color.RED);
```

Working with Paint Antialiasing

Antialiasing makes many graphics—whether they are shapes or typefaces—look smoother on the screen. This property is set within the `Paint` of an object.

For example, the following code instantiates a `Paint` object with antialiasing enabled:

```
Paint aliasedPaint = new Paint(Paint.ANTI_ALIAS_FLAG);
```

Working with Paint Styles

`Paint` style controls how an object is filled with color. For example, the following code instantiates a `Paint` object and sets the Style to `STROKE`, which signifies that the object should be painted as a line drawing and not filled (the default):

```
Paint linePaint = new Paint();
linePaint.setStyle(Paint.Style.STROKE);
```

Working with Paint Gradients

You can create a gradient of colors using one of the gradient subclasses. The different gradient classes (see Figure 9.2), including `LinearGradient`, `RadialGradient`, and `SweepGradient`, are available under the superclass `android.graphics.Shader`.

All gradients need at least two colors—a start color and an end color—but might contain any number of colors in an array. The different types of gradients are differentiated by the direction in which the gradient "flows." Gradients can be set to mirror and repeat as necessary.

You can set the `Paint` gradient using the `setShader()` method.

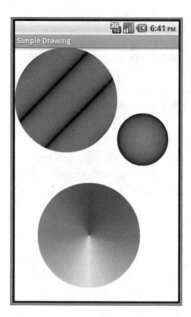

Figure 9.2   An example of a **LinearGradient**
(top), a **RadialGradient** (right), and a
SweepGradient (bottom).

Working with Linear Gradients

A linear gradient is one that changes colors along a single straight line. The top-left circle
in Figure 9.2 is a linear gradient between black and red, which is mirrored.

You can achieve this by creating a `LinearGradient` and setting the `Paint` method
`setShader()` before drawing on a `Canvas`, as follows:

```
import android.graphics.Canvas;
import android.graphics.Color;
import android.graphics.LinearGradient;
import android.graphics.Paint;
import android.graphics.Shader;
...
Paint circlePaint = new Paint(Paint.ANTI_ALIAS_FLAG);
LinearGradient linGrad = new LinearGradient(0, 0, 25, 25,
    Color.RED, Color.BLACK,
    Shader.TileMode.MIRROR);
circlePaint.setShader(linGrad);
canvas.drawCircle(100, 100, 100, circlePaint);
```

Working with Radial Gradients

A radial gradient is one that changes colors starting at a single point and radiating outward in a circle. The smaller circle on the right in Figure 9.2 is a radial gradient between green and black.

You can achieve this by creating a `RadialGradient` and setting the `Paint` method `setShader()` before drawing on a `Canvas`, as follows:

```
import android.graphics.Canvas;
import android.graphics.Color;
import android.graphics.RadialGradient;
import android.graphics.Paint;
import android.graphics.Shader;
...
Paint circlePaint = new Paint(Paint.ANTI_ALIAS_FLAG);
RadialGradient radGrad = new RadialGradient(250,
    175, 50, Color.GREEN, Color.BLACK,
    Shader.TileMode.MIRROR);
circlePaint.setShader(radGrad);
canvas.drawCircle(250, 175, 50, circlePaint);
```

Working with Sweep Gradients

A sweep gradient is one that changes colors using slices of a pie. This type of gradient is often used for a color *chooser*. The large circle at the bottom of Figure 9.2 is a sweep gradient between red, yellow, green, blue, and magenta.

You can achieve this by creating a `SweepGradient` and setting the `Paint` method `setShader()` before drawing on a `Canvas`, as follows:

```
import android.graphics.Canvas;
import android.graphics.Color;
import android.graphics.SweepGradient;
import android.graphics.Paint;
import android.graphics.Shader;
...
Paint circlePaint = new Paint(Paint.ANTI_ALIAS_FLAG);
SweepGradient sweepGrad = new
    SweepGradient(canvas.getWidth()-175,
    canvas.getHeight()-175,
    new int[] { Color.RED, Color.YELLOW, Color.GREEN,
    Color.BLUE, Color.MAGENTA }, null);

circlePaint.setShader(sweepGrad);
canvas.drawCircle(canvas.getWidth()-175,
    canvas.getHeight()-175, 100,
    circlePaint);
```

Working with Paint Utilities for Drawing Text

The `Paint` class includes a number of utilities and features for rendering text to the screen in different typefaces and styles. Now is a great time to start drawing some text to the screen.

Working with Text

Android provides several default font typefaces and styles. Applications can also use custom fonts by including font files as application assets and loading them using the `AssetManager`, much as one would use resources.

Using Default Fonts and Typefaces

By default, Android uses the Sans Serif typeface, but Monospace and Serif typefaces are also available. The following code excerpt draws some antialiased text in the default typeface (Sans Serif) to a `Canvas`:

```
import android.graphics.Canvas;
import android.graphics.Color;
import android.graphics.Paint;
import android.graphics.Typeface;
...
Paint mPaint = new Paint(Paint.ANTI_ALIAS_FLAG);
Typeface mType;

mPaint.setTextSize(16);
mPaint.setTypeface(null);

canvas.drawText("Default Typeface", 20, 20, mPaint);
```

You can instead load a different typeface, such as Monotype:

```
Typeface mType = Typeface.create(Typeface.MONOSPACE,
    Typeface.NORMAL);
```

Perhaps you would prefer *italic* text, in which case you can simply set the style of the typeface and the font family:

```
Typeface mType = Typeface.create(Typeface.SERIF,
    Typeface.ITALIC);
```

Warning

Not all typeface styles are supported by all typeface families. You need to check to make sure the typeface and style desired exists on the device.

You can set certain properties of a typeface such as antialiasing, underlining, and strike-through using the `setFlags()` method of the `Paint` object:

```
mPaint.setFlags(Paint.UNDERLINE_TEXT_FLAG);
```

Figure 9.3 shows some of the `Typeface` families and styles available by default on Android.

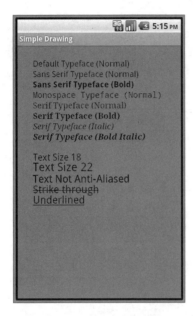

Figure 9.3   Some typefaces and typeface styles
available on Android.

Using Custom Typefaces

You can easily use custom typefaces with your application by including the font file as an application asset and loading it on demand. Fonts might be used for a custom look-and-feel, for implementing language symbols that are not supported natively, or for custom symbols.

For example, you might want to use a handy chess font to implement a simple, scalable chess game. A chess font includes every symbol needed to implement a chessboard, including the board and the pieces. Hans Bodlaender has kindly provided a free chess font called *Chess Utrecht*. Using the *Chess Utrecht* font, the letter Q draws a black queen on a white square, whereas a q draws a white queen on a white square, and so on. This nifty font is available at www.chessvariants.com/d.font/utrecht.html as chess1.ttf.

To use a custom font, such as *Chess Utrecht*, simply download the font from the website and copy the chess1.ttf file from your hard drive to the project directory /assets/fonts/chess1.ttf.

Now you can load the `Typeface` object programmatically much as you would any resource:

```
import android.graphics.Typeface;
import android.graphics.Color;
import android.graphics.Paint;
...
Paint mPaint = new Paint(Paint.ANTI_ALIAS_FLAG);
Typeface mType =
    Typeface.createFromAsset(getContext().getAssets(),
    "fonts/chess1.ttf");
```

You can then use the *Chess Utrecht* typeface to "draw" a chessboard (see Figure 9.4) using the appropriate character sequences.

Figure 9.4   Using the *Chess Utrecht* font to draw
a chessboard.

Measuring Text Screen Requirements

You can measure how large text with a given `Paint` is and how big of a rectangle you need to encompass it using the `measureText()` and `getTextBounds()` methods.

Working with Bitmaps

You can find lots of goodies for working with graphics such as bitmaps (including `NinePatch`) in the `android.graphics` package. The core class for bitmaps is `android.graphics.Bitmap`.

Drawing Bitmap Graphics on a Canvas

You can draw bitmaps onto a valid `Canvas`, such as within the `onDraw()` method of a `View`, using one of the `drawBitmap()` methods. For example, the following code loads a `Bitmap` resource and draws it on a canvas:

```
import android.graphics.Bitmap;
import android.graphics.BitmapFactory;
...
Bitmap pic = BitmapFactory.decodeResource(getResources(),
    R.drawable.bluejay);
canvas.drawBitmap(pic, 0, 0, null);
```

Scaling Bitmap Graphics

Perhaps you want to scale your graphic to a smaller size. In this case, you can use the `createScaledBitmap()` method, like this:

```
Bitmap sm = Bitmap.createScaledBitmap(pic, 50, 75, false);
```

You can preserve the aspect ratio of the `Bitmap` by checking the `getWidth()` and `getHeight()` methods and scaling appropriately.

Transforming Bitmaps Using Matrixes

You can use the helpful `Matrix` class to perform transformations on a `Bitmap` graphic (see Figure 9.5). Use the `Matrix` class to perform tasks such as mirroring and rotating graphics, among other actions.

The following code uses the `createBitmap()` method to generate a new `Bitmap` that is a mirror of an existing `Bitmap` called `pic`:

```
import android.graphics.Bitmap;
import android.graphics.Matrix;
...
Matrix mirrorMatrix = new Matrix();
mirrorMatrix.preScale(-1, 1);

Bitmap mirrorPic = Bitmap.createBitmap(pic, 0, 0,
    pic.getWidth(), pic.getHeight(), mirrorMatrix, false);
```

You can perform a 30-degree rotation in addition to mirroring by using this `Matrix` instead:

```
Matrix mirrorAndTilt30 = new Matrix();
mirrorAndTilt30.preRotate(30);
mirrorAndTilt30.preScale(-1, 1);
```

You can see the results of different combinations of tilt and mirror `Matrix` transforms in Figure 9.5. When you're no longer using a `Bitmap`, you can free its memory using the `recycle()` method:

```
pic.recycle();
```

Figure 9.5   A single-source bitmap: scaled, tilted, and mirrored using Android **Bitmap** classes.

There are a variety of other **Bitmap** effects and utilities available as part of the Android SDK, but they are numerous and beyond the scope of this book. See the **android.graphics** package for more details.

Working with Shapes

You can define and draw primitive shapes such as rectangles and ovals using the **ShapeDrawable** class in conjunction with a variety of specialized **Shape** classes. You can define **Paintable** drawables as XML resource files, but more often, especially with more complex shapes, this is done programmatically.

Tip

Many of the code examples provided in this section are taken from the SimpleShapes application. This source code for the SimpleShapes application is provided for download on the book website.

Defining Shape Drawables as XML Resources

In Chapter 6, "Managing Application Resources," we show you how to define primitive shapes such as rectangles using specially formatted XML files within the **/res/drawable/** resource directory.

The following resource file called `/res/drawable/green_rect.xml` describes a simple, green rectangle shape drawable:

```
<?xml version="1.0" encoding="utf-8"?>
<shape xmlns:android=
    "http://schemas.android.com/apk/res/android"
    android:shape="rectangle">
    <solid android:color="#0f0"/>
</shape>
```

You can then load the shape resource and set it as the `Drawable` as follows:

```
ImageView iView = (ImageView)findViewById(R.id.ImageView1);
iView.setImageResource(R.drawable.green_rect);
```

You should note that many `Paint` properties can be set via XML as part of the `Shape` definition. For example, the following `Oval` shape is defined with a linear gradient (red to white) and stroke style information:

```
<?xml version="1.0" encoding="utf-8"?>
<shape xmlns:android="http://schemas.android.com/apk/res/android"
    android:shape="oval">
    <solid android:color="#f00"/>
    <gradient android:startColor="#f00"
        android:endColor="#fff"
        android:angle="180"/>
    <stroke android:width="3dp" android:color="#00f"
        android:dashWidth="5dp" android:dashGap="3dp"/>
</shape>
```

Defining Shape Drawables Programmatically

You can also define these `ShapeDrawable` instances programmatically. The different shapes are available as classes within the `android.graphics.drawable.shapes` package. For example, you can programmatically define the aforementioned green rectangle as follows:

```
import android.graphics.drawable.ShapeDrawable;
import android.graphics.drawable.shapes.RectShape;
...
ShapeDrawable rect = new ShapeDrawable(new RectShape());
rect.getPaint().setColor(Color.GREEN);
```

You can then set the `Drawable` for the `ImageView` directly:

```
ImageView iView = (ImageView)findViewById(R.id.ImageView1);
iView.setImageDrawable(rect);
```

The resulting green rectangle is shown in Figure 9.6.

Drawing Different Shapes

Some of the different shapes available within the `android.graphics.drawable.shapes` package include

- Rectangles (and squares)
- Rectangles with rounded corners
- Ovals (and circles)
- Arcs and lines
- Other shapes defined as paths

Figure 9.6   A green rectangle.

You can create and use these shapes as `Drawable` resources directly within `ImageView` views, or you can find corresponding methods for creating these primitive shapes within a `Canvas`.

Drawing Rectangles and Squares

Drawing rectangles and squares (rectangles with equal height/width values) is simply a matter of creating a `ShapeDrawable` from a `RectShape` object. The `RectShape` object has no dimensions but is bound by the container object—in this case, the `ShapeDrawable`. You can set some basic properties of the `ShapeDrawable`, such as the Paint color and the default size.

For example, here we create a magenta-colored rectangle that is 100-pixels long and 2-pixels wide, which looks like a straight, horizontal line. We then set the shape as the drawable for an `ImageView` so the shape can be displayed:

```
import android.graphics.drawable.ShapeDrawable;
import android.graphics.drawable.shapes.RectShape;
...
```

```
ShapeDrawable rect = new ShapeDrawable(new RectShape());
rect.setIntrinsicHeight(2);
rect.setIntrinsicWidth(100);
rect.getPaint().setColor(Color.MAGENTA);


ImageView iView = (ImageView)findViewById(R.id.ImageView1);
iView.setImageDrawable(rect);
```

Drawing Rectangles with Rounded Corners

You can create rectangles with rounded corners, which can be nice for making custom buttons. Simply create a `ShapeDrawable` from a `RoundRectShape` object. The `RoundRectShape` requires an array of eight float values, which signify the radii of the rounded corners. For example, the following creates a simple cyan-colored, rounded-corner rectangle:

```
import android.graphics.drawable.ShapeDrawable;
import android.graphics.drawable.shapes.RoundRectShape;
...
ShapeDrawable rndrect = new ShapeDrawable(
    new RoundRectShape( new float[] { 5, 5, 5, 5, 5, 5, 5, 5 },
    null, null));
rndrect.setIntrinsicHeight(50);
rndrect.setIntrinsicWidth(100);
rndrect.getPaint().setColor(Color.CYAN);
ImageView iView = (ImageView)findViewById(R.id.ImageView1);
iView.setImageDrawable(rndrect);
```

The resulting round-corner rectangle is shown in Figure 9.7.

You can also specify an inner-rounded rectangle within the outer rectangle, if you so choose. The following creates an inner rectangle with rounded edges within the outer white rectangle with rounded edges:

```
import android.graphics.drawable.ShapeDrawable;
import android.graphics.drawable.shapes.RoundRectShape;
...
float[] outerRadii = new float[]{ 6, 6, 6, 6, 6, 6, 6, 6 };
RectF insetRectangle = new RectF(8, 8, 8, 8);
float[] innerRadii = new float[]{ 6, 6, 6, 6, 6, 6, 6, 6 };

ShapeDrawable rndrect = new ShapeDrawable(
    new RoundRectShape(
    outerRadii,insetRectangle , innerRadii));

rndrect.setIntrinsicHeight(50);
rndrect.setIntrinsicWidth(100);
rndrect.getPaint().setColor(Color.WHITE);
ImageView iView = (ImageView)findViewById(R.id.ImageView1);
iView.setImageDrawable(rndrect);
```

Figure 9.7   A cyan rectangle with rounded corners.

The resulting round rectangle with an inset rectangle is shown in Figure 9.8.

Figure 9.8   A white rectangle with rounded corners, with an inset rounded rectangle.

Drawing Ovals and Circles

You can create ovals and circles (which are ovals with equal height/width values) by creating a `ShapeDrawable` using an `OvalShape` object. The `OvalShape` object has no dimensions but is bound by the container object—in this case, the `ShapeDrawable`. You can set some basic properties of the `ShapeDrawable`, such as the Paint color and the default size. For example, here we create a red oval that is 40-pixels high and 100-pixels wide, which looks like a Frisbee:

```
import android.graphics.drawable.ShapeDrawable;
import android.graphics.drawable.shapes.OvalShape;
...
ShapeDrawable oval = new ShapeDrawable(new OvalShape());
oval.setIntrinsicHeight(40);
oval.setIntrinsicWidth(100);
oval.getPaint().setColor(Color.RED);
ImageView iView = (ImageView)findViewById(R.id.ImageView1);
iView.setImageDrawable(oval);
```

The resulting red oval is shown in Figure 9.9.

Figure 9.9   A red oval.

Drawing Arcs

You can draw arcs, which look like pie charts or Pac-Man, depending on the sweep angle you specify. You can create arcs by creating a `ShapeDrawable` by using an `ArcShape` object. The `ArcShape` object requires two parameters: a `startAngle` and a `sweepAngle`. The startAngle begins at 3 o'clock. Positive sweepAngle values sweep clockwise; negative values sweep counterclockwise. You can create a circle by using the values 0 and 360.

The following code creates an arc that looks like a magenta Pac-Man:

```
import android.graphics.drawable.ShapeDrawable;
import android.graphics.drawable.shapes.ArcShape;
...
ShapeDrawable pacMan =
    new ShapeDrawable(new ArcShape(0, 345));
pacMan.setIntrinsicHeight(100);
pacMan.setIntrinsicWidth(100);
pacMan.getPaint().setColor(Color.MAGENTA);
ImageView iView = (ImageView)findViewById(R.id.ImageView1);
iView.setImageDrawable(pacMan);
```

The resulting arc is shown in Figure 9.10.

Figure 9.10   A magenta arc of 345 degrees
(resembling Pac-Man).

Drawing Paths

You can specify any shape you want by breaking it down into a series of points along a path. The android.graphics.Path class encapsulates a series of lines and curves that make up some larger shape.

For example, the following `Path` defines a rough five-point star shape:

```
import android.graphics.Path;
...
Path p = new Path();
p.moveTo(50, 0);
p.lineTo(25,100);
p.lineTo(100,50);
p.lineTo(0,50);
p.lineTo(75,100);
p.lineTo(50,0);
```

You can then encapsulate this star `Path` in a `PathShape`, create a `ShapeDrawable`, and paint it yellow.

```
import android.graphics.drawable.ShapeDrawable;
import android.graphics.drawable.shapes.PathShape;
...
ShapeDrawable star =
    new ShapeDrawable(new PathShape(p, 100, 100));
star.setIntrinsicHeight(100);
star.setIntrinsicWidth(100);
star.getPaint().setColor(Color.YELLOW);
```

By default, this generates a star shape filled with the `Paint` color yellow (see Figure 9.11).
Or, you can set the `Paint` style to `Stroke` for a line drawing of a star.

```
star.getPaint().setStyle(Paint.Style.STROKE);
```

The resulting star would look something like Figure 9.12.

Tip

The graphics support available within the Android SDK could be the subject of an entire book. After you have familiarized yourself with the basics, we recommend that you check out the APIDemos sample application provided with the Android SDK.

Working with Animation

The Android platform supports three types of graphics animation:

- Animated GIF images
- Frame-by-frame animation
- Tweened animation

Figure 9.11   A yellow star.

Figure 9.12   A yellow star using the stroke style
of Paint.

Animated GIFs store the animation frames within the image, and you simply include these GIFs like any other graphic drawable resource. For frame-by-frame animation, the developer must provide all graphics frames of the animation. However, with tweened animation, only a single graphic is needed, upon which transforms can be programmatically applied.

Tip

Many of the code examples provided in this chapter are taken from the ShapeShifter application. This source code for the ShapeShifter application is provided for download on the book website.

Working with Frame-by-Frame Animation

You can think of frame-by-frame animation as a digital flipbook in which a series of similar images display on the screen in a sequence, each subtly different from the last. When you display these images quickly, they give the illusion of movement. This technique is called frame-by-frame animation and is often used on the Web in the form of animated GIF images.

Frame-by-frame animation is best used for complicated graphics transformations that are not easily implemented programmatically.

For example, we can create the illusion of a genie juggling gifts using a sequence of three images, as shown in Figure 9.13.

Figure 9.13   Three frames for an animation of a genie juggling.

In each frame, the genie remains fixed, but the gifts are repositioned slightly. The smoothness of the animation is controlled by providing an adequate number of frames and choosing the appropriate speed on which to swap them.

The following code demonstrates how to load three `Bitmap` resources (our three genie frames) and create an `AnimationDrawable`. We then set the `AnimationDrawable` as the background resource of an `ImageView` and start the animation:

```
ImageView img = (ImageView)findViewById(R.id.ImageView1);

BitmapDrawable frame1 = (BitmapDrawable)getResources().
    getDrawable(R.drawable.f1);
```

```
BitmapDrawable frame2 = (BitmapDrawable)getResources().
    getDrawable(R.drawable.f2);
BitmapDrawable frame3 = (BitmapDrawable)getResources().
    getDrawable(R.drawable.f3);

int reasonableDuration = 250;
AnimationDrawable mAnimation = new AnimationDrawable();

mAnimation.addFrame(frame1, reasonableDuration);
mAnimation.addFrame(frame2, reasonableDuration);
mAnimation.addFrame(frame3, reasonableDuration);

img.setBackgroundDrawable(mAnimation);
```

To name the animation loop continuously, we can call the `setOneShot()` method:

```
mAnimation.setOneShot(false);
```

To begin the animation, we call the `start()` method:

```
mAnimation.start();
```

We can end our animation at any time using the `stop()` method:

```
mAnimation.stop();
```

Although we used an `ImageView` background in this example, you can use a variety of different `View` widgets for animations. For example, you can instead use the `ImageSwitcher` view and change the displayed `Drawable` resource using a timer. This sort of operation is best done on a separate thread. The resulting animation might look something like Figure 9.14—you just have to imagine it moving.

Working with Tweened Animations

With tweened animation, you can provide a single `Drawable` resource—it is a `Bitmap` graphic (see Figure 9.15, left), a `ShapeDrawable`, a `TextView` (see Figure 9.15, right), or any other type of `View` object—and the intermediate frames of the animation are rendered by the system. Android provides tweening support for several common image transformations, including alpha, rotate, scale, and translate animations. You can apply tweened animation transformations to any `View`, whether it is an `ImageView` with a `Bitmap` or shape `Drawable`, or a layout such as a `TableLayout`.

Defining Tweening Transformations

You can define tweening transformations as XML resource files or programmatically. All tweened animations share some common properties, including when to start, how long to animate, and whether to return to the starting state upon completion.

Figure 9.14   The genie animation in the Android emulator.

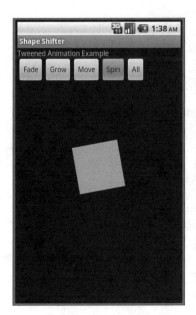

Figure 9.15   Rotating a green rectangle shape **drawable** (left) and a **TableLayout** (right).

Defining Tweened Animations as XML Resources

In Chapter 6, we showed you how to store animation sequences as specially formatted XML files within the `/res/anim/` resource directory. For example, the following resource file called `/res/anim/spin.xml` describes a simple five-second rotation:

```
<?xml version="1.0" encoding="utf-8" ?>
<set xmlns:android
    = "http://schemas.android.com/apk/res/android"
    android:shareInterpolator="false">
    <rotate
        android:fromDegrees="0"
        android:toDegrees="360"
        android:pivotX="50%"
        android:pivotY="50%"
        android:duration="5000" />
</set>
```

Defining Tweened Animations Programmatically

You can programmatically define these animations. The different types of transformations are available as classes within the `android.view.animation` package. For example, you can define the aforementioned rotation animation as follows:

```
import android.view.animation.RotateAnimation;
...
RotateAnimation rotate = new RotateAnimation(
    0, 360, RotateAnimation.RELATIVE_TO_SELF, 0.5f,
    RotateAnimation.RELATIVE_TO_SELF, 0.5f);

rotate.setDuration(5000);
```

Defining Simultaneous and Sequential Tweened Animations

Animation transformations can happen simultaneously or sequentially when you set the `startOffset` and `duration` properties, which control when and for how long an animation takes to complete. You can combine animations into the `<set>` tag (programmatically, using `AnimationSet`) to share properties.

For example, the following animation resource file `/res/anim/grow.xml` includes a set of two scale animations: First, we take 2.5 seconds to double in size, and then at 2.5 seconds, we start a second animation to shrink back to our starting size:

```
<?xml version="1.0" encoding="utf-8" ?>
<set xmlns:android=
    http://schemas.android.com/apk/res/android
    android:shareInterpolator="false">
    <scale
        android:pivotX="50%"
        android:pivotY="50%"
```

```
        android:fromXScale="1.0"
        android:fromYScale="1.0"
        android:toXScale="2.0"
        android:toYScale="2.0"
        android:duration="2500" />
    <scale
        android:startOffset="2500"
        android:duration="2500"
        android:pivotX="50%"
        android:pivotY="50%"
        android:fromXScale="1.0"
        android:fromYScale="1.0"
        android:toXScale="0.5"
        android:toYScale="0.5" />
</set>
```

Loading Animations

Loading animations is made simple by using the `AnimationUtils` helper class. The following code loads an animation XML resource file called `/res/anim/grow.xml` and applies it to an `ImageView` whose source resource is a green rectangle shape `drawable`:

```
import android.view.animation.Animation;
import android.view.animation.AnimationUtils;
...
ImageView iView = (ImageView)findViewById(R.id.ImageView1);
iView.setImageResource(R.drawable.green_rect);
Animation an =
    AnimationUtils.loadAnimation(this, R.anim.grow);
iView.startAnimation(an);
```

We can listen for `Animation` events, including the animation start, end, and repeat events, by implementing an `AnimationListener` class, such as the `MyListener` class shown here:

```
class MyListener implements Animation.AnimationListener {

    public void onAnimationEnd(Animation animation) {
        // Do at end of animation
    }

    public void onAnimationRepeat(Animation animation) {
        // Do each time the animation loops
    }

    public void onAnimationStart(Animation animation) {
        // Do at start of animation
    }
}
```

You can then register your `AnimationListener` as follows:

```
an.setAnimationListener(new MyListener());
```

Exploring the Four Different Tweening Transformations

Now let's look at each of the four types of tweening transformations individually. These types are

- Transparency changes (Alpha)
- Rotations (Rotate)
- Scaling (Scale)
- Movement (Translate)

Working with Alpha Transparency Transformations

Transparency is controlled using Alpha transformations. Alpha transformations can be used to fade objects in and out of view or to layer them on the screen.

Alpha values range from 0.0 (fully transparent or invisible) to 1.0 (fully opaque or visible). Alpha animations involve a starting transparency (`fromAlpha`) and an ending transparency (`toAlpha`).

The following XML resource file excerpt defines a transparency-change animation, taking five seconds to fade in from fully transparent to fully opaque:

```
<alpha
    android:fromAlpha="0.0"
    android:toAlpha="1.0"
    android:duration="5000">
</alpha>
```

Programmatically, you can create this same animation using the `AlphaAnimation` class within the `android.view.animation` package.

Working with Rotating Transformations

You can use rotation operations to spin objects clockwise or counterclockwise around a pivot point within the object's boundaries.

Rotations are defined in terms of degrees. For example, you might want an object to make one complete clockwise rotation. To do this, you set the `fromDegrees` property to 0 and the `toDegrees` property to 360. To rotate the object counterclockwise instead, you set the `toDegrees` property to -360.

By default, the object pivots around the (0,0) coordinate, or the top-left corner of the object. This is great for rotations such as those of a clock's hands, but much of the time, you want to pivot from the center of the object; you can do this easily by setting the pivot point, which can be a fixed coordinate or a percentage.

The following XML resource file excerpt defines a rotation animation, taking five seconds to make one full clockwise rotation, pivoting from the center of the object:

```
<rotate
    android:fromDegrees="0"
    android:toDegrees="360"
    android:pivotX="50%"
    android:pivotY="50%"
    android:duration="5000" />
```

Programmatically, you can create this same animation using the `RotateAnimation` class within the `android.view.animation` package.

Working with Scaling Transformations

You can use scaling operations to stretch objects vertically and horizontally. Scaling operations are defined as relative scales. Think of the scale value of 1.0 as 100 percent, or full-size. To scale to half-size, or 50 percent, set the target scale value of 0.5.

You can scale horizontally and vertically on different scales or on the same scale (to preserve aspect ratio). You need to set four values for proper scaling: starting scale (`fromXScale`, `fromYScale`) and target scale (`toXScale`, `toYScale`). Again, you can use a pivot point to stretch your object from a specific (x,y) coordinate such as the center or another coordinate.

The following XML resource file excerpt defines a scaling animation, taking five seconds to double an object's size, pivoting from the center of the object:

```
<scale
    android:pivotX="50%"
    android:pivotY="50%"
    android:fromXScale="1.0"
    android:fromYScale="1.0"
    android:toXScale="2.0"
    android:toYScale="2.0"
    android:duration="5000" />
```

Programmatically, you can create this same animation using the `ScaleAnimation` class within the `android.view.animation` package.

Working with Moving Transformations

You can move objects around using translate operations. Translate operations move an object from one position on the (x,y) coordinate to another coordinate.

To perform a translate operation, you must specify the change, or delta, in the object's coordinates. You can set four values for translations: starting position (`fromXDelta`, `fromYDelta`) and relative target location (`toXDelta`, `toYDelta`).

The following XML resource file excerpt defines a translate animation, taking 5 seconds to move an object up (negative) by 100 on the y-axis. We also set the `fillAfter` property to be true, so the object doesn't "jump" back to its starting position when the animation finishes:

```
<translate android:toYDelta="-100"
    android:fillAfter="true"
    android:duration="2500" />
```

Programmatically, you can create this same animation using the `TranslateAnimation` class within the `android.view.animation` package.

Working with Different Interpolators

The animation interpolator determines the rate at which a transformation happens in time. There are a number of different interpolators provided as part of the Android SDK framework. Some of these interpolators include

- `AccelerateDecelerateInterpolator`: Animation starts slowly, speeds up, and ends slowly
- `AccelerateInterpolator`: Animation starts slowly and then accelerates
- `AnticipateInterpolator`: Animation starts backward, and then flings forward
- `AnticipateOvershootInterpolator`: Animation starts backward, flings forward, overshoots its destination, and then settles at the destination
- `BounceInterpolator`: Animation "bounces" into place at its destination
- `CycleInterpolator`: Animation is repeated a certain number of times smoothly transitioning from one cycle to the next
- `DecelerateInterpolator`: Animation begins quickly, and then decelerates
- `LinearInterpolator`: Animation speed is constant throughout
- `OvershootInterpolator`: Animation overshoots its destination, and then settles at the destination

You can specify the interpolator used by an animation programmatically using the `setInterpolator()` method or in the animation XML resource using the `android:interpolator` attribute.

Summary

The Android SDK comes with the `android.graphics` package, which includes powerful classes for drawing graphics and text to the screen in a variety of different ways. Some features of the graphics library include `Bitmap` graphics utilities, `Typeface` and font style support, `Paint` colors and styles, different types of gradients, and a variety of primitive and not-so-primitive shapes that can be drawn to the screen and even animated using tweening and frame-by-frame animation mechanisms.

In Chapter 17, "Using Android 3D Graphics with OpenGL ES," we dive further into using the OpenGL ES library for 2D and 3D rendering.

## 10

Using Android Data and Storage APIs

Applications are about functionality and data. In this chapter, we explore the various ways you can store, manage, and share application data with Android. Applications can store and manage data in different ways. For example, applications can use a combination of application preferences, the file system, and built-in SQLite database support to store information locally. The methods your application uses depend on your requirements. In this chapter, you learn how to use each of these mechanisms to store, retrieve, and interact with data.

Working with Application Preferences

Many applications need a lightweight data storage mechanism called shared preferences for storing application state, simple user information, configuration options, and other such information.

Tip

Many of the code examples provided in this section are taken from the SimplePreferences application. This source code for the SimplePreferences application is provided for download on the book website.

Android provides a simple preferences system for storing primitive application data at the `Activity` level and preferences shared across all of an application's activities. You cannot share preferences outside of the package. Preferences are stored as groups of key/value pairs. The following data types are supported as preference settings:

- Boolean values
- Float values
- Integer values
- Long values
- String values

Preference functionality can be found in the `SharedPreferences` interface of the `android.content` package. To add preferences support to your application, you must take the following steps:

1. Retrieve an instance of a `SharedPreferences` object.

2. Create a `SharedPreferences.Editor` to modify preference content.

3. Make changes to the preferences using the Editor.

4. Commit your changes.

Creating Private and Shared Preferences

Individual activities can have their own private preferences. These preferences are for the specific `Activity` only and are not shared with other activities within the application. The activity gets only one group of private preferences.

The following code retrieves the activity's private preferences:

```
import android.content.SharedPreferences;
...
SharedPreferences settingsActivity = getPreferences(MODE_PRIVATE);
```

Creating shared preferences is similar. The only two differences are that we must name our preference set and use a different call to get the preference instance:

```
import android.content.SharedPreferences;
...
SharedPreferences settings =
    getSharedPreferences("MyCustomSharedPreferences", 0);
```

You can access shared preferences by name from any activity in the application. There is no limit to the number of different shared preferences you can create. You can have some shared preferences called `UserNetworkPreferences` and another called `AppDisplayPreferences`. How you organize shared preferences is up to you, the developer. However, you want to declare your preference name as a variable (in a base class or header) so that you can reuse the name across multiple activities. For example

```
public static final String PREFERENCE_FILENAME = "AppPrefs";
```

Searching and Reading Preferences

Reading preferences is straightforward. Simply retrieve the `SharedPreferences` instance you want to read. You can check for a preference by name, retrieve strongly typed preferences, and register to listen for changes to the preferences. Table 10.1 describes some helpful methods in the `SharedPreferences` interface.

Table 10.1   Important **android.content.SharedPreferences** Methods

Method	Purpose
`SharedPreferences.contains()`	Sees whether a specific preference exists by name
`SharedPreferences.edit()`	Retrieves the editor to change these preferences
`SharedPreferences.getAll()`	Retrieves a map of all preference key/value pairs
`SharedPreferences.getBoolean()`	Retrieves a specific Boolean-type preference by name
`SharedPreferences.getFloat()`	Retrieves a specific Float-type preference by name
`SharedPreferences.getInt()`	Retrieves a specific Integer-type preference by name
`SharedPreferences.getLong()`	Retrieves a specific Long-type preference by name
`SharedPreferences.getString()`	Retrieves a specific String-type preference by name

Adding, Updating, and Deleting Preferences

To change preferences, you need to open the preference `Editor`, make your changes, and commit them. Table 10.2 describes some helpful methods in the `SharedPreferences.Editor` interface.

Table 10.2   Important **android.content.SharedPreferences.Editor** Methods

Method	Purpose
`SharedPreferences.Editor.clear()`	Removes all preferences. This operation happens first, regardless of when it is called within an editing session; then all other changes are made and committed.
`SharedPreferences.Editor.remove()`	Removes a specific preference by name. This operation happens first, regardless of when it is called within an editing session; then all other changes are made and committed.
`SharedPreferences.Editor.putBoolean()`	Sets a specific Boolean-type preference by name.
`SharedPreferences.Editor.putFloat()`	Sets a specific Float-type preference by name.
`SharedPreferences.Editor.putInt()`	Sets a specific Integer-type preference by name.

TABLE 10.2   **Continued**

Method	Purpose
`SharedPreferences.Editor.putLong()`	Sets a specific Long-type preference by name.
`SharedPreferences.Editor.putString()`	Sets a specific String-type preference by name.
`SharedPreferences.Editor.commit()`	Commits all changes from this editing session.

The following block of code retrieves the activity's private preferences, opens the preference editor, adds a long preference called `SomeLong`, and saves the change:

```
import android.content.SharedPreferences;
...
SharedPreferences settingsActivity = getPreferences(MODE_PRIVATE);
SharedPreferences.Editor prefEditor = settingsActivity.edit();
prefEditor.putLong("SomeLong", java.lang.Long.MIN_VALUE);
prefEditor.commit();
```

Finding Preferences Data on the Android File System

Internally, application preferences are stored as XML files. You can access the preferences file using DDMS using the File Explorer. You find these files on the Android file system in the following directory:

```
/data/data/<package name>/shared_prefs/<preferences filename>.xml
```

The preferences filename is the Activity's class name for private preferences or the name you give for the shared preferences. Here is an example of the file contents of a simple preference file with a preference in each data type:

```
<?xml version="1.0" encoding="utf-8" standalone="yes" ?>
<map>
    <string name="String_Pref">Test String</string>
    <int name="Int_Pref" value="-2147483648" />
    <float name="Float_Pref" value="-Infinity" />
    <long name="Long_Pref" value="9223372036854775807" />
    <boolean name="Boolean_Pref" value="false" />
</map>
```

Understanding the application preferences file format can be helpful for testing purposes. You can use Dalvik Debug Monitor Service (DDMS) to copy the preferences files to and from the device.

Note

For more information about using DDMS and the File Explorer, please see Appendix B, "The Android DDMS Quick-Start Guide."

Working with Files and Directories

Remember from Chapter 1, "Introducing Android," that each Android application is its own user on the underlying Linux operating system. It has its own private application directory and files. Within the Android SDK, you can also find a variety of standard Java file utility classes (such as `java.io`) for handling different types of files, such as text files, binary files, and XML files.

In Chapter 6, "Managing Application Resources," you also learned that Android applications can also include static raw and XML files as resources. Although retrieving the file is handled slightly differently when accessing resources, the file can be read like any other file.

Android application files are stored in a standard directory hierarchy on the Android file system. You can browse an application's directory structure using the DDMS File Explorer.

> **Tip**
>
> Many of the code examples provided in this section are taken from the SimpleFiles and FileStreamOfConsciousness applications. The SimpleFiles application demonstrates basic file and directory operations; it has no user interface (see the LogCat output instead). The FileStreamOfConsciousness application demonstrates how to log strings to a file as a chat stream; this application is multi-threaded. The source code for these applications is provided for download on the book website.

Exploring with the Android Application Directories

Android application data is stored on the Android file system in the following top-level directory:

```
/data/data/<package name>/
```

Several default subdirectories are created for storing databases, preferences, and files as necessary. You can also create other custom directories as needed. File operators all begin by interacting with the application `Context` object. Table 10.3 lists some important methods available for application file management. You can use all the standard `java.io` package utilities to work with `FileStream` objects and such.

Table 10.3   Important **android.content.Context** File and Directory Management Methods

Method	Purpose
`Context.openFileInput()`	Opens an application file for reading. These files are located in the `/files` subdirectory.
`Context.openFileOutput()`	Creates or opens an application file for writing. These files are located in the `/files` subdirectory.
`Context.deleteFile()`	Deletes an application file by name. These files must be located in the `/files` subdirectory.

Table 10.3   **Continued**

Method	Purpose
Context.fileList()	Gets a list of all files in the /files subdirectory.
Context.getFilesDir()	Retrieves the application /files subdirectory object.
Context.getCacheDir()	Retrieves the application /cache subdirectory object.
Context.getDir()	Creates or retrieves an application subdirectory by name.

Creating and Writing to Files to the Default Application Directory

Android applications that require only the occasional file rely upon the helpful method called openFileOutput(). Use this method to create files in the default location under the application data directory:

```
/data/data/<package name>/files/
```

For example, the following code snippet creates and opens a file called Filename.txt. We write a single line of text to the file and then close the file:

```
import java.io.FileOutputStream;
...
FileOutputStream fos;
String strFileContents = "Some text to write to the file.";
fos = openFileOutput("Filename.txt", MODE_PRIVATE);
fos.write(strFileContents.getBytes());
fos.close();
```

We can append data to the file by opening it with the mode set to MODE_APPEND:

```
import java.io.FileOutputStream;
...
FileOutputStream fos;
String strFileContents = "More text to write to the file.";
fos = openFileOutput("Filename.txt", MODE_APPEND);
fos.write(strFileContents.getBytes());
fos.close();
```

The file we created has the following path on the Android file system:

```
/data/data/<package name>/files/Filename.txt
```

Reading from Files in the Default Application Directory

Again we have a shortcut for reading files stored in the default /files subdirectory. The following code snippet opens a file called Filename.txt for read operations:

```
import java.io.FileInputStream;
...
String strFileName = "Filename.txt";
FileInputStream fis = openFileInput(strFileName);
```

Reading Raw Files Byte-by-Byte

You handle file-reading and -writing operations using standard Java methods. Check out the subclasses of `java.io.InputStream` for reading bytes from different types of primitive file types. For example, `DataInputStream` is useful for reading one line at a time.

Here's a simple example of how to read a text file, line by line, and store it in a `StringBuffer`:

```
FileInputStream fis = openFileInput(filename);
StringBuffer sBuffer = new StringBuffer();
DataInputStream dataIO = new DataInputStream(fis);
String strLine = null;

while ((strLine = dataIO.readLine()) != null) {
    sBuffer.append(strLine + "\n");
}

dataIO.close();
fis.close();
```

Reading XML Files

The Android SDK includes several utilities for working with XML files, including SAX, an XML Pull Parser, and limited DOM, Level 2 Core support. Table 10.4 lists the packages helpful for XML parsing on the Android platform.

Table 10.4   **Important XML Utility Packages**

Method	Purpose
`android.sax.*`	Framework to write standard SAX handlers.
`android.util.Xml.*`	XML utilities including the `XMLPullParser`.
`org.xml.sax.*`	Core SAX functionality. Project: www.saxproject.org/.
`javax.xml.*`	SAX and limited DOM, Level 2 Core support.
`org.w3c.dom`	Interfaces for DOM, Level 2 Core.
`org.xmlpull.*`	`XmlPullParser` and `XMLSerializer` interfaces as well as a SAX2 Driver class. Project: www.xmlpull.org/.

Tip

The ResourceRoundup project in Chapter 6 provides an example of parsing a static XML file included as an application resource using the `XmlPullParser` called `XmlResourceParser`.

Working with Other Directories and Files on the Android File System

Using `Context.openFileOutput()` and `Context.openFileInput()` are great if you have a few files and you want them stored in the `/files` subdirectory, but if you have more sophisticated file-management needs, you need to set up your own directory structure. To do this, you must interact with the Android file system using the standard `java.io.File` class methods.

The following code gets a `File` object for the `/files` application subdirectory and retrieves a list of all filenames in that directory:

```
import java.io.File;
...
File pathForAppFiles = getFilesDir();
String[] fileList = pathForAppFiles.list();
```

Here is a more generic method to create a file on the file system. This method works anywhere on the Android file system you have permission to access, not the `/files` directory:

```
import java.io.File;
import java.io.FileOutputStream;
...
File fileDir = getFilesDir();
String strNewFileName = "myFile.dat";
String strFileContents = "Some data for our file";

File newFile = new File(fileDir, strNewFileName);
newFile.createNewFile();

FileOutputStream fo =
    new FileOutputStream(newFile.getAbsolutePath());
fo.write(strFileContents.getBytes());
fo.close();
```

You can use `File` objects to manage files within a desired directory and create subdirectories. For example, you might want to store "track" files within "album" directories. Or perhaps you want to create a file in a directory other than the default.

Tip

Applications should store large amounts of data on external storage (using the SD card) rather than limited internal storage.

Let's say you want to cache some data to speed up your application's performance and how often it accesses the network. In this instance, you might want to create a cache file. There is also a special application directory for storing cache files. Cache files are stored in the following location on the Android file system:

```
/data/data/<package name>/cache/
```

> **Warning**
>
> Applications are responsible for managing their own cache directory and keeping it to a reasonable size (1MB is commonly recommended). The Android file system deletes cache files as needed when internal storage space is low, or when the user uninstalls the application.

The following code gets a `File` object for the `/cache` application subdirectory, creates a new file in that specific directory, writes some data to the file, closes the file, and then deletes it:

```
File pathCacheDir = getCacheDir();
String strCacheFileName = "myCacheFile.cache";
String strFileContents = "Some data for our file";

File newCacheFile = new File(pathCacheDir, strCacheFileName);
newCacheFile.createNewFile();

FileOutputStream foCache =
    new FileOutputStream(newCacheFile.getAbsolutePath());
foCache.write(strFileContents.getBytes());
foCache.close();

newCacheFile.delete();
```

Storing Structured Data Using SQLite Databases

For occasions when your application requires a more robust data storage mechanism, the Android file system includes support for application-specific relational databases using SQLite. SQLite databases are lightweight and file-based, making them ideally suited for embedded devices.

> **Tip**
>
> Many of the code examples provided in this section are taken from the SimpleDatabase application. This source code for the SimpleDatabase application is provided for download on the book website.

These databases and the data within them are private to the application. To share application data with other applications, you must expose the data you want to share by making your application a content provider (discussed later in this chapter).

The Android SDK includes a number of useful SQLite database management classes. Many of these classes are found in the `android.database.sqlite` package. Here you can find utility classes for managing database creation and versioning, database management, and query builder helper classes to help you format proper SQL statements and queries. The package also includes specialized `Cursor` objects for iterating query results. You can also find all the specialized exceptions associated with SQLite.

Here we focus on creating databases within our Android applications. For that, we use the built-in SQLite support to programmatically create and use a SQLite database to store application information. However, if your application works with a different sort of database, you can also find more generic database classes (within the `android.database` package) to help you work with data from other providers.

In addition to programmatically creating and using SQLite databases, developers can also interact directly with their application's database using the `sqlite3` command-line tool that's accessible through the ADB shell interface. This can be an extremely helpful debugging tool for developers and quality assurance personnel, who might want to manage the database state (and content) for testing purposes.

> **Note**
>
> For more information about designing SQLite databases and interacting with them via the sqlite3 command-line tool, please see Appendix E, "The SQLite Quick-Start Guide." This appendix is divided into two parts: the first half is an overview of the most commonly used features of the `sqlite3` command-line interface and the limitations of SQLite compared to other flavors of SQL; the second half of the appendix includes a fully functional tutorial in which you build a SQLite database from the ground up and then use it. If you are new to SQLite or a bit rusty on your syntax, this appendix is for you.

Creating a SQLite Database

You can create a SQLite database for your Android application in several ways. To illustrate how to create and use a simple SQLite database, let's create an Android project called SimpleDatabase.

Creating a SQLite Database Instance Using the Application Context

The simplest way to create a new `SQLiteDatabase` instance for your application is to use the `openOrCreateDatabase()` method of your application `Context`, like this:

```
import android.database.sqlite.SQLiteDatabase;
...
SQLiteDatabase mDatabase;
mDatabase = openOrCreateDatabase(
    "my_sqlite_database.db",
    SQLiteDatabase.CREATE_IF_NECESSARY,
    null);
```

Finding the Application's Database File on the Device File System

Android applications store their databases (SQLite or otherwise) in a special application directory:

```
/data/data/<application package name>/databases/<databasename>
```

So, in this case, the path to the database would be

```
/data/data/com.androidbook.SimpleDatabase/databases/my_sqlite_database.db
```

You can access your database using the `sqlite3` command-line interface using this path.

Configuring the SQLite Database Properties

Now that you have a valid `SQLiteDatabase` instance, it's time to configure it. Some important database configuration options include version, locale, and the thread-safe locking feature.

```
import java.util.Locale;
...
mDatabase.setLocale(Locale.getDefault());
mDatabase.setLockingEnabled(true);
mDatabase.setVersion(1);
```

Creating Tables and Other SQLite Schema Objects

Creating tables and other SQLite schema objects is as simple as forming proper SQLite statements and executing them. The following is a valid `CREATE TABLE` SQL statement. This statement creates a table called `tbl_authors`. The table has three fields: a unique `id` number, which auto-increments with each record and acts as our primary key, and `firstname` and `lastname` text fields:

```
CREATE TABLE tbl_authors (
id INTEGER PRIMARY KEY AUTOINCREMENT,
firstname TEXT,
lastname TEXT);
```

You can encapsulate this `CREATE TABLE` SQL statement in a static final String variable (called `CREATE_AUTHOR_TABLE`) and then execute it on your database using the `execSQL()` method:

```
mDatabase.execSQL(CREATE_AUTHOR_TABLE);
```

The `execSQL()` method works for nonqueries. You can use it to execute any valid SQLite SQL statement. For example, you can use it to create, update, and delete tables, views, triggers, and other common SQL objects. In our application, we add another table called `tbl_books`. The schema for `tbl_books` looks like this:

```
CREATE TABLE tbl_books (
id INTEGER PRIMARY KEY AUTOINCREMENT,
title TEXT,
dateadded DATE,
authorid INTEGER NOT NULL CONSTRAINT authorid REFERENCES tbl_authors(id) ON DELETE
CASCADE);
```

Unfortunately, SQLite does not enforce foreign key constraints. Instead, we must enforce them ourselves using custom SQL triggers. So we create triggers, such as this one that enforces that books have valid authors:

```
private static final String CREATE_TRIGGER_ADD =
"CREATE TRIGGER fk_insert_book BEFORE INSERT ON tbl_books
FOR EACH ROW
BEGIN
```

```
SELECT RAISE(ROLLBACK, 'insert on table \"tbl_books\" violates foreign key
constraint \"fk_authorid\"') WHERE  (SELECT id FROM tbl_authors WHERE id =
NEW.authorid) IS NULL;
END;";
```

We can then create the trigger simply by executing the CREATE TRIGGER SQL statement:

```
mDatabase.execSQL(CREATE_TRIGGER_ADD);
```

We need to add several more triggers to help enforce our link between the author and book tables, one for updating `tbl_books` and one for deleting records from `tbl_authors`.

Creating, Updating, and Deleting Database Records

Now that we have a database set up, we need to create some data. The SQLiteDatabase class includes three convenience methods to do that. They are, as you might expect, `insert()`, `update()`, and `delete()`.

Inserting Records

We use the `insert()` method to add new data to our tables. We use the ContentValues object to pair the column names to the column values for the record we want to insert. For example, here we insert a record into `tbl_authors` for J.K. Rowling:

```
import android.content.ContentValues;
...
ContentValues values = new ContentValues();
values.put("firstname", "J.K.");
values.put("lastname", "Rowling");
long newAuthorID = mDatabase.insert("tbl_authors", null, values);
```

The `insert()` method returns the id of the newly created record. We use this author id to create book records for this author.

Tip

There is also another helpful method called `insertOrThrow()`, which does the same thing as the `insert()` method but throws a SQLException on failure, which can be helpful, especially if your inserts are not working and you'd really like to know why.

You might want to create simple classes (that is, class Author and class Book) to encapsulate your application record data when it is used programmatically.

Updating Records

You can modify records in the database using the `update()` method. The `update()` method takes four arguments:

- The table to update records
- A ContentValues object with the modified fields to update
- An optional WHERE clause, in which ? identifies a WHERE clause argument

- An array of WHERE clause arguments, each of which is substituted in place of the ?'s from the second parameter

Passing `null` to the WHERE clause modifies all records within the table, which can be useful for making sweeping changes to your database.

Most of the time, we want to modify individual records by their unique identifier. The following function takes two parameters: an updated book title and a `bookId`. We find the record in the table called `tbl_books` that corresponds with the `id` and update that book's title. Again, we use the `ContentValues` object to bind our column names to our data values:

```
public void updateBookTitle(Integer bookId, String newtitle) {
    ContentValues values = new ContentValues();
    values.put("title", newtitle);
    mDatabase.update("tbl_books",
        values, "id=?", new String[] { bookId.toString() });
}
```

Because we are not updating the other fields, we do not need to include them in the `ContentValues` object. We include only the title field because it is the only field we change.

Deleting Records

You can remove records from the database using the `remove()` method. The `remove()` method takes three arguments:

- The table to delete the record from
- An optional WHERE clause, in which ? identifies a WHERE clause argument
- An array of WHERE clause arguments, each of which is substituted in place of the ?'s from the second parameter

Passing `null` to the WHERE clause deletes all records within the table. For example, this function call deletes all records within the table called `tbl_authors`:

```
mDatabase.delete("tbl_authors", null, null);
```

Most of the time, though, we want to delete individual records by their unique identifiers. The following function takes a parameter `bookId` and deletes the record corresponding to that unique `id` (primary key) within the table called `tbl_books`:

```
public void deleteBook(Integer bookId) {
    mDatabase.delete("tbl_books", "id=?",
        new String[] { bookId.toString() });
}
```

You need not use the primary key (`id`) to delete records; the WHERE clause is entirely up to you. For instance, the following function deletes all book records in the table `tbl_books` for a given author by the author's unique `id`:

```
public void deleteBooksByAuthor(Integer authorID) {
```

```
    int numBooksDeleted = mDatabase.delete("tbl_books", "authorid=?",
        new String[] { authorID.toString() });
}
```

Working with Transactions

Often you have multiple database operations you want to happen all together or not at all. You can use SQL Transactions to group operations together; if any of the operations fails, you can handle the error and either recover or roll back all operations. If the operations all succeed, you can then commit them. Here we have the basic structure for a transaction:

```
mDatabase.beginTransaction();
try {
    // Insert some records, updated others, delete a few
    // Do whatever you need to do as a unit, then commit it

    mDatabase.setTransactionSuccessful();
} catch (Exception e) {
    // Transaction failed. Failed! Do something here.
    // It's up to you.
} finally {
    mDatabase.endTransaction();
}
```

Now let's look at the transaction in a bit more detail. A transaction always begins with a call to `beginTransaction()` method and a `try/catch` block. If your operations are successful, you can commit your changes with a call to the `setTransactionSuccessful()` method. If you do not call this method, all your operations are rolled back and not committed. Finally, you end your transaction by calling `endTransaction()`. It's as simple as that.

In some cases, you might recover from an exception and continue with the transaction. For example, if you have an exception for a read-only database, you can open the database and retry your operations.

Finally, note that transactions can be nested, with the outer transaction either committing or rolling back all inner transactions.

Querying SQLite Databases

Databases are great for storing data in any number of ways, but retrieving the data you want is what makes databases powerful. This is partly a matter of designing an appropriate database schema, and partly achieved by crafting SQL queries, most of which are SELECT statements.

Android provides many ways in which you can query your application database. You can run raw SQL query statements (strings), use a number of different SQL statement builder utility classes to generate proper query statements from the ground up, and bind specific user interface controls such as container views to your backend database directly.

Working with Cursors

When results are returned from a SQL query, you often access them using a `Cursor` found in the `android.database.Cursor` class. `Cursor` objects are rather like file pointers; they allow random access to query results.

You can think of query results as a table, in which each row corresponds to a returned record. The `Cursor` object includes helpful methods for determining how many results were returned by the query the `Cursor` represents and methods for determining the column names (fields) for each returned record. The columns in the query results are defined by the query, not necessarily by the database columns. These might include calculated columns, column aliases, and composite columns.

`Cursor` objects are generally kept around for a time. If you do something simple (such as get a count of records or in cases when you know you retrieved only a single simple record), you can execute your query and quickly extract what you need; don't forget to close the `Cursor` when you're done, as shown here:

```
// SIMPLE QUERY: select * from tbl_books
Cursor c = mDatabase.query("tbl_books",null,null,null,null,null,null);
// Do something quick with the Cursor here...
c.close();
```

Managing Cursors as Part of the Application Lifecycle

When a `Cursor` returns multiple records, or you do something more intensive, you need to consider running this operation on a thread separate from the UI thread. You also need to manage your `Cursor`.

`Cursor` objects must be managed as part of the application lifecycle. When the application pauses or shuts down, the `Cursor` must be deactivated with a call to the `deactivate()` method, and when the application restarts, the `Cursor` should refresh its data using the `requery()` method. When the `Cursor` is no longer needed, a call to `close()` must be made to release its resources.

As the developer, you can handle this by implementing `Cursor` management calls within the various lifecycle callbacks, such as `onPause()`, `onResume()`, and `onDestroy()`.

If you're lazy, like us, and you don't want to bother handling these lifecycle events, you can hand off the responsibility of managing `Cursor` objects to the parent `Activity` by using the `Activity` method called `startManagingCursor()`. The `Activity` handles the rest, deactivating and reactivating the `Cursor` as necessary and destroying the `Cursor` when the `Activity` is destroyed. You can always begin manually managing the `Cursor` object again later by simply calling `stopManagingCursor()`.

Here we perform the same simple query and then hand over `Cursor` management to the parent `Activity`:

```
// SIMPLE QUERY: select * from tbl_books
Cursor c = mDatabase.query("tbl_books",null,null,null,null,null,null);
startManagingCursor(c);
```

Note that, generally, the managed `Cursor` is a member variable of the class, scope-wise.

Iterating Rows of Query Results and Extracting Specific Data

You can use the Cursor to iterate those results, one row at a time using various navigation methods such as moveToFirst(), moveToNext(), and isAfterLast().

On a specific row, you can use the Cursor to extract the data for a given column in the query results. Because SQLite is not strongly typed, you can always pull fields out as Strings using the getString() method, but you can also use the type-appropriate extraction utility function to enforce type safety in your application.

For example, the following method takes a valid Cursor object, prints the number of returned results, and then prints some column information (name and number of columns). Next, it iterates through the query results, printing each record.

```
public void logCursorInfo(Cursor c) {
    Log.i(DEBUG_TAG, "*** Cursor Begin *** " + " Results:" +
        c.getCount() + " Columns: " + c.getColumnCount());

    // Print column names
    String rowHeaders = "|| ";
    for (int i = 0; i < c.getColumnCount(); i++) {
        rowHeaders = rowHeaders.concat(c.getColumnName(i) + " || ");
    }

    Log.i(DEBUG_TAG, "COLUMNS " + rowHeaders);

    // Print records
    c.moveToFirst();
    while (c.isAfterLast() == false) {

        String rowResults = "|| ";
        for (int i = 0; i < c.getColumnCount(); i++) {
            rowResults = rowResults.concat(c.getString(i) + " || ");
        }

        Log.i(DEBUG_TAG,
            "Row " + c.getPosition() + ": " + rowResults);

        c.moveToNext();
    }
    Log.i(DEBUG_TAG, "*** Cursor End ***");
}
```

The output to the LogCat for this function might look something like Figure 10.1.

Executing Simple Queries

Your first stop for database queries should be the query() methods available in the SQLiteDatabase class. This method queries the database and returns any results as in a Cursor object.

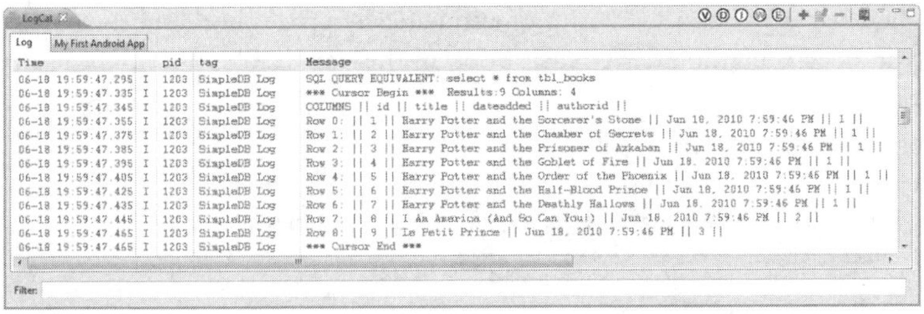

Figure 10.1   Sample log output for the **logCursorInfo()** method.

The `query()` method we mainly use takes the following parameters:

- [String]: The name of the table to compile the query against
- [String Array]: List of specific column names to return (use `null` for all)
- [String] The WHERE clause: Use `null` for all; might include selection args as ?'s
- [String Array]: Any selection argument values to substitute in for the ?'s in the earlier parameter
- [String] GROUP BY clause: `null` for no grouping
- [String] HAVING clause: `null` unless GROUP BY clause requires one
- [String] ORDER BY clause: If `null`, default ordering used
- [String] LIMIT clause: If `null`, no limit

Previously in the chapter, we called the `query()` method with only one parameter set to the table name.

```
Cursor c = mDatabase.query("tbl_books",null,null,null,null,null,null);
```

This is equivalent to the SQL query

```
SELECT * FROM tbl_books;
```

Tip

The individual parameters for the clauses (WHERE, GROUP BY, HAVING, ORDER BY, LIMIT) are all Strings, but you do not need to include the keyword, such as WHERE. Instead, you include the part of the clause after the keyword.

Add a `WHERE` clause to your query, so you can retrieve one record at a time:

```
Cursor c = mDatabase.query("tbl_books", null,
    "id=?", new String[]{"9"}, null, null, null);
```

This is equivalent to the SQL query

```
SELECT * tbl_books WHERE id=9;
```

Selecting all results might be fine for tiny databases, but it is not terribly efficient. You should always tailor your SQL queries to return only the results you require with no extraneous information included. Use the powerful language of SQL to do the heavy lifting for you whenever possible, instead of programmatically processing results yourself. For example, if you need only the titles of each book in the book table, you might use the following call to the `query()` method:

```
String asColumnsToReturn[] = { "title", "id" };
String strSortOrder = "title ASC";
Cursor c = mDatabase.query("tbl_books", asColumnsToReturn,
    null, null, null, null, strSortOrder);
```

This is equivalent to the SQL query

```
SELECT title, id FROM tbl_books ORDER BY title ASC;
```

Executing More Complex Queries Using `SQLiteQueryBuilder`

As your queries get more complex and involve multiple tables, you should leverage the `SQLiteQueryBuilder` convenience class, which can build complex queries (such as joins) programmatically.

When more than one table is involved, you need to make sure you refer to columns within a table by their fully qualified names. For example, the title column within the `tbl_books` table is `tbl_books.title`. Here we use a `SQLiteQueryBuilder` to build and execute a simple INNER JOIN between two tables to get a list of books with their authors:

```
import android.database.sqlite.SQLiteQueryBuilder;
...
SQLiteQueryBuilder queryBuilder = new SQLiteQueryBuilder();

queryBuilder.setTables("tbl_books, tbl_authors");
queryBuilder.appendWhere("tbl_books.authorid=tbl_authors.id");

String asColumnsToReturn[] = {
    "tbl_books.title",
    "tbl_books.id",
    "tbl_authors.firstname",
    "tbl_authors.lastname",
    "tbl_books.authorid" };
String strSortOrder = "title ASC";

Cursor c = queryBuilder.query(mDatabase, asColumnsToReturn,
    null, null, null, null,strSortOrder);
```

First, we instantiate a new `SQLiteQueryBuilder` object. Then we can set the tables involved as part of our JOIN and the WHERE clause that determines how the JOIN occurs. Then, we call the `query()` method of the `SQLiteQueryBuilder` that is similar to the `query()` method we have been using, except we supply the `SQLiteDatabase` instance instead of the table name. The earlier query built by the `SQLiteQueryBuilder` is equivalent to the SQL query:

```
SELECT tbl_books.title,
```

```
tbl_books.id,
tbl_authors.firstname,
tbl_authors.lastname,
tbl_books.authorid
FROM tbl_books
INNER JOIN tbl_authors on tbl_books.authorid=tbl_authors.id
ORDER BY title ASC;
```

Executing Raw Queries Without Builders and Column-Mapping

All these helpful Android query utilities can sometimes make building and performing a nonstandard or complex query too verbose. In this case, you might want to consider the `rawQuery()` method. The `rawQuery()` method simply takes a SQL statement `String` (with optional selection arguments if you include ?'s) and returns a `Cursor` of results. If you know your SQL and you don't want to bother learning the ins and outs of all the different SQL query building utilities, this is the method for you.

For example, let's say we have a UNION query. These types of queries are feasible with the `QueryBuilder`, but their implementation is cumbersome when you start using column aliases and the like.

Let's say we want to execute the following SQL UNION query, which returns a list of all book titles and authors whose name contains the substring ow (that is *Hallows, Rowling*), as in the following:

```
SELECT title AS Name,
'tbl_books' AS OriginalTable
FROM tbl_books
WHERE Name LIKE '%ow%'
UNION
SELECT (firstname||' '|| lastname) AS Name,
'tbl_authors' AS OriginalTable
FROM tbl_authors
WHERE Name LIKE '%ow%'
ORDER BY Name ASC;
```

We can easily execute this by making a string that looks much like the original query and executing the `rawQuery()` method.

```
String sqlUnionExample = "SELECT title AS Name, 'tbl_books' AS
    OriginalTable from tbl_books WHERE Name LIKE ? UNION SELECT
    (firstname||' '|| lastname) AS Name, 'tbl_authors' AS OriginalTable
    from tbl_authors WHERE Name LIKE ? ORDER BY Name ASC;";

Cursor c = mDatabase.rawQuery(sqlUnionExample,
    new String[]{ "%ow%", "%ow%"});
```

We make the substrings (ow) into selection arguments, so we can use this same code to look for other substrings searches).

Closing and Deleting a SQLite Database

Although you should always close a database when you are not using it, you might on occasion also want to modify and delete tables and delete your database.

Deleting Tables and Other SQLite Objects

You delete tables and other SQLite objects in exactly the same way you create them. Format the appropriate SQLite statements and execute them. For example, to drop our tables and triggers, we can execute three SQL statements:

```
mDatabase.execSQL("DROP TABLE tbl_books;");
mDatabase.execSQL("DROP TABLE tbl_authors;");
mDatabase.execSQL("DROP TRIGGER IF EXISTS fk_insert_book;");
```

Closing a SQLite Database

You should close your database when you are not using it. You can close the database using the `close()` method of your `SQLiteDatabase` instance, like this:

```
mDatabase.close();
```

Deleting a SQLite Database Instance Using the Application Context

The simplest way to delete a `SQLiteDatabase` is to use the `deleteDatabase()` method of your application `Context`. You delete databases by name and the deletion is permanent. You lose all data and schema information.

```
deleteDatabase("my_sqlite_database.db");
```

Designing Persistent Databases

Generally speaking, an application creates a database and uses it for the rest of the application's lifetime—by which we mean until the application is uninstalled from the phone. So far, we've talked about the basics of creating a database, using it, and then deleting it.

In reality, most mobile applications do not create a database on-the-fly, use them, and then delete them. Instead, they create a database the first time they need it and then use it. The Android SDK provides a helper class called `SQLiteOpenHelper` to help you manage your application's database.

To create a SQLite database for your Android application using the `SQLiteOpenHelper`, you need to extend that class and then instantiate an instance of it as a member variable for use within your application. To illustrate how to do this, let's create a new Android project called PetTracker.

Tip

Many of the code examples provided in this section are taken from the PetTracker application. This source code for the PetTracker application is provided for download on the book website. We build upon this example in this and future chapters.

Keeping Track of Database Field Names

You've probably realized by now that it is time to start organizing your database fields programmatically to avoid typos and such in your SQL queries. One easy way you do this is to make a class to encapsulate your database schema in a class, such as `PetDatabase`, shown here:

```
import android.provider.BaseColumns;

public final class PetDatabase {

    private PetDatabase() {}

    public static final class Pets implements BaseColumns {
        private Pets() {}
        public static final String PETS_TABLE_NAME="table_pets";
        public static final String PET_NAME="pet_name";
        public static final String PET_TYPE_ID="pet_type_id";
        public static final String DEFAULT_SORT_ORDER="pet_name ASC";
    }

    public static final class PetType implements BaseColumns {
        private PetType() {}
        public static final String PETTYPE_TABLE_NAME="table_pettypes";
        public static final String PET_TYPE_NAME="pet_type";
        public static final String DEFAULT_SORT_ORDER="pet_type ASC";
    }
}
```

By implementing the `BaseColumns` interface, we begin to set up the underpinnings for using database-friendly user interface controls in the future, which often require a specially named column called `_id` to function properly. We rely on this column as our primary key.

Extending the `SQLiteOpenHelper` Class

To extend the `SQLiteOpenHelper` class, we must implement several important methods, which help manage the database versioning. The methods to override are `onCreate()`, `onUpgrade()`, and `onOpen()`. We use our newly defined `PetDatabase` class to generate appropriate SQL statements, as shown here:

```
import android.content.Context;
import android.database.sqlite.SQLiteDatabase;
import android.database.sqlite.SQLiteOpenHelper;

import com.androidbook.PetTracker.PetDatabase.PetType;
import com.androidbook.PetTracker.PetDatabase.Pets;

class PetTrackerDatabaseHelper extends SQLiteOpenHelper {
```

```
private static final String DATABASE_NAME = "pet_tracker.db";
private static final int DATABASE_VERSION = 1;

PetTrackerDatabaseHelper(Context context) {
    super(context, DATABASE_NAME, null, DATABASE_VERSION);
}

@Override
public void onCreate(SQLiteDatabase db) {
    db.execSQL("CREATE TABLE " +PetType.PETTYPE_TABLE_NAME+" ("
        + PetType._ID + " INTEGER PRIMARY KEY AUTOINCREMENT ,"
        + PetType.PET_TYPE_NAME + " TEXT"
        + ");");
    db.execSQL("CREATE TABLE " + Pets.PETS_TABLE_NAME + " ("
        + Pets._ID + " INTEGER PRIMARY KEY AUTOINCREMENT ,"
        + Pets.PET_NAME + " TEXT,"
        + Pets.PET_TYPE_ID + " INTEGER" // FK to pet type table
        + ");");
}

@Override
public void onUpgrade(SQLiteDatabase db, int oldVersion,
    int newVersion){
    // Housekeeping here.
    // Implement how "move" your application data
    // during an upgrade of schema versions
    // Move or delete data as required. Your call.
}

@Override
public void onOpen(SQLiteDatabase db) {
    super.onOpen(db);
}
}
```

Now we can create a member variable for our database like this:

```
PetTrackerDatabaseHelper mDatabase = new
    PetTrackerDatabaseHelper(this.getApplicationContext());
```

Now, whenever our application needs to interact with its database, we request a valid database object. We can request a read-only database or a database that we can also write to. We can also close the database. For example, here we get a database we can write data to:

```
SQLiteDatabase db = mDatabase.getWritableDatabase();
```

Binding Data to the Application User Interface

In many cases with application databases, you want to couple your user interface with the data in your database. You might want to fill drop-down lists with values from a database table, or fill out form values, or display only certain results. There are various ways to bind database data to your user interface. You, as the developer, can decide whether to use built-in data-binding functionality provided with certain user interface controls, or you can build your own user interfaces from the ground up.

Working with Database Data Like Any Other Data

If you peruse the PetTracker application provided on the book website, you notice that its functionality includes no magical data-binding features, yet the application clearly uses the database as part of the user interface.

Specifically, the database is leveraged:

- When you fill out the Pet Type field, the `AutoComplete` feature is seeded with pet types already in listed in the `table_pettypes` table (Figure 10.2, left).

Figure 10.2   The PetTracker application: Entry Screen (left, middle) and Pet Listing Screen (right).

- When you save new records using the Pet Entry Form (Figure 10.2, middle).
- When you display the Pet List screen, you query for all pets and use a `Cursor` to programmatically build a TableLayout on-the-fly (Figure 10.2, right).

This might work for small amounts of data; however, there are various drawbacks to this method. For example, all the work is done on the main thread, so the more records you add, the slower your application response time becomes. Second, there's quite a bit of custom code involved to map the database results to the individual user interface components. If you decide you want to use a different control to display your data, you have quite a lot of rework to do. Third, we constantly requery the database for fresh results, and we might be requerying far more than necessary.

Note

Yes, we really named our pet bunnies after data structures and computer terminology. We are that geeky. Null, for example, is a rambunctious little black bunny. Shane enjoys pointing at him and calling himself a Null pointer.

Binding Data to Controls Using Data Adapters

Ideally, you'd like to bind your data to user interface controls and let them take care of the data display. For example, we can use a fancy `ListView` to display the pets instead of building a `TableLayout` from scratch. We can spin through our `Cursor` and generate `ListView` child items manually, or even better, we can simply create a data adapter to map the `Cursor` results to each `TextView` child within the `ListView`.

We included a project called PetTracker2 on the book website that does this. It behaves much like the PetTracker sample application, except that it uses the `SimpleCursorAdapter` with `ListView` and an `ArrayAdapter` to handle `AutoCompleteTextView` features.

Tip

The source code for subsequent upgrades to the PetTracker application (for example, PetTracker2, PetTracker3, and so on) is provided for download on the book website.

Binding Data Using `SimpleCursorAdapter`

Let's now look at how we can create a data adapter to mimic our Pet Listing screen, with each pet's name and species listed. We also want to continue to have the ability to delete records from the list.

Remember from Chapter 8, "Designing User Interfaces with Layouts," that the `ListView` container can contain children such as `TextView` objects. In this case, we want to display each Pet's name and type. We therefore create a layout file called `pet_item.xml` that becomes our `ListView` item template:

```xml
<?xml version="1.0" encoding="utf-8"?>
<RelativeLayout
    xmlns:android="http://schemas.android.com/apk/res/android"
    android:id="@+id/RelativeLayoutHeader"
    android:layout_height="wrap_content"
    android:layout_width="fill_parent">
    <TextView
        android:id="@+id/TextView_PetName"
        android:layout_width="wrap_content"
        android:layout_height="?android:attr/listPreferredItemHeight"
        android:layout_alignParentLeft="true" />
    <TextView
```

```
        android:id="@+id/TextView_PetType"
        android:layout_width="wrap_content"
        android:layout_height="?android:attr/listPreferredItemHeight"
        android:layout_alignParentRight="true" />
</RelativeLayout>
```

Next, in our main layout file for the Pet List, we place our `ListView` in the appropriate place on the overall screen. The `ListView` portion of the layout file might look something like this:

```
<ListView
    android:layout_width="wrap_content"
    android:layout_height="wrap_content"
    android:id="@+id/petList" android:divider="#000" />
```

Now to programmatically fill our `ListView`, we must take the following steps:

1. Perform our query and return a valid `Cursor` (a member variable).

2. Create a data adapter that maps the `Cursor` columns to the appropriate `TextView` controls within our `pet_item.xml` layout template.

3. Attach the adapter to the `ListView`.

In the following code, we perform these steps:

```
SQLiteQueryBuilder queryBuilder = new SQLiteQueryBuilder();
queryBuilder.setTables(Pets.PETS_TABLE_NAME +", " +
    PetType.PETTYPE_TABLE_NAME);

queryBuilder.appendWhere(Pets.PETS_TABLE_NAME + "." +
    Pets.PET_TYPE_ID + "=" + PetType.PETTYPE_TABLE_NAME + "." +
    PetType._ID);

String asColumnsToReturn[] = { Pets.PETS_TABLE_NAME + "." +
    Pets.PET_NAME, Pets.PETS_TABLE_NAME +
    "." + Pets._ID, PetType.PETTYPE_TABLE_NAME + "." +
    PetType.PET_TYPE_NAME };

mCursor = queryBuilder.query(mDB, asColumnsToReturn, null, null,
    null, null, Pets.DEFAULT_SORT_ORDER);

startManagingCursor(mCursor);

ListAdapter adapter = new SimpleCursorAdapter(this,
    R.layout.pet_item, mCursor,
    new String[]{Pets.PET_NAME, PetType.PET_TYPE_NAME},
    new int[]{R.id.TextView_PetName, R.id.TextView_PetType });

ListView av = (ListView)findViewById(R.id.petList);
av.setAdapter(adapter);
```

Notice that the _id column as well as the expected name and type columns appears in the query. This is required for the adapter and ListView to work properly.

Using a ListView (Figure 10.3, left) instead of a custom user interface enables us to take advantage of the ListView control's built-in features, such as scrolling when the list becomes longer, and the ability to provide context menus as needed. The _id column is used as the unique identifier for each ListView child node. If we choose a specific item on the list, we can act on it using this identifier, for example, to delete the item.

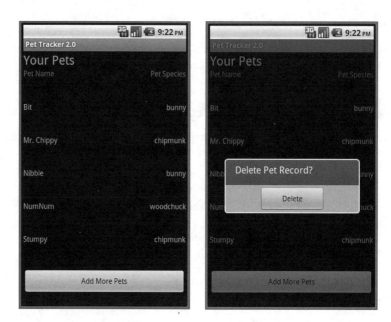

Figure 10.3   The PetTracker2 application: Pet Listing Screen **ListView**
(left) with Delete feature (right).

Now we re-implement the Delete functionality by listening for onItemClick() events and providing a Delete Confirmation dialog (Figure 10.3, right):

```
av.setOnItemClickListener(new AdapterView.OnItemClickListener() {
    public void onItemClick( AdapterView<?> parent, View view,
        int position, long id) {

        final long deletePetId =  id;

        new AlertDialog.Builder(PetTrackerListActivity.this).setMessage(
            "Delete Pet Record?").setPositiveButton(
            "Delete", new DialogInterface.OnClickListener() {
```

```
        @Override
        public void onClick(DialogInterface dialog,int which) {
            deletePet(deletePetId);
            mCursor.requery();
    }}).show();
  }
});
```

You can see what this would look like on the screen in Figure 10.3.

Note that within the PetTracker2 sample application, we also use an `ArrayAdapter` to bind the data in the `pet_types` table to the `AutoCompleteTextView` on the Pet Entry screen. Although our next example shows you how to do this in a preferred manner, we left this code in the PetTracker sample to show you that you can always intercept the data your `Cursor` provides and do what you want with it. In this case, we create a `String` array for the AutoText options by hand. We use a built-in Android layout resource called `android.R.layout.simple_dropdown_item_1line` to specify what each individual item within the AutoText listing looks like. You can find the built-in layout resources provided within your appropriate Android SDK version's resource subdirectory.

Storing Nonprimitive Types (Such as Images) in the Database

Because SQLite is a single file, it makes little sense to try to store binary data within the database. Instead store the *location* of data, as a file path or a URI in the database, and access it appropriately. We show an example of storing image URIs in the database in the next chapter.

Summary

There are a variety of different ways to store and manage application data on the Android platform. The method you use depends on what kind of data you need to store. With these skills, you are well on your way to leveraging one of the more powerful and unique features of Android.

Your application can store data using the following mechanisms:

- Lightweight application preferences (Activity-level and Application-wide)
- Android file system file and directory support with XML file format support
- Application-specific SQLite databases for structured storage

You learned how to design persistent data-access mechanisms within your Android application, and you understand how to bind data from various sources to user interface controls, such as `ListView` objects.

References and More Information

SQLite website:
   http://www.sqlite.org/index.html
SQLzoo.net:
   http://sqlzoo.net/

## 11

Sharing Data Between Applications with Content Providers

Applications can access data within other applications on the Android system through content provider interfaces and expose internal application data to other applications by becoming a content provider.

First, we take a look at some of the other content providers available on the Android platform and what you can do with them. Next, you see some examples of how to use content providers to improve the sample applications used in previous chapters. Finally, you learn how applications can become content providers to share information—for example, with `LiveFolders`.

Exploring Android's Content Providers

Android devices ship with a number of built-in applications, many of which expose their data as content providers. Your application can access content provider data from a variety of sources. You can find the content providers included with Android in the package `android.provider`. Table 11.1 lists some useful content providers in this package.

Table 11.1 **Useful Built-In Content Providers**

Provider	Purpose
MediaStore	Audio-visual data on the phone and external storage
CallLog	Sent and received calls
Browser	Browser history and bookmarks
ContactsContract	Phone contact database or phonebook
Settings	System-wide device settings and preferences
UserDictionary	A dictionary of user-defined words for use with predictive text input

Now let's look at the individual content providers in more detail.

> **Tip**
>
> Many of the code examples provided in this section are taken from the SimpleContent-
> Provider application. This source code for the SimpleContentProvider application is provided
> for download on the book website.

Using the `MediaStore` Content Provider

You can use the `MediaStore` content provider to access media on the phone and on external storage devices. The primary types of media that you can access are audio, images, and video. You can access these different types of media through their respective content provider classes under `android.provider.MediaStore`.

Most of the `MediaStore` classes allow full interaction with the data. You can retrieve, add, and delete media files from the device. There are also a handful of helper classes that define the most common data columns that can be requested.

Table 11.2 lists some commonly used classes that you can find under `android.provider.MediaStore`.

Table 11.2   **Common `MediaStore` Classes**

Class	Purpose
`Video.Media`	Manages video files on the device
`Images.Media`	Manages image files on the device
`Images.ThumbNails`	Retrieves thumbnails for the images
`Audio.Media`	Manages audio files on the device
`Audio.Albums`	Manages audio files organized by the album
`Audio.Artists`	Manages audio files by the artist who created them
`Audio.Genres`	Manages audio files belonging to a particular genre
`Audio.Playlists`	Manages audio files that are part of a particular playlist

The following code demonstrates how to request data from a content provider. A query is made to the `MediaStore` to retrieve the titles of all the audio files on the SD card of the handset and their respective durations. This code requires that you load some audio files onto the virtual SD card in the emulator.

```
String[] requestedColumns = {
    MediaStore.Audio.Media.TITLE,
    MediaStore.Audio.Media.DURATION
};
```

```
Cursor cur = managedQuery(
    MediaStore.Audio.Media.EXTERNAL_CONTENT_URI,
    requestedColumns, null, null, null);

Log.d(DEBUG_TAG, "Audio files: " + cur.getCount());
Log.d(DEBUG_TAG, "Columns: " + cur.getColumnCount());

String[] columns = cur.getColumnNames();

int name = cur.getColumnIndex(MediaStore.Audio.Media.TITLE);
int size = cur.getColumnIndex(MediaStore.Audio.Media.DURATION);

cur.moveToFirst();
while (!cur.isAfterLast()) {
    Log.d(DEBUG_TAG, "Title" + cur.getString(name));
    Log.d(DEBUG_TAG, "Length: " +
        cur.getInt(size) / 1000 + " seconds");
    cur.moveToNext();
}
```

The `MediaStore.Audio.Media` class has predefined strings for every data field (or column) exposed by the content provider. You can limit the audio file data fields requested as part of the query by defining a string array with the column names required. In this case, we limit the results to only the track title and the duration of each audio file.

We then use a `managedQuery()` method call. The first parameter is the predefined URI of the content provider you want to query (in most cases, the primary external storage is the SD card). The second parameter is the list of columns to return (audio file titles and durations). The third and fourth parameters control any selection filtering arguments, and the fifth parameter provides a sort method for the results. We leave these null, as we want all audio files at this location. By using the `managedQuery()` method, we get a managed `Cursor` as a result. We then examine our `Cursor` for the results.

Using the `CallLog` Content Provider

Android provides a content provider to access the call log on the handset via the class `android.provider.CallLog`. At first glance, the `CallLog` might not seem to be a useful provider for developers, but it has some nifty features. You can use the `CallLog` to filter recently dialed calls, received, and missed calls. The date and duration of each call is logged and tied back to the Contact application for caller identification purposes.

The `CallLog` is a useful content provider for customer relationship management (CRM) applications. The user can also tag specific phone numbers with custom labels within the Contact application.

To demonstrate how the `CallLog` content provider works, let's look at a hypothetical situation where we want to generate a report of all calls to a number with the custom labeled `HourlyClient123`. Android allows for custom labels on these numbers, which we leverage for this example:

```
String[] requestedColumns = {
    CallLog.Calls.CACHED_NUMBER_LABEL,
    CallLog.Calls.DURATION
};

Cursor calls = managedQuery(
    CallLog.Calls.CONTENT_URI, requestedColumns,
    CallLog.Calls.CACHED_NUMBER_LABEL
    + " = ?", new String[] { "HourlyClient123" } , null);

Log.d(DEBUG_TAG, "Call count: " + calls.getCount());

int durIdx = calls.getColumnIndex(CallLog.Calls.DURATION);
int totalDuration = 0;

calls.moveToFirst();
while (!calls.isAfterLast()) {
    Log.d(DEBUG_TAG, "Duration: " + calls.getInt(durIdx));
    totalDuration += calls.getInt(durIdx);
    calls.moveToNext();
}

Log.d(DEBUG_TAG, "HourlyClient123 Total Call Duration: " + totalDuration);
```

This code is similar to the code shown for the `MediaStore` audio files. Again, we start with listing our requested columns: the call label and the duration of the call. This time, however, we don't want to get every call in the log, only those with a label of `HourlyClient123`. To filter the results of the query to this specific label, it is necessary to specify the third and fourth parameters of the `managedQuery()` call. Together, these two parameters are equivalent to a database WHERE clause. The third parameter specifies the format of the WHERE clause with the column name with selection parameters (shown as ?s) for each selection argument value. The fourth parameter, the `String` array, provides the values to substitute for each of the selection arguments (?s) in order as you would do for a simple SQLite database query.

As before, the `Activity` manages the `Cursor` object lifecycle. We use the same method to iterate the records of the `Cursor` and add up all the call durations.

Accessing Content Providers That Require Permissions

Your application needs a special permission to access the information provided by the `CallLog` content provider. You can declare the `uses-permission` tag using the Eclipse Wizard or by adding the following to your `AndroidManifest.xml` file:

```
<uses-permission
    xmlns:android="http://schemas.android.com/apk/res/android"
```

```
        android:name="android.permission.READ_CONTACTS">
</uses-permission>
```

Although it's a tad confusing, there is no `CallLog` permission. Instead, applications that access the `CallLog` use the `READ_CONTACTS` permission. Although the values are cached within this content provider, the data is similar to what you might find in the contacts provider.

Tip

You can find all available permissions in the class `android.Manifest.permission`.

Using the Browser Content Provider

Another useful, built-in content provider is the `Browser`. The `Browser` content provider exposes the user's browser site history and their bookmarked websites. You access this content provider via the `android.provider.Browser` class. As with the `CallLog` class, you can use the information provided by the `Browser` content provider to generate statistics and to provide cross-application functionality. You might use the `Browser` content provider to add a bookmark for your application support website.

In this example, we query the `Browser` content provider to find the top five most frequently visited bookmarked sites.

```
String[] requestedColumns = {
    Browser.BookmarkColumns.TITLE,
    Browser.BookmarkColumns.VISITS,
    Browser.BookmarkColumns.BOOKMARK
};

Cursor faves = managedQuery(Browser.BOOKMARKS_URI, requestedColumns,
    Browser.BookmarkColumns.BOOKMARK + "=1", null,
    Browser.BookmarkColumns.VISITS + " DESC limit 5");

Log.d(DEBUG_TAG, "Bookmarks count: " + faves.getCount());

int titleIdx = faves.getColumnIndex(Browser.BookmarkColumns.TITLE);
int visitsIdx = faves.getColumnIndex(Browser.BookmarkColumns.VISITS);
int bmIdx = faves.getColumnIndex(Browser.BookmarkColumns.BOOKMARK);

faves.moveToFirst();

while (!faves.isAfterLast()) {
    Log.d("SimpleBookmarks", faves.getString(titleIdx) + " visited "
        + faves.getInt(visitsIdx) + " times : "
        + (faves.getInt(bmIdx) != 0 ? "true" : "false"));
    faves.moveToNext();
}
```

Again, the requested columns are defined, the query is made, and the cursor iterates through the results.

Note that the `managedQuery()` call has become substantially more complex. Let's take a look at the parameters to this method in more detail. The first parameter, `Browser.BOOKMARKS_URI`, is a URI for all browser history, not only the Bookmarked items. The second parameter defines the requested columns for the query results. The third parameter specifies that the bookmark property must be true. This parameter is needed in order to filter within the query. Now the results are only browser history entries that have been bookmarked. The fourth parameter, selection arguments, is used only when replacement values are used, which is not used in this case, so the value is set to `null`. Lastly, the fifth parameter specifies an order to the results (most visited in descending order). Retrieving browser history information requires setting the `READ_HISTORY_BOOKMARKS` permission.

Tip

Notice that we also tacked on a LIMIT statement to the fifth parameter of `managedQuery()`. Although not specifically documented, we've found limiting the query results in this way works well and might even improve application performance in some situations where the query results are lengthy.

Using the Contacts Content Provider

The Contacts database is one of the most commonly used applications on the mobile phone. People always want phone numbers handy for calling friends, family, coworkers, and clients. Additionally, most phones show the identity of the caller based on the contacts application, including nicknames, photos, or icons.

Android provides a built-in Contact application, and the contact data is exposed to other Android applications using the content provider interface. As an application developer, this means you can leverage the user's contact data within your application for a more robust user experience.

Note

The content provider for accessing user contacts was originally called `Contacts`. Android 2.0 introduced an enhanced contacts management content provider class to manage the data available from the user's contacts. This class, called `ContactsContract`, includes a sub-class called `ContactsContract.Contacts`. This is the preferred contacts content provider, as of API Level 5. However, as Contacts are a commonly used feature across all Android platform versions, we include only the original Contacts content provider method for backward compatibility. For use of the new ContactsContract method, please see the related article on our website (http://androidbook.blogspot.com/2010/09/contacts-contract.html).

Accessing Private Contact Data

Your application needs special permission to access the private user information provided by the `Contacts` content provider. You must declare a `uses-permission` tag using the permission `READ_CONTACTS` to read this information.

The code to start reading contact data from the Contacts application should look familiar.

```
Cursor oneContact = managedQuery( People.CONTENT_URI, null, null, null,
    "name desc LIMIT 1");

Log.d(debugTag, "Count: " + oneContact.getCount());
```

This short example simply shows querying for a single contact. We used LIMIT to retrieve one contact record. If you actually look at the returned columns of data, you find that there is little more than the contact name and some indexes. The data fields are not explicitly returned. Instead, the results include the values needed to build specific URIs to those pieces of data. We need to request the data for the contact using these indexes.

Specifically, we retrieve the primary email and primary phone number for this contact.

```
int nameIdx = oneContact.getColumnIndex(Contacts.People.NAME);
int emailIDIdx = oneContact
    .getColumnIndex(Contacts.People.PRIMARY_EMAIL_ID);

int phoneIDIdx = oneContact
    .getColumnIndex(Contacts.People.PRIMARY_PHONE_ID);

oneContact.moveToFirst();
int emailID = oneContact.getInt(emailIDIdx);
int phoneID = oneContact.getInt(phoneIDIdx);
```

Now that we have the column index values for the contact's name, primary email address, and primary phone number, we need to build the Uri objects associated with those pieces of information and query for the primary email and primary phone number.

```
Uri emailUri = ContentUris.withAppendedId(
    Contacts.ContactMethods.CONTENT_URI,
    emailID);

Uri phoneUri = ContentUris.withAppendedId(
    Contacts.Phones.CONTENT_URI, phoneID);

Cursor primaryEmail = managedQuery(emailUri,
    new String[] {
        Contacts.ContactMethods.DATA
    },
    null, null, null);

Cursor primaryNumber = managedQuery(phoneUri,
    new String[] {
        Contacts.Phones.NUMBER
    },
    null, null, null);
```

After retrieving the appropriate column indexes for a contact's specific email and phone number, we call `ContentUris.withAppendedId()` to create the new `Uri` objects from existing ones and the identifiers we now have. This enables direct selection of a particular row from the table when the index of that row is known. You can use a selection parameter to do this, as well. Lastly, we used the two new `Uri` objects to perform two calls to `managedQuery()`.

Now we take a shortcut with the requested columns `String` array because each query only has one column:

```
String name = oneContact.getString(nameIdx);
primaryEmail.moveToFirst();
String email = primaryEmail.getString(0);
primaryNumber.moveToFirst();
String number = primaryNumber.getString(0);
```

If an email or phone number doesn't exist, an exception called `android.database.CursorIndexOutOfBoundsException` is thrown. This can be caught, or you can check to see that a result was actually returned in the `Cursor` first.

Querying for a Specific Contact

If that seemed like quite a lot of coding to get a phone number, you're not alone. For getting a quick piece of data, there is a faster way. The following block of code demonstrates how we can get the primary number and name for one contact. The primary number for a contact is designated as the default number within the contact manager on the handset. It might be useful to use the primary number field if you don't get any results back from the query.

```
String[] requestedColumns = {
    Contacts.Phones.NAME,
    Contacts.Phones.NUMBER,
};

Cursor contacts = managedQuery(
    Contacts.Phones.CONTENT_URI,
    requestedColumns,
    Contacts.Phones.ISPRIMARY + "<>0",
    null, "name desc limit 1");

Log.d(debugTag, "Contacts count: "
    + contacts.getCount());

int nameIdx = contacts
    .getColumnIndex(Contacts.Phones.NAME);
int phoneIdx = contacts
    .getColumnIndex(Contacts.Phones.NUMBER);
```

```
contacts.moveToFirst();
Log.d(debugTag, "Name: " + contacts.getString(nameIdx));
Log.d(debugTag, "Phone: " + contacts.getString(phoneIdx));
```

This block of code should look somewhat familiar, yet it is a much shorter and more straightforward method to query for phone numbers by Contact name. The `Contacts.Phones.CONTENT_URI` contains phone numbers but it also happens to have the contact name. This is similar to the `CallLog` content provider.

Using the `UserDictionary` Content Provider

Another useful content provider is the `UserDictionary` provider. You can use this content provider for predictive text input on text fields and other user input mechanisms. Individual words stored in the dictionary are weighted by frequency and organized by locale. You can use the `addWord()` method within the `UserDictionary.Words` class to add words to the custom user dictionary.

Using the `Settings` Content Provider

Another useful content provider is the `Settings` provider. You can use this content provider to access the device settings and user preferences. Settings are organized much as they are in the `Settings` application—by category. You can find information about the `Settings` content provider in the `android.provider.Settings` class.

Modifying Content Providers Data

Content providers are not only static sources of data. They can also be used to add, update, and delete data, if the content provider application has implemented this functionality. Your application must have the appropriate permissions (that is, `WRITE_CONTACTS` as opposed to `READ_CONTACTS`) to perform some of these actions.

Adding Records

Using the `Contacts` content provider, we can, for example, add a new record to the contacts database programmatically.

```
ContentValues values = new ContentValues();

values.put(Contacts.People.NAME, "Sample User");

Uri uri = getContentResolver().insert(
    Contacts.People.CONTENT_URI, values);

Uri phoneUri = Uri.withAppendedPath(uri,
    Contacts.People.Phones.CONTENT_DIRECTORY);
```

```
values.clear();

values.put(Contacts.Phones.NUMBER, "2125551212");
values.put(Contacts.Phones.TYPE, Contacts.Phones.TYPE_WORK);

getContentResolver().insert(phoneUri, values);

values.clear();

values.put(Contacts.Phones.NUMBER, "3135551212");
values.put(Contacts.Phones.TYPE, Contacts.Phones.TYPE_MOBILE);

getContentResolver().insert(phoneUri, values);
```

Just as we used the `ContentValues` class to insert records into an application's SQLite database, we use it again here. The first action we take is to provide a name for the `Contacts.People.NAME` column. We need to create the contact with a name before we can assign information, such as phone numbers. Think of this as creating a row in a table that provides a one-to-many relationship to a phone number table.

Next, we insert the data in the database found at the `Contacts.People.CONTENT_URI` path. We use a call to `getContentResolver()` to retrieve the `ContentResolver` associated with our `Activity`. The return value is the `Uri` of our new contact. We need to use it for adding phone numbers to our new contact. We then reuse the `ContentValues` instance by clearing it and adding a `Contacts.Phones.NUMBER` and the `Contacts.Phones.TYPE` for it. Using the `ContentResolver`, we insert this data into the newly created `Uri`.

Tip

At this point, you might be wondering how the structure of the data can be determined. The best way is to thoroughly examine the documentation from the specific content provider with which you want to integrate your application.

Updating Records

Inserting data isn't the only change you can make. You can update one or more rows, as well. The following block of code shows how to update data within a content provider. In this case, we update a note field for a specific contact, using its unique identifier.

```
ContentValues values = new ContentValues();
values.put(People.NOTES, "This is my boss");
Uri updateUri = ContentUris.withAppendedId(People.CONTENT_URI, rowId);
int rows = getContentResolver().update(updateUri, values, null, null);
Log.d(debugTag, "Rows updated: " + rows);
```

Again, we use an instance of the `ContentValues` object to map the data field we want to update with the data value—in this case, the note field. This replaces any current note stored in the NOTES field currently stored with the contact. We then create the Uri for the specific contact we are updating. A simple call to the update() method of the ContentResolver class completes our change. We can then confirm that only one row was updated.

Tip

You can use the filter values when updating rows. This enables you to make changes to values across many rows at the same time. The content provider must support this, though. We have found that the Contacts Provider blocks this on the People URI, preventing developers from making sweeping or global changes to contacts.

Deleting Records

Now that you cluttered up your contacts application with sample user data, you might want to delete some of it. Deleting data is fairly straightforward.

Deleting All Records

The following code deletes all rows at the given URI, although you should execute operations like this with extreme care:

```
int rows = getContentResolver().delete(People.CONTENT_URI, null, null);
Log.d(debugTag, "Rows: "+ rows);
```

The delete() method deletes all rows at a given URI filtered by the selection parameters, which, in this case, includes all rows at the People.CONTENT_URI location; in other words, all contact entries.

Deleting Specific Records

Often you want to select specific rows to delete by adding the unique identifier index to the end of the URI or remove rows matching a particular pattern.

For example, the following deletion matches all contact records with the name Sample User, which we used when we created sample contacts previously in the chapter.

```
int rows = getContentResolver().delete(People.CONTENT_URI,
    People.NAME + "=?",
    new String[] {"Sample User"});
Log.d(debugTag, "Rows: "+ rows);
```

Enhancing Applications Using Content Providers

The concept of a content provider is complex and best understood by working through an example. The Pet Tracker series of applications from the previous chapter are nice and all, but the application could really use some graphics. Wouldn't it be great if we could include photos for each pet record? Well, let's do it! There's only one catch: We need to access pictures provided through another application on the Android system—the Media Store application.

Tip

Many of the code examples provided in this section are taken from the PetTracker3 application. This source code for the PetTracker3 application is provided for download on the book website.

In Figure 11.1, you can see the results of extending the previous Pet Tracking projects using the Media Store content provider.

Figure 11.1   Pet Tracker application: Entry Screen (left, middle) and Pet Listing Screen (right).

Accessing Images on the Device

Now that you can visualize what adding photos looks like, let's break down the steps needed to achieve this feature. The PetTracker3 application has the same basic structure as our previous Pet Tracker projects, with several key differences:

- On the Pet Entry screen, you can choose a photo from a `Gallery` control, which displays all the images available on the SD card, or simulated SD card on the emulator, by accessing the `MediaStore` content provider (Figure 11.1, left).
- On the Pet Listing screen, each picture is displayed in the `ListView` control (Figure 11.1, right), again using the `MediaStore` content provider to access specific images.
- On the Pet Listing screen, each item in the `ListView` (Figure 11.1, right) is a custom layout. The new PetTracker3 sample application provides two methods to achieve this: by inflating a custom layout XML file, and by generating the layout programmatically.
- Internally, we extend `BaseAdapter` on two different occasions to successfully bind pet data to the `ListView` and `Gallery` with our own custom requirements.

- Finally, we provide custom implementations of the methods for `SimpleCursorAdapter.CursorToStringConverter` and `FilterQueryProvider` to allow the `AutoCompleteTextView` to bind directly to the internal SQLite database table called `pet_types` (Figure 11.1, middle), and change the `AutoCompleteTextView` behavior to match all substrings, not only the beginning of the word. Although we won't go into detail about this in the subsequent text, check out the sample code for more information on the specific details of implementation.

First, we need to decide where we are going to get our photos. We can take pictures with the built-in camera and access those, but for simplicity's sake with the emulator (which can only take "fake pictures"), it is easier if we download those cute, fuzzy pictures from the browser onto the SD card and access them that way.

Tip

For the PetTracker3 sample application to work, you need to configure your emulator to use a virtual SD card. To keep the code simple and readable, we do not provide error handling for when this is not set up or where there are no images, nor do we check the content type of the media.

You'll know you've set things up correctly when you can launch the browser on the emulator, browse to a website, and download some pictures. You can view these photographs in the Gallery application.

To download an image through the Browser application, select an image to download by choosing it (pressing with the mouse works), and then selecting the Save Image option. Go ahead and download your own pet (or kid or whatever) images from whatever website you like and save them onto the SD card. If you don't have pets (or kids or whatever), you can borrow our personal bunny pictures, which we use in our example, from http://tinyurl.com/geekybuns.

Locating Content on the Android System Using URIs

Most access to content providers comes in the form of queries: a list of contacts, a list of bookmarks, a list of calls, a list of pictures, and a list of audio files. Applications make these requests much as they would access a database, and they get the same type of structured results. The results of a query are often iterated through using a cursor. However, instead of crafting queries, we use URIs.

You can think of a URI as an "address" to the location where content exists. URI addresses are hierarchical. Most content providers, such as the `Contacts` and the `MediaStore`, have URI addresses predefined. For example, to access images the External Media Device (also known as the SD card), we use the following URI defined in the `MediaStore.Images.Media` class:

```
Uri mMedia = Media.EXTERNAL_CONTENT_URI;
```

Retrieving Content Provider Data with `managedQuery()`

We can query the Media Store content provider using the URI much like we would query a database. We now use the `managedQuery()` method to return a managed `Cursor` containing all image media available on the SD card.

```
String[] projection = new String[] { Media._ID, Media.TITLE };


Uri mMedia = Media.EXTERNAL_CONTENT_URI;


Cursor mCursorImages = managedQuery(mMedia, projection, null, null,
    Media.DATE_TAKEN + " ASC"); // Order-by clause.
```

We have retrieved the records for each piece of media available on the SD card.

Now we have this `Cursor`, but we still have some legwork to get our `Gallery` widget to display the individual images.

Data-Binding to the Gallery Control

We need to extend the `BaseAdapter` class for a new type of data adapter called `ImageUriAdapter` to map the URI data we retrieved to the `Gallery` widget. Our custom `ImageUriAdapter` maps the `Cursor` results to an array of `GalleryRecord` objects, which correspond to the child items within the `Gallery` widget. Although the code for the `ImageUriAdapter` is too long to show here, we go over some of the methods you must implement for the adapter to work properly.

- The `ImageUriAdapter()` constructor is responsible for mapping the `Cursor` to an array of `GalleryRecord` objects, which encapsulate the base URI and the individual image's `id`. The image `id` is tacked on to the end of the URI, resulting in a fully qualified URI for the individual image.

- The `getItem()` and `getItemId()` methods return the unique identifier for the specific image. This is the value we require when the user clicks on a specific image within the `Gallery`. We save this information in our database so that we know which image corresponds to which pet.

- The `getView()` method returns the custom `View` widget that corresponds to each child `View` within the `Gallery`. In this case, we return an `ImageView` with the corresponding image. We set each view's `Tag` property to the associated `GalleryRecord` object, which includes all our `Cursor` information we mapped for that record. This is a nifty trick for storing extra information with widgets for later use.

After all this magic has been implemented, we can set our newly defined custom adapter to the adapter used by the `Gallery` with our new `Cursor`.

```
ImageUriAdapter iAdapter = new ImageUriAdapter(this,
    mCursorImages, mMedia);


final Gallery pictureGal = (Gallery) findViewById(R.id.GalleryOfPics);
    pictureGal.setAdapter(iAdapter);
```

Retrieving Gallery Images and Saving Them in the Database

Notice that we added two new columns to our SQLite database: the base URI for the image and the individual image id, which is the unique identifier tacked to the end of the URI. We do not save the image itself in the database, only the URI information to retrieve it.

When the user presses the Save button on the Pet Entry screen, we examine the Gallery item selected and extract the information we require from the Tag property of the selected View, like this:

```
final Gallery gall = (Gallery) findViewById(R.id.GalleryOfPics);

ImageView selectedImageView = (ImageView) gall.getSelectedView();

GalleryRecord galleryItem;

if (selectedImageView != null) {
    galleryItem = (GalleryRecord)selectedImageView.getTag();
    long imageId = galleryItem.getImageId();
    String strImageUriPathString = galleryItem.getImageUriPath();
}
```

We can then save our Pet Record as we have before.

Displaying Images Retrieved from the SD Card Using URIs

Now that our Pet Entry form is saved properly, we must turn our attention to the Pet Listing screen. Our ListView is getting more complicated; each item needs to contain an ImageView and two TextView widgets for the pet name and species. We begin by defining a custom layout template for each ListView item called pet_item.xml. This should be familiar; it contains an ImageView and two TextView objects.

We want to make sure this implementation is scalable, in case we want to add new features to individual ListView items in the future. So instead of taking shortcuts and using standard adapters and built-in Android layout templates, we implement another custom adapter called PetListAdapter.

The PetListAdapter is similar to the ImageUriAdapter we previously implemented for the Gallery widget. This time, instead of Gallery child items, we work with the ListView child records, which correspond to each pet. Again, the constructor maps the Cursor data to an array of PetRecord objects.

The getView() method of the PetListAdapter is where the magic occurs. Here we use a LayoutInflater to inflate our custom layout file called pet_item.xml for each ListView item. Again we use the Tag property of the view to store any information about the record that we might use later. It is here that we use the URI information we stored in our database to rebuild the fully qualified image URI using the Uri.parse() and ContentUris.withAppendedId() utility methods and assign this URI to the ImageView widget using the setImageURI() method.

Now that we've set up everything, we assign the `PetListAdapter` to our `ListView`:

```
String asColumnsToReturn[] = {
    Pets.PETS_TABLE_NAME + "." + Pets.PET_NAME,
    Pets.PETS_TABLE_NAME + "." + Pets.PET_IMAGE_URI,
    Pets.PETS_TABLE_NAME + "." + Pets._ID,
    Pets.PETS_TABLE_NAME + "." + Pets.PET_IMAGE_ID,
    PetType.PETTYPE_TABLE_NAME + "." + PetType.PET_TYPE_NAME };

mCursor = queryBuilder.query(mDB, asColumnsToReturn, null, null,
    null, null, Pets.DEFAULT_SORT_ORDER);
startManagingCursor(mCursor);

SetListAdapter adapter = new PetListAdapter(this, mCursor);
ListView av = (ListView) findViewById(R.id.petList);
av.setAdapter(adapter);
```

That's about it. Note that you can also create the `ListView` item layout programmatically (see the `PetListItemView` class and the `PetListAdapter.getView()` method comments for more information).

Now you've seen how to leverage a content provider to make your application more robust, but this example has scratched only the surface of how powerful content providers can be.

Acting as a Content Provider

Do you have data in your application? Can another application do something interesting with that data? To share the information within your application with other applications, you need to make the application a content provider by providing the standardized content provider interface for other applications; then you must register your application as a content provider within the Android manifest file. The most straightforward way to make an application a content provider is to store the information you want to share in a SQLite database.

One example is a content provider for GPS track points. This content provider enables users of it to query for points and store points. The data for each point contains a time stamp, the latitude and longitude, and the elevation.

Tip

Some of the code examples provided in this section are taken from the Tracks application. This source code for the Tracks application is provided for download on the book website. In order to use this application, you need to get your own Google Maps API key: http://code. google.com/android/maps-api-signup.html.

Implementing a Content Provider Interface

Implementing a content provider interface is relatively straightforward. The following code shows the basic interface that an application needs to implement to become a content provider, requiring implementations of five important methods:

Tip

You can use Eclipse to easily create a new class and include the basic overrides that you need. To do this, right-click on the package you want to add the new class to, choose New, and then Class. Type the name of your content provider in the Name field, choose `android.content.ContentProvider` as your superclass, and check the box next to Inherited abstract methods.

```java
public class TrackPointProvider extends ContentProvider {

    public int delete(Uri uri,
        String selection, String[] selectionArgs) {
        return 0;
    }

    public String getType(Uri uri) {
        return null;
    }

    public Uri insert(Uri uri, ContentValues values) {
        return null;
    }

    public boolean onCreate() {
        return false;
    }

    public Cursor query(Uri uri, String[] projection,
        String selection, String[] selectionArgs, String sortOrder) {
        return null;
    }

    public int update(Uri uri, ContentValues values,
        String selection, String[] selectionArgs) {
        return 0;
    }
}
```

Defining the Data URI

The provider application needs to define a base URI that other applications will use to access this content provider. This must be in the form of a `public static final Uri` named `CONTENT_URI`, and it must start with `content://`. The URI must be unique. The best practice for this naming is to use the fully qualified class name of the content provider. Here, we have created a URI name for our GPS track point provider book example:

```
public static final Uri CONTENT_URI =
    Uri.parse("content://com.androidbook.TrackPointProvider");
```

Defining Data Columns

The user of the content provider needs to know what columns the content provider has available to it. In this case, the columns used are timestamp, latitude and longitude, and the elevation. We also include a column for the record number, which is called _id.

```
public final static String _ID = "_id";
public final static String TIMESTAMP = "timestamp";
public final static String LATITUDE = "latitude";
public final static String LONGITUDE = "longitude";
public final static String ELEVATION = "elevation";
```

Users of the content provider use these same strings. A content provider for data such as this often stores the data within a SQLite database. If this is the case, matching these columns' names to the database column names simplifies the code.

Implementing Important Content Provider Methods

This section shows example implementations of each of the methods that are used by the system to call this content provider when another application wants to use it. The system, in this case, is the `ContentResolver` interface that was used indirectly in the previous section when built-in content providers were used.

Some of these methods can make use of a helper class provided by the Android SDK, `UriMatcher`, which is used to match incoming `Uri` values to patterns that help speed up development. The use of `UriMatcher` is described and then used in the implementation of these methods.

Implementing the `query()` Method

Let's start with a sample query implementation. Any query implementation needs to return a `Cursor` object. One convenient way to get a `Cursor` object is to return the `Cursor` from the underlying SQLite database that many content providers use. In fact, the interface to `ContentProvider.query()` is compatible with the `SQLiteQueryBuilder.query()` call. This example uses it to quickly build the query and return a `Cursor` object.

```
public Cursor query(Uri uri, String[] projection,
    String selection, String[] selectionArgs,
    String sortOrder) {

    SQLiteQueryBuilder qBuilder = new SQLiteQueryBuilder();

    qBuilder.setTables(TrackPointDatabase.TRACKPOINTS_TABLE);

    if ((sURIMatcher.match(uri)) == TRACKPOINT_ID) {
        qBuilder.appendWhere("_id=" + uri.getLastPathSegment());
    }

    Cursor resultCursor = qBuilder.query(mDB
        .getReadableDatabase(), projection,
        selection, selectionArgs, null, null,
        sortOrder, null);

    resultCursor.setNotificationUri(getContext()
        .getContentResolver(), uri);
    return resultCursor;
}
```

First, the code gets an instance of a `SQLiteQueryBuilder` object, which builds up a query with some method calls. Then, the `setTables()` method configures which table in the database is used. The `UriMatcher` class checks to see which specific rows are requested. `UriMatcher` is discussed in greater detail later.

Next, the actual query is called. The content provider query has fewer specifications than the SQLite query, so the parameters are passed through and the rest is ignored. The instance of the SQLite database is read-only. Because this is only a query for data, it's acceptable.

Finally, the `Cursor` needs to know if the source data has changed. This is done by a call to the `setNotificationUri()` method telling it which URI to watch for data changes. The call to the application's `query()` method might be called from multiple threads, as it calls to `update()`, so it's possible the data can change after the `Cursor` is returned. Doing this keeps the data synchronized.

Exploring the `UriMatcher` Class

The `UriMatcher` class is a helper class for pattern matching on the URIs that are passed to this content provider. It is used frequently in the implementations of the content provider functions that must be implemented. Here is the `UriMatcher` used in these sample implementations:

```
public static final String AUTHORITY =
    "com.androidbook.TrackPointProvider"

private static final int TRACKPOINTS = 1;
private static final int TRACKPOINT_ID = 10;
```

```
private static final UriMatcher sURIMatcher =
    new UriMatcher(UriMatcher.NO_MATCH);
static {
    sURIMatcher.addURI(AUTHORITY, "points", TRACKPOINTS);
    sURIMatcher.addURI(AUTHORITY, "points/#", TRACKPOINT_ID);
}
```

First, arbitrary numeric values are defined to identify each different pattern. Next, a static `UriMatcher` instance is created for use. The code parameter that the constructor wants is merely the value to return when there is no match. A value for this is provided for use within the `UriMatcher` class itself.

Next, the URI values are added to the matcher with their corresponding identifiers. The URIs are broken up in to the authority portion, defined in `AUTHORITY`, and the path portion, which is passed in as a literal string. The path can contain patterns, such as the "#" symbol to indicate a number. The "*" symbol is used as a wildcard to match anything.

Implementing the `insert()` Method

The `insert()` method is used for adding data to the content provider. Here is a sample implementation of the `insert()` method:

```
public Uri insert(Uri uri, ContentValues values) {

    int match = sURIMatcher.match(uri);
    if (match != TRACKPOINTS) {
        throw new IllegalArgumentException(
            "Unknown or Invalid URI " + uri);
    }

    SQLiteDatabase sqlDB = mDB.getWritableDatabase();

    long newID = sqlDB.
        insert(TrackPointDatabase.TRACKPOINTS_TABLE, null, values);

    if (newID > 0) {
        Uri newUri = ContentUris.withAppendedId(uri, newID);
        getContext()
            .getContentResolver().notifyChange(newUri, null);
        return newUri;
    }

    throw new SQLException("Failed to insert row into " + uri);
}
```

The `Uri` is first validated to make sure it's one where inserting makes sense. A `Uri` targeting a particular row would not, for instance. Next, a writeable database object instance is retrieved. Using this, the database `insert()` method is called on the table defined by the incoming `Uri` and with the values passed in. At this point, no error checking is performed on the values. Instead, the underlying database implementation throws exceptions that can be handled by the user of the content provider.

If the insert was successful, a `Uri` is created for notifying the system of a change to the underlying data via a call to the `notifyChange()` method of the `ContentResolver`. Otherwise, an exception is thrown.

Implementing the `update()` Method

The `update()` method is used to modify an existing row of data. It has elements similar to the `insert()` and `query()` methods. The update is applied to a particular selection defined by the incoming `Uri`.

```
public int update(Uri uri, ContentValues values,
    String selection, String[] selectionArgs) {

    SQLiteDatabase sqlDB = mDB.getWritableDatabase();
    int match = sURIMatcher.match(uri);
    int rowsAffected;

    switch (match) {
        case TRACKPOINTS:
            rowsAffected = sqlDB.update(
                TrackPointDatabase.TRACKPOINTS_TABLE,
                values, selection, selectionArgs);
            break;

        case TRACKPOINT_ID:
            String id = uri.getLastPathSegment();
            if (TextUtils.isEmpty(selection)) {
                rowsAffected = sqlDB.update(
                    TrackPointDatabase.TRACKPOINTS_TABLE,
                    values, _ID + "=" + id, null);
            } else {
                rowsAffected = sqlDB.update(
                    TrackPointDatabase.TRACKPOINTS_TABLE,
                    values, selection + " and " + _ID + "="
                    + id, selectionArgs);
            }
            break;
        default:
            throw new IllegalArgumentException(
                "Unknown or Invalid URI " + uri);
    }

    getContext().getContentResolver().notifyChange(uri, null);
    return rowsAffected;
}
```

In this block of code, a writable `SQLiteDatabase` instance is retrieved and the `Uri` type the user passed in is determined with a call to the `match()` method of the `UriMatcher`. No checking of values or parameters is performed here. However, to block updates to a specific `Uri`, such as a `Uri` affecting multiple rows or a match on `TRACKPOINT_ID`, `java.lang.UnsupportedOperationException` can be thrown to indicate this. In this example, though, trust is placed in the user of this content provider.

After calling the appropriate `update()` method, the system is notified of the change to the URI with a call to the `notifyChange()` method. This tells any observers of the URI that data has possibly changed. Finally, the affected number of rows is returned, which is information conveniently returned from the call to the `update()` method.

Implementing the `delete()` Method

Now it's time to clean up the database. The following is a sample implementation of the `delete()` method. It doesn't check to see if the user might be deleting more data than they should. You also notice that this is similar to the `update()` method.

```
public int delete(Uri uri, String selection, String[] selectionArgs) {
    int match = sURIMatcher.match(uri);

    SQLiteDatabase sqlDB = mDB.getWritableDatabase();
    int rowsAffected = 0;
    switch (match) {

        case TRACKPOINTS:
            rowsAffected = sqlDB.delete(
                TrackPointDatabase.TRACKPOINTS_TABLE,
                selection, selectionArgs);
            break;

        case TRACKPOINT_ID:
            String id = uri.getLastPathSegment();
            if (TextUtils.isEmpty(selection)) {
            rowsAffected =
                sqlDB.delete(TrackPointDatabase.TRACKPOINTS_TABLE,
                _ID+"="+id, null);
            } else {
                rowsAffected =
                    sqlDB.delete(TrackPointDatabase.TRACKPOINTS_TABLE,
                    selection + " and " +_ID+"="+id, selectionArgs);
            }
            break;
        default:
            throw new IllegalArgumentException(
                "Unknown or Invalid URI " + uri);
    }
```

```
getContext().getContentResolver().notifyChange(uri, null);

    return rowsAffected;
}
```

Again, a writable database instance is retrieved and the `Uri` type is determined using the match method of `UriMatcher`. If the result is a directory `Uri`, the delete is called with the selection the user passed in. However, if the result is a specific row, the row index is used to further limit the delete, with or without the selection. Allowing this without a specific selection enables deletion of a specified identifier without having to also know exactly where it came from.

As before, the system is then notified of this change with a call to the `notifyChange()` method of `ContentResolver`. Also as before, the number of affect rows is returned, which we stored after the call to the `delete()` method.

Implementing the `getType()` Method

The last method to implement is the `getType()` method. The purpose of this method is to return the MIME type for a particular `Uri` that is passed in. It does not need to return MIME types for specific columns of data.

```
public static final String CONTENT_ITEM_TYPE =
    ContentResolver.CURSOR_ITEM_BASE_TYPE +
    "/track-points";

public static final String CONTENT_TYPE =
    ContentResolver.CURSOR_DIR_BASE_TYPE +
    "/track-points";

public String getType(Uri uri) {
    int matchType = sURIMatcher.match(uri);
    switch (matchType) {

        case TRACKPOINTS:
            return CONTENT_TYPE;

        case TRACKPOINT_ID:
            return CONTENT_ITEM_TYPE;

        default:
            throw new
                IllegalArgumentException("Unknown or Invalid URI "
                + uri);
    }
}
```

To start, a couple of MIME types are defined. The Android SDK provides some guideline values for single items and directories of items, which are used here. The corresponding string for each is `vnd.android.cursor.item` and `vnd.android.cursor.dir`, respectively. Finally, the `match()` method is used to determine the type of the provided `Uri` so that the appropriate MIME type can be returned.

Updating the Manifest File

Finally, you need to update your application's `AndroidManifest.xml` file so that it reflects that a content provider interface is exposed to the rest of the system. Here, the class name and the authorities, or what might considered the domain of the `content://` URI, need to be set. For instance, `content://com.androidbook.TrackPointProvider` is the base URI used in this content provider example, which means the authority is `com.androidbook.TrackPointProvider`. The following XML shows an example of this:

```
<provider
    android:authorities="com.androidbook.gpx.TrackPointProvider"
    android:multiprocess="true"
    android:name="com.androidbook.gpx.TrackPointProvider"
</provider>
```

The value of `multiprocess` is set to true because the data does not need to be synchronized between multiple running versions of this content provider. It's possible that two or more applications might access a content provider at the same time, so proper synchronization might be necessary.

> **Note**
>
> We frequently reference notifications that are sent to observers. In Chapter 20, "Working with Notifications," you learn about notifications that are sent to the device.

Working with Live Folders

A `LiveFolder` (`android.provider.LiveFolders`) is a powerful feature that complements the content provider interface. A `LiveFolder` is a special folder containing content generated by a content provider. For example, a user might want to create a `LiveFolder` with favorite contacts ("Fave Five"), most frequently viewed emails in a custom email application, or high-priority tasks in a task management application.

When the user chooses to create a `LiveFolder`, the Android system provides a list of all activities that respond to the `ACTION_CREATE_LIVE_FOLDER` Intent. If the user chooses your `Activity`, that `Activity` creates the `LiveFolder` and passes it back to the system using the `setResult()` method.

The `LiveFolder` consists of the following components:

- Folder name
- Folder icon
- Display mode (grid or list)
- Content provider URI for the folder contents

The first task when enabling a content provider to serve up data to a `LiveFolder` is to provide an `<intent-filter>` for an `Activity` that handles enabling the `LiveFolder`. This is done within the `AndroidManifest.xml` file as follows:

```
<intent-filter>
    <action android:name=
        "android.intent.action.CREATE_LIVE_FOLDER" />
    <category
        android:name="android.intent.category.DEFAULT" />
</intent-filter>
```

Next, this action needs to be handled within the `onCreate()` method of the `Activity` it has been defined for. Within the preceding provider example, you can place the following code to handle this action:

```
super.onCreate(savedInstanceState);

final Intent intent = getIntent();
final String action = intent.getAction();
if (LiveFolders.ACTION_CREATE_LIVE_FOLDER.equals(action)) {

    final Intent resultIntent = new Intent();

    resultIntent.setData(TrackPointProvider.LIVE_URI);
    resultIntent.putExtra(
        LiveFolders.EXTRA_LIVE_FOLDER_NAME, "GPX Sample");
    resultIntent.putExtra(LiveFolders.EXTRA_LIVE_FOLDER_ICON,
        Intent.ShortcutIconResource.fromContext(
        this, R.drawable.icon));
    resultIntent.putExtra(LiveFolders.EXTRA_LIVE_FOLDER_DISPLAY_MODE,
        LiveFolders.DISPLAY_MODE_LIST);

    setResult(RESULT_OK, resultIntent);
} // ... rest of onCreate()
```

This defines the core components of the `LiveFolder`: its name, icon, display mode, and `Uri`. The `Uri` is not the same as one that already existed because it needs certain specific fields to work properly. This leads directly to the next task: modifying the content provider to prepare it for serving up data to the `LiveFolder`.

First, you define a new `Uri`. In this case, you add `"/live"` to the end of the existing `CONTENT_URI`. For example:

```
public static final Uri LIVE_URI = Uri.parse("content://"
    + AUTHORITY + "/" + TrackPointDatabase.TRACKPOINTS_TABLE
    + "/live");
```

You add this new `Uri` pattern the `UriMatcher`. Next, modify the `query()` implementation to recognize this new `Uri` and add a projection, which is defined next:

```
switch (sURIMatcher.match(uri)) {
case TRACKPOINT_ID:
    qBuilder.appendWhere("_id=" + uri.getLastPathSegment());
    break;
case TRACKPOINTS_LIVE:
    qBuilder.setProjectionMap(
        TRACKPOINTS_LIVE_FOLDER_PROJECTION_MAP);
    break;
// ... other cases
}
Cursor c = qBuilder.query( // ...
```

The projection is critical for a working `LiveFolder` provider. There are two mandatory fields that must be in the resulting `Cursor`: `LiveFolder._ID` and `LiveFolder.NAME`. In addition to these, other fields, such as `LiveFolder.DESCRIPTION`, are available to modify the look and behavior of the view. In this example, we use `TIMESTAMP` for the name, as shown here in the following projection implementation:

```
private static final HashMap<String,String>
    TRACKPOINTS_LIVE_FOLDER_PROJECTION_MAP;
static {
    TRACKPOINTS_LIVE_FOLDER_PROJECTION_MAP =
        new HashMap<String,String>();
    TRACKPOINTS_LIVE_FOLDER_PROJECTION_MAP.put(
        LiveFolders._ID, _ID + " as " + LiveFolders._ID);
    TRACKPOINTS_LIVE_FOLDER_PROJECTION_MAP.put(
        LiveFolders.NAME, TIMESTAMP + " as " + LiveFolders.NAME);
}
```

After this is done, the `LiveFolder` should be, well, live. In this example, only a list of dates is shown, as in Figure 11.2.

Figure 11.2   Sample **LiveFolder** list with
dates.

Summary

Your application can leverage the data available within other Android applications, if they
expose that data as a content provider. Content providers such as MediaStore, Browser,
CallLog, and Contacts can be leveraged by other Android applications, resulting in a robust, immersive experience for users. Applications can also share data among themselves
by becoming content providers. Becoming a content provider involves implementing a
set of methods that manage how and what data you expose for use in other applications
or even directly on the Home screen through the use of LiveFolders.

References and More Information

Android Dev Guide: Content Providers:
    http://developer.android.com/guide/topics/providers/content-providers.html

## 12

Using Android Networking APIs

Applications written with networking components are far more dynamic and content-rich than those that are not. Applications leverage the network for a variety of reasons: to deliver fresh and updated content, to enable social networking features of an otherwise standalone application, to offload heavy processing to high-powered servers, and to enable data storage beyond what the user can achieve on the device.

Those accustomed to Java networking will find the `java.net` package familiar. There are also some helpful Android utility classes for various types of network operations and protocols. This chapter focuses on Hypertext Transfer Protocol (HTTP), the most common protocol for networked mobile applications.

Understanding Mobile Networking Fundamentals

Networking on the Android platform is standardized, using a combination of powerful yet familiar technologies and libraries such as `java.net`. Network implementation is generally straightforward, but mobile application developers need to plan for less stable connectivity than one might expect in a home or office network setting—connectivity depends on the location of the users and their devices. Users demand stable, responsive applications. This means that you must take extra care when designing network-enabled applications. Luckily, the Android SDK provides a number of tools and classes for ensuring just that.

Warning

Recall that developers must agree to a number of network best practices as part of the Android Software Development Kit (SDK) License Agreement. If you plan to use network support in your application, you might want to review these contractual points to ensure that your application complies with the agreement.

Accessing the Internet (HTTP)

The most common way to transfer data to and from the network is to use HTTP. You can use HTTP to encapsulate almost any type of data and to secure the data with Secure Sockets Layer (SSL), which can be important when you transmit data that falls under privacy requirements. Also, most common ports used by HTTP are typically open from the phone networks.

> **Tip**
>
> Many of the code examples provided in this chapter are taken from the SimpleNetworking application. This source code for the SimpleNetworking application is provided for download on the book website.

Reading Data from the Web

Reading data from the Web can be extremely simple. For example, if all you need to do is read some data from a website and you have the web address of that data, you can leverage the URL class (available as part of the `java.net` package) to read a fixed amount of text from a file on a web server, like this:

```java
import java.io.InputStream;
import java.net.URL;

// ...

URL text = new URL(
    "http://api.flickr.com/services/feeds/photos_public.gne" +
    "?id=26648248@N04&lang=en-us&format=atom");

InputStream isText = text.openStream();
byte[] bText = new byte[250];
int readSize = isText.read(bText);
Log.i("Net", "readSize = " + readSize);
Log.i("Net", "bText = "+ new String(bText));
isText.close();
```

First, a new URL object is created with the URL to the data we want to read. A stream is then opened to the URL resource. From there, we read the data and close the `InputStream`. Reading data from a server can be that simple.

> **Note**
>
> As we state in the book's introduction, exception handling has been stripped from book code examples for readability. However, when it comes to networking code, you often need to add this handling for the code examples to compile. See the sample code provided on the book website for examples of how to implement exception handling properly.

However, remember that because we work with a network resource, errors can be more common. Our phone might not have network coverage; the server might be down for maintenance or disappear entirely; the URL might be invalid; and network users might experience long waits and timeouts.

This method might work in some instances—for example, when your application has lightweight, noncritical network features—but it's not particularly elegant. In many cases, you might want to know more about the data before reading from it from the URL. For instance, you might want to know how big it is.

Finally, for networking to work in any Android application, permission is required. Your application needs to have the following statement in its `AndroidManifest.xml` file:

```
<uses-permission
    android:name="android.permission.INTERNET" />
```

Using `HttpURLConnection`

We can use the `HttpURLConnection` object to do a little reconnaissance on our URL before we transfer too much data. `HttpURLConnection` retrieves some information about the resource referenced by the URL object, including HTTP status and header information.

Some of the information you can retrieve from the `HttpURLConnection` includes the length of the content, content type, and date-time information so that you can check to see if the data changed since the last time you accessed the URL.

Here is a short example of how to use `HttpURLConnection` to query the same URL previously used:

```
import java.io.InputStream;
import java.net.HttpURLConnection;
import java.net.URL;

// ...

URL text = new URL(
    "http://api.flickr.com/services/feeds/photos_public.gne
➥?id=26648248@N04&lang=en-us&format=atom");
HttpURLConnection http =
    (HttpURLConnection)text.openConnection();
Log.i("Net", "length = " + http.getContentLength());
Log.i("Net", "respCode = " + http.getResponseCode());
Log.i("Net", "contentType = "+ http.getContentType());
Log.i("Net", "content = "+http.getContent());
```

The log lines demonstrate a few useful methods with the `HttpURLConnection` class. If the URL content is deemed appropriate, you can then call `http.getInputStream()` to get the same `InputStream` object as before. From there, reading from the network resource is the same, but more is known about the resource.

Parsing XML from the Network

A large portion of data transmitted between network resources is stored in a structured fashion in Extensible Markup Language (XML). In particular, RSS feeds are provided in a standardized XML format, and many web services provide data using these feeds.

Android SDK provides a variety of XML utilities. We dabble with the XML Pull Parser in Chapter 6, "Managing Application Resources." We also cover the various SAX and DOM support available in Chapter 10, "Using Android Data and Storage APIs."

Parsing XML from the network is similar to parsing an XML resource file or a raw file on the file system. Android provides a fast and efficient XML Pull Parser, which is a parser of choice for networked applications.

The following code demonstrates how to use the XML Pull Parser to read an XML file from flickr.com and extract specific data from within it. A `TextView` called `status` is assigned before this block of code is executed and displays the status of the parsing operation.

```
import java.net.URL;

import org.xmlpull.v1.XmlPullParser;
import org.xmlpull.v1.XmlPullParserFactory;

// ...

URL text = new URL(
    "http://api.flickr.com/services/feeds/photos_public.gne
➥?id=26648248@N04&lang=en-us&format=atom");

XmlPullParserFactory parserCreator =
    XmlPullParserFactory.newInstance();
XmlPullParser parser = parserCreator.newPullParser();

parser.setInput(text.openStream(), null);

status.setText("Parsing...");
int parserEvent = parser.getEventType();
while (parserEvent != XmlPullParser.END_DOCUMENT) {
    switch(parserEvent) {
        case XmlPullParser.START_TAG:
            String tag = parser.getName();

            if (tag.compareTo("link") == 0) {
                String relType =
                    parser.getAttributeValue(null, "rel");

                if (relType.compareTo("enclosure") == 0 ) {
                    String encType =
                        parser.getAttributeValue(null, "type");
```

```
            if (encType.startsWith("image/")) {
                String imageSrc =
                    parser.getAttributeValue(null, "href");
                Log.i("Net",
                    "image source = " + imageSrc);
            }
        }
    }
    break;
}
parserEvent = parser.next();
}
status.setText("Done...");
```

After the URL is created, the next step is to retrieve an `XmlPullParser` instance from the `XmlPullParserFactory`. A Pull Parser has a main method that returns the next event. The events returned by a Pull Parser are similar to methods used in the implementation of a SAX parser handler class. Instead, though, the code is handled iteratively. This method is more efficient for mobile use.

In this example, the only event that we check for is the `START_TAG` event, signifying the beginning of an XML tag. Attribute values are queried and compared. This example looks specifically for image URLs within the XML from a flickr feed query. When found, a log entry is made.

You can check for the following XML Pull Parser events:

- `START_TAG`: Returned when a new tag is found (that is, `<tag>`)
- `TEXT`: Returned when text is found (that is, `<tag>text</tag>` where text has been found)
- `END_TAG`: Returned when the end of tag is found (that is, `</tag>`)
- `END_DOCUMENT`: Returned when the end of the XML file is reached

Additionally, the parser can be set to validate the input. Typically, parsing without validation is used when under constrained memory environments, such as a mobile environment. Compliant, nonvalidating parsing is the default for this XML Pull Parser.

Processing Asynchronously

Users demand responsive applications, so time-intensive operations such as networking should not block the main UI thread. The style of networking presented so far causes the UI thread it runs on to block until the operation finishes. For small tasks, this might be acceptable. However, when timeouts, large amounts of data, or additional processing, such as parsing XML, is added into the mix, you should move these time-intensive operations off of the main UI thread.

Offloading intensive operations such as networking provides a smoother, more stable experience to the user. The Android SDK provides two easy ways to manage offload processing from the main UI thread: the `AsyncTask` class and the standard Java `Thread` class.

The `AsyncTask` class is a special class for Android development that encapsulates background processing and helps facilitate communication to the UI thread while managing the lifecycle of the background task within the context of the activity lifecycle. Developers can also construct their own threading solutions using the standard Java methods and classes—but they are then responsible for managing the entire thread lifecycle as well.

Working with `AsyncTask`

`AsyncTask` is an abstract helper class for managing background operations that eventually post back to the UI thread. It creates a simpler interface for asynchronous operations than manually creating a Java Thread class.

Instead of creating threads for background processing and using messages and message handlers for updating the UI, you can create a subclass of `AsyncTask` and implement the appropriate event methods. The `onPreExecute()` method runs on the UI thread before background processing begins. The `doInBackground()` method handles background processing, whereas `publishProgress()` informs the UI thread periodically about the background processing progress. When the background processing finishes, the `onPostExecute()` method runs on the UI thread to give a final update.

The following code demonstrates an example implementation of `AsyncTask` to perform the same functionality as the code for the `Thread`:

```
private class ImageLoader extends
    AsyncTask<URL, String, String> {

@Override
protected String doInBackground(
    URL... params) {
    // just one param
    try {
        URL text = params[0];

        // ... parsing code {

        publishProgress(
            "imgCount = " + curImageCount);

        // ... end parsing code }

    }
    catch (Exception e ) {
        Log.e("Net",
            "Failed in parsing XML", e);
        return "Finished with failure.";
```

```
   }

      return "Done...";
}


protected void onCancelled() {
   Log.e("Net", "Async task Cancelled");
}

protected void onPostExecute(String result) {
    mStatus.setText(result);
}


protected void onPreExecute() {
    mStatus.setText("About to load URL");
}

protected void onProgressUpdate(
    String... values) {
    // just one value, please
    mStatus.setText(values[0]);
}}
```

When launched with the `AsyncTask.execute()` method, `doInBackground()` runs in a background thread while the other methods run on the UI thread. There is no need to manage a `Handler` or post a `Runnable` object to it. This simplifies coding and debugging.

Using Threads for Network Calls

The following code demonstrates how to launch a new thread that connects to a remote server, retrieves and parses some XML, and posts a response back to the UI thread to change a `TextView`:

```
import java.net.URL;


import org.xmlpull.v1.XmlPullParser;
import org.xmlpull.v1.XmlPullParserFactory;

// ...


new Thread() {
    public void run() {
        try {
            URL text = new URL(
                "http://api.flickr.com/services/feeds/photos_public.gne?
➡id=26648248@N04&lang=en-us&format=atom");
```

```
XmlPullParserFactory parserCreator =
    XmlPullParserFactory.newInstance();
XmlPullParser parser =
    parserCreator.newPullParser();

parser.setInput(text.openStream(), null);

mHandler.post(new Runnable() {
    public void run() {
        status.setText("Parsing...");
    }
});

int parserEvent = parser.getEventType();
while (parserEvent !=
    XmlPullParser.END_DOCUMENT) {

    // Parsing code here ...

    parserEvent = parser.next();
}

mHandler.post(new Runnable() {
    public void run() {
        status.setText("Done...");
    }
});

} catch (Exception e) {
    Log.e("Net", "Error in network call", e);
}
}
}.start();
```

For this example, an anonymous `Thread` object will do. We create it and call its `start()` method immediately. However, now that the code runs on a separate thread, the user interface updates must be posted back to the main thread. This is done by using a `Handler` object on the main thread and creating `Runnable` objects that execute to call `setText()` on the `TextView` widget named `status`.

The rest of the code remains the same as in the previous examples. Executing both the parsing code and the networking code on a separate thread allows the user interface to continue to behave in a responsive fashion while the network and parsing operations are done behind the scenes, resulting in a smooth and friendly user experience. This also allows for handling of interim actions by the user, such as canceling the transfer. You can accomplish this by implementing the `Thread` to listen for certain events and check for certain flags.

Displaying Images from a Network Resource

Now that we have covered how you can use a separate thread to parse XML, let's take our example a bit deeper and talk about working with non-primitive data types.

Continuing with the previous example of parsing for image locations from a flickr feed, let's display some images from the feed. The following example reads the image data and displays it on the screen, demonstrating another way you can use network resources:

```
import java.io.InputStream;
import java.net.URL;

import org.xmlpull.v1.XmlPullParser;
import org.xmlpull.v1.XmlPullParserFactory;
import android.os.Handler;

// ...

final String imageSrc =
    parser.getAttributeValue(null, "href");

final String currentTitle = new String(title);
imageThread.queueEvent(new Runnable() {
    public void run() {
        InputStream bmis;
        try {
            bmis = new URL(imageSrc).openStream();
            final Drawable image = new BitmapDrawable(
                BitmapFactory.decodeStream(bmis));
            mHandler.post(new Runnable() {
                public void run() {
                    imageSwitcher.setImageDrawable(image);
                    info.setText(currentTitle);
                }
            });
        } catch (Exception e) {
            Log.e("Net", "Failed to grab image", e);
        }
    }
});
```

You can find this block of code within the parser thread, as previously described. After the image source and title of the image have been determined, a new `Runnable` object is queued for execution on a separate image handling thread. The thread is merely a queue that receives the anonymous `Runnable` object created here and executes it at least 10 seconds after the last one, resulting in a slideshow of the images from the feed.

> ### Warning
>
> Although the preceding code is sound for local resources and URLs, for sources over slow connections, it might not work properly. This is a known issue with the Android SDK caused by a buffering issue with loading large bitmaps over slow connections. There is a relatively straightforward workaround that you can find in the code provided for this chapter.

As with the first networking example, a new `URL` object is created and an `InputStream` retrieved from it. You need a `Drawable` object to assign to the `ImageSwitcher`. Then you use the `BitmapFactory.decodeStream()` method, which takes an `InputStream`.

Finally, from this `Runnable` object, which runs on a separate queuing thread, spacing out image drawing, another anonymous `Runnable` object posts back to the main thread to actually update the `ImageSwitcher` with the new image. Figure 12.1 shows what the screen might look like showing decoding status and displaying the current image.

Figure 12.1   Screen showing a flickr image and
decoding status of feed.

Although all this continues to happen while the feed from flickr is decoded, certain operations are slower than others. For instance, while the image is decoded or drawn on the screen, you can notice a distinct hesitation in the progress of the decoding. This is to be expected on current mobile devices because most have only a single thread of execution available for applications. You need to use careful design to provide a reasonably smooth and responsive experience to the user.

Retrieving Android Network Status

The Android SDK provides utilities for gathering information about the current state of the network. This is useful to determine if a network connection is even available before trying to use a network resource. The `ConnectivityManager` class provides a number of methods to do this. The following code determines if the mobile (cellular) network is available and connected. In addition, it determines the same for the Wi-Fi network:

```
import android.net.ConnectivityManager;
import android.net.NetworkInfo;

// ...

ConnectivityManager cm = (ConnectivityManager)
    getSystemService(Context.CONNECTIVITY_SERVICE);
NetworkInfo ni =
    cm.getNetworkInfo(ConnectivityManager.TYPE_WIFI);
boolean isWifiAvail = ni.isAvailable();
boolean isWifiConn = ni.isConnected();
ni = cm.getNetworkInfo(ConnectivityManager.TYPE_MOBILE);
boolean isMobileAvail = ni.isAvailable();
boolean isMobileConn = ni.isConnected();

status.setText("WiFi\nAvail = "+ isWifiAvail +
    "\nConn = " + isWifiConn +
    "\nMobile\nAvail = "+ isMobileAvail +
    "\nConn = " + isMobileConn);
```

First, an instance of the `ConnectivityManager` object is retrieved with a call to the `getSystemService()` method, available as part of your application `Context`. Then this instance retrieves `NetworkInfo` objects for both `TYPE_WIFI` and `TYPE_MOBILE` (for the cellular network). These objects are queried for their availability but can also be queried at a more detailed status level to learn exactly what state of connection (or disconnection) the network is in. Figure 12.2 shows the typical output for the emulator in which the mobile network is simulated but Wi-Fi isn't available.

If the network is available, this does not necessarily mean the server that the network resource is on is available. However, a call to the `ConnectivityManager` method `requestRouteToHost()` can answer this question. This way, the application can give the user better feedback when there are network problems.

For your application to read the status of the network, it needs explicit permission. The following statement is required to be in its `AndroidManifest.xml` file:

```
<uses-permission
    android:name="android.permission.ACCESS_NETWORK_STATE"/>
```

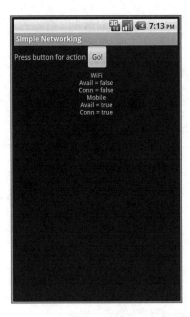

Figure 12.2   Typical network status of the
Android SDK emulator.

Tip

Use the emulator networking settings to simulate various types of cellular networks, from GSM to HSDPA (and unlimited) data rates. Additionally, you can control the latency of the network to be similar to that of the cellular networks. Although this is useful for testing how your application behaves in good conditions for the chosen network type, it can't simulate the real behavior of the network out in the field when the user is in bad coverage, goes on an elevator, or is on a train rapidly losing and reacquiring network coverage. Only physical handset testing can truly reveal these results.

Summary

Many applications use networking to enhance and improve the features they can provide to the user. However, a user's network connectivity is not a guaranteed, always-available service. Application developers need to design and implement networking features carefully to ensure a stable and responsive application. Integrating networking features into your mobile application needs to be considered at the design level. Deciding how much networking support your application should contain is part of the application design process—something we talk more about in Chapter 26, "The Mobile Software Development Process."

References and More Information

Java.net package:

http://developer.android.com/reference/java/net/package-summary.html

Android.net package:

http://developer.android.com/reference/android/net/package-summary.html

XML Pull Parsing:

http://www.xmlpull.org/

Android XML Pull Parser:

http://developer.android.com/reference/org/xmlpull/v1/XmlPullParser.html

13

Using Android Web APIs

Mobile developers often rely upon web technologies to enrich their applications, provide fresh content, and integrate with popular web services such as social networks. Android application can harness the power of the Internet in a variety of ways, including adding browser functionality to applications using the special `WebView` control and extending web-based functionality using standard WebKit libraries. Newer Android devices can also run Flash applications. In this chapter, we discuss the web technologies available on the Android platform.

Browsing the Web with `WebView`

Applications that retrieve and display content from the Web often end up displaying that data on the screen. Instead of customizing various screens with custom controls, Android applications can simply use the `WebView` control to display web content to the screen. You can think of the `WebView` control as a browser-like view.

The `WebView` control uses the WebKit rendering engine to draw HTML content on the screen. This content could be HTML pages on the Web or it can be locally sourced. WebKit is an open source browser engine. You can read more about it on its official website at http://webkit.org.

Tip

Many of the code examples provided in this section are taken from the SimpleWeb application. The source code for this application is provided for download on the book's website.

Using the `WebView` control requires the `android.permission.INTERNET` permission. You can add this permission to your application's Android manifest file as follows:

```
<uses-permission android:name="android.permission.INTERNET" />
```

When deciding if the `WebView` control is right for your application, consider that you can always launch the Browser application using an `Intent`. When you want the user to have full access to all Browser features, such as bookmarking and browsing, you're better off launching into the Browser application to a specific website, letting users do their browsing, and having them return to your application when they're done. You can do this as follows:

```
Uri uriUrl = Uri.parse("http://androidbook.blogspot.com/");
Intent launchBrowser = new Intent(Intent.ACTION_VIEW, uriUrl);
startActivity(launchBrowser);
```

Launching the Browser via an Intent does not require any special permissions. This means that your application is not required to have the `android.permission.INTERNET` permission. In addition, because Android transitions from your application's current activity to a specific Browser application's activity, and then returns when the user presses the back key, the experience is nearly as seamless as implementing your own `Activity` class with an embedded `WebView`.

Designing a Layout with a `WebView` Control

The `WebView` control can be added to a layout resource file like any other view. It can take up the entire screen or just a portion of it. A typical `WebView` definition in a layout resource might look like this:

```
<WebView
    android:id="@+id/web_holder"
    android:layout_height="wrap_content"
    android:layout_width="fill_parent"
/>
```

Generally speaking, you should give your `WebView` controls ample room to display text and graphics. Keep this in mind when designing layouts using the `WebView` control.

Warning

The Eclipse Layout Resource Editor does not display the WebView control properly. You need to run either the Android emulator or a device to make sure the layout displays properly.

Loading Content into a `WebView` Control

You can load content into a `WebView` control in a variety of ways. For example, a `WebView` control can load a specific website or render raw HTML content. Web pages can be stored on a remote web server or stored on the device.

Here is an example of how to use a `WebView` control to load content from a specific website:

```
final WebView wv = (WebView) findViewById(R.id.web_holder);
wv.loadUrl("http://www.perlgurl.org/");
```

You do not need to add any additional code to load the referenced web page on the screen. Similarly, you could load an HTML file called webby.html stored in the application's assets directory like this:

```
wv.loadUrl("file:///android_asset/webby.html");
```

If, instead, you want to render raw HTML, you can use the `loadData()` method:

```
String strPageTitle = "The Last Words of Oscar Wilde";
String strPageContent = "<h1>" + strPageTitle +
    ": </h1>\"Either that wallpaper goes, or I do.\"";
String myHTML = "<html><title>" + strPageTitle
    +"</title><body>"+ strPageContent +"</body></html>";
wv.loadData(myHTML, "text/html", "utf-8");
```

The resulting `WebView` control is shown in Figure 13.1.

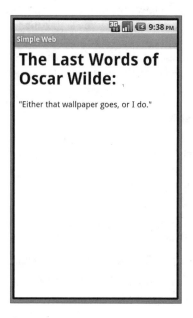

Figure 13.1   A **WebView** control used to display
HTML.

Unfortunately, not all websites are designed for mobile devices. It can be handy to change the scale of the web content to fit comfortably within the `WebView` control. You can achieve this by setting the initial scale of the control, like this:

```
wv.setInitialScale(30);
```

The call to the `setInitialScale()` method scales the view to 30 percent of the original size. For pages that specify absolute sizes, scaling the view is necessary to see the entire page on the screen. Some text might become too small to read, though, so you might need to test and make page design changes (if the web content is under your control) for a good user experience.

> **Tip**
>
> If you want an entire screen to be a `WebView` control, you can simply create a `WebView` pro-grammatically and pass it into the `setContentView()` method within the `onCreate()` method of your `Activity`.

Adding Features to the `WebView` Control

You might have noticed that the `WebView` control does not have all the features of a full browser. For example, it does not display the title of a webpage or provide buttons for re-loading pages. In fact, if the user clicks on a link within the `WebView` control, that action does not load the new page within the view. Instead, it fires up the Browser application.

By default, all the `WebView` control does is display the web content provided by the de-veloper using its internal rendering engine, WebKit. You can enhance the `WebView` control in a variety of ways, though. You can use three classes, in particular, to help modify the be-havior of the control: the `WebSettings` class, the `WebViewClient` class, and the `WebChromeClient` class.

Modifying `WebView` Settings with `WebSettings`

By default, a `WebView` control has various default settings: no zoom controls, JavaScript disabled, default font sizes, user-agent string, and so on. You can change the settings of a `WebView` control using the `getSettings()` method. The `getSettings()` method returns a `WebSettings` object that can be used to configure the desired `WebView` settings. Some useful settings include

- Enabling and disabling zoom controls using the `setSupportZoom()` and `setBuiltInZoomControls()` methods
- Enabling and disabling JavaScript using the `setJavaScriptEnabled()` method
- Enabling and disabling mouseovers using the `setLightTouchEnabled()` method
- Configuring font families, text sizes, and other display characteristics

You can also use the `WebSettings` class to configure `WebView` plug-ins and allow for mul-tiple windows.

Handling `WebView` Events with `WebViewClient`

The `WebViewClient` class enables the application to listen for certain `WebView` events, such as when a page is loading, when a form is submitted, and when a new URL is about to be loaded. You can also use the `WebViewClient` class to determine and handle any errors that occur with page loading. You can tie a valid `WebViewClient` object to a `WebView` using the `setWebViewClient()` method.

The following is an example of how to use `WebViewClient` to handle the `onPageFinished()` method to draw the title of the page on the screen:

```
WebViewClient webClient = new WebViewClient() {

    public void onPageFinished(WebView view, String url) {
```

```
        super.onPageFinished(view, url);
        String title = wv.getTitle();
        pageTitle.setText(title);
    }};

wv.setWebViewClient(webClient);
```

When the page finishes loading, as indicated by the call to `onPageFinished()`, a call to the `getTitle()` method of the `WebView` object retrieves the title for use. The result of this call is shown in Figure 13.2.

Figure 13.2   A **WebView** control with micro-
browser features such as title display.

Adding Browser Chrome with `WebChromeClient`

You can use the `WebChromeClient` class in a similar way to the `WebViewClient`. However, `WebChromeClient` is specialized for the sorts of items that will be drawn outside the region in which the web content is drawn, typically known as *browser chrome*. The `WebChromeClient` class also includes callbacks for certain JavaScript calls, such as `onJsBeforeUnload()`, to confirm navigation away from a page. A valid `WebChromeClient` object can be tied to a `WebView` using the `setWebChromeClient()` method.

The following code demonstrates using `WebView` features to enable interactivity with the user. An `EditText` and a `Button` control are added below the `WebView` control, and a `Button` handler is implemented as follows:

```
Button go = (Button) findViewById(R.id.go_button);
go.setOnClickListener(new View.OnClickListener() {
    public void onClick(View v) {
        wv.loadUrl(et.getText().toString());
    }
});
```

Calling the `loadUrl()` method again, as shown, is all that is needed to cause the `WebView` control to download another HTML page for display, as shown in Figure 13.3. From here, you can build a generic web browser in to any application, but you can apply restrictions so that the user is restricted to browsing relevant materials.

Figure 13.3 **WebView** with **EditText** allowing
entry of arbitrary URLs.

Using `WebChromeClient` can help add some typical chrome on the screen. For instance, you can use it to listen for changes to the title of the page, various JavaScript dialogs that might be requested, and even for developer-oriented pieces, such as the console messages.

```
WebChromeClient webChrome = new WebChromeClient() {
    @Override
```

```
    public void onReceivedTitle
        (WebView view, String title) {
        Log.v(DEBUG_TAG, "Got new title");
        super.onReceivedTitle(view, title);
        pageTitle.setText(title);
    }
};
wv.setWebChromeClient(webChrome);
```

Here the default `WebChromeClient` is overridden to receive changes to the title of the page. This title of the web page is then set to a `TextView` visible on the screen.

Whether you use `WebView` to display the main user interface of your application or use it sparingly to draw such things as help pages, there are circumstances where it might be the ideal control for the job to save coding time, especially when compared to a custom screen design. Leveraging the power of the open source engine, `WebKit`, `WebView` can provide a powerful, standards-based HTML viewer for applications. Support for `WebKit` is widespread because it is used in various desktop browsers, including Apple Safari and Google Chrome, a variety of mobile browsers, including those on the Apple iOS, Nokia, Palm WebOS, and BlackBerry handsets, and various other platforms, such as Adobe AIR.

Building Web Extensions Using WebKit

All HTML rendering on the Android platform is done using the WebKit rendering engine. The `android.webkit` package provides a number of APIs for browsing the Internet using the powerful `WebView` control. You should be aware of the WebKit interfaces and classes available, as you are likely to need them to enhance the `WebView` user experience.

These are not classes and interfaces to the Browser app (although you can interact with the Browser data using contact providers). Instead, these are the classes and interfaces that you must use to control the browsing abilities of `WebView` controls you implement in your applications.

Browsing the WebKit APIs

Some of the most helpful classes of the `android.webkit` package are

- The `CacheManager` class gives you some control over cache items of a `WebView`.
- The `ConsoleMessage` class can be used to retrieve JavaScript console output from a `WebView`.
- The `CookieManager` class is used to set and retrieve user cookies for a `WebView`.
- The `URLUtil` class is handy for validating web addresses of different types.
- The `WebBackForwardList` and `WebHistoryItem` classes can be used to inspect the web history of the `WebView`.

Now let's take a quick look at how you might use some of these classes to enhance a `WebView`.

Extending Web Application Functionality to Android

Let's take some of the WebKit features we have discussed so far in this chapter and work through an example. It is fairly common for mobile developers to design their applications as web applications in order to reach users across a variety of platforms. This minimizes the amount of platform-specific code to develop and maintain. However, on its own, a web application cannot call into native platform code and take advantage of the features that native apps (such as those written in Java for the Android platform) can, such as using a built-in camera or accessing some other underlying Android feature.

Developers can enhance web applications by designing a lightweight shell application in Java and using a `WebView` control as a portal to the web application content. Two-way communication between the web application and the native Java application is possible through scripting languages such as JavaScript.

> **Tip**
>
> Many of the code examples provided in this section are taken from the SimpleWebExtension application. The source code for this application is provided for download on the book website.

Let's create a simple Android application that illustrates communication between web content and native Android code. This example requires that you understand JavaScript.

To create this application, take the following steps:

1. Create a new Android application.

2. Create a layout with a `WebView` control called `html_viewer` and a `Button` control called `call_js`. Set the `onClick` attribute of the `Button` control to a method called `setHTMLText`.

3. In the `onCreate()` method of your application activity, retrieve the `WebView` control using the `findViewById()` method.

4. Enable JavaScript within the `WebView` by retrieving its `WebSettings` and calling the `setJavaScriptEnabled()` method.

5. Create a `WebChromeClient` object and implement its `onConsoleMessage()` method in order to monitor the JavaScript console messages.

6. Add the `WebChromeClient` object to the `WebView` using the `setWebChromeClient()` method.

7. Allow the JavaScript interface to control your application by calling the `addJavascriptInterface()` method of the `WebView` control. You will need to define the functionality that you want the JavaScript interface to be able to control and within what namespace the calls will be available. In this case, we allow the JavaScript to initiate `Toast` messages.

8. Load your content into the `WebView` control using one of the standard methods, such as the `loadUrl()` method. In this case, we load an HTML asset we defined within the application package.

If you followed these steps, you should end up with your activity's `onCreate()` method looking something like this:

```
@Override
public void onCreate(Bundle savedInstanceState) {
    super.onCreate(savedInstanceState);
    setContentView(R.layout.main);
    final WebView wv = (WebView) findViewById(R.id.html_viewer);
    WebSettings settings = wv.getSettings();
    settings.setJavaScriptEnabled(true);
    WebChromeClient webChrome = new WebChromeClient() {
        @Override
        public boolean onConsoleMessage(ConsoleMessage consoleMessage) {
            Log.v(DEBUG_TAG, consoleMessage.lineNumber()
                + ": " + consoleMessage.message());
            return true;
        }
    };

    wv.setWebChromeClient(webChrome);
    wv.addJavascriptInterface(new JavaScriptExtensions(), "jse");
    wv.loadUrl("file:///android_asset/sample.html");
}
```

A custom `WebChromeClient` class is set so that any JavaScript `console.log` messages go out to LogCat output, using a custom debug tag as usual to enable easy tracking of log output specific to the application. Next, a new JavaScript interface is defined with the namespace called `jse`—the namespace is up to you. To call from JavaScript to this Java class, the JavaScript calls must all start with namespace `jse.`, followed by the appropriate exposed method—for instance, `jse.javaMethod()`.

You can define the `JavaScriptExtensions` class as a subclass within the activity as a subclass with a single method that can trigger Android `Toast` messages:

```
class JavaScriptExtensions {
    public static final int TOAST_LONG = Toast.LENGTH_LONG;
    public static final int TOAST_SHORT = Toast.LENGTH_SHORT;
    public void toast(String message, int length) {
        Toast.makeText(SimpleWebExtension.this, message, length).show();
    }
}
```

The JavaScript code has access to everything in the `JavaScriptExtensions` class, including the member variables as well as the methods. Return values work as expected from the methods, too.

Now switch your attention to defining the web page to load in the `WebView` control. For this example, simply create a file called sample.html in the /assets directory of the application. The contents of the sample.html file are shown here:

```html
<html>
<head>
<script type="text/javascript">

function doToast() {
    jse.toast("'"+document.getElementById('form_text').value +
        "' -From Java!", jse.TOAST_LONG);
}

function doConsoleLog() {
    console.log("Console logging.");
}

function doAlert() {
    alert("This is an alert.");
}

function doSetFormText(update) {
    document.getElementById('form_text').value = update;
}

</script>
</head>
<body>
<h2>This is a test.</h2>
<input type="text" id="form_text" value="Enter something here..." />
<input type="button" value="Toast" onclick="doToast();" /><br />
<input type="button" value="Log" onclick="doConsoleLog();" /><br />
<input type="button" value="Alert" onclick="doAlert();" />
</body>
</html>
```

The sample.html file defines four JavaScript functions and displays the form shown within the `WebView`:

- The `doToast()` function calls into the Android application using the `jse` object defined earlier with the call to the `addJavaScriptInterface()` method. The `addJavaScriptInterface()` method, for all practical intents and purposes, can be treated literally as the `JavaScriptExtensions` class as if that class had been written in JavaScript. If the `doToast()` function had returned a value, we could assign it to a variable here.

- The `doConsoleLog()` function writes into the JavaScript console log, which is picked up by the `onConsoleMessage()` callback of the `WebChromeClient`.

- The `doAlert()` function illustrates how alerts work within the `WebView` control by launching a dialog. If you want to override what the alert looks like, you can override the `WebChromeClient.onJSAlert()` method.

- The `doSetFormText()` function illustrates how native Java code can communicate back through the JavaScript interface and provide data to the web application.

Finally, to demonstrate making a call from Java back to JavaScript, you need to define the click handler for the `Button` control within your `Activity` class. Here, the `onClick` handler, called `setHTMLText()`, executes some JavaScript on the currently loaded page by calling a JavaScript function called `doSetFormText()`, which we defined earlier in the web page. Here is an implementation of the `setHTMLText()` method:

```
public void setHTMLText(View view) {
    WebView wv = (WebView) findViewById(R.id.html_viewer);
    wv.loadUrl("javascript:doSetFormText('Java->JS call');");
}
```

This method of making a call to the JavaScript on the currently loaded page does not allow for return values. There are ways, however, to structure your design to allow checking of results, generally by treating the call as asynchronous and implementing another method for determining the response.

Warning

Keep in mind that opening up the Android application to JavaScript control using the `addJavascriptInterface()` method must be done securely. Make sure your `WebView` only loads content under your control—not just any content on the Web. Also, the JavaScript interface does not run on the UI thread, so you need to employ normal cross-thread communication techniques, such as using a handler to post messages back to the other thread in order to communicate.

Figure 13.4 shows how this application might behave on an Android device.

This style of development has been popularized by the open source PhoneGap project, which aims to provide a set of standard JavaScript interfaces to native code across a variety of platforms, including iOS, Android, BlackBerry, Symbian, and Palm. Learn more about PhoneGap at http://phonegap.com.

Working with Flash

For those web developers wanting to bring their Flash applications to mobile, Android is the only smart phone platform currently supporting desktop Flash 10.1 (as opposed to Flash Lite, a common mobile variant of Flash that's very limited). However, there are both benefits and drawbacks to including Flash technology on the platform. Let's look at some of the facts:

- Flash might not be the "future," but it's the "status quo" in some web circles. There are millions of Flash applications and websites out there that can now be accessed from Android devices. This makes users happy, which should make the rest of us happy.

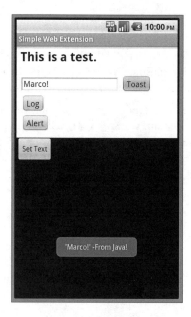

Figure 13.4   A simple Android application with a
JavaScript interface.

- Native Android applications are always going to perform better, use fewer resources (read: drain the battery slower), provide tighter platform integration, have fewer platform prerequisites, and support more Android devices than Flash applications.

- Deciding to build Flash applications for the Android platform instead of native Java applications is a design decision that should not be taken lightly. There are performance and security tradeoffs as well as limited device support (and no backward compatibility) for Flash.

- You can't expect all Flash applications to just be loaded up work. All the usual mobile constraints and UI paradigms apply. This includes designing around such constraints as a touch interface on a small screen, a relatively slow processor, and interruptions (such as phone calls) being the norm.

Still, there are those millions of great Flash applications out there. Let's look at how you can bring these applications to the Android platform.

Enabling Flash Applications

Android devices with Android 2.2 and higher can run Flash applications (currently Flash 10.1). In order to run Flash, the Android device must have Adobe's Flash Player for Android installed.

Users can download the Adobe's Flash Player for Android application from the Android Market. Android handsets might also ship with the Adobe application pre-loaded. Keep in mind that only the faster, more powerful Android devices are likely to run Flash smoothly and provide a positive user experience. After it's installed, the Flash Player for Android application behaves like a typical browser plug-in (see Figure 13.5). Users can enable or disable it, and you can control whether plug-ins are enabled or not within your screens that use the `WebView` control.

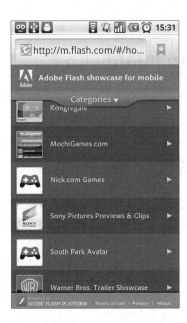

Figure 13.5   The Nexus One running a Flash application showing many mobile Flash applications available.

Building AIR Applications for Android

Adobe has created tools for developing cross-platform applications using their AIR tool suite in ActionScript 3, which is Adobe's web scripting language for web and Flash applications. The company recently announced Adobe AIR for Android, which enables developers to create AIR applications that can be compiled into native Android APK files that can then be published like any other Android application. Developers use Adobe's Flash Professional CS5 tools with a special extension to develop AIR applications that can be compiled into Android package files and distributed like native Android applications.

Note

As of this writing, the Adobe AIR for Android program is in prerelease. Developers can sign up to be part of the beta program at http://labs.adobe.com/technologies/air2/android/.

Summary

Android developers can add browser support to their applications using the versatile `WebView` control. Applications that require more control can enhance their applications with web features using powerful yet familiar technologies such as `WebKit`. In Android 2.2, Flash support was introduced to the Android platform in the form of an Adobe application. Adobe has also developed a tool suite that allows ActionScript applications to be compiled into Android APK files and distributed as native Android applications.

References and More Information

WebKit Open Source Project:
   http://www.webkit.org
W3School's JavaScript Tutorial:
   http://www.w3schools.com/js/js_intro.asp
Adobe AIR Tool Suite:
   http://www.adobe.com/products/air/tools/

14

Using Location-Based Services (LBS) APIs

Whether for safety or for convenience, location-based features on cell phones are mostly standard these days. As such, incorporating location information, navigation, and mapping features into your project can make your application much more robust.

In this chapter, you learn how to leverage location-based services available within the Android SDK. You learn how to determine the location of the handset using a particular device hardware provider, such as a built-in Global Positioning Systems (GPS) unit. You also learn how to translate raw location coordinates into descriptive location names—and how to do the reverse. Finally, we explore a couple of different methods for mapping and utilities that work with the maps.

Using Global Positioning Services (GPS)

The Android SDK provides means for accessing location via a built-in GPS hardware, when it's available. Generally speaking, just about every Android phone has some LBS capabilities. For example, in the United States, mobile phone location information is used by emergency services. That said, not all Android devices are phones, nor do all phones enable consumer-usage of LBS services. If GPS features are disabled, or an Android device does not have LBS hardware, the Android SDK provides additional APIs for determining alternate location providers. These other providers might have advantages and disadvantages in terms of power use, speed, and accuracy of reporting.

Tip

Many of the code examples provided in this chapter are taken from the SimpleLocation application. The source code for this application is provided for download on the book website.

Using GPS Features in Your Applications

LBS services and hardware such as a built-in precision GPS are optional features for Android devices. In addition to requiring the appropriate permissions, you can specify which optional features your application requires within the Android Manifest file. You can declare that your application uses or requires specific LBS services using the `<uses-feature>` tag of the Android Manifest file. Although this tag is not enforced by the Android operating system, it enables popular publication mechanisms such as the Android Market to filter your app and provide it only to users with appropriate devices. If your application will only function well on devices with some sort of method for determining the current location, you could use the following `<uses-feature>` tag in your application's manifest file:

```
<uses-feature android:name="android.hardware.location" />
```

If your application requires a precise location fix (that is, the device has functional GPS hardware, not just cell tower triangulation or other such mechanisms), you could use the following `<uses-feature>` tag instead:

```
<uses-feature android:name="android.hardware.location.gps" />
```

Note

New settings for the `<uses-feature>` tag have been added in recent Android SDK releases. For example, the values we've discussed, such as `android.hardware.location`, were added in Android 2.2 (API Level 8).

Finding Your Location

To determine device location, you need to perform a few steps and make some choices. The following list summarizes this process:

1. Retrieve an instance of the `LocationManager` using a call to the `getSystemService()` method using the `LOCATION_SERVICE`.

2. Add an appropriate permission to the `AndroidManifest.xml` file, depending on what type of location information the application needs.

3. Choose a provider using either the `getAllProviders()` method or the `getBestProvider()` method.

4. Implement a `LocationListener` class.

5. Call the `requestLocationUpdates()` method with the chosen provider and the `LocationListener` object to start receiving location information.

Specific permissions are not needed to retrieve an instance of the `LocationManager` object. Instead, the permissions determine the available providers. The following code retrieves an instance of the `LocationManager` object:

```
import android.location.*;
...
LocationManager location =
    (LocationManager)getSystemService(Context.LOCATION_SERVICE);
```

The following block of XML provides the application with both coarse and fine location permissions when added within the AndroidManifest.xml permissions file:

```
<uses-permission
    android:name="android.permission.ACCESS_FINE_LOCATION" />
<uses-permission
    android:name="android.permission.ACCESS_COARSE_LOCATION" />
```

Now that the application has permissions to use location information and the LocationManager object is valid, we must determine what provider to use for location information. The following code configures a Criteria object and requests the provider based on this information:

```
Criteria criteria = new Criteria();
criteria.setAccuracy(Criteria.NO_REQUIREMENT);
criteria.setPowerRequirement(Criteria.NO_REQUIREMENT);

String bestProvider = location.getBestProvider(criteria, true);
```

The setAccuracy() method can take values for ACCURACY_COARSE and ACCURACY_FINE that can be used (along with the appropriate permissions) to request a provider that the application has permissions to use. You can use the setPowerRequirement() method to find a provider that fits certain power use requirements, such as POWER_HIGH or POWER_LOW. The Criteria object also enables us to specify if the provider can incur a monetary cost to the user, whether altitude is needed, and some other details. If the application has specific requirements, this is where you set them. However, setting these criteria doesn't imply that the provider is available to the user. Some flexibility might be required to allow use on a broad range of devices. A Boolean parameter of the getBestProvider() method enables the application to ask for only enabled providers.

Using the provider returned by the getBestProvider() method, the application can request the location. Before doing so, however, the application needs to provide an implementation of LocationListener. The LocationListener implementation consists of four methods: To tell the application whether the provider has been disabled or enabled; to give the status about the provider (such as the number of satellites the GPS receiver can see); and to tell the application location information. The following is a sample implementation for the last method, the onLocationChanged() method:

```
public void onLocationChanged(Location location) {
    String locInfo = String.
        format("Current loc = (%f, %f) @ (%f meters up)",
        location.getLatitude(), location.getLongitude(),
        location.getAltitude() );
```

```
    if (lastLocation != null) {
        float distance = location.distanceTo(lastLocation);
        locInfo += String.
            format("\n Distance from last = %f meters", distance);
    }
    lastLocation = location;
    status.setText(locInfo);
}
```

The onLocationChanged() method receives a Location object with the most recent location information from the chosen provider. In this example, the application merely prints out the location, including the altitude, which might or might not be returned by the provider. Then, it uses a utility method of the Location object, distanceTo(), to calculate how far the handset has moved since the last time onLocationChanged() was called.

It is up to the application to determine how to use this location information. The application might want to turn the location information into an address, display the location on an embedded map, or launch the built-in Maps application (if the Google applications are installed) centered at the location.

Tip

To use many LBS services, you should use Android Virtual Device (AVD) configurations that target the Android SDK with the Google APIs. Using the Google APIs target puts applications like the Maps on the emulator. Other times, LBS design and testing is best done on a real Android device.

Locating Your Emulator

The Android emulator can simulate location-based services, but as you would expect, it does not have any "underlying hardware" to get a real satellite fix. The Android SDK provides a means to simulate location data with the use of a single location point, GPX file, or KML file. This works only with the emulator, not the physical handset, but it can be useful for testing your location-based application.

For more information on this, see Appendix A, "The Android Emulator Quick-Start Guide."

Geocoding Locations

Determining the latitude and longitude is useful for precise location, tracking, and measurements; however, it's not usually descriptive to users. The Android SDK provides some helper methods to turn raw location data into addresses and descriptive place names. These methods can also work in reverse, turning place names or addresses into raw location coordinates.

Warning

According to the Android documentation, AVDs that target the Google APIs enable developers to test on emulator instances with the "Google experience." The Google APIs provide the
ability to use Google Maps as well as a back-end geocoder service. Although it is not documented, not all AVD API Levels support these geocoder services. For example, AVDs for API
Level 6 with the Google APIs provide geocoder services, whereas AVDs with API Levels 7 and
8 plus Google APIs do not (as of this writing). When you use an AVD without back-end
geocoder services, you simply get an exception stating there is no back-end service. The
code in this chapter is best run in an emulator running an AVD with API Level 6 plus the
Google APIs, or on a real device with true geocoder back-end services.

The `Geocoder` object can be used without any special permissions. The following block of
code demonstrates using the `Geocoder` object to get the location names of a `Location`
object passed in to the `onLocationChanged()` method of a `LocationListener`:

```
Geocoder coder = new Geocoder(this);
try {
    Iterator<Address> addresses = coder
        .getFromLocation(location.getLatitude(),
        location.getLongitude(), 3).iterator();
    if (addresses != null) {
        while (addresses.hasNext()) {
            Address namedLoc = addresses.next();
            String placeName = namedLoc.getLocality();
            String featureName = namedLoc.getFeatureName();
            String country = namedLoc.getCountryName();
            String road = namedLoc.getThoroughfare();
            locInfo += String.format("\n[%s][%s][%s][%s]",
                placeName, featureName, road, country);
            int addIdx = namedLoc.getMaxAddressLineIndex();
            while (addIdx >= 0 ) {
                String addLine = namedLoc.getAddressLine(addIdx);
                locInfo += String.
                    format("\nLine %d: %s", addIdx, addLine);
                addIdx--;
            }
        }
    }
} catch (IOException e) {
    Log.e("GPS", "Failed to get address", e);
}
```

You can extract information from the results of the call to the `getFromLocation()`
method in two ways, both of which are demonstrated. Note that a particular location
might have multiple `Address` results in the form of a `List<Address>` object. Typically, the
first `Address` is the most detailed, and the subsequent `Address` objects have less detail and
describe a broader region.

The first method is to query for specific information, such as by using the `getFeatureName()` method or the `getLocality()` method. These methods are not guaranteed to return useful information for all locations. They are useful, though, when you know you need only a specific piece of general information, such as the country.

The second method for querying information is by "address lines." This is generally used for displaying the "address" of a location to the user. It might also be useful to use the location in directions and in other cases where a street address is desired. That said, the addresses returned might not be complete. Simply use the `getMaxAddressLineIndex()` and `getAddressLine()` methods to iterate through the addresses. Figure 14.1 shows a sample location with three resulting addresses.

Figure 14.1   Image showing location geocoded
to three "addresses."

The `Geocoder` object also supports using named locations or address lines to generate latitude and longitude information. The input is forgiving and returns reasonable results in most cases. For instance, all the following returns valid and correct results: "Eiffel Tower," "London, UK," "Iceland," "BOS," "Yellowstone," and "1600 Pennsylvania Ave, DC."

The following code demonstrates a button handler for computing location data based on user input of this kind:

```
public void onClick(View v) {
    String placeName = name.getText().toString();
```

```
try {
    List<Address> geocodeResults =
        coder.getFromLocationName(placeName, 3);

    Iterator<Address> locations = geocodeResults.iterator();
    String locInfo = "Results:\n";

    while (locations.hasNext()) {
        Address loc = locations.next();
        locInfo += String.format("Location: %f, %f\n",
            loc.getLatitude(), loc.getLongitude());
    }

    results.setText(locInfo);
} catch (IOException e) {
    Log.e("GeoAddress", "Failed to get location info", e);
}
}
```

The result of the call to the getFromLocationName() method is a List of Address
objects, much like the previous example. Figure 14.2 shows the results for entering
Eiffel Tower.

Figure 14.2   The results for geocoding
the term Eiffel Tower.

Always assume that you will get more than one result. It is good form to provide a picker for the user to select from the results and choose the most appropriate location. Another good way to confirm with the user that they entered the correct location is to map it. We now discuss a couple of different methods for mapping locations using Google Maps.

Warning

Geocoding operations typically require a network connection and therefore should not be run on the main UI thread. Instead, perform geocoding tasks in a separate thread so as not to cause your application responsiveness to degrade.

Mapping Locations

The Android SDK provides two different methods to show a location with Google Maps. The first method is to use a location `Uri` to launch the built-in Google Maps application with the specified location. The second method is to use a `MapView` embedded within your application to display the map location.

Mapping Intents

In the previous section, we demonstrated how to determine the latitude and longitude for a place name. Now we map the location using the built-in maps application. The following block of code demonstrates how to perform this:

```
String geoURI = String.format("geo:%f,%f", lat, lon);
Uri geo = Uri.parse(geoURI);
Intent geoMap = new Intent(Intent.ACTION_VIEW, geo);
startActivity(geoMap);
```

The first task is to create a `String` that conforms to the URI handled by the mapping application. In this case, it's `geo:` followed by the latitude and longitude. This URI is then used to create a new `Uri` object for creating a new `ACTION_VIEW Intent`. Finally, we call the `startActivity()` method. If the latitude and longitude are valid, such as the location for the `Acropolis`, the screen would look like Figure 14.3.

Using this method of mapping launches the user into a built-in mapping application—in this case, Google Maps. If the application does not want to bother with the details of a full mapping application or does not need to provide any further control over the map, this is a fast-and-easy method to use. Users are typically accustomed to the controls of the mapping application on their handset, too.

Mapping Views

Sometimes, though, we want to have the map integrated into our application for a more seamless user experience. Let's add a small map to our geocoding example to show the location immediately to the users when they enter a place name.

Figure 14.3   The resulting map for geocoding the
term `Acropolis` and launching a geo URI.

The following block of XML shows the change needed within the layout file to
include a widget called the `MapView`:

```
<com.google.android.maps.MapView
    android:id="@+id/map"
    android:apiKey="yourMapKey"
    android:layout_width="fill_parent"
    android:layout_height="wrap_content" />
```

As you might have already noticed, the `MapView` XML is a little different. First, the tag
name is the fully qualified name. And second, an `apiKey` attribute is needed. We get to the
key in a moment.

The `AndroidManifest.xml` file also needs to be modified to allow for using the
`MapView` with Google Maps. Here are the two changes needed:

```
<application
...
    <uses-library
        android:name="com.google.android.maps" />
</application>
<uses-permission
    android:name="android.permission.INTERNET" />
```

Both of these permission lines are required. The `MapView` object specifically requires the `INTERNET` permission and its library must be referenced explicitly. Otherwise, an error occurs.

Finally, you can use a `MapView` only within a `MapActivity`. Accessing a `MapView` from outside a `MapActivity` results in an error. The `MapActivity` is similar to a normal `Activity`, but it requires implementing the `isRouteDisplayed()` method. This method must return true if a route will be displayed. Otherwise, false must be returned. Here is the default implementation for when no route is displayed:

```
@Override
protected boolean isRouteDisplayed() {
    // we do not display routes
    return false;
}
```

Now the application can use the `MapView` to display locations to the user. The following block of code demonstrates retrieval of a `MapController` object, which is used to control the location that the `MapView` displays:

```
MapView map = (MapView) findViewById(R.id.map);
map.setSatellite(true);
final MapController mapControl = map.getController();
mapControl.setZoom(17);
```

These lines of code set the display to show the satellite view, which is visually interesting. The `MapController` object then sets the zoom level of the map. Larger values are zoomed in farther, with 1 zoomed all the way out. The given value, 17, usually shows a few city blocks, but there are some areas where even this is too close for the data available. In a moment, we talk about how to easily give control of this to the user.

Building on the previous example, the following lines of code are added to the button handler for geocoding a place name:

```
GeoPoint newPoint = new
    GeoPoint((int)(lat * 1E6), (int)(lon * 1E6));
mapControl.animateTo(newPoint);
```

In this case, we create a new `GeoPoint` to use with the `animateTo()` method. A `GeoPoint` object uses microdegrees, so we must multiply the result of the geocoding by `1E6` (1,000,000 or one million). The `animateTo()` method smoothly animates the `MapView` to the new location. How much of the interim mapping data displays depends on the speed of the Internet connection and what mode the `MapView` is in. The `setCenter()` method can set the center of the map.

Finally, this is almost enough to test the results. However, there is one last thing you need to take care of. You need to get a Google Maps API Key from Google to use its API and mapping services.

Getting Your Debug API Key

To use a `MapView` within your applications, you must obtain a Google Maps API Key from Google. The key is generated from an MD5 fingerprint of a certificate that you use to sign your applications.

For production distribution, you need to follow these steps, substituting your release distribution signing certificate. You can read more about this in Chapter 29, "Selling Your Android Application." For testing purposes, you can use the debug certificate that is created by the Android SDK.

You need to do the following to generate the appropriate API key:

1. Generate an MD5 fingerprint for your debug certificate.

2. Sign in to http://code.google.com/android/maps-api-signup.html with a Google account.

3. Accept the Terms of Service.

4. Paste in the fingerprint from Step 1.

5. Save the Android Maps API key presented on the next screen.

The first step is performed on your development machine. Locate the debug certificate used by the Android SDK. On all platforms, the filename is `debug.keystore` by default. If you use Eclipse, the location of the file is listed under the Android Build preferences. Using this file, you then need to execute the following command (make sure the Java tools are in your path):

```
keytool -list -keystore /path/to/debug.keystore -storepass android
```

The result is the fingerprint that you must paste into the form on step 4. Read the terms of service carefully before proceeding. Although the terms allow many types of applications, you need to make sure your application is allowed and that your anticipated usage is acceptable to Google.

Tip

The default debug keystore on the Android SDK lasts for only one year and is unique to a developer's computer. We highly recommend making a debug key that lasts longer and can be shared among team members. This enables your Google Maps API key to last much longer. In addition, you won't have to uninstall apps from a shared handset before you can install one with someone else's debug key. Luckily, it's easy to do this using the keytool command-line tool using the following command:

```
keytool -genkey -keypass android -keystore debug.keystore
➥-alias androiddebugkey -storepass android
➥-validity 10000
➥-dname "CN=Android Debug,O=Android,C=US"
```

This command generates a valid debug keystore that can be shared among team members and lasts for 10,000 days. After creating it, make sure you reference it from Eclipse if it's not in the default location.

When you have successfully completed the steps to get your key, you can then reference your map key in the `Layout` file definition for the `MapView` you use. Now, when you execute the code, you should be presented with a screen that looks like Figure 14.4.

Figure 14.4   `MapView` results for geocoding
the term `Sydney Opera House`.

Tip

If you work on multiple development machines or work as part of a team, you need to have an API key for everyone's debug certificate. Alternatively, you can copy the debug certificate from one machine to other machines so that the signing and check against the Android Maps API key is successful. This can save you time because you don't have to modify the code or layout files for each developer on the team.

Panning the Map View

Sometimes the locations returned either do not show the exact location that the user wants or the user might want to determine where in the world they are by exploring the map a bit. One way to do this is through panning the map. Luckily, this is as easy as enabling clicking from within the layout file:

```
<com.google.android.maps.MapView
    android:id="@+id/map"
    android:clickable="true"
    android:apiKey="mapApiKey"
    android:layout_width="fill_parent"
    android:layout_height="wrap_content" />
```

Now, if the user searches for `Great Pyramids`, he could then pan east a tad to see the Great Pyramid, as shown in Figure 14.5.

Figure 14.5   Results for `Great Pyramids` on the left, panned east to the Great Pyramid on the right.

Zooming the Map View

Other times, panning won't help users. They might want to zoom in or out from the same location. Our application does not have to re-implement the zoom controls, though. Instead, simply enable the built-in zoom controls as follows:

```
map.setBuiltInZoomControls(true);
```

When the user clicks on the map, the zoom controls fade in to view and are functional, as shown in Figure 14.6.

Marking the Spot

Now that panning and zooming works, users may lose track of their position. Sure, they could just search again, but wouldn't it be more helpful if we marked the point of interest directly on the map? The Android SDK provides a few different ways to do this. One way is to use the `MapView` as a container for an arbitrary `View` object that can be assigned using a `GeoPoint` instead of typical screen or `View` coordinates. Another way is to use `ItemizedOverlay`, which is especially useful if you have more than one place to mark.

Finally, you can manually draw items over the map using the `Overlay` and implement the `onDraw()` method.

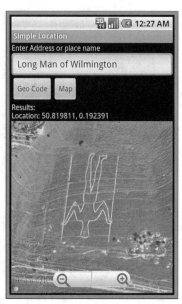

Figure 14.6   On the left, you see a bird's eye view of the town of Wilmington, but zoom in to the south and you see The Long Man of Wilmington as shown on the right.

For the place name finder example, we use the first method. Assuming you have a suitable map marker as a drawable resource, the following code demonstrates how to do this:

```
GeoPoint newPoint = new GeoPoint((int)(lat * 1E6), (int)(lon*1E6));

// add a view at this point
MapView.LayoutParams mapMarkerParams = new
    MapView.LayoutParams(LayoutParams.WRAP_CONTENT,
    LayoutParams.WRAP_CONTENT,
    newPoint, MapView.LayoutParams.TOP_LEFT );

ImageView mapMarker = new ImageView(getApplicationContext());
mapMarker.setImageResource(R.drawable.paw);
map.addView(mapMarker, mapMarkerParams);
```

The `MapView` layout parameters enable you to set a `GeoPoint`. Doing this enables the added `View` to stay put at a geographic location and pan with the map, as shown in Figure 14.7.

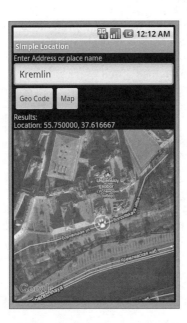

Figure 14.7   The Kremlin at the top left of the
marker (paw print in a circle).

Keep in mind that the added `View` sticks around as long as the `MapView` does. If the
application needs to present multiple locations to the user, though, there is a simpler way.
Just use the `ItemizedOverlay` object.

In this example, a static `ItemizedOverlay` is created to represent the chain of back-
packer huts in the White Mountains along the Appalachian Trail:

```
private class HutsItemizedOverlay
    extends ItemizedOverlay<OverlayItem> {

    public HutsItemizedOverlay(Drawable defaultMarker) {}

    protected OverlayItem createItem(int i) {}
    public int size() {}
}
```

To do this, we provide implementations for each of the required methods of
`ItemizedOverlay<OverlayItem>`. First, we define the constructor:

```
public HutsItemizedOverlay(Drawable defaultMarker) {
    super(defaultMarker);

    boundCenterBottom(defaultMarker);

    populate();
}
```

The `Drawable` passed in is one that we define later in the `onCreate()` method of
`MapActivity`. The system does not provide a default marker. The call to the
`boundCenterBottom()` method is made so that the map coordinates are at the center bottom and the shadow is cast from the bottom of the marker, which is a more natural look.
The default shadow is from the top. If, however, we'd rather turn off the shadow completely, you can override the `draw()` method, as follows:

```
@Override
public void draw(Canvas canvas, MapView mapView, boolean shadow) {
    super.draw(canvas, mapView, false);
}
```

Finally, within the constructor we call the `populate()` method. This should be done as
soon as the location data is available. Because we have it statically compiled into the application, we call it before returning. The `populate()` method calls our implementation of
the `createItem()` method for as many items as we defined in our implementation of the
`size()` method. Here is the implementation of our `createItem()` method, along with a
small array of hut locations, in no particular order:

```
public GeoPoint hutPoints[] = new GeoPoint[] {
    // Lakes of the Clouds
    new GeoPoint(44258793, -71318940),
    // Zealand Falls
    new GeoPoint(44195798, -71494402),
    // Greanleaf
    new GeoPoint(44160372, -71660385),
    // Galehead
    new GeoPoint(44187866, -71568734),
    // Carter Notch
    new GeoPoint(44259224, -71195633),
    // Mizpah Spring
    new GeoPoint(44219362, -71369473),
    // Lonesome Lake
    new GeoPoint(44138452, -71703064),
    // Madison Spring
    new GeoPoint(44327751, -71283283)
};

@Override
protected OverlayItem createItem(int i) {

    OverlayItem item = new OverlayItem(hutPoints[i], null, null);
    return item;
}
```

In the array, we've multiplied all the location values by one million so that they are in
microdegrees, as required by the `GeoPoint` object. Within the `createItem()` method, the

location array is indexed with the passed-in value. Neither of the two text fields, Title and Snippet, are used at this time, so they are set to null. The maximum index value is determined by the size() method, which, in this case, merely has to return the length of the array:

```
@Override
public int size() {
    return hutPoints.length;
}
```

The necessary ItemizedOverlay<OverlayItem> class is now implemented. Next, the application needs to tell the MapView about it. The following code demonstrates how to do this in the onCreate() method of our MapActivity:

```
@Override
protected void onCreate(Bundle data) {
    super.onCreate(data);
    setContentView(R.layout.huts);

    Drawable marker = getResources().getDrawable(R.drawable.paw);

    HutsItemizedOverlay huts = new HutsItemizedOverlay(marker);

    MapView map = (MapView)findViewById(R.id.map);
    map.setSatellite(true);

    List<Overlay> overlays = map.getOverlays();
    overlays.add(huts);

    FrameLayout zoomFrame = (FrameLayout)
        findViewById(R.id.map_zoom_holder);
    zoomFrame.addView(map.getZoomControls());
}
```

First, the Drawable is retrieved from the resources. Next, we instantiate the HutsItemizedOverlay object. The OverlayItems in it need to be added to the ones that might already exist within the MapView. The getOverlays() method of MapView returns a list of the current Overlay objects. Calling the add() method on this list inserts our new ones for each hut. Finally, the zoom controls are added to the MapView so that the user can zoom in and out. After launching this application and zooming in on New Hampshire, the user should see a screen like Figure 14.8.

Forcing the user to pan and zoom to the location of the huts is not user-friendly. Two utility methods that the ItemizedOverlay<OverlayItem> class provides return values for the span of the location of the items. Combining this functionality with an override to the default behavior of the getCenter() method, which normally returns the location of the first item, enables the map to start to draw at a convenient zoom level covering all the huts. You can add this block of code to the onCreate() method to do just that:

```
MapController mapControl = map.getController();

mapControl.setCenter(huts.getCenter());
mapControl.zoomToSpan(
    huts.getLatSpanE6(), huts.getLonSpanE6());
```

Figure 14.8   A map with markers at each of the
Appalachian Mountain Huts of New Hampshire.

The getCenter() method computes the average latitude and the average longitude across all the given hut locations. You could provide a central point, or you could place the first item near the center of all the points requiring no override of the getCenter() method.

Doing More with Location-Based Services

You have been introduced to a number of different location tools provided on Android; however, you should be aware of several more.

The LocationManager supports Proximity Alerts, which are alerts that trigger a PendingIntent when the handset comes within some distance of a location. This can be useful for warning the user of an upcoming turn in directions, for scavenger hunts, or help in geocaching.

You saw how to do `ItemizedOverlays`. In general, you can assign your own `Overlays` to draw custom objects and `Views` on the given `Canvas`. This is useful for drawing pop-up information for locations, putting logos over the map that don't move with the map, or putting hints for scavenger hunts over the map. This functionality is similar to displaying photos at a given location, which are often provided on Google Maps at famous locations.

The `GpsStatus`, `GpsStatus.Listener`, and `GpsSatellite` classes provide more detailed information about the GPS satellites used by the GPS engine. The `GpsStatus` and its `Listener` subclass monitors the GPS engine and gets a list of the satellites used. The `GpsSatellite` class represents the current state of an individual satellite used by the GPS engine with state information such as satellite elevation and whether the particular satellite was used in the most recent GPS fix.

Tip

LBS applications are a popular category of Android applications. LBS services are like networking services: sometimes unreliable or unresponsive. Make sure to consider application responsiveness when designing LBS applications. This means completing LBS-related tasks asynchronously using threads or `ASyncTask` as well as considering Android services (more about these in Chapter 21).

Summary

The Android SDK, with Google Maps support available to developers that register for a key, can be used to enhance Android applications with location-rich information. Some applications want to build in seamless map support, whereas others might just launch the built-in map application for the user to leverage. Developers can add to the information provided on the map by using various types of overlays to include even more information to the user. The opportunities for using location-based services to improve Android applications are only just beginning to be explored.

References and More Information

Android Dev Guide: Location and Maps:
    http://developer.android.com/guide/topics/location/index.html
Get Your Own Google Maps API Key:
    http://code.google.com/android/add-ons/google-apis/mapkey.html

## 15

Using Android Multimedia APIs

Multimedia—whether it's images, videos, or audio—has become a key driver of mobile device sales. The modern "smart" mobile handset has a camera to capture and display still images and video as well as sophisticated music playback abilities.

In this chapter, you learn how to capture still images using the camera, as well as record and play back audio and video files.

Working with Multimedia

The Android SDK provides a variety of methods for applications to incorporate audio and visual media, including support for many different media types and formats. Individual Android devices and developers can extend the list of supported media to other formats. Not every Android handset has the same multimedia capabilities. Always verify the capabilities of target devices before publication.

The multimedia features of the Android platform generally fall into three categories:

- Still images (recorded with the camera)
- Audio (recorded with the microphone, played back with speakers or audio output)
- Video (recorded with the camera and microphone, played back with speakers or audio output)

Multimedia hardware such as a built-in camera, speakers, and audio or video output ports are optional features for Android devices.

In addition to requiring the appropriate permissions, you can specify which optional features your application requires within the Android Manifest file. You can do this using the `<uses-feature>` tag of the Android Manifest file declare that your application uses the camera. Remember, though, that the `<uses-feature>` tag is not enforced by the Android platform. Instead, application stores such as the Android Market use this data to filter which applications to sell to certain devices.

Any application that requests the `CAMERA` permission is assumed to use all camera features. If your application accesses the camera, but can function properly without it, you can also set the `android:required` field of `<uses-feature>` to `false`. However, if your application requires a microphone and a camera with autofocus but not a flash to be present on the device, you can set the camera features your application requires specifically, like this:

```
<uses-feature android:name="android.hardware.microphone" />
<uses-feature android:name="android.hardware.camera" />
<uses-feature android:name="android.hardware.camera.autofocus" />
```

Tip

Many of the code examples provided in this chapter are taken from the SimpleMultimedia application. The source code for this application is provided for download on the book website.

Working with Still Images

We illustrated how to display still images such as bitmaps by using the `ImageView` widget in Chapter 7, "Exploring User Interface Screen Elements." If the user's handset has built-in camera hardware, the user can also capture still images using the `Camera` object of the Android SDK. In addition, you can assign images as the home screen wallpaper using the `WallpaperManager` class.

Capturing Still Images Using the Camera

The `Camera` object (`android.hardware.Camera`) controls the camera on handsets that have camera support enabled. The preview feature of the camera relies on the assignment of a `SurfaceHolder` of an appropriate type. This enables applications to control the placement and size of the preview area that the camera can use.

Follow these steps to add camera capture capability to an application without having to draw preview frames (the `CameraSurfaceView` displays the camera view):

1. Create a new class extending `SurfaceView` and implement `SurfaceHolder.Callback`. For this example, we name this class `CameraSurfaceView`.

2. In the `surfaceCreated()` method, get an instance of the `Camera` object.

3. In the `surfaceChanged()` method, configure and apply the `Camera.Parameters`; then call the `startPreview()` method.

4. Add a method in `CameraSurfaceView` for capturing images.

5. Add the `CameraSurfaceView` to an appropriate layout.

6. Include some way, such as a button, for the user to trigger the capturing of images.

7. Implement a `PictureCallback` class to handle storing of the captured image.

8. Add the `android.permission.CAMERA` permission to the `AndroidManifest.xml` file.

9. Release the `Camera` object in the `surfaceDestroyed()` method.

Let's start by looking at the `CameraSurfaceView` class:

```java
import android.hardware.Camera;
import android.view.SurfaceHolder;
import android.view.SurfaceView;

private class CameraSurfaceView extends SurfaceView
    implements SurfaceHolder.Callback {

    private SurfaceHolder mHolder;
    private Camera camera = null;

    public CameraSurfaceView(Context context) {
        super(context);
        mHolder = getHolder();
        mHolder.addCallback(this);
        mHolder.setType(
            SurfaceHolder.SURFACE_TYPE_PUSH_BUFFERS);
    }

    public void surfaceChanged(SurfaceHolder holder,
        int format, int width, int height) {
    }

    public void surfaceCreated(SurfaceHolder holder) {
    }

    public void surfaceDestroyed(SurfaceHolder holder) {
    }

    public boolean capture(Camera.PictureCallback
        jpegHandler) {
    }
}
```

The constructor for the `CameraSurfaceView` configures the `SurfaceHolder`, including setting the `SurfaceHolder` type to `SURFACE_TYPE_PUSH_BUFFERS`, which is used by the camera internals. The constructor is appropriate for calling from an activity's `onCreate()` method. When the display is ready, the `surfaceCreated()` method is called. Here we instantiate the `Camera` object:

```java
public void surfaceCreated(SurfaceHolder holder) {
    camera = Camera.open();
    camera.setPreviewDisplay(mHolder);
}
```

The `Camera` object has a static method to retrieve a usable instance. Because the `Surface` is now available, the configured holder can now be assigned to it. Information about the `Surface` might not yet be available, but at the next call to the `surfaceChanged()` method, the camera parameters will be assigned and the preview will start, as shown here:

```
public void surfaceChanged(SurfaceHolder holder,
    int format, int width, int height) {
    List<Camera.Size> sizes = params.getSupportedPreviewSizes();

    Camera.Size pickedSize = getBestFit(sizes, width, height);
    if (pickedSize != null) {
        params.setPreviewSize(pickedSize.width, pickedSize.height);
        camera.setParameters(params);
    }
    camera.startPreview();
}
```

The `surfaceChanged()` method provides the application with the proper width and height for use with the camera preview. After assigning this to the `Camera` object, the preview starts. At this point, the users see whatever is in front of the camera on their device. If, however, you debug this within the emulator, you see a black-and-white checkerboard with an animated square on it, as shown in Figure 15.1. This is the simulated camera preview, so camera testing can take place, to some extent, on the emulator.

Note

The format parameter passed in to the `surfaceChanged()` method is not related to the format parameter of the `setPreviewFormat()` method of the `Camera` object.

When the `Surface` is no longer displayed, the `surfaceDestroyed()` method is called. Here is an implementation of the `surfaceDestroyed()` method suitable for this example:

```
public void surfaceDestroyed(SurfaceHolder holder) {
    camera.stopPreview();
    camera.release();
    camera = null;
}
```

In the `surfaceDestroyed()` method, the application stops the preview and releases the `Camera` object. If the `CameraSurfaceView` is used again, the `surfaceCreated()` method is called again, so this is the appropriate place to perform this operation.

The final step required to capture a still image is to add some way to call the `takePicture()` method of the `Camera` object. `CameraSurfaceView` could provide public access to the `Camera` object, but in this example, we provide a method to perform this within the `CameraSurfaceView` class:

```
public boolean capture(Camera.PictureCallback jpegHandler) {
    if (camera != null) {
        camera.takePicture(null, null, jpegHandler);
        return true;
    } else {
        return false;
    }
}
```

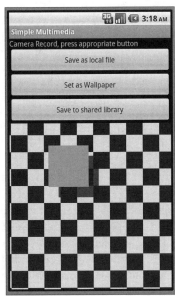

Figure 15.1   Emulator screen showing simulated
camera view.

You can also use the `takePicture()` method to assign a callback suitable to play a shutter sound, or any other action just before the image is collected from the sensor. In addition, you can assign a `PictureCallback` to get raw data from the camera.

Note

The format of the raw camera data can vary from device to device.

The `CameraSurfaceView` object is now ready for use within an `Activity`. For this example, an `Activity` with a layout that contains a `FrameLayout` widget for positioning the preview is used. Here is a sample implementation of assigning the `cameraView` to the layout:

```
final CameraSurfaceView cameraView = new
    CameraSurfaceView(getApplicationContext());
FrameLayout frame = (FrameLayout) findViewById(R.id.frame);
frame.addView(cameraView);
```

Next, a button click handler calls the `capture()` method of the `CameraSurfaceView`
object. A sample implementation is shown here:

```
public void onClick(View v) {
    cameraView.capture(new Camera.PictureCallback() {

        public void onPictureTaken(byte[] data,
            Camera camera) {
            FileOutputStream fos;

            try {
                String filename = "capture.jpg";
                fos = openFileOutput("capture.jpg",
                    MODE_WORLD_READABLE);

                fos.write(data);
                fos.close();

            } catch (Exception e) {
                Log.e("Still", "Error writing file", e);
            }
        }
    });
}
```

The data that comes back from the callback can be written out directly to a JPEG file
within the application file directory. If written as shown, though, the captured image is usable only by the application. In some cases, this might be suitable. However, the application
might want to share the image with the rest of the handset, for example, by including it
within the Pictures application, which uses the `MediaStore` content provider. You do this
by using the `ContentResolver` object to place an entry for the image in the media library.

Warning

As with all lengthy operations, you should perform large file system writes from a separate
thread to keep the application interface as responsive as possible.

Configuring Camera Mode Settings

You can use the `Camera` class to configure the specific capture settings for a picture. Many
of the capture settings are stored in the `Camera.Parameters` class, and set in the Camera
using the `setParameters()` method.

Working with Common Camera Parameters

Let's take a closer look at the `Camera.Parameters` class. Some of the most interesting camera parameters are

- Flash modes (where flash hardware is available)
- Focus types (fixed point, depth of field, infinity, and so on)
- White balance settings (fluorescent, incandescent, and so on)
- Scene modes (snow, beach, fireworks, and so on)
- Effects (photo negative, sepia, and so on)
- Anti-banding settings (noise reduction)

Different parameters are supported by different devices, so always check for support before trying to enable parameters. Use the `Camera.Parameters` class to determine what camera features are supported. For example, you can use the set of methods called `getSupportedFlashModes()`, `getSupportedFocusModes()`, and so on. Also, the `Camera.Parameters` class contains methods to access more technical camera settings, such as exposure compensation and EXIF information.

Zooming the Camera

The camera zoom setting is controlled using the `startSmoothZoom()` and `stopSmoothZoom()` methods of the `Camera` class. As you might expect, you can set zoom parameters using the `Camera.Parameters` class. Useful zoom methods in the `Camera.Parameters` class include

- Determining if zooming is supported with `isZoomSupported()`
- Determining if smooth zooming is supported with `isSmoothZoomSupported()`
- Determining the maximum zoom value with `getMaxZoom()`
- Retrieving the current zoom value with `getZoom()`
- Setting the current zoom value with `setZoom()`
- Calculating the zoom increments (for example, 1x, 2x, 10x) with `getZoomRatios()`

Depending on the features available for a specific camera, zoom might be digital, optical, or some combination of the two.

Sharing Images

Storing an image in the local application directory, as demonstrated, might work for some applications; however, other applications might find it useful if the image goes in the shared image library on the device. The `ContentResolver` can be used in conjunction with the `MediaStore` object to push the image into the shared image library. The following example demonstrates storing the still image taken by the camera as an image file within the `MediaStore` content provider, using the same camera image callback:

```
public void onPictureTaken(byte[] data, Camera camera) {
    Log.v("Still", "Image data received from camera");
    try {
        Bitmap bm = BitmapFactory.decodeByteArray(
            data, 0, data.length);
        String fileUrl = MediaStore.Images.Media.
            insertImage(getContentResolver(), bm,
            "Camera Still Image",
            "Camera Pic Sample App Took");

        if (fileUrl == null) {
            Log.d("Still", "Image Insert failed");
            return;
        } else {
            Uri picUri = Uri.parse(fileUrl);
            sendBroadcast(new Intent(
                Intent.ACTION_MEDIA_SCANNER_SCAN_FILE,
                picUri));
        }
    } catch (Exception e) {
        Log.e("Still", "Error writing file", e);
    }
}
```

The image is turned into a `Bitmap` object, which is passed into the `insertImage()` method. This method creates an entry in the shared image library. After the image is inserted, we use the returned URL to create a `Uri` object representing the new image's location, which we instruct the Media Scanner to pick up by broadcasting a specialized intent. To determine if the scan completed successfully, you can make a call to the static `MediaScannerConnection.scanFile()` method, and provide a `MediaScannerConnection.OnScanCompletedListener` class implementation.

Now the image is available to all applications that use the `MediaStore` content provider, such as the Pictures application.

Warning

To use the `MediaStore` with the emulator, you must have a mounted SD card image.

Additionally, although it's technically not necessary to force the media scanner to scan for new images, we've found that the Pictures application on the emulator and handset might crash if the `MediaStore` does not perform a scan before trying to access the image. It's a good idea to send the `Intent` or use the `MediaScannerConnection` class.

Assigning Images as Wallpapers

Wallpapers are a great way for users to personalize their phones with interesting and fun images. The `WallpaperManager` class is used for all wallpaper interaction. You learn more about it in Chapter 22, "Extending Android Reach," when you create Live Wallpaper. For now, use it to set still image wallpapers.

The current wallpaper can be retrieved with a call to the `getDrawable()` or `peekDrawable()` methods. The methods `getDesiredMinimumHeight()` and `getDesiredMinimumWidth()` enable the application to programmatically determine the size that a wallpaper should be on the particular handset. Finally, you can assign wallpaper through the `setResource()`, `setBitmap()`, and `setStream()` methods.

The following callback of the `Camera` object sets the wallpaper:

```
public void onPictureTaken(byte[] data, Camera camera) {
    Bitmap recordedImage =
        BitmapFactory.decodeByteArray(data, 0, data.length);
    try {
        WallpaperManager wpManager = WallpaperManager
            .getInstance(StillImageActivity.this);
        wpManager.setBitmap(recordedImage);
    } catch (Exception e) {
        Log.e("Still", "Setting wallpaper failed.", e);
    }
}
```

The image is copied locally for the wallpaper, so the original doesn't need to be kept, which is good in this case because it was never written to disk. You can remove the wallpaper completely with a call to the `clear()` method.

Finally, your application needs the `android.permission.SET_WALLPAPER` permission within the `AndroidManifest.xml` file.

Note

Prior to API Level 5 (Android 2.0), simple wallpaper commands were handled directly through the `Context` object. See the Android SDK documentation on the `Context.setWallpaper()` and `Context.getWallpaper()` methods for further information.

Working with Video

In recent years, video has become commonplace on handsets. Most handsets on the market now can record and play back video, and this is no different with Android, although the specific video features might vary from handset to handset.

Recording Video

Android applications can record video using the `MediaRecorder` class. Using `MediaRecorder` is a matter of following a few simple steps:

1. Instantiate a new `MediaRecorder` object.

2. Set the video source.

3. Set the video output format.

4. Set the video size to record (optional).

5. Set the video frame rate (optional).

6. Set the video encoder.

7. Set the file to record to. (The extension must match output format.)

8. Set the preview surface.

9. Prepare the object for recording.

10. Start the recording.

11. Stop and release the recording object when finished.

Using some standard button controls, you can create an `Activity` to record and play back video using the preceding steps. The `onClick()` method for a record button might look like this:

```
public void onClick(View v) {
    if (videoRecorder == null) {
        videoRecorder = new MediaRecorder();
    }
    String pathForAppFiles =
        getFilesDir().getAbsolutePath();
    pathForAppFiles += RECORDED_FILE;

    videoRecorder.setVideoSource(
        MediaRecorder.VideoSource.CAMERA);

    videoRecorder.setOutputFormat(
        MediaRecorder.OutputFormat.MPEG4 );

    videoRecorder.setVideoSize(640, 480);
    videoRecorder.setVideoFrameRate(30);
    videoRecorder.setVideoEncoder(
        MediaRecorder.VideoEncoder.H264);

    videoRecorder.setOutputFile(pathForAppFiles);
    videoRecorder.setPreviewDisplay(surface);

    videoRecorder.prepare();
    videoRecorder.start();

    // button handling and other behavior here
}
```

The `videoRecorder` object is instantiated and given some video configuration values for the recording source. There are several values for each video configuration setting; however, supported values can vary by device.

A stop button configured with an `onClick()` handler might look like this:

```java
public void onClick(View v) {
    if (videoRecorder!= null) {
        videoRecorder.stop();
        videoRecorder.release();
        videoRecorder = null;
    }
    // button handling and other behavior here
}
```

Finally, applications wanting to record video require the explicit permission `android.permission.CAMERA` set within the `AndroidManifest.xml` file.

Now it is time to add the playback functionality, so we can watch the video we just recorded.

Playing Video

The simplest way to play back video with the Android SDK is to use the `VideoView` widget along with the `MediaController` widget to provide basic video controls. The following is an implementation of an `onCreate()` method within an `Activity` that demonstrates a workable video playback solution:

```java
@Override
protected void onCreate(Bundle savedInstanceState) {
    super.onCreate(savedInstanceState);
    setContentView(R.layout.moving);

    VideoView vv = (VideoView) findViewById(R.id.video);
    MediaController mc = new MediaController(this);
    Uri video = Uri.parse(MOVIE_URL);

    vv.setMediaController(mc);
    vv.setVideoURI(video);
}
```

Note

The Android emulator doesn't play video files particularly well in all screen resolutions. Instead, it's best to test video code on the device.

A simple layout file with these controls might look like Figure 15.2. The `MediaController` presents a nice `ProgressBar` that shows download completion and current location. The use of the `setAnchorView()` method of the `MediaController` is not needed when used with the `setMediaController()` method of `VideoView`—it's automatically set to the `VideoView`.

Figure 15.2   Screen showing video playback with
default media controller displayed.

The call to the setVideoURI() method automatically starts playback. You can create a
listener for when playback finishes using the setOnCompletionListener() method of the
ViewView. The VideoView object has several other helpful methods, such as
getDuration() and direct control over playback through methods such as pause(). For
finer control over the media, or for an alternate way to play back media, you can use the
MediaPlayer object. Use of it is similar to using the Camera—you need a
SurfaceHolder.

> **Warning**
>
> The MediaController can't be retrieved from a layout file XML definition by a call to
> findViewById(). It must be instantiated programmatically and uses the Activity Con-
> text, not the Application Context.

Working with Audio

Much like video, the Android SDK provides methods for audio playback and recording.
Audio files can be resources, local files, or Uri objects to shared or network resources. Audio recording takes place through the built-in microphone on the device, if one is present
(typically a requirement for a phone because one speaks into it quite often).

Recording Audio

The `MediaRecorder` object of the Android SDK provides audio recording functionality. Using it is a matter of following a few simple steps you should now find familiar:

1. Instantiate a new `MediaRecorder` object.

2. Set the audio source.

3. Set the audio format to record with.

4. Set the file format to store the audio in.

5. Set the file to record to.

6. Prepare the object for recording.

7. Start the recording.

8. Stop and release the recording object when finished.

Using a couple simple buttons, you can create a simple `Activity` to record and play back audio using the preceding steps. The `onClick()` method for a record button might look like this:

```
public void onClick(View v) {
    if (audioRecorder == null) {
        audioRecorder = new MediaRecorder();
    }
    String pathForAppFiles =
        getFilesDir().getAbsolutePath();
    pathForAppFiles += RECORDED_FILE;

    audioRecorder.setAudioSource(
        MediaRecorder.AudioSource.MIC);
    audioRecorder.setOutputFormat(
        MediaRecorder.OutputFormat.DEFAULT);
    audioRecorder.setAudioEncoder(
        MediaRecorder.AudioEncoder.DEFAULT);

    audioRecorder.setOutputFile(pathForAppFiles);

    audioRecorder.prepare();
    audioRecorder.start();

    // button handling and other behavior here
}
```

The `audioRecorder` object is instantiated, if necessary. The default values for the recording source and output file work fine for our purposes. Of note are the values for `CAMCORDER`, which uses a microphone in the direction of the camera, and various voice values that can be used to record calls (beware of local laws) and choose the proper microphone for voice recognition uses.

Warning

If you find that recording does not start, check the file extension used. For instance, when using the MPEG4 container, the Android SDK requires that the file extension is `.mp4`; otherwise, the recording does not start.

A stop button is configured with an `onClick()` handler that looks like this:

```
public void onClick(View v) {
    if (audioRecorder != null) {
        audioRecorder.stop();
        audioRecorder.release();
        audioRecorder = null;
    }
    // button handling and other behavior here
}
```

Finally, applications wanting to record audio require the explicit permission `android.permission.RECORD_AUDIO` set within the `AndroidManifest.xml` file.

Now it is time to add the playback functionality, so we can listen to the audio we just recorded.

Playing Audio

The `MediaPlayer` object can be used to play audio. The following steps are required to prepare a file for playback:

1. Instantiate a new `MediaPlayer` object.

2. Set the path to the file using the `setDataSource` method.

3. Call the `prepare()` method of the `MediaPlayer` object.

4. Call the `start()` method to begin playback.

5. Playback can then be stopped with a call to the `stop()` method.

The `onClick()` handler for a button to play the recorded audio from the previous example might look like the following:

```
public void onClick(View v) {
    if (player == null) {
        player = new MediaPlayer ();
    }
    try {
```

```
    String audioFilePath =
        getFilesDir().getAbsolutePath();
    audioFilePath += RECORDED_FILE;

    player.setDataSource(audioFilePath);

    player.prepare();
    player.start();
} catch (Exception e) {
    Log.e("Audio", "Playback failed.", e);
}
}
```

The audio data source can be a local file path, valid file object, or valid `Uri` to an audio resource. You can programmatically stop the sound playback by a call to the `stop()` method. You can set a `MediaPlayer.OnCompletionListener` object to get a callback when the playback finishes. When done with the `MediaPlayer` object, you should use a call to the `release()` method to free up any resources it might be using, much like the releasing of the `MediaRecorder` object.

Tip

The `AudioManager` (`android.media.AudioManager`) is a system service. You can request the `AudioManager` by calling the `getSystemService(Context.AUDIO_SERVICE)` method. You can use the `AudioManager` to inspect, manage, and modify device-wide audio settings. A number of new APIs were added to the `AudioManager` in the Android 2.2 SDK for managing audio focus—that is, how multiple audio sources playing at the same time give one another "right of way", and so forth. This functionality can be crucial for audio-streaming applications like podcast and music players.

Sharing Audio

Audio can be shared with the rest of the system. The `ContentResolver` can send the file to the `MediaStore` content provider. The following code snippet shows how to configure an audio entry in the audio library on the device:

```
ContentValues values = new ContentValues(9);


values.put(MediaStore.MediaColumns.TITLE, "RecordedAudio");
values.put(MediaStore.Audio.Media.ALBUM,
    "Your Groundbreaking Album");
values.put(MediaStore.Audio.Media.ARTIST, "Your Name");
values.put(MediaStore.Audio.Media.DISPLAY_NAME,
    "The Audio File You Recorded In Media App");
values.put(MediaStore.Audio.Media.IS_RINGTONE, 1);
values.put(MediaStore.Audio.Media.IS_MUSIC, 1);
values.put(MediaStore.MediaColumns.DATE_ADDED,
    System.currentTimeMillis() / 1000);
```

```
values.put(MediaStore.MediaColumns.MIME_TYPE, "audio/mp4");
values.put(MediaStore.Audio.Media.DATA, pathForAppFiles);

Uri audioUri = getContentResolver().insert(
    MediaStore.Audio.Media.EXTERNAL_CONTENT_URI, values);
if (audioUri == null) {
    Log.d("Audio", "Content resolver failed");
    return;
}
```

Setting these values enables the recorded audio to be used by different audio-oriented applications on the handset. For example, setting the `IS_MUSIC` flag enables the audio file to appear in the various sections of the music player and be sorted by its Album information. Setting the `IS_RINGTONE` flag enables the audio file to appear in the list of ringtones for the device.

Periodically, the handset scans for new media files. However, to speed up this process, a `BroadcastIntent` can be sent telling the system about new audio files. The following code demonstrates this for the audio added to the content library:

```
sendBroadcast(new Intent(
    Intent.ACTION_MEDIA_SCANNER_SCAN_FILE,audioUri));
```

After this broadcast `Intent` is handled, the audio file immediately appears in the designated applications.

Searching for Multimedia

You can use the search intent called `android.intent.action.MEDIA_SEARCH` to search for multimedia on a given device. You can also register an intent filter with your application to show up as a source for multimedia with this action. For example, you could perform a search for a specific artist and song like this:

```
Intent searchMusic = new Intent(
    android.provider.MediaStore.INTENT_ACTION_MEDIA_SEARCH);
searchMusic.putExtra(android.provider.MediaStore.EXTRA_MEDIA_ARTIST,
    "Cyndi Lauper");
searchMusic.putExtra(android.provider.MediaStore.EXTRA_MEDIA_TITLE,
    "I Drove All Night");
searchMusic.putExtra(android.provider.MediaStore.EXTRA_MEDIA_FOCUS,
    "audio/*");
startActivity(searchMusic);
```

If you load up a bunch of music on your device (such as Cyndi Lauper's "I Drove All Night") and launch this intent, you are then directed straight to the song you requested. Note that if you have many music apps installed, you might need to select an appropriate one (such as the Music application) the first time you send the Intent.

Working with Ringtones

Much like wallpapers, ringtones are a popular way to personalize a handset. The Android SDK provides a variety of ways to manage ringtones through the `RingtoneManager` object. You can assign the recorded audio from the previous example as the current ringtone with the following static method call:

```
RingtoneManager.setActualDefaultRingtoneUri(
    getApplicationContext(),
    RingtoneManager.TYPE_RINGTONE, audioUri);
```

The type can also be `TYPE_ALARM` or `TYPE_NOTIFICATION` to configure sounds of other system events that use audio tones. To successfully perform this operation, though, the application must have the `android.permission.WRITE_SETTINGS` permission set in the `AndroidManifest.xml` file. You can also query the default ringtone with a call to the static `RingtoneManager.getActualDefaultRingtoneUri()` method. You can use the resulting `Uri` to play the ringtone, which might be useful within applications that want to alert the user.

Summary

Use of multimedia within many applications can dramatically increase their appeal, usefulness, and even usability. The Android SDK provides a variety of APIs for recording audio, video, and images using the camera and microphone hardware; it also provides the ability to play audio and video and display still images. Multimedia can be private to a specific application or shared among all applications using the `MediaStore` content provider.

References and More Information

Android Dev Guide: Audio and Video:
    http://developer.android.com/guide/topics/media/index.html
Android Supported Media Formats:
    http://developer.android.com/guide/appendix/media-formats.html

## 16

Using Android Telephony APIs

Although the Android platform has been designed to run on almost any type of device, the Android devices available on the market are primarily phones. Applications can take advantage of this fact by integrating phone features into their feature set.

This chapter introduces you to the telephony-related APIs available within the Android SDK.

Working with Telephony Utilities

The Android SDK provides a number of useful utilities for applications to integrate phone features available on the device. Generally speaking, developers should consider an Android device first and foremost as a phone. Although these devices might also run applications, phone operations generally take precedence. Your application should not interrupt a phone conversation, for example. To avoid this kind of behavior, your application should know something about what the user is doing, so that it can react differently. For instance, an application might query the state of the phone and determine that the user is talking on the phone and then choose to vibrate instead of play an alarm.

In other cases, applications might need to place a call or send a text message. Phones typically support a Short Message Service (SMS), which is popular for texting (text messaging). Enabling the capability to leverage this feature from an application can enhance the appeal of the application and add features that can't be easily replicated on a desktop environment. Because many Android devices are phones, applications frequently deal with phone numbers and the contacts database; some might want to access the phone dialer to place calls or check phone status information. Adding telephony features to an application enables a more integrated user experience and enhances the overall value of the application to the users.

Tip

Many of the code examples provided in this chapter are taken from the SimpleTelephony application. The source code for this application is provided for download on the book website.

Gaining Permission to Access Phone State Information

Let's begin by looking at how to determine telephony state of the device, including the ability to request the hook state of the phone, information of the phone service, and utilities for handling and verifying phone numbers. The `TelephonyManager` object within the `android.telephony` package is a great place to start.

Many of the method calls in this section require explicit permission set with the Android application manifest file. The `READ_PHONE_STATE` permission is required to retrieve information such as the call state, handset phone number, and device identifiers or serial numbers. The `ACCESS_COARSE_LOCATION` permission is required for cellular location information. Recall that we cover location-based services in detail in Chapter 14, "Using Location-Based Services (LBS) APIs."

The following block of XML is typically needed in your application's `AndroidManifest.xml` file to access basic phone state information:

```
<uses-permission
    android:name="android.permission.READ_PHONE_STATE" />
```

Requesting Call State

You can use the `TelephonyManager` object to retrieve the state of the phone and some information about the phone service itself, such as the phone number of the handset.

You can request an instance of `TelephonyManager` using the `getSystemService()` method, like this:

```
TelephonyManager telManager = (TelephonyManager)
    getSystemService(Context.TELEPHONY_SERVICE);
```

With a valid `TelephonyManager` instance, an application can now make several queries. One important method is `getCallState()`. This method can determine the voice call status of the handset. The following block of code shows how to query for the call state and all the possible return values:

```
int callStatus = telManager.getCallState();
String callState = null;

switch (callStatus) {
        case TelephonyManager.CALL_STATE_IDLE:
            callState = "Phone is idle.";
            break;
        case TelephonyManager.CALL_STATE_OFFHOOK:
            callState = "Phone is in use.";
            break;
        case TelephonyManager.CALL_STATE_RINGING:
            callState = "Phone is ringing!";
            break;
        }
Log.i("telephony", callState);
```

The three call states can be simulated with the emulator through the Dalvik Debug Monitor Service (DDMS) tool, which is discussed in detail in Appendix B, "The Android DDMS Quick-Start Guide."

Querying for the call state can be useful in certain circumstances. However, listening for changes in the call state can enable an application to react appropriately to something the user might be doing. For instance, a game might automatically pause and save state information when the phone rings so that the user can safely answer the call. An application can register to listen for changes in the call state by making a call to the `listen()` method of `TelephonyManager`.

```
telManager.listen(new PhoneStateListener() {
    public void onCallStateChanged(
        int state, String incomingNumber) {
            String newState = getCallStateString(state);
        if (state == TelephonyManager.CALL_STATE_RINGING) {
            Log.i("telephony", newState +
                " number = " + incomingNumber);
        } else {
            Log.i("telephony", newState);
        }
    }
}, PhoneStateListener.LISTEN_CALL_STATE);
```

The listener is called, in this case, whenever the phone starts ringing, the user makes a call, the user answers a call, or a call is disconnected. The listener is also called right after it is assigned so an application can get the initial state.

Another useful state of the phone is determining the state of the service. This information can tell an application if the phone has coverage at all, if it can only make emergency calls, or if the radio for phone calls is turned off as it might be when in airplane mode. To do this, an application can add the `PhoneStateListener.LISTEN_SERVICE_STATE` flag to the listener described earlier and implement the `onServiceStateChanged` method, which receives an instance of the `ServiceState` object. Alternatively, an application can check the state by constructing a `ServiceState` object and querying it directly, as shown here:

```
int serviceStatus = serviceState.getState();
String serviceStateString = null;
switch (serviceStatus) {

    case ServiceState.STATE_EMERGENCY_ONLY:
        serviceStateString = "Emergency calls only";
        break;

    case ServiceState.STATE_IN_SERVICE:
        serviceStateString = "Normal service";
        break;
```

```
    case ServiceState.STATE_OUT_OF_SERVICE:
        serviceStateString = "No service available";
        break;

    case ServiceState.STATE_POWER_OFF:
        serviceStateString = "Telephony radio is off";
        break;
    }
Log.i("telephony", serviceStateString);
```

In addition, a status such as whether the handset is roaming can be determined by a call to the `getRoaming()` method. A friendly and frugal application can use this method to warn the user before performing any costly roaming operations such as data transfers within the application.

Requesting Service Information

In addition to call and service state information, your application can retrieve other information about the device. This information is less useful for the typical application but can diagnose problems or provide specialized services available only from certain provider networks. The following code retrieves several pieces of service information:

```
String opName = telManager.getNetworkOperatorName();
Log.i("telephony", "operator name = " + opName);

String phoneNumber = telManager.getLine1Number();
Log.i("telephony", "phone number = " + phoneNumber);

String providerName = telManager.getSimOperatorName();
Log.i("telephony", "provider name = " + providerName);
```

The network operator name is the descriptive name of the current provider that the handset connects to. This is typically the current tower operator. The SIM operator name is typically the name of the provider that the user is subscribed to for service. The phone number for this application programming interface (API) is defined as the MSISDN, typically the directory number of a GSM handset (that is, the number someone would dial to reach that particular phone).

Monitoring Signal Strength and Data Connection Speed

Sometimes an application might want to alter its behavior based upon the signal strength or service type of the device. For example, a high-bandwidth application might alter stream quality or buffer size based on whether the device has a low-speed connection (such as 1xRTT or EDGE) or a high-speed connection (such as EVDO or HSDPA). `TelephonyManager` can be used to determine such information.

If your application needs to react to changes in telephony state, you can use the `listen()` method of `TelephonyManager` and implement a `PhoneStateListener` to receive changes in service, data connectivity, call state, signal strength, and other phone state information.

Working with Phone Numbers

Applications that deal with telephony, or even just contacts, frequently have to deal with the input, verification, and usage of phone numbers. The Android SDK includes a set of helpful utility functions that simplify handling of phone number strings. Applications can have phone numbers formatted based on the current locale setting. For example, the following code uses the `formatNumber()` method:

```
String formattedNumber =
    PhoneNumberUtils.formatNumber("9995551212");
Log.i("telephony", formattedNumber);
```

The resulting output to the log would be the string 999-555-1212 in my locale. Phone numbers can also be compared using a call to the `PhoneNumberUtils.compare()` method. An application can also check to see if a given phone number is an emergency phone number by calling `PhoneNumberUtils.isEmergencyNumber()`, which enables your application to warn users before they call an emergency number. This method is useful when the source of the phone number data might be questionable.

> ### Tip
> There are a number of formatting utilities for formatting phone numbers based upon locale. Keep in mind that different countries format their numbers in different ways. For example, there is a utility method called `formatJapaneseNumber()` for formatting numbers with special prefixes in the Japanese style.

The `formatNumber()` method can also take an `Editable` as a parameter to format a number in place. The useful feature here is that you can assign the `PhoneNumberFormattingTextWatcher` object to watch a `TextView` (or `EditText` for user input) and format phone numbers as they are entered. The following code demonstrates the ease of configuring an `EditText` to format phone numbers that are entered:

```
EditText numberEntry = (EditText) findViewById(R.id.number_entry);
numberEntry.addTextChangedListener(
    new PhoneNumberFormattingTextWatcher());
```

While the user is typing in a valid phone number, the number is formatted in a way suitable for the current locale. Just the numbers for 19995551212 were entered on the `EditText` shown in Figure 16.1.

Using SMS

SMS usage has become ubiquitous in the last several years. Integrating messaging services, even if only outbound, to an application can provide familiar social functionality to the user. SMS functionality is provided to applications through the `android.telephony` package.

Figure 16.1   Screen showing formatting results
after entering only digits.

Gaining Permission to Send and Receive SMS Messages

SMS functionality requires two different permissions, depending on if the application sends or receives messages. The following XML, to be placed with `AndroidManifest.xml`, shows the permissions needed for both actions:

```
<uses-permission
    android:name="android.permission.SEND_SMS" />
<uses-permission
    android:name="android.permission.RECEIVE_SMS" />
```

Sending an SMS

To send an SMS, an application first needs to get an instance of the `SmsManager`. Unlike other system services, this is achieved by calling the static method `getDefault()` of `SmsManager`:

```
final SmsManager sms = SmsManager.getDefault();
```

Now that the application has the `SmsManager`, sending SMS is as simple as a single call:

```
sms.sendTextMessage(
    "9995551212", null, "Hello!", null, null);
```

The application does not know if the actual sending of the SMS was successful without providing a `PendingIntent` to receive the broadcast of this information. The following code demonstrates configuring a `PendingIntent` to listen for the status of the SMS:

```
Intent msgSent = new Intent("ACTION_MSG_SENT");


final PendingIntent pendingMsgSent =
    PendingIntent.getBroadcast(this, 0, msgSent, 0);
registerReceiver(new BroadcastReceiver() {
    public void onReceive(Context context, Intent intent) {
        int result = getResultCode();
        if (result != Activity.RESULT_OK) {
            Log.e("telephony",
                "SMS send failed code = " + result);
            pendingMsgReceipt.cancel();
        } else {
            messageEntry.setText("");
        }
    }
}, new IntentFilter("ACTION_MSG_SENT"));
```

The `PendingIntent` `pendingMsgSent` can be used with the call to the `sendTextMessage()`. The code for the message-received receipt is similar but is called when the sending handset receives acknowledgment from the network that the destination handset received the message.

If we put all this together with the preceding phone number formatting `EditText`, a new entry field for the message, and a button, we can create a simple form for sending an SMS message. The code for the button handling looks like the following:

```
Button sendSMS = (Button) findViewById(R.id.send_sms);
sendSMS.setOnClickListener(new View.OnClickListener() {
    public void onClick(View v) {
        String destination =
            numberEntry.getText().toString();

        String message =
            messageEntry.getText().toString();

        sms.sendTextMessage(destination, null, message,
            pendingMsgSent, pendingMsgReceipt);

        registerReceiver(...);
    }
}
```

After this code is hooked in, the result should look something like Figure 16.2. Within this application, we used the emulator "phone number" trick (its port number). This is a great way to test sending SMS messages without using hardware or without incurring charges by the handset operator.

 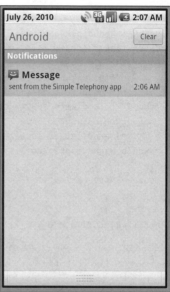

Figure 16.2   Two emulators, one sending an SMS from an application and one receiving an SMS.

A great way to extend this would be to set the sent receiver to modify a graphic on the screen until the sent notification is received. Further, you could use another graphic to indicate when the recipient has received the message. Alternatively, you could use `ProgressBar` widgets track the progress to the user.

Receiving an SMS

Applications can also receive SMS messages. To do so, your application must register a `BroadcastReceiver` to listen for the `Intent` action associated with receiving an SMS. An application listening to SMS in this way doesn't prevent the message from getting to other applications.

Expanding on the previous example, the following code shows how any incoming text message can be placed within a `TextView` on the screen:

```
final TextView receivedMessage = (TextView)findViewById(
    R.id.received_message);
```

```
rcvIncoming = new BroadcastReceiver() {

    public void onReceive(Context context, Intent intent) {
        Log.i("telephony", "SMS received");
        Bundle data = intent.getExtras();
        if (data != null) {
            Object pdus[] =
                (Object[]) data.get("pdus");

            String message = "New message:\n";
            String sender = null;

            for (Object pdu : pdus) {
                SmsMessage part = SmsMessage.
                    createFromPdu((byte[])pdu);

                message += part.
                    getDisplayMessageBody();

                if (sender == null) {
                    sender = part.
                        getDisplayOriginatingAddress();
                }
            }
            receivedMessage.setText(
                message + "\nFrom: "+sender);
            numberEntry.setText(sender);
        }
    }
};

registerReceiver(rcvIncoming, new IntentFilter(
    "android.provider.Telephony.SMS_RECEIVED"));
```

This block of code is placed within the onCreate() method of the Activity. First, the message Bundle is retrieved. In it, an array of Objects holds several byte arrays that contain PDU data—the data format that is customarily used by wireless messaging protocols. Luckily, the Android SDK can decode these with a call to the static SmsMessage.createFromPdu() utility method. From here, we can retrieve the body of the SMS message by calling getDisplayMessageBody().

The message that comes in might be longer than the limitations for an SMS. If it is, it will have been broken up in to a multipart message on the sending side. To handle this, we loop through each of the received Object parts and take the corresponding body from each, while only taking the sender address from the first.

Tip

When dealing with multipart text messages, it's important to know that the user might be charged the full texting charge for each part of the message. This can add up quickly. Care should be taken to warn users that applications that use any text messaging, sending or receiving, might incur charges by their operator.

An application can send a similar multipart message by taking advantage of the `SmsManager.divideMessage()` method. This method breaks up a `String` into parts no larger than the maximum size allowed by the SMS specification. The application could then use the method called `sendMultipartTextMessage()`, passing in the result of the call to `divideMessage()`.

Next, the code updates the text string in the `TextView` to show the user the received message. The sender address is also updated so that the recipient can respond with less typing. Finally, we register the `BroadcastReceiver` with the system. The `IntentFilter` used here, `android.provider.Telephony.SMS_RECEIVED`, is a well-known but undocumented `IntentFilter` used for this. As such, we have to use the string literal for it.

Warning

We strongly recommend watching for updates to the Android SDK in relation to this functionality. Future versions of the SDK might either add this string officially or remove the feature entirely.

Making and Receiving Phone Calls

It might come as a surprise to the younger generation (they usually just text), but phones are often still used for making and receiving phone calls. Any application can be made to initiate calls and answer incoming calls; however, these abilities should be used judiciously so as not to unnecessarily disrupt the calling functionality of the user's device.

Tip

You can also use two emulator instances to test calling to another handset. As with the SMS sending, the port number of the emulator is the phone number that can be called.

Making Phone Calls

You've seen how to find out if the handset is ringing. Now let's look at how to enable your application to make phone calls as well.

Building on the previous example, which sent and received SMS messages, we now walk through similar functionality that adds a call button to the screen to call the phone number instead of messaging it.

The Android SDK enables phone numbers to be passed to the dialer in two different ways. The first way is to launch the dialer with a phone number already entered. The user then needs to press the Send button to actually initiate the call. This method does not require any specific permissions. The second way is to actually place the call. This method requires the `android.permission.CALL_PHONE` permission to be added to the application's `AndroidManifest.xml` file.

Let's look at an example of how to enable an application to take input in the form of a phone number and launch the Phone dialer after the user presses a button, as shown in Figure 16.3.

Figure 16.3   The user can enter a phone number in the **EditText** control and press the Call button to initiate a phone call from within the application.

We extract the phone number the user entered in the EditText field (or the most recently received SMS when continuing with the previous example). The following code demonstrates how to launch the dialer after the user presses the Call button:

```
Button call = (Button) findViewById(R.id.call_button);
call.setOnClickListener(new View.OnClickListener() {
    public void onClick(View v) {
        Uri number = Uri.parse("tel:" +
            numberEntry.getText().toString());
        Intent dial = new Intent(
            Intent.ACTION_DIAL, number);
        startActivity(dial);
    }
});
```

First, the phone number is requested from the EditText and tel: is prepended to it, making it a valid Uri for the Intent. Then, a new Intent is created with

`Intent.ACTION_DIAL` to launch in to the dialer with the number dialed in already. You can also use `Intent.ACTION_VIEW`, which functions the same. Replacing it with `Intent.ACTION_CALL`, however, immediately calls the number entered. This is generally not recommended; otherwise, calls might be made by mistake. Finally, the `startActivity()` method is called to launch the dialer, as shown in Figure 16.4.

Figure 16.4   One emulator calling the other after the Call button is pressed within the application.

Receiving Phone Calls

Much like applications can receive and process incoming SMS messages, an application can register to answer incoming phone calls. To enable this within an application, you must implement a broadcast receiver to process intents with the action `Intent.ACTION_ANSWER`.

Remember, too, that if you're not interested in the call itself, but information about the incoming call, you might want to consider using the `CallLog.Calls` content provider (`android.provider.CallLog`) instead. You can use the `CallLog.calls` class to determine recent call information, such as

- Who called
- When they called

- Whether it was an incoming or outgoing call
- Whether or not anyone answered
- The duration of the call

Summary

The Android SDK provides many helpful telephony utilities to handle making and receiving phone calls and SMS messages (with appropriate permissions) and tools to help with formatting phone numbers entered by the user or from other sources.

These telephony utilities enable applications to work seamlessly with the device's core phone features. Developers might also integrate voice calls and messaging features into their own applications, resulting in compelling new features. Messaging is more popular than ever, so integrating text messaging into an application can add a familiar and exciting social feature that users will likely enjoy.

References and More Information

3GPP Specifications (SMS):
    http://www.3gpp.org/specifications
Wikipedia's Write-Up on SMS:
    http://en.wikipedia.org/wiki/SMS

## 17

Using Android 3D Graphics with OpenGL ES

The world around us is not two-dimensional but rich with depth. Although the phone display is a flat surface, presenting games and applications with visual depth has long been a way to enhance and add realism to them. For this purpose, developers can use the OpenGL ES implementations provided within the Android SDK.

OpenGL ES is a graphics application programming interface (API) for embedded systems based on the OpenGL desktop standard. It is popular on wireless platforms and is supported on all major mobile phone platforms, including Windows Mobile, Symbian, MeeGo, BREW, Apple iOS, Palm WebOS, and now Android. Android devices support different versions of OpenGL ES depending on the platform version.

This chapter discusses how to use OpenGL ES in the Android SDK. Familiarity with OpenGL concepts can be helpful. This chapter does not teach you OpenGL, but it shows you how to perform a variety of common tasks with OpenGL ES on Android devices. These include configuring EGL (Embedded-System Graphics Library) and GL (Graphics Libraries), drawing objects, animating objects and scenes, lighting a scene, and texturing objects.

Working with OpenGL ES

Before 1992, Silicon Graphics (SGI) had a proprietary graphics standard called Integrated Raster Imaging System Graphics Library (IRIS GL) and known typically as just GL. In 1992, to clean up the code and make GL more maintainable, SGI created OpenGL and set up a consortium of companies to maintain the open standard form of GL. Today, this consortium is known as the nonprofit Khronos Group, with more than 100 member companies. OpenGL ES was developed in the early 2000s to extend this open library to embedded devices. OpenGL ES is a subset of OpenGL. EGL was developed shortly thereafter to provide a common interface layer to native platform graphics.

Within the interfaces, OpenGL is simply referred to as GL. This is true for OpenGL ES, as well. Within the text of this chapter, GL typically refers to the underlying objects and interfaces within OpenGL to be consistent with the naming conventions within the code. OpenGL ES typically refers to the Android implementation of the OpenGL ES subset of OpenGL. Finally, OpenGL is used in a more generic fashion to refer to the generic concept or library.

Leveraging OpenGL ES in Android

Android developers can implement 3D graphics applications in two ways:

- The Android SDK provides OpenGL ES functionality within the `android.opengl` package in conjunction with the Khronos `javax.microedition.khronos.opengles` and `javax.microedition.khronos.egl` packages.
- The Android Native Development Kit (NDK) can be used to leverage OpenGL ES 1.1 and 2.0 native libraries for optimum performance.

Note

In this chapter, we focus on how to use the Android SDK to develop OpenGL ES applications. We discuss the Android Native Development Kit in Chapter 18, "Using the Android NDK."

The Android SDK has support for different versions of OpenGL ES, depending on the API Level or platform version:

- OpenGL ES 1.0 functionality (`android.opengl`) is fully supported on devices running Android 1.0 (API Level 1) and higher.
- OpenGL ES 1.1 (`android.opengl.GLES11`) is fully supported by devices running Android 1.6 (API Level 4) and higher.
- OpenGL ES 2.0 (`android.opengl.GLES20`) is fully supported by devices running Android 2.2 (API Level 8) and higher.

Ensuring Device Compatibility

Applications that require OpenGL functionality should declare this fact within the Android Manifest file using the `<uses-feature>` tag with the `android:glEsVersion` attribute. This enables stores like the Android Market to filter the application and provide it only to devices that support the OpenGL version required by the application. The `android:glEsVersion` attribute is a 32-bit number where the high bits specify the major version and the low bits specify the minor version.

- If the application requires OpenGL ES 1.0, then you do not need to declare any `<uses-feature>` tag, as this is the default for all applications. All Android devices support OpenGL ES 1.0.
- If the application requires OpenGL ES 1.1, then you should declare a `<uses-feature>` tag as follows: `<uses-feature android:glEsVersion =" 0x00010001" />`.
- If the application requires OpenGL ES 2.0, then you should declare a `<uses-feature>` tag as follows: `<uses-feature android:glEsVersion =" 0x00020000" />`.

Only one OpenGL ES version should be listed in the Android Manifest file. Applications that can function using different versions of OpenGL ES by checking for the supported graphics libraries at runtime should specify the lowest version supported by their application. It's also safe to assume that if a platform supports a newer version of OpenGL ES, say 2.0, then it also supports all older versions (such as 1.1 and 1.0).

Using OpenGL ES APIs in the Android SDK

Using OpenGL ES on Android is a mix of using Android `View` object concepts and regular OpenGL ES concepts. There are a number of different ways to initialize and use the OpenGL ES functionality provided as part of the Android SDK.

- Developers can implement their own OpenGL ES solutions, handling the initialization of EGL and GL, managing a separate worker thread for OpenGL ES calls, and drawing on a `SurfaceView` control.
- As of Android 1.5, developers can take advantage of the `GLSurfaceView` and `GLSurfaceView.Renderer` classes to help handle EGL initialization and threading. Calls are made into a user-defined `Renderer` class. The `Renderer` class handles the drawing and GL initialization and is run outside of the UI thread.

In this chapter, we give examples of both of these methods. Although the second method (using `GLSurfaceView`) is indeed simpler, you gain a more complete understanding of the fundamentals of Android OpenGL ES by following along as we describe the "manual" way first. In addition, many developers will be porting their code over from a platform where they normally go through this configuration and might have the need to customize many pieces. Therefore, we start with the "manual" method so that we can review the steps necessary to set up, draw, and tear down OpenGL ES correctly. The concepts and classes used for both methods are very similar, though, making this discussion useful even if you choose to use only the included `GLSurfaceView` method for your projects.

Tip

Many of the code examples provided in this chapter are taken from the SimpleOpenGL application. The source code for this application is provided for download on the book website.

Handling OpenGL ES Tasks Manually

We have provided a custom implementation leveraging OpenGL without using `GLSurfaceView` for users who need to develop for Android versions previous to Android 1.5 or who have a need for tighter control of the rendering pipeline and initialization. The following steps to initialize OpenGL ES enable you to start drawing on the screen via the OpenGL interface:

1. Initialize `SurfaceView` with a surface of type `SURFACE_TYPE_GPU`.
2. Start a thread for OpenGL; all OpenGL calls will be performed on this thread.

3. Initialize EGL.

4. Initialize GL.

5. Start drawing!

Warning

When OpenGL ES is initialized on a particular thread of your application, all subsequent calls must be on this same thread; otherwise, they will fail. You should not use your application's main thread for OpenGL ES calls, as the extra processing and loops can cause your application to become less responsive. This does introduce some thread synchronization consequences that you must handle, and we discuss those later in this chapter.

Creating a `SurfaceView`

The first step to drawing fancy 3D graphics on the screen is to create your `SurfaceView`. This involves extending `SurfaceView` and implementing callbacks for `SurfaceHolder.Callback`. The following is an empty implementation that we complete shortly:

```
private class BasicGLSurfaceView
    extends SurfaceView
    implements SurfaceHolder.Callback {

    SurfaceHolder mAndroidHolder;

    BasicGLSurfaceView(Context context) {
        super(context);
        mAndroidHolder = getHolder();
        mAndroidHolder.addCallback(this);
        mAndroidHolder.setType(
            SurfaceHolder.SURFACE_TYPE_GPU);
    }

    public void surfaceChanged(SurfaceHolder holder,
        int format, int width, int height) {}

    public void surfaceCreated(SurfaceHolder holder) {}

    public void surfaceDestroyed(SurfaceHolder holder) {}
}
```

First, within the constructor, `getHolder()` is called to get and store the `SurfaceHolder`. Because the `SurfaceView` implements the `SurfaceHolder.Callback` interface, this `SurfaceView` is assigned for receiving callbacks for those events. Finally, you must set the surface type to `SURFACE_TYPE_GPU` for OpenGL ES calls to work on it. This class is initialized and set as the content `View` for the activity as follows:

```
protected void onCreate(Bundle savedInstanceState) {
    super.onCreate(savedInstanceState);
    mAndroidSurface = new BasicGLSurfaceView(this);
    setContentView(mAndroidSurface);
}
```

Although setting the `SurfaceView` as the entire content View works fine, it isn't flexible if you want other functionality on the screen besides the 3D area. One way to place the `SurfaceView` on your screen and still have the benefits of using an XML layout file is to use one of the container widgets, such as `FrameLayout`, and add this View to it. For instance, consider this `FrameLayout` definition, which can exist anywhere within a layout:

```
<FrameLayout
    android:id="@+id/gl_container"
    android:layout_height="100px"
    android:layout_width="100px" />
```

This puts a 100×100 pixel square container somewhere on the screen, depending on the rest of the layout. Now, the following code uses the identifier for this `FrameLayout` to place the child `SurfaceView` within the `FrameLayout`:

```
mAndroidSurface = new TextureGLSurfaceView(this);
setContentView(R.layout.constrained);
FrameLayout v = (FrameLayout) findViewById(R.id.gl_container);
v.addView(mAndroidSurface);
```

In this example, `R.layout.constrained` is our layout resource, which contains the `FrameLayout` with the particular identifier we used. You see why this works regardless of what is drawn in the OpenGL surface as we continue through the initialization of OpenGL ES on Android.

Starting Your OpenGL ES Thread

Within Android, you can update only the screen from the main thread of your application, sometimes referred to as the UI thread. The `SurfaceView` widget, however, is used so that we can offload graphics processing to a secondary thread, which can update this part of the screen. This is our OpenGL thread. Like updating the screen from the UI thread, all OpenGL calls must be within the same thread.

Recall that the `SurfaceView` presented also implemented the `SurfaceHolder.Callback` interface. You can access the underlying surface of the `SurfaceView` only after calling `surfaceCreated()` and before calling `surfaceDestroyed()`. Between these two calls is the only time that we have a valid surface for our OpenGL instance to draw to.

As such, we won't bother creating the OpenGL thread until `surfaceCreated()` is called. The following is an example implementation of `surfaceCreate()`, which starts up the OpenGL thread:

```
public void surfaceCreated(SurfaceHolder holder) {
    mGLThread = new BasicGLThread(this);
    mGLThread.start();
}
```

As promised, little more than launching the thread takes place here. The `SurfaceView` is passed to the thread. This is done because the OpenGL calls need to know which `SurfaceView` to draw upon.

The `BasicGLThread` class is an implementation of a `Thread` that contains the code we run in the OpenGL thread described. The following code block shows which functionality is placed where. The `BasicGLThread` is placed as a private member of the `Activity` class.

```
private class BasicGLThread extends Thread {
    SurfaceView sv;
    BasicGLThread(SurfaceView view) {
        sv = view;
    }

    private boolean mDone = false;
    public void run() {
        initEGL();
        initGL();
        while (!mDone) {
            // drawing code
        }
    }

    public void requestStop() {
        mDone = true;
        try {
            join();
        } catch (InterruptedException e) {
            Log.e("GL", "failed to stop gl thread", e);
        }
        cleanupGL();
    }

    public void cleanupGL() {}
    public void initGL() {}
    public void initEGL() {}

    // main OpenGL variables
}
```

During creation, the `SurfaceView` is saved for later use. In the `run()` method, EGL and GL are initialized, which we describe later in this chapter. Then, the drawing code is executed either once or, as shown here, in a loop. Finally, the thread can safely be stopped from outside the thread with a call to the `requestStop()` method. This also cleans up the OpenGL resources. More on this is found in the section "Cleaning Up OpenGL ES" later in this chapter.

Initializing EGL

Up to this point, the application has a `SurfaceView` with a valid `Surface` and an OpenGL thread that has just been launched. The first step with most OpenGL implementations is to initialize EGL, or the native hardware. You do this in basically the same way each time, and this is a good block of code to write once and reuse. The following steps must be performed to initialize EGL on Android:

1. Get the EGL object.

2. Initialize the display.

3. Get a configuration.

4. Link the `EGLSurface` to an Android `SurfaceView`.

5. Create the EGL context.

6. Tell EGL which display, surface, and context to use.

7. Get our GL object for use in rendering.

The Android SDK provides some utility classes for use with OpenGL ES. The first of these is the `GLDebugHelper` class. OpenGL calls don't directly return errors. Instead, they set an error internally that can be queried. You can use the `GLDebugHelper` class to wrap all EGL and GL calls and have the wrapper check for errors and throw an exception. The first call for getting the EGL object uses this wrapper, as shown here:

```
mEGL = (EGL10) GLDebugHelper.wrap(
    EGLContext.getEGL(),
    GLDebugHelper.CONFIG_CHECK_GL_ERROR |
    GLDebugHelper.CONFIG_CHECK_THREAD,
    null);
```

Here, the `EGL10` object is retrieved and wrapped. Turning on the `CONFIG_CHECK_GL_ERROR` flag checks for all GL Errors. In addition, the wrapper makes sure all our GL and EGL calls are made from the correct thread because `CONFIG_CHECK_THREAD` is enabled.

Now we can proceed with initializing the display, as shown here:

```
mGLDisplay = mEGL.eglGetDisplay(EGL10.EGL_DEFAULT_DISPLAY);
```

The default display, `EGL10.EGL_DEFAULT_DISPLAY`, is configured by the internals of the Android implementation of OpenGL ES. Now that we have the display, we can initialize EGL and get the version of the implementation:

```
int[] curGLVersion = new int[2];
mEGL.eglInitialize(mGLDisplay, curGLVersion);
```

The current GL version varies by device. With the display initialized, we can request which configuration is closest to the one we require:

```
int[] mConfigSpec = { EGL10.EGL_RED_SIZE, 5,
                      EGL10.EGL_GREEN_SIZE, 6,
                      EGL10.EGL_BLUE_SIZE, 5,
                      EGL10.EGL_DEPTH_SIZE, 16,
                      EGL10.EGL_NONE };
EGLConfig[] configs = new EGLConfig[1];
int[] num_config = new int[1];
mEGL.eglChooseConfig(mGLDisplay, mConfigSpec,
                     configs, 1, num_config);
mGLConfig = configs[0];
```

The preceding configuration works on the emulator and the current hardware. If you are unsure that the configuration you've chosen works with your application's target platforms, this is a good way to check the resulting list of configurations.

Now we can create the EGL surface based on this configuration:

```
mGLSurface = mEGL.eglCreateWindowSurface
    (mGLDisplay, mGLConfig, sv.getHolder(), null);
```

Recall that we stored our `SurfaceView` for use later. Here, we use it to pass the native Android surface to EGL so they can be linked correctly. We still need to get the EGL context before we can finalize and get our instance of the GL object.

```
mGLContext = mEGL.eglCreateContext(
    mGLDisplay, mGLConfig,EGL10.EGL_NO_CONTEXT, null);
```

Now that we have our display, surface, and context, we can get our GL object.

```
mEGL.eglMakeCurrent(mGLDisplay, mGLSurface,
    mGLSurface, mGLContext);
mGL = (GL10) GLDebugHelper.wrap(
    mGLContext.getGL(),
    GLDebugHelper.CONFIG_CHECK_GL_ERROR |
    GLDebugHelper.CONFIG_CHECK_THREAD, null);
```

Once again, we use `GLDebugHelper` to wrap the GL object so that it checks errors and confirms the thread for us. This completes the initialization of EGL on Android. Next, we can initialize GL to set up our projection and other rendering options.

Initializing GL

Now the fun begins. We have EGL fully initialized, and we have a valid GL object, so we can initialize our drawing space. For this example, we won't be drawing anything complex. We leave most options at their default values.

Typically, one of the first calls made to initialize GL is to set the viewport. Here is an example of how to set the viewport to the same dimensions as our `SurfaceView`:

```
int width = sv.getWidth();
int height = sv.getHeight();
mGL.glViewport(0, 0, width, height);
```

The location of the surface on the screen is determined internally by EGL. We also use the following width and height of the `SurfaceView` to determine the aspect ratio for GL to render in. In the following code, we complete the configuration of a basic GL projection setup:

```
mGL.glMatrixMode(GL10.GL_PROJECTION);
mGL.glLoadIdentity();
float aspect = (float) width/height;
GLU.gluPerspective(mGL, 45.0f, aspect, 1.0f, 30.0f);
mGL.glClearColor(0.5f,0.5f,0.5f,1);
```

The Android SDK provides a few helpers similar to those found in GLUT (OpenGL Utility Toolkit). Here, we use one of them to define a perspective in terms of the vertical angle of view, aspect ratio, and near and far clipping planes. The `gluPerspective()` method is useful for configuring the projection matrix, which transforms the 3D scene into a flat surface. Finally, we clear the screen to gray.

Drawing on the Screen

Now that EGL and GL are initialized, objects can be drawn to the screen. For this example, to demonstrate that we've set up everything to actually draw, we put a simple three-vertex flat surface (in layman's terms, a triangle) on the screen. Here is some sample code to do this:

```
mGL.glMatrixMode(GL10.GL_MODELVIEW);
mGL.glLoadIdentity();
GLU.gluLookAt(mGL, 0, 0, 10f, 0, 0, 0, 0, 1, 0f);
mGL.glColor4f(1f, 0f, 0f, 1f);
while (!mDone) {
    mGL.glClear(GL10.GL_COLOR_BUFFER_BIT |
        GL10.GL_DEPTH_BUFFER_BIT);
    mGL.glRotatef(1f, 0, 0, 1f);
    triangle.draw(mGL);
    mEGL.eglSwapBuffers(mGLDisplay, mGLSurface);
}
```

If it looks like something is missing, you are correct. This code doesn't actually show the draw command for the triangle. However, it does use an Android SDK utility method to transform the model view matrix with the intuitive `gluLookAt()` method. Here, it sets the eye point 10 units away from the origin and looks toward the origin. The up value is, as usual, set to the positive y-axis. Within the loop, notice that the identity matrix is not assigned. This gives the `glRotatef()` method a compounding effect, causing the triangle to rotate in a counter-clockwise direction. In the next section, "Drawing 3D Objects," we discuss the details of drawing with OpenGL ES in Android.

When launched, a screen similar to that in Figure 17.1 should display.

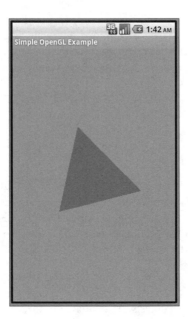

Figure 17.1   A red triangle rendered using
OpenGL ES on the Android emulator.

You now have a working OpenGL ES environment within the Android SDK. We continue from this point to talk more about drawing within the environment.

Drawing 3D Objects

Now that you have the OpenGL ES environment working within Android, it's time to do some actual drawing. This section leads you through a number of examples, each building upon the previous. In doing so, these examples introduce new Android-specific concepts with OpenGL ES.

Drawing Your Vertices

OpenGL ES supports two primary drawing calls, `glDrawArrays()` and `glDrawElements()`. Both of these methods require the use of a vertex buffer assigned through a call to `glVertexPointer`. Because Android runs on top of Java, though, an arbitrary array cannot be passed in as the array contents might move around in memory. Instead, we have to use a `ByteBuffer`, `FloatBuffer`, or `IntBuffer` so the data stays at the same location in memory. Converting various arrays to buffers is common, so we have

implemented some helper methods. Here is one for converting a float array into a
`FloatBuffer`:

```
FloatBuffer getFloatBufferFromFloatArray(float array[]) {
    ByteBuffer tempBuffer =
        ByteBuffer.allocateDirect(array.length * 4);
    tempBuffer.order(ByteOrder.nativeOrder());
    FloatBuffer buffer = tempBuffer.asFloatBuffer();
    buffer.put(array);
    buffer.position(0);
    return buffer;
}
```

This creates a buffer of 32-bit float values with a stride of 0. You can then store the resulting `FloatBuffer` and assign it to OpenGL calls. Here is an example of doing this, using
the triangle we showed previously in this chapter:

```
float[] vertices = {
    -0.559016994f, 0, 0,
    0.25f, 0.5f, 0f,
    0.25f, -0.5f, 0f
};
mVertexBuffer = getFloatBufferFromFloatArray(vertices);
```

With the buffer assigned, we can now draw the triangle, as shown here:

```
void drawTriangle(GL10 gl) {
    gl.glEnableClientState(GL10.GL_VERTEX_ARRAY);
    gl.glVertexPointer(3, GL10.GL_FLOAT, 0, mVertexBuffer);
    gl.glDrawArrays(GL10.GL_TRIANGLES, 0, 3);
}
```

We have to enable the `GL_VERTEX_ARRAY` state, though you could do this in GL configuration, as it is required to draw anything with OpenGL ES. We then assign the vertex
buffer through a call to `glVertexPointer()`, also telling GL that we're using float values.
Fixed point values, through `GL_FIXED`, can also be used and might be faster with some
Android implementations. Finally, a call to `glDrawArrays()` is made to draw the triangles
using three vertices from the first one. The result of this can be seen in Figure 17.1.

Coloring Your Vertices

In OpenGL ES, you can use an array of colors to individually assign colors to each vertex
that is drawn. This is accomplished by calling the `glColorPointer()` method with a
buffer of colors. The following code sets up a small buffer of colors for three vertices:

```
float[] colors = {
    1f, 0, 0, 1f,
    0, 1f, 0, 1f,
    0, 0, 1f, 1f
    };
mColorBuffer = getFloatBufferFromFloatArray(colors);
```

With the buffer available, we can now use it to color our triangle, as shown in the following code:

```
void drawColorful(GL10 gl) {
    gl.glEnableClientState(GL10.GL_COLOR_ARRAY);
    gl.glColorPointer(4,GL10.GL_FLOAT, 0, mColorBuffer);
    draw(gl);
    gl.glDisableClientState(GL10.GL_COLOR_ARRAY);
}
```

First, the client state for GL_COLOR_ARRAY is enabled. Then, calling the glColorPointer method sets the preceding color buffer created. The call to draw() draws the triangle like the colorful one seen in Figure 17.2.

Figure 17.2   A triangle with red, green, and blue
vertices smoothly blended.

Drawing More Complex Objects

A standard cube has eight vertices. However, in OpenGL ES, each of the six faces needs to be drawn with two triangles. Each of these triangles needs three vertices. That's a total of 36 vertices to draw an object with just 8 of its own vertices. There must be a better way.

OpenGL ES supports index arrays. An index array is a list of vertex indexes from the current vertex array. The index array must be a buffer, and in this example we use a ByteBuffer because we don't have many vertices to indicate. The index array lists the order that the vertices should be drawn when used with glDrawElements(). Note that the color arrays (and normal arrays that we get to shortly) are still relative to the vertex array and not the index array. Here is some code that draws an OpenGL cube using just eight defined vertices:

```
float vertices[] = {
    -1,1,1, 1,1,1, 1,-1,1, -1,-1,1,
    1,1,-1, -1,1,-1, -1,-1,-1, 1,-1,-1
};
byte indices[] = {
    0,1,2, 2,3,0,  1,4,7, 7,2,1,  0,3,6, 6,5,0,
    3,2,7, 7,6,3,  0,1,4, 4,5,0,  5,6,7, 7,4,5
};
FloatBuffer vertexBuffer =
    getFloatBufferFromFloatArray(vertices);
ByteBuffer indexBuffer =
    getByteBufferFromByteArray(indices);
gl.glVertexPointer(3, GL10.GL_FLOAT, 0, vertexBuffer);
gl.glDrawElements(GL10.GL_TRIANGLES, indices.length,
    GL10.GL_UNSIGNED_BYTE, indexBuffer);
```

The vertices define the typical shape for a cube. Then, however, we use the index array to define in what order the vertices are drawn to create the cube out of the 12 triangles that we need (recalling that OpenGL ES does not support quads). Now you have a red shape on your screen that looks like Figure 17.3 (left). It doesn't actually look much like a cube, though, does it? Without some shading, it looks too much like a random polygon. If, however, you switch the `glDrawElements()` to GL_LINE_LOOP instead of GL_TRIANGLES, you see a line-drawing version of the shape, like Figure 17.3 (right). Now you can see that it really is a cube. You can reuse the vertices buffer with different index buffers, too. This is useful if you can define multiple shapes using the same set of vertices and then draw them in their own locations with transformations.

Lighting Your Scene

The last 3D object that we drew was a cube that looked like some strange polygon on your flat 2D screen. The colors of each face could be made different by applying coloring between each call to draw a face. However, that will still produce a fairly flat-looking cube. Instead, why not shine some light on the scene and let the lighting give the cube some additional depth?

Before you can provide lighting on a scene, each vertex of each surface needs a vector applied to it to define how the light will reflect and, thus, how it will be rendered. Although this vector can be anything, most often it is perpendicular to the surface defined by the vertices; this is called the normal of a surface. Recalling our cube from the preceding example, we see now that a cube can't actually be created out of eight vertices as each vertex can carry only one normal array, and we would need three per vertex because each vertex belongs to three faces. Instead, we have to use a cube that does, in fact, contain the entire lot of 24 vertices. (Technically, you could define a bunch of index arrays and change the normal array between calls to each face, but it's more commonly done with a large list of vertices and a single list of normal vectors.)

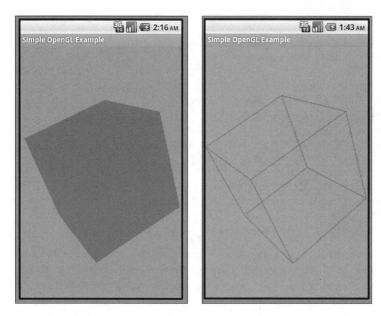

Figure 17.3   (Left) A solid cube with no shading and (right) the same cube with only lines.

Like the color array, the normal array is applied to each vertex in the vertex array in order. Lighting is a fairly complex topic and if it's unfamiliar, you need to check out the References and More Information section at the end of this chapter where you can learn more. For now, we just give an example of how to use the lighting features of Open GL ES within Android.

Here is some code for enabling simple lighting:

```
mGL.glEnable(GL10.GL_LIGHTING);
mGL.glEnable(GL10.GL_LIGHT0);
mGL.glLightfv(GL10.GL_LIGHT0, GL10.GL_AMBIENT,
    new float[] {0.1f, 0.1f, 0.1f, 1f}, 0);
mGL.glLightfv(GL10.GL_LIGHT0, GL10.GL_DIFFUSE,
    new float[] {1f, 1f, 1f, 1f}, 0);
mGL.glLightfv(GL10.GL_LIGHT0, GL10.GL_POSITION,
    new float[] {10f, 0f, 10f, 1f}, 0);
mGL.glEnable(GL10.GL_COLOR_MATERIAL);
mGL.glShadeModel(GL10.GL_SMOOTH);
```

This code enables lighting, enables GL_LIGHT0, and then sets the color and brightness of the light. Finally, the light is positioned in 3D space. In addition, we enable

GL_COLOR_MATERIAL so the color set for drawing the objects is used with the lighting. We also enable the smooth shading model, which helps remove the visual transition between triangles on the same face. You can use color material definitions for fancier lighting and more realistic-looking surfaces, but that is beyond the scope of this book.

Here is the drawing code for our cube, assuming we now have a full vertex array of all 24 points and an index array defining the order in which they should be drawn:

```
gl.glEnableClientState(GL10.GL_NORMAL_ARRAY);
gl.glVertexPointer(3, GL10.GL_FLOAT, 0, mVertexBuffer);
gl.glNormalPointer(GL10.GL_FLOAT, 0, mNormalBuffer);
gl.glDrawElements(GL10.GL_TRIANGLES, indices.length,
GL10.GL_UNSIGNED_BYTE, mIndexBuffer);
```

Notice that the normal array and normal mode are now turned on. Without this, the lighting won't look right. As with the other arrays, this has to be assigned through a fixed buffer in Java, as this code demonstrates:

```
float normals[] = {
    // front
    0, 0, 1, 0, 0, 1, 0, 0, 1, 0, 0, 1,
    // back
    0, 0, -1, 0, 0, -1, 0, 0, -1, 0, 0, -1,
    // top
    0, 1, 0, 0, 1, 0, 0, 1, 0, 0, 1, 0,
    // bottom
    0, -1, 0, 0, -1, 0, 0, -1, 0, 0, -1, 0,
    // right
    1, 0, 0, 1, 0, 0, 1, 0, 0, 1, 0, 0,
    // left
    -1, 0, 0, -1, 0, 0, -1, 0, 0, -1, 0, 0 };
mNormalBuffer = getFloatBufferFromFloatArray(normals);
```

The preceding code uses one of the helper methods we talked about previously to create a FloatBuffer. We use a floating point array for the normals. This also shows the normals and how each vertex must have one. (Recall that we now have 24 vertices for the cube.) You can create various lighting effects by making the normals not actually perpendicular to the surface, but for more accurate lighting, it's usually better to just increase the polygon count of your objects or add textures. Figure 17.4 shows the solid cube, now shaded to show depth better.

Texturing Your Objects

Texturing surfaces, or putting images on surfaces, is a rather lengthy and complex topic. It's enough for our purposes to focus on learning how to texture with Android, so we use the previously lit and colored cube and texture it.

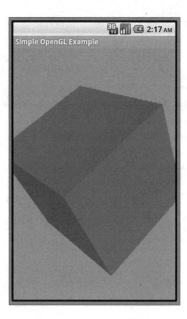

Figure 17.4   A cube with a light shining from the
right to shade it.

First, texturing needs to be enabled, as shown in the following code:

```
mGL.glEnable(GL10.GL_TEXTURE_2D);
int[] textures = new int[1];
mGL.glGenTextures(1, textures, 0);
```

This code enables texturing and creates an internally named slot for one texture. We use
this slot to tell OpenGL what texture we operate on in the next block of code:

```
gl.glBindTexture(GL10.GL_TEXTURE_2D, textures[0]);
Bitmap bitmap = BitmapFactory.decodeResource(
    c.getResources(), R.drawable.android);
Bitmap bitmap256 = Bitmap.createScaledBitmap(
    bitmap, 256, 256, false);
GLUtils.texImage2D(GL10.GL_TEXTURE_2D, 0, bitmap256, 0);
bitmap.recycle();
bitmap256.recycle();
```

You've probably begun to wonder what happened to Android-specific code. Well, it's back.
OpenGL ES needs bitmaps to use as textures. Lucky for us, Android comes with a `Bitmap`
class that can read in nearly any format of image, including PNG, GIF, and JPG files. You
can do this straight from a Drawable resource identifier, too, as demonstrated in the preceding code. OpenGL requires that textures be square and have sides that are powers of
two, such as 64×64 or 256×256. Because the source image might or might not be in

one of these exact sizes, we scale it again with just a single Android method call. If the source image weren't square, though, the original aspect ratio is not kept. Sometimes it is easier to scale down with the original aspect ratio and add colored padding around the edges of the image instead of stretching it, but this is beyond the scope of this example.

Finally, `GLUtils.texImage2D()` assigns an Android `Bitmap` to an OpenGL texture. OpenGL keeps the image internally, so we can clean up the `Bitmap` objects with a call to the `recycle()` method.

Now that OpenGL ES knows about the texture, the next step is to tell it where to draw the texture. You can accomplish this through using a texture coordinate buffer. This is similar to all the other buffer arrays in that it must be assigned to a fixed Java buffer and enabled. Here is the code to do this with our cube example:

```
float texCoords[] = {
    1,0, 1,1, 0,1, 0,0,
    1,0, 1,1, 0,1, 0,0,
    1,0, 1,1, 0,1, 0,0,
    1,0, 1,1, 0,1, 0,0,
    1,0, 1,1, 0,1, 0,0,
    1,0, 1,1, 0,1, 0,0,
    };
mCoordBuffer = getFloatBufferFromFloatArray(texCoords);
gl.glEnableClientState(GL10.GL_TEXTURE_COORD_ARRAY);
gl.glTexCoordPointer(2, GL10.GL_FLOAT, 0, mCoordBuffer);

draw(gl);
```

As promised, this code creates a fixed buffer for the texture coordinates. We set the same ones on each face of the cube, so each vertex has a texture coordinate assigned to it. (0,0 is the lower-left portion of the texture and 1,1 is the upper-right.) Next, we enable the `GL_TEXTURE_COORD_ARRAY` state and then tell OpenGL which buffer to use. Finally, we draw the cube. Now, we left the code the same as before, which produces the output you see in Figure 17.5 (left). The coloring does still apply, even with textures. If coloring is not applied, the output looks like what you see in Figure 17.5 (right).

Interacting with Android Views and Events

Now that you have gone through this introduction to OpenGL ES on Android, you have seen how to draw 3D objects on the screen. Actually, these 3D objects are drawn on a `SurfaceView`, which has all the typical Android attributes found on `View` widgets. We now use these attributes to interact with the rest of the application.

First, we show you how to send information from the OpenGL thread back to the main thread to monitor performance. Then, we give an example of how to forward key events from the main thread to the OpenGL thread to control the animation on the screen.

Figure 17.5   (Left) A red colored cube with texture and (right)
the same cube without red coloring.

Enabling the OpenGL Thread to Talk to the Application Thread

The Android SDK provides a helper class for running code on another thread. The
`Handler` class can allow a piece of code to run on a target thread—the thread that the
`Handler` was instantiated in. For the purpose of this example, you do this within the
`Activity` class:

```
public final Handler mHandler = new Handler();
```

This enables the OpenGL thread to execute code on the `Activity` thread by calling the
`post()` method of the `Handler`. This enables us to act on other `View` objects on the screen
that we can't act on from outside of the `Activity` thread on the OpenGL thread. For this
example, the frame rate of the scene rendered is calculated in the OpenGL thread and
then posted back to the `Activity` thread. Here is a method that does just that:

```
public void calculateAndDisplayFPS() {
    if (showFPS) {
        long thisTime = System.currentTimeMillis();
        if (thisTime - mLastTime < mSkipTime) {
            mFrames++;
        } else {
            mFrames++;
            final long fps =
                mFrames / ((thisTime-mLastTime)/1000);
            mFrames = 0;
```

```
        mLastTime = thisTime;
        mHandler.post(new Runnable() {
            public void run() {
                mFPSText.setText("FPS = " + fps);
            }
        });
    }
  }
}
```

The `calculateAndDisplayFPS()` method is called from within the animation loop of the OpenGL thread. The math is fairly straightforward: the number of frames divided by the duration for those frames in seconds. Then, we take that and post it to the `Handler` for the `Activity` thread by creating a new `Runnable` object that applies a `String` to the `TextView` that holds the current frame rate.

However, doing this every iteration causes the performance to drop substantially. Instead, a counter tracks the number of frames drawn, and we do the calculation and display every time the duration of `mSkipTime` has gone by. A value of 5000ms has worked well to avoid influencing the performance too much by simply measuring the performance. Figure 17.6 shows the display with the frame rate.

Figure 17.6   A textured, lit, shaded cube with the
frame rate displayed.

Enabling the Application Thread to Talk to the OpenGL Thread

Now let's look at the reverse situation. We want the main application thread to communicate with the OpenGL thread. We could use a `Handler` to post code to the OpenGL thread for execution. However, if we are not going to execute any OpenGL code, we aren't required to run it within the OpenGL thread context. Instead, we can add a key event handler to the `SurfaceView` to either speed up or stop the animation within the OpenGL thread.

A `SurfaceView` needs to be the current focus before it receives key events. A couple of method calls configure this:

```
setFocusable(true);
setFocusableInTouchMode(true);
```

Setting focusable for both touch modes enables key events to come in regardless of the mode. Now, within the `SurfaceView`, key event handlers need to be implemented. First, we implement a handler for toggling the frame rate on and off. The following is a sample implementation of the `onKeyDown()` method override:

```
public boolean onKeyDown(int keyCode, KeyEvent event) {
    switch (keyCode) {
        case KeyEvent.KEYCODE_F:
            mGLThread.toggleFPSDisplay();
            return true;
    }
    return super.onKeyDown(keyCode, event);
}
```

When the user presses the F key, a call to the `toggleFPSDisplay()` method of the OpenGL ES thread is made. This merely changes the state of the `boolean` flag and then updates the text field status. The `onKeyDown()` method is called multiple times if the key is held, toggling the display until the key is released. There are multiple methods to prevent this, such as just handling it within `onKeyUp()` or using different keys to enable and disable the state.

The next control we provide to the user is the ability to pause the animation while the P key is held down. Add the following case statement to `onKeyDown()`:

```
case KeyEvent.KEYCODE_P:
    mGLThread.setAnim(false);
    return true;
```

Here, the state is forced to false regardless of how many times `onKeyDown()` is called. Next, an implementation of `onKeyUp()` is needed to resume the animation when the user lifts his finger:

```
public boolean onKeyUp(int keyCode, KeyEvent event) {
    switch (keyCode) {
        case KeyEvent.KEYCODE_P:
            mGLThread.setAnim(true);
```

```
        return true;
    }
    return super.onKeyUp(keyCode, event);
}
```

Again, the value is forced and set to true so that when the user lifts his finger off the key, the animation resumes regardless of the current state. An `if` statement around the inner part of the entire `while()` animation loop can pause the entire rendering in this example.

In these examples, the code does not actually run in the OpenGL thread to change the state of the flags. This is acceptable for the following reasons:

- The values are set in this way exclusively (no concurrency problems).
- The exact state of the flags is unimportant during the loop.
- No calls to OpenGL are made.

The first two reasons mean that we don't have to perform thread synchronization for the functionality to work acceptably and safely. The last reason means that we don't need to create a `Handler` on the OpenGL thread to execute OpenGL calls in the proper thread. There are many circumstances where these aren't met. Discussing thread synchronization is not within the scope of this chapter, however. Standard Java methods are available for doing this, though.

Cleaning Up OpenGL ES

It is necessary for your application to clean up OpenGL when your application is done using it. This happens when the application is quitting or the `Activity` has changed in some way. The recommended process for gracefully shutting down OpenGL is to reset the surface and context, destroy the surface and context you configured, and then terminate the EGL instance. You can do this with the following code:

```
private void cleanupGL() {
    mEGL.eglMakeCurrent(mGLDisplay, EGL10.EGL_NO_SURFACE,
        EGL10.EGL_NO_SURFACE, EGL10.EGL_NO_CONTEXT);
    mEGL.eglDestroySurface(mGLDisplay, mGLSurface);
    mEGL.eglDestroyContext(mGLDisplay, mGLContext);
    mEGL.eglTerminate(mGLDisplay);
}
```

First, `eglMakeCurrent()` removes the surface and context that were used. Next, `eglDestroySurface()` and `eglDestroyContext()` release any resources held by OpenGL for the surface and the context. Finally, OpenGL is terminated through a call to `eglTerminate()`. If OpenGL runs in a separate thread, the thread can now be terminated as well.

It is up to the application to clean up OpenGL properly. There are no helper methods available for managing all of it automatically within the Android lifecycle as there are with `Cursor` objects and the like.

Using GLSurfaceView (Easy OpenGL ES)

Several new classes were introduced with Android 1.5 (API Level 3) that you can use to simplify application OpenGL ES implementation. The GLSurfaceView and GLSurfaceView.Renderer classes effectively require less code to write so that you can focus on the actual GL drawing process instead of the implementation details and upkeep necessary to handle OpenGL ES calls. Essentially, the GLSurfaceView class handles the EGL initialization, threading, and calls in to a user-defined Renderer class. The Renderer class handles the drawing and GL initialization.

Tip

The code examples provided in this section are taken from ShowAndroidGLActivity.java class within the SimpleOpenGL application. The source code for this application is provided for download on the book website.

To use the GLSurfaceView class, you must either extend it or instantiate it directly. Either way, you then need to provide an implementation of a GLSurfaceView.Renderer class. The Renderer class must contain appropriate callbacks for drawing and GL initialization. Additionally, the Activity must pass onPause() and onResume() events on to the GLSurfaceView. The EGL initialization is handled by the GLSurfaceView object, and threading is used to offload the processing away from the main thread.

The following code demonstrates an entire Activity that duplicates the colorful triangle we drew earlier in this chapter, as shown in Figure 17.2:

```
public class AndroidOpenGL extends Activity {
CustomSurfaceView mAndroidSurface = null;

protected void onPause() {
    super.onPause();
    mAndroidSurface.onPause();
}

protected void onResume() {
    super.onResume();
    mAndroidSurface.onResume();
}

protected void onCreate(Bundle savedInstanceState) {
    super.onCreate(savedInstanceState);

    mAndroidSurface = new CustomSurfaceView(this);
    setContentView(mAndroidSurface);
}

private class CustomSurfaceView extends GLSurfaceView {
    final CustomRenderer mRenderer = new CustomRenderer();
```

```java
    public CustomSurfaceView(Context context) {
        super(context);
        setFocusable(true);
        setFocusableInTouchMode(true);
        setRenderer(mRenderer);
    }

    public boolean onKeyDown(int keyCode, KeyEvent event) {
        switch (keyCode) {
        case KeyEvent.KEYCODE_P:
            queueEvent(new Runnable() {
                public void run() {
                    mRenderer.togglePause();
                }
            });
            return true;
        }
        return super.onKeyDown(keyCode, event);
    }
}

private class CustomRenderer implements
    GLSurfaceView.Renderer {
    TriangleSmallGLUT mTriangle = new TriangleSmallGLUT(3);
    boolean fAnimPaused = false;

    public void onDrawFrame(GL10 gl) {
        if (!fAnimPaused) {
            gl.glClear(GL10.GL_COLOR_BUFFER_BIT |
                GL10.GL_DEPTH_BUFFER_BIT);
            gl.glRotatef(1f, 0, 0, 1f);

            if (mTriangle != null) {
                mTriangle.drawColorful(gl);
            }
        }
    }

    public void togglePause() {
        if (fAnimPaused == true) {
            fAnimPaused = false;
        } else {
            fAnimPaused = true;
        }
    }

    public void onSurfaceChanged(GL10 gl, int width,
```

```
        int height) {
        gl.glViewport(0, 0, width, height);

        // configure projection to screen
        gl.glMatrixMode(GL10.GL_PROJECTION);
        gl.glLoadIdentity();
        gl.glClearColor(0.5f, 0.5f, 0.5f, 1);
        float aspect = (float) width / height;
        GLU.gluPerspective(gl, 45.0f, aspect, 1.0f, 30.0f);
    }

    public void onSurfaceCreated(GL10 gl,
        EGLConfig config) {
        gl.glEnableClientState(GL10.GL_VERTEX_ARRAY);

        // configure model space
        gl.glMatrixMode(GL10.GL_MODELVIEW);
        gl.glLoadIdentity();
        GLU.gluLookAt(gl, 0, 0, 10f, 0, 0, 0, 0, 1, 0f);
        gl.glColor4f(1f, 0f, 0f, 1f);
    }
}}
```

As you can see, this code demonstrates creating a new GLSurfaceView and a new
GLSurfaceView.Renderer. The end result, with proper implementation of the triangle
drawing class (included with the book code and discussed earlier in this chapter), is a spinning triangle that the user can pause with the press of the P key. The GLSurfaceView
implementation contains its own renderer, which is less generic than assigning it externally, but with the key handling we implemented. The two classes must work closely
together.

The GLSurfaceView implements key handling by overriding the onKeyDown() method
of the regular View class. The action is passed on to the Renderer through a helper
method called queueEvent(). The queueEvent() method passes the Runnable object on
to the Renderer thread held by the GLSurfaceView.

Next, the Renderer implementation provides the drawing in the onDrawFrame()
method. This is either called continuously or on demand, depending on the render mode
set via a call to the GLSurfaceView.setRenderMode() method. The implementation of
onSurfaceChanged() is now where we set up the screen projection—an appropriate
place because this method is called on orientation or size changes of the surface. Then, in
onSurfaceCreated(), the basic GL configuration is performed, including setting client
states and static data, such as the model view.

All EGL configuration is now performed internally to GLSurfaceView, so the application need not worry about it. If, however, the application needs to perform custom configuration of the EGL, the EGLConfig object is passed to the onSurfaceCreated()
method and is used to perform such custom configuration.

If you choose to use this method to bring up a GL surface on Android, the implementation of the rendering code doesn't need to change at all.

Using OpenGL ES 2.0

Android began supporting Open GL ES 2.0 in Android 2.2 (API Level 8), although applications that leveraged the Android NDK could use 2.0 features as early as API Level 5 with NDK Release 3. In this section, we discuss the Android Java API support for OpenGL ES 2.0. Support also remains for OpenGL ES 1.x, and for good reason. Open GL ES 2.0 is not backward compatible with OpenGL ES 1.x. The different OpenGL ES versions provide different methods of handling 3D graphics:

- OpenGL ES 1.x provides a fixed function rendering and texturing pipeline. That is to say, the math used to transform, light, and color a scene is all the same—fixed functions.
- OpenGL ES 2.0 replaced the fixed functions with vertex and fragment shader programs written, of course, by you, the developer. Writing the shader programs provides much more flexibility, but does incur a bit more overhead on the development side.

The choice of which version of OpenGL ES to use is yours. In this section, we show you how to initialize and get a basic OpenGL ES 2.0 program up and running. Using the NDK method is discussed in Chapter 18.

Tip

Many of the code examples provided in this section are taken from the SimpleOpenGL2 application. The source code for this application is provided for download on the book website.

Configuring Your Application for OpenGL ES 2.0

If you're going to use the Android OpenGL ES 2.0 APIs, and aren't planning on supporting alternate code paths, you need to specify two items within your manifest file: that your application requires Android 2.2 or higher using the `<uses-sdk>` tag and that it requires OpenGL ES 2.0 using the `<uses-feature>` tag.

```
<uses-sdk
    android:targetSdkVersion="8"
    android:minSdkVersion="8" />
<uses-feature
    android:glEsVersion="0x00020000" />
```

Requesting an OpenGL ES 2.0 Surface

Start by creating your custom `SurfaceView`, which you usually do within the `Activity` class `onCreate()` method, as follows:

```
mAndroidSurface = new CustomGL2SurfaceView(this);
setContentView(mAndroidSurface);
```

Of course, you need to implement the `CustomGL2SurfaceView` class. In our sample project, we did this as an inner class of the `Activity`, for convenience:

```
private class CustomGL2SurfaceView extends GLSurfaceView {
    final CustomRenderer renderer;

    public CustomGL2SurfaceView(Context context) {
        super(context);
        setEGLContextClientVersion(2);
        renderer = new CustomRenderer();
        setRenderer(renderer);
    }
}
```

The most important line of code here is the call to the `setEGLContextClientVersion()` method. This call is made in order to request an EGL context for OpenGL ES 1.x (when the parameter is 1) or OpenGL ES 2.x (when the parameter is 2). Then the custom renderer is set.

Although it might seem confusing, the `Renderer` methods take `GL10` objects. How, then, are you to make OpenGL ES 2.0 calls? The answer turns out to be simple: The new `GLES20` class is entirely static. Just ignore the `GL10` parameters and make calls directly to the `GLES20` class.

The `CustomRenderer` class starts out by initializing the vertices, much as we did earlier. Then, when the `onSurfaceCreate()` method is called, we can initialize the shader programs, as follows:

```
@Override
public void onSurfaceCreated(GL10 unused, EGLConfig unused2) {
    try {
        initShaderProgram(R.raw.simple_vertex, R.raw.simple_fragment);
        initialized = true;
    } catch (Exception e) {
        Log.e(DEBUG_TAG, "Failed to init GL");
    }
}
```

The two resource identifiers, `simple_vertex` and `simple_fragment`, simply reference two text files stored as a raw resources. Now, let's look at the initialization of the shaders:

```
private int shaderProgram = 0;
private void initShaderProgram(int vertexId, int fragmentId)
    throws Exception {
    int vertexShader =
        loadAndCompileShader(GLES20.GL_VERTEX_SHADER, vertexId);
    int fragmentShader =
        loadAndCompileShader(GLES20.GL_FRAGMENT_SHADER, fragmentId);
    shaderProgram = GLES20.glCreateProgram();
    if (shaderProgram == 0) {
```

```
        throw new Exception("Failed to create shader program");
    }
    // attach the shaders to the program
    GLES20.glAttachShader(shaderProgram, vertexShader);
    GLES20.glAttachShader(shaderProgram, fragmentShader);
    // bind attribute in our vertex shader
    GLES20.glBindAttribLocation(shaderProgram, 0, "vPosition");
    // link the shaders
    GLES20.glLinkProgram(shaderProgram);
    // check the linker status
    int[] linkerStatus = new int[1];
    GLES20.glGetProgramiv(shaderProgram, GLES20.GL_LINK_STATUS,
        linkerStatus, 0);
    if (GLES20.GL_TRUE != linkerStatus[0]) {
        Log.e(DEBUG_TAG, "Linker Failure: "
            + GLES20.glGetProgramInfoLog(shaderProgram));
        GLES20.glDeleteProgram(shaderProgram);
        throw new Exception("Program linker failed");
    }
    GLES20.glClearColor(0.5f, 0.5f, 0.5f, 1);
}
```

This process does not change substantially for different shaders. Recall that OpenGL ES 2.0 requires both a vertex shader and a fragment shader. First, we load the text for each shader and compile them. Then, we create a new shader program reference, attach both shaders to it, assign an attribute position to our only input parameter, and link the program. Finally, checks are made to confirm that the program linked successfully.

The loading of each shader is handled by our `loadAndCompileShader()` method. Here is a sample implementation of this method:

```
private int loadAndCompileShader(int shaderType, int shaderId)
    throws Exception {
    InputStream inputStream =
        AndroidGL2Activity.this.getResources().openRawResource(shaderId);
    String shaderCode = inputStreamToString(inputStream);
    int shader = GLES20.glCreateShader(shaderType);
    if (shader == 0) {
        throw new Exception("Can't create shader");
    }
    // hand the code over to GL
    GLES20.glShaderSource(shader, shaderCode);
    // compile it
    GLES20.glCompileShader(shader);
    // get compile status
    int[] status = new int[1];
    GLES20.glGetShaderiv(shader, GLES20.GL_COMPILE_STATUS, status, 0);
    if (status[0] == 0) {
```

```
        // failed
        Log.e(DEBUG_TAG, "Compiler Failure: "
            + GLES20.glGetShaderInfoLog(shader));
        GLES20.glDeleteShader(shader);
        throw new Exception("Shader compilation failed");
    }
    return shader;
}
```

The loadAndCompileShader() method reads in the raw resource as a string. Then the
source is handed over to GLES20 via a call to the glShaderSource() method. Finally, the
shader is compiled with a call to glCompileShader(). The result is checked to make sure
the compile was successful. OpenGL ES 2.0 holds the binary results internally so that
they can be used later during linking.

The onSurfaceChanged() method should look quite familiar—it changes little. The
viewport is reconfigured for the new display metrics and then the clear color is set. Note
again that you can simply use the static GLES20 calls rather than the GL10 parameter.

```
@Override
public void onSurfaceChanged(GL10 unused, int width, int height) {
    Log.v(DEBUG_TAG, "onSurfaceChanged");
    GLES20.glViewport(0, 0, width, height);
    GLES20.glClearColor(0.5f, 0.5f, 0.5f, 1);
}
```

Finally, we're ready to render the triangle. The scene is rendered each time the system calls
our onDrawFrame() implementation.

```
@Override
public void onDrawFrame(GL10 unused) {
    if (!initialized) {
        return;
    }
    GLES20.glClear(GLES20.GL_COLOR_BUFFER_BIT);
    GLES20.glUseProgram(shaderProgram);
    GLES20.glVertexAttribPointer(0, 3, GLES20.GL_FLOAT, false, 12,
        verticesBuffer);
    GLES20.glEnableVertexAttribArray(0);
    GLES20.glDrawArrays(GLES20.GL_TRIANGLES, 0, 3);
}
```

At this point, the code should also appear familiar. The primary difference here is the call
to the glUseProgram() method, where we must pass in the numeric identifier of the
program we compiled and linked. The final result is simply a static (motionless) triangle
on the screen. It's not very exciting, considering the amount of code required. The flexibility of the shaders is powerful, but many applications don't need the extra flexibility that
comes with using OpenGL ES 2.0, either.

By now, you might be wondering what the shaders look like. Because the resource system of Android just uses the part of the file name before the extension, we decided to name our shader files very clearly so we could easily tell what they were: simple_vertex.shader and simple_fragment.shader. These are two of the simplest shaders one can define.

First, let's look at the vertex shader because it's first in the pipeline:

```
attribute vec4 vPosition;
void main()
{
    gl_Position = vPosition;
}
```

This has a single input, `vPosition`, which is simply assigned to the output. No transformations are applied, and we're not doing any texturing. Now let's turn our attention to the fragment shader:

```
precision mediump float;
void main()
{
    gl_FragColor = vec4(0.0, 1.0, 0.0, 1.0);
}
```

This shader is even simpler. It's assigning a fixed color to the output. In this case, it's assigning green to the output.

Shader definitions can be quite complex. Implementing lighting, texturing, fog effects, and other interesting OpenGL ES 2.0 features that can't be fashioned using the fixed pipeline of OpenGL ES 1.x is far beyond the scope of this book. However, we'd recommend picking up a book on OpenGL ES 2.0, such as *OpenGL ES 2.0 Programming Guide* by Aaftab Munshi, Dan Gisnburg, and Dave Shreiner (ISBN: 0321502795) or *OpenGL SuperBible* by Richard S. Wright, Jr., Nicholas Haemel, Graham Sellers, and Benjamin Lipchak (ISBN: 0321712617), or finding resources online.

Summary

In this chapter, you learned the basics for using OpenGL ES from within an Android application. You also learned about the different versions of OpenGL ES supported by the Android platform.

You learned about several ways to use OpenGL ES in your Android applications. You learned how to initialize OpenGL ES within its own thread. Then you learned how to draw, color, and light objects using a variety of OpenGL and Android helper methods. You then learned how your application thread and the OpenGL thread can interact with each other. Finally, you learned how to clean up OpenGL.

Creating fully functional 3D applications and games is a vast topic, more than enough to fill entire books. You have learned enough to get started drawing in three dimensions on Android and can use the knowledge to apply general OpenGL concepts to Android. The reference section that follows contains links to more information to help you deepen your OpenGL ES knowledge.

References and More Information

Khronos OpenGL ES Overview:
  http://www.khronos.org/opengles/
OpenGL ES 1.1 API Documentation:
  http://www.khronos.org/opengles/sdk/1.1/docs/man/
OpenGL ES 2.0 API Documentation:
  http://www.khronos.org/opengles/sdk/2.0/docs/man/
OpenGL ES Information:
  http://www.opengl.org

## 18

Using the Android NDK

Although Android applications are primarily written in Java, there are times when developers need or prefer to leverage native C or C++ libraries. The Android Native Development Kit (NDK) provides the tools necessary to include and use native libraries within your Android applications. In this chapter, you learn under what circumstances the Android NDK should be considered, as well as how to configure and use it.

Determining When to Use the Android NDK

Most Android applications are written solely in Java using the Android SDK and run within the Dalvik VM. Most applications run smoothly and efficiently in this fashion. However, there are situations when calling into native code from Java can be preferable. The Android NDK provides tool-chain support for compiling and using native C and C++ libraries in conjunction with your Android Java applications. This is usually done for one of two reasons:

- To perform processor-intensive operations such as complex physics, which can be implemented more efficiently in C and C++, offering substantial performance improvements.
- To leverage existing code, usually in the form of shared or proprietary C or C++ libraries, when porting is not ideal. This is often the case when trying to support multiple platforms with a single code base.

Warning

The native libraries created by the Android NDK can be used only on devices running Android 1.5 and higher. You cannot develop applications that use the Android NDK for older platform versions.

Calling into native code from within Java involves some tradeoffs. Application developers must consider their application design carefully, weighing the benefits of using the NDK versus the drawbacks, which include

- Increased code complexity

- Increased debugging complexity
- Performance overhead for each native code call
- More complex build process
- Developers required to be versed in both Java and C/C++

Although developers cannot write entire applications in C or C++, they can leverage the benefits of these compiled languages from Java when the situation merits. If your application requires complex math, physics, graphics algorithms, or other intensive operations, the Android NDK might be right for your project. Your libraries can take advantage of a number of stable native C and C++ APIs, including

- C library headers (libc)
- Math library headers (libm)
- The zlib compression library headers (libz)
- 3D graphics library headers (OpenGL ES 1.1 and 2.0)
- A cpufeatures library for detecting device cpu features at runtime
- Other headers for C++, logging, JNI, and more

Installing the Android NDK

You can install the Android NDK on Windows, Mac OSX, or Linux operating systems that have the Android SDK and tools properly installed. You also need to install

- GNU Make 3.81 or later (http://www.gnu.org/software/make/)
- GNU Awk (Gawk) or Nawk (http://www.gnu.org/software/gawk/)
- Cygwin 1.7 or later (Windows only, http://www.cygwin.com)

You can download the Android NDK from the Android developer website at http://developer.android.com/sdk/ndk/.

Exploring the Android NDK

The Android NDK contains a number of different tools and files, specifically

- Native system libraries and headers that are forward-compatible with the Android platform (1.5 and beyond)
- Tools for compiling and linking native libraries for ARMv5TE and ARMv7-A devices (x86 coming soon)
- Build files for embedding native libraries into Android applications
- Native debugging using ndk-gdb
- NDK documentation in the /docs subdirectory
- NDK sample applications in the /samples subdirectory

Running an Android NDK Sample Application

The best way to familiarize yourself with the Android NDK is to build one of the sample applications provided, such as hello-jni. To do this, take the following steps:

1. Build the hello-jni native library, located in the NDK `/samples/hello-jni` subdirectory, by typing the following on the command line (within Cygwin on Windows): `ndk-build`.

2. Within Eclipse, import the existing project from the `/samples/hello-jni/project/` subdirectory of the NDK installation directory by choosing New, Android Project and then choosing the Create from Existing Source option. Do a clean build on the project.

3. Create a Debug Configuration for the project.

4. Create an appropriate AVD if necessary. Run the application as normal.

5. If you get errors, you might need to do a "Clean project" within Eclipse after running an `ndk-build clean` and `ndk-build` again. It's not uncommon for Eclipse's state to get out of sync with the build status of the native library.

Creating Your Own NDK Project

Now let's look at an example of how to set up and use the NDK for your own Android applications using Eclipse. To create a new Android application that calls into native code, take the following steps:

1. Begin by creating a new Android Project in Eclipse.

2. Navigate to your project directory and create a subdirectory called `/jni`.

3. Within the `/jni` subdirectory, create a file called `Android.mk`. A sample `Android.mk` file might look like this, the one used in our sample application:

```
LOCAL_PATH := $(call my-dir)
include $(CLEAR_VARS)
LOCAL_LDLIBS := -llog -lGLESv2
LOCAL_MODULE    := simplendk
LOCAL_SRC_FILES := native_basics.c native_opengl2.c
include $(BUILD_SHARED_LIBRARY)
```

4. Edit the `Android.mk` file and make any build changes necessary. By default, only the ARMv5TE instruction set will be targeted. For our sample, this is not necessary. You might want to target a narrower number of handsets, but use ARMv7 code to gain native floating point operations to possibly improve math performance.

5. Build the native library and embed it in your Android application by navigating back to the project directory and running the `ndk-build` script. You might need to set up the path to this batch file; the `ndk-build` script is located in the ndk install directory.

6. In Eclipse, update your application manifest file. Be sure to set the `<uses-sdk>` tag with its `android:minSdkVersion` attribute set to a value of 3 or higher. In our sample, we ultimately add OpenGL ES 2.0, so we've set these to `8`.

7. Create an Eclipse Debug Configuration and any necessary AVDs as normal.

Tip

Many of the code examples provided in this chapter are taken from the SimpleNDK application. The source code for this application is provided for download on the book website.

Calling Native Code from Java

There are three main steps necessary to add a call from Java to native code, as follows:

1. Add a declaration for the new function in your Java class file as a native type.

2. Add a static initializer for the library that the native function will be compiled into.

3. Add the function of the appropriate name, following a very specific naming scheme to the native source file.

This isn't as complex as it sounds, but we go through each step now. The SimpleNDK project has a class called `NativeBasicsActivity.java`. Let's start there by adding the declaration for the native function. The following declaration must be added to the class:

```
private native void basicNativeCall();
```

Now, make sure that the native library with this function is loaded. This doesn't need to happen for every call, just for each library. In the Android.mk file, we identified the library as simplendk, so we load that library. Add this static initializer to the `NativeBasicsActivity` class:

```
static {
    System.loadLibrary("simplendk");
}
```

Finally, the function needs to be added to one of the C files in the native library that's being compiled. Each function must follow a very specific naming convention. Instead of dots, each part of the function name is separated using an underscore, as follows:

```
Java_package_name_ClassName_functionName
(JNIEnv *env, jobject this, your vars...);
```

For the example, that means our function looks like this:

```
void Java_com_androidbook_simplendk_NativeBasicsActivity_basicNativeCall
    (JNIEnv *env, jobject this)
{
    // do something interesting here
}
```

That's a lengthy function name, but you get errors if you name it incorrectly. This function is now called whenever the Java method declared as `basicNativeCall()` is invoked. But how will you know? Add the following line to the function and then make sure to `include "android/log.h"` in the C file:

```
__android_log_print(ANDROID_LOG_VERBOSE, DEBUG_TAG, "Basic call");
```

And there you have it! Your first call from Android Java to C native. If you're familiar with JNI, you might realize that it's mostly the same. The main difference is which libraries are available. If you're familiar with JNI, you should find using the NDK fairly straightforward.

Handling Parameters and Return Values

Now that you can make a basic native call, let's pass some parameters in to C and then return something. We make a simple little C function that takes a format string that works with the `stdio sprintf()` call and two numbers to add. The numbers are added, placed in the format string, and a new string is returned. Although simplistic, this demonstrates the handling of Java objects and reminds us that we need to manage memory properly in native C code.

```c
jstring Java_com_androidbook_simplendk_NativeBasicsActivity_formattedAddition
    (JNIEnv *env, jobject this, jint number1,
    jint number2, jstring formatString)
{
    // get a C string from a Java string object
    jboolean fCopy;
    const char * szFormat =
        (*env)->GetStringUTFChars(env, formatString, &fCopy);
    char * szResult;
    // add the two values
    jlong nSum = number1+number2;
    // make sure there's ample room for nSum
    szResult = malloc(sizeof(szFormat)+30);
    // make the call
    sprintf(szResult, szFormat, nSum);
    // get a Java string object
    jstring result = (*env)->NewStringUTF(env, szResult);

    // free the C strings
    free(szResult);
    (*env)->ReleaseStringUTFChars(env, formatString, szFormat);
    // return the Java string object
    return(result);
}
```

The JNI environment object is used for interacting with Java objects. Regular C functions are used for regular C memory management.

Using Exceptions with Native Code

Native code can throw exceptions that the Java side can catch as well as check for exceptions when making calls to Java code. This makes heavy use of the JNIEnv object and might be familiar to those with JNI experience. The following native function throws an exception if the input number parameter isn't a certain value:

```
void Java_com_androidbook_simplendk_NativeBasicsActivity_throwsException
    (JNIEnv * env, jobject this, jint number)
{
    if (number < NUM_RANGE_MIN || number > NUM_RANGE_MAX) {
        // throw an exception
        jclass illegalArgumentException =
            (*env)->FindClass(env, "java/lang/IllegalArgumentException");
        if (illegalArgumentException == NULL) {
            return;
        }
        (*env)->ThrowNew(env, illegalArgumentException,
            "What an exceptional number.");
    } else {
        __android_log_print(ANDROID_LOG_VERBOSE, DEBUG_TAG,
            "Nothing exceptional here");
    }
}
```

The Java declaration for this, as you might expect, needs a throws clause.

```
private native void throwsException(int num)
    throws IllegalArgumentException;
```

Basically, the exception class is found through reflection. Then, the ThrowNew() method of the JNIEnv object is used to do the actual throwing of the exception.

To show how to check for an exception in native C code, we need to also show how to call a Java method from C. The following block of code does just that:

```
void Java_com_androidbook_simplendk_NativeBasicsActivity_checksException
    (JNIEnv * env, jobject this, jint number)
{
    jthrowable exception;
    jclass class = (*env)->GetObjectClass(env, this);
    jmethodID fnJavaThrowsException =
        (*env)->GetMethodID(env, class, "javaThrowsException", "(I)V");
    if (fnJavaThrowsException != NULL) {
        (*env)->CallVoidMethod(env, this, fnJavaThrowsException, number);
        exception = (*env)->ExceptionOccurred(env);
        if (exception) {
```

```
            (*env)->ExceptionDescribe(env);
            (*env)->ExceptionClear(env);
            __android_log_print(ANDROID_LOG_ERROR,
                DEBUG_TAG, "Exception occurred. Check LogCat.");
        }
    } else {
        __android_log_print(ANDROID_LOG_ERROR,
            DEBUG_TAG, "No method found");
    }
}
```

The call to the `GetMethodID()` function is best looked up in your favorite JNI reference or online. It's basically a reflective way of getting a reference to the method, but the fourth parameter must be supplied correctly. In this case, it takes a single integer and returns a void.

Because the method returns a void, use the `CallVoidMethod()` function to actually call it and then use the `ExceptionOccurred()` function to check to see if the method threw an exception. If it did, the `ExceptionDescribe()` function actually writes the exception out to LogCat, but it looks slightly different from a normal exception output. Then the exception is cleared so it doesn't go any further.

The Java method being called, `javaThrowsException()`, is defined as follows:

```
@SuppressWarnings("unused") // is called from native
private void javaThrowsException(int num)
    throws IllegalArgumentException {
    if (num == 42) {
        throw new IllegalArgumentException("Anything but that number!");
    } else {
        Log.v(DEBUG_TAG, "Good choice in numbers.");
    }
}
```

The use of the `@SuppressWarnings` option is due to the fact that the method is never called directly from Java, only from native code. You can use this process of calling Java methods for Android SDK methods, as well. However, remember that the idea of using NDK is generally to increase performance. If you find yourself doing many Android calls, the performance might be improved by simply staying on the Java side of things and leaving algorithmically heavy functionality on the native side.

Improving Graphics Performance

One of the most common reasons to use the Android NDK is to leverage the OpenGL ES 1.1 and 2.0 native libraries, to perform complex math calculations that would benefit from native code, and speed up the porting process. Although you can use the Java APIs within the Android SDK to provide OpenGL ES support, some developers with core graphics libraries built in C or C++ might prefer to use the NDK. Here are some tips for developing and using graphics libraries provided with the Android NDK:

- OpenGL ES 1.1 native libraries are guaranteed on Android 1.6 (API Level 4) and higher; OpenGL ES 2.0 native libraries are guaranteed on Android 2.0 (API Level 5) and higher. Make sure you include "GLES2/gl2.h" and, optionally, include "GLES2/gl2ext.h" to get access to the functions. They are named in the standard OpenGL way (for example, glClearColor).

- Use the <uses-sdk> manifest tag to enforce the minimum SDK supported by the OpenGL ES version your application leverages.

- Use the <uses-feature> manifest tag to specify which version of OpenGL ES your application leverages so that the Android Market can filter your application and provide it only to compatible devices.

For example, the following block of code is how the drawFrame() method from the OpenGL chapter would look in the NDK. You can find this code in the SimpleNDK project:

```
const GLfloat gVertices[] =  {
    0.0f, 0.5f, 0.0f,
    -0.5f, -0.5f, 0.0f,
    0.5f, -0.5f, 0.0f
};


void Java_com_androidbook_simplendk_NativeOpenGL2Activity_drawFrame
    (JNIEnv * env, jobject this, jint shaderProgram)
{
    glClear(GL_COLOR_BUFFER_BIT);
    glUseProgram(shaderProgram);
    glVertexAttribPointer(0, 3, GL_FLOAT, GL_FALSE, 12, gVertices);
    glEnableVertexAttribArray(0);
    glDrawArrays(GL_TRIANGLES, 0, 3);
}
```

This is called from the onDrawFrame() method of our CustomRenderer class. Because this is the code that runs in a tight loop, it makes sense to implement it with native code. Of course, this particular implementation doesn't benefit at all, but if we had done a bunch of complex math, transformations, and other algorithmically heavy code, it could possibly be faster. Only testing on actual handsets can determine for each case what is or isn't faster, though.

Summary

The Android NDK provides helpful tools that enable developers to call into native C and C++ libraries on devices running Android 1.5 and higher. Installing the Android NDK toolset is a relatively straightforward process. Using the Android NDK involves creating build scripts in order to include shared native libraries within your Android application package files. Although using the Android NDK is not necessary for every application, certain types of applications might benefit greatly from its use.

References and More Information

Android NDK Download Site:
   http://developer.android.com/sdk/ndk/index.html
Google Discussion Group: Android NDK:
   http://groups.google.com/group/android-ndk

19

Using Android's Optional Hardware APIs

The Android Software Development Kit (SDK) provides a variety of application programming interfaces (APIs) for accessing low-level hardware features on the handset. In addition to the camera, Android devices might have a number of other sensors and hardware. Some popular device sensors include the magnetic and orientation sensors, light and temperature sensors, as well as hardware support for Wi-Fi and Bluetooth radios. Applications can also access battery state information. In this chapter, you explore the optional hardware APIs provided as part of the Android SDK.

Interacting with Device Hardware

The Android platform allows unprecedented access to the device's underlying hardware in a secure and robust manner. Because not all Android devices support or contain all hardware options, it is very important to follow these guidelines when accessing underlying device hardware:

- Make no assumptions about the existence or availability of underlying hardware in code or otherwise.
- Always check and verify optional features before trying to access hardware programmatically.
- Pay special attention to exception handling as well as error and return value checking when working with hardware APIs.
- Understand that hardware features are device resources. Acquire them late, and release them as soon as you're done. In other words, play nice with the other apps. Don't hog the hardware or drain the device battery by misusing hardware resources.

Warning

The Android emulator has very limited support for simulating hardware sensors, Wi-Fi, Bluetooth, and the device battery. These are cases when testing on real devices is crucial. Much of the code and APIs discussed in this chapter work only on Android hardware, and do little or nothing in the Android emulator.

The optional hardware features of different Android devices are key market differentiators to consumers. For example, some might want a device that can act as a Wi-Fi hotspot. Others might require Bluetooth. Still others might be interested in the data that can be collected from various sensors on the device. Finally, applications can access data about the battery and the power management state. Also recall that we talked about other hardware-related features, such as the camera and location-based services, in Chapter 14, "Using Location-Based Services (LBS) APIs," and Chapter 15, "Using Android Multimedia APIs," respectively.

Tip

Many of the code examples provided in this chapter are taken from the SimpleHardware application. The source code for this application is provided for download on the book website.

Using the Device Sensor

The Android SDK provides access to raw data from sensors on the device. The sensors, and their precision and features, will vary from device to device. Some of the sensors that applications can interact with include the magnetic sensor, which can be used as a compass, and the accelerometer sensor that can detect motion.

You can access the device sensors through the `SensorManager` object (`android.hardware.SensorManager`). The `SensorManager` object listens for data from the sensors. It is a system service, and you can retrieve an instance retrieved with the `getSystemService()` method, as shown here:

```
SensorManager sensors =
    (SensorManager) getSystemService(Context.SENSOR_SERVICE);
```

Working with Different Sensors

The `Sensor` class (`android.hardware.Sensor`) defines a number of identifiers for the various sensors that you might find on a device. Not all sensors are available on each device. The most interesting sensors are listed here:

- `TYPE_ACCELEROMETER`: Measures acceleration in three directions (values are SI units (m/s^2))

- `TYPE_GYROSCOPE`: Measures angular orientation in three directions (values are angles in degrees)

- `TYPE_ORIENTATION`: Measures orientation in three directions (values are angles in degrees) (deprecated)

- **TYPE_LIGHT**: Measures ambient light (values are SI lux units)
- **TYPE_MAGNETIC_FIELD**: Measures magnetism in three directions; the compass (values are micro-Tesla (uT))
- **TYPE_PRESSURE**: Measures barometric pressure
- **TYPE_PROXIMITY**: Measures the distance to an object (values in centimeters, or "near" vs. "far")
- **TYPE_TEMPERATURE**: Measures temperature

The `SensorManager` class also has a number of constants that can be useful with certain sensors. For instance, you can use the `STANDARD_GRAVITY` constant with the accelerometer and the `LIGHT_SUNLIGHT` constant with the light sensor.

Tip

Not all sensors are available on all devices. For instance, the HTC Evo 4G Android handset has an accelerometer, magnetic sensor, and proximity sensor, but no temperature, pressure, or gyroscope sensors.

Unfortunately, the emulator does not provide any sensor data. All sensor testing must be done on a physical device. Alternatively, OpenIntents.org also provides a handy Sensor Simulator (http://code.google.com/p/openintents/wiki/SensorSimulator). This tool simulates accelerometer, compass, and temperature sensors and transmits data to the emulator.

Acquiring Access to a Sensor

You can acquire access to a specific sensor using the `SensorManager` class method called `getDefaultSensor()`. This method takes a sensor type parameter. For example, you could acquire the default accelerometer sensor as follows:

```
Sensor accelSensor = sensors.getDefaultSensor(Sensor.TYPE_ACCELEROMETER);
```

Reading Sensor Data

After you have a valid `Sensor` object, you can read the sensor data periodically. Sensor values are sent back to an application using a `SensorEventListener` object that the application must implement and register using the `registerListener()` method.

```
boolean isAvailable = sensors.registerListener(SensorsActivity.this,
    accelSensor, SensorManager.SENSOR_DELAY_NORMAL);
```

In this case, the accelerometer sensor is watched. The `onSensorChanged()` method is called at particular intervals defined by the delay value in `registerListener()`, which is the default value in this case.

The `SensorEventListener` interface has two required methods you must implement: `onAccuracyChanged()` and `onSensorChanged()`. The `onAccuracyChanged()` method is called whenever the accuracy of a given sensor changes. The `onSensorChanged()` method is called whenever the values of the sensor change. The `onSensorChanged()` method is generally used to inspect sensor information.

Here is a sample implementation of onSensorChanged() that works for displaying various types of sensor data (not just the accelerometer):

```
@Override
public void onSensorChanged(SensorEvent event) {
    StringBuilder sensorMessage =
        new StringBuilder(event.sensor.getName()).append(" new values: ");

    for (float value : event.values) {
        sensorMessage.append("[").append(value).append("]");
    }

    sensorMessage.append(" with accuracy ").append(event.accuracy);
    sensorMessage.append(" at timestamp ").append(event.timestamp);

    sensorMessage.append(".");

    Log.i(DEBUG_TAG, sensorMessage);
}
```

The onSensorChanged() method has a single parameter: a SensorEvent object. The SensorEvent class contains all the data about the sensor, including which sensor caused the event, the accuracy of the sensor, the sensor's current readings and a timestamp. For details about what data to expect for each type of sensor, see the SensorEvent class documentation provided with the Android SDK.

The accelerometer sensor provides three values corresponding to the acceleration minus Gravity on the x, y, and z axes. Output from a typical Android device with an accelerometer sensor is shown in Figure 19.1.

Warning

Depending on the sensor in use, the rate of sensor data might be very high. Be aware that your application should do as little as possible within the onSensorChanged() method.

Calibrating Sensors

The sensor values won't be useful to the application until they are calibrated. One way to calibrate is to ask the user to click a button to calibrate the sensor. The application can then store the current values. Then new values can be compared against the original values to see how they have changed from their original values (delta). Although the phone sensors have a specific orientation, this enables the user to use the app in either portrait or landscape mode, regardless of how the user is holding the device.

When registering a sensor, the registerListener() method returns true if the sensor is available and can be activated. It returns false if the sensor isn't available or cannot be activated.

The sensor values are typically quite sensitive. For most uses, an application probably wants to provide some smoothing of the values to reduce the effects of any noise or shaking. How this is done depends on the purpose of the application. For instance, a simulated bubble level might need less smoothing than a game where too much sensitivity can be frustrating.

Figure 19.1   Sensor sample application
showing accelerometer values.

The orientation values might be appropriate in cases where only the handset's orientation is needed but not the rate at which it is changed (accelerometer) or specific direction it's pointing (compass).

Determining Device Orientation

You can use the `SensorManager` class to determine the orientation of the device. Although the `Sensor.TYPE_ORIENTATION` sensor value is deprecated, it is still valid on most popular devices. However, the newest recommended way is to use the `getOrientation()` method of the `SensorManager` class instead.

Note

We say newest way because the recommended method for determining device orientation has changed several times since Android was initially developed.

The `getOrientation()` method takes two parameters: a rotation matrix and an array of three float values (azimuth [z], pitch [x], and roll [y]).

Finding True North

In addition to the `SensorManager`, there is a helpful class called `GeomagneticField` available within the `android.hardware` package. The `GeomagneticField` class uses the World Magnetic Model to estimate the magnetic field anywhere on the planet, which is typically used to determine magnetic variation between compass north and true north. This model, developed by the United States National Geospatial-Intelligence Agency (NGA), is updated for precision every five years. This model expires in 2015, although results will be accurate enough for most purposes for some time after that date, at which point the Android `GeomagneticField` class will likely be updated to the latest model.

Working with Wi-Fi

The Wi-Fi sensor can read network status and determine nearby wireless access points. The Android SDK provides a set of APIs for retrieving information about the Wi-Fi networks available to the device and Wi-Fi network connection details. These APIs are separate from the `SensorManager` APIs. This information can be used for tracking signal strength, finding access points of interest, or performing actions when connected to specific access points. This section describes how to get Wi-Fi information. However, if you are looking for information on networking, that is more thoroughly discussed as part of Chapter 12, "Using Android Networking APIs."

The following samples require two explicit permissions in the `AndroidManifest.xml` file. The `CHANGE_WIFI_STATE` permission is needed when an application is accessing information about Wi-Fi networks that can turn on the Wi-Fi radio, thus changing its state. The `ACCESS_WIFI_STATE` permission is needed, as well, to request any information from the Wi-Fi device. You can add these to the `AndroidManifest.xml` file as follows:

```
<uses-permission
    android:name="android.permission.CHANGE_WIFI_STATE" />
<uses-permission
    android:name="android.permission.ACCESS_WIFI_STATE" />
```

The next thing the application needs is an instance of the `WifiManager` object. It is a system service, so the `getSystemService()` method works.

```
WifiManager wifi =
    (WifiManager) getSystemService(Context.WIFI_SERVICE);
```

Now that the `WifiManager` object is available, the application can do something interesting or useful with it. First, the application performs a Wi-Fi scan to see what access points are available in the local area. You need to complete a few steps to perform a scan:

1. Start the scan with the `startScan()` method of the `WifiManager` object.

2. Register a `BroadcastReceiver` for the `SCAN_RESULTS_AVAILABLE` Intent.

3. Call `getScanResults()` to get a list of `ScanResult` objects.

4. Iterate over the results and do something with them.

You can perform the first two steps with the following code:

```
wifi.startScan();

registerReceiver(rcvWifiScan,
    new IntentFilter(WifiManager.SCAN_RESULTS_AVAILABLE_ACTION));
```

The sample `BroadcastReceiver` object, shown here, performs the last two steps. It is called regularly until the `stopScan()` method is called on the `WifiManager` object.

```
rcvWifiScan = new BroadcastReceiver() {

    public void onReceive(Context context, Intent intent) {
        List<ScanResult> resultList = wifi.getScanResults();
        int foundCount = resultList.size();

        Toast.makeText(WiFi.this,
            "Scan done, " + foundCount + " found",
            Toast.LENGTH_SHORT).show();
        ListIterator<ScanResult> results = resultList.listIterator();
        String fullInfo = "Scan Results : \n";
        while (results.hasNext()) {
            ScanResult info = results.next();
            String wifiInfo = "Name: " + info.SSID +
                "; capabilities = " + info.capabilities +
                "; sig str = " + info.level + "dBm";

            Log.v("WiFi", wifiInfo);

            fullInfo += wifiInfo + "\n";
        }

        status.setText(fullInfo);
    }
};
```

The `ScanResult` object contains a few more fields than demonstrated here. However, the `SSID`, or name, property is probably the most recognizable to users. The `capabilities` property lists such things as what security model can be used (such as "WEP"). The signal strength (`level`), as given, isn't all that descriptive for most users.

However, the `WifiManager` object provides a couple of helper methods for dealing with signal levels. The first is the `calculateSignalLevel()` that effectively turns the number into a particular number of "bars" of strength. You can use the second, `compareSignalLevel()`, to compare the relative signal strengths of two results.

Note

The emulator does not provide Wi-Fi emulation but the `WifiManager` APIs do work. However, there are not any results when you use them. Perform testing of Wi-Fi APIs on actual hardware that has a functional Wi-Fi radio.

You can use the `WifiManager` object to list known access points. These are typically access points that the user has configured or connected to in the past. The following code demonstrates the use of the `getConfiguredNetworks()` method:

```
ListIterator<WifiConfiguration> configs =
    wifi.getConfiguredNetworks().listIterator();

String allConfigs = "Configs: \n";
while (configs.hasNext()) {
    WifiConfiguration config = configs.next();
    String configInfo = "Name: " + config.SSID +
        "; priority = " + config.priority;

    Log.v("WiFi", configInfo);

    allConfigs += configInfo + "\n";
}

status.setText(allConfigs);
```

The returned `WifiConfiguration` object does not include all the fields that it could. For instance, it does not fill any network key fields. It does, however, fill in similar fields to those found in the `ScanResults` object. This could be used, for instance, to notify the users when they are in range of known Wi-Fi networks if their devices are set to not automatically connect.

You can use the `WifiManager` object to configure Wi-Fi networks, get the state of the Wi-Fi radio, and more. See the `android.net.wifi` package for more information.

Working with Bluetooth

Bluetooth APIs were made available as part of the Android 2.0 SDK. Clearly, that means that not all Android devices have Bluetooth hardware. However, this is a popular consumer feature that Android developers can use to their advantage. When Bluetooth hardware is present, Android applications can

- Scan for and discover Bluetooth devices and interact with the Bluetooth adapter.
- Establish RFCOMM connections and transfer data to and from devices via data streams.
- Maintain point-to-point and multipoint connections with Bluetooth devices and manage multiple connections.

The Bluetooth APIs are part of the `android.bluetooth` package. As you might expect, the application must have permission to use the Bluetooth services. The `android.permission.BLUETOOTH` permission is required to connect to Bluetooth devices. Similarly, Android applications must have the `android.permission.BLUETOOTH_ADMIN` permission in order to administer Bluetooth hardware and related services, including tasks enabling or disabling the hardware and performing discovery scans.

The Bluetooth APIs are divided into several useful classes, including

- The `BluetoothAdapter` class represents the Bluetooth radio hardware on the local device.

- The `BluetoothDevice` class represents a remote Bluetooth device.

- The `BluetoothServerSocket` class is used to open a socket to listen for incoming connections and provides a `BluetoothSocket` object when a connection is made.

- The `BluetoothSocket` class is used by the client to establish a connection to a re-mote device. After the device is connected, `BluetoothSocket` object is used by both sides to handle the connection and retrieve the input and output streams.

Checking for the Existence of Bluetooth Hardware

The first thing to do when trying to enable Bluetooth functionality within your applica-tion is to establish whether or not the device has a Bluetooth radio. You can do this by calling and checking the return value of the `BluetoothAdapter` class's static method called `getDefaultAdapter()`.

```
BluetoothAdapter btAdapter = BluetoothAdapter.getDefaultAdapter();
if (btAdapter == null) {
    Log.d(DEBUG_TAG, "No bluetooth available.");
    // ...
} else {
    // bt available
}
```

Enabling Bluetooth

After you have determined that the device has a Bluetooth radio, you need to check to see if it is enabled using the `BluetoothAdapter` class method called `isEnabled()`. If the Bluetooth adapter is enabled, you can proceed. Otherwise, you need to request that it is turned on. This can be done in several ways:

- Fire off the `BluetoothAdapter.ACTION_REQUEST_ENABLE` Intent using the `startActivityForResult()` method. This launches an `Activity` that enables the user to choose to turn on the Bluetooth adapter. If the result is `RESULT_OK`, then Bluetooth has been enabled; otherwise, the user canceled the Bluetooth-enabling process.

- Call the `BluetoothAdapter enable()` method. This method should only be used by applications that need to explicitly enable the Bluetooth radio and requires the `BLUETOOTH_ADMIN` permission. In addition, it should only be performed as the result of a direct request from the user, such as through a button, menu item, and query dialog.

- The process of making an Android device discoverable also automatically enables Bluetooth. This can be achieved by firing off the `BluetoothAdapter.ACTION_REQUEST_DISCOVERABLE` Intent using the `startActivityForResult()` method. This launches an `Activity` that presents the user with a choice to make their device discoverable for a set amount of time.

Querying for Paired Devices

You can use the `BluetoothAdapter` to query for available Bluetooth devices to connect to. The `getBondedDevices()` method returns a set of `BluetoothDevice` objects that represent the devices paired to the Bluetooth adapter.

```
Set<BluetoothDevice> pairedBtDevices = btAdapt.getBondedDevices();
```

Discovering Devices

New Bluetooth devices must be discovered and paired to the adapter before use. You can use the `BluetoothAdapter` to start and stop the discovery process for available Bluetooth devices to connect to. The `startDiscovery()` method starts the discovery process asynchronously. This method requires the `android.permission.BLUETOOTH_ADMIN` permission.

After you have initiated the discovery process, your application needs to register to receive broadcasts for the following Intents:

- `ACTION_DISCOVERY_STARTED`: Occurs when the discovery process initiates
- `ACTION_FOUND`: Occurs each time a remote Bluetooth device is found
- `ACTION_DISCOVERY_FINISHED`: Occurs when the discovery process completes

The discovery process is resource and time-intensive. You can use the `isDiscovering()` method to test if the discovery process is currently underway. The `cancelDiscovery()` method can be used to stop the discovery process. This method should also be used any time a connection is about to be established with a remote Bluetooth device.

Establishing Connections Between Devices

The general idea behind connecting two devices via Bluetooth is for one device to find the other device via whatever means necessary, depending upon whether it be a previously paired device or found through discovery. After it's found, the device calls the `connect()` method. Both devices then have a valid `BluetoothSocket` object that can be used to retrieve the `InputStream` and `OutputStream` objects for initiating data communications between the two devices.

Now, that's where the theory ends and reality sets in. If it's the same application running on both devices, as it usually is, this means both devices should find a remote device and both should be discoverable so they can also be found, as well as open a listening socket via the `BluetoothServerSocket` object so they can receive incoming connection requests, and be able to connect to the other device. Add to that the fact that both the calls to the `accept()` method of the `BluetoothServerSocket` class and to the `connect()` method of the `BluetoothSocket` class are blocking synchronous calls, and you can quickly see you need to use some threads here. Discovery also uses a fair amount of the Bluetooth hardware resources, so you need to cancel and then later restart this process as appropriate. Performing discovery during a connection or even while attempting a connection likely leads to negative device performance.

Tip

The short code listings provided in the Bluetooth section are taken from the SimpleBluetooth application. The full source code for this application is provided for download on the book website. The code required to establish and maintain connections between two devices is very lengthy. Therefore, we have chosen to discuss it broadly here and not to include full Bluetooth code listings in this section. Instead, please consult the sample project for a complete implementation of Bluetooth, including the ability to cause one device to make a "ping" sound (sonar style) on the other device.

Figure 19.2 shows a reasonable layout for a Bluetooth implementation, as well as labeling the threads used within the SimpleBluetooth project.

Monitoring the Battery

Mobile devices operate with the use of the battery. Although many applications do not need to know the state of the battery, some types of applications might want to change their behavior based on the battery level, charging state or power management settings. For instance, a monitoring application can reduce the monitoring frequency when the battery is low and can increase it if the handset is powered by an external power source. The battery levels could also monitor the efficiency of an application and find areas where behavior can be modified to improve battery life, which is appreciated by users.

To monitor the battery, the application must have the `BATTERY_STATS` permission. The following XML added to the `AndroidManifest.xml` file is sufficient:

```
<uses-permission
    android:name="android.permission.BATTERY_STATS" />
```

Then the application needs to register for a particular `BroadcastIntent`. In this case, it must be `Intent.ACTION_BATTERY_CHANGED`. The following code demonstrates this:

```
registerReceiver(batteryRcv,
    new IntentFilter(Intent.ACTION_BATTERY_CHANGED));
```

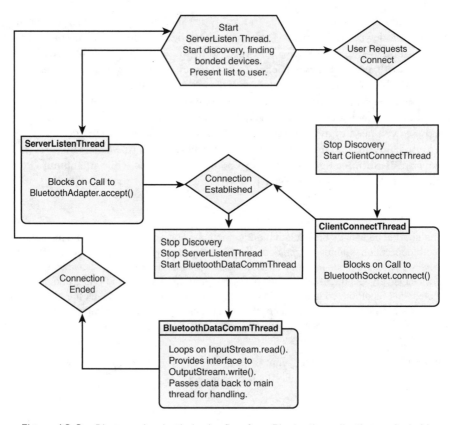

Figure 19.2   Diagram showing behavior flow for a Bluetooth application on Android.

Next, the application needs to provide an implementation of the `BroadcastReceiver`.
The following is an example of a `BroadcastReceiver`:

```
batteryRcv = new BroadcastReceiver() {

    public void onReceive(Context context, Intent intent) {
        int level =
            intent.getIntExtra(BatteryManager.EXTRA_LEVEL, -1);
        int maxValue =
            intent.getIntExtra(BatteryManager.EXTRA_SCALE, -1);
        int batteryStatus =
            intent.getIntExtra(BatteryManager.EXTRA_STATUS, -1);
        int batteryHealth =
            intent.getIntExtra(BatteryManager.EXTRA_HEALTH, -1);
        int batteryPlugged =
            intent.getIntExtra(BatteryManager.EXTRA_PLUGGED, -1);
```

```
String batteryTech =
    intent.getStringExtra(BatteryManager.EXTRA_TECHNOLOGY);
int batteryIcon =
    intent.getIntExtra(BatteryManager.EXTRA_ICON_SMALL, -1);
float batteryVoltage =
    (float) intent.getIntExtra(BatteryManager.EXTRA_VOLTAGE,
        -1) / 1000;
boolean battery =
    intent.getBooleanExtra(BatteryManager.EXTRA_PRESENT,
        false);
float batteryTemp =
    (float) intent.getIntExtra(
        BatteryManager.EXTRA_TEMPERATURE, -1) / 10;
int chargedPct = (level * 100)/maxValue ;

String batteryInfo = "Battery Info:\nHealth=" +
    (String)healthValueMap.get(batteryHealth)+"\n" +
    "Status="+(String)statusValueMap.get(batteryStatus)+"\n" +
    "Charged % = "+chargedPct+"%\n"+
    "Plugged = " + pluggedValueMap.get(batteryPlugged) + "\n" +
    "Type = " + batteryTech + "\n"         +
    "Voltage = " + batteryVoltage + " volts\n" +
    "Temperature = " + batteryTemp + "°C\n"+
    "Battery present = " + battery + "\n";

status.setText(batteryInfo);
icon.setImageResource(batteryIcon);

Toast.makeText(Battery.this, "Battery state changed",
    Toast.LENGTH_LONG).show();
    }

};
```

There are a couple of interesting items here. First, notice that the battery level isn't used
directly. Instead, it's used with the scale, or maximum value, to find the percentage
charged. The raw value wouldn't have much meaning to the user. The next property is the
status. The values and what they mean are defined in the `android.os.BatteryManager`
object. This is typically the charging state of the battery. Next, the health of the battery,
also defined in the `android.os.BatteryManager` object, is an indication of how worn
out the battery is. It can also indicate other issues, such as overheating. Additionally, the
plugged value indicates whether the device is plugged in and, if it is, whether it is using
AC or USB power.

Warning

On specific devices, not all this information might be available or accurate. For instance, even though we see good data for most fields, we have noted in several instances that devices are returning false for the `present` field. Proper testing might be required before relying on battery data for a particular device.

Some other information is returned as well, including an icon identifier that can visually display the state of the battery and some technical details, such as the type of battery, current voltage, and temperature. All displayed, this information looks something like what is shown in Figure 19.3.

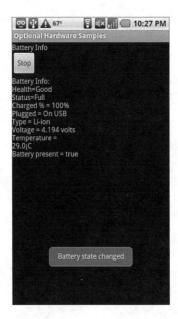

Figure 19.3   Screen capture showing values
from the battery monitor from a physical handset.

Tip

Testing of the battery information can be partially done with the emulator. See Appendix A, "The Android Emulator Quick-Start Guide," for more information on the power controls.

Summary

Unlike many other mobile platforms, Android allows complete access to the underlying hardware on the device, including the capability to read raw device sensor data, use built-in Wi-Fi and Bluetooth hardware and services, and monitor battery usage. It is important to remember that different devices have different underlying hardware. Always verify the functionality available on each target phone platform during the planning stage of your Android project.

References and More Information

Android API Reference: Sensor Data Details:
   http://developer.android.com/reference/android/hardware/SensorEvent.html#values
NOAA: World Magnetic Model:
   http://www.ngdc.noaa.gov/geomag/WMM/DoDWMM.shtml
Android Dev Guide: Bluetooth:
   http://developer.android.com/guide/topics/wireless/bluetooth.html
Android Sample Application: Bluetooth Chat:
   http://developer.android.com/resources/samples/BluetoothChat/index.html

## 20

Working with Notifications

Applications often need to communicate with the user even when the application isn't actively running. Applications can alert users with text notifications, vibration, blinking lights, and even audio. In this chapter, you learn how to build different kinds of notifications into your Android applications.

Notifying the User

Applications can use notifications to greatly improve the user's experience. For example:

- An email application might notify a user when new messages arrive. A news reader application might notify a user when there are new articles to read.
- A game might notify a user when a friend has signed in, or sent an invitation to play, or beat a high score.
- A weather application might notify a user of special weather alerts.
- A stock market application might notify the user when certain stock price targets are met. (Sell now! Before it's too late!)

Users appreciate these notifications because they help drive application workflow, reminding the users when they need to launch the application. However, there is a fine line between just enough and too many notifications. Application designers need to consider carefully how they should employ the use of notifications so as not to annoy the user or interrupt them without good reason. Each notification should be appropriate for the specific application and the event the user is being notified of. For example, an application should not put out an emergency style notification (think flashing lights, ringing noises, and generally making a "to-do") simply to notify the user that his picture has been uploaded to a website or that new content has been downloaded.

The Android platform provides a number of different ways of notifying the user. Notifications are often displayed on the status bar at the top of the screen. Notifications may involve

- Textual information
- Graphical indicators
- Sound indicators
- Vibration of the device
- Control over the indicator light

Warning

Although the Android SDK provides APIs for creating a variety of notifications, not all notifications are supported by all devices. For example, the indicator light and vibrate features
are not available on all Android devices. There is also a degree of variation between how different devices handle notifications. Always test any notification implementations on target
devices.

Now let's look at how to use these different kinds of notifications within your
application.

Notifying with the Status Bar

The standard location for displaying notifications and indicators on an Android device is
the status bar that runs along the top of the screen. Typically, the status bar shows information such as the current date and time. It also displays notifications (like incoming SMS
messages) as they arrive—in short form along the bar and in full if the user pulls down the
status bar to see the notification list. The user can clear the notifications by pulling down
the status bar and hitting the Clear button.

Developers can enhance their applications by using notifications from their applications
to inform the user of important events. For example, an application might want to send a
simple notification to the user whenever new content has been downloaded. A simple
notification has a number of important components:

- An icon (appears on status bar and full notification)
- Ticker text (appears on status bar)
- Notification title text (appears in full notification)
- Notification body text (appears in full notification)
- An intent (launches if the user clicks on the full notification)

In this section, you learn how to create this basic kind of notification.

Tip

Many of the code examples provided in this chapter are taken from the SimpleNotifica-
tions application. The source code for this application is provided for download on the
book website.

Using the `NotificationManager` Service

All notifications are created with the help of the `NotificationManager`. The `NotificationManager` (within the `android.app` package) is a system service that must be requested. The following code demonstrates how to obtain a valid `NotificationManager` object using the `getSystemService()` method:

```
NotificationManager notifier = (NotificationManager)
    getSystemService(Context.NOTIFICATION_SERVICE);
```

The `NotificationManager` is not useful without having a valid `Notification` object to use with the `notify()` method. The `Notification` object defines what information displays to the user when the `Notification` is triggered. This includes text that displays on the status bar, a couple of lines of text that display on the expanded status bar, an icon displayed in both places, a count of the number of times this `Notification` has been triggered, and a time for when the last event that caused this `Notification` took place.

Creating a Simple Text Notification with an Icon

You can set the icon and ticker text, both of which display on the status bar, through the constructor for the `Notification` object, as follows:

```
Notification notify = new Notification(
    R.drawable.android_32, "Hello!", System.currentTimeMillis());
```

Additionally, you can set notification information through public member variable assignment, like this:

```
notify.icon = R.drawable.android_32;
notify.tickerText = "Hello!";
notify.when = System.currentTimeMillis();
```

You need to set a couple more pieces of information before the call to the `notify()` method takes place. First, we need to make a call to the `setLastEventInfo()` method, which configures a `View` that displays in the expanded status bar. Here is an example:

```
Intent toLaunch = new Intent
    (SimpleNotificationsActivity.this,
    SimpleNotificationsActivity.class);
PendingIntent intentBack = PendingIntent.getActivity
    (SimpleNotificationsActivity.this, 0, toLaunch, 0);

notify.setLatestEventInfo(SimpleNotificationsActivity.this,
    "Hi there!", "This is even more text.", intentBack);
```

Next, use the `notify()` method to supply the notification's title and body text as well as the `Intent` triggered when the user clicks on the notification. In this case, we're using our own `Activity` so that when the user clicks on the notification, our `Activity` launches again.

Note

When the expanded status bar is pulled down, the current `Activity` lifecycle is still treated as if it were the top (displayed) `Activity`. Triggering system notifications while running in the foreground, though, isn't particularly useful. An application that is in the foreground would be better suited using a `Dialog` or `Toast` to notify the user, not by using notifications.

Working with the Notification Queue

Now the application is ready to actually notify the user of the event. All that is needed is a call to the `notify()` method of the `NotificationManager` with an identifier and the `Notification` we configured. This is demonstrated with the following code:

```
private static final int NOTIFY_1 = 0x1001;
// ...
notifier.notify(NOTIFY_1, notify);
```

The identifier matches up a `Notification` with any previous `Notification` instances of that type. When the identifiers match, the old `Notification` is updated instead of creating a new one. You might have a `Notification` that some file is being downloaded. You could update the `Notification` when the download is complete, instead of filling the `Notification` queue with a separate `Notification`, which quickly becomes obsolete. This `Notification` identifier only needs to be unique within your application.

The notification displays as an icon and ticker text showing up on the status bar. This is shown at the top of Figure 20.1.

Figure 20.1   Status bar notification showing
an icon and ticker text.

Shortly after the ticker text displays, the status bar returns to normal with each notification icon shown. If the users expand the status bar, they see something like what is shown in Figure 20.2.

Figure 20.2   Expanded status bar showing
the icon, both text fields, and the time
of the notification.

Updating Notifications

You don't want your application's notifications piling up in the notification bar. Therefore, you might want to reuse or update notifications to keep the notification list manageable. For example, there is no reason to keep a notification informing the user that the application is downloading File X when you now want to send another notification saying File X has finished downloading. Instead, you can simply update the first notification with new information.

When the notification identifiers match, the old notification is updated. When a notification with matching identifier is posted, the ticker text does not draw a second time. To show the user that something has changed, you can use a counter. The value of the number member variable of the Notification object tracks and displays this. For instance, we can set it to the number 4, as shown here:

```
notify.number = 4;
```

This is displayed to the user as a small number over the icon. This is only displayed in the status bar and not in the expanded status bar, although an application could update the text to also display this information. Figure 20.3 shows what this might look like in the status bar.

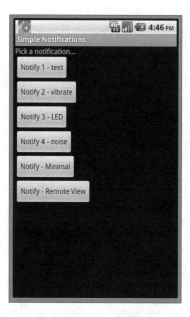

Figure 20.3   Status bar notification with the count of "4" showing over the icon.

Clearing Notifications

When a user clicks on the notification, the Intent assigned is triggered. At some point after this, the application might want to clear the notification from the system notifications queue. This is done through a call to the cancel() method of the NotificationManager object. For instance, the notification we created earlier could be canceled with the following call:

```
notifier.cancel(NOTIFY_1);
```

This cancels the notification that has the same identifier. However, if the application doesn't care what the user does after clicking on the notification, there is an easier way to cancel notifications. Simply set a flag to do so, as shown here:

```
notify.flags |= Notification.FLAG_AUTO_CANCEL;
```

Setting the Notification.FLAG_AUTO_CANCEL flag causes notifications to be canceled when the user clicks on them. This is convenient and easy for the application when just launching the Intent is good enough.

The Notification object is a little different from other Android objects you might have encountered. Most of the interaction with it is through direct access to its public variables instead of through helper methods. This is useful for a background application or service, discussed in Chapter 21, "Working with Services." The Notification object can be kept around and only the values that need to be changed can be modified. After any change, the Notification needs to be posted again by calling the notify() method.

Vibrating the Phone

Vibration is a great way to enable notifications to catch the attention of a user in noisy environments or alert the user when visible and audible alerts are not appropriate (though a vibrating phone is often noisy on a hard desktop surface). Android notifications give a fine level of control over how vibration is performed. However, before the application can use vibration with a notification, an explicit permission is needed. The following XML within your application's AndroidManifest.xml file is required to use vibration:

```
<uses-permission
    android:name="android.permission.VIBRATE" />
```

Warning

The vibrate feature must be tested on the handset. The emulator does not indicate vibration in any way. Also, some Android devices do not support vibration.

Without this permission, the vibrate functionality will not work nor will there be any error. With this permission enabled, the application is free to vibrate the phone however it wants. This is accomplished by describing the vibrate member variable, which determines the vibration pattern. An array of long values describes the vibration duration. Thus, the following line of code enabled a simple vibration pattern that occurs whenever the notification is triggered:

```
notify.vibrate = new long[] {0, 200, 200, 600, 600};
```

This vibration pattern vibrates for 200 milliseconds and then stops vibrating for 200 milliseconds. After that, it vibrates for 600 milliseconds and then stops for that long. To repeat the Notification alert, a notification flag can be set so it doesn't stop until the user clears the notification.

```
notify.flags |= Notification.FLAG_INSISTENT;
```

An application can use different patterns of vibrations to alert the user to different types of events or even present counts. For instance, think about a grandfather clock with which you can deduce the time based on the tones that are played.

Tip

Using short, unique patterns of vibration can be useful, and users become accustomed to them.

Blinking the Lights

Blinking lights are a great way to pass information silently to the user when other forms of alert are not appropriate. The Android SDK provides reasonable control over a multi-colored indicator light, when such a light is available on the device. Users might recognize this light as a service indicator or battery level warning. An application can take advantage of this light as well, by changing the blinking rate or color of the light.

Warning

Indicator lights are not available on all Android devices. Also, the emulator does not display the light's state. This mandates testing on actual hardware.

You must set a flag on the `Notification` object to use the indicator light. Then, the color of the light must be set and information about how it should blink. The following block of code configures the indicator light to shine green and blink at rate of 1 second on and 1 second off:

```
notify.flags |= Notification.FLAG_SHOW_LIGHTS;


notify.ledARGB = Color.GREEN;
notify.ledOnMS = 1000;
notify.ledOffMS = 1000;
```

Although you can set arbitrary color values, a typical physical implementation of the indicator light has three small LEDs in red, green, and blue. Although the colors blend reasonably well, they won't be as accurate as the colors on the screen. For instance, on the T-Mobile G1, the color white looks a tad pink.

Warning

On some devices, certain notifications appear to take precedence when it comes to using the indicator light. For instance, the light on the T-Mobile G1 is always solid green when plugged in to a USB port, regardless of other applications are trying to use the indicator light. Additionally, on the Nexus One, the color trackball is not lit unless the screen is off. You must unplug the phone from the USB port for the colors to change.

An application can use different colors and different blinking rates to indicate different information to the user. For instance, the more times an event occurs, the more urgent the indicator light could be. The following block of code shows changing the light based on the number of notifications that have been triggered:

```
notify.number++;
notify.flags |= Notification.FLAG_SHOW_LIGHTS;

if (notify.number < 2) {
    notify.ledARGB = Color.GREEN;
    notify.ledOnMS = 1000;
    notify.ledOffMS = 1000;
```

```
} else if (notify.number < 3) {
   notify.ledARGB = Color.BLUE;
   notify.ledOnMS = 750;
   notify.ledOffMS = 750;
} else if (notify.number < 4) {
   notify.ledARGB = Color.WHITE;
   notify.ledOnMS = 500;
   notify.ledOffMS = 500;
} else {
   notify.ledARGB = Color.RED;
   notify.ledOnMS = 50;
   notify.ledOffMS = 50;
}
```

The blinking light continues until the Notification is cleared by the user. The use of the Notification.FLAG_INSISTENT flag does not affect this as it does vibration effects.

Color and blinking rates could also be used to indicate other information. For instance, temperature from a weather service could be indicated with red and blue plus blink rate. Use of such colors for passive data indication can be useful even when other forms would work. It is far less intrusive than annoying, loud ringers or harsh, vibrating phone noises. For instance, a simple glance at the handset could tell the user some useful piece of information without the need to launch any applications or change what they are doing.

Making Noise

Sometimes, the handset has to make noise to get the user's attention. Luckily, the Android SDK provides a means for this using the Notification object. Begin by configuring the audio stream type to use when playing a sound. Generally, the most useful stream type is STREAM_NOTIFICATION. You can configure the audio stream type on your notification as follows:

```
notify.audioStreamType = AudioManager.STREAM_NOTIFICATION;
```

Now, assign a valid Uri object to the sound member variable and that sound plays when the notification is triggered. The following code demonstrates how to play a sound that is included as a project resource:

```
notify.sound = Uri.parse(
   "android.resource://com.androidbook.simplenotifications/" +
   R.raw.fallbackring);
```

By default, the audio file is played once. As with the vibration, the Notification.FLAG_INSISTENT flag can be used to repeat incessantly until the user clears the notification. No specific permissions are needed for this form of notification.

Note

The sound file used in this example is included within the project as a raw resource. However, you could use any sound file on the device. Keep in mind that the sound files available on a given Android device vary.

Customizing the Notification

Although the default notification behavior in the expanded status bar tray is sufficient for most purposes, developers can customize how notifications are displayed if they so choose. To do so, developers can use the `RemoteViews` object to customize the look and feel of a notification.

The following code demonstrates how to create a `RemoteViews` object and assign custom text to it:

```
RemoteViews remote =
    new RemoteViews(getPackageName(), R.layout.remote);

remote.setTextViewText(R.id.text1, "Big text here!");
remote.setTextViewText(R.id.text2, "Red text down here!");
notify.contentView = remote;
```

To better understand this, here is the layout file `remote.xml` referenced by the preceding code:

```
<LinearLayout
    xmlns:android="http://schemas.android.com/apk/res/android"
    android:orientation="vertical"
    android:layout_width="fill_parent"
    android:layout_height="fill_parent">
    <TextView
        android:id="@+id/text1"
        android:layout_width="fill_parent"
        android:layout_height="wrap_content"
        android:textSize="31dp"
        android:textColor="#000" />
    <TextView
        android:id="@+id/text2"
        android:layout_width="fill_parent"
        android:layout_height="wrap_content"
        android:textSize="18dp"
        android:textColor="#f00" />
</LinearLayout>
```

This particular example is similar to the default notification but does not contain an icon. The `setLatestEventInfo()` method is normally used to assign the text to the default layout. In this example, we use our custom layout instead. The `Intent` still needs to be assigned, though, as follows:

```
Intent toLaunch = new Intent
    (SimpleNotificationsActivity.this, SimpleNotificationsActivity.class);
PendingIntent intentBack = PendingIntent.getActivity
    (SimpleNotificationsActivity.this, 0, toLaunch, 0);

notify.contentIntent = intentBack;
notifier.notify(NOTIFY_5, notify);
```

The end result looks something like Figure 20.4.

Figure 20.4   Custom notification showing
with just two lines of text.

Using a custom notification layout can provide better control over the information on
the expanded status bar. Additionally, it can help differentiate your application's notifications from other applications by providing a themed or branded appearance.

Note

The size of the area that a layout can use on the expanded status bar is fixed for a given
device. However, the exact details might change from device to device. Keep this in mind
when designing a custom notification layout. Additionally, be sure to test the layout on all
target devices in all modes of screen operation so that you can be sure the notification layout draws properly.

The default layout includes two fields of text: an icon and a time field for when the notification was triggered. Users are accustomed to this information. An application, where feasible and where it makes sense, should try to conform to at least this level of information when using custom notifications.

Designing Useful Notifications

As you can see, the notification capabilities on the Android platform are quite robust—so robust that it is easy to overdo it and make your application tiresome for the user. Here are some tips for designing useful notifications:

- Only use notifications when your application is not in the foreground. When in the foreground, use `Toast` or `Dialog` controls.
- Allow the user to determine what types (text, lights, sound, vibration) and frequency of notifications she will receive, as well as what events to trigger notifications for.
- Whenever possible, update and reuse an existing notification instead of creating a new one.
- Clear notifications regularly so as not to overwhelm the user with dated information.
- When in doubt, generate "polite" notifications (read: quiet).
- Make sure your notifications contain useful information in the ticker, title, and body text fields and launch sensible intents.

The notification framework is lightweight yet powerful. However, some applications such as alarm clocks or stock market monitors might also need to implement their own alert windows above and beyond the notification framework provided. In this case, they may use a background service and launch full Activity windows upon certain events. In Android 2.0 and later, developers can use the `WindowManager.LayoutParams` class to enable activity windows to display, even when the screen is locked with a keyguard.

Summary

Applications can interact with their users outside the normal activity boundaries by using notifications. Notifications can be visual, auditory, or use the vibrate feature of the device. Various methods can customize these notifications to provide rich information to the user. Special care must be taken to provide the right amount of appropriate information to the user without the application becoming a nuisance or the application being installed and forgotten about.

References and More Information

Android Dev Guide: Notifying the User:
   http://developer.android.com/guide/topics/ui/notifiers/index.html
Android Dev Guide: Creating Status Bar Notifications:
   http://developer.android.com/guide/topics/ui/notifiers/notifications.html
Android Reference: The NotificationManager Class:
   http://developer.android.com/reference/android/app/NotificationManager.html

21

Working with Services

One important Android application component that can greatly enhance an application is a service. An Android service might be used to perform functions that do not require user input in the background, or to supply information to other applications. In this chapter, you learn how to create and interact with an Android service. You also learn how to define a remote interface using the Android Interface Definition Language (AIDL). Finally, you learn how to pass objects through this interface by creating a class that implements a `Parcelable` object.

Determining When to Use Services

A service within the Android Software Development Kit (SDK) can mean one of two things. First, a service can mean a background process, performing some useful operation at regular intervals. Second, a service can be an interface for a remote object, called from within your application. In both cases, the service object extends the `Service` class from the Android SDK, and it can be a stand-alone component or part of an application with a complete user interface.

Certainly, not all applications require or use services. However, you might want to consider a service if your application meets certain criteria, such as the following:

- The application performs lengthy or resource-intensive processing that does not require input from the user.

- The application must perform certain functions routinely, or at regular intervals, such as uploading or downloading fresh content or logging the current location.

- The application performs a lengthy operation that, if cancelled because the application exits, would be wasteful to restart. An example of this is downloading large files.

- The application needs to expose and provide data or information services (think web services) to other Android applications without the need of a user interface.

Note

Android Cloud to Device Messaging (C2DM) is a service that was introduced in Android 2.2. This service provides developers with the ability to initiate application events remotely, effectively waking up the application when needed instead of requiring each application to implement a background service itself (improving battery life). Instead, the C2DM service runs on the device and is shared by interested applications. Developers send messages from remote servers through to the device's C2DM service, which delivers the message to the target application. For devices running 2.2 and higher, consider if the C2DM solution is more appropriate for your application than services. For more information about Cloud to Device Messaging, see the Google Project website: http://code.google.com/android/c2dm/.

Understanding the Service Lifecycle

Before we get into the details of how to create a service, let's look at how services interact with the Android operating system. First, it should be noted that a service implementation must be registered in that application's manifest file using the <service> tag. The service implementation might also define and enforce any permissions needed for starting, stopping, and binding to the service, as well as make specific service calls.

After it's been implemented, an Android service can be started using the `Context.startService()` method. If the service was already running when the `startService()` method was called, these subsequent calls don't start further instances of the service. The service continues to run until either the `Context.stopService()` method is called, or the service completes its tasks and stops itself using the `stopSelf()` method.

To connect to a service, interested applications use the `Context.bindService()` method to obtain a connection. If that service is not running, it is created at that time. After the connection is established, the interested applications can begin making requests of that service, if the applications have the appropriate permissions. For example, a Magic Eight Ball application might have an underlying service that can receive yes-or-no questions and provide Yoda-style answers. Any interested application could connect to the Magic Eight Ball service, ask a question ("Will my app flourish on the Android Market?") and receive the result ("Signs point to Yes."). The application can then disconnect from the service when finished using the `Context.unbindService()` method.

Warning

Like applications, services can be killed by the Android operating system under low-memory conditions. Also like applications, services have a main thread that can be blocked, causing the system to become unresponsive. Always offload intensive processing to worker threads, even when implementing a service.

Creating a Service

Creating an Android service involves extending the `Service` class and adding a service block to the `AndroidManifest.xml` permissions file. The `GPXService` class overrides the `onCreate()`, `onStart()`, `onStartCommand()`, and `onDestroy()` methods to begin with. Defining the service name enables other applications to start the service that runs in the background and stop it. Both the onStart() and onStartCommand() methods are essentially the same, with the exception that onStart() is deprecated in API Levels 5 and above. (The default implementation of the onStartCommand() on API Level 5 or greater is to call onStart() and returns an appropriate value such that behavior will be compatible to previous versions.) In the following example, both methods are implemented.

Tip

Many of the code examples provided in this chapter are taken from the SimpleService and UseService applications. The source code for these applications is provided for download on the book website.

For this example, we implement a simple service that listens for GPS changes, displays notifications at regular intervals, and then provides access to the most recent location data via a remote interface. The following code gives a simple definition to the Service class called GPXService:

```
public class GPXService extends Service {
    public static final String GPX_SERVICE =
        "com.androidbook.GPXService.SERVICE";

    private LocationManager location = null;
    private NotificationManager notifier = null;

    @Override
    public void onCreate() {
        super.onCreate();
    }
    @Override
    public void onStart(Intent intent, int startId) {
        super.onStart(intent, startId);
    }

    @Override
    public void onStartCommand(Intent intent, int flags, int startId) {
        super.onStart(intent, startId);
    }

    @Override
    public void onDestroy() {
        super.onDestroy();
    }
}
```

You need to understand the lifecycle of a service because it's different from that of an activity. If a service is started by the system with a call to the Context.StartService() method, the onCreate() method is called just before the onStart() or onStartCommand() methods. However, if the service is bound to with a call to the

Context.bindService() method, the onCreate() method is called just before the
onBind() method. The onStart() or onStartCommand() methods are not called in this
case. We talk more about binding to a service later in this chapter. Finally, when the service is finished—that is, it is stopped and no other process is bound to it—the onDestroy()
method is called. Everything for the service must be cleaned up in this method.

With this in mind, here is the full implementation of the onCreate() method for the
GPXService class previously introduced:

```java
public void onCreate() {
    super.onCreate();

    location = (LocationManager)
        getSystemService(Context.LOCATION_SERVICE);
    notifier = (NotificationManager)
        getSystemService(Context.NOTIFICATION_SERVICE);
}
```

Because the object doesn't yet know if the next call is to either of the start methods or
the onBind() method, we make a couple of quick initialization calls, but no background
processing is started. Even this might be too much if neither of these objects were used by
the interface provided by the binder.

Because we can't always predict what version of Android our code is running on, we
can simple implement both the onStart() and onStartCommand() methods and have
them call a third method that provides a common implementation. This enables us to customize behavior on later Android versions while being compatible with earlier versions.
To do this, the project needs to be built for an SDK of Level 5 or higher, while having a
minSdkValue of whatever earlier versions are supported. Of course, we highly recommend
testing on multiple platform versions to verify that the behavior is as you expect. Here are
sample implementations of the onStartCommand() and onStart() methods:

```java
@Override
public int onStartCommand(Intent intent, int flags, int startId ) {
    Log.v(DEBUG_TAG, "onStartCommand() called, must be on L5 or later");

    if (flags != 0) {
        Log.w(DEBUG_TAG, "Redelivered or retrying service start: "+flags);
    }

    doServiceStart(intent, startId);
    return Service.START_REDELIVER_INTENT;
}

@Override
public void onStart(Intent intent, int startId) {
    super.onStart(intent, startId);
    Log.v(DEBUG_TAG, "onStart() called, must be on L3 or L4");
    doServiceStart(intent,startId);
}
```

Next, let's look at the implementation of the `doStartService()` method in greater detail:

```
@Override
public void doServiceStart(Intent intent, int startId) {
    super.onStart(intent, startId);
    updateRate = intent.getIntExtra(EXTRA_UPDATE_RATE, -1);
    if (updateRate == -1) {
        updateRate = 60000;
    }

    Criteria criteria = new Criteria();
    criteria.setAccuracy(Criteria.NO_REQUIREMENT);
    criteria.setPowerRequirement(Criteria.POWER_LOW);

    location = (LocationManager)
        getSystemService(Context.LOCATION_SERVICE);

    String best = location.getBestProvider(criteria, true);

    location.requestLocationUpdates(best,
        updateRate, 0, trackListener);

    Notification notify = new
        Notification(android.R.drawable.stat_notify_more,
        "GPS Tracking", System.currentTimeMillis());
    notify.flags |= Notification.FLAG_AUTO_CANCEL;

    Intent toLaunch = new Intent(getApplicationContext(),
        ServiceControl.class);
    PendingIntent intentBack =
        PendingIntent.getActivity(getApplicationContext(),
        0, toLaunch, 0);

    notify.setLatestEventInfo(getApplicationContext(),
        "GPS Tracking", "Tracking start at " +
        updateRate+"ms intervals with [" + best +
        "] as the provider.", intentBack);
    notifier.notify(GPS_NOTIFY, notify);
}
```

The background processing starts within the two start methods. In this example, though, the background processing is actually just registering for an update from another service. For more information about using location-based services and the `LocationManager`, see Chapter 14, "Using Location-Based Services (LBS) APIs," and for more information on `Notification` calls, see Chapter 20, "Working with Notifications."

> **Tip**
>
> The use of a callback to receive updates is recommended over doing background process-ing to poll for updates. Most mobile devices have limited battery life. Continual running in the background, or even just polling, can use a substantial amount of battery power. In addi-tion, implementing callbacks for the users of your service is also more efficient for the same reasons.

In this case, we turn on the GPS for the duration of the process, which might affect battery life even though we request a lower power method of location determination. Keep this in mind when developing services.

The `Intent` extras object retrieves data passed in by the process requesting the service. Here, we retrieve one value, `EXTRA_UPDATE_RATE`, for determining the length of time be-tween updates. The string for this, `update-rate`, must be published externally, either in developer documentation or in a publicly available class file so that users of this service know about it.

The implementation details of the `LocationListener` object, `trackListener`, are not interesting to the discussion on services. However, processing should be kept to a mini-mum to avoid interrupting what the user is doing in the foreground. Some testing might be required to determine how much processing a particular phone can handle before the user notices performance issues.

There are two common methods to communicate data to the user. The first is to use `Notifications`. This is the least-intrusive method and can be used to drive users to the application for more information. It also means the users don't need to be actively using their phone at the time of the notification because it is queued. For instance, a weather application might use notifications to provide weather updates every hour.

The other method is to use `Toast` messages. From some services, this might work well, especially if the user expects frequent updates and those updates work well overlaid briefly on the screen, regardless of what the user is currently doing. For instance, a background music player could briefly overlay the current song title when the song changes.

The `onDestroy()` method is called when no clients are bound to the service and a re-quest for the service to be stopped has been made via a call to the `Context.stopService()` method, or a call has been made to the `stopSelf()` method from within the service. At this point, everything should be gracefully cleaned up because the service ceases to exist.

Here is an example of the `onDestroy()` method:

```
@Override
public void onDestroy() {
    if (location != null) {
        location.removeUpdates(trackListener);
        location = null;
    }

    Notification notify = new
        Notification(android.R.drawable.stat_notify_more,
```

```
        "GPS Tracking", System.currentTimeMillis());
    notify.flags |= Notification.FLAG_AUTO_CANCEL;

    Intent toLaunch = new Intent(getApplicationContext(),
        ServiceControl.class);
    PendingIntent intentBack =
        PendingIntent.getActivity(getApplicationContext(),
        0, toLaunch, 0);
    notify.setLatestEventInfo(getApplicationContext(),
        "GPS Tracking", "Tracking stopped", intentBack);

    notifier.notify(GPS_NOTIFY, notify);
    super.onDestroy();
}
```

Here, we stop updates to the `LocationListener` object. This stops all our background processing. Then, we notify the user that the service is terminating. Only a single call to the `onDestroy()` method happens, regardless of how many times the start methods are called.

The system does not know about a service unless it is defined within the `AndroidManifest.xml` permissions file using the `<service>` tag. Here is the `<service>` tag we must add to the Android Manifest file:

```
<service
    android:enabled="true"
    android:name="GPXService">
    <intent-filter>
        <action android:name=
            "com.androidbook.GPXService.SERVICE" />
    </intent-filter>
</service>
```

This block of XML defines the service name, `GPXService`, and that the service is enabled. Then, using an `Intent` filter, we use the same string that we defined within the class. This is the string that is used later on when controlling the service. With this block of XML inside the application section of the manifest, the system now knows that the service exists and it can be used by other applications.

Controlling a Service

At this point, the example code has a complete implementation of a `Service`. Now we write code to control the service we previously defined.

```
Intent service = new Intent("com.androidbook.GPXService.SERVICE");
service.putExtra("update-rate", 5000);
startService(service);
```

Starting a service is as straightforward as creating an Intent with the service name and calling the `startService()` method. In this example, we also set the `update-rate`

`Intent` extra parameter to 5 seconds. That rate is quite frequent but works well for testing. For practical use, we probably want this set to 60 seconds or more. This code triggers a call to the `onCreate()` method, if the `Service` isn't bound to or running already. It also triggers a call to the `onStart()` or `onStartCommand()` methods, even if the service is already running.

Later, when we finish with the service, it needs to be stopped using the following code:

```
Intent service = new Intent("com.androidbook.GPXService.SERVICE");
stopService(service);
```

This code is essentially the same as starting the service but with a call to the `stopService()` method. This calls the `onDestroy()` method if there are no bindings to it. However, if there are bindings, `onDestroy()` is not called until those are also terminated. This means background processing might continue despite a call to the `stopService()` method. If there is a need to control the background processing separate from these system calls, a remote interface is required.

Implementing a Remote Interface

Sometimes it is useful to have more control over a service than just system calls to start and stop its activities. However, before a client application can bind to a service for making other method calls, you need to define the interface. The Android SDK includes a useful tool and file format for remote interfaces for this purpose.

To define a remote interface, you must declare the interface in an AIDL file, implement the interface, and then return an instance of the interface when the `onBind()` method is called.

Using the example `GPXService` service we already built in this chapter, we now create a remote interface for it. This remote interface has a method, which can be called especially for returning the last location logged. You can use only primitive types and objects that implement the `Parcelable` protocol with remote service calls. This is because these calls cross process boundaries where memory can't be shared. The AIDL compiler handles the details of crossing these boundaries when the rules are followed. The `Location` object implements the `Parcelable` interface so it can be used.

Here is the AIDL file for this interface, `IRemoteInterface`:

```
package com.androidbook.services;


interface IRemoteInterface {
    Location getLastLocation();
}
```

When using Eclipse, you can add this AIDL file, `IRemoteInterface.aidl`, to the project under the appropriate package and the Android SDK plug-in does the rest. Now we must implement the code for the interface. Here is an example implementation of this interface:

```
private final IRemoteInterface.Stub
    mRemoteInterfaceBinder = new IRemoteInterface.Stub() {
        public Location getLastLocation() {
            Log.v("interface", "getLastLocation() called");
            return lastLocation;
        }
    };
```

The service code already stored off the last location received as a member variable, so we can simply return that value. With the interface implemented, it needs to be returned from the onBind() method of the service:

```
@Override
public IBinder onBind(Intent intent) {
    // we only have one, so no need to check the intent
    return mRemoteInterfaceBinder;
}
```

If multiple interfaces are implemented, the Intent passed in can be checked within the onBind() method to determine what action is to be taken and which interface should be returned. In this example, though, we have only one interface and don't expect any other information within the Intent, so we simply return the interface.

We also add the class name of the binder interface to the list of actions supported by the intent filter for the service within the AndroidManifest.xml file. Doing this isn't required but is a useful convention to follow and allows the class name to be used. The following block is added to the service tag definition:

```
<action android:name =
    "com.androidbook.services.IRemoteInterface" />
```

The service can now be used through this interface. This is done by implementing a ServiceConnection object and calling the bindService() method. When finished, the unbindService() method must be called so the system knows that the application is done using the service. The connection remains even if the reference to the interface is gone.

Here is an implementation of a ServiceConnection object's two main methods, onServiceConnected() and onServiceDisconnected():

```
public void onServiceConnected(ComponentName name,
    IBinder service) {

    mRemoteInterface =
        IRemoteInterface.Stub.asInterface(service);
    Log.v("ServiceControl", "Interface bound.");
}
```

```
public void onServiceDisconnected(ComponentName name) {
    mRemoteInterface = null;
    Log.v("ServiceControl",
        "Remote interface no longer bound");
}
```

When the `onServiceConnected()` method is called, an `IRemoteInterface` instance that can be used to make calls to the interface we previously defined is retrieved. A call to the remote interface looks like any call to an interface now:

```
Location loc = mRemoteInterface.getLastLocation();
```

> **Tip**
>
> Remember that remote interface calls operate across process boundaries and are completed synchronously. If a call takes a while to complete, you should place it within a separate thread, as any lengthy call would be.

To use this interface from another application, you should place the AIDL file within the project and appropriate package. The call to `onBind()` triggers a call to the `onServiceConnected()` after the call to the service's `onCreate()` method. Remember, the `onStart()` or `onStartCommand()` methods are not called in this case.

```
bindService(new Intent(IRemoteInterface.class.getName()),
    this, Context.BIND_AUTO_CREATE);
```

In this case, the Activity we call from also implements the `ServiceConnection` interface. This code also demonstrates why it is a useful convention to use the class name as an intent filter. Because we have both intent filters and we don't check the action on the call to the `onBind()` method, we can also use the other intent filter, but the code here is clearer.

When done with the interface, a call to `unbindService()` disconnects the interface. However, a callback to the `onServiceDisconnected()` method does not mean that the service is no longer bound; the binding is still active at that point, just not the connection.

Implementing a Parcelable Class

In the example so far, we have been lucky in that the `Location` class implements the `Parcelable` interface. What if a new object needs to be passed through a remote interface?

Let's take the following class, `GPXPoint`, as an example:

```
public final class GPXPoint {

    public int latitude;
    public int longitude;
    public Date timestamp;
    public double elevation;

    public GPXPoint() {
    }
}
```

The GPXPoint class defines a location point that is similar to a GeoPoint but also includes the time the location was recorded and the elevation. This data is commonly found in the popular GPX file format. On its own, this is not a basic format that the system recognizes to pass through a remote interface. However, if the class implements the Parcelable interface and we then create an AIDL file from it, the object can be used in a remote interface.

To fully support the Parcelable type, we need to implement a few methods and a Parcelable.Creator<GPXPoint>. The following is the same class now modified to be a Parcelable class:

```java
public final class GPXPoint implements Parcelable {

    public int latitude;
    public int longitude;
    public Date timestamp;
    public double elevation;

    public static final Parcelable.Creator<GPXPoint>
        CREATOR = new Parcelable.Creator<GPXPoint>() {

        public GPXPoint createFromParcel(Parcel src) {
            return new GPXPoint(src);
        }

        public GPXPoint[] newArray(int size) {
            return new GPXPoint[size];
        }

    };

    public GPXPoint() {
    }

    private GPXPoint(Parcel src) {
        readFromParcel(src);
    }

    public void writeToParcel(Parcel dest, int flags) {
        dest.writeInt(latitude);
        dest.writeInt(longitude);
        dest.writeDouble(elevation);
        dest.writeLong(timestamp.getTime());
    }
```

```
    public void readFromParcel(Parcel src) {
        latitude = src.readInt();
        longitude = src.readInt();
        elevation = src.readDouble();
        timestamp = new Date(src.readLong());
    }

    public int describeContents() {
        return 0;
    }
}
```

The `writeToParcel()` method is required and flattens the object in a particular order
using supported primitive types within a `Parcel`. When the class is created from a
`Parcel`, the Creator is called, which, in turn, calls the private constructor. For readability,
we also created a `readFromParcel()` method that reverses the flattening, reading the
primitives in the same order that they were written and creating a new `Date` object.

Now you must create the AIDL file for this class. You should place it in the same directory as the Java file and name it `GPXPoint.aidl` to match. You should make the contents look like the following:

```
package com.androidbook.services;

parcelable GPXPoint;
```

Now the `GPXPoint` class can be used in remote interfaces. This is done in the same way as
any other native type or `Parcelable` object. You can modify the
`IRemoteInterface.aidl` file to look like the following:

```
package com.androidbook.services;

import com.androidbook.services.GPXPoint;

interface IRemoteInterface {
    Location getLastLocation();
    GPXPoint getGPXPoint();
}
```

Additionally, we can provide an implementation for this method within the interface, as
follows:

```
public GPXPoint getGPXPoint() {
    if (lastLocation == null) {
        return null;
    } else {
        Log.v("interface", "getGPXPoint() called");
        GPXPoint point = new GPXPoint();
```

```
            point.elevation = lastLocation.getAltitude();
            point.latitude =
                (int) (lastLocation.getLatitude() * 1E6);
            point.longitude =
                (int) (lastLocation.getLongitude() * 1E6);
            point.timestamp =
                new Date(lastLocation.getTime());

            return point;
    }
}
```

As can be seen, nothing particularly special needs to happen. Just by making the object `Parcelable`, it can now be used for this purpose.

Summary

The Android SDK provides the `Service` mechanism that can be used to implement background tasks and to share functionality across multiple applications. By creating an interface through the use of AIDL, a `Service` can expose functionality to other applications without having to distribute libraries or packages. Creating objects with the `Parcelable` interface enables developers to extend the data that can be passed across process boundaries, as well.

Care should be taken when creating a background service. Poorly designed background services might have substantial negative impact on handset performance and battery life. In addition to standard testing, you should test a `Service` implementation with respect to these issues.

Prudent creation of a `Service`, though, can dramatically enhance the appeal of an application or service you might provide. `Service` creation is a powerful tool provided by the Android SDK for designing applications simply not possible on other mobile platforms.

References and More Information

Android Reference: The Service Class:
    http://developer.android.com/reference/android/app/Service.html
Android Dev Guide: Service Lifecycle:
    http://developer.android.com/guide/topics/fundamentals.html#servlife
Android Dev Guide: Processes and Threads:
    http://developer.android.com/guide/topics/fundamentals.html#procthread
Android Application Framework FAQ:
    http://developer.android.com/guide/appendix/faq/framework.html

22

Extending Android Application Reach

Android applications can be extended far beyond traditional functional boundaries to integrate tightly with the rest of the operating system. Developers can use a number of other platform features to improve the usefulness of an application. In this chapter, you learn about the various ways to enhance your applications and extend their reach, making them even more powerful and compelling to your users.

Enhancing Your Applications

One of Android's most compelling features as a platform is its approach to application interoperability. Unlike the mobile development platforms of the past, which simply allowed each simple application to run in its own little bubble, Android allows applications to share data and functionality with other applications and the rest of the operating system in a secure and reasonable fashion. After you've developed your core application, it's time to give some thought as to how to extend the application's reach beyond the traditional use case, which is

1. User launches the app.

2. User runs the app.

3. User closes the app.

Although it's certainly necessary to support that particular scenario, it's not the only way that users can interact with your app or its features. The Android framework includes a number of ways to move beyond this paradigm. You can extend and enhance Android applications in a variety of ways, including

- Exposing small segments of application functionality in the form of App Widgets, which can reside on the user's Home screen.

- Providing users with an interactive background associated with your application in the form of a live wallpaper.

- Enabling users to organize application data for quick and easy access using live folders.

- Making application content searchable across the device.

- Enabling your application to act as a content type handler, exposing the ability to process common types of data such as pictures or videos.

- Acting as content providers, thus exposing internal data for use by other applications, as well as taking advantage of other content providers to enhance your applications, as discussed in Chapter 11, "Sharing Data Between Applications with Content Providers."

- Enabling different application entry points using intent filters above and beyond the default Activity to launch.

- Acting as a broadcast receiver to react to important events that occur and by broadcasting application events of interest to other applications.

- By acting as a service, providing data services and special functionality to other applications, and enhancing your application with other services (system services or other applications' services), as discussed in Chapter 21, "Working with Services."

This is where we encourage you to think outside the box and consider how to extend the reach of your applications. By doing so, you keep your application fresh in your users' minds so they continually rely on your application and don't forget about it. Now let's look at some of the options listed in more detail.

Working with App Widgets

Introduced officially in API Level 3, the App Widget provides a new level of application integration with the Android operating system previously not available to mobile developers. Applications that publish App Widgets are called App Widget *providers*. A component that can contain an App Widget is called an App Widget *host*. An App Widget is a lightweight, simply featured application (such as a desktop plug-in) that can be installed on a host such as the Home screen.

An App Widget is normally tied back to some underlying application. For example, a calendar application might have an App Widget that shows the current date and enables the user to view the scheduled events of the day. Clicking on a specific event might launch the full calendar application to that date, enabling the user to access the full range of application features. Similarly, a music application might provide a simple set of controls within an App Widget, enabling the user to easily start and stop music playback from his Home screen. We provide a simple App Widget implementation as part of the code that accompanies this book; this App Widget displays information about the United States

Homeland Security Advisory System's threat level (red/severe, orange/high, yellow/elevated, blue/guarded, green/low)—this type of App Widget might be appropriate for a travel application.

An App Widget can be updated at regular intervals with fresh content. This makes App Widgets ideal for secondary application features, whereas notifications that launch into the full application functionality might be more appropriate for events that require a speedy user response.

Creating an App Widget

Consider whether or not your application should include App Widget functionality. Although App Widgets are small in size and light on functionality, they allow the user access to application functionality straight from the Home screen. App Widgets also serve to keep users using the application, by reminding them that they installed it. Some applications allow only one instance of an App Widget to run (such as the music player), whereas others might allow multiple instances of the same App Widget to be placed simultaneously, though generally showing different content (such as a picture frame).

You need to make the following changes to your application in order to support App Widgets:

- Provide an XML App Widget configuration.
- Determine whether the App Widget requires a configuration activity.
- Provide an `AppWidgetProvider` class implementation.
- Provide a `Service` class implementation to handle App Widget content updates, as needed.
- Update the application Android manifest file to register the App Widget provider information, as well as any information about the update service.

Now let's look at some of these requirements in greater detail.

Tip

The code examples provided in this section are taken from the SimpleAppWidget application. The source code for this application is provided for download on the book website.

Creating an App Widget Configuration

First, your application must provide an XML App Widget definition. You can store this definition within the project's resources in the `/res/xml` directory. Let's take a closer look at an example of an App Widget definition, as defined in `/res/xml/simple_widget_info.xml`:

```xml
<?xml version="1.0" encoding="utf-8"?>
<appwidget-provider
    xmlns:android="http://schemas.android.com/apk/res/android"
    android:minWidth="146dp"
    android:minHeight="72dp"
    android:updatePeriodMillis="28800000"
    android:initialLayout="@layout/widget">
</appwidget-provider>
```

This simple App Widget definition is encapsulated within the `<appwidget-provider>`
XML tag. The `minWidth` and `minHeight` attributes dictate the size of the App Widget (a
dimension, here in `dp`), and the `updatePeriodMillis` attribute is used to define how
often the App Widget content is refreshed (using the App Widget update service)—in this
case, once every eight hours. Finally, the App Widget layout definition is referenced using
the `initialLayout` attribute—we talk more about this layout file in a few moments.

> **Note**
>
> An App Widget cannot be updated more frequently than every 30 minutes (1,800,000 mil-
> liseconds). Ensure that the `updatePeriodMillis` attribute of your App Widget provider
> reflects this limitation. This limit has testing implications. You might consider a tool to force
> an update or some sort of refresh button that users might benefit from, as well.
>
> If your widget must break this limit, which you should only do for a very good reason, you
> must implement the timer yourself. Keep in mind the effect on battery life and performance
> this decision might have.

To draw nicely on the Home screen, the App Widget dimensions must follow certain
guidelines. The Home screen is divided into cells of a particular size. When the user
attempts to install an App Widget, the system checks to make sure there is enough space
(as dictated by the minimum width and height values of the App Widget).

> **Tip**
>
> The basic formula for determining the size of your App Widget is to multiply the number of
> cells you want by 74, and then subtract two. In our case, we want an App Widget two cells
> high and two cells wide. Therefore, we use a size of ((74*2)-2) or 146. For a nice write-up on
> App Widget design guidelines, see the Android website: http://developer.android.com/
> guide/practices/ui_guidelines/widget_design.html.

There are a number of other attributes available within the `<appwidget-provider>` tag.
For example, you could specify the `Activity` class used to configure the App Widget
using the `configure` attribute, which is especially useful when you support multiple
simultaneous App Widget instances (see the App Widget write-ups on our book blog for
more advanced App Widget implementations). For a complete list of available App Widget
provider configuration details, see the class documentation for the
`android.appwidget.AppWidgetProviderInfo` class.

Determining if the App Widget Requires a Configuration Activity

Generally speaking, if there is more than one instance of an App Widget, each instance should look or behave differently. This isn't a strict requirement; if each instance of the App Widget looks and acts the same, users quickly catch on and only install one instance at a time.

However, if you want to differentiate between App Widget instances, you need to provide each with settings, and thus you must create a configuration activity. This configuration activity is a normal activity, but it will read in certain `Intent` extras upon launch. The configuration activity must be defined within the App Widget XML configuration.

Each time a new App Widget instance is created, the configuration `Activity` is launched. The `Activity` is launched with the unique App Widget identifier, passed in via the launch intent's `EXTRA_APPWIDGET_ID` extra. The `Activity`, on completion, must set this value back in the result intent along with result status, such as `RESULT_OK`.

The configuration activity should not only let the user configure options on this particular App Widget instance, but it should also update the `RemoteViews` object, as the App Widget will not receive an update event when it's first created with a configuration `Activity` set in the XML configuration. Subsequent updates receive the update event, though.

Creating an App Widget Provider

An App Widget is basically a `BroadcastReceiver` that handles particular actions. As with a broadcast receiver, the primary interaction with an App Widget happens through the `onReceive()` method. However, the default `AppWidgetProvider` class handles `onReceive()` and, in turn, delegates operations to the its other methods, which you then implement.

Implementing the AppWidgetProvider Class

The `AppWidgetProvider` class simplifies the handling of these actions by providing a framework for developers to implement App Widgets. An `AppWidgetProvider` implementation requires the following methods:

- The `onEnabled()` method is called when the App Widget is created. This is a good place to perform any configuration shared for the entire widget provider. This method is called once for the first App Widget instance added to the widget host (usually the home screen).

- The `onDisabled()` method is called when the App Widget is disabled. This method is called only after all App Widget instances for this provider are removed from the App Widget host. For example, if there were five App Widgets for this provider on the home screen, this method would only be called after the user removed the fifth and final App Widget.

- The `onUpdate()` method is called at regular intervals, depending on the update frequency specified in the App Widget configuration file. This frequency uses an in-exact timer, so do not rely on this frequency being precise. If you need precision updates, consider scheduling updates using the `AlarmManager` class. This method is called with a list of widget identifiers. Each identifier references a unique App Widget instance within the App Widget host. The App Widget provider implementation must differentiate between each instance and, typically, store different configuration values for each as well.

- The `onDeleted()` method is called when a particular instance of this App Widget is deleted.

Warning

A well-documented defect exists with the `onDelete()` method that requires overriding of the `onReceived()` method to create a suitable fix. This problem only exists on the Android 1.5 platform. If Android 1.5 is one of your target platforms, you'll want to implement the solution found at http://developer.android.com/guide/topics/appwidgets/index.html#AppWidgetProvider.

Using Remote Views

Android App Widgets do not run within the application process, but in the host's process. Therefore, the App Widget uses the `RemoteViews` class in order to define its user interface. The `RemoteViews` class supports a subset of the overall `View` hierarchy, for display within another process. Generally speaking, you want to configure the `RemoteViews` object and send it to the App Widget Manager during the `onUpdate()` method. However, you'll also need to update it when an instance is created and a configuration activity exists.

View hierarchies defined using `RemoteViews` can only contain a limited set of controls, including `Button`, `ImageButton`, `ImageView`, `TextView`, `AnalogClock`, `Chronometer`, and `ProgressBar` controls and only within `FrameLayout`, `LinearLayout`, or `RelativeLayout` layouts. Objects derived from these controls cannot be used, either. The `RemoteViews` configuration should be kept as simple as possible because access to its view hierarchy is controlled through helper methods, such as `setImageViewResource()`, `setTextViewText()`, `setProgressbar()`, `setShort()`, `setString()`, and `setChronometer()`. In short, you can generate an XML layout definition for an App Widget, but you must be careful only to use controls that are supported by the `RemoteViews` class.

Let's look at the incredibly simple layout definition used by the threat level App Widget, as defined in the resource file `/res/layout/widget.xml`:

```xml
<?xml version="1.0" encoding="utf-8"?>
<RelativeLayout
    xmlns:android="http://schemas.android.com/apk/res/android"
    android:layout_height="match_parent"
    android:layout_width="match_parent"
    android:id="@+id/widget_view">
    <TextView
        android:layout_width="wrap_content"
        android:layout_height="wrap_content"
        android:id="@+id/widget_text_threat"
        android:layout_centerInParent="true">
    </TextView>
</RelativeLayout>
```

Nothing too complex in this layout, eh? A single `TextView` control, which displays the threat level information, is encapsulated within a `RelativeLayout` control. Now your layout can be loaded programmatically into a `RemoteViews` object for use within the App Widget provider. Don't worry, things get more complex when we cram that layout into a `RemoteViews` object and act upon it across processes.

In order to load a layout resource (such as widget.xml defined earlier) into a `RemoteViews` object, you can use the following code:

```
RemoteViews remoteView =
    new RemoteViews(context.getPackageName(), R.layout.widget);
```

When you want to update the text in that layout's `TextView` control, you need to use the `setTextViewText()` method of the `RemoteViews` class, like this:

```
remoteView.setTextViewText(R.id.widget_text_threat, "Red alert!");
```

If you want the user to be able to click within the `RelativeLayout` control of the App Widget display and to launch the underlying application, use the `setOnClickPendingIntent()` method of the `RemoteViews` class. For example, the following code creates a pending intent that can launch the `SimpleAppWidgetActivity` activity:

```
Intent launchAppIntent =
    new Intent(context, SimpleAppWidgetActivity.class);
PendingIntent launchAppPendingIntent = PendingIntent.getActivity(
    context, 0, launchAppIntent,
    PendingIntent.FLAG_UPDATE_CURRENT);
remoteView.setOnClickPendingIntent
    (R.id.widget_view, launchAppPendingIntent);
```

Finally, when the `RemoteViews` object is all set up, the App Widget provider needs to tell the App Widget Manager about the updated `RemoteViews` object:

```
ComponentName simpleWidget = new ComponentName(context,
    SimpleAppWidgetProvider.class);
AppWidgetManager appWidgetManager =
    AppWidgetManager.getInstance(context);
appWidgetManager.updateAppWidget(simpleWidget, remoteView);
```

To update the appropriate App Widget, the `AppWidgetManager` object requires its component name. The App Widget Manager will then update the content of the specific named App Widget using the contents of the `RemoteViews` object you provide in the `updateAppWidget()` method. Each time the `RemoteViews` object is updated, it is rebuilt. Although this usually happens infrequently, keep them simple for good performance.

Note

Unfortunately, the complete implementation of the `AppWidgetProvider` class provided in `SimpleAppWidget` is too lengthy for print. See the `SimpleAppWidgetProvider` class within that sample project for the full details of how the threat level App Widget works.

Updating an App Widget

When the `onUpdate()` method of the App Widget provider is called, a list of identifiers are passed in. Each identifier references a particular App Widget instance for this provider. That is, a user can add any number of App Widgets of a particular kind to a host. It's up to you, though, how they will differ. During the update event, each identifier must be iterated over and update each of the `RemoteViews` objects individually (that is, if you support different instances simultaneously).

An App Widget must be very responsive during the update event because it is being executed from the UI thread of the host process. When the updates are done, there is no guarantee that the App Widget Provider object stays around. Therefore, if an App Widget refresh requires any lengthy blocking operations, it must use a service so that it can create a thread to perform these operations in the background.

In our threat level App Widget example, we already have a service that performs some network operations in order to download updated threat level data. This service is perfect for the needs of an App Widget as well as the application, so they can share this service. Convenient, huh?

Creating a App Widget Update Service

Most App Widgets do not contain static content, but are updated from time to time. Normally, an Android service is used to enable App Widget content updates. The service performs any necessary update-related tasks, including spawning threads, connecting to the Internet, and so on. The App Widget provider's `onUpdate()` method, which is called at the App Widget update interval, is a great place to start this update service. After the service has done its job, it should shut itself down until the next time fresh content is needed. Let's revisit the threat level App Widget, which uses two services:

- The `SimpleDataUpdateService` class runs at the App Widget update interval (started in the `onUpdate()` method of the App Widget provider). The service connects to the Internet, checks the current threat level, and stores the result in the application's shared preferences. Finally, the service shuts itself down. It might be helpful to consider the application as the "owner" of this service—it provides information for both the application and the App Widget by saving data to the shared preferences.

- The `PrefListenerService` class listens for changes in the application's shared preferences. In addition to using the `onUpdate()` method, this service is started when the App Widget is enabled, thus allowing it to be updated whenever the data changes (for example, when the underlying application modifies the shared preference by checking the threat level itself). When the threat level preference changes, this service triggers a call to the `updateAppWidget()` method of the App Widget provider, which updates the `RemoteViews` object for the App Widget—bypassing the frequency limitations of the App Widget Manager. It might be helpful to consider the App Widget as the "owner" of this service—it runs within the App Widget lifecycle and exists only to update the content of the App Widget.

Certainly, there are simpler ways to update your App Widget. For example, the App Widget could use its one service to do all the work of downloading the threat level data and updating the App Widget content, but then the application is left to do its own thing. The method described here illustrates how you can bypass some of the update frequency limitations of App Widgets and still share content between App Widgets and their underlying application.

Tip

Updating the `RemoteViews` object need not happen from within the App Widget provider. It can be called directly from the application, too. In this example, the service created for downloading the threat level data is used by the application and App Widget alike. Using a service for downloading online data is a good practice for a number of reasons. However, if there was no download service to leverage, we could have gotten away with just one service. In this service, fully controlled by the App Widget, we would have not only done the download but also then updated the `RemoteViews` object directly. Doing this would have eliminated the need for listening to the shared preferences changes from the App Widget service, too.

Configuring the Android Manifest File for App Widgets

In order for the Android system to know about your application's App Widget, you must include a `<receiver>` tag in the application's Android manifest file to register it as an App Widget provider. App Widgets often use services, and these services must be registered within the Android manifest file with a `<service>` tag like any other service. Here is an excerpt of the Android manifest file from the `SimpleAppWidget` project:

```
<receiver android:name="SimpleAppWidgetProvider"
    android:label="@string/widget_desc"
    android:icon="@drawable/threat_levels_descriptions">
    <intent-filter>
        <action android:name=
            "android.appwidget.action.APPWIDGET_UPDATE" />
    </intent-filter>
    <meta-data
        android:name="android.appwidget.provider"
        android:resource="@xml/simple_widget_info" />
</receiver>
<service android:name="SimpleDataUpdateService" />
<service android:name="SimpleAppWidgetProvider$PrefListenerService" />
```

Notice that, unlike a typical `<receiver>` definition, a `<meta-data>` section references an XML file resource. The `<receiver>` tag includes several bits of information about the App Widget configuration, including a label and icon for the App Widget, which is displayed on the App Widget picker (where the user chooses from available App Widgets on the system). The `<receiver>` tag also includes an intent filter to handle the `android.appwidget.action.APPWIDGET_UPDATE` intent action, as well as a `<meta-data>` tag that references the App Widget configuration file stored in the XML resource directory. Finally, the services used to update the App Widget are registered.

Installing an App Widget

After your application has implemented App Widget functionality, a user (who has installed your application) can install it to the Home screen using the following steps:

1. Long-press on the Home Screen.

2. From the menu, choose the Widgets option, as shown in Figure 22.1 (left).

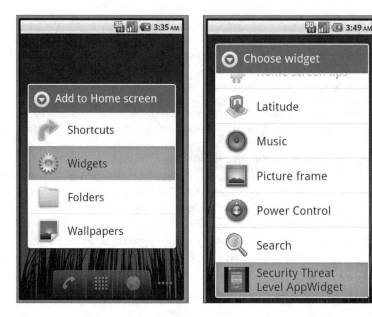

Figure 22.1   Using the Widget picker to install an App Widget
on the Home screen.

3. From the Widget menu, choose the App Widget you want to include, as shown in Figure 22.1 (right).

4. Provided there is room for it, the App Widget is placed on the screen, as shown in Figure 22.2. You can move the App Widget around on the screen or remove it by dragging it onto the trash icon at the bottom of the Home screen.

Becoming an App Widget Host

Although somewhat less common, applications might also become App Widget hosts. App Widget hosts (`android.appWidget.AppWidgetHost`) are simply containers that can embed and display App Widgets. The most commonly used App Widget host is the Home screen. For more information on developing an App Widget host, see the Android SDK documentation.

Current Threat Level is
ELEVATED, which was
last updated at Fri Aug 27
03:50:04 GMT+00:00
2010.

Figure 22.2   A Simple App Widget on the Home
screen that displays the security threat level.

Working with Live Wallpapers

In addition to still image wallpapers, Android supports the notion of a live wallpaper.
Instead of displaying a static background image on the Home screen, the user can set an
interactive, or live, wallpaper that can display anything that can be drawn on a surface, such
as graphics and animations. Live wallpapers were introduced in Android 2.1 (API Level 7).

Your applications can provide live wallpapers that use 3D graphics and animations as
well as display interesting application content. Some examples of live wallpapers include

- A 3D display showing an animated scene portraying abstract shapes
- A service that animates between images found on an online image-sharing service
- An interactive pond with water that ripples with touch
- Wallpapers that change based on the actual season, weather, and time of day

Tip

Programmatic installation of still image wallpapers is discussed in Chapter 15, "Using
Android Multimedia APIs."

Creating a Live Wallpaper

A live wallpaper is similar to an Android Service, but its result is a surface that the host can display. You need to make the following changes to your application in order to support live wallpapers:

- Provide an XML wallpaper configuration.
- Provide a `WallpaperService` implementation.
- Update the application Android manifest file to register the wallpaper service with the appropriate permissions.

Now let's look at some of these requirements in greater detail.

Tip

The code examples provided in this section are taken from the SimpleLiveWallpaper application. The source code for this application is provided for download on the book website.

Creating a Live Wallpaper Service

The guts of the live wallpaper functionality are provided as part of a `WallpaperService` implementation, and most of the live wallpaper functionality is driven by its `WallpaperService.Engine` implementation.

Implementing a Wallpaper Service

Your application needs to extend the `WallpaperService` class. The most important method the class needs to override is the `onCreateEngine()` method. Here is a sample implementation of a wallpaper service called `SimpleDroidWallpaper`:

```
public class SimpleDroidWallpaper extends WallpaperService {
    private final Handler handler = new Handler();

    @Override
    public Engine onCreateEngine() {
        return new SimpleWallpaperEngine();
    }
    class SimpleWallpaperEngine extends WallpaperService.Engine {
        // Your implementation of a wallpaper service engine here...
    }
}
```

There's not much to this wallpaper service. The `onCreateEngine()` method simply returns your application's custom wallpaper engine, which provides all the functionality for a specific live wallpaper. You could also override the other wallpaper service methods, as necessary. A `Handler` object is initialized for posting wallpaper draw operations.

Implementing a Wallpaper Service Engine

Now let's take a closer look at the wallpaper service engine implementation. The wallpaper service engine handles all the details regarding the lifecycle of a specific instance of a live wallpaper. Much like the graphics examples used in Chapter 17, "Using Android 3D

Graphics with OpenGL ES," live wallpaper implementations use a `Surface` object to draw to the screen.

There are a number of callback methods of interest within the wallpaper service engine:

- You can override the `onCreate()` and `onDestroy()` methods to set up and tear down the live wallpaper. The `Surface` object is not valid during these parts of the lifecycle.

- You can override the `onSurfaceCreated()` and `onSurfaceDestroyed()` methods (convenience methods for the `Surface` setup and teardown) to set up and tear down the `Surface` used for live wallpaper drawing.

- You should override the `onVisibilityChanged()` method to handle live wallpaper visibility. When invisible, a live wallpaper must not remain running. This method should be treated much like an `Activity` pause or resume event.

- The `onSurfaceChanged()` method is another convenience method for `Surface` management.

- You can override the `onOffsetsChanged()` method to enable the live wallpaper to react when the user swipes between Home screens.

- You can override the `onTouchEvent()` method to handle touch events. The incoming parameter is a `MotionEvent` object—we talk about the `MotionEvent` class in detail in the gestures section of Chapter 24, "Handling Advanced User Input." You also need to enable touch events (off by default) for the live wallpaper using the `setTouchEventsEnabled()` method.

The implementation details of the live wallpaper are up to the developer. Often, a live wallpaper implementation uses OpenGL ES calls to draw to the screen. For example, the sample live wallpaper project included with this book includes a live wallpaper service that creates a Bitmap graphic of a droid, which floats around the screen, bouncing off the edges of the wallpaper boundaries. It also responds to touch events by changing its drift direction. Its wallpaper engine uses a thread to manage drawing operations, posting them back to the system using the Handler object defined in the wallpaper service.

Tip

Your live wallpaper can respond to user events, such as touch events. It can also listen for events where the user drops items on the screen. For more information, see the documentation for the `WallpaperService.Engine` class.

Note

Unfortunately, the wallpaper engine implementation of the sample application, SimpleLive-Wallpaper, is far too lengthy for print due to all the OpenGL ES drawing code. However, you can see its implementation as part of the sample code provided for download. Specifically, check the `SimpleDroidWallpaper` class.

Warning

You should take into account handset responsiveness and battery life when designing live wallpapers.

Creating a Live Wallpaper Configuration

Next, your application must provide an XML wallpaper definition. You can store this definition within the project's resources in the `/res/xml` directory. For example, here is a simple wallpaper definition called `/res/xml/droid_wallpaper.xml`:

```
<?xml version="1.0" encoding="utf-8"?>
<wallpaper xmlns:android="http://schemas.android.com/apk/res/android"
    android:thumbnail="@drawable/live_wallpaper_android"
    android:description="@string/wallpaper_desc" />
```

This simple wallpaper definition is encapsulated within the `<wallpaper>` XML tag. The `description` and `thumbnail` attributes are displayed on the wallpaper picker, where the user is prompted to select a specific wallpaper to use.

Configuring the Android Manifest File for Live Wallpapers

Finally, you need to update the application's Android manifest file to expose the live wallpaper service. Specifically, the `WallpaperService` needs to be registered using the `<service>` tag. The `<service>` tag must include several important bits of information:

- The `WallpaperService` class
- The `BIND_WALLPAPER` permission
- An intent filter for the `WallpaperService` action
- Wallpaper metadata to reference the live wallpaper configuration

Let's look at an example. Here is the `<service>` tag implementation for a simple live wallpaper:

```
<service
    android:label="@string/wallpaper_name"
    android:name="SimpleDroidWallpaper"
    android:permission="android.permission.BIND_WALLPAPER">
    <intent-filter>
        <action
            android:name="android.service.wallpaper.WallpaperService" />
    </intent-filter>
    <meta-data
        android:name="android.service.wallpaper"
        android:resource="@xml/droid_wallpaper" />
</service>
```

In addition to the service definition, you also need to limit installation of your application to API Level 7 and higher (where support for live wallpapers exists) using the `<uses-sdk>` manifest tag:

```
<uses-sdk android:minSdkVersion="7" android:targetSdkVersion="8" />
```

Keep in mind that your live wallpaper might use APIs (such as OpenGL ES 2.0 APIs) that require a higher `minSdkVersion` than API Level 7. You might also want to use the `<uses-feature>` tag to specify that your application includes live folder support, for use within Android Market filters:

```
<uses-feature android:name="android.software.live_wallpaper" />
```

Installing a Live Wallpaper

After you've implemented live wallpaper support within your application, you can set a live wallpaper on your Home screen using the following steps:

1. Long-press on the Home Screen.
2. From the menu, choose the Wallpapers option, as shown in Figure 22.3 (left).

Figure 22.3   Installing a live wallpaper on the Home screen.

3. From the Wallpaper menu, choose the Live wallpapers option, as shown in Figure 22.3 (middle).
4. From the Live Wallpaper menu, choose the live wallpaper you want to include, as shown in Figure 22.3 (right).

5. After you've chosen a wallpaper, it is shown in preview mode. Simply choose the
    Set Wallpaper button to confirm you want to use that live wallpaper. The live wall-
    paper is now visible on your Home screen, as shown in Figure 22.4.

Figure 22.4   A Simple AppWidget on the Home
screen that displays the security threat level.

Acting as a Content Type Handler

Your application can act as a content type filter—that is, handle common intent actions
such as VIEW, EDIT, or SEND for specific MIME types.

> **Tip**
>
> See the `android.content.Intent` class for a list of standard activity actions.

A photo application might act as a content type handler for VIEW actions for any graphic
formats, such as JPG, PNG, or RAW image file MIME types. Similarly, a social networking
application might want to handle intent SEND actions when the underlying data has a
MIME type associated with typical social content (for example, text, graphic, or video).
This means that any time the user tries to send data (with the MIME types that the social
networking application was interested in) from an Android application using an Intent
with action SEND, the social networking application is listed as a choice for completing the
SEND action request. If the user chooses to send the content using the social networking
application, that application has to launch an Activity to handle the request (for example,
an Activity that uploads the content to the social networking website to share).

Finally, content type handlers make it easier to extend the application to act as a content provider, provide search capabilities, or include live folder features. Define data records using custom MIME types, so that no matter how an Intent fires (inside or outside the application), the action is handled by the application in a graceful fashion.

To enable your application to act as a content type handler, you need to make several changes to your application:

- Determine which Intent actions and MIME types your application needs to be able to handle.

- You need to implement an `Activity` that can process the Intent action or actions that you want to handle.

- You need to register that `Activity` in your application's Android Manifest file using the `<activity>` tag as you normally would. You then need to configure an `<intent-filter>` tag for that Activity within your application's Android Manifest file, providing the appropriate intent action and MIME types your application can process.

Determining Intent Actions and MIME Types

Let's look at a simple example. For the remainder of this chapter, we make various modifications to a simple field notes application that uses a content provider to expose African game animal field notes; each note has a title and text body (the content itself comes from field notes on African game animals that we wrote up years ago on our nature blog, which is very popular with grade-schoolers). Throughout these examples, the application acts as a content type handler for VIEW requests for data with a custom MIME type:

```
vnd.android.cursor.item/vnd.androidbook.live.fieldnotes
```

Tip

MIME types come in two forms. Most developers are familiar with MIME types, such as `text/plain` or `image/jpeg` (as defined in RFC2045 & RFC2046), which are standards used globally. The Internet Assigned Numbers Authority (IANA, at http://www.iana.org) manages these global MIME types.

Developers frequently need to create their own MIME types, but without the need for them to become global standards. These types must still be sufficiently unique that MIME type namespace collisions do not occur. When you're dealing with Android content providers, there are two well-defined prefixes that you can use for creating MIME types. The `ContentResolver.CURSOR_DIR_BASE_TYPE` prefix ("vnd.android.cursor.dir") is for use with directories or folders of items. The `ContentResolver.CURSOR_ITEM_BASE_TYPE` prefix ("vnd.android.cursor.item") is for use with a single type. The part after the slash must then be unique. It's not uncommon to pattern MIME types after package names or other such unique qualifiers.

Implementing the Activity to Process the Intents

Next the application needs an `Activity` class to handle the Intents it receives. For the sample, we simply need to load a page capable of viewing a field note. Here is a sample implementation of an `Activity` that can parse the `Intent` data and show a screen to displays the field note for a specific animal:

```
public class SimpleViewDetailsActivity extends Activity {
    @Override
    protected void onCreate(Bundle savedInstanceState) {
        super.onCreate(savedInstanceState);
        setContentView(R.layout.details);
        try {
            Intent launchIntent = getIntent();
            Uri launchData = launchIntent.getData();
            String id = launchData.getLastPathSegment();
            Uri dataDetails = Uri.withAppendedPath
                (SimpleFieldnotesContentProvider.CONTENT_URI, id);
            Cursor cursor =
                managedQuery(dataDetails, null, null, null, null);
            cursor.moveToFirst();
            String fieldnoteTitle = cursor.getString(cursor
                .getColumnIndex(SimpleFieldnotesContentProvider
                .FIELDNOTES_TITLE));
            String fieldnoteBody = cursor.getString(cursor
                .getColumnIndex(SimpleFieldnotesContentProvider
                .FIELDNOTES_BODY));
            TextView fieldnoteView = (TextView)
                findViewById(R.id.text_title);
            fieldnoteView.setText(fieldnoteTitle);
            TextView bodyView = (TextView) findViewById(R.id.text_body);
            bodyView.setLinksClickable(true);
            bodyView.setAutoLinkMask(Linkify.ALL);
            bodyView.setText(fieldnoteBody);
        } catch (Exception e) {
            Toast.makeText(this, "Failed.", Toast.LENGTH_LONG).show();
        }
    }
}
```

The `SimpleViewDetailsActivity` class retrieves the Intent that was used to launch the `Activity` using the `getIntent()` method. It then inspects the details of that intent, extracting the specific field note identifier using the `getLastPathSegment()` method. The rest of the code simply involves querying the underlying content provider for the appropriate field note record and displaying it using a layout.

Registering the Intent Filter

Finally, the Activity class must be registered in the application's Android manifest file and the intent filter must be configured so that the application only accepts Intents for specific actions and specific MIME types. For example, the `SimpleViewDetailsActivity` would be registered as follows:

```
<activity
    android:name="SimpleViewDetailsActivity">
    <intent-filter>
      <action
          android:name="android.intent.action.VIEW" />
      <category
          android:name="android.intent.category.DEFAULT" />
      <data android:mimeType =
          "vnd.android.cursor.item/vnd.androidbook.live.fieldnotes" />
    </intent-filter>
</activity>
```

The `<activity>` tag remains the same as any other. The `<intent-filter>` tag is what's interesting here. First, the action that the application wants to handle is defined using an `<action>` tag that specifies the action the application can handle is the `VIEW` action. The `<category>` tag is set to DEFAULT, which is most appropriate, and finally the `<data>` tag is used to filter `VIEW` Intents further to only those of the custom MIME type associated with field notes.

Tip

The rest of the sample applications used in this chapter (SimpleSearchIntegration and SimpleLiveFolder) act as content type handlers for field note content as described in this section. The source code for these applications is provided in full for download on the book website. However, read on for more information regarding the implementation of these applications.

Making Application Content Searchable

If your application is content rich, either with content created by users or with content provided by you, the developer, then integrating with the search capabilities of Android can provide many benefits and add value to the user. The application data becomes part of the overall handset experience, is more accessible, and your application may be presented to the user in more cases than just when they launch it.

Most Android devices share a set of common hardware buttons: Home (⌂), Menu
(MENU), Back (↩), and Search (🔍). Applications can implement powerful search features
within their applications using the Android framework. There are two ways that search
capabilities are generally added to Android applications:

- Applications implement a search framework that enables their activities to react to
  the user pressing the Search button and perform searches on data within that
  application.
- Applications can expose their content for use in global, system-wide searches that
  include application and web content.

Search framework features include the ability to search for and access application data as
search results, as well as the ability to provide suggestions as the user is typing search criteria. Applications can also provide an Intent to launch when a user selects specific search
suggestions.

Tip

The code examples provided in this section are taken from the SimpleSearchIntegration application. The source code for this application is provided for download on the book website.

Let's consider the African field notes application we discussed in the previous section.
This application uses a simple content provider to supply information about game
animals. Enabling search support within this application seems rational; it would enable
the user to quickly find information about a specific animal simply by pressing the Search
button. When a result is found, the application needs to be able to apply an `Intent` for
launching the appropriate screen to view that specific field note—the perfect time to
implement a simple content type handler that enables the application to handle "view
field note" actions, as shown in Figure 22.5.

Enabling Searches Within Your Application

You need to make a number of changes within your application to enable searches.
Although these changes might seem complex, the good news is that if you do it right,
enabling global searches later is very simple. Searching content generally necessitates that
your application acts as a content provider, or at the very least has some sort of underlying
database that can be searched in a systematic fashion.

Note

The search framework provided by the `SearchManager` class
(`android.app.SearchManager`) does not actually perform the search queries—that is up
to you, the developer. The `SearchManager` class simply manages search services and the
search dialog controls. How and what data is searched and which results are returned are
implementation details.

Figure 22.5   Handling in-application searches and search suggestions.

To enable in-application searches, you need to

- Develop an application with data, ideally exposed as a content provider.
- Create an XML search configuration file.
- Implement an `Activity` class to handle searches.
- Configure the application's Android manifest file for searches.

Now let's look at each of these requirements in more detail.

Creating a Search Configuration

Creating a search configuration for your application simply means that you need to create an XML file with special search tags. This search configuration file is normally stored in the xml resource directory (for example, `/res/xml/searchable.xml`) and referenced in the searchable application's Android manifest file.

Enabling Basic Searches

The following is a sample search configuration the field notes application might use, stored as an application resource file called

```
<?xml version="1.0" encoding="utf-8"?>
<searchable
    xmlns:android="http://schemas.android.com/apk/res/android"
```

```
    android:label="@string/app_name"
    android:hint="@string/search_hint"
    android:searchSettingsDescription="@string/search_settings_help">
</searchable>
```

The basic attributes of the search configuration are fairly straightforward. The `label` field is generally set to the name of your application (the application providing the search result). The `hint` field is the text that shows in the `EditText` control of the search box when no text has been entered—a prompt. You can further customize the search dialog by customizing the search button text and input method options, if desired.

Enabling Search Suggestions

If your application acts as a content provider and you want to enable search suggestions—those results provided in a list below the search box as the user types in search criteria—then you must include several additional attributes within your search configuration. You need to specify information about the content provider used to supply the search suggestions, including its authority, path information, and the query to use to return search suggestions. You also need to provide information for the `Intent` to trigger when a user clicks on a specific suggestion.

Again, let's go back to the field notes example. Here are the search configuration attributes required in order to support search suggestions that query field note titles:

```
android:searchSuggestAuthority =
    "com.androidbook.simplesearchintegration.SimpleFieldnotesContentProvider"
android:searchSuggestPath="fieldnotes"
android:searchSuggestSelection="fieldnotes_title LIKE ?"
android:searchSuggestIntentAction="android.intent.action.VIEW"
android:searchSuggestIntentData = "content://com.androidbook.simplesearch
integration.SimpleFieldnotesContentProvider/fieldnotes"
```

The first attribute, `searchSuggestAuthority`, sets the content provider to use for the search suggestion query. The second attribute defines the path appended to the `Authority` and right before `SearchManager.SUGGEST_URI_PATH_QUERY` is appended to the `Authority`, as well. The third attribute supplies the SQL WHERE clause of the search query (here, only the field note titles, not their bodies, are queried to keep search suggestion performance reasonably fast). Next, an `Intent` action is provided for when a user clicks a search suggestion and then finally the intent, the `Uri` used to launch the `Intent`, is defined.

You can also set a threshold (`android:searchSuggestThreshold`) on the number of characters the user needs to type before a search suggestion query is performed. Consider setting this value to a reasonable number like 3 or 4 characters to keep queries to a minimum (the default is 0). At a value of zero, even an empty search field shows suggestions—but these are not filtered at all.

Each time the user begins to type in search criteria, the system performs a content provider query to retrieve suggestions. Therefore, the application's content provider interface needs to be updated to handle these queries. In order to make this all work properly, you need to define a projection in order to map the content provider data columns to those that the search framework expects to use to fill the search suggestion list with content. For example, the following code defines a project to map the field notes unique identifiers and titles to the _ID, SUGGEST_COLUMN_TEXT_1 and SUGGEST_COLUMN_INTENT_DATA_ID fields for the search suggestions:

```
private static final HashMap<String, String>
FIELDNOTES_SEARCH_SUGGEST_PROJECTION_MAP;
static {
    FIELDNOTES_SEARCH_SUGGEST_PROJECTION_MAP =
        new HashMap<String, String>();
    FIELDNOTES_SEARCH_SUGGEST_PROJECTION_MAP.put(_ID, _ID);
    FIELDNOTES_SEARCH_SUGGEST_PROJECTION_MAP.put(
        SearchManager.SUGGEST_COLUMN_TEXT_1, FIELDNOTES_TITLE + " AS "
        + SearchManager.SUGGEST_COLUMN_TEXT_1);
    FIELDNOTES_SEARCH_SUGGEST_PROJECTION_MAP.put(
        SearchManager.SUGGEST_COLUMN_INTENT_DATA_ID, _ID + " AS "
        + SearchManager.SUGGEST_COLUMN_INTENT_DATA_ID);
}
```

Each time search suggestions need to be displayed, the system executes a query using the Uri provided as part of the search configuration. Don't forget to define this Uri and register it in the content provider's UriMatcher object (using the addURI() method). For example, the field notes application used the following Uri for search suggestion queries:

```
content:// com.androidbook.simplesearchintegration.
SimpleFieldnotesContentProvider/fieldnotes/search_suggestion_query
```

By providing a special search suggestion Uri for the content provider queries, you can simply update the content provider's query() method to handle the specialized query, including building the projection, performing the appropriate query and returning the results. Let's take a closer look at the field notes content provider query() method:

```
@Override
public Cursor query(Uri uri, String[] projection, String selection,
    String[] selectionArgs, String sortOrder) {
    SQLiteQueryBuilder queryBuilder = new SQLiteQueryBuilder();
    queryBuilder.setTables(SimpleFieldnotesDatabase.FIELDNOTES_TABLE);
    int match = sURIMatcher.match(uri);
    switch (match) {
    case FIELDNOTES_SEARCH_SUGGEST:
        selectionArgs = new String[] { "%" + selectionArgs[0] + "%" };
        queryBuilder.setProjectionMap(
            FIELDNOTES_SEARCH_SUGGEST_PROJECTION_MAP);
        break;
    case FIELDNOTES:
        break;
```

```
case FIELDNOTE_ITEM:
    String id = uri.getLastPathSegment();
    queryBuilder.appendWhere(_ID + "=" + id);
    break;
default:
    throw new IllegalArgumentException("Invalid URI: " + uri);
}
SQLiteDatabase sql = database.getReadableDatabase();
Cursor cursor =
    queryBuilder.query(sql, projection, selection,
    selectionArgs, null, null, sortOrder);
cursor.setNotificationUri(getContext().getContentResolver(), uri);
return cursor;
}
```

This `query()` method implementation handles both regular content queries and special search suggestion queries (those that come in with the search suggestion `Uri`). When the search suggestion query occurs, we wrap the search criteria in wildcards and use the handy `setProjectionMap()` method of the `QueryBuilder` object to set and execute the query as normal. Because we want to return results quickly, we only search for titles matching the search criteria for suggestions, not the full text of the field notes.

> **Tip**
>
> Instead of using wildcards and a slow LIKE expression in SQLite, we could have used the SQLite FTS3 extension, which enables fast full-text queries. With a limited number of rows of data, this is not strictly necessary in our case and it requires creating tables in a different and much less relational way. Indices are not supported, so query performance might suffer. See the SQLite FTS3 documentation at http://www.sqlite.org/fts3.html.

Enabling Voice Search

You can also add voice search capabilities to your application. This enables the user to speak the search criteria instead of type it. There are several attributes you can add to your search configuration to enable voice searches. The most important attribute is `voiceSearchMode`, which enables voice searches and sets the appropriate mode: The `showVoiceSearchButton` value enables the little voice recording button to display as part of the search dialog, the `launchRecognizer` value tells the Android system to use voice recording activity, and the `launchWebSearch` value initiates the special voice web search activity.

To add simple voice support to the field notes sample application can be done simply by adding the following line to the search configuration:

```
android:voiceSearchMode="showVoiceSearchButton|launchRecognizer"
```

Other voice search attributes you can set include the voice language model (free form or web search), the voice language, the maximum voice results, and a text prompt for the voice recognition dialog. See the Android SDK documentation regarding Searchable

Configuration for more details: http://developer.android.com/guide/topics/search/searchable-config.html.

Creating a Search Activity

Next, you need to implement an `Activity` class that actually performs the requested searches. This `Activity` is launched whenever your application receives an intent with the action value of `ACTION_SEARCH`.

The search request contains the search string in the extra field called `SearchManager.QUERY`. The `Activity` takes this value, performs the search, and then responds with the results.

Let's look at the search `Activity` from our field notes example. You can implement its search activity, `SimpleSearchableActivity`, as follows:

```java
public class SimpleSearchableActivity extends ListActivity {
    @Override
    protected void onCreate(Bundle savedInstanceState) {
        super.onCreate(savedInstanceState);
        Intent intent = getIntent();
        checkIntent(intent);
    }

    @Override
    protected void onNewIntent(Intent newIntent) {
        // update the activity launch intent
        setIntent(newIntent);
        // handle it
        checkIntent(newIntent);
    }

    private void checkIntent(Intent intent) {
        String query = "";
        String intentAction = intent.getAction();
        if (Intent.ACTION_SEARCH.equals(intentAction)) {
            query = intent.getStringExtra(SearchManager.QUERY);
            Toast.makeText(this,
                "Search received: " + query, Toast.LENGTH_LONG)
                .show();
        } else if (Intent.ACTION_VIEW.equals(intentAction)) {
            // pass this off to the details view activity
            Uri details = intent.getData();
            Intent detailsIntent =
                new Intent(Intent.ACTION_VIEW, details);
            startActivity(detailsIntent);
            finish();
            return;
        }
```

```
        fillList(query);
    }


    private void fillList(String query) {
        String wildcardQuery = "%" + query + "%";
        Cursor cursor =
            managedQuery(
                SimpleFieldnotesContentProvider.CONTENT_URI,
                null,
                SimpleFieldnotesContentProvider.FIELDNOTES_TITLE
                + " LIKE ? OR "
                + SimpleFieldnotesContentProvider.FIELDNOTES_BODY
                + " LIKE ?",
                new String[] { wildcardQuery, wildcardQuery }, null);
        ListAdapter adapter =
            new SimpleCursorAdapter(
                this,
                android.R.layout.simple_list_item_1,
                cursor,
                new String[] {
                    SimpleFieldnotesContentProvider.FIELDNOTES_TITLE },
                new int[] { android.R.id.text1 });
        setListAdapter(adapter);
    }


    @Override
    protected void onListItemClick(
        ListView l, View v, int position, long id) {
        Uri details = Uri.withAppendedPath(
            SimpleFieldnotesContentProvider.CONTENT_URI, "" + id);
        Intent intent =
            new Intent(Intent.ACTION_VIEW, details);
        startActivity(intent);
    }
}
```

Both the `onCreate()` and `onNewIntent()` methods are implemented because the
`Activity` is flagged with a `launchMode` set to `singleTop`. This `Activity` is capable of
bringing up the search dialog when the user presses the Search button, like the rest of the
activities in this example. When the user performs a search, the system launches the
`SimpleSearchableActivity`—the same activity the user was already viewing. We don't
want to create a huge stack of search result activities, so we don't let it have more than one
instance on top of the stack—thus the `singleTop` setting.

Handling the search is fairly straightforward. We use the search term provided for us to
create a query. Using the `managedQuery` call, the results are obtained as a `Cursor` object

that is then used with the `SimpleCursorAdapter` object to fill the `ListView` control of the `Activity` class.

For list item click handling, the implementation here simply creates a new `VIEW` intent and, effectively, lets the system handle the item clicking. In this case, the details activity handles the displaying of the proper field note. Why do this instead of launching the class activity directly? No reason other than it's simple and it's well tested from other uses of this launch style.

When a user clicks on a suggestion in the list, instead of an `ACTION_SEARCH`, this activity receives the usual `ACTION_VIEW`. Instead of handling it here, though, it's passed on to the details view `Activity` as that activity is already designed to handle the drawing of the details for each item—no reason to implement it twice.

Configuring the Android Manifest File for Search

Now it's time to register your searchable Activity class within the application manifest file, including configuring the intent filter associated with the `ACTION_SEARCH` action. You also need to mark your application as searchable using a `<meta-data>` manifest file tag.

Here is the Android manifest file excerpt for the searchable activity registration:

```
<activity
    android:name="SimpleSearchableActivity"
    android:launchMode="singleTop">
    <intent-filter>
        <action android:name="android.intent.action.SEARCH" />
    </intent-filter>
    <intent-filter>
        <action android:name="android.intent.action.VIEW" />
    </intent-filter>
    <meta-data
        android:name="android.app.searchable"
        android:resource="@xml/searchable" />
</activity>
```

The main difference between this `<activity>` tag configuration and a typical activity is the addition of the intent filter for intents with an action type of `SEARCH`. In addition, some metadata is provided so that the system knows where to find the search configuration details.

Next, let's look at an example of how to enable the Search button for all activities within the application. This `<meta-data>` block needs to be added to the `<application>` tag, outside any `<activity>` tags.

```
<meta-data
    android:name="android.app.default_searchable"
    android:value =
        "com.androidbook.simplesearchintegration.SimpleSearchableActivity" />
```

This `<meta-data>` tag configures the default activity that handles the search results for the entire application. This way, pressing the Search button brings up the search dialog from any activity within the application. If you don't want this functionality in every activity, you need to add this definition to each activity for which you do want the Search button enabled.

> **Note**
>
> Not all Android devices have a Search button. If you want to guarantee search abilities within the application, consider adding other ways to initiate a search, such as adding a Search button to the application screen or providing the search option on the Option menu.

Enabling Global Search

After you have enabled your application for searches, you can make it part of the global device search features with a few extra steps. Global searches are often invoked using the Quick Search Box. In order to enable your application for global search, you need to

- Begin with an application that already has in-application search abilities as described earlier.
- Update the search configuration file to enable global searches.
- Include your application in global searches by updating the Search settings of the device.

Now let's look at these requirements in a bit more detail. Let's assume we're working with the same sample application—the field notes. Figure 22.6 shows the global search box, as initiated from the Home screen.

Updating a Search Configuration for Global Searches

Updating an existing search configuration is very simple. All you need to do is add the `includeInGlobalSearch` attribute in your configuration and set it to `true` as follows:

```
android:includeInGlobalSearch="true"
```

At this point, you should also ensure that your application is acting as a content type handler for the results you provide as part of global searches (if you haven't already). That way, users can select search suggestions provided by your application. Again, you probably want to leverage the content type handler functionality again, in order to launch the application when a search suggestion is chosen.

> **Tip**
>
> You can initiate a global search using the `SearchManager.INTENT_ACTION_GLOBAL_SEARCH` Intent.

Updating Search Settings for Global Searches

However, the user has ultimate control over what applications are included as part of the global search. Your application is not included in global searches by default. The user must include your application explicitly. In order for your application's content to show up as part of global searches, the user must adjust the device Search settings. The user makes this configuration from the Settings, Search, Searchable Items menu, as shown in Figure 22.7.

Figure 22.6   Application content is included in global
search results, such as when the user presses the
search button while on the Home screen.

If your application has content that is appropriate for global searches, you might want
to include a shortcut to these settings so that users can easily navigate to them without
feeling like they've left your application. The `SearchManager` class has an intent called
`INTENT_ACTION_SEARCH_SETTINGS` for this purpose:

```
Intent intent = new Intent(SearchManager.INTENT_ACTION_SEARCH_SETTINGS);
startActivity(intent);
```

This intent launches the Settings application on the Search settings screen, as shown in
Figure 22.7 (left).

As you can see, searches—whether they are in-application searches or global searches—
allow application content to be exposed in new and interesting ways so that the user's data
is always just a few keystrokes (or spoken words) away. But wait! There's more! Check out
the Search Dev Guide on the Android developer website to learn more about the sophisticated features available as part of the Android search framework: http://developer.android.
com/guide/topics/search/index.html.

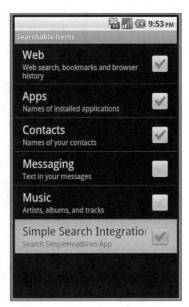

Figure 22.7   Configuring device search settings to include
content from your application.

Working with Live Folders

Another way you can make content-rich applications more readily available to users is with the use of live folders. Introduced in Android 1.5 (API Level 3), a live folder is a special type of folder that the user can place in various areas such as the Home screen and, when clicked, displays its content by querying an application that acts as a content provider. Each piece of data in the folder can be paired with an intent. You could also think of it as a folder of shortcuts into your application. For example, a music application might allow the user to create live folders for favorite music. Similarly, a to-do list application might include support for a live folder of the day's tasks. Finally, a game might have a live folder for saved game points. When the user clicks on an item, the application launches to play the appropriate song, show the appropriate to-do list item, or start the game at that save point. Applications can support live folders with different types of content—it all depends on the content the application has to expose.

Let's return to the example of the African field notes application and update it so that users can create live folders with field note titles. Clicking on a specific field note launches the application with an action VIEW for the full field note contents (again, by acting as a content type handler, as discussed earlier in this chapter).

Tip

Many of the code examples provided in this section are taken from the SimpleLiveFolder application. The source code for this application is provided for download on the book website.

Creating Live Folders

To enable in-application live folder creation within your application, you need

- An application with data exposed as a content provider
- An application that acts as a content type handler for the type of data that is exposed in the live folder (for example, VIEW field notes)
- To implement an `Activity` class to handle live folder creation
- To update the application's content provider interface to handle live folder queries
- To configure the application's Android manifest file for live folders

Now let's look at some of these requirements in more detail.

Creating a Live Folder Activity

An application that supports live folders must include a live folder creation activity. This activity is launched anytime the application reacts to the intent action `ACTION_CREATE_LIVE_FOLDER`. The live folder creation activity is responsible for one thing: responding with a specific instance of a live folder configuration. If you recall how the `startActivityForResult()` method works, this is exactly how the live folder creation activity is called. The activity needs to retrieve the incoming intent that performed the live folder creation request, craft a new live folder (as an `Intent` object with suitable extras to specify the live folder configuration details) and set the Activity result using the `setResult()` method. The `setResult()` method parameters can be used to communicate whether or not the live folder creation was successful as the `resultCode` parameter and pass back the specific instance of the live folder as the accompanying result Intent `data` parameter.

Sounds a tad complex, eh? Well, let's look at a specific example. Here is the implementation of the live folder creation activity for the field notes application:

```
import android.app.Activity;
import android.content.Intent;
import android.os.Bundle;
import android.provider.LiveFolders;

public class SimpleLiveFolderCreateActivity extends Activity {
    @Override
    protected void onCreate(Bundle savedInstanceState) {
        super.onCreate(savedInstanceState);
        final Intent intent = getIntent();
        final String action = intent.getAction();
        if (LiveFolders.ACTION_CREATE_LIVE_FOLDER.equals(action)) {
            final Intent baseIntent = new Intent(Intent.ACTION_VIEW,
                SimpleFieldnotesContentProvider.CONTENT_URI);
            final Intent resultIntent = new Intent();
            resultIntent.setData(
                SimpleFieldnotesContentProvider.LIVE_URI);
```

```
                resultIntent.putExtra(LiveFolders.EXTRA_LIVE_FOLDER_NAME,
                    getResources().getString(R.string.livefolder_label));
                resultIntent.putExtra(LiveFolders.EXTRA_LIVE_FOLDER_ICON,
                    Intent.ShortcutIconResource.fromContext(
                    this, R.drawable.foldericon));
                resultIntent.putExtra(
                    LiveFolders.EXTRA_LIVE_FOLDER_DISPLAY_MODE,
                    LiveFolders.DISPLAY_MODE_LIST);
                resultIntent.putExtra(
                    LiveFolders.EXTRA_LIVE_FOLDER_BASE_INTENT,
                    baseIntent);
                setResult(RESULT_OK, resultIntent);
            } else {
                setResult(RESULT_CANCELED);
            }
            finish();
        }
}
```

As you can see, the SimpleLiveFolderCreateActivity has a very short lifespan. It waits
for ACTION_CREATE_LIVE_FOLDER requests and then crafts the appropriate Intent object
to return as part of the activity result. The most important code in this activity is the code
that creates the new intent called resultIntent. This Intent object contains all the configuration details for the new live folder instance. The setData() method is used to supply the live Uri (the Uri to query to fill the folder with data).

Several extras are set to provide the live folder instance with a label and icon, as well
as specify the display mode of the live folder. Live folders have several canned display
modes: The DISPLAY_MODE_LIST value causes all live folder content to display in
ListView control (ideal for text content) and the DISPLAY_MODE_GRID displays live folder
content in a GridView control—more appropriate if the live folder contents are graphics.
Finally, the base Intent object for each live folder item is set. In this case, the base intent
has an action type of VIEW, as you might expect, and therefore is compatible with the content type handler technique. For more information on the configuration details that can
be applied to a live folder, see the Android SDK documentation for the
android.provider.LiveFolders package.

Handling Live Folder Content Provider Queries

Each time the user opens the live folder, the system performs a content provider query.
Therefore, the application's content provider interface needs to be updated to handle
queries to fill the live folder with data. As with search suggestions, you need to define a
projection in order to map the content provider data columns to those that the live folder
expects to use to fill the list or grid (depending on the display mode) within the folder.

For example, the following code defines a project to map the field notes' unique identi-fiers and titles to the ID and name fields for the live folder items:

```
private static final HashMap<String, String>
FIELDNOTES_LIVE_FOLDER_PROJECTION_MAP;
static {
    FIELDNOTES_LIVE_FOLDER_PROJECTION_MAP = new HashMap<String, String>();
    FIELDNOTES_LIVE_FOLDER_PROJECTION_MAP
        .put(LiveFolders._ID, _ID + " AS "
        + LiveFolders._ID);
    FIELDNOTES_LIVE_FOLDER_PROJECTION_MAP.put(
        LiveFolders.NAME, FIELDNOTES_TITLE
        + " AS " + LiveFolders.NAME);
}
```

Whenever the live folder is opened by the user, the system executes a query on the Uri provided as part of the live folder configuration. Don't forget to define the live Uri address and register it in the content provider's UriMatcher object (using the addURI() method). For example, the field notes application used the Uri:

```
content:// com.androidbook.simplelivefolder.
SimpleFieldnotesContentProvider/fieldnotes/live
```

By providing a special live folder Uri for the content provider queries, you can simply update the content provider's query method to handle the specialized query, including building the projection, performing the appropriate query, and returning the results for display in the live folder. Let's take a closer look at the field notes content provider query() method:

```
@Override
public Cursor query(Uri uri, String[] projection, String selection,
    String[] selectionArgs, String sortOrder) {
    SQLiteQueryBuilder queryBuilder = new SQLiteQueryBuilder();
    queryBuilder.setTables(SimpleFieldnotesDatabase.FIELDNOTES_TABLE);
    int match = sURIMatcher.match(uri);
    switch (match) {
    case FIELDNOTE_ITEM:
        String id = uri.getLastPathSegment();
        queryBuilder.appendWhere(_ID + "=" + id);
        break;
    case FIELDNOTES_LIVE:
        queryBuilder.setProjectionMap(
            FIELDNOTES_LIVE_FOLDER_PROJECTION_MAP);
        break;
    default:
        throw new IllegalArgumentException("Invalid URI: " + uri);
    }
    SQLiteDatabase sql = database.getReadableDatabase();
    Cursor cursor = queryBuilder.query(sql,
```

```
        projection, selection, selectionArgs, null,
        null, sortOrder);
    cursor.setNotificationUri(getContext().getContentResolver(), uri);
    return cursor;
}
```

This `query()` method implementation handles both regular content queries and special live folder queries (those that come in with the live `Uri`). When the live folder query occurs, we simply use the handy `setProjectionMap()` method of the `QueryBuilder` object to set and execute the query as normal.

Configuring the Android Manifest File for Live Folders

Finally, the live folder Activity class needs to be registered within the application Android manifest file with an intent filter with the `CREATE_LIVE_FOLDER` action. For example, here is an excerpt from the field notes Android manifest file that does just that:

```
<activity
    android:name="SimpleLiveFolderCreateActivity"
    android:label="@string/livefolder_label"
    android:icon="@drawable/foldericon">
    <intent-filter>
        <action
            android:name="android.intent.action.CREATE_LIVE_FOLDER" />
        <category
            android:name="android.intent.category.DEFAULT" />
    </intent-filter>
</activity>
```

This type of `Activity` registration should look familiar. The `SimpleLiveFolderCreateActivity` class is responsible for handling the `CREATE_LIVE_FOLDER` intent (as dictated by the intent filter). You can also set the live folder's text `label` and `icon` using the attributes for the creation activity.

> **Note**
>
> The icon and text label shown in the Live Folder picker is set separately from the icon and label shown for a given instance of a live folder. You can set the information for the Live Folder in the picker using the `android:label` and `android:icon` attributes of the `<activity>` tag corresponding to the activity that handles the intent filter for `android.intent.action.CREATE_LIVE_FOLDER` action in the Android manifest file. The icon and label for each Live Folder instance on the Home screen (or other live folder host) is set as part intent extra fields when your `Activity` class handles the action `LiveFolders.ACTION_CREATE_LIVE_FOLDER`.

Installing a Live Folder

After the application is capable of handling the creation of a live folder, your development work is done. As a user, you can install a live folder on the Home screen using the following steps:

1. Long-press on an empty space in the Home Screen.
2. From the menu, choose the Folders option, as shown in Figure 22.8 (left).

 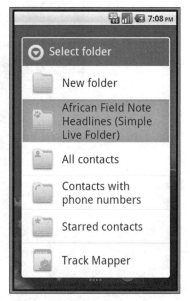

Figure 22.8   Installing a live folder on the Home screen.

3. From the Select folder menu, choose the folder to add, as shown in Figure 22.8 (right).
4. The live folder is now visible on your Home Screen, as shown in Figure 22.9.
5. If you click on the live folder, it opens and shows its contents (as dictated by the developer). Choosing an item from the live folder launches the underlying application. For example, choosing one of the field note titles from the list launches the `Activity` used to view that specific item and its details, as shown in Figure 22.10.

Figure 22.9   A live folder on the Home screen.

Figure 22.10   Choosing a specific field note from the live folder (left)
launches the application to display its content (right).

Summary

The Android platform provides a number of ways to integrate your applications tightly into the operating system, enabling you to extend your reach beyond traditional application boundaries. In this chapter, you learned how to extend your application by creating simple App Widgets, live wallpapers, live folders, and more. You also learned how to enable search within your applications, as well as how to include your application content in global searches.

References and More Information

Our Series of Articles on App Widgets:
    http://j.mp/a8mpdH
Android Dev Guide: App Widgets:
    http://developer.android.com/guide/topics/appwidgets/index.html
Android Dev Guide: Search:
    http://developer.android.com/guide/topics/search/index.html
Android Technical Articles: Live Wallpapers:
    http://developer.android.com/resources/articles/live-wallpapers.html
Android Technical Articles: Live Folders:
    http://developer.android.com/resources/articles/live-folders.html

## 23

Managing User Accounts and Synchronizing User Data

Android is cloud-friendly. Android applications can integrate tightly with remote services, helping users transition seamlessly. Android applications can synchronize data with remote cloud-based (Internet) services using sync adapters. Developers can also take advantage of Android's cloud-based backup service to protect and migrate application data safely and effectively. In this chapter, you learn about the account and synchronization features to sync data to built-in applications as well as protect application data using the backup and restore features available in Android.

Managing Accounts with the Account Manager

From a user perspective, the Android 2.0 platform introduced many exciting new device features. For instance, the user can register and use multiple accounts for email and contact management. This feature was provided through a combination of new synchronization and account services that are also available to developers. Although you can use the account and synchronization packages with any kind of data, the intention seems to be to provide a way for developers and companies to integrate their business services with the system that synchronizes data to the built-in Android applications.

Android user accounts are manipulated using the classes available within the `android.accounts` package. This functionality is primarily designed for accounts with services that contain contact, email, or other such information in them. A good example of this type of online service is a social networking application that contains friends' contact information, as well as other relevant information such as their statuses. This information is often delivered and used on an Android device using the synchronization service (we talk more about synchronization later in the chapter).

First, we talk about accounts. Accounts registered with the Android account manager should provide access to the same sort of information—contact information, for the most part. Different accounts can be registered for a given user using the Android `AccountManager` class. Each account contains authentication information for a service, usually credentials for a server account somewhere online. Android services, such as the synchronization services built-in to the platform, can access these accounts, mining them for the appropriate types of information (again, primarily contact details, but also other bits of data such as social networking status).

Let's look at how using account information provided via the `AccountManager` and `Account` classes works. An application that needs to access the server can request a list of accounts from the system. If one of the accounts contains credentials for the server, the application can request an authentication token for the account. The application would then use this token as a way to log in to the remote server to access its services. This keeps the user credentials secure and private while also providing a convenience to the user in that they only need to provide their credentials once, regardless of how many applications use the information. All these tasks are achieved using the `AccountManager` class. A call to the `getAccountByType()` method retrieves a list of accounts and then a call to the `getAuthToken()` method retrieves the token associated with a specific account, which the application can use to communicate with a password-protected resource, such as a web service.

On the other side of this process, authenticating credentials against the back-end server are the account providers. That is, the services that provide users with accounts and with which user information is authenticated so the applications can get the auth tokens. In order to do all of this (handle system requests to authenticate an `Account` object against the remote server), the account provider must implement an account authenticator. Through the authenticator, the account provider requests appropriate credentials and then confirms them with whatever account authentication operations are necessary—usually an online server. To implement an account authenticator, you need to make several modifications to your application. Begin by implementing the `AbstractAccountAuthenticator` class. You also need to update the application's Android Manifest file, provide an authenticator configuration file (XML), and provide an authenticator preference screen configuration in order to make the authentication experience as seamless as possible for the user.

Tip

Learn more about creating system-wide accounts in the Android SDK documentation for the `AbstractAccountAuthenticator` class. Learn more about using accounts in the Android SDK documentation for the `AccountManager` class.

Synchronizing Data with Sync Adapters

The synchronization feature available in the Android SDK requires the use of the accounts classes we talked about earlier. This service is principally designed to enable syncing of contact, email, and calendar data to the built-in applications from a back-end datastore—you're "adapting" back-end server data to the existing content providers. That is, the service is not generally used for syncing data specific to your typical Android application. In theory, applications could use this service to keep data in sync, but they might be better served by implementing synchronization internally. You could do this using the

`AlarmManager` class to schedule systematic data synchronization via the network, perhaps using an Android service.

If, however, you are working with data that is well suited to syncing to the internal applications, such as contacts or calendar information that you want to put in the built-in applications and content providers, implementing a sync adapter makes sense. This enables the Android system to manage synchronization activities.

The account service must provide the sync adapter by extending the `AbstractThreadedSyncAdapter` class. When the sync occurs, the `onPerformSync()` method of the sync adapter is called. The parameters to this method tell the adapter what account (as defined by the `Account` parameter) is being used, thus providing necessary authentication tokens (auth token, for short) for accessing protected resources without the need for asking the user for credentials. The adapter is also told which content provider to write the data to and for which authority, in the content provider sense, the data belongs to.

In this way, synchronization operations are performed on their own thread at a time requested by the system. During the sync, the adapter gets updated information from the server and synchronizes it to the given content provider. The implementation details for this are flexible, and up to the developer.

Tip

Learn more about creating sync adapters by checking out the Sync Adapter sample application on the Android developer website: http://developer.android.com/resources/samples/SampleSyncAdapter/.

Using Backup Services

Android backup services were introduced in Android 2.2 (API Level 8). Applications can use the backup system service to request that application data such as shared preferences and files be backed up or restored. The backup service handles things from there, sending or retrieving the appropriate backup archives to a remote backup service.

Backup services should not be used for syncing application content. Backup and restore operations do not occur on demand. Use a synchronization strategy such as the sync adapter discussed earlier in this chapter in this case. Use Android backup services only to back up important application data.

Tip

Many of the code examples provided in this section are taken from the SimpleBackup application. The source code for this application is provided for download on the book website. Also, you need to use the `adb bmgr` command to force backups and restores to occur. For more information on `adb`, see Appendix C, "The Android Debug Bridge Quick-Start Guide."

Choosing a Remote Backup Service

One of the most important decisions when it comes to backing up application data is deciding where to back it up to. The remote backup service you choose should be secure, reliable, and always available. Many developers will likely choose the solution provided by Google: Android Backup Service.

Note

Other third-party remote backup services might be available. If you want complete control over the backup process, you might want to consider creating your own. However, this is beyond the scope of this book.

In order for your application to use Android Backup Service, you must register your application with Google and acquire a unique backup service key for use within the application's manifest file.

You can sign up for Google's backup service at the Android Backup Service website: http://code.google.com/android/backup/signup.html.

Warning

Backup services are available on most, but not all, Android devices running Android 2.2 and higher. The underlying implementation might vary. Also, different remote backup services might impose additional limitations on the devices supported. Test your specific target devices and backup solution thoroughly to determine that backup services function properly with your application.

Registering with Android Backup Service

After you have chosen a remote backup service, you might need to jump through a few more hoops. With Google's Android Backup Service, you need to register for a special key to use. After you've acquired this key, you can use it within your application's manifest file using the `<meta-data>` tag within the `<application>` block, like this:

```
<meta-data android:name="com.google.android.backup.api_key"
    android:value="KEY HERE" />
```

Implementing a Backup Agent

The backup system service relies upon an application's backup agent to determine what application data should be archived for backup and restore purposes.

Providing a Backup Agent Implementation

Now it's time to implement the backup agent for your particular application. The backup agent determines what application data to send to the backup service. If you only want to back up shared preference data and application files, you can simply use the `BackupAgentHelper` class.

Tip

If you need to customize how your application backs up its data, you need to extend the `BackupAgent` class, which requires you to implement two callback methods. The `onBackup()` method is called when your application requests a backup and provides the backup service with the appropriate application data to back up. The `onRestore()` method is called when a restore is requested. The backup service supplies the archived data and the `onRestore()` method handles restoring the application data.

Here is a sample implementation of a backup agent class:

```
public class SimpleBackupAgent extends BackupAgentHelper {
    @Override
    public void onCreate() {
        // Register helpers here
    }
}
```

Your application's backup agent needs to include a backup helper for each type of data it wants to back up.

Implementing a Backup Helper for Shared Preferences

To back up shared preferences files, you need to use the `SharedPreferencesBackupHelper` class. Adding support for shared preferences is very straightforward. Simply update the backup agent's `onCreate()` method, create a valid `SharedPreferencesBackupHelper` object, and use the `addHelper()` method to add it to the agent:

```
SharedPreferencesBackupHelper prefshelper = new
SharedPreferencesBackupHelper(this,
    PREFERENCE_FILENAME);
addHelper(BACKUP_PREFERENCE_KEY, prefshelper);
```

This particular helper backs up all shared preferences by name. In this case, the `addHelper()` method takes two parameters:

- A unique name for this helper (in this case, the backup key is stored as a `String` variable called `BACKUP_PREFERENCE_KEY`).
- A valid `SharedPreferencesBackupHelper` object configured to control backups and restores on a specific set of shared preferences by name (in this case, the preference filename is stored in a `String` variable called `PREFERENCE_FILENAME`).

That's it. In fact, if your application is only backing up shared preferences, you don't even need to implement the `onBackup()` and `onRestore()` methods of your backup agent class.

Tip

Got more than one set of preferences? No problem. The constructor for `SharedPreferencesBackupHelper` can take any number of preference filenames. You still need only one unique name key for the helper.

Implementing a Backup Helper for Files

To back up application files, use the `FileBackupHelper` class. Files are a bit trickier to handle than shared preferences because they are not thread-safe. Begin by updating the backup agent's `onCreate()` method, create a valid `FileBackupHelper` object, and use the `addHelper()` method to add it to the agent:

```
FileBackupHelper filehelper = new FileBackupHelper(this, APP_FILE_NAME);
addHelper(BACKUP_FILE_KEY, filehelper);
```

The file helper backs up specific files by name. In this case, the `addHelper()` method takes two parameters:

- A unique name for this helper (in this case, the backup key is stored as a `String` variable called `BACKUP_FILE_KEY`).

- A valid `FileBackupHelper` object configured to control backups and restores on a specific file by name (in this case, the filename is stored in a `String` variable called `APP_FILE_NAME`).

Tip

Got more than one file to back up? No problem. The constructor for `FileBackupHelper` can take any number of filenames. You still need only one unique name key for the helper. The services were designed to back up configuration data, not necessarily all files or media. There are currently no guidelines for the size of the data that can be backed up. For instance, a book reader application might back up book titles and reading states, but not the book contents. Then, after a restore, the data could be used to download the book contents again. To the user, the state appears the same.

You also need to make sure that all file operations within your application are thread-safe as it's possible a backup will be requested while a file is being accessed. The Android website suggests the following method for defining a lock from a simple `Object` array within your `Activity`, as follows:

```
static final Object[] fileLock = new Object[0];
```

Use this lock each and every time you are performing file operations, either in your application logic, or within the backup agent. For example:

```
synchronized(fileLock){
    // Do app logic file operations here
}
```

Finally, you need to override the `onBackup()` and `onRestore()` methods of your backup agent, if only to make sure all file operations are synchronized using your lock for thread-safe access. Here we have the full implementation of a backup agent that backs up one set of shared preferences called AppPrefs and a file named appfile.txt:

```java
public class SimpleBackupAgent extends BackupAgentHelper {
    private static final String PREFERENCE_FILENAME = "AppPrefs";
    private static final String APP_FILE_NAME = "appfile.txt";
    static final String BACKUP_PREFERENCE_KEY = "BackupAppPrefs";
    static final String BACKUP_FILE_KEY = "BackupFile";

    @Override
    public void onCreate() {
        SharedPreferencesBackupHelper prefshelper = new
            SharedPreferencesBackupHelper(this,
            PREFERENCE_FILENAME);
        addHelper(BACKUP_PREFERENCE_KEY, prefshelper);
        FileBackupHelper filehelper =
            new FileBackupHelper(this, APP_FILE_NAME);
        addHelper(BACKUP_FILE_KEY, filehelper);
    }
    @Override
    public void onBackup(ParcelFileDescriptor oldState,
        BackupDataOutput data, ParcelFileDescriptor newState)
        throws IOException {
            synchronized (SimpleBackupActivity.fileLock) {
                super.onBackup(oldState, data, newState);
            }
    }
    @Override
    public void onRestore(BackupDataInput data, int appVersionCode,
        ParcelFileDescriptor newState) throws IOException {
            synchronized (SimpleBackupActivity.fileLock) {
                super.onRestore(data, appVersionCode, newState);
            }
    }
}
```

To make the doBackup() and doRestore() methods thread-safe, we simply wrapped the super class call with a synchronized block using your file lock.

Registering the Backup Agent in the Application Manifest File

Finally, you need to register your backup agent class in your application's manifest file using the android:backupAgent attribute of the <application> tab. For example, if your backup agent class is called SimpleBackupAgent, you would register it using its fully-qualified path name as follows:

```
<application
    android:icon="@drawable/icon"
    android:label="@string/app_name"
    android:backupAgent="com.androidbook.simplebackup.SimpleBackupAgent">
```

Backing Up and Restoring Application Data

The `BackupManager` system service manages backup and restore requests. This service works in the background, on its own schedule. Applications that implement a backup agent can request a backup or restore, but the operations might not happen immediately. To get an instance of the `BackupManager`, simply create one within your `Activity` class, as follows:

```
BackupManager mBackupManager = new BackupManager(this);
```

Requesting a Backup

An application can request a backup using the `dataChanged()` method. Generally, this method should be called any time application data that is to be archived changes. It can be called any number of times, but when it's time to back up, the backup takes place only one time, regardless of how many times `dataChanged()` was called before the backup.

```
mBackupManager.dataChanged();
```

Normally, the user does not initiate a backup. Instead, whenever important application data changes, the `dataChanged()` method should be called as part of the data saving process. At some point in the future, a backup is performed "behind the scenes" by the backup manager.

> ### Warning
>
> Avoid backing up sensitive data to remote servers. Ultimately, you, the developer, are responsible for securing user data, not the backup service you employ.

Requesting a Restore

Restore operations occur automatically when a user resets his device or upgrades after "accidentally" dropping his old one in a hot tub or runs it through the washing machine (happens more often than you'd think). When a restore occurs, the user's data is fetched from the remote backup service and the application's backup agent refreshes the data used by the application, overwriting any data that was there.

An application can directly request a restore using the `requestRestore()` method as well. The `requestRestore()` method takes one parameter: a `RestoreObserver` object. The following code illustrates how to request a restore:

```
RestoreObserver obs = new RestoreObserver(){
    @Override
    public void onUpdate(int nowBeingRestored, String currentPackage) {
        Log.i(DEBUG_TAG, "RESTORING: " + currentPackage);
    }
```

```
    @Override
    public void restoreFinished(int error) {
        Log.i(DEBUG_TAG, "RESTORE FINISHED! ("+error+")");
    }

    @Override
    public void restoreStarting(int numPackages) {
        Log.i(DEBUG_TAG, "RESTORE STARTING...");
    }
};

try {
    mBackupManager.requestRestore(obs);
} catch (Exception e) {
    Log.i(DEBUG_TAG,
        "Failed to request restore. Try adb bmgr restore...");
}
```

Warning

Backup services are a fairly new feature within the Android SDK. There are currently some issues (exceptions thrown, services missing) with running backup services on the emulator. Testing of backup services is best done on a device running Android 2.2 or later, in conjunction with the `adb bmgr` command, which can force an immediate backup or restore to occur.

Summary

Android applications do not exist in a vacuum. Users demand that their data be accessible (securely, of course) across any and all technologies they use regularly. Phones fall into hot tubs (more often than you'd think) and users upgrade to newer devices. The Android platform provides services for keeping local application data synchronized with remote cloud services, as well as protecting application data using remote backup and restore services.

References and More Information

Wikipedia on Cloud Computing:
   http://en.wikipedia.org/wiki/Cloud_computing
Android Reference: The AccountManager Class:
   http://developer.android.com/reference/android/accounts/AccountManager.html
Android Sample App: Sample Sync Adapter:
   http://developer.android.com/resources/samples/SampleSyncAdapter/
Android Dev Guide: Data Backup:
   http://developer.android.com/guide/topics/data/backup.html
Google's Android Backup Service:
   http://code.google.com/android/backup/index.html

## 24

Handling Advanced User Input

Users interact with Android devices in many ways, including using keyboards, trackballs, touch-screen gestures, and even voice. Different devices support different input methods and have different hardware. For example, certain devices have hardware keyboards, and others rely only upon software keyboards. In this chapter, you learn about the different input methods available to developers and how you can use them to great effect within your applications.

Working with Textual Input Methods

The Android SDK includes input method framework classes that enable interested developers to use powerful input methods as well as create their own input methods, such as custom software keyboards and other Input Method Editors (IMEs). Users can download custom IMEs to use on their devices. For example, there's nothing stopping a developer from creating a custom keyboard with Lord of the Rings-style Elvish characters, smiley faces, or Greek symbols.

> **Tip**
>
> Most device settings related to input methods are available under the Settings, Language & Keyboard menu. Here users can select the language as well as configure the custom user dictionary and make changes to how their keyboards function. The user can change the input method on the device by press-and-holding an `EditText` control, for example. A context menu comes up, allowing the user to change the input method (Android keyboard is usually the default).

Working with Software Keyboards

Because text input methods are locale-based (different countries use different alphabets and keyboards) and situational (numeric vs. alphabetic vs. special keys), the Android platform has trended toward software keyboards as opposed to relying on hardware manufacturers to deliver specialized hardware keyboards.

Choosing the Appropriate Software Keyboard

The Android platform has a number of software keyboards available for use. One of the easiest ways to enable your users to enter data efficiently is to specify the type of input expected in each text input field.

Tip

Many of the code examples provided in this section are taken from the SimpleTextInput-Types application. The source code for this application is provided for download on the book website.

For example, to specify an `EditText` that should take only capitalized textual input, you could set the `inputType` attribute as follows:

```
<EditText android:layout_height="wrap_content"
    android:layout_width="fill_parent"
    android:inputType="text|textCapCharacters">
</EditText>
```

Figure 24.1 shows a number of `EditText` controls with different `inputType` configurations.

Figure 24.1   EditText Controls with
different input types.

The input type dictates which software keyboard is used by default and it enforces appropriate rules, such as limiting input to certain characters.

Figure 24.2 (left) illustrates what the software keyboard looks like for an `EditText` control with its `inputType` attribute set to all capitalized text input. Note how the software keyboard keys are all capitalized. If you were to set the `inputType` to `textCapWords` instead, the keyboard switches to lowercase after the first letter of each word and then back to uppercase after a space. Figure 24.2 (middle) illustrates what the software keyboard looks like for an `EditText` control with its `inputType` attribute set to `number`. Figure 24.2 (right) illustrates what the software keyboard looks like for an `EditText` control with its `inputType` attribute set to textual input, where each sentence begins with a capital letter and the text can be multiple lines.

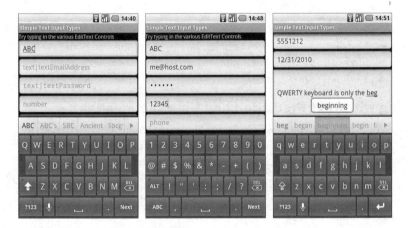

Figure 24.2   The software keyboards associated with specific input types.

Depending on the user's keyboard settings (specifically, if the user has enabled the Show Suggestions and Auto-complete options in the Android Keyboard settings of his device), the user might also see suggested words or spelling fixes while typing.

For a complete list of `inputType` attribute values and their uses, see http://developer. android.com/reference/android/R.attr.html#inputType.

Tip

You can also have your `Activity` react to the display of software keyboards (to adjust where fields are displayed, for example) by requesting the `WindowManager` as a system service and modifying the layout parameters associated with the `softInputMode` field.

For more fine-tuned control over input methods, see the
`android.view.inputmethod.InputMethodManager` class.

Providing Custom Software Keyboards

If you are interested in developing your own software keyboards, we highly recommend
the following references:

- IMEs are implemented as an Android service. Begin by reviewing the Android
  packages called `android.inputmethodservice` and `android.view.inputmethod`,
  which can be used to implement custom input methods.
- The SoftKeyboard sample application in the Android SDK provides an implementation of a software keyboard.
- The Android Developer technical articles on onscreen input methods (http://de-
  veloper.android.com/resources/articles/on-screen-inputs.html) and creating an input method (http://developer.android.com/resources/articles/
  creating-input-method.html).

Working with Text Prediction and User Dictionaries

Text prediction is a powerful and flexible feature available on Android devices. We've
already talked about many of these technologies in other parts of this book, but they merit
mentioning in this context as well.

- In Chapter 7, "Exploring User Interface Screen Elements," you learned how to use
  `AutoCompleteTextView` and `MultiAutoCompleteTextView` controls to help users
  input common words and strings.
- In Chapter 10, "Using Android Data and Storage APIs," you learned how to tie an
  `AutoCompleteTextView` control to an underlying SQLite database table.
- In Chapter 11, "Sharing Data Between Applications with Content Providers," you
  learned about the `UserDictionary` content provider
  (`android.provider.UserDictionary`), which can be used to add words for the
  user's custom dictionary of commonly used words.

Exploring the Accessibility Framework

The Android SDK includes numerous features and services for the benefit of users with
visual and hearing impairments. Those users without such impairments also benefit from
these features, especially when they are not paying complete attention to the device (such
as when driving). Many of the most powerful accessibility features were added in
Android 1.6 and 2.0, so check the API level for a specific class or method before using it
within your application. Some of the accessibility features available within the Android
SDK include

- The Speech Recognition Framework.
- The Text-To-Speech (TTS) Framework.

- The ability to enable haptic feedback (that vibration you feel when you press a button, rather like a rumble pack game controller) on any `View` object (API Level 3 and higher). See the `setHapticFeedbackEnabled()` method of the `View` class.

- The ability to set associated metadata, such as a text description of an `ImageView` control on any `View` object (API Level 4 and higher). This feature is often very helpful for the visually impaired. See the `setContentDescription()` method of the `View` class.

- The ability to create and extend accessibility applications in conjunction with the Android Accessibility framework. See the following packages to get started writing accessibility applications: `android.accessibilityservice` and `android.view.accessibility`. There are also a number of accessibility applications, such as KickBack, SoundBack, and TalkBack, which ship with the platform. For more information, see the device settings under Settings, Accessibility.

Tip

Give some thought to providing accessibility features, such as providing View metadata, within your applications. There's really no excuse for not doing so. Your users appreciate these small details, which make all the difference in terms of whether or not certain users can use your application at all. Also, make sure your quality assurance team verifies accessibility features as part of their testing process.

Because speech recognition and Text-To-Speech applications are all the rage, and their technologies are often used for navigation applications (especially because many states are passing laws making driving while using a mobile device without hands-free operation illegal), let's look at these two technologies in a little more detail.

Android applications can leverage speech input and output. Speech input can be achieved using speech recognition services and speech output can be achieved using Text-To-Speech services. Not all devices support these services. However, certain types of applications—most notably hands-free applications such as directional navigation—often benefit from the use of these types of input.

Speech services are available within the Android SDK in the `android.speech` package. The underlying services that make these technologies work might vary from device to device; some services might require a network connection to function properly.

Tip

Many of the code examples provided in this section are taken from the SimpleSpeech application. The source code for this application is provided for download on the book website. Speech services are best tested on a real Android device. We used an HTC Nexus One running Android 2.2 in our testing.

Leveraging Speech Recognition Services

You can enhance an application with speech recognition support by using the speech recognition framework provided within the Android SDK. Speech recognition involves speaking into the device microphone and enabling the software to detect and interpret that speech and translate it into a string. Speech recognition services are intended for use with short command-like phrases without pauses, not for long dictation. If you want more robust speech recognition, you need to implement your own solution.

On Android SDK 2.1 and higher, access to speech recognition is built in to most pop-up keyboards. Therefore, an application might already support speech recognition, to some extent, without any changes. However, directly accessing the recognizer can allow for more interesting spoken-word control over applications.

You can use the `android.speech.RecognizerIntent` intent to launch the built-in speech recorder. This launches the recorder (shown in Figure 24.3), allowing the user to record speech.

Figure 24.3   Recording speech with the **RecognizerIntent**.

The sound file is sent to an underlying recognition server for processing, so this feature is not really practical for devices that don't have a reasonable network connection. You can then retrieve the results of the speech recognition processing and use them within your application. Note that you might receive multiple results for a given speech segment.

Note

Speech recognition technology is continually evolving and improving. Be sure to enunciate clearly when speaking to your device. Sometimes it might take several tries before the speech recognition engine interprets your speech correctly.

The following code demonstrates how an application could be enabled to record speech using the `RecognizerIntent` intent:

```java
public class SimpleSpeechActivity extends Activity
{
    private static final int VOICE_RECOGNITION_REQUEST = 1;
```

```
@Override
public void onCreate(Bundle savedInstanceState) {
    super.onCreate(savedInstanceState);
    setContentView(R.layout.main);
}
public void recordSpeech(View view) {
    Intent intent =
        new Intent(RecognizerIntent.ACTION_RECOGNIZE_SPEECH);
    intent.putExtra(RecognizerIntent.EXTRA_LANGUAGE_MODEL,
        RecognizerIntent.LANGUAGE_MODEL_FREE_FORM);
    intent.putExtra(RecognizerIntent.EXTRA_PROMPT,
        "Please speak slowly and clearly");
    startActivityForResult(intent, VOICE_RECOGNITION_REQUEST);
}

@Override
protected void onActivityResult(int requestCode,
    int resultCode, Intent data) {
    if (requestCode == VOICE_RECOGNITION_REQUEST &&
        resultCode == RESULT_OK) {
        ArrayList<String> matches = data.getStringArrayListExtra(
            RecognizerIntent.EXTRA_RESULTS);
        TextView textSaid = (TextView) findViewById(R.id.TextSaid);
        textSaid.setText(matches.get(0));
    }
    super.onActivityResult(requestCode, resultCode, data);
}
}
```

In this case, the intent is initiated through the click of a Button control, which causes the recordSpeech() method to be called. The RecognizerIntent is configured as follows:

- The intent action is set to ACTION_RECOGNIZE_SPEECH in order to prompt the user to speak and send that sound file in for speech recognition.

- An intent extra called EXTRA_LANGUAGE_MODEL is set to LANGUAGE_MODEL_FREE_FORM to simply perform standard speech recognition. There is also another language model especially for web searches called LANGUAGE_MODEL_WEB_SEARCH.

- An intent extra called EXTRA_PROMPT is set to a string to display to the user during speech input.

After the RecognizerIntent object is configured, the intent can be started using the startActivityForResult() method, and then the result is captured in the onActivityResult() method. The resulting text is then displayed in the TextView control called TextSaid. In this case, only the first result provided in the results is displayed to the user. So, for example, the user could press the button initiating the recordSpeech()

method, say "We're going to need a bigger boat," and that text is then displayed in the application's `TextView` control, as shown in Figure 24.4.

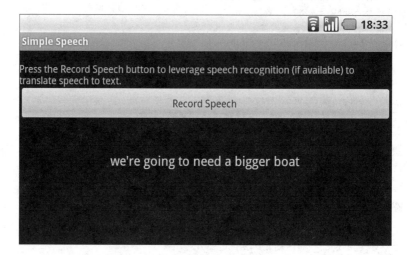

Figure 24.4 The text string resulting from the `RecognizerIntent`.

Leveraging Text-To-Speech Services

The Android platform includes a TTS engine (`android.speech.tts`) that enables devices to perform speech synthesis. You can use the TTS engine to have your applications "read" text to the user. You might have seen this feature used frequently with location-based services (LBS) applications that allow for hands-free directions. Other applications use this feature for users who have reading or sight problems. The synthesized speech can be played immediately or saved to an audio file, which can be treated like any other audio file.

> **Note**
>
> To provide TTS services to users, an Android device must have both the TTS engine (available in Android SDK 1.6 and higher) and the appropriate language resource files. In some cases, the user must install the appropriate language resource files (assuming that the user has space for them) from a remote location. The users can install the language resource files by going to Settings, Voice Input & Output Settings, Text-to-Speech, Install Voice Data. Unlike some other settings pages, this one doesn't have a specific intent action defined under `android.provider.Settings`. You might also need to do this on your devices. Additionally, the application can verify that the data is installed correctly or trigger the installation if it's not.

For a simple example, let's have the device read back the text recognized in our earlier speech recognition example. First, we must modify the activity to implement the `TextToSpeech.OnInitListener` interface, as follows:

```
public class SimpleSpeechActivity extends Activity
    implements TextToSpeech.OnInitListener
{
    // class implementation
}
```

Next, you need to initialize TTS services within your activity:

```
TextToSpeech mTts = new TextToSpeech(this, this);
```

Initializing the TTS engine happens asynchronously. The `TextToSpeech.OnInitListener` interface has only one method, `onInit()`, that is called when the TTS engine has finished initializing successfully or unsuccessfully. Here is an implementation of the `onInit()` method:

```
@Override
public void onInit(int status) {
    Button readButton = (Button) findViewById(R.id.ButtonRead);
    if (status == TextToSpeech.SUCCESS) {
        int result = mTts.setLanguage(Locale.US);
        if (result == TextToSpeech.LANG_MISSING_DATA
            || result == TextToSpeech.LANG_NOT_SUPPORTED) {
            Log.e(DEBUG_TAG, "TTS Language not available.");
            readButton.setEnabled(false);
        } else {
            readButton.setEnabled(true);
        }
    } else {
        Log.e(DEBUG_TAG, "Could not initialize TTS Engine.");
        readButton.setEnabled(false);
    }
}
```

We use the `onInit()` method to check the status of the TTS engine. If it was initialized successfully, the `Button` control called `readButton` is enabled; otherwise, it is disabled. The `onInit()` method is also the appropriate time to configure the TTS engine. For example, you should set the language used by the engine using the `setLanguage()` method. In this case, the language is set to American English. The voice used by the TTS engine uses American pronunciation.

Note

The Android TTS engine supports a variety of languages, including English (in American or British accents), French, German, Italian, and Spanish. You could just as easily have enabled British English pronunciation using the following language setting in the `onInit()` method implementation instead:

```
int result = mTts.setLanguage(Locale.UK);
```

> We amused ourselves trying to come up with phrases that illustrate how the American and British English TTS services differ. The best phrase we came up with was: *"We adjusted our schedule to search for a vase of herbs in our garage."*
>
> Feel free to send us your favorite locale-based phrases, and we will post them on the book website. Also, any amusing misinterpretations of the voice recognition are also welcome (for example, we often had "our garage" come out as "nerd haha").

Finally, you are ready to actually convert some text into a sound file. In this case, we grab the text string currently stored in the `TextView` control (where we set using speech recognition in the previous section) and pass it to TTS using the `speak()` method:

```
public void readText(View view) {
    TextView textSaid = (TextView) findViewById(R.id.TextSaid);
    mTts.speak((String) textSaid.getText(),
        TextToSpeech.QUEUE_FLUSH, null);
}
```

The `speak()` method takes three parameters: the string of text to say, the queuing strategy and the speech parameters. The queuing strategy can either be to add some text to speak to the queue or to flush the queue—in this case, we use the `QUEUE_FLUSH` strategy, so it is the only speech spoken. No special speech parameters are set, so we simply pass in `null` for the third parameter. Finally, when you are done with the `TextToSpeech` engine (such as in your activity's `onDestroy()` method), make sure to release its resources using the `shutdown()` method:

```
mTts.shutdown();
```

Now, if you wire up a `Button` control to call the `readText()` method when clicked, you have a complete implementation of TTS. When combined with the speech recognition example discussed earlier, you can develop an application that can record a user's speech, translate it into a string, display that string on the screen, and then read that string back to the user. In fact, that is exactly what the sample project called SimpleSpeech does.

Working with Gestures

Android devices often rely upon touch screens for user input. Users are now quite comfortable using common finger gestures to operate their devices. Android applications can detect and react to one-finger (single-touch) and two-finger (multi-touch) gestures.

> **Note**
>
> Even early Android devices supported simple single touch gestures. Support for multi-touch gestures was added in the Android 2.2 SDK and is available only on devices with capacitive touch screen hardware.

One of the reasons that gestures can be a bit tricky is that a gesture can be made of multiple touch events, or motions. Different sequences of motion add up to different gestures. For example, a fling gesture involves the user pressing his finger down on the screen, swiping across the screen, and lifting his finger up off the screen while the swipe is still in motion (that is, without slowing down to stop before lifting his finger). Each of these steps can trigger motion events that applications can react to.

Detecting User Motions Within a View

By now you've come to understand that Android application user interfaces are built using different types of `View` controls. Developers can handle gestures much like they do click events within a `View` control using the `setOnClickListener()` and `setOnLongClickListener()` methods. Instead, the `onTouchEvent()` callback method is used to detect that some motion has occurred within the `View` region.

The `onTouchEvent()` callback method has a single parameter: a `MotionEvent` object. The `MotionEvent` object contains all sorts of details about what kind of motion is occurring within the `View`, enabling the developer to determine what sort of gesture is happening by collecting and analyzing many consecutive `MotionEvent` objects. You could use all of the `MotionEvent` data to recognize and detect every kind of gesture you could possibly imagine. Alternately, you can use built-in gesture detectors provided in the Android SDK to detect common user motions in a consistent fashion. Android currently has two different classes that can detect navigational gestures:

- The `GestureDetector` class can be used to detect common single-touch gestures.
- The `ScaleGestureDetector` can be used to detect multi-touch scale gestures.

It is likely that more gesture detectors will be added in future versions of the Android SDK. You can also implement your own gesture detectors to detect any gestures not supported by the built-in gesture detectors. For example, you might want to create a two-fingered rotate gesture to, say, rotate an image or a three-fingered swipe gesture that brings up an option menu.

In addition to common navigational gestures, you can use the `android.gesture` package with the `GestureOverlayView` to recognize command-like gestures. For instance, you could create an S-shaped gesture that brings up a search, or a zig-zag gesture that clears a screen on a drawing app. Tools are available for recording and creating libraries of this style gesture. As it uses an overlay for detection, it isn't well suited for all types of applications. This package was introduced in API Level 4.

Warning

The type and sensitivity of the touch screen can vary by device. Different devices can detect different numbers of touch points simultaneously, which affects the complexity of gestures you can support.

Handling Common Single-Touch Gestures

Introduced in API Level 1, the `GestureDetector` class can be used to detect gestures made by a single finger. Some common single finger gestures supported by the `GestureDetector` class include:

- `onDown`: Called when the user first presses on the touch screen.

- `onShowPress`: Called after the user first presses the touch screen but before he lifts his finger or moves it around on the screen; used to visually or audibly indicate that the press has been detected.

- `onSingleTapUp`: Called when the user lifts up (using the up `MotionEvent`) from the touch screen as part of a single-tap event.

- `onSingleTapConfirmed`: Called when a single-tap event occurs.

- `onDoubleTap`: Called when a double-tap event occurs.

- `onDoubleTapEvent`: Called when an event within a double-tap gesture occurs, including any down, move, or up `MotionEvent`.

- `onLongPress`: Similar to `onSingleTapUp`, but called if the user holds down his finger long enough to not be a standard click but also without any movement.

- `onScroll`: Called after the user presses and then moves his finger in a steady motion before lifting his finger. This is commonly called dragging.

- `onFling`: Called after the user presses and then moves his finger in an accelerating motion before lifting it. This is commonly called a flick gesture and usually results in some motion continuing after the user lifts his finger.

You can use the interfaces available with the `GestureDetector` class to listen for specific gestures such as single and double taps (see `GestureDetector.OnDoubleTapListener`), as well as scrolls and flings (see `GestureDetector.OnGestureListener`). The scrolling gesture involves touching the screen and moving your finger around on it. The fling gesture, on the other hand, causes (though not automatically) the object to continue to move even after the finger has been lifted from the screen. This gives the user the impression of throwing or flicking the object around on the screen.

Tip

You can use the `GestureDetector.SimpleOnGestureListener` class to listen to any and all of the gestures recognized by the `GestureDetector`.

Let's look at a simple example. Let's assume you have a game screen that enables the user to perform gestures to interact with a graphic on the screen. We can create a custom `View` class called `GameAreaView` that can dictate how a bitmap graphic moves around within the game area based upon each gesture. The `GameAreaView` class can use the `onTouchEvent()` method to pass along `MotionEvent` objects to a `GestureDetector`. In this way, the `GameAreaView` can react to simple gestures, interpret them, and make the appropriate changes to the bitmap, including moving it from one location to another on the screen.

Tip

How the gestures are interpreted and what actions they cause is completely up to the developer. You could, for example, interpret a fling gesture and make the bitmap graphic disappear... but does that make sense? Not really. It's important to always make the gesture jive well with the resulting operation within the application so that users are not confused. Users are now accustomed to specific screen behavior based on certain gestures, so it's best to use the expected convention, too.

In this case, the `GameAreaView` class interprets gestures as follows:

- A double-tap gesture causes the bitmap graphic to return to its initial position.
- A scroll gesture causes the bitmap graphic to "follow" the motion of the finger.
- A fling gesture causes the bitmap graphic to "fly" in the direction of the fling.

Tip

Many of the code examples provided in this section are taken from the SimpleGestures application. The source code for this application is provided for download on the book website.

To make these gestures work, the `GameAreaView` class needs to include the appropriate gesture detector, which triggers any operations upon the bitmap graphic. Based upon the specific gestures detected, the `GameAreaView` class must perform all translation animations and other graphical operations applied to the bitmap. To wire up the `GameAreaView` class for gesture support, we need to implement several important methods:

- The class constructor must initialize any gesture detectors and bitmap graphics.
- The `onTouchEvent()` method must be overridden to pass the `MotionEvent` data to the gesture detector for processing.
- The `onDraw()` method must be overridden to draw the bitmap graphic in the appropriate position at any time.
- Various methods are needed to perform the graphics operations required to make a bitmap move around on the screen, fly across the screen, reset its location based upon the data provided by the specific gesture.

All these tasks are handled by our `GameAreaView` class definition:

```
public class GameAreaView extends View {

    private static final String DEBUG_TAG =
        "SimpleGesture->GameAreaView";
    private GestureDetector gestures;
    private Matrix translate;
    private Bitmap droid;
    private Matrix animateStart;
    private Interpolator animateInterpolator;
    private long startTime;
    private long endTime;
```

```
private float totalAnimDx;
private float totalAnimDy;

public GameAreaView(Context context, int iGraphicResourceId) {
    super(context);
    translate = new Matrix();
    GestureListener listener = new GestureListener(this);
    gestures = new GestureDetector(context, listener, null, true);
    droid = BitmapFactory.decodeResource(getResources(),
        iGraphicResourceId);
}

@Override
public boolean onTouchEvent(MotionEvent event) {
    boolean retVal = false;
    retVal = gestures.onTouchEvent(event);
    return retVal;
}

@Override
protected void onDraw(Canvas canvas) {
    Log.v(DEBUG_TAG, "onDraw");
    canvas.drawBitmap(droid, translate, null);
}

public void onResetLocation() {
    translate.reset();
    invalidate();
}

public void onMove(float dx, float dy) {
    translate.postTranslate(dx, dy);
    invalidate();
}

public void onAnimateMove(float dx, float dy, long duration) {
    animateStart = new Matrix(translate);
    animateInterpolator = new OvershootInterpolator();
    startTime = System.currentTimeMillis();
    endTime = startTime + duration;
    totalAnimDx = dx;
    totalAnimDy = dy;
    post(new Runnable() {
        @Override
        public void run() {
            onAnimateStep();
        }
```

```
        });
    }

    private void onAnimateStep() {
        long curTime = System.currentTimeMillis();
        float percentTime = (float) (curTime - startTime) /
            (float) (endTime - startTime);
        float percentDistance = animateInterpolator
            .getInterpolation(percentTime);
        float curDx = percentDistance * totalAnimDx;
        float curDy = percentDistance * totalAnimDy;
        translate.set(animateStart);
        onMove(curDx, curDy);

        if (percentTime < 1.0f) {
            post(new Runnable() {
                @Override
                public void run() {
                    onAnimateStep();
                }
            });
        }
    }
}
```

As you can see, the GameAreaView class keeps track of where the bitmap graphic should be drawn at any time. The onTouchEvent() method is used to capture motion events and pass them along to a gesture detector whose GestureListener we must implement as well (more on this in a moment). Typically, each method of the GameAreaView applies some operation to the bitmap graphic and then calls the invalidate() method, forcing the view to be redrawn. Now we turn our attention to the methods required to implement specific gestures:

- For double-tap gestures, we implement a method called onResetLocation() to draw the bitmap graphic in its original location.

- For scroll gestures, we implement a method called onMove() to draw the bitmap graphic in a new location. Note that scrolling can occur in any direction—it simply refers to a finger swipe on the screen.

- For fling gestures, things get a little tricky. To animate motion on the screen smoothly, we used a chain of asynchronous calls and a built-in Android interpolator to calculate the location to draw the graphic based upon how long it had been since the animation started. See the onAnimateMove() and onAnimateStep() methods for the full implementation of fling animation.

Now we need to implement our `GestureListener` class to interpret the appropriate gestures and call the `GameAreaView` methods we just implemented. Here's an implementation of the `GestureListener` class that our `GameAreaView` class can use:

```
private class GestureListener extends
    GestureDetector.SimpleOnGestureListener  {

    GameAreaView view;

    public GestureListener(GameAreaView view) {
        this.view = view;
    }

    @Override
    public boolean onDown(MotionEvent e) {
        return true;
    }

    @Override
    public boolean onFling(MotionEvent e1, MotionEvent e2,
        final float velocityX, final float velocityY) {
        final float distanceTimeFactor = 0.4f;
        final float totalDx = (distanceTimeFactor * velocityX / 2);
        final float totalDy = (distanceTimeFactor * velocityY / 2);

        view.onAnimateMove(totalDx, totalDy,
            (long) (1000 * distanceTimeFactor));
        return true;
    }

    @Override
    public boolean onDoubleTap(MotionEvent e) {
        view.onResetLocation();
        return true;
    }

    @Override
    public boolean onScroll(MotionEvent e1, MotionEvent e2,
        float distanceX, float distanceY) {
        view.onMove(-distanceX, -distanceY);
        return true;
    }
}
```

Note that you must return true for any gesture or motion event that you want to detect. Therefore, you must return true in the `onDown()` method as it happens at the beginning of a scroll-type gesture. Most of the implementation of the `GestureListener` class methods involves our interpretation of the data for each gesture. For example:

- We react to double taps by resetting the bitmap to its original location using the `onResetLocation()` method of our `GameAreaView` class.

- We use the distance data provided in the `onScroll()` method to determine the direction to use in the movement to pass into the `onMove()` method of the `GameAreaView` class.

- We use the velocity data provided in the `onFling()` method to determine the direction and speed to use in the movement animation of the bitmap. The `timeDistanceFactor` variable with a value of 0.4 is subjective, but gives the resulting slide-to-a-stop animation enough time to be visible but is short enough to be controllable and responsive. You could think of it as a high-friction surface. This information is used by the animation sequence implemented within the `onAnimateMove()` method of the `GameAreaView` class.

Now that we have implemented the `GameAreaView` class in its entirety, you can display it on a screen. For example, you might create an `Activity` that has a user interface with a `FrameLayout` control and add an instance of a `GameAreaView` using the `addView()` method. The resulting scroll and fling gestures look something like Figure 24.5.

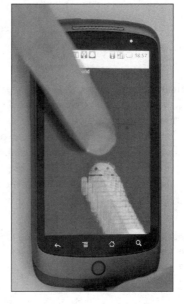

Figure 24.5   Scroll (left) and Fling (right) gestures.

Tip

To support the broadest range of devices, we recommend supporting simple, one-fingered gestures and providing alternate navigational items for devices that don't support multi-touch gestures. However, users are beginning to expect multi-touch gesture support now, so use them where you can and where they make sense. Resistive touch-screens remain somewhat uncommon on lower-end devices.

Handling Common Multi-Touch Gestures

Introduced in API Level 8 (Android 2.2), the `ScaleGestureDetector` class can be used to detect two-fingered scale gestures. The scale gesture enables the user to move two fingers toward and away from each other. When the fingers are moving apart, this is considered scaling up; when the fingers are moving together, this is considered scaling down. This is the "pinch-to-zoom" style often employed by map and photo applications.

Tip

You can use the `ScaleGestureDetector.SimpleOnScaleGestureListener` class to detect scale gestures detected by the `ScaleGestureDetector`.

Let's look at another example. Again, we use the custom view class called `GameAreaView`, but this time we handle the multi-touch scale event. In this way, the `GameAreaView` can react to scale gestures, interpret them, and make the appropriate changes to the bitmap, including growing or shrinking it on the screen.

Tip

Many of the code examples provided in this section are taken from the SimpleMulti-TouchGesture application. The source code for this application is provided for download on the book website.

In order to handle scale gestures, the `GameAreaView` class needs to include the appropriate gesture detector: a `ScaleGestureDetector`. The `GameAreaView` class needs to be wired up for scale gesture support in a similar fashion as when we implemented single touch gestures earlier, including initializing the gesture detector in the class constructor, overriding the `onTouchEvent()` method to pass the `MotionEvent` objects to the gesture detector, and overriding the `onDraw()` method to draw the view appropriately as necessary. We also need to update the `GameAreaView` class to keep track of the bitmap graphic size (using a `Matrix`) and provide a helper method for growing or shrinking the graphic. Here is the new implementation of the `GameAreaView` class with scale gesture support:

```
public class GameAreaView extends View {
    private ScaleGestureDetector multiGestures;
    private Matrix scale;
    private Bitmap droid;

    public GameAreaView(Context context, int iGraphicResourceId) {
        super(context);
        scale = new Matrix();
```

```
        GestureListener listener = new GestureListener(this);
        multiGestures = new ScaleGestureDetector(context, listener);
        droid = BitmapFactory.decodeResource(getResources(),
            iGraphicResourceId);
    }

    public void onScale(float factor) {
        scale.preScale(factor, factor);
        invalidate();
    }

    @Override
    protected void onDraw(Canvas canvas) {
        Matrix transform = new Matrix(scale);
        float width = droid.getWidth() / 2;
        float height = droid.getHeight() / 2;
        transform.postTranslate(-width, -height);
        transform.postConcat(scale);
        transform.postTranslate(width, height);
        canvas.drawBitmap(droid, transform, null);
    }

    @Override
    public boolean onTouchEvent(MotionEvent event) {
        boolean retVal = false;
        retVal = multiGestures.onTouchEvent(event);
        return retVal;
    }
}
```

As you can see, the `GameAreaView` class keeps track of what size the bitmap should be at any time using the `Matrix` variable called `scale`. The `onTouchEvent()` method is used to capture motion events and pass them along to a `ScaleGestureDetector` gesture detector. As before, the `onScale()` helper method of the `GameAreaView` applies some scaling to the bitmap graphic and then calls the `invalidate()` method, forcing the view to be redrawn.

Now let's take a look at the `GestureListener` class implementation necessary to interpret the scale gestures and call the `GameAreaView` methods we just implemented. Here's the implementation of the `GestureListener` class:

```
private class GestureListener implements
    ScaleGestureDetector.OnScaleGestureListener {

    GameAreaView view;

    public GestureListener(GameAreaView view) {
        this.view = view;
    }
```

```
@Override
public boolean onScale(ScaleGestureDetector detector) {
    float scale = detector.getScaleFactor();
    view.onScale(scale);
    return true;
}

@Override
public boolean onScaleBegin(ScaleGestureDetector detector) {
    return true;
}

@Override
public void onScaleEnd(ScaleGestureDetector detector) {
}
}
```

Remember that you must return `true` for any gesture or motion event that you Want to detect. Therefore, you must return true in the `onScaleBegin()` method as it happens at the beginning of a scale-type gesture. Most of the implementation of the `GestureListener` methods involves our interpretation of the data for the scale gesture. Specifically, we use the scale factor (provided by the `getScaleFactor()` method) to calculate whether we should shrink or grow the bitmap graphic, and by how much. We pass this information to the `onScale()` helper method we just implemented in the `GameAreaView` class.

Now, if you were to use the `GameAreaView` class within your application, scale gestures might look something like Figure 24.6.

Note

The Android emulator does not currently support multi-touch input. You will have to run and test multi-touch support such as the scale gesture using a device running Android 2.2 or higher.

Making Gestures Look Natural

Gestures can enhance your Android application user interfaces in new, interesting, and intuitive ways. Closely mapping the operations being performed on the screen to the user's finger motion makes a gesture feel natural and intuitive. Making application operations look natural requires some experimentation on the part of the developer. Keep in mind that devices vary in processing power, and this might be a factor in making things seem natural.

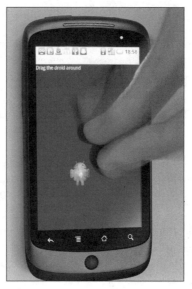

Figure 24.6   Scale up (left) and scale down (right) gestures.

Working with the Trackball

Some Android devices have hardware trackballs, but not all. Developers can handle trackball events within a `View` control in a similar fashion to click events or gestures. To handle
trackball events, you can leverage the `View` class method called `onTrackballEvent()`. This
method, like a gesture, has a single parameter: a `MotionEvent` object. You can use the
`getX()` and `getY()` methods of the `MotionEvent` class to determine the relative movement of the trackball. Optical track-pads such as those available on the Droid Incredible
can be supported in the same way.

| Tip

If your application requires the device to have a trackball, you should set the `<uses-con-
figuration>` tag to specify that a trackball is required within your application's Android
manifest file.

Handling Screen Orientation Changes

Many Android devices on the market today have landscape and portrait modes and can
seamlessly transition between these orientations. The Android operating system automatically handles these changes for your application, if you so choose. You can also provide
alternative resources, such as different layouts, for portrait and landscape modes (more on

this in Chapter 25, "Targeting Different Device Configurations and Languages"). Also, you can directly access device sensors such as the accelerometer, as we talked about in Chapter 19, "Using Android's Optional Hardware APIs," to capture device orientation along three axes.

However, if you want to listen for simple screen orientation changes programmatically and have your application react to them, you can use the `OrientationEventListener` class to do this within your activity.

Tip

Many of the code examples provided in this section are taken from the SimpleOrientation application. The source code for this application is provided for download on the book website. Orientation changes are best tested on devices, not the emulator.

Implementing orientation event handling within your activity is simple. Simply instantiate an `OrientationEventListener` and provide its implementation. For example, the following activity class called `SimpleOrientationActivity` logs orientation information to LogCat:

```
public class SimpleOrientationActivity extends Activity {

    OrientationEventListener mOrientationListener;

    @Override
    public void onCreate(Bundle savedInstanceState) {
        super.onCreate(savedInstanceState);
        setContentView(R.layout.main);

        mOrientationListener = new OrientationEventListener(this,
            SensorManager.SENSOR_DELAY_NORMAL) {

            @Override
            public void onOrientationChanged(int orientation) {
                Log.v(DEBUG_TAG,
                    "Orientation changed to " + orientation);
            }
        };

        if (mOrientationListener.canDetectOrientation() == true) {
            Log.v(DEBUG_TAG, "Can detect orientation");
            mOrientationListener.enable();
        } else {
            Log.v(DEBUG_TAG, "Cannot detect orientation");
            mOrientationListener.disable();
        }
    }
```

```
@Override
protected void onDestroy() {
    super.onDestroy();
    mOrientationListener.disable();
}
}
```

You can set the rate to check for orientation changes to a variety of different values. There are other rate values appropriate for game use and other purposes. The default rate, SENSOR_DELAY_NORMAL, is most appropriate for simple orientation changes. Other values, such as SENSOR_DELAY_UI and SENSOR_DELAY_GAME, might make sense for your application.

After you have a valid OrientationEventListener object, you can check if it can detect orientation changes using the canDetectOrientation() method, and enable and disable the listener using its enable() and disable() methods.

The OrientationEventListener has a single callback method, which enables you to listen for orientation transitions: the onOrientationChanged() method. This method has a single parameter, an integer. This integer normally represents the device tilt as a number between 0 and 359:

- A result of ORIENTATION_UNKNOWN (–1) means the device is flat (perhaps on a table) and the orientation is unknown.
- A result of 0 means the device is in its "normal" orientation, with the top of the device facing in the up direction. (What "normal" means is defined by the manufacturer. You need to test on the device to find out for sure what it means.)
- A result of 90 means the device is tilted at 90 degrees, with the left side of the device facing in the up direction.
- A result of 180 means the device is tilted at 180 degrees, with the bottom side of the device facing in the up direction (upside down).
- A result of 270 means the device is tilted at 270 degrees, with the right side of the device facing in the up direction.

Figure 24.7 shows an example of how the device orientation might read when the device is tilted to the right by 90 degrees.

Warning

Early versions of the Android SDK included a class called OrientationListener, which many early developers of the platform used to handle screen orientation transitions. This class is now deprecated, and you should not use it.

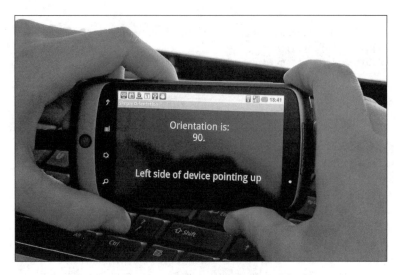

Figure 24.7   Orientation of the device as reported by an
`OrientationEventListener`.

Summary

The Android platform enables great flexibility when it comes to ways that users can provide input to the device. Developers benefit from the fact that many powerful input
methods are built into the view controls themselves, just waiting to be leveraged. Applications can take advantage of built-in input methods, such as software keyboards, or can
customize them for special purposes. The Android framework also includes powerful features, such as gesture support, as well as extensive accessibility features, including speech
recognition and text-to-speech support. It is important to support a variety of input
methods within your applications, as users often have distinct preferences and not all
methods are available on all devices.

References and More Information

Android Reference: Faster Orientation Changes:
    http://j.mp/9P3yTy
Android Reference: Screen Orientation and Direction:
    http://j.mp/b2zY1t

## 25

Targeting Different Device Configurations and Languages

There are now more than 60 different Android devices on the market worldwide. In this chapter, you learn how to design and develop Android applications that are compatible with a variety of devices despite differences in screen size, hardware, or platform version. We offer numerous tips for designing and developing your application to be compatible with many different devices. Finally, you learn how to internationalize your applications for foreign markets.

Maximizing Application Compatibility

With almost two dozen manufacturers developing Android devices, we've seen an explosion of different models—each with its own market differentiators and unique characteristics. Users now have choices, but these choices come at a cost. This proliferation of devices has led to what some developers call *fragmentation* and others call *compatibility issues*. Terminology aside, it has become a challenging task to develop Android applications that support a broad range of devices. Developers must contend with different platform versions, devices with and without optional hardware such as cameras and keyboards, and variations in screen sizes and resolutions (see Figure 25.1). The list of device differentiators is lengthy, and grows with each new device.

Although fragmentation makes the Android app developer's life more complicated, it's still possible to develop for and support a variety of devices—even all devices—within a single application. When it comes to maximizing compatibility, you'll always want to use the following strategies:

- Whenever possible, choose the development option that is supported by the widest variety of devices.

- Whenever a development decision limits the compatibility of your application (for example, using an API that was introduced in a later API Level or introducing a hardware requirement such as camera support), assess the risk and document this limitation. Determine whether you are going to provide an alternative solution for devices that do not support this requirement.

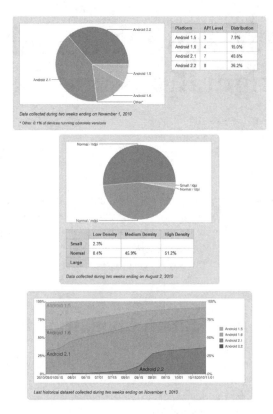

Figure 25.1   Some Android device statistics regarding
platform version and screen density
(source: http://j.mp/bnW7OV).

- Consider screen size and resolution differences when designing application user interfaces. It is often possible to design very flexible layouts that look reasonable in both portrait and landscape modes, as well as different screen resolutions and sizes. However, if you don't consider this early, you will likely have to make changes (sometimes painful ones) later on to accommodate these differences.
- Test on a wide range of devices early in the development process to avoid unpleasant surprises late in the game. Make sure the devices have different hardware and software, including different versions of the Android platform, different screen sizes, and different hardware capabilities.

- Whenever necessary, provide alternative resources to help smooth over differences between device characteristics (we talk extensively about alternative resources later in this chapter).

- If you do introduce software and hardware requirements to your application, make sure you register this information in the Android manifest file using the appropriate tags. These tags, used by the Android platform as well as third parties such as the Android Market, help ensure that your application is only installed on devices that are capable of meeting your application's requirements.

Now let's look at some of the strategies you can use to target different device configurations and languages.

Designing User Interfaces for Compatibility

Before we show you the many ways in which you can provide custom application resources and code to support specific device configurations, it's important to remember that you can often avoid needing them in the first place. The trick is to design your initial default solution to be flexible enough to cover any variations. When it comes to user interfaces, keep them simple and don't overcrowd them. Also, take advantage of the many powerful tools at your disposal:

- As a rule of thumb, design for medium- to large-size screens and medium resolutions. Over time, devices trend toward larger screens with higher resolutions.

- For `View` and `Layout` control width and height attributes, use `fill_parent` (now `match_parent`) and `wrap_content` so that controls scale for different screen sizes and orientation changes.

- For dimensions, use the flexible units, such as `dp` and `sp`, as opposed to fixed unit types, such as `px`, `mm`, and `in`.

- Avoid using `AbsoluteLayout` and other pixel-perfect settings and attributes.

- Use flexible layout controls such as `RelativeLayout`, `LinearLayout`, `TableLayout`, and `FrameLayout` to design a screen that looks great in both portrait and landscape modes and on a variety of different screen sizes and resolutions. Try the working square principle for organizing screen content—we talk more about this in a moment.

- Encapsulate screen content in scalable container controls such as `ScrollView` and `ListView`. Generally, you should scale and grow screens in only one direction (vertically or horizontally), but not both.

- Don't provide exact positions for screen elements, sizes, and dimensions. Instead, use relative positions, weights, and gravity. Spending time up-front to get these right saves time later.

- Provide application graphics of reasonable quality and always keep the original (larger) sizes around in case you need different versions for different resolutions at a later time. There is always a tradeoff in terms of graphic quality versus file size. Find the sweet spot where the graphic scales reasonably well for changes in screen characteristics, without bulking up your application or taking too long to display. Whenever possible, use stretchable graphics, such as Nine-Patch, which allow a graphic to change size based upon the area in which it is displayed in.

Tip

Looking for information about the device screen? Check out the `DisplayMetrics` utility class, which, when used in conjunction with the window manager, can determine all sorts of information about the display characteristics of the device at runtime:

```
DisplayMetrics currentMetrics = new DisplayMetrics();

WindowManager wm = getWindowManager();

wm.getDefaultDisplay().getMetrics(currentMetrics);
```

Supporting Specific Screen Types

Although you generally want to try to develop your applications to be screen independent (support all types of screens, small and large, high density and low), you can specify the types of screens your application can support explicitly when necessary using the `<supports-screens>` Android manifest file tag. By default, your application supports all screen types. You might want to consider this configuration option if your application—say a video app or an eBook reader—does not run well at all on small screens. For more information on this Android Manifest tag, see the Android SDK documentation: http://developer.android.com/guide/topics/manifest/supports-screens-element.html.

Tip

The Android operating system uses a combination of scaling techniques to help smooth differences in screen size, density, and aspect ratio. For more details, see the Android Best Practices article on supporting multiple screens, referenced in the Resources and More Information section at the end of this chapter.

Working with Nine-Patch Stretchable Graphics

Phone screens come in various dimensions. It can be handy to use stretchable graphics to allow a single graphic that can scale appropriately for different screen sizes and orientations or different lengths of text. This can save you a lot of time in creating graphics for many different screen sizes. Android supports Nine-Patch Stretchable Graphics for this purpose. Nine-Patch Stretchable Graphics are simply PNG graphics that have patches, or areas of the image, defined to scale appropriately, instead of scaling the entire image as one unit. Often the center segment is transparent. Figure 25.2 illustrates how the image (shown as the square) is divided into nine patches.

Nine-Patch Stretchable Graphics can be created from PNG files using the `draw9patch` tool included with the `Tools` directory of the Android SDK. The interface for the `draw9patch` tool (see Figure 25.3) is straightforward. In the left pane, you can define the Nine-Patch guides to your graphic to define how it scales when stretched. In the right pane, you can preview how your graphic behaves when scaled with the patches you defined.

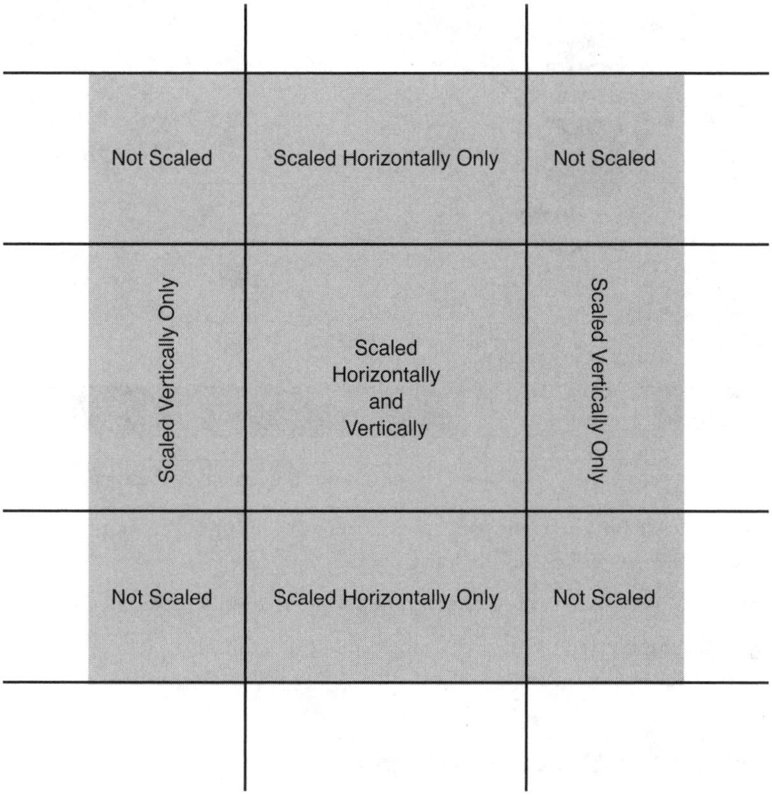

Not Scaled	Scaled Horizontally Only	Not Scaled
Scaled Vertically Only	Scaled Horizontally and Vertically	Scaled Vertically Only
Not Scaled	Scaled Horizontally Only	Not Scaled

Figure 25.2   How a Nine-Patch Graphic of a square is scaled.

To create a Nine-Patch Stretchable Graphic file from a PNG file using the `draw9patch` tool, perform the following steps:

1. Launch `draw9patch.bat` in your Android SDK `tools` directory.

2. Drag a PNG file into the left pane (or use File, Open Nine-Patch).

3. Click the Show Patches check box at the bottom of the left pane.

4. Set your Patch Scale appropriately (higher to see more marked results).

5. Click along the left edge of your graphic to set a horizontal patch guide.

6. Click along the top edge of your graphic to set a vertical patch guide.

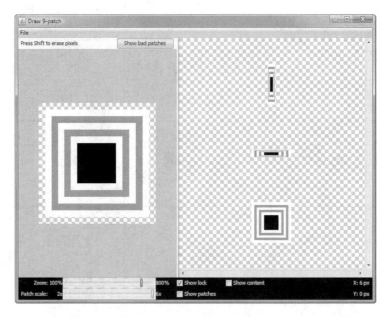

Figure 25.3   A simple PNG file before Nine-Patch processing.

7. View the results in the right pane; move patch guides until the graphic stretches as desired, as shown in Figures 25.4 and 25.5.

8. To delete a patch guide, press Shift, and click on the guide pixel (black).

9. Save your graphic with the extension `.9.png` (for example, `little_black_box.9.png`).

Using the Working Square Principle

Another way to design for different screen orientations is to try to keep a "working square" area where most of your application's user activity (meaning, where they look and click on the screen) takes place. This area remains unchanged (or changes little beyond just rotating) when the screen orientation changes. Only functionality displayed outside of the "working square" changes substantially when screen orientation changes (see Figure 25.6).

One clever example of a "working square," which turns the idea on its head, is the Camera application on the HTC Evo 4G. In Portrait mode, the camera controls are on the bottom of the viewfinder (see Figure 25.7, left); when rotated clockwise into Landscape mode, the camera controls stay in the same place but now they are to the left of the viewfinder (see Figure 25.7, right). The viewfinder area would be considered the working square—the area that remains uncluttered. The controls and sliding drawer with settings are kept outside that area, so the user can compose their photos and videos.

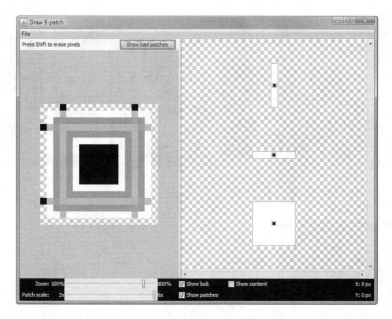

Figure 25.4   A Nine-Patch PNG file after Nine-Patch processing
with some patch guides defined.

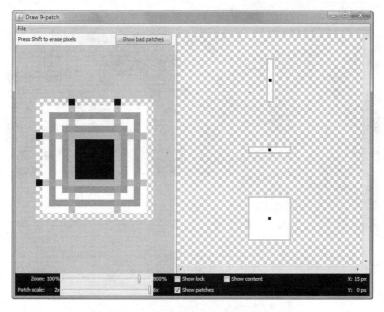

Figure 25.5   A Nine-Patch PNG file after Nine-Patch processing
with different patch guides defined.

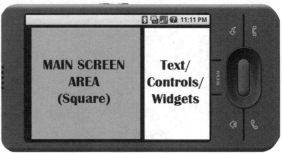

Figure 25.6   The "working square" principle.

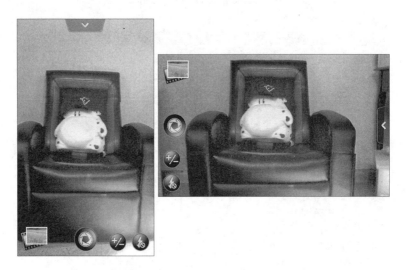

Figure 25.7   Evo 4G Camera application using a form of the
"working square" principle.

When you're using the application, visually the rotation looks as if it has had little effect. The controls moved from being below the viewfinder to being to the left of the viewfinder. It just so happens, though, that they remain in the same location on the screen. This is part of the elegance of the "working square" principal.

Providing Alternative Application Resources

Each time a screen is drawn within an Android application, the Android operating system attempts to match the best possible resource for the job. In many cases, applications provide only one set of resources—the default resources. Developers can include alternative versions of those same resources as part of their application packages. The Android operating system always attempts to load the most specific resources available—the developer does not have to worry about determining which resources to load because the operating system handles this task.

Working with Alternative Resource Qualifiers

Alternative resources can be created for many different criteria, including, but not limited to, screen characteristics, device input methods, and language or regional differences. These alternative resources are organized hierarchically within the `/res` resource project directory. You use directory qualifiers (in the form of directory name suffixes) to specify a resource as an alternative resource to load in specific situations.

A simple example might help to drive this concept home. The most common example of when alternative resources are used has to do with the default application icon resources created as part of a new Android project in Eclipse. An application could simply provide a single application icon graphic resource, stored in the `/res/drawable` directory. However, different Android devices have different screen resolutions. Therefore, alternative resources are used instead: `/res/drawable-hdpi/icon.png` is an application icon suitable for high-density screens, the `/res/drawable-ldpi/icon.png` is the application icon suitable for low-density screens, and the `/res/drawable-mdpi/icon.png` is the application icon suitable for medium-density screens. Note that in each case, the alternative resource is named the same. This is important. Alternative resources *must* use the same names as the default resources. This is how the Android system can match the appropriate resource to load—by its name.

Ironically, this example is also one of the only times you do not also see a default resource (that is, an `icon.png` resource file stored in the `/res/drawable` directory), which the system could fall back on if the device environment did not match an `hdpi`, `mdpi,` or `ldpi` qualifier for resolution screen. The reason you can get away with this is because, by definition, all Android devices fall into one of these three categories, so a fallback is unnecessary.

Note

No, we don't like that explanation either. As developers, we are taught to implement the `default` case in a `switch` statement simply for safety's sake. Alternative resources are no different. We prefer to err on the safe side and try to always define default resources, so that the application has a resource to load, no matter what the device settings claim. We want to avoid the theoretical situation in which some device forgets to specify its dpi setting, thus putting our application in a position of not having an appropriate resource to load. One way to work around this issue is to store most compatible resources (those that won't cause any harm) as your default resources and only use alternative resources for secondary cases. For example, you could put the mdpi version of your icon in the `/res/drawable` directory as your default resources and then only create alternative resources in the `/res/drawable-ldpi` and `/res/drawable-hdpi` directories. That said, how you organize your resources is up to you (more on this later in the chapter).

Here are some additional important facts about alternative resources:

- Alternative resource directory qualifiers are always applied to the default resource directory name. For example, `/res/drawable-qualifier`, `/res/values-qualifier`, `/res/layout-qualifier`.

- Alternative resource directory qualifiers (and resource filenames) must always be lowercase, with one exception: region qualifiers.

- Only one directory qualifier of a given type may be included in a resource directory name. Sometimes this has unfortunate consequences—you might be forced to include the same resource in multiple directories. For example, you cannot create an alternative resource directory called `/res/drawable-ldpi-mdpi` to share the same icon graphic. Instead, you must create two directories: `/res/drawable-ldpi` and `/res/drawable/mpdi`. Frankly, when you want different qualifiers to share resources instead of providing two copies of the same resource, you're often better off making those your default resources, and then providing alternative resources for those that do not match `ldpi` and `mdpi`—that is, `hdpi`. As we said, it's up to you how you go about organizing your resources; these are just our suggestions for keeping things under control.

- Alternative resource directory qualifiers can be combined or chained with each qualifier being separated by a dash. This enables developers to create very specific directory names and therefore very specialized alternative resources. These qualifiers must be applied in a very specific order and the Android operating system always attempts to load the most specific resource (that is, the resource with the longest matching path). For example, you can create an alternative resource directory for French language (qualifier `fr`), Canadian region (qualifier `rCA`—this is a region qualifier and is therefore capitalized) string resources (stored in the values directory) as follows: `/res/values-fr-rCA/strings.xml`.

- You only need to create alternative resources for the specific resources you require—not every resource in a given file. If you only need to translate half the strings in the default strings.xml file, then only provide alternative strings for those specific string resources. In other words, the default strings.xml resource file might contain a superset of string resources with the alternative string resource files containing a subset—only the strings requiring translation. Common examples of strings that do not get localized are company or brand names.

- No custom directory names or qualifiers are allowed. You may only use the qualifiers defined as part of the Android SDK. Most of these qualifiers are listed in Table 25.1.

Table 25.1   **Important Alternative Resource Qualifiers**

Directory Qualifier	Example Values	Description
Mobile country code and mobile network code	`mcc310` (United States) `mcc310-mnc004` (United States, Verizon) `mcc208-mnc00` (France, Orange)	The mobile country code (MCC), optionally followed by a dash and a mobile network code (MNC) from the SIM card in the device.
Language and region code	`en` (English) `ja` (Japanese) `de` (German) `en-rUS` (American English) `en-rGB` (British English)	The language code (ISO 639-1 2-letter language code), optionally followed by a dash and the region code (a lowercase "r" followed by the region code, as defined by ISO 3166-1-alpha-2).

Screen size	`small`
	 `normal`
	 `large`
		Generalized screen size.
		
		 A `small` screen is generally a low-density QVGA or higher-density VGA screen.
		
		 A `normal` screen is generally a medium-density HVGA screen or similar.
		
		 A `large` screen has at least a medium-density VGA screen or other screen with more pixels than an HVGA display.
		
		 Added in API Level 4.

Table 25.1   Continued

Directory Qualifier	Example Values	Description
Screen aspect ratio	`long` `notlong`	Whether or not the device is a wide-screen device. WQVGA, WVGA, and FWVGA screens are `long` screens. QVGA, HVGA, and VGA screens are `notlong` screens. Added in API Level 4.
Screen orientation	`port` `land`	When a device is in portrait mode, the `port` resources are loaded. When the device is in landscape mode, the `land` resources are loaded.
Dock mode	`car` `desk`	Load specific resources when the device is in a car or desk dock. Added in API Level 8.
Night mode	`night` `notnight`	Load specific resources when the device is in a night mode or not. Added in API Level 8.

Screen pixel density	`ldpi`
	`mdpi`
	`hdpi`
	`nodpi`
		Low-density screen resources (approx. 120dpi) should use the `ldpi` option.
		Medium-density screen resources (approx. 160dpi) should use the `mdpi` option.
		High-density screen resources (approx. 240dpi) should use the `hdpi` option.
		Use the `nodpi` option to specify resources that you do not want to be scaled to match the screen density of the device.
		Added in API Level 4.

Table 25.1   Continued

Directory Qualifier	Example Values	Description

Touch screen type	`notouch`
	`stylus`
	`finger`
		Resources for devices without touch screens should use the `notouch` option.
		Resources for devices with a stylus-style (resistive) touch screen should use the `stylus` option.
		Resources for devices with finger-style (capacitive) touch screens should use the `finger` option.

Keyboard type and availability	`keysexposed`
	`keyshidden`
	`keyssoft`
		Use the `keysexposed` option for resources when a keyboard is available (hardware or soft keyboard).
		Use the `keyshidden` option for resources when no hardware or software keyboard is available.
		Use the `keyssoft` option for resources when the software keyboard is available.

Text input method	`nokeys`
	`qwerty`
	`12key`
		Use the `nokeys` option for resources when the device has no hardware keys for text input.
		Use the `qwerty` option for resources when the device has a QWERTY hardware keyboard for text input.
		Use the `12key` option for resources when the device has a 12-key numeric keypad for text input.

Navigation key availability	`navexposed` `navhidden`	Use `navexposed` for resources when the navigational hardware buttons are available to the user. Use `navhidden` for resources when the navigational hardware buttons are not available to the user (such as when the phone case is slid shut).

Table 25.1   Continued

Directory Qualifier	Example Values	Description

Navigation method	`nonav`
	`dpad`
	`trackball`
	`wheel`
		Use `nonav` if the device has no navigation buttons other than a touch screen.
		
		Use `dpad` for resources where the primary nav method is a directional pad.
		
		Use `trackball` for resources where the primary nav method is a trackball.
		
		Use `wheel` for resources where the primary nav method is a directional wheel.

Android platform	`v3` (Android 1.5) `v4` (Android 1.6) `v5` (Android 2.0) `v7` (Android 2.1) `v8` (Android 2.2) `v9` (Gingerbread)	Load resources based upon the Android platform version, as specified by the API Level. This qualifier loads resources for the specified API level or *higher*. Note: There are some known issues for this qualifier. See the Android documentation for details.

- Always try to include default resources—that is, those resources saved in directories without any qualifiers. These are the resources that the Android operating system will fall back upon when no specific alternative resource matches the criteria. If you don't, the system falls back on the closest matching resource based upon the directory qualifiers—one that might not make sense.

Now that you understand how alternative resources work, let's look at some of the directory qualifiers you can use to store alternative resources for different purposes. Qualifiers are tacked on to the existing resource directory name in a strict order, shown in descending order in Table 25.1.

Good examples of alternative resource directories with qualifiers are

```
/res/values-en-rUS-port-finger
/res/drawables-en-rUS-land-mdpi
/res/values-en-qwerty
```

Bad examples of alternative resource directories with qualifiers are

```
/res/values-en-rUS-rGB
/res/values-en-rUS-port-FINGER-wheel
/res/values-en-rUS-port-finger-custom
/res/drawables-rUS-en
```

The first bad example does not work because you can have only one qualifier of a given type, and this one violates that rule by including both rUS and rGB. The second bad example violates the rule that qualifiers (with the exception of the Region) are always lowercase. The third bad example includes a custom attribute defined by the developer, but these are not currently supported. The last bad example violates the order in which the qualifiers must be placed: Language first, then Region, and so on.

Providing Resources for Different Orientations

Let's look at a very simple application that uses alternative resources to customize screen content for different orientations.

Tip

The code provided in this section is taken from the SimpleAltResources application. The source code for this application is provided for download on the book website.

This application has no real code to speak of—check the Activity class if you don't believe us. Instead, all interesting functionality depends upon the resource folder qualifiers. These resources are

- The default resources for this application include the application icon and a picture graphic stored in the /res/drawable directory, the layout file stored in the /res/layout directory, and the color and string resources stored in the /res/values directory. These resources are loaded whenever a more specific resource is not available to load. They are the fallbacks.

- There is a portrait-mode alternative picture graphic stored in the /res/drawable-port directory. There are also portrait-mode–specific string and color resources stored in the /res/values-port directory. If the device is in portrait orientation, these resources—the portrait picture graphic, the strings, and colors—are loaded and used by the default layout.

- There is a landscape-mode alternative picture graphic stored in the /res/drawable-land directory. There are landscape-mode–specific string and color (basically reversed background and foreground colors) resources stored in the /res/values-land directory as well. If the device is in landscape orientation, these resources—the landscape picture graphic, the strings, and the colors—are loaded and used by the default layout.

In this way, the application loads different resources based upon the orientation of the device at runtime, as shown in Figure 25.8. This figure shows the project layout, in terms of resources, as well as what the screen might look like when the device is in different orientations.

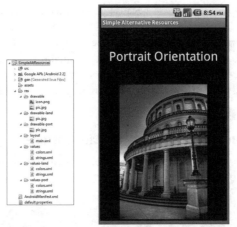

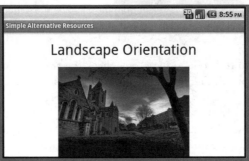

Figure 25.8   Using alternative resources for
portrait and landscape orientations.

Using Alternative Resources Programmatically

There is currently no way to request resources of a specific configuration programmatically. For example, the developer cannot programmatically request the French or English version of the string resource. Instead, the Android system determines the resource at runtime, and developers refer only to the general resource variable name.

Organizing Application Resources Efficiently

It's easy to go too far with alternative resources. You could provide custom graphics for every different permutation of device screen, language, or input method. However, each time you include an application resource in your project, the size of your application package grows.

There are also performance issues with swapping out resources too frequently—generally when runtime configuration transitions occur. Each time a runtime event such as an orientation or keyboard state change occurs, the Android operating system restarts the underlying `Activity` and reloads the resources. If your application is loading a lot of resources and content, these changes come at a cost to application performance and responsiveness.

Choose your resource organization scheme carefully. Generally, you should put the most commonly used resources as your defaults and then carefully overlay alternative resources only when necessary. For example, if you are writing an application that routinely shows videos or displays a game screen, you might want to make landscape mode resources your defaults and provide alternative portrait mode resources because they are not as likely to be used.

Retaining Data Across Configuration Changes

An Activity can keep data around through these transitions by using the `onRetainNonConfigurationInstance()` method to save data and the `getLastNonConfigurationInstance()` method to restore this data after the transition. This functionality can be especially helpful when your `Activity` has a lot of setup or preloading to do.

Handling Configuration Changes

In cases where your Activity does not need to reload alternative resources on a specific transition, you might want to consider having the Activity class handle the transition to avoid having your Activity restart. The camera application mentioned earlier uses this technique to handle orientation changes without having to reinitialize the camera hardware internals, redisplay the viewfinder window, or redisplay the camera controls (the `Button` controls simply rotate in place to the new orientation—very slick).

For an `Activity` class to handle its own configuration changes, your application must

- Update the `<activity>` tag in the Android manifest file for that specific `Activity` class to include the `android:configChanges` attribute. This attribute must specify the types of changes the `Activity` class handles itself.

- Implement the `onConfigurationChanged()` method of the `Activity` class to handle the specific changes (by type).

Internationalizing Applications

Android users hail from many different parts of the world. They speak different languages, use different currencies, and format their dates in different ways—just to name a few examples. Android application internationalization generally falls into three categories:

- Providing alternative resources such as strings or graphics for use when the application is running in different languages

- Implementing locale-independent or locale-specific code and other programmatic concerns

- Configuring your application for sale in foreign markets—a topic we discuss further in Chapter 29, "Selling Your Android Application"

We already discussed how to use alternate resources, but perhaps another example is in order—let's look at an application that loads resources based upon the device language settings. Specifically, let's consider a simple application that loads different string and graphic resources based upon the language and region settings of the device.

Internationalization Using Alternative Resources

Let's look at two examples of how to use alternative resources—this time, to localize an application for a variety of different languages and locales. By language, we mean the linguistic variety such as English, French, Spanish, German, Japanese, and so on. By locale, we are getting more specific, such as English (United States) versus English (United Kingdom) or English (Australia). There are times when you can get away with just providing language resources (English is English is English, right?) and times when this just won't fly.

Our first example is theoretical. If you want your application to support both English and French strings (in addition to the default strings), you can simply create two additional resource directories called /res/values-en (for the English strings.xml) and /res/values-fr (for the French strings.xml). Within the strings.xml files, the resource names are the same. For example, the /res/values-en/strings.xml file could look like this:

```
<?xml version="1.0" encoding="utf-8"?>
<resources>
    <string name="hello">Hello in English!</string>
</resources>
```

Whereas, the /res/values-fr/strings.xml file would look like this:

```
<?xml version="1.0" encoding="utf-8"?>
<resources>
    <string name="hello">Bonjour en Français!</string>
</resources>
```

A default layout file in the /res/layout directory that displays the string refers to the string by the variable name @string/hello, without regard to which language or directory the string resource is in. The Android operating system determines which version of the string (French, English, or default) to load at runtime. A layout with a TextView control to display the string might look like this:

```
<?xml version="1.0" encoding="utf-8"?>
<LinearLayout
    xmlns:android="http://schemas.android.com/apk/res/android"
    android:orientation="vertical"
    android:layout_width="fill_parent"
    android:layout_height="fill_parent">
    <TextView
        android:layout_width="fill_parent"
        android:layout_height="fill_parent"
        android:text="@string/hello" >
</LinearLayout>
```

The string is accessed programmatically in the normal way:

```
String str = getString(R.string.hello);
```

It's as easy as that. So, we move on to a more complex example, which illustrates how you can organize alternative application resources in order to provide functionality based upon the device language and locale.

Tip

The code examples provided in this chapter are taken from the SimpleInternationalization application. The source code for this application is provided for download on the book website.

Again, this application has no real code to speak of. Instead, all interesting functionality depends upon the judicious and clever use of resource folder qualifiers to specify resources to load. These resources are

- The default resources for this application include the application icon stored in the `/res/drawable` directory, the layout file stored in the `/res/layout` directory, and the strings.xml string resources stored in the `/res/values` directory. These resources are loaded whenever there isn't a more specific resource available to load. They are the fallbacks.

- There are English string resources stored in the `/res/values-en` directory. If the device language is English, these strings load for use within the default layout.

- There are French Canadian string resources stored in the `/res/values-fr-rCA` directory. If the device language and locale are set to French (Canada), these strings load for use within the layout. But wait! There's also an alternative layout stored in the `/res/layout-fr-rCA` directory, and this alternative layout uses a special drawable graphic (the Quebec flag) stored in the `/res/drawable-fr-rCA` directory.

- Finally, there are French string resources stored in the `/res/values-fr` directory. If the device language is French (any locale except Canada), these strings load for use within the default layout.

In this way, the application loads different resources based upon the language and locale information, as shown in Figure 25.9. This figure shows the project layout, in terms of resources, as well as what the screen might look like when the device settings are set to different languages and locales.

Changing the Language Settings

Generally, a device ships in a default language. In the United States, this language is English (United States). Users who purchase devices in France, however, are likely to have a default language setting of French (France), while those in Britain and many British territories would likely have the language set to English (United Kingdom)—that said, Australia and New Zealand have their very own English settings and Canada has both an English (Canada) option and a French (Canada) language option.

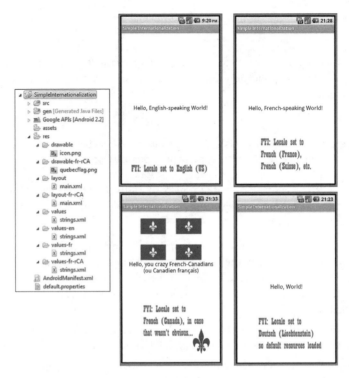

Figure 25.9   Using alternative resources for different
language string resources.

To change the locale setting on the emulator or the device, you need to perform the
following steps:

1. Navigate to the Home screen.

2. Press the Menu button.

3. Choose the Settings option.

4. Scroll down and choose the Language & keyboard settings (see Figure 25.10, left).

5. Choose the Select Language option (see Figure 25.10, middle).

6. Select the locale you want to change the system to, for example, French (France),
   English (United States), or English (United Kingdom) (see Figure 25.10, right).

Make sure you memorize the steps (and related icons, such as the Settings icon, shown in
Figure 25.11) required to change the language settings, as you need to navigate back to
this screen in that foreign language, in order to change the settings back.

Figure 25.10   Changing device language settings.

Figure 25.11   The Settings icon in English and French
(left) and the Settings menu in French (right).

Tip

You can also create custom locales for testing using the Custom Locale application, available on the Android Emulator. For example, you might want to create a Spanish locale for Mexico. When you use a custom locale, the emulator displays in its default language but the current locale is detected as your custom locale, allowing you to localize your application.

Internationalization forces design choices on the development team. For example, will you build one big project for all languages, or will you break the applications up by region? For some projects with light internationalization, you might be able to get away with one project with all internationalized resources. For deep internationalization, you might need to reorganize projects so that no application becomes too large or cumbersome for the user.

Because much of the work for application localization revolves around alternative resources, this means that this work might fall not to a developer who knows how to use Eclipse and the Android tools well, but to a designer who needs some training on how Android internationalization works, how resources can be layered, and the drawbacks of over-internationalizing (resulting in very large package files with many graphics and such). On the plus side, this leaves developers free to do what they do best: developing code.

Finally, you've likely noticed that the Android alternative resource structure isn't perfect—especially for countries with multiple official (and unofficial) languages. It is possible to work around these issues, when necessary, by loading graphics programmatically based upon the current locale setting on the device, but this should only be attempted when absolutely necessary.

Implementing Locale Support Programmatically

There are times in which you should ensure that your application code is "locale-aware." Often, this means writing code that is flexible enough to run smoothly regardless of the locale. However, when your application needs to be locale-aware—for example, to download appropriate content from a remote application server—you should rely upon locale-friendly methods.

Tip

To determine the device locale, developers can use the `getDefault()` method of the `java.util.Locale` class. Similarly, you can use the `getAvailableLocales()` method to retrieve a list of locales available on the device. Not all locales are supported on all devices; device manufacturers and operators might include only a subset of all locales supported by the Android operating system. For example, you might see devices sold in the United States that support only English and Spanish. You might also want to check out the `android.content.res.Configuration` class for more information on device configuration, including locale settings.

Here are some pointers for developing applications that work in a variety of locales:

- Begin by accepting that different parts of the world have different ways of expressing common information. Respect these differences and support them when feasible.
- Apply standard methods for internationalizing Java applications.
- Most localization issues with application code revolve around the use and formatting of strings, numbers, currencies, dates, and times. Audio and video containing speech is also routinely localized.
- Don't make assumptions about character encodings or what locale your application is running in.
- Always use locale-friendly methods, when they are available. Often, a class has two versions of a method: one that uses the current locale, and another that includes a locale parameter that you can use when necessary to override behavior.

Tip

There are a number of utility classes and methods provided within the Android SDK for locale- and region-specific string (start with the `String.format()` method) and date manipulation (start with the `java.text.DateFormat` utility class) and phone number formatting (start with the `android.telephony.PhoneNumberUtils` class). Note also that many classes have methods that take a Locale parameter, enabling the developer to override behavior for other than the current locale.

Targeting Different Device Configurations

Android devices come in all colors, shapes, and sizes. Sometimes you want to try to support all devices with a single application, and other times you want to limit the types of device configurations that your application can support. Really, it all comes down to knowing your user audience, so that they have positive experience (without excluding anyone unnecessarily).

Developers can target different device configurations using a number of Android Manifest tags, including `<supports-screen>`, `<uses-configuration>`, `<uses-feature>`, and `<uses-sdk>`. Developers can also use certain programming techniques to help ensure that applications are both forward and backward compatible.

Supporting Hardware Configurations

Let's take a closer look at some of the Android manifest file tags that you can use in your application to help identify target device configurations and how they work:

- You can use the `<supports-screen>` tag to limit what types of screens your application supports, as discussed earlier in the chapter.
- You can use the `<uses-configuration>` tag to indicate the device configurations (generally related to input methods) used by the application, as well as whether or not they are required for the application to run properly.

- You can use the `<uses-feature>` tag to indicate more features used by the application, as well as whether or not they are required for the application to run properly. Use this tag to specify what version of OpenGL ES your application supports as well as the optional hardware used (cameras, microphones, sensors). For a complete list of features available for use with this tag, see the feature constants defined in the `PackageManager` class documentation.

- You can use the `<uses-sdk>` tag to limit what platforms can install your application to a specific range of SDK versions (as defined by API levels). This information is enforced by the Android operating system.

For more details on each tag, see the Android SDK documentation: http://developer. android.com/guide/topics/manifest/manifest-intro.html.

Tip

Developers that publish their applications through the Android Market can also control which countries to deploy to, among other options. The Android Market is discussed in detail in Chapter 29, "Selling Your Android Application."

Targeting Different Android SDK Versions

When a new version of the Android version is released, developers must take note of the new SDK components added as well as those that were deprecated. First and foremost, you want to make sure you use the `<uses-sdk>` tag correctly in your application's Android manifest file.

Tip

To determine details about the device build at runtime, you can use the `Build` class (`android.os.Build.VERSION`, to be specific).

You can also use some other techniques to help ensure compatibility with different Android SDKs, including

- Determine whether or not to use a specific feature of the Android SDK based upon its API Level (the Android SDK version in which it was introduced)

- Use Java reflection to conditionally load newer SDK features, while supporting devices that run older versions of the platform

Determining When SDK Features Were Introduced

When developing an application that targets multiple platform versions, developers need to pay special attention to the API Level associated with a given package, class, method, or constant in the SDK. The API Level in which a given class, interface, or method was introduced is usually listed in the Android SDK documentation, as shown in Figure 25.12.

The API Level for a given SDK component might be shown in different places in the documentation:

- For packages, classes, and interfaces, the API level is displayed in the top-right corner of the Java documentation (at the top).

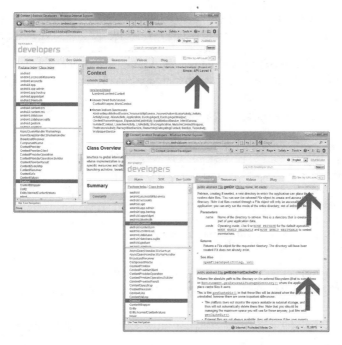

Figure 25.12   How to determine the API Level for a
specific package, class, or method.

- For methods and constants, the API level is shown to the right of the method name in its *description* (toward the bottom of the class documentation).

Using Java Reflection to Ensure Backward Compatibility

Luckily, Android applications are written in Java, and the Java programming language supports reflection. What this means is that developers can programmatically retrieve methods and classes by name at runtime, if necessary.

This is especially helpful when you want your application to take advantage of new parts of the Android SDK while still supporting older versions. When using this technique, you must build your project against the older SDK version while running on the new SDK version. The reason this technique works is because you never reference new methods or classes that don't exist directly in code. Instead, they're conditionally loaded by passing in strings to the Java reflection methods.

Tip

Read more about Java Reflection for backward compatibility at the Android developer website (http://developer.android.com/resources/articles/backward-compatibility.html) and the Android development blog (http://android-developers.blogspot.com/2010/06/allowing-applications-to-play-nicer.html).

Let's look at a quick example. To get a method by name, use the `getMethod()` method (say that ten times, fast) of the static class object of the specific class you are interested in. The following code retrieves a reference to the `getExternalStoragePublicDirectory()` method of the `Environment` class using Java reflection. This particular method was introduced in API Level 8 (Android 2.2) and therefore not available in previous versions of the platform:

```
Method methodExternalStoragePublicDirectory;
try{
    methodExternalStoragePublicDirectory =
        Environment.class.getMethod(
        "getExternalStoragePublicDirectory",
        new Class[] {String.class});
} catch (Exception e) {
    // failed, not running API Level 8
    // plan to provide alternate functionality
}
```

If the method is available, calls can then be made using the `methodExternalStoragePublicDirectory` object, via its `invoke()` method. You could invoke the method as follows:

```
methodExternalStoragePublicDirectory.invoke(null, picture_directory);
```

Using these techniques enables the developer to maintain backward compatibility in her applications while taking advantage of the great new features crammed into newer versions of the Android SDK. Used judiciously, this technique can save time and effort and avoid the need to provide different versions of the application for different platform versions (often confusing to users).

It's best not to over-use this technique—at some point, the application might be using so many of these features that the effort to implement and use Java reflection to support special cases becomes too great. Java reflection also introduces a performance penalty. Making a method call through the `invoke()` method is slower than a regular method call and common patterns involve placing all the reflection logic in a new class to abstract and simplify the use of it. This adds yet another layer to the call stack, though. This technique also makes your code harder to read and maintain.

> **Tip**
>
> The Android Developer's blog has some handy tricks for maximizing backward compatibility without the overhead of reflection. You can read more at http://android-developers.blogspot.com/2010/07/how-to-have-your-cupcake-and-eat-it-too.html.

Summary

Compatibility is a vast topic, and we've given you a lot to think about. During design and implementation, always consider if your choices are going to introduce roadblocks to device compatibility. Quality assurance personnel should always vary the devices used for testing as much as possible. The goal might or might not be to have a single application that supports every device configuration under the sun. Instead, use practices that encourage compatibility and do your best to keep compatibility-related resources and code streamlined and manageable.

If you take only one concept away from this chapter, it should be that alternative resources can be used to great effect. They enable a flexibility that can go a long way toward achieving compatibility, whether it's for screen differences or internationalization. Additionally, certain Android manifest file tags can help ensure that your applications are installed only on devices that meet certain prerequisites, or requirements, such as a certain version of OpenGL ES, or availability of camera hardware.

References and More Information

Android Dev Guide: Alternative Resources:
   http://developer.android.com/guide/topics/resources/providing-resources.html#AlternativeResources.
Android Dev Guide: How Android Finds the Best-Matching Resource:
   http://developer.android.com/guide/topics/resources/providing-resources.html#BestMatch
Android Dev Guide: Handling Runtime Changes:
   http://developer.android.com/guide/topics/resources/runtime-changes.html
ISO 639-1 Languages:
   http://www.loc.gov/standards/iso639-2/php/code_list.php
ISO 3166-1-alpha-2 Regions:
   http://www.iso.org/iso/country_codes/iso_3166_code_lists/
Android Best Practices: Compatibility:
   http://developer.android.com/guide/practices/compatibility.html
Android Best Practices: Supporting Multiple Screens:
   http://developer.android.com/guide/practices/screens_support.html

## 26

The Mobile Software Development Process

The mobile development process is much like the traditional desktop software process with a couple of distinct differences. Understanding how these differences affect your team is critical to running a successful mobile development project. This insight into the mobile development process is invaluable to those new to mobile development and veteran developers alike, to those in management and planning, as well as the developers and testers in the trenches. In this chapter, you learn about the peculiarities of mobile development as they pertain to each stage of the software development process.

An Overview of the Mobile Development Process

Mobile development teams are often small in size and project schedules are short in length. The entire project lifecycle is often condensed, and whether you're a team of one or one hundred, understanding the mobile development considerations for each part of the development process can save you a lot of wasted time and effort. Some hurdles a mobile development team must overcome include

- Choosing an appropriate software methodology for your mobile project
- Understanding how target devices dictate the functionality of your application
- Performing thorough, accurate, and ongoing feasibility analyses
- Mitigating the risks associated with preproduction devices
- Keeping track of device functionality through configuration management
- Designing a responsive, stable application on a memory restrictive system
- Designing user interfaces for a variety of devices with different user experiences
- Testing the application thoroughly on the target devices
- Incorporating third-party requirements that affect where you can sell your application
- Deploying and maintaining a mobile application

Choosing a Software Methodology

Developers can easily adapt most modern software methodologies to mobile development. Whether your team opts for traditional Rapid Application Development (RAD) principles or more modern variants of Agile software development, such as Scrum, mobile applications have some unique requirements.

Understanding the Dangers of Waterfall Approaches

The short development cycle might tempt some to use a waterfall approach, but developers should beware of the inflexibility that comes with this choice. It is generally a bad idea to design and develop an entire mobile application without taking into account the many changes that tend to occur during the development cycle (see Figure 26.1). Changes to target devices (especially preproduction models), ongoing feasibility, and performance concerns and the need for quality assurance to test early and often on the target devices (not just the emulator) make it difficult for strict waterfall approaches to succeed with mobile projects.

Figure 26.1   The dangers of waterfall development.
(Graphic courtesy of Amy Tam Badger.)

Understanding the Value of Iteration

Because of the speed at which mobile projects tend to progress, iterative methods have been the most successful strategies adapted to mobile development. Rapid prototyping enables developers and quality assurance personnel ample opportunity to evaluate the feasibility and performance of the mobile application on the target devices and adapt as needed to the change that inevitably occurs over the course of the project.

Gathering Application Requirements

Requirements analyses for mobile applications can be more complex than that of traditional desktop applications. You must often tailor requirements to work across a number of devices—devices that might have vastly different user interfaces and input methods. Having great variation in target platforms makes development assumptions tricky. It's not unlike the differences web developers might need to accommodate when developing for different web browsers (and versions of web browsers).

Determining Project Requirements

When multiple devices are involved (which is almost always the case with Android), here are two approaches we have found to be helpful for determining project requirements:

- The lowest common denominator method
- The customization method

Each method has its benefits and its drawbacks. With the lowest common denominator method, you design the application to run *sufficiently* well across a number of devices. In this case, the primary target for which you develop is the device configuration with the fewest features—basically, the most inferior device. Only requirements that can be met by all devices are included in the specification in order to reach the broadest range of devices—requirements such as input methods, screen resolution, and the platform version.

> **Note**
>
> The lowest common denominator method is roughly equivalent to developing a desktop application with the following minimum system requirements: (1) Windows 2000 and (2) 128 megabytes of RAM, on the assumption that the application will be forward compatible with the latest version of Windows (and every other version in between). It's not ideal, but in some cases, the trade-offs are acceptable.

Some light customization, such as resources and the final compiled binary (and the version information) is usually feasible with the lowest common denominator method. The main benefit of this method is that there is only one major source code tree to work with; bugs are fixed in one place and apply for all devices. You can also easily add other devices without changing much code, provided they too meet the minimum hardware requirements. The drawbacks include the fact that the resulting generalized application does not maximize any device-specific features nor can it take advantage of new platform features.

Also, if a device-specific problem arises or you misjudge the lowest common denominator and later find that an individual device lacks the minimum requirements, the team might be forced to implement a workaround (hack) or branch the code at a later date, losing the early benefits of this method but keeping all the drawbacks.

Tip

The Android tools make it easy for developers to target multiple platform versions within a single application package. Developers should take care to identify target platforms early in the design phase. That said, over-the-air firmware updates to users are a fairly regular occurrence, so the platform version on a given device is likely to change over time. Always design your applications with forward compatibility in mind and make contingency plans for distributing application upgrades to existing applications as necessary.

Using the customization method, the application is tailored for specific devices or a class of devices (such as all devices capable of OpenGL ES 2.0, for example). This method works well for specialized applications with a small number of target devices but does not scale well from a resource management perspective. There is generally a core application framework (classes or packages) shared across all versions of the application. All versions of a client-server application would likely share the same server and interact with it in the same way, but the client implementation is tailored to take advantage of specific device features. That is the key benefit of this approach. Some drawbacks include source code fragmentation (many branches of the same code), increased testing requirements, and the fact that it can be more difficult to add new devices in the future.

In truth, mobile development teams usually use a hybrid approach incorporating some of the aspects from both methods. It's pretty common to see developers define classes of devices based on functionality. For example, a game application might group devices based on graphics performance, screen resolution, or input methods. A location-based service (LBS) application might group devices based on the available internal sensors. Other applications might develop one version for devices with built-in front-facing cameras and one version for those without. These groupings are arbitrary and set by the developer to keep the code and testing manageable. They will, in large part, be driven by the details of a particular application and any support requirements. In many cases, these features can be detected at runtime as well, but add enough of them together and the code paths can become overly complex when having two or more applications would actually be easier.

Tip

A single, unified version of an application is cheaper to support than multiple versions. However, a game might sell better with custom versions that leverage the distinct advantages and features of a specific class of devices. A vertical business application would likely benefit more from a unified approach that works the same, is easier to train users across multiple devices, and would thus have lower support costs for the business.

Developing Use Cases for Mobile Applications

You should first write use cases in general terms for the application before adapting them to specific device classes, which impose their own limitations. For example, a high-level use case for an application might be "Enter Form Data," but the individual devices might use different input methods, such as hardware versus software keyboards, and so on.

Tip

Developing an application for multiple devices is much like developing an application for different operating systems and input devices (such as handling Mac keyboard shortcuts versus those on Windows)—you must account for subtle and not-so-subtle differences. These differences might be obvious, such as not having a keyboard for input, or not so obvious, such as device-specific bugs or different conventions for soft keys. See Chapter 25, "Targeting Different Device Configurations and Languages," for a discussion on device compatibility.

Incorporating Third-Party Requirements

In addition to the requirements imposed by your internal requirements analyses, your team needs to incorporate any requirements imposed by others. Third-party requirements can come from any number of sources, including

- Android License Agreement Requirements
- Google Maps API License Agreement Requirements (if applicable)
- Third-Party API Requirements (if applicable)
- Android Market Requirements (if applicable)
- Mobile Carrier/Operator Requirements (if applicable)
- Other Application Store Requirements (if applicable)
- Application Certification Requirements (if applicable)

Incorporating these requirements into your project plan early is essential not only for keeping your project on schedule but also so that these requirements are built into the application from the ground up, as opposed to applied as afterthoughts that can be risky.

Managing a Device Database

As your mobile development team builds applications for a growing number of devices, it becomes more and more important to keep track of the target device information for revenue estimation and maintenance purposes. Creating a device database is a great way to keep track of both marketing and device specification details for target devices. When we say "database," we mean anything from a Microsoft Excel spreadsheet to a little SQL database. The point is that the information is shared across the team or company and kept up to date. It can also be helpful to break devices into classes, such as those that support OpenGL ES 2.0 or those without camera hardware.

The device database is best implemented early, when project requirements are just determined and target devices are determined. Figure 26.2 illustrates how you can track device information and how different members of the application development team can use it.

Determining Which Devices to Track

Some companies track only the devices they actively develop for, whereas others also track devices they might want to include in the future, or lower priority devices. You can include devices in the database during the Requirements phase of a project but also later as a change in project scope. You can also add devices as subsequent porting projects long after the initial application has been released.

Storing Device Data

You should design the device database to contain any information about a given device that would be helpful for developing and selling applications. This might require that someone be tasked with keeping track of a continual stream of information from carrier and manufacturers. Still, this information can be useful for all mobile projects at a company. This data should include

- Important device technical specification details (screen resolution, hardware details, supported media formats, input methods, localization)
- Any known issues with devices (bugs and important limitations)
- Device carrier information (any firmware customizations, release and sunset dates, expected user statistics, such as if a device is highly anticipated and expected to sell a lot, or well received for vertical market applications, and so on)
- Firmware upgrade information (as it becomes available, changes might have no impact on the application or warrant an entirely separate device entry)
- Actual testing device information (which devices have been purchased or loaned through manufacturer or carrier loaner programs, how many are available)

You can also cross-reference the device carrier information with sales figures from the carrier, application store, and internal metrics.

The actual testing device information is often best implemented as a library check-out system. Team members can reserve devices for testing and development purposes. When a loaner device needs to be returned to the manufacturer, it's easy to track. This also facilitates sharing devices across teams.

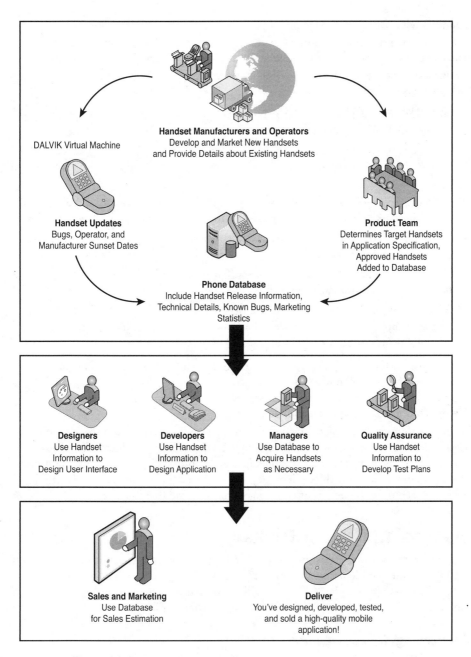

Figure 26.2   How a development team uses the device database.

Using Device Data

Remember that the database can be used for multiple mobile development projects. Device resources can be shared, and sales statistics can be compared to see upon which devices your applications perform best. Different team members (or roles) can use the device database in different ways:

- Product designers use the database to develop the most appropriate application user interface for the target devices.
- Media artists use the database to generate application assets such as graphics, videos, and audio in supported media file formats and resolutions appropriate for the target devices.
- Project managers use the database to determine the devices that must be acquired for development and testing purposes on the project and development priorities.
- Software developers use the database to design and develop applications compatible with target device specifications.
- Quality assurance personnel use the database to design and develop test plans' target device specifications and to test the application thoroughly.
- Marketing and sales professionals use the database to estimate sales figures for released applications. For example, it is important to be aware that application sales will drop as device availability drops.

The information in the database can also help determine the most promising target devices for future development and porting.

Using Third-Party Device Databases

There are third-party databases for device information including screen size and internal device details and carrier support details, but subscribing to such information can be costly for a small company. Many mobile developers instead choose to create a custom device database with only the devices they are interested in and the specific data they need for each device, which is often absent from open and free databases.

Assessing Project Risks

In addition to the normal risks any software project must identify, mobile projects need to be aware of the outside influences that can affect their project schedule and whether the project requirements can be met. Some of the risk factors include identifying and acquiring target devices and continually reassessing application feasibility.

Identifying Target Devices

Just as most sane software developers wouldn't write a desktop application without first deciding what operating systems (and their versions) the application would run on, mobile developers must consider the target devices their application will run on. Each device has different capabilities, a different user interface, and unique limitations.

Target devices are generally determined in one of two ways:

- There's a popular "killer" device you want to develop for.
- You want to develop an application for maximum coverage.

In the first instance, you have your initial target device (or class of devices) figured out; in the second instance, you want to look at the available (and soon to be available) devices on the market and adjust your application specification to cover as many as is reasonably feasible.

Tip

On the Android platform, you normally do not target individual devices specifically, but device features (for example, those running a specific platform version or having specific hardware configurations). You can limit the devices upon which your application will be installed using Android Manifest tags, which act as market filters. You learn about Android Manifest tags and market filters in Chapters 5, "Defining Your Application Using the Android Manifest File," 25, and 29, "Selling Your Android Application."

Understanding How Manufacturers and Operators Fit In

It's also important to note that we've seen popular product lines, such as the Droid line of Android devices, customized by a number of manufacturers. A carrier often ships its custom version of a device, including a different user experience or skin, as well as big bundles of custom applications (taking up a bunch of space on the device). The carrier might also disable specific device features (such as Bluetooth or Wi-Fi), which effectively makes it impossible for your application to run. You must take all these factors into account when considering your application requirements and abilities. Your application's running requirements must match the features shared across all target devices and handle optional feature use appropriately in all cases.

Understanding How Devices Come and Go Over Time

New devices are developed all the time. Carriers and manufacturers retire (sunset) devices all the time. Different carriers might carry the same (or similar) device but might sunset (retire) the devices at a different time.

Tip

Developers should set a policy, made clear to users, of how long an application will be supported after the carrier or manufacturer stops supporting a specific device. This policy might need to be different for various carriers because carriers impose their own support requirements.

Developers need to understand how different kinds of device models can move through the worldwide marketplace. Some devices are available (or become popular) only in certain geographic regions. Sometimes devices are released worldwide, but often they are released regionally. The T-Mobile G1, for example, was first released in the United

States but later released worldwide. Similarly, the Motorola Droid was only available in the United States, whereas the similar Motorola Milestone was available only outside the United States.

Historically, it's been common for a device (or new generation of devices) to become available initially in market-driving regions of eastern Asia, including South Korea and Japan, and then show up in Europe, North America, and Australia, where device users often upgrade every year or two and pay premium rates for applications. Finally, these same devices become available in Central and South America, China, and India, where subscribers often don't have landlines nor do they have the same levels of income. Regions such as China and India must often be treated as entirely separate mobile marketplaces—with more affordable devices requiring vastly different revenue models. Here applications sell for less, but revenue is instead derived from the huge and growing subscriber base.

Acquiring Target Devices

The earlier you can get your hands on the target devices, the better off you are. Sometimes this is as easy as going to the store and buying a new device. Other times, you need to acquire devices in other ways.

It is quite common for an application developer to target upcoming devices—devices not yet shipping or available to consumers. There is a great competitive advantage to having your application ready to run the moment consumers have the device in their hands for the first time. For preproduction devices, you can join manufacturer and operator developer programs. These programs help you keep abreast of changes to the device lines (upcoming models, discontinued models). Many of these programs also include preproduction device loan programs, enabling developers to get their hands on the device before consumers do.

Tip

If you are just getting started acquiring Android devices, consider an Android Dev Phone, such as the Google Nexus One. Android Dev Phones are SIM-unlocked, contract-free devices, meaning you can use them on any GSM network. Android Dev Phones also feature a bootloader so you can install custom system images. See the link in the "Resources and More Information" section for details on how to purchase these devices.

There are risks for developers writing applications for specific preproduction devices because device shipment dates often slide and the platform might have unstable or bug-prone firmware. Devices are delayed or canceled. Device features (especially new and interesting ones) are not set in stone until the device ships and the developer verifies that those features work as expected. Exciting new devices are announced all the time—devices you might want your application to support. Your project plan must be flexible enough to change and adapt with the market as necessary.

Determining Feasibility of Application Requirements

Mobile developers are at the mercy of the device limitations, which vary in terms of memory and processing power, screen type, and platform version. Mobile developers do not really have the luxury traditional desktop application developers have of saying an application requires "more memory" or "more space." Device limitations are pretty much fixed, and if a mobile application is to run, it runs within the device's limitations, or not at all. Technically speaking, most Android devices have some hardware flexibility, such as the ability to use external storage devices such as SD cards, but we're still talking about limited resources.

You can do true feasibility assessment only on the physical device, not the software emulator. Your application might work beautifully in the emulator but falter on the actual device. Mobile developers most constantly revisit feasibility, application responsiveness, and performance throughout the development process.

Understanding Quality Assurance Risks

The quality assurance team has its work cut out for it because the testing environment is generally less than ideal.

Testing Early, Testing Often

Get those target devices in-hand as early as possible. For preproduction devices, it can take months to get the hardware in hand from the manufacturer. Cooperating with carrier device loaner programs and buying devices from retail locations is frustrating but some-times necessary. Don't wait until the last minute to gather the test hardware.

Testing on the Device

It cannot be said enough: *Testing on the emulator is helpful, but testing on the device is essential.* In reality, it doesn't matter if the application works on the emulator—no one uses an emulator in the real world.

Although you can perform factory resets on devices and wipe user data, there is often no easy way to completely "wipe" a device and return it to a clean starting state, so the quality assurance team needs to determine and stick to a testing policy of what is consid-ered a clean state on the device. Testers might need to learn to flash devices with different firmware versions and understand subtle differences between platform versions, as well as how underlying application data is stored on the device (for example, SQLite databases, private application files, and cache usage).

Mitigating the Risk of Limited Real-World Testing Opportunities

In some ways, every quality assurance tester works within a controlled environment. This is doubly true for mobile testers. They often work with devices not on real networks and preproduction devices that might not match those in the field. Add to this that because testing generally takes place in a lab, the location (including primary cell tower, satellite fixes and related device signal strength, availability of data services, LBS information, and locale information) is fixed. The quality assurance team needs to get creative to mitigate the risks of testing too narrow a range of these factors. For example, it is essential to test all applications when the device has no signal (and in airplane mode, and such) to make sure they don't crash and burn under such conditions that we all experience at some point in time.

Testing Client-Server and Cloud-Friendly Applications

Make sure the quality assurance team understands its responsibilities. Mobile applications often have network components and server-side functionality. Make sure thorough server and service testing is part of the overall test plan—not just the client portion of the overall solution that is implemented on the device. This might require the development of desktop or web applications to exercise network portions of the overall solution.

Writing Essential Project Documentation

You might think that with its shorter schedules, smaller teams, and simpler functionality, mobile software project documentation would be less onerous. Unfortunately, this is not the case—quite the opposite. In addition to the traditional benefits any software project enjoys, good documentation serves a variety of purposes in mobile development. Consider documenting the following for your project:

- Requirements analysis and prioritization
- Risk assessment and management
- Application architecture and design
- Feasibility studies including performance benchmarking
- Technical specifications (overall, server, device-specific client)
- Detailed user-interface specifications (general, service-specific)
- Test plans, test scripts, test cases (general, device-specific)
- Scope change documentation

Much of this documentation is common in your average software development project. But perhaps your team finds that skimping on certain aspects of the documentation process has been doable in the past. Before you think of cutting corners in a mobile development project, consider some of these documentation requirements for a successful project. Some project documentation might be simpler than that of larger-scale software projects, but other portions might need to be fleshed out in finer detail—especially user interface and feasibility studies.

Developing Test Plans for Quality Assurance Purposes

Quality assurance relies heavily on the functional specification documentation and the user interface documentation. Screen real estate is valuable on the small screens of mobile devices, and user experience is vital to the successful mobile project.

Understanding the Importance of User Interface Documentation

There's no such thing as a killer application with a poorly designed user interface. Thoughtful user interface design is one of the most important details to nail down during the design phase of any mobile software project. You must thoroughly document application workflow (application state) at the screen-by-screen level and can include detailed specifications for key usage patterns and how to gracefully fall back when certain keys or features are missing. You should clearly define usage cases in advance.

Leveraging Third-Party Testing Facilities

Some companies opt to have quality assurance done offsite by a third party; most quality assurance teams require detailed documentation including use case workflow diagrams to determine correct application behavior. If you do not provide adequate and detailed documentation to the testing facility, you will not get deep and detailed testing. By providing detailed documentation, you raise the bar from "it works" to "it works correctly." What might seem straightforward to some people might not be to others.

Providing Documentation Required by Third Parties

If you are required to submit your application to a software certification program or even, in some cases, to a mobile application store, part of your submission is likely to require some documentation about your application. Some stores require, for example, that your application include a Help feature or technical support contact information. Certification programs might require you to provide detailed documentation on application functionality, user interface workflow, and application state diagrams.

Providing Documentation for Maintenance and Porting

Mobile applications are often ported to additional devices and other mobile platforms. This porting work is frequently done by a third party, making the existence of thorough functional and technical specifications even more crucial.

Leveraging Configuration Management Systems

There are many wonderful source control systems out there for developers, and most that work well for traditional development work fine for a mobile project. Versioning your application, on the other hand, is not necessarily as straightforward as you might think.

Choosing a Source Control System

Mobile development considerations impose no surprise requirements for source control systems. Some considerations for developers evaluating how they handle configuration management for a mobile project are

- Ability to keep track of source code (Java) and binaries (Android packages, and so on)
- Ability to keep track of application resources by device configuration (graphics, and so on)
- Integration with the developer's chosen development environment (Eclipse)

One point to consider is integration between the development environment (such as Eclipse) and your source control system. Common source control systems such as Perforce, Subversion, and CVS work well with Eclipse.

Implementing an Application Version System That Works

Developers should also make an early decision on a versioning scheme that takes into account the device particulars and the software build. It is often not sufficient to version the software by build alone (that is, Version 1.0.1).

Mobile developers often combine the traditional versioning scheme with the target device configuration or device class supported (Version 1.0.1.Important Characteristic/Device Class Name). This helps quality assurance, technical support personnel, and end users who might not know the model names or features of their devices or only know them by marketing names developers are often unaware of. For example, an application developed with camera support might be versioned 1.0.1.Cam, where Cam stands for "Camera Support," whereas the same application for a device without camera support might have a version such as 1.0.1.NoCam, where NoCam stands for "No Camera Support" source branch. If you had two different maintenance engineers supporting the different source code trees, you would know just by the version name who to assign bugs to.

Just to make things a tad more confusing, you need to plan your upgrade versions as well. If an upgrade spawns a rebuild of your application, you might want to version it appropriately: Version 1.0.1.NoCam.Upg1, and such. Yes, this can get out of control, so don't go overboard, but if you design your versioning system intelligently upfront, it can be useful later when you have different device builds floating around internally and with users. Finally, you also have to keep track of the `versionCode` attribute associated with your application.

Designing Mobile Applications

When designing an application for mobile, the developer must consider the constraints the device imposes and decide what type of application framework is best for a given project.

Understanding Mobile Device Limitations

Applications are expected to be fast, responsive, and stable, but developers must work with limited resources. You must keep in mind the memory and processing power constraints of all target devices when designing and developing mobile applications.

Exploring Common Mobile Application Architectures

Mobile applications have traditionally come in two basic models: stand-alone applications and network-driven applications.

Stand-alone applications are packaged with everything they require and rely on the device to do all the heavy lifting. All processing is done locally, in memory, and is subject to the limitations of the device. Stand-alone applications might use network functions, but they do not rely on them for core application functionality. An example of a reasonable stand-alone application is a basic Solitaire game. A user can play the game when the device is in Airplane Mode without issue.

Network-driven applications provide a lightweight client on the device but rely on the network (or "the cloud") to provide a good portion of its content and functionality. Network-driven applications are often used to offload intensive processing to a server. Network-driven applications also benefit from the ability to deliver additional content or functionality on-the-fly long after the application has been installed. Developers also like network-driven applications because this architecture enables them to build one smart application server or cloud service with device clients for many different operating systems to support a larger audience of users. Good examples of network-driven applications include

- Applications that leverage cloud-based services, application servers, or web services
- Customizable content such as ringtone and wallpaper applications
- Applications with noncritical process and memory-intensive operations that can be offloaded to a powerful server and the results delivered back to the client
- Any application that provides additional features at a later date without a full update to the binary

How much you rely on the network to assist in your application's functionality is up to you. You can use the network to provide only content updates (popular new ringtones), or you can use it to dictate how your application looks and behaves (for instance, adding new menu options or features on-the-fly).

Designing for Extensibility and Maintenance

Applications can be written with a fixed user interface and a fixed feature set, but they need not be. Network-driven applications can be more complex to design but offer flexibility for the long term—here's an example: Let's say you want to write a wallpaper application. Your application can be a stand-alone version, partially network-driven or completely network-driven. Regardless, your application has two required functions:

- Display a set of images and allow the user to choose one
- Take the chosen image and set it as the wallpaper on the device

A super simple stand-alone wallpaper application might come with a fixed set of wallpapers. If they're a generic size for all target devices, you might need to reformat them for the specific device. You could write this application, but it would waste space and processing. You can't update the wallpapers available, and it is generally just a bad design.

The partially network-driven wallpaper application might enable the user to browse a fixed menu of wallpaper categories, which show images from a generic image server. The application downloads a specific graphic and then formats the image for the device. As the developer, you can add new wallpaper images to the server anytime, but you need to build a new application every time you want to add a new device configuration or screen size. If you want to change the menu to add live wallpapers at a later date, you need to write a new version of your application. This application design is feasible, but it isn't using its resources wisely either and isn't particularly extensible. However, you could use the single application server and write applications for Android, iPhone, BREW, J2ME, and Blackberry clients, so we are still in a better position than we were with the stand-alone wallpaper application.

The fully network-driven version of the wallpaper application does the bare minimum it needs to on the device. The client enables the server to dictate what the client user interface looks like, what menus to display, and where to display them. The user browses the images from the application server just like the partially network-driven version does, but when the user chooses a wallpaper, the mobile application just sends a request to the server: "I want this wallpaper and I am this kind of device, with such and such screen resolution." The server formats and resizes the image (any process-intensive operations) and sends the perfectly tailored wallpaper down to the application, which the application then sets as the wallpaper. Adding support for more devices is straightforward—simply deploy the lightweight client with any necessary changes and add support for that device configuration to the server. Adding a new menu item is just a server change, resulting in all devices (or whichever devices the server dictates) getting that new category. You only need to update the client when a new function requires the client to change, such as to add support for live wallpapers. The response time of this application depends upon network performance, but the application is the most extensible and dynamic. However, this application is basically useless when the device is in Airplane Mode.

Stand-alone applications are straightforward and great for one-shot applications and those that are meant to be network-independent. Network-driven applications require a bit more forethought and are sometimes more complicated to develop but might save a lot of time and provide users with fresh content and features for the long run.

Designing for Application Interoperability

Mobile application designers should consider how they will interface with other applications on the device, including other applications written by the same developer. Some issues to address are

- Will your application rely on other content providers?
- Are these content providers guaranteed to be installed on the device?
- Will your application act as a content provider? What data will it provide?

- Will your application have background features? Act as a service?
- Will your application rely on third-party services or optional components?
- Will your application expose its functionality through a remote interface (AIDL)?

Developing Mobile Applications

Mobile application implementation follows the same design principles as other platforms. The steps mobile developers take during implementation are fairly straightforward:

- Write and compile the code.
- Run the application in the software emulator.
- Test and debug the application in the software emulator.
- Package and deploy the application to the target device.
- Test and debug the application on the target device.
- Incorporate changes from the team and repeat until the application is complete.

Note

We talk more about development strategies for building solid Android applications in Chapter 27, "Designing and Developing Bulletproof Android Applications."

Testing Mobile Applications

Testers face many challenges, including device fragmentation (many devices, each with different features—some call this "compatibility"), defining device states (what is a clean state?), and handling real-world events (device calls, loss of coverage). Gathering the devices needed for testing can be costly and difficult.

Note

We discuss testing Android applications in detail in Chapter 28, "Testing Android Applications."

The good news for mobile QA teams is that the Android SDK includes a number of useful tools for testing applications both on the emulator and the device. There are many opportunities for leveraging white box testing.

You must modify defect tracking systems to handle testing across device configurations and carriers. For thorough testing, QA team members generally cannot be given the device and told to "try to break it." There are many shades of gray for testers, between black box and white box testing. Testers should know their way around the Android emulator and the other utilities provided with the Android SDK.

Tip

The tools discussed in the appendices of this book (especially Appendices A, B, C, and D) are valuable not only to developers; the tools provide testers much more control over the device configuration.

Mobile quality assurance involves a lot of edge case testing and, again, a preproduction model of a device might not be exactly the same as what eventually ships to consumers.

Deploying Mobile Applications

Developers need to determine what methods they use to distribute applications. With Android, you have a number of options. You can market applications yourself and leverage third-party marketplaces such as the Android Market. Consolidated mobile marketplaces, such as Handango, also have Android distribution channels of which you can take advantage.

Note

We discuss publication of Android applications in detail in Chapter 29.

Determining Target Markets

Developers must take into account any requirements imposed by third parties offering application distribution mechanisms. Specific distributers might impose rules for what types of applications they distribute on your behalf. They might impose quality requirements such as testing certifications (although there are none specific to Android applications at the time this book went to print) and accompanying technical support, and documentation and adherence to common user interface workflow standards (that is, the Back button should behave like this) and performance metrics for responsive applications. Distributers might also impose content restrictions such as barring objectionable content.

Supporting and Maintaining Mobile Applications

Generally speaking, mobile application support requirements are minimal if you come from a traditional software background, but they do exist. Carriers and operators generally serve as the front line of technical support to end users. As a developer, you aren't usually required to have 24/7 responsive technical support staff or toll-free device numbers and such. In fact, the bulk of application maintenance can fall on the server side and be limited to content maintenance—such as posting new media such as ringtones, wallpapers, videos, or other content.

That said, the hardware on the market changes quickly, and mobile development teams need to stay on top of the market. Here are some of the maintenance and support considerations unique to mobile application development.

Warning

Developers cannot just develop an application, publish it, and forget about it—even the simplest of applications likely require some maintenance and the occasional upgrade.

Track and Address Crashes Reported by Users

The Android Market—the most popular way to distribute Android applications—has built-in features enabling users to submit crash and bug reports regarding your application. Monitor your developer account and address these issues in a timely fashion in order to maintain your credibility and keep your users happy.

Testing Firmware Upgrades

Android handsets receive frequent (some say *too* frequent) firmware upgrades. This means that the Android platform versions you initially tested and supported become obsolete and the handsets your application is installed upon can suddenly run new versions of the Android firmware. Although upgrades are supposed to be backward compatible, this hasn't always proven true. In fact, many developers have fallen victim to poor upgrade scenarios, in which their applications suddenly cease to function properly. Always retest your applications after a major or minor firmware upgrade occurs in the field.

Maintaining Adequate Application Documentation

Maintenance is often not performed by the same engineers who developed the application in the first place. Here, keeping adequate development and testing documentation, including specifications and test scripts, is even more vital.

Managing Live Server Changes

Always treat any live server and web or cloud service with the care it deserves. This means you need to appropriately time backups and upgrades. You need to safeguard data and maintain user privacy at all times. You should manage rollouts carefully because live mobile application users might rely on its availability. Do not underestimate the server-side development or testing needs. Always test server rollouts and service upgrades in a safe testing environment before "going live."

Identifying Low-Risk Porting Opportunities

If you've implemented the device database we previously talked about in the chapter, now is the ideal time to analyze device similarities to identify easy porting projects. For example, you might discover the following: An application was originally developed for a specific class of device, but now there are several popular devices on the market with similar specifications. Porting an existing application to these new devices is sometimes as straightforward as generating a new build (with appropriate versioning) and testing the application on the new devices. If you defined your device classes well, you might even get lucky and not have to make any changes at all when new devices come out.

Summary

Mobile software development has evolved over time and differs in some important ways from traditional desktop software development. In this chapter, you gained some practical advice to adapting traditional software processes to mobile, from identifying target devices to testing and deploying your application to the world. There's always room for improvement when it comes to software process. Hopefully some of these insights can help you avoid the pitfalls new mobile companies sometimes fall into or simply improve the processes of veteran teams.

References and More Information

Wikipedia on Software Process:
    http://en.wikipedia.org/wiki/Software_development_process
Wikipedia on Rapid Application Development (RAD):
    http://en.wikipedia.org/wiki/Rapid_application_development
Wikipedia on Iterative Development:
    http://en.wikipedia.org/wiki/Iterative_and_incremental_development
Wikipedia on Waterfall Development Process:
    http://en.wikipedia.org/wiki/Waterfall_model
Extreme Programming:
    http://www.extremeprogramming.org
Purchase Nexus One and Android Dev Phones:
    http://android.brightstarcorp.com/index.htm

## 27

Designing and Developing Bulletproof Android Applications

In this chapter, we cover tips and techniques from our years in the trenches of mobile software design and development. We also warn you—the designers, developers, and managers of mobile applications—of the various and sundry pitfalls you should do your best to avoid. Reading this chapter all at one time when you're new to mobile development might be a bit overwhelming. Instead, consider reading specific sections when planning the parts of the overall process. All our advice might not be appropriate for your particular project, and processes can always be improved. Hopefully this information about how mobile development projects succeed (or fail) gives you some insight into how you might improve the chances of success for your own projects.

Best Practices in Designing Bulletproof Mobile Applications

The "rules" of mobile application design are straightforward and apply across all platforms. These rules were crafted to remind us that our applications play a secondary role on the device. Often Android devices are, at the end of the day, phones first. These rules also make it clear that we do operate, to some extent, because of the infrastructure managed by the carriers and device manufacturers. These rules are echoed throughout the Android Software Development Kit (SDK) License Agreement and those of third-party application marketplace terms and conditions.

These "rules" are as follows:

- Don't interfere with device phone and messaging services.
- Don't break or otherwise tamper with or exploit the device hardware, firmware, software, or OEM components.

- Don't abuse or cause problems on operator networks.
- Don't abuse the user's trust.

Now perhaps these rules sound like no-brainers, but even the most well-intentioned developer can accidentally fall into some of these categories if they aren't careful and don't test the application thoroughly before distribution. This is especially true for applications that leverage networking support and low-level hardware APIs on the device, and those that store private user data such as names, locations, and contact information.

Meeting Mobile Users' Demands

Mobile users also have their own set of demands for applications they install on their devices. Applications are expected to

- Be responsive, stable, and secure
- Have straightforward, intuitive user interfaces that are easy to get up and running
- Get the job done with minimal frustration to the user
- Be available 24 hours a day, 7 days a week (remote servers or services always on, always available)
- Include a Help and/or About Screen for feedback and support contact information

Designing User Interfaces for Mobile Devices

Designing effective user interfaces for mobile devices, especially applications that run on a number of different devices, is something of a black art. We've all seen bad mobile application user interfaces. A frustrating user experience can turn a user off your brand forever, and a good experience can win a user's loyalty for the long term. It can also give your application an edge over the competition, even if your functionality is similar. A great user interface can win over users even when the functionality is behind the competition. Here are some tips for designing great mobile user interfaces:

- Fill screens sparingly; too much information on one screen overwhelms the user.
- Be consistent with user interface workflows, menu types, and buttons. Consider the device norms with this consistency, as well.
- Make Touch Mode "hit areas" large enough and spaced appropriately.
- Streamline common use cases with clear, consistent, and straightforward interfaces.
- Use big, readable fonts and large icons.
- Integrate tightly with other applications on the system using standardized controls, such as the quick Contact badge, content providers, and search adapters.
- Keep localization in mind when designing text-heavy user interfaces. Some languages are lengthier than others.
- Reduce keys or clicks needed as much as possible.

- Do not assume that specific input mechanisms (such as specific buttons or the existence of a keyboard) are available on all devices.

- Try to design the default use case of each screen to require only the user's thumb. Special cases might require other buttons or input methods, but encourage "thumbing" by default.

- Size graphics appropriately for phones. Do not include oversized resources and assets because they use valuable device resources and load more slowly, even if they resize appropriately. Also consider stripping out unnecessary information, such as EXIF or IPTC metadata, using tools such as ImageMagick or PNGOptimizer. You can also use the Draw 9 Patch tool to help optimize your Android graphics files.

- In terms of "friendly" user interfaces, assume that users do not read the application permissions when they approve them to install your application. If your application does anything that could cause the user to incur significant fees or shares private information, consider informing them again (as appropriate) when your application performs such actions.

Note

We discuss how to design Android applications that are compatible with a wide range of devices, including how to develop for different screen sizes and resolutions, in Chapter 25, "Targeting Different Device Configurations and Languages."

Designing Stable and Responsive Mobile Applications

Mobile device hardware has come a long way in the past few years, but developers must still work with limited resources. Users do not usually have the luxury of upgrading the RAM and other hardware in Android devices such as phones. Android users can, however, take advantage of removable storage devices such as SD cards to provide some "extra" space for application and media storage. Spending some time upfront to design a stable and responsive application is important for the success of the project. The following are some tips for designing robust and responsive mobile applications:

- Don't perform resource intensive operations on the main UI thread. Always use asynchronous tasks or threads to offload blocking operations.

- Use efficient data structures and algorithms; these choices manifest themselves in app responsiveness and happy users.

- Use recursion with care; these functional areas should be code reviewed and performance tested.

- Keep application state at all times. Android activity stack makes this work well, but you should take extra care to go above and beyond.

- Save your state and assume that your application will be suspended or stopped at any moment. If your application is suspended or closed, you cannot expect a user to verify anything (click a button, and so on). If your application resumes gracefully, your users will be grateful.

- Start up fast and resume fast. You cannot afford to have the user twiddling thumbs waiting for your application to start. Instead, you need to strike a delicate balance between preloading and on-demand data because your application might be suspended (or closed) with no notice.

- Inform users during long operations by using progress bars. Consider offloading heavy processing to a server instead of performing these operations on the device because these operations might drain battery life beyond the limits users are willing to accept.

- Ensure that long operations are likely to succeed before embarking upon them. For example, if your application downloads large files, check for network connectivity, file size, and available space before attempting the download.

- Minimize use of local storage, as most devices have very limited amounts. Use external storage, when appropriate. Be aware that SD cards (the most common external storage option) can be ejected and swapped; your application should handle this gracefully.

- Understand that data calls to content providers and across the AIDL barrier come at a cost to performance, so make these calls judiciously.

- Verify that your application resource consumption model matches your target audience. Gamers might anticipate shorter battery life on graphics-intensive games, but productivity applications should not drain the battery unnecessarily and should be lightweight for people "on the go" who do not always have their phone charging.

Tip

Written by the Google Android team, Android Developers blog (http://android-developers. blogspot.com) is a fantastic resource. This blog provides detailed insight into the Android platform, often covering topics not discussed in the Android platform documentation. Here you can find tips, tricks, best practices, and shortcuts on relevant Android development topics such as memory management (such as Context management), view optimization (avoiding deep view hierarchies), and layout tricks to improve UI speed. Savvy Android developers visit this blog regularly and incorporate these practices and tips into their projects.

Designing Secure Mobile Applications

Many mobile applications integrate with core applications such as the Phone, Camera, and Contacts. Make sure you take all the precautions necessary to secure and protect private user data such as names, locations, and contact information used by your application. This includes safeguarding personal user data on application servers and during network transmission.

Tip

If your application accesses or uses private data, especially usernames, passwords, or contact information, it's a good idea to include an End User License Agreement (EULA) and a Privacy Policy with your application.

Handling Private Data

To begin with, limit the private or sensitive data your application stores as much as possible. Don't store this information in plain text, and don't transmit it without safeguards. Do not try to work around any security mechanisms imposed by the Android framework. Store private user data in private application files, which are private to the application, and not in shared parts of the operating system. Do not expose application data in content providers without enforcing appropriate permissions on other applications. Use the encryption classes available in the Android framework when necessary.

Transmitting Private Data

The same cautions should apply to any remote network data storage (such as application servers or cloud storage) and network transmission. Make sure any servers or services that your application relies upon are properly secured against identity or data theft and invasion of privacy. Treat any servers your application uses like any other part of the application—test these areas thoroughly. Any private data transmitted should be secured using typical security mechanisms such as SSL. The same rules apply when enabling your application for backups using services such as Android Backup Service.

Designing Mobile Applications for Maximum Profit

For billing and revenue generation, mobile applications generally fall into one of four categories:

- Free applications (including those with advertising revenue)
- Single payment (pay once)
- Subscription payments (pay on a schedule, often seen with productivity and service applications)
- In-application payment for content (pay for specific content, such as a ringtone, a Sword of Smiting, or a new level pack)

Applications can use multiple types of billing, depending on which marketplaces and billing APIs they use (Android Market, for example, limits billing methods to Google Checkout). Although there are currently no billing APIs in the Android framework, there are rumblings that this might change in a future version. With Android in general, third parties can provide billing methods or APIs, so technically the sky's the limit.

When designing your mobile applications, consider the functional areas where billing can come into play and factor this into your design. Consider the transactional integrity of specific workflow areas of the application that can be charged for. For example, if your application has the capability to deliver data to the device, make sure this process is transactional in nature so that if you decide to charge for this feature, you can drop in the billing code, and when the user pays, the delivery occurs, or the entire transaction is rolled back.

Note

You learn more about the different methods currently available to market your application in Chapter 29, "Selling Your Android Application."

Leveraging Third-Party Standards for Android Application Design

There are no certification programs specifically designed for Android applications. However, as more applications are developed, third-party standards might be designed to differentiate quality applications from the masses. For example, mobile marketplaces could impose quality requirements and certainly programs could be created with some recognized body's endorsement or stamp of approval. Developers with an eye on financial applications would do well to consider conformance requirements.

Warning

With Android, the market is expected to manage itself. Do not make the mistake of interpreting that as "no rules" when it really means "few rules imposed by the system." There are strong licensing terms to keep malware and other malicious code out of users' hands.

It can be highly beneficial to examine the certification programs available in other mobile platforms and adjust them for Android. You might also want to examine the certification programs for desktop applications and other mobile platforms; consider how the requirements from these programs can be applied to Android applications. For example, if a specific type of encryption is recommended to meet certification requirements, and that type of encryption is feasible within Android, you should consider using it within your application.

Designing Mobile Applications for Ease of Maintenance and Upgrades

Generally speaking, it's best to make as few assumptions about the device configurations as possible when developing a mobile application. You'll be rewarded later when you want to port your application or provide an easy upgrade. You should carefully consider what assumptions you make.

Leveraging Network Diagnostics

In addition to developing adequate documentation and easy-to-decipher code, you can leverage some tricks to help maintain and monitor mobile applications in the field. Many of these tricks work best with mobile applications leveraging an application server, but you can sometimes gather information from third-party reports, such as application sales figures from mobile marketplaces or by including optional feedback gathering features in your application. Developers can also gather statistics from the bug reports that users can send in when a crash occurs on the device.

For networked applications, it can be highly useful to build in some lightweight auditing, logging, and reporting on the server side to keep your own statistics and not rely solely on third-party information. For example, you can easily keep track of

- How many users launch the application for the first time?
- How many users regularly use the application?
- What are the most popular usage patterns and trends?
- What are the least popular usage patterns and features?
- What devices (determined by application versioning or other relevant metrics) are the most popular?

Often you can translate these figures into rough estimates of expected sales, which you can later compare with actual sales figures from third-party marketplaces. You can streamline and make more efficient the most popular usage. You can review and improve the least popular features. Sometimes you can even identify potential bugs, such as features that are not working at all, just by noting that a feature has never been used in the field. Finally, you can determine which device targets are most appropriate for your specific application and user base.

Tip

Never collect personal data without the user's knowledge and consent. Gathering anonymous diagnostics is fairly commonplace, but avoid keeping any data that can be considered private. Make sure your sample sizes are large enough to obfuscate any personal user details, and make sure to factor out any live QA testing data from your results (especially when considering sales figures).

Designing for Easy Updates and Upgrades

Android applications can easily be upgraded in the field. The application update and upgrade processes do pose some challenges to developers, though. By update, we're talking about modifying the Android manifest version information and re-deploying the updated application on users' devices. By upgrading, we're talking about creating an entirely new application package with new features and deploying it as a separate application that the user needs to choose to install.

From an update perspective, you need to consider what conditions necessitate an update in the field. For example, do you draw the line at crashes or feature requests? You also want to consider the frequency in which you deploy updates—you need to schedule updates such that they come up frequently enough to be truly useful, but not so often that the users are constantly updating their application.

Tip

You should build application content updates into the application functionality as a feature (often network-driven) as opposed to necessitating an over-the-air actual application update. By enabling your applications to retrieve fresh content on-the-fly, you keep your users happy longer and applications stay relevant.

When considering upgrades, decide what manner you will migrate users from one version of your application to the next. Will you leverage Android backup features so that your users can transition seamlessly from one device to the next or will you provide your own solution? Consider how you will inform users of existing applications that a major new version is available.

Leveraging Android Tools for Application Design

The Android SDK and developer community provide a number of useful tools and resources for application design. You might want to leverage the following tools during this phase of your development project:

- The Android emulator is a good place to start for rapid proof of concept, before you have specific devices. You can use different Android Virtual Device (AVD) configurations to simulate different device configurations and platform versions.
- The DDMS tool is very useful for memory profiling.
- The Hierarchy Viewer in Pixel Perfect View enables accurate user interface design.
- The Draw Nine Patch tool can create stretchable graphics for mobile use.
- Use real devices for feasibility research and application proof-of-concept work, whenever possible. Do not design solely using the emulator.
- The technical specifications for specific devices, often available from manufacturers and carriers, can be invaluable for determining the configuration details of target devices.

Avoiding Silly Mistakes in Android Application Design

Last but not least, here is a list of some of the silly mistakes Android designers should do their best to steer clear of:

- Designing or developing for months without performing feasibility testing on the device
- Designing for a single device, platform, language, or hardware
- Designing as if your device has a large amount of storage and processing power and is always plugged in to a power source
- Developing for the wrong version of the Android SDK (verify device SDK version)
- Trying to adapt applications to smaller screens after the fact by having the phone "scale"
- Deploying oversized graphics and media assets with an application instead of sizing them appropriately

Best Practices in Developing Bulletproof Mobile Applications

Developing applications for mobile is not that different from traditional desktop development. However, developers might find developing mobile applications more restrictive, especially resource constrained. Again, let's start with some best practices or "rules" for mobile application development:

- Test assumptions regarding feasibility early and often on the target devices.
- Keep application size as small and efficient as possible.
- Choose efficient data structures and algorithms appropriate to mobile.
- Exercise prudent memory management.
- Assume that devices are running primarily on battery power.

Designing a Development Process That Works for Mobile Development

A successful project's backbone is a good software process. It ensures standards, good communication, and reduces risks. We talked about the overall mobile development process in Chapter 26. Again, here are a few general tips of successful mobile development processes:

- Use an iterative development process.
- Use a regular, reproducible build process with adequate versioning.
- Communicate scope changes to all parties—changes often affect testing most of all.

Testing the Feasibility of Your Application Early and Often

It cannot be said enough: You must test developer assumptions on real devices. There is nothing worse than designing and developing an application for a few months only to find that it needs serious redesign to work on an actual device. Just because your application works on the emulator does not, *in any way*, guarantee that it will run properly on the device. Some functional areas to examine carefully for feasibility include

- Functionality that interacts with peripherals and device hardware
- Network speed and latency
- Memory footprint and usage
- Algorithm efficiency
- User interface suitability for different screen sizes and resolutions
- Device input method assumptions
- File size and storage usage

We know; we sound like a broken record but, truly, we've seen this mistake happen over and over again. Projects are especially vulnerable to this when target devices aren't yet available. What happens is that engineers are forced closer to the waterfall method of software development with a big, bad surprise after weeks or months of development on some vanilla-style emulator.

We don't need to explain again why waterfall approaches are dangerous, do we? You can never be too cautious about this stuff. Think of this as the preflight safety speech of mobile software development.

Using Coding Standards, Reviews, and Unit Tests to Improve Code Quality

Developers who spend the time and effort necessary to develop efficient mobile application are rewarded by their users. The following is a representative list of some of the efforts that you can take:

- Centralizing core features in shared Java packages (or, if you have shared C or C++ libraries, consider using the Android NDK)
- Developing for compatible versions of the Android SDK (know your target devices)
- Using built-in controls and widgets appropriate to the application, customizing only where needed

You can use system services to determine important device characteristics (screen type, language, date, time, input methods, available hardware, and so on). If you make any changes to system settings from within your application, be sure to change the settings back when your application exits or pauses, if appropriate.

Defining Coding Standards

Developing a set of well-communicated coding standards for the development team can help drive home some of the important requirements of mobile applications. Some standards might include

- Implementing robust error handling and handle exceptions gracefully.
- Moving lengthy, process-intensive, or blocking operations off the main UI thread.
- Releasing objects and resources you aren't actively using.
- Practicing prudent memory management. Memory leaks can render your application useless.
- Using resources appropriately for future localization. Don't hardcode strings and other assets in code or layout files.
- Avoiding obfuscation in the code itself; comments are worthwhile. However, you should consider obfuscation later in the development process to protect against software piracy. Ideally, use obfuscation settings that preserve filename and line number details, so that you can easily track down application defects.

- Considering using standard document generation tools, such as Javadoc.
- Instituting and enforce naming conventions—in code and in database schema design.

Performing Code Reviews

Performing code inspections can improve the quality of project code, help enforce coding standards, and identify problems before QA gets their hands on a build and spends time and resources testing it.

It can also be helpful to pair developers with the QA tester who tests their specific functional areas to build a closer relationship between the teams. If testers understand how the application and Android operating system functions, they can test the application more thoroughly and successfully. This might or might not be done as part of a formal code review process. For example, a tester can identify defects related to type-safety just by noting the type of input expected (but not validated) on a form field of a layout or by reviewing Submit or Save button handling function with the developer.

Developing Code Diagnostics

The Android SDK provides a number of packages related to code diagnostics. Building a framework for logging, unit testing, and exercising your application to gather important diagnostic information, such as the frequency of method calls and performance of algorithms, can help you develop a solid, efficient, and effective mobile application. It should be noted that diagnostic hooks are almost always removed prior to application publication because they impose significant performance reductions and greatly reduce responsiveness.

Using Application Logging

In Chapter 3, "Writing Your First Android Application," we discuss how to leverage the built-in logging class `android.util.Log` to implement diagnostic logging, which can be monitored via a number of Android tools, such as the LogCat utility (available within DDMS, ADB, and Android Development Plug-in for Eclipse).

Developing Unit Tests

Unit testing can help developers move one step closer to the elusive 100 percent of code coverage testing. The Android SDK includes extensions to the JUnit framework for testing Android applications. Automated testing is accomplished by creating test cases, in Java code, that verify that the application works the way you designed it. You can do this automated testing for both unit testing and functional testing, including user interface testing.

Basic JUnit support is provided through the `junit.framework` and `junit.runner` packages. Here you find the familiar framework for running basic unit tests with helper classes for individual test cases. You can combine these test cases into test suites. There are utility classes for your standard assertions and test result logic.

The Android-specific unit testing classes are part of the `android.test` package, which includes an extensive array of testing tools designed specifically for Android applications.

This package builds upon the JUnit framework and adds many interesting features, such as the following:

- Simplified Hooking of Test Instrumentation (`android.app.Instrumentation`) with `android.test.InstrumentationTestRunner`, which you can run via ADB shell commands
- Performance Testing (`android.test.PerformanceTestCase`)
- Single `Activity` (or `Context`) Testing (`android.test.ActivityUnitTestCase`)
- Full Application Testing (`android.test.ApplicationTestCase`)
- Services Testing (`android.test.ServiceTestCase`)
- Utilities for generating events such as Touch events (`android.test.TouchUtils`)
- Many more specialized assertions (`android.test.MoreAsserts`)
- `View` validation (`android.test.ViewAsserts`)

If you are interested in designing and implementing a unit test framework for your Android application, we suggest working through our tutorial called "Android SDK: Unit Testing with the JUnit Testing Framework." You can find this tutorial online on our blog at http://androidbook.blogspot.com/2010/08/unit-testing-with-android-junit.html.

Tip

For more information on JUnit, check out http://www.junit.org, or books on the subject.

Handling Defects Occurring on a Single Device

Occasionally, you have a situation in which you need to provide code for a specific device. Google and the Android team tell you that when this happens, it's a bug, so you should tell them about it. By all means, do so. However, this won't help you in the short term. Handling bugs that occur only on a single device can be tricky. You don't want to branch code unnecessarily, so here are some of your choices:

- If possible, keep the client generic, and use the server to serve up device-specific items.
- If the conditions can be determined programmatically on the client, try to craft a generic solution that enables developers to continue to develop under one source code tree, without branching.
- If the device is not a high-priority target, consider dropping it from your requirements if the cost-benefit ratio suggests that a workaround is not cost effective.
- If required, branch the code to implement the fix. Make sure to set your Android manifest file settings such that the branched application version is installed only on the appropriate devices.
- If all else fails, document the problem only and wait for the underlying "bug" to be addressed. Keep your users in the loop.

Leveraging Android Tools for Development

The Android SDK comes with a number of useful tools and resources for application development. The development community adds even more useful utilities to the mix. You might want to leverage the following tools during this phase of your development project:

- The Eclipse development environment with the ADT plug-in
- The Android emulator and physical devices for testing
- The Android Dalvik Debug Monitor Service (DDMS) tool for debugging and interaction with the emulator or device
- The Android Debug Bridge (ADB) tool for logging, debugging, and shell access tools
- The `sqlite3` command-line tool for application database access (available via the ADB shell)
- The Hierarchy Viewer for user interface debugging of views

There are also numerous other tools available as part of the Android SDK. See the Android documentation for more details.

Avoiding Silly Mistakes in Android Application Development

Here are some of the frustrating and silly mistakes Android developers should try to avoid:

- Forgetting to add new application activities and necessary permissions to the `AndroidManifest.xml` file
- Forgetting to display `Toast` messages using the `show()` method
- Hard-coding information such as network information, test user information, and other data into the application
- Forgetting to disable diagnostic logging before release
- Distributing live applications with debug mode enabled

Summary

Be responsive, stable, and secure—these are the tenets of Android development. In this chapter, we armed you, the software designers, developers, and project managers, with tips, tricks, and best practices for mobile application design and development based upon real-world knowledge and experience from veteran mobile developers. Feel free to pick and choose which information works well for your specific project, and keep in mind that the software process, especially the mobile software process, is always open to improvement.

References and More Information

Android Best Practices: Designing for Performance:
    http://developer.android.com/guide/practices/design/performance.html
Android Best Practices: Designing for Responsiveness:
    http://developer.android.com/guide/practices/design/responsiveness.html
Android Best Practices: Designing for Seamlessness:
    http://developer.android.com/guide/practices/design/seamlessness.html
Android Best Practices: User Interface Guidelines:
    http://developer.android.com/guide/practices/ui_guidelines/index.html

## 28

Testing Android Applications

Test early, test often, test on the device. That is the quality assurance mantra we consider most important when it comes to testing mobile applications. Testing applications need not be an onerous process. Instead, you can adapt traditional quality assurance techniques such as automation and unit testing to Android with relative ease. In this chapter, we discuss our tips and tricks for testing Android applications. We also warn you—the project managers, software developers, and testers of mobile applications—of the various and sundry pitfalls to do your best to avoid.

Best Practices in Testing Mobile Applications

Like all QA processes, mobile development projects benefit from a well-designed defect tracking system, regularly scheduled builds, and planned, systematic testing. There are also plentiful opportunities for white box (or gray box) testing and some limited opportunities for automation.

Designing a Mobile Application Defect Tracking System

You can customize most defect tracking systems to work for the testing of mobile applications. The defect tracking system must encompass tracking of issues for specific device defects and problems related to any centralized application servers (if applicable).

Logging Important Defect Information

A good mobile defect tracking system includes the following information about a typical device defect:

- Build version information, language, and so on.
- Device configuration and state information including device type, platform version, screen orientation, network state, and carrier information.

- Steps to reproduce the problem using specific details about exactly which input methods were used (touch versus click).

- Device screenshots that can be taken using DDMS or the Hierarchy Viewer tool provided with the Android SDK.

Tip

It can be helpful to develop a simple glossary of standardized terms for certain actions on the devices, such as touch mode gestures, and click versus tap, long-click versus press-and-hold, clear versus back, and so on. This helps make the steps to reproduce a defect more precise to all parties involved.

Redefining the Term Defect for Mobile Applications

It's also important to consider the larger definition of the term *defect*. Defects might occur on all devices or on only some devices. Defects might also occur in other parts of the application environment, such as on a remote application server. Some types of defects typical on mobile applications include

- Crashing and unexpected terminations.

- Features not functioning correctly (improper implementation).

- Using too much disk space/memory on the device.

- Inadequate input validation (typically, button mashing).

- State management problems (startup, shutdown, suspend, resume, power off).

- Responsiveness problems (slow startup, shutdown, suspend, resume).

- Inadequate state change testing (failures during inter-state changes, such as an unexpected interruption during resume).

- Usability issues related to input methods, font sizes, and cluttered screen real estate. Cosmetic problems that cause the screen to display incorrectly.

- Pausing or "freezing" on the main UI thread (failure to implement asynchronous threading).

- Feedback indicators missing (failure to indicate progress).

- Integration with other applications on the device causing problems.

- Application "not playing nicely" on the device (draining battery, disabling power-saving mode, overusing networking resources, incurring extensive user charges, obnoxious notifications).

- Using too much memory, not freeing memory or releasing resources appropriately, and not stopping worker threads when tasks are finished.

- Not conforming to third-party agreements, such as Android SDK License Agreement, Google Maps API terms, marketplace terms, or any other terms that apply to the application.

- Application client or server not handling protected/private data securely. This includes ensuring that remote servers or services have adequate uptime and security measures taken.

Managing the Testing Environment

Testing mobile applications poses a unique challenge to the QA team, especially in terms of configuration management. The difficulty of such testing is often underestimated. Don't make the mistake of thinking that mobile applications are easier to test because they have fewer features than desktop applications and are, therefore, simpler to validate. The vast variety of Android devices available on the market today makes testing different installation environments tricky.

> **Warning**
>
> Ensure that all changes in project scope are reviewed by the quality assurance team. Adding new devices sometimes has little impact on the development schedule but can have significant consequences in terms of testing schedules.

Managing Device Configurations

Device fragmentation is perhaps the biggest challenge the mobile tester faces. Android devices come in various form-factors with different screens, platform versions, and underlying hardware. They come with a variety of input methods such as buttons and touch screens. They come with optional features, such as cameras and enhanced graphics support. Many Android devices are smartphones, but not all. Keeping track of all the devices, their abilities, and so on is a big job, and much of the work falls on the test team.

QA personnel must have a detailed understanding of the functionality available of each target device, including familiarity with what features are available and any device-specific idiosyncrasies that exist. Whenever possible, testers should test each device as it is used in the field, which might not be the device's default configuration or language. This means changing input modes, screen orientation, and locale settings. It also means testing with battery power, not just plugged in while sitting at a desk.

> **Tip**
>
> Be aware of how third-party firmware modifications can affect how your application works on the device. For example, let's assume you've gotten your hands on an unbranded version of a target phone and testing has gone well. However, if certain carriers take that same device, but remove some default applications and load it up with others, this is valuable information to the tester. Just because your application runs flawlessly on the "vanilla" device doesn't mean that this is how most users' devices are configured by default. Do your best to get test devices that closely resemble the devices users will have in the field.

One hundred percent testing coverage is impossible, so QA must develop priorities thoughtfully. As we discuss in Chapter 26, developing a device database can greatly reduce the confusion of mobile configuration management, help determine testing priorities, and keep track of physical hardware available for testing. Using AVD configurations, the emulator is also an effective tool for extending coverage to simulate devices and situations that would not be covered otherwise.

Tip

If you have trouble configuring devices for real-life situations, you might want to look into the device "labs" available through some carriers. Instead of loaner programs, the developer visits the carrier's onsite lab where they can rent time on specific devices. Here, the developer installs the application and tests it—not ideal for recurring testing but much better than no testing, and some labs are staffed with experts to help out with device-specific issues.

Determining Clean Starting State on a Device

There is currently no good way to "image" a device so that you can return to the same starting state again and again. The QA test team needs to define what a "clean" device is for the purposes of test cases. This can involve a specific uninstall process, some manual clean-up, or sometimes a factory reset.

Tip

Using the Android SDK tools such as DDMS and ADB enables developers and testers access to the Android file system, including application SQLite databases. You can use these tools to monitor and manipulate data on the device and the emulator. For example, testers might use the `sqlite3` command-line interface to "wipe" an application database or fill it with test data for specific test scenarios.

Mimicking Real-World Activities

It is nearly impossible (and certainly not cost-effective for most companies) to set up a complete isolated environment for mobile application testing. It's fairly common for networked applications to be tested against test (mock) application servers and then go "live" on production servers with similar configurations. However, in terms of device configuration, mobile software testers must use real devices with real service to test mobile applications properly. If the device is a phone, then it needs to be able to make and receive phone calls, send and receive text messages, determine location using LBS services, and basically do anything a phone would normally do.

Testing a mobile application involves more than just making sure the application works properly. In the real world, your application does not exist in a vacuum but is one of many installed on the device. Testing a mobile application involves ensuring that the software integrates well with other device functions and applications. For example, let's say you were developing a game. Testers must verify that calls received while playing the game caused the game to automatically pause (keep state) and allow calls to be answered or ignored without issue.

This also means testers must install other applications on to the device. A good place to start is with the most popular applications for the device. Testing your application not only with these applications installed, but also with real use, can reveal integration issues or usage patterns that don't mesh well with the rest of the device.

Sometimes testers need to be creative when it comes to reproducing certain types of events. For example, testers must ensure that their application behaves appropriately when mobile handsets lose network or phone coverage.

> **Tip**
>
> Unlike some other mobile platforms, testers actually have to take special steps to make most Android devices lose coverage above and beyond holding them wrong. To test loss of signal, you could go out and test your application in a highway tunnel or elevator, or you could just place the device in the refrigerator. Don't leave it in the cold too long, though, or it will drain the battery. Tin cans work great, too, especially those that have cookies in them: First, eat the cookies; then place the phone in the can to seal off the signal.

Maximizing Testing Coverage

All test teams strive for 100 percent testing coverage, but most also realize such a goal is not reasonable or cost-effective (especially with dozens of Android devices available around the world). Testers must do their best to cover a wide range of scenarios, the depth and breadth of which can be daunting—especially for those new to mobile. Let's look at several specific types of testing and how QA teams have found ways—some tried-and-true and others new and innovative—to maximize coverage.

Validating Builds and Designing Smoke Tests

In addition to a regular build process, it can be helpful to institute a build acceptance test policy (also sometimes called build validation, smoke testing, or sanity testing). Build acceptance tests are short and targeted at key functionality to determine if the build is good enough for more thorough testing to be completed. This is also an opportunity to quickly verify bug fixes expected to be in the build before a complete retesting cycle occurs. Consider developing build acceptance tests for multiple Android platform versions to run simultaneously.

Automating Functional Testing for Build Acceptance

Mobile build acceptance testing is typically done manually on the highest-priority target device; however, this is also an ideal situation for an automated "sanity" test. By creating a bare-bones functional test for the emulator that, as desktop software, can be used with typical QA automation platforms such as Borland SilkTest (www.borland.com/us/products/silk/silktest/index.html), the team can increase its level of confidence that a build is worth further testing, and the number of bad builds delivered to QA can be minimized.

Testing on the Emulator Versus the Device

When you can get your hands on the actual device your users have, focus your testing there. However, devices and the service contracts that generally come with them can be expensive. Your test team cannot be expected to set up test environments on every carrier or every country where your users use your application. There are times when the Android emulator can reduce costs and improve testing coverage. Some of the benefits of using the emulator include

- Ability to simulate devices when they are not available or in short supply
- Ability to test difficult test scenarios not feasible on live devices
- Ability to be automated like any other desktop software

Testing Before Devices Are Available Using the Emulator

Developers often target up-and-coming devices or platform versions not yet available to the general public. These devices are often highly anticipated and developers who are ready with applications for these devices on Day 1 of release often experience a sales bump because fewer applications are available to these users—less competition, more sales.

The latest version of the Android SDK is usually released to developers several months prior to when the general public receives over-the-air updates. Also, developers can sometimes gain access to preproduction phones through carrier and manufacturer developer programs. However, developers and testers should be aware of the dangers of testing on preproduction phones: These phones are beta-quality. The final technical specifications and firmware can change without notice. These phone release dates can slip, and the phone might never reach production.

When preproduction phones cannot be acquired, testers can do some functional testing using emulator configurations that attempt to closely match the target platform, lessening the risks for a compact testing cycle when these devices go live, allowing developers to release applications faster.

Leveraging Automated Testing Opportunities Using the Emulator

Android testers have a number of different automation options available to choose from. It's certainly possible to rig up automated testing software to exercise the software emulator and there are a number of testing tools (monkey, for example) that can help with the testing process. Unfortunately, there are not really a lot of options for automated hardware testing, beyond those used with the unit testing framework. We can certainly *imagine* someone coming up with a hardware testing solution—in our minds, the device looks a lot like the automated signature machine U.S. presidents use to sign pictures and Christmas cards. The catch is that every device looks and acts differently, so any animatronic hand would need to be recalibrated for each device. The other problem is how to determine when the application has failed or succeeded. If anyone is developing mobile software automated testing tools, it's likely a mobile software testing consultancy company. For the typical mobile software developer, the costs are likely prohibitive.

Understanding the Dangers of Relying on the Emulator

Unfortunately, the emulator is more of a "generic" Android device that pretends at many of the device internals—despite all the options available within the AVD configuration.

Tip

Consider developing a document describing the specific AVD configurations used for testing different device configurations as part of the test plan.

The emulator does not represent the specific implementation of the Android platform that is unique to a given device. It does not use the same hardware to determine signal, networking, or location information. The emulator can pretend to make and receive calls and messages, or take pictures or video. At the end of the day, it doesn't matter if the application works on the emulator if it doesn't work on the actual device.

Testing Strategies: White Box Testing

The Android tools provide ample tools for black box and white box testing:

- Black box testers might require only testing devices and test documentation. For black box testing, it is even more important that the testers have a working knowledge of the specific devices, so providing device manuals and technical specifications also aids in more thorough testing. In addition to such details, knowing device nuances as well as device standards can greatly help with usability testing. For example, if a dock is available for the device, knowing that it's either landscape or portrait mode is useful.

- White box testing has never been easier on mobile. White box testers can leverage the many affordable tools including the Eclipse development environment, which is free, and the many debugging tools available as part of the Android SDK. White box testers use the Android Emulator, DDMS, and ADB especially. They can also take advantage of the powerful unit testing framework, which we discussed in detail in the previous chapter. For these tasks, testers require a computer with a development environment similar to the developer's.

Testing Mobile Application Servers and Services

Although testers often focus on the client portion of the application, they sometimes neglect to thoroughly test the server portion. Many mobile applications rely on networking or "the cloud." If your application depends on a server or remote service to operate, testing the server side of your application is vital. Even if the service is not your own, you need to test thoroughly against it so you know it behaves as the application expects it to behave.

Warning

Users expect applications to be available any time, day or night, 24/7. Minimize server or service down times and make sure the application notifies the users appropriately (and doesn't crash and burn) if the services are unavailable. If the service is outside your control, it might be worthwhile to look at what Service Level Agreements are offered.

Here are some guidelines for testing remote servers or services:

- Version your server builds. You should manage server rollouts like any other part of the build process. The server should be versioned and rolled out in a reproducible way.

- Use test servers. Often, QA tests against a mock server in a controlled environment. This is especially true if the live server is already operational with real users.

- Verify scalability. Test the server or service under load, including stress testing (many users, simulated clients).
- Test the server security (hacking, SQL injection, and such).
- Ensure that your application handles remote server maintenance or service interruptions gracefully—scheduled or otherwise.
- Test server upgrades and rollbacks and develop a plan for how you are going to inform users if and when services are down.

These types of testing offer yet another opportunity for automated testing to be employed.

Testing Application Visual Appeal and Usability

Testing a mobile application is not only about finding dysfunctional features, but also about evaluating the usability of the application. Report areas of the application that lack visual appeal or are difficult to navigate or use. We like to use the walking-and-chewing-gum analogy when it comes to mobile user interfaces. Mobile users frequently do not give the application their full attention. Instead, they walk or do something else while they use it. Applications should be as easy for the user as chewing gum.

Tip

Consider conducting usability studies to collect feedback from people who are not familiar with the application. Relying solely on the product team members, who see the application regularly, can blind the team to application flaws.

Leveraging Third-Party Standards for Android Testing

Make a habit to try to adapt traditional software testing principles to mobile. Encourage quality assurance personnel to develop and share these practices within your company.

Again, no certification programs are specifically designed for Android applications at this time; however, nothing is stopping the mobile marketplaces from developing them. Consider looking over the certification programs available in other mobile platforms, such as the extensive testing scripts and acceptance guidelines used by Apple iPhone and BREW platforms and adjusting them for your Android applications. Whether you plan to apply for a specific certification, making an attempt to conform to well-recognized quality guidelines can improve your application's quality.

Handling Specialized Test Scenarios

In addition to functional testing, there are a few other specialized testing scenarios that any QA team should consider.

Testing Application Integration Points

It's necessary to test how the application behaves with other parts of the Android operating system. For example:

- Ensuring that interruptions from the operating system are handled properly (incoming messages, calls, and powering off)

- Validating Content Provider data exposed by your application, including such uses as through a Live Folder
- Validating functionality triggered in other applications via an `Intent`
- Validating any known functionality triggered in your application via an `Intent`
- Validating any secondary entry points to your application as defined in the `AndroidManifest.xml`, such as application shortcuts
- Validating alternate forms of your application, such as App Widgets
- Validating service-related features, if applicable

Testing Upgrades

When possible, perform upgrade tests of both the client and the server or service side of things. If upgrade support is planned, have development create a mock upgraded Android application so that QA can validate that data migration occurs properly, even if the upgraded application does nothing with the data.

Tip

Users receive Android platform updates over-the-air on a regular basis. The platform version your application is installed on might change over time. Some developers have found that firmware upgrades have broken their applications, necessitating upgrades. Always re-test your applications when a new version of the SDK is released, so that you can upgrade users before your applications have a chance to break in the field.

Testing Product Internationalization

It's a good idea to test internationalization support early in the development process—both the client and the server or services. You're likely to run into some problems in this area related to screen real-estate and issues with strings, dates, times, and formatting.

Tip

If your application will be localized for multiple languages, test in a foreign language—especially on a verbose one. The application might look flawless in English but be unusable in German where words are generally longer.

Testing for Conformance

Make sure to review any policies, agreements, and terms to which your application must conform and make sure your application complies. For example, Android applications must by default conform to the Android Developer Agreement and the Google Maps terms of service (if applicable).

Installation Testing

Generally speaking, installation of Android applications is straightforward; however, you need to test installations on devices with low resources and low memory and test installation from the specific marketplaces when your application "goes live." If the manifest install location allows external media, be sure to test various low or missing resource scenarios.

Backup Testing

Don't forget to test features that are not readily apparent to the user, such as the backup and restore services and sync features discussed in Chapter 23, "Managing User Accounts and Synchronizing User Data."

Performance Testing

Application performance matters in the mobile world. The Android SDK has support for calculating performance benchmarks within an application and monitoring memory and resource usage. Testers should familiarize themselves with these utilities and use them often to help identify performance bottlenecks and dangerous memory leaks and misused resources.

Testing Application Billing

Billing is too important to leave to guesswork. Test it. You notice a lot of test applications on the Android Market. Remember to specify that your application is a test app.

Testing for the Unexpected

Regardless of the workflow you design, understand that users do random, unexpected things—on purpose and by accident. Some users are "button mashers," whereas others forget to set the keypad lock before putting the phone in their pocket, resulting in a weird set of key presses. A phone call or text message inevitably comes in during the far-thest, most-remote edge cases. Your application must be robust enough to handle this. The Exerciser Monkey command-line tool is a good way to test for this type of event.

Testing to Increase Your Chances of Being a "Killer App"

Every mobile developer wants to develop a "killer app"—those applications that go viral, rocket to the top of the charts, and make millions a month. Most people think that if they just find the right idea, they'll have a killer app on their hands. Developers are always scouring the top-ten lists, trying to figure out how to develop the next big thing. But let us tell you a little secret: If there's one thing that all "killer apps" share, it's a higher-than-average quality standard. No clunky, slow, obnoxious, or difficult-to-use application ever makes it to the big leagues. Testing and enforcing quality standards can mean the differ-ence between a mediocre application and a killer app.

If you spend any time examining the mobile marketplace, you notice a number of larger mobile development companies publish a variety of high-quality applications with a shared look and feel. These companies leverage user interface consistency, shared and above-average quality standards to build brand loyalty and increase market share, while hedging their bets that perhaps just one of their many applications will have that magical combination of great idea and quality design. Other, smaller companies often have the great ideas but struggle with the quality aspects of mobile software development. The inevitable result is that the mobile marketplace is full of fantastic application ideas badly executed with poor user interfaces and crippling defects.

Leveraging Android Tools for Android Application Testing

The Android SDK and developer community provide a number of useful tools and resources for application testing and quality assurance. You might want to leverage these tools during this phase of your development project:

- The physical devices for testing and bug reproduction
- The Android emulator for automated testing and testing of builds when devices are not available
- The Android DDMS tool for debugging and interaction with the emulator or device, as well as taking screenshots
- The ADB tool for logging, debugging, and shell access tools
- The Exerciser Monkey command-line tool for stress testing of input (available via ADB shell)
- The `sqlite3` command-line tool for application database access (available via ADB shell)
- The Hierarchy Viewer for user interface navigation and verification and for pixel-perfect screenshots of the device
- The Eclipse development environment with the ADT and related logging and debugging tools for white box testing

It should be noted that although we have used the Android tools such as the Android emulator and DDMS debugging tools with Eclipse, these are stand-alone tools that can be used by quality assurance personnel without the need for source code or a development environment.

Avoiding Silly Mistakes in Android Application Testing

Here are some of the frustrating and silly mistakes and pitfalls that Android testers should try to avoid:

- Not testing the server or service components used by an application as thoroughly as the client side.
- Not testing with the appropriate version of the Android SDK (device versus development build versions).
- Not testing on the device and assuming the emulator is enough.
- Not testing the live application using the same system that users use (billing, installation, and such). Buy your own app.
- Neglecting to test all entry points to the application.
- Neglecting to test in different coverage areas and network speeds.
- Neglecting to test using battery power. Don't always have the device plugged in.

Outsourcing Testing Responsibilities

Mobile quality assurance can be outsourced. Remember, though, that the success of outsourcing your QA responsibilities depends on the quality and detail of the documentation you can provide. Outsourcing makes it more difficult to form the close relationships between QA and developers that help ensure thorough and comprehensive testing.

Summary

In this chapter, we armed you—the keepers of application quality—with real-world knowledge for testing Android applications. Whether you're a team of one or one hundred, testing your applications is critical for project success. Luckily, the Android SDK provides a number of tools for testing applications, as well as a powerful unit testing framework. By following standard quality assurance techniques and leveraging these tools, you can ensure that the application you deliver to your users is the best it can be.

References and More Information

Android Dev Guide: Testing & Instrumentation:
    http://developer.android.com/guide/topics/testing/testing_android.html
Android Dev Guide: Testing:
    http://developer.android.com/guide/developing/testing/index.html
Android Tools: UI/Application Exerciser Monkey:
    http://developer.android.com/guide/developing/tools/monkey.html
Wikipedia on Software Testing:
    http://en.wikipedia.org/wiki/Software_testing
Software Testing Help:
    http://www.softwaretestinghelp.com

## 29

Selling Your Android Application

After you've developed an application, the next logical step is to publish it so that other people can enjoy it. You might even want to make some money. There are a variety of distribution opportunities available to Android application developers. Many developers choose to sell their applications through mobile marketplaces such as Google's Android Market. Others develop their own distribution mechanisms—for example, they might sell their applications from a website. Regardless, developers should consider which distribution options they plan to use during the application design and development process, as some distribution choices might require code changes or impose restrictions on content.

Choosing the Right Distribution Model

The application distribution methods you choose to employ depend on your goals and target users. Some questions you should ask yourself are

- Is your application ready for prime time or are you considering a beta period to iron out the kinks?
- Are you trying to reach the broadest audience, or have you developed a vertical market application? Determine who your users are, which devices they are using, and their preferred methods for seeking out and downloading applications.
- How will you price your application? Is it freeware or shareware? Are the payment models (single payment versus subscription model versus ad-driven revenue) you require available on the distribution mechanisms you want to leverage?
- Where do you plan to distribute? Verify that any application markets you plan to use are capable of distributing within those countries or regions.
- Are you willing to share a portion of your profits? Distribution mechanisms such as the Android Market take a percentage of each sale in exchange for hosting your application for distribution and collecting application revenue on your behalf.
- Do you require complete control over the distribution process or are you willing to work within the boundaries and requirements imposed by third-party marketplaces? This might require compliance with further license agreements and terms.

- If you plan to distribute yourself, how will you do so? You might need to develop more services to manage users, deploy applications and collect payments. If so, how will you protect user data? What trade laws must you comply with?

- Have you considered creating a free trial version of your application? If the distribution system under consideration has a return policy, consider the ramifications. You need to ensure that your application has safeguards to minimize the number of users that buy your app, use it, and return it for a full refund. For example, a game might include safeguards such as a free trial version and a full-scale version with more game levels than could possibly be completed within the refundable time period.

Now let's look at the steps you need to take to package and publish your application.

Packaging Your Application for Publication

There are several steps developers must take when preparing an Android application for publication and distribution. Your application must also meet several important requirements imposed by the marketplaces. The following steps are required for publishing an application:

1. Prepare and perform a release candidate build of the application.

2. Verify that all requirements for marketplace are met, such as configuring the Android manifest file properly. For example, make sure the application name and version information is correct and the debuggable attribute is set to false.

3. Package and digitally sign the application.

4. Test the packaged application release thoroughly.

5. Publish the application.

The preceding steps are required but not sufficient to guarantee a successful deployment. Developers should also

1. Thoroughly test the application on all target handsets.

2. Turn off debugging, including Log statements and any other logging.

3. Verify permissions, making sure to add ones for services used and remove any that aren't used, regardless of whether they are enforced by the handsets.

4. Test the final, signed version with all debugging and logging turned off.

Now, let's explore each of these steps in more detail, in the order they might be performed.

Preparing Your Code to Package

An application that has undergone a thorough testing cycle might need changes made to it before it is ready for a production release. These changes convert it from a debuggable, preproduction application into a release-ready application.

Setting the Application Name and Icon

An Android application has default settings for the icon and label. The icon appears in the application Launcher and can appear in various other locations, including marketplaces. As such, an application is required to have an icon. You should supply alternate icon drawable resources for various screen resolutions. The label, or application name, is also displayed in similar locations and defaults to the package name. You should choose a user-friendly name.

Versioning the Application

Next, proper versioning is required, especially if updates could occur in the future. The version name is up to the developer. The version code, though, is used internally by the Android system to determine if an application is an update. You should increment the version code for each new update of an application. The exact value doesn't matter, but it must be greater than the previous version code. Versioning within the Android manifest file is discussed in Chapter 5, "Defining Your Application Using the Android Manifest File."

Verifying the Target Platforms

Make sure your application sets the `<uses-sdk>` tag in the Android manifest file correctly. This tag is used to specify the minimum and target platform versions that the application can run on. This is perhaps the most important setting after the application name and version information.

Configuring the Android Manifest for Market Filtering

If you plan to publish through the Android Market, you should read up on how this distribution system uses certain tags within the Android manifest file to filter applications available to users. Many of these tags, such as `<supports-screens>`, `<uses-configuration>`, `<uses-feature>`, `<uses-library>`, `<uses-permission>`, and `<uses-sdk>`, were discussed in Chapter 5. Set each of these settings carefully, as you don't want to accidentally put too many restrictions on your application. Make sure you test your application thoroughly after configuring these Android manifest file settings. For more information on how Android Market filters work, see http://developer.android.com/guide/appendix/market-filters.html.

Preparing Your Application Package for the Android Market

The Android Market has strict requirements on application packages. When you upload your application to the Android Market website, the package is verified and any problems are communicated to you. Most often, problems occur when you have not properly configured your Android manifest file.

The Android Market uses the `android:versionName` attribute of the `<manifest>` tag within the Android manifest file to display version information to users. It also uses the `android:versionCode` attribute internally to handle application upgrades. The `android:icon` and `android:label` attributes must also be present because both are used by the Android Market to display the application name to the user with a visual icon.

Warning

The Android SDK allows the `android:versionName` attribute to reference a string resource. The Android Market, however, does not. An error is generated if a string resource is used.

Disabling Debugging and Logging

Next, you should turn off debugging and logging. Disabling debugging involves removing the `android:debuggable` attribute from the `<application>` tag of the `AndroidManifest.xml` file or setting it to `false`. You can turn off the logging code within Java in a variety of different ways, from just commenting it out to using a build system that can do this automatically.

Tip

A common method for conditionally compiling debug code is to use a class interface with a single, public, static, final Boolean set to true or false. When used with an `if` statement and set to false, because it's immutable, the compiler should not include the unreachable code, and it certainly won't be executed. We recommend using some method other than just commenting out the Log lines and other debug code, even if you don't.

Verifying Application Permissions

Finally, the permissions used by the application should be reviewed. Include all permissions that the application requires, and remove any that are not used. Users appreciate this.

Packing and Signing Your Application

Now that the application is ready for publication, the file package—the `.apk` file—needs to be prepared for release. The package manager of an Android device will not install a package that has not been digitally signed. Throughout the development process, the Android tools have accomplished this through signing with a debug key. The debug key cannot be used for publishing an application to the wider world. Instead, you need to use a true key to digitally sign the application. You can use the private key to digitally sign the release package files of your Android application, as well as any upgrades. This ensures that the application (as a complete entity) is coming from you, the developer, and not some other source (imposters!).

Warning

A private key identifies the developer and is critical to building trust relationships between developers and users. It is very important to secure private key information.

The Android Market requires that your application's digital signature validity period end after October 22, 2033. This date might seem like a long way off and, for mobile, it certainly is. However, because an application must use the same key for upgrading and applications that want to work closely together with special privileges and trust relationships must also be signed with the same key, the key could be chained forward through many applications. Thus, Google is mandating that the key be valid for the foreseeable future so application updates and upgrades are performed smoothly for users.

Note

Finding a third-party certificate authority that will issue a key valid for such a long duration can be a challenge, so self-signing is the most straightforward signing solution. Within the Android Market, there is no benefit to using a third-party certificate authority.

Although self-signing is typical of Android applications, and a certificate authority is not required, creating a suitable key and securing it properly is critical. The digital signature for Android applications can impact certain functionality. The expiry of the signature is verified at installation time, but after it's installed, an application continues to function even if the signature has expired.

You can export and sign your Android package file from within Eclipse using the Android Development plug-in, or you can use the command-line tools. You can export and sign your Android package file from within Eclipse by taking the following steps:

1. In Eclipse, right-click the appropriate application project and choose the Export option.

2. Under the Export menu, expand the Android section and choose Export Android Application.

3. Click the Next button.

4. Select the project to export (the one you right-clicked before is the default).

5. On the keystore selection screen, choose the Create New Keystore option and enter a file location (where you want to store the key) as well as a password for managing the keystore. (If you already have a keystore, choose browse to pick your keystore file, and then enter the correct password.)

Warning

Make sure you choose strong passwords for the keystore. Remember where the keystore is located, too. The same one is required to publish an upgrade to your application. If it's checked in to a revision control system, the password helps protect it, but consider adding an extra layer of privilege required to get to it.

6. Click the Next button.

7. On the Key Creation screen, enter the details of the key, as shown in Figure 29.1.

Figure 29.1   Exporting and signing an Android
application in Eclipse.

8. Click the Next button.

9. On the Destination and Key/Certificate Checks screen, enter a destination for the application package file.

10. Click the Finish button.

You have now created a fully signed and certified application package file. The application package is ready for publication.

Note

If you are not using Eclipse and the Android Development plug-in, you can use the `keytool` and `jarsigner` command-line tools available within the JDK in addition to the `zipalign` utility provided with the Android SDK to create a suitable key and sign an application package file (.apk). Although `zipalign` is not directly related to signing, it optimizes the application package for more efficient use on Android. The ADT plug-in for Eclipse runs `zipalign` automatically after the signing step.

Testing the Release Version of Your Application Package

Now that you have configured your application for production, you should perform a full final testing cycle paying special attention to subtle changes to the installation process. An important part of this process is to verify that you have disabled all debugging features and logging has no negative impact on the functionality and performance of the application.

Certifying Your Android Application

If you're familiar with other mobile platforms, you might be familiar with the many strict certification programs found on platforms, such as the TRUE BREW or Symbian Signed programs. These programs exist to enforce a lower bound on the quality of an application.

As of this writing, Android does not have any certification or testing requirements. It is an open market with only a few content guidelines and rules to follow. This does not mean, however, that certification won't be required at some point or that certain distribution means won't require certification.

Typically, certification programs require rigorous and thorough testing, certain usability conventions must be met, and various other constraints that might be good common practice or operator-specific rules are enforced. The best way to prepare for any certification program is to incorporate its requirements into the design of your specific project. Following best practices for Android development and developing efficient, usable, dynamic, and robust applications always pay off in the end—whether your application requires certification.

Distributing Your Applications

Now that you've prepared your application for publication, it's time to get your application out to users—for fun and profit. Unlike other mobile platforms, most Android distribution mechanisms support free applications and price plans.

Selling Your Application on the Android Market

The Android Market is the primary mechanism for distributing Android applications at this time. This is where your typical user purchases and downloads applications. As of this writing, it's available to most, but not all, Android devices. As such, we show you how to check your package for preparedness, sign up for a developer account, and submit your application for sale on the Android Market.

Note

The Android Market supports a licensing service. This is available as a Google API add-on, but works on Android versions 1.5 and higher. It only works with paid applications and only for applications distributed through Android Market. It requires application support—code additions—to be fully utilized and you should seriously consider obfuscating your code. The service's primary purpose is to verify that a paid application installed on a device was properly purchased by the user. Read more about it at http://developer.android.com/guide/publishing/licensing.html. To learn more about creating an implementation that is difficult to crack, visit http://j.mp/9HoP4t and http://j.mp/9A0cRv. Dan Galpin's article on Proguard, Android, and the Licensing Server (available at http://android-developers.blogspot.com/ 2010/09/proguard-android-and-licensing-server.html) offers some practical advice on using the Proguard tool for obfuscation purposes.

Signing Up for a Developer Account on the Android Market

To publish applications through the Android Market, you must register as a developer. This accomplishes two things. It verifies who you are to Google and signs you up for a Google Checkout account, which is used for billing of Android applications.

Note

As of this writing, only developers ("Merchants") residing in Argentina, Australia, Austria, Belgium, Brazil, Canada, Denmark, Finland, France, Germany, Hong Kong, Ireland, Israel, Italy, Japan, Mexico, Netherlands, New Zealand, Norway, Portugal, Russia, Singapore, South Korea, Spain, Sweden, Switzerland, Taiwan, the UK, and the United States may sell priced applications on the Android Market, as described here: http://market.android.com/support/bin/answer.py?hl=en&answer=150324.

Developers from many other countries can register for Publisher accounts, but they may only publish free applications at this time. For a complete list of supported publisher countries, see http://market.android.com/support/bin/answer.py?hl=en&answer=136758. These lists are subject to change at any time.

To sign up for an Android Market developer account, you need to follow these steps:

1. Go to the Android Market sign-up website at http://market.android.com/publish/ signup, as shown in Figure 29.2.

2. Sign in with the Google Account you want to use. (At this time, you cannot change the associated Google Account, but you can change the contact email addresses for applications independently.)

3. Enter your developer information, including your name, email address, and website, as shown in Figure 29.3.

4. Confirm your registration payment (as of this writing, $25 USD). Note that Google Checkout is used for registration payment processing.

5. Signing up and paying to be an Android Developer also creates a mandatory Google Checkout Merchant account for which you also need to provide information. This account is used for payment processing purposes.

6. Agree to link your credit card and account registration to the Android Market Developer Distribution Agreement. The basic agreement (U.S. version) is available for review at http://www.android.com/us/developer-distribution-agreement.html. Always print out the actual agreement you sign as part of the registration process, in case it changes in the future.

Figure 29.2   The Android Market publisher sign-up page.

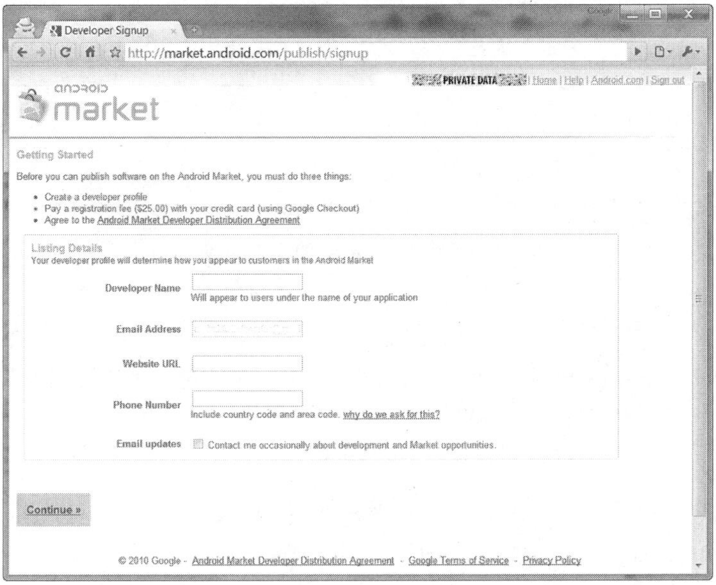

Figure 29.3   The Android Market publisher profile page.

When you successfully complete these steps, you are presented with the home screen of the Android Market, which also confirms that the Google Checkout Merchant account was created.

Uploading Your Application to the Android Market

Now that you have an account registered for publishing applications through Android Market and a signed application package, you are ready to upload it for publication. From the main page of the Android Market website (http://market.android.com/publish), sign in with your developer account information. After you are logged in, you see a webpage with your developer account information, as shown in Figure 29.4.

Figure 29.4   Android Market developer application listings.

From this page, you can configure developer account settings, see your payment trans-action history, and manage your published applications. In order to publish a new applica-tion, press the Upload Application button on this page. A form is presented for uploading the application package (see Figure 29.5).

Let's look at some of the important fields you must enter on this form:

- The application package file (.apk)
- Promotional screenshots and graphics for the market listing
- The application title and description in several languages
- Application type and category

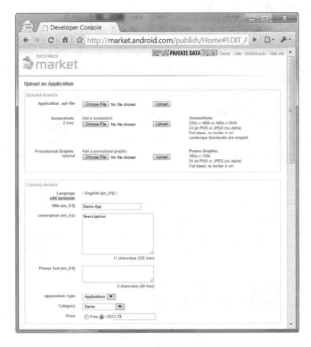

Figure 29.5   Android Market application upload form.

Warning

Spend the time to set the application type and category fields appropriately so that your application reaches its intended audience. Incorrectly categorized applications do not sell well. For a complete list of types and categories, see the Android Market Help listing at http://market.android.com/support/bin/answer.py?hl=en&answer=113475.

- Application price—Free or Paid (this cannot be changed later)

Note

The Android Market currently imposes a 30% transaction fee for hosting applications within the Android Market. Prices can range from $0.99 to $200 USD, and similar ranges are available in other supported currencies. Only single payment pricing models exist at the time of this writing.

- Copy protection information—Choosing this option might help prevent the application from being copied from the device and distributed without your knowledge or permission. This option is likely to change in the near future, as Google adds a new licensing service.
- Locations to distribute to—Choose the countries where the application should be published.

Note

These locations are subject to export compliance laws, so choose your locations carefully. As of this writing, nearly 50 locations are available and new locations are being added regularly. In addition, you can choose specific carriers for each location to further limit application distribution. Alternatively, you can choose to make your application available in specific countries or All Current and Future Locations. Not all locations support priced applications; some might not even have shipping Android devices yet. Generally, free applications are enabled for countries first, with billing capabilities becoming enabled later on, if possible. For a list of locations where qualified merchants can ship free versus priced applications, see the Android Market Help page listing at http://market.android.com/support/bin/answer.py?hl=en&answer=138294.

- Support contact information—This option defaults to the information you provided for the developer account. You can change it on an app-by-app basis, though, which allows for great support flexibility when you're publishing multiple applications.
- Consent—You must click the checkboxes to agree to the terms of the current (at the time you click) Android Content Guidelines, as well as the export laws of the United States, regardless of your location or nationality.

Tip

After the application package has been successfully uploaded, the preceding information can be saved as a draft, which is great for verification before final publishing. Also, the application icon, name, version, localization information, and required permissions are shown so that you can verify you have properly configured the Android manifest file.

Publishing Your Application on the Android Market

Finally, you are ready to press the Publish button. Your application appears in the Android Market almost immediately. After publication, you can see statistics including ratings, reviews, downloads, and active installs in the Your Android Market Listings section of the main page on your developer account. These statistics aren't updated as frequently as the publish action is, and you can't see review details directly from the listing. Clicking on the application listing enables you to edit the various fields.

Understanding the Android Market Application Return Policy

Although it is a matter of no small controversy, the Android Market has a 24-hour refund policy on applications. That is to say, a user can use an application for 24 hours and then return it for a full refund. As a developer, this means that sales aren't final until after the first 24 hours. However, this only applies to the first download and first return. If a particular user has already returned your application and wants to "try it again," he or she must make a final purchase—and can't return it a second time. Although this limits abuse, you should still be aware that if your application has limited reuse appeal or if all its value can come from just a few hours (or less) of use, you might find that you have a return rate that's too high and need to pursue other methods of monetization.

Upgrading Your Application on the Android Market

You can upgrade existing applications from the Market from the developer account page. Simply upload a new version of the same application using the Android manifest file tag, `android:versionCode`. When you publish it, users receive an Update Available notification, prompting them to download the upgrade.

> **Warning**
>
> Application updates must be signed with the same private key as the original application. For security reasons, the Android package manager does not install the update over the existing application if the key is different. This means you need to keep the key corresponding with the application in a secure, easy-to-find location for future use.

Removing Your Application from the Android Market

You can also use the unpublish action to remove the application from the Market from the developer account. The unpublish action is also immediate, but the application entry on the Market application might be cached on handsets that have viewed or downloaded the application.

Using Other Developer Account Benefits

In addition to managing your applications on the Android Market, an additional benefit to have a registered Android developer account is the ability to purchase development versions of Android handsets. These handsets are useful for general development and testing but might not be suitable for final testing on actual target handsets because some functionality might be limited, and the firmware version might be different than that found on consumer handsets.

Selling Your Application on Your Own Server

You can distribute Android applications directly from a website or server. This method is most appropriate for vertical market applications, content companies developing mobile marketplaces, and big brand websites wanting to drive users to their branded Android applications. It can also be a good way to get beta feedback from end users.

Although self-distribution is perhaps the easiest method of application distribution, it might also be the hardest to market, protect, and make money. The only requirement for self-distribution is to have a place to host the application package file.

The downside of self-distribution is that end users must configure their devices to allow packages from unknown sources. This setting is found under the Applications section of the device Settings application, as shown in Figure 29.6. This option is not available on all consumer devices in the market. Most notably, Android devices on U.S. carrier AT&T can only install applications from the Android Market—no third-party sources are allowed.

Figure 29.6   Settings application showing
required check box for downloading from
unknown sources.

After that, the final step the user must make is to enter the URL of the application package in to the web browser on the handset and download the file (or click on a link to it). When downloaded, the standard Android install process occurs, asking the user to confirm the permissions and, optionally, confirm an update or replacement of an existing application if a version is already installed.

Selling Your Application Using Other Alternatives

The Android Market is not the only consolidated market available for selling Android applications. Android is an open platform, which means there is nothing preventing a handset manufacturer or an operator (or even you) from running an Android market website or building another Android application that serves as a market. Many of the mobile-focused stores, such as Handango, have been adding Android applications to their offerings.

Here are a few alternate marketplaces where you might consider distributing your Android applications:

- **Handango** distributes mobile applications across a wide range of devices with various billing models (http://www.handango.com).
- **SlideME** is an Android-specific distribution community for free and commercial applications using an on-device store (http://slideme.org).

- **AndAppStore** is an Android-specific distribution for free applications using an on-device store (http://www.andappstore.com).
- **MobiHand** distributes mobile applications for a wide range of devices for free and commercial applications (http://www.mobihand.com).

This list is not complete, nor do we endorse any of these markets. That said, we feel it is important to demonstrate that there are a number of alternate distribution mechanisms available to developers. Application requirements vary by store. Third-party application stores are free to enforce whatever rules they want on the applications they accept, so read the fine print carefully. They might enforce content guidelines, require additional technical support, and enforce digital signing requirements. Only you and your team can determine which are suitable for your specific needs.

Tip

Another way to get great distribution is to partner with device manufacturers and mobile operators, who often select applications to pre-load onto devices prior to purchase. Look for special developer programs that can help you foster partnerships and other distribution relationships with manufacturers, carriers, and the like.

Protecting Your Intellectual Property

You've spent time, money, and effort to build a valuable Android application. Now you want to distribute it but perhaps you are concerned about reverse engineering of trade secrets and software piracy. As technology rapidly advances, it's impossible to perfectly protect against both.

If you're accustomed to developing Java applications, you might be familiar with code obfuscation tools. These are designed to strip easy-to-read information from compiled Java byte codes making the decompiled application more difficult to understand. For Android, though, applications are compiled for the Dalvik virtual machine. As such, existing Java tools might not work directly and might need to be updated. Some tools, such as ProGuard (http://proguard.sourceforge.net), support Android applications because they can run after the `jar` file is created and before it's converted to the final package file used with Android.

Android Market supports a form of copy protection via a check box when you publish your application. The method that this uses isn't well documented currently. However, you can also use your own copy protection methods or those available through other markets if this is a huge concern for you or your company.

Billing the User

Unlike some other mobile platforms you might have used, Android does not currently provide built-in billing APIs that work directly from within applications or charge directly to the users' cell phone bill. Instead, Android Market uses Google checkout for processing payments. When an application is purchased, the user owns it (although any paid application can be returned within 24 hours for a full refund).

Billing Recurring Fees or Content-Specific Fees

If your application requires a service fee and sells other goods within the application (that is, ringtones, music, e-books, and more), the application developer must develop a custom billing mechanism. Most Android devices can leverage the Internet, so using online billing services and APIs—Paypal, Google, and Amazon, to name a few—are likely to be the common choice. Check with your preferred billing service to make sure it specifically allows mobile use and that the billing methods your application requires are available, feasible, and legal for your target users.

Leveraging Ad Revenue

Another method to make money from users is to have an ad-supported mobile business model. This is a relatively new model for use within applications because many older application distribution methods specifically disallowed it. However, Android has no specific rules against using advertisements within applications. This shouldn't come as too much of a surprise, considering the popularity of Google's AdSense.

Summary

You've now learned how to design, develop, test, and deploy professional-grade Android applications. In this final chapter, you learned how to prepare your application package for publication using a variety of revenue-models. Whether you publish through your own website, the Android Market, use one of the many alternative methods available, or some combination of these options, you can now build a robust application from the ground up and distribute it for profit (or fame!).

So, now it's time to go out there, fire up Eclipse, and build some amazing applications. We want to encourage you to think outside of the box. The Android platform leaves the developer with a lot more freedom and flexibility than most mobile platforms. Take advantage of this. Use what works and reinvent what doesn't. You might just find yourself with a killer app.

Finally, if you're so inclined, we'd love to know about all the exciting applications you're building. You'll find our contact information in the Introduction at the beginning of this book. Best of luck!

References and More Information

The Android Market Website:
   http://market.android.com/
Android Dev Guide: Market Filters:
   http://developer.android.com/guide/appendix/market-filters.html

The Android Emulator Quick-Start Guide

The most useful tool provided with the Android Software Development Kit (SDK) is the emulator. Developers use the emulator to quickly develop Android applications for a variety of hardware. This Quick-Start Guide is not a complete documentation of the emulator commands. Instead, it is designed to get you up and running with common tasks. Please see the emulator documentation provided with the Android SDK for a complete list of features and commands.

The Android emulator is integrated with Eclipse using the Android Development Tools Plug-in for the Eclipse integrated development environment (IDE). The emulator is also available within the /tools directory of the Android SDK, and you can launch it as a separate process.

Simulating Reality: The Emulator's Purpose

The Android emulator (shown in Figure A.1) simulates a real device environment where your applications run. As a developer, you can configure the emulator to closely resemble the devices on which you plan to deploy your applications.

Here are some tips for using the emulator effectively from the start:

- You can use keyboard commands to easily interact with the emulator.
- Mouse clicking within the emulator window works, as does scrolling and dragging. So do the keyboard arrow buttons. Don't forget the side buttons, such as the volume control. These work, too.
- If your computer has an Internet connection, so does your emulator. The browser works. You can toggle networking using the F8 key.
- Different platform versions run slightly different underlying user experiences (the basics of the Android operating system). For example, older platforms use an application drawer to store installed applications, whereas the newer platforms use sleeker controls and an improved Home screen. The emulator uses the basic

"Google Experience" UI, which is frequently overridden by manufacturers and carriers. In other words, the operating system features might not match what real users see.

Figure A.1   A typical Android emulator.

- The Settings application can be useful for managing system settings. You can use the Settings application to configure the Wireless controls, Call Settings, Sound & Display (ringtones, brightness, and so on), Data synchronization settings, Security & Location, Manage Applications, SD Card and phone storage, Date & Time, Text Input settings, and About Phone (phone status/software version, and such). The Dev Tools application can be useful for setting development options.

- To switch between portrait and landscape modes of the emulator, use the 7 key and 9 key on the numeric keypad of the host machine (or Ctrl+F11 and Ctrl+F12 keys).

- The Menu button is a context menu for the given screen, replacing traditional buttons along the bottom of the screen for features such as Add, Edit, and Delete.

- Application lifecycle-wise: To easily pause an application, just press Home. To resume, launch the application again. It should begin where you left off (if the phone hasn't run low on memory and killed your application behind the scenes).

- Notifications such as incoming SMS messages appear in the white notification bar at the top of the screen, along with battery life, and so on.

Warning

The Android emulator is a powerful tool but no substitute for testing on the true target device.

Working with Android Virtual Devices (AVDs)

The Android emulator is a not a real device, but a generic Android system simulator for testing purposes. Developers can simulate different types of Android devices by creating Android Virtual Device (AVD) configurations. Using AVD configurations, Android emulators can simulate

- Different target platform versions
- Different screen sizes and resolutions
- Different input methods
- Different underlying hardware configurations
- Different external storage configurations

Each emulator configuration is unique, as described within its AVD and stores its data persistently on its emulated SD card. A number of emulators with different AVD configurations are shown in Figure A.2.

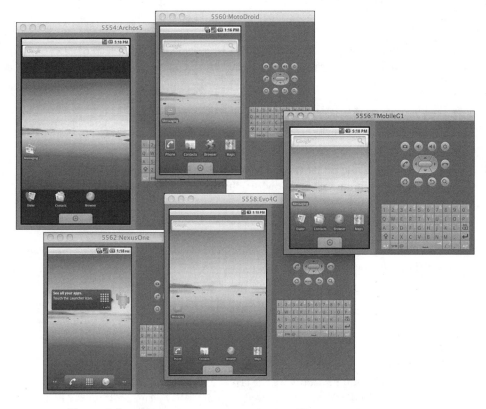

Figure A.2   AVD configurations described in different emulator settings.

Tip

It can be helpful to think of an AVD as providing the emulator's personality. Without an AVD, an emulator is an empty shell.

Using the Android SDK and AVD Manager

To run an application in the Android emulator, you must configure an Android Virtual Device (AVD). To create and manage AVDs, you can use the Android SDK and AVD Manager from within Eclipse (available as part of the ADT plug-in) or use the `android` command-line tool provided with the Android SDK in the `/tools` subdirectory.

Note

For the purposes of this book, we assume you are using the popular Eclipse development environment and the Android SDK and AVD Manager to manage AVD configurations. However, if you are not using Eclipse or the plug-in, you need to use the `emulator` tool from the command line, the `android` tool to create and manage AVDs, and the `mksdcard` command-line tool to create virtual SD card images. You can find help for using these tools by running the tools on the command line and at the Android website: http://developer.android.com/guide/developing/tools/.

Regardless of which tools you use or the way in which you use them, each AVD configuration contains important information describing a specific type of Android device, including

- The friendly, descriptive name for the configuration
- The target Android operating system
- The screen size, aspect ratio, and resolution
- Hardware configuration details and features, including how much RAM is available, which input methods exist, and optional hardware details such as cameras and location sensor support
- Simulated external storage (virtual SD cards)

Figure A.3 illustrates how you can use the Android SDK and AVD Manager to create and manage AVD configurations.

Creating an AVD

Follow these steps to create an AVD configuration within Eclipse:

1. Launch the Android SDK and AVD Manager from within Eclipse by clicking on the little green Android icon with the arrow ( ) on the toolbar. You can also launch it by selecting Window, Android SDK and AVD Manager from the Eclipse menu.

Figure A.3   The Android SDK and AVD Manager (left) can be used
to create AVD configurations (right).

2. Click the Virtual Devices menu item on the left menu (Figure A.3, left). The configured AVDs are displayed as a list.

3. Click the New button to create a new AVD (Figure A.3, right).

4. Choose a name for the AVD. If you are trying to simulate a specific device, you
   might want to name it as such. For example, a name such as "NexusOne2.2_Style"
   might refer to an AVD that simulates the Nexus One handset running Android 2.2
   platform with the Google APIs.

5. Choose a build target. This represents the version of the Android platform running
   on the emulator. The platform is represented by the API Level. For example, to support Android 2.2 is API Level 8. However, this is also where you choose whether or
   not to include the optional Google APIs. If your application relies upon the Maps
   application and other Google Android services, you should choose the target with
   the Google APIs.

6. Choose an SD card capacity. Capacity can be configured in kibibytes or mibibytes.

Tip

Each SD card image takes up space on your hard drive and takes a long time to generate;
don't make your card capacities too large, or they will hog your hard drive space. Choose a
reasonable size, such as a 1024MiB or less. The minimum is 9MiB.

7. Choose a skin. This determines the screen characteristics to emulate. For each target
   platform, there are a number of predefined skins (HVGA, and so on) that represent
   common Android device characteristics to make this easy. You can also use your
   own screen settings if none of the predefined skins match your requirements.

8. Configure or modify any hardware characteristics that do not match the defaults (more on this in a moment). Sometimes the predefined skins automatically set some of these characteristics for you, such as screen density.

9. Click the Create AVD button and wait for the operation to complete.

10. Click Finish.

Note

Because the Android Virtual Device Manager formats the memory allocated for SD card images, creating an AVD configuration sometimes takes a few moments.

Exploring AVD Skin Choices

Different Android devices have different screen characteristics. Testing your application in emulators configured to simulate appropriate screen sizes and resolutions is crucial. Let's take a look at some of the predefined skins available to AVD configurations. These skins are described in Table A.1. You can also create custom skins to emulate other devices, like Android tablets.

Table A.1   **Important Default Emulator Skin Options**

Skin Name	Description
HVGA	320×480 Pixel Screen
	LCD Density: 160
QVGA	240×320 Pixel Screen
	LCD Density: 120
WQVGA400	240×400 Pixel Screen
	LCD Density: 120
WQVGA432	240×432 Pixel Screen
	LCD Density: 120
WVGA800	480×800 Pixel Screen
	LCD Density: 240
	Maximum VM Application Heap: 24
WVGA854	480×854 Pixel Screen
	LCD Density: 240
	Maximum VM Application Heap: 24

Creating AVDs with Custom Hardware Settings

As mentioned earlier, you can specify specific hardware configuration settings within your AVD configurations. You need to know what the default settings are to know if you need to override them. The hardware options available are shown in Table A.2.

Table A.2   **Hardware Profile Options**

Hardware Property Option	Description	Default Value
Device RAM Size `hw.ramSize`	Physical RAM on the device in megabytes	96
Touch-screen Support `hw.touchScreen`	Touch screen exists on the device	Yes
Trackball Support `hw.trackBall`	Trackball exists on the device	Yes
Keyboard Support `hw.keyboard`	QWERTY keyboard exists on the device	Yes
DPad Support `hw.dPad`	Directional Pad exists on the device	Yes
GSM Modem Support `hw.gsmModem`	GSM modem exists in the device	Yes
Camera Support `hw.camera`	Camera exists on the device	No Note: This setting does not appear to do anything. We always see a camera. In fact, one is generally required on Android 2.0+.

Camera Pixels (Horizontal)
`hw.camera.`
`maxHorizontalPixels`
	Maximum horizontal camera pixels	640

Camera Pixels (Vertical)
`hw.camera.`
`maxVerticalPixels`
	Maximum vertical camera pixels	480

GPS Support `hw.gps`	GPS exists on the device	Yes
Battery Support `hw.battery`	Device can run on a battery	Yes
Accelerometer Support `hw.accelerometer`	Accelerometer exists on the device	Yes
Audio Recording Support `hw.audioInput`	Device can record audio	Yes

Table A.2   **Continued**

Hardware Property Option	Description	Default Value
Audio Playback Support `hw.audioOutput`	Device can play audio	Yes
SD Card Support `hw.sdCard`	Device supports removable SD cards	Yes
Cache Partition Support `disk.cachePartition`	Device supports cache partition	Yes
Cache Partition Size `disk.cachePartition.size`	Device cache partition size in megabytes	66
Abstracted LCD Density `hw.lcd.density`	Generalized screen density	160
Max VM App Heap Size `vm.heapSize`	Maximum heap size an application can allocate before being killed by the operating system	16

Tip

You can save time, money, and a lot of grief by spending a bit of time upfront configuring AVDs that closely match the hardware upon which your application will run. Share the specific settings with your fellow developers and testers. For example, our article on commonly used Android device configurations is available here: http://androidbook.blogspot.com/2010/08/creating-useful-avds.html.

Launching the Emulator with a Specific AVD

After you have configured the AVD you want to use, you are ready to launch the emulator. There are a number of ways to do this, but there are four main ways you will likely do so on a regular basis:

- From within Eclipse, you can configure application's Debug or Run configurations to use a specific AVD.
- From within Eclipse, you can configure application's Debug or Run configuration to enable the developer to choose an AVD manually upon launch.
- From within Eclipse, you can launch an emulator directly from within the Android SDK and AVD Manager.
- The emulator is available within the /tools directory of the Android SDK and can be launched as a separate process from the command line (generally only necessary if you are not using Eclipse).

Tip

During development, keep the emulator running between debugging sessions in order to quickly reinstall and debug your applications. This saves several minutes of waiting for the emulator to boot up. Instead, simply launch the Debug configuration from Eclipse and the debugger reattaches.

Configuring Emulator Startup Options

The Android emulator has a number of configuration options above and beyond those set in the AVD profile. These options are configured in the Eclipse Debug and Run configurations for your specific applications, or when launching the emulator from the command-line. Some emulator start-up settings include network speed and latency, media settings, the ability to disable boot animation upon startup and numerous other system settings. There are also debugging settings, such as support for proxy servers, DNS addresses, and other details. For a complete list of emulator startup options, consult the Android emulator documentation.

Launching an Emulator to Run an Application

The most common way you launch the emulator involves launching a specific emulator instance (with a specific AVD configuration) and installing or reinstalling the latest incarnation of your application. This is achieved within Eclipse using Run and Debug configurations, as described in Chapter 3, "Writing Your First Android Application."

Tip

Remember that you can create Run configurations and Debug configurations separately, with different options, using different startup options and even different AVDs.

To create a Debug configuration for a specific project within Eclipse, take the following steps:

1. Choose Run, Debug Configurations (or right-click the Project and Choose Debug As...).
2. Double-click on Android Application.
3. Name your Debug configuration (we often use the project name).
4. Choose the Project by clicking on the Browse button.
5. Switch to the Target tab and choose the appropriate Deployment Target Selection Mode. Either choose a specific AVD to use with the emulator (only those matching your application's target SDK are shown), or select the Manual option to be prompted upon launch to choose an AVD on-the-fly.
6. Configure any emulator startup options on the Target tab. You can enter any options not specifically shown on the tab as normal command-line options in the Additional Emulator Command-Line Options field.

The resulting Debug configuration might look something like Figure A.4.

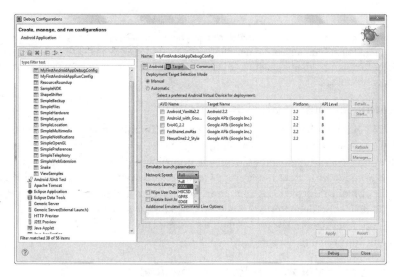

Figure A.4   Creating a Debug configuration in Eclipse.

You can create Run configurations in a very similar fashion. If you set a specific AVD for use in the Deployment Target Selection Mode settings, that AVD is used with the emulator whenever you debug your application in Eclipse. However, if you chose the Manual option, you are prompted to select an AVD from the Android Device Chooser when you first try to debug the application, as shown in Figure A.5. After you have launched that emulator, Eclipse pairs it to your project for the duration of your debugging session.

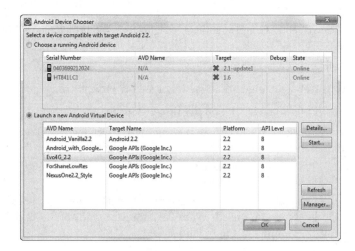

Figure A.5   The Android Device Chooser.

Note

If you have Android devices connected via USB when you attempt to run or debug your application from Eclipse, you might be prompted to choose your target at runtime despite having selected a specific AVD. This enables you to redirect the install or reinstall operation to a device other than an emulator.

Launching an Emulator from the Android SDK and AVD Manager

Sometimes you just want to launch an emulator on the fly, such as to have a second emulator running to interact with your first emulator to simulate calls, text messages, and such. In this case, you can simply launch it from the Android SDK and AVD Manager. To do this, take the following steps:

1. Launch the Android SDK and AVD Manager from within Eclipse by clicking on the little green Android icon with the arrow (📦) on the toolbar. You can also launch it by selecting Window, Android SDK and AVD Manager from the Eclipse menu.

2. Click the Virtual Devices menu item on the left menu. The configured AVDs are displayed as a list.

3. Select an existing AVD configuration from the list or create a new AVD that matches your requirements.

4. Hit the Start button.

5. Configure any launch options necessary.

6. Hit the Launch button. The emulator now launches with the AVD you requested.

Warning

You cannot run multiple instances of the same AVD configuration simultaneously. If you think about it, this makes sense because the AVD configuration keeps the state and persistent data.

Configuring the GPS Location of the Emulator

To develop and test applications that use Google Maps support with location-based services, you need to begin by creating an AVD with a target that includes the Google APIs. After you have created the appropriate AVD and launched the emulator, you need to configure its location. The emulator does not have location sensors, so the first thing you need to do is seed your emulator with GPS coordinates. To do this, launch your emulator and follow these steps:

1. Launch the emulator. If you're running an application, press the Home button or navigate to the Home screen.

2. Choose the Maps application. If you did not include the Google APIs as part of the AVD platform target, you do not have the Maps application.

3. Within the Maps application, click the Menu button.

4. Choose the My Location menu item. (It looks like a target.)

5. Within Eclipse, click the Dalvik Debug Monitor Service (DDMS) perspective in the top-right corner of Eclipse.

6. In the top-left pane, select the emulator instance to which you want to send location information (if there is more than one emulator running).

7. Within the Emulator Control pane, scroll down to the Location Controls.

8. Manually enter the longitude and latitude coordinates you want to send to the emulator. For example, Yosemite Valley has the coordinates Longitude: -119.588542 and Latitude: 37.746761.

9. Click Send.

Back in the emulator, notice that the map now shows the location you seeded. Your screen should now display your location as Yosemite, as shown in Figure A.6. This location persists across emulator launches.

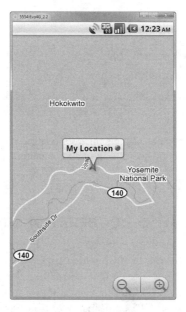

Figure A.6   Setting the location of the emulator to Yosemite Valley.

You can also use GPX coordinate files to send a series of GPS locations through DDMS to the emulator, if you prefer.

Tip

To find a specific set of GPS coordinates, you can go to http://maps.google.com. Navigate to the location you want and center the map on the location by right-clicking the map. Choose Link to Map and copy the URL. Take a closer look at the URL and weed out the "ll" variable, which represents the latitude/longitude of the location. For example, Yosemite Valley link has the value ll=37.746761,-119.588542, which stands for Latitude: 37.746761 and Longitude: -119.588542.

Calling Between Two Emulator Instances

You can have two emulator instances call each other using the Dialer application provided on the emulator. The emulator's "phone number" is its port number, which can be found in the title bar of the emulator window. To simulate a phone call between two emulators, you must perform the following steps:

1. Launch two different AVDs so two emulators are running simultaneously. (Using the Android AVD and SDK Manager is easiest.)
2. Note the port number of the emulator you want to receive the call.
3. In the emulator that makes the call, launch the Dialer application.
4. Type the port number you noted as the number to call. Press Enter (or Send).
5. You see (and hear) an incoming call on the receiving emulator instance. Figure A.7 shows an emulator with port 5554 (left) using the Dialer application to call the emulator on port 5556 (right).
6. Answer the call by pressing Send or swiping across the Dialer app.
7. Pretend to chat for a bit. Figure A.8 shows a call in progress.
8. You can end either emulator call at any time by pressing the End key.

Messaging Between Two Emulator Instances

You can send SMS messages between two emulators exactly as previously described for simulating calls using the emulator port numbers as SMS addresses. To simulate a text message between two emulators, you must perform the following steps:

1. Launch two instances of the emulator.
2. Note the port number of the emulator you want to receive the text message.
3. In the emulator that sends the text, launch the Messaging application.
4. Type the port number you noted as the "To" field for the text message. Enter a text message, as shown in Figure A.9. Press the Send button.
5. You see (and hear) an incoming text message on the receiving emulator instance. Figure A.10 shows an emulator with port 5554 receiving a text message from the emulator on port 5556.

Figure A.7   Simulating a phone call between two emulators.

Figure A.8   Two emulators with a phone call in progress.

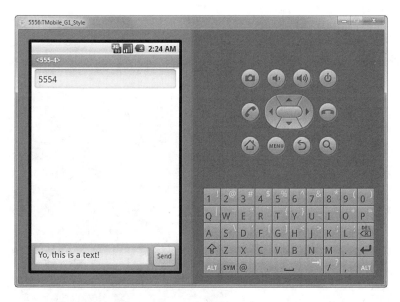

Figure A.9   Emulator at port 5556 crafting a text message
to send to another emulator at port 5554.

Figure A.10   Incoming text message in an
emulator with port 5554.

6. View the text message by pulling down the notification bar or launching the Messaging app.

7. Pretend to chat for a bit. Figure A.11 shows a text message conversation in progress.

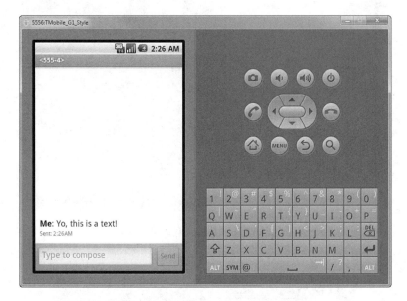

Figure A.11   A text message thread between two emulators.

Note
You can also use DDMS or the console to send SMS messages to emulator instances.

Interacting with the Emulator Through the Console

In addition to using the DDMS tool to interact with the emulator, you can also connect directly to the emulator console using a telnet connection, and then issue commands. For example, to connect to the Emulator console of the emulator using port 5554, you would do the following:

```
telnet localhost 5554
```

You can use the Emulator console to issue commands to the emulator. To end the session, just type quit or exit. You can shut this instance of the emulator using the kill command.

Using the Console to Simulate Incoming Calls

You can simulate incoming calls to the emulator from specified numbers. The console command for issuing an incoming call is

```
gsm call <number>
```

For example, to simulate an incoming call from the number 555-1212, you would issue the following console command:

```
gsm call 5551212
```

The result of this command in the emulator is shown in Figure A.12.

Figure A.12   Incoming call from 555-1212
(configured as a contact named Anne Droid),
prompted via the Emulator console.

Tip

You can control inbound and outbound phone calls, busy signals, and such using other `gsm` subcommands. Gsm subcommands include `list`, `call`, `busy`, `hold`, `accept`, `cancel`, `data`, `voice`, and `status`.

Using the Console to Simulate SMS Messages

You can simulate SMS messages to the emulator from specified numbers. The command for issuing an incoming SMS is

```
sms send <number> <message>
```

For example, to simulate an incoming SMS from the number 555-1212 asking "How are you?" in SMS slang, you would issue the following command:

```
sms send 5551212 HRU?
```

In the emulator, you get a notification on the white status bar informing you of a new message. It even displays the contents on the bar for a moment and then rolls away, showing the Message icon. You can pull down the notification bar to see the new message or launch the Messaging application. The result of the preceding command in the emulator is shown in Figure A.13.

Figure A.13   An incoming SMS from 555-1212 (configured as a contact named Anne Droid), prompted via the emulator console.

Warning

The `sms send` command does not work as expected on all the platforms we tested. For example, if you include multiple words in your SMS message, you might want to enclose them in quotes to avoid the message displaying in the wrong encoding on the emulator. Unfortunately, the quotes might display in the message.

Using the Console to Send GPS Coordinates

You can use the Emulator console to issue commands to the emulator. The command for a simple GPS fix is

```
geo fix <longitude> <latitude> [<altitude>]
```

For instance, to set the fix for the emulator to the top of Mount Everest, launch the Maps application in the emulator by selecting Menu, My Location. Then, within the Emulator console, issue the following command to set the device's coordinates appropriately:

```
geo fix 86.929837 27.99003 8850
```

Using the Console to Monitor Network Status

You can monitor network status of the emulator and change the network speed and latency on-the-fly. The command for displaying network status is

```
network status
```

Typical results from this request look something like this:

```
network status
Current network status:
  download speed:        0 bits/s (0.0 KB/s)
  upload speed:          0 bits/s (0.0 KB/s)
  minimum latency: 0 ms
  maximum latency: 0 ms
OK
```

Using the Console to Manipulate Power Settings

You can manage "fake" power settings on the emulator using the power commands. You can turn the battery capacity to 99 percent charged as follows:

```
power capacity 99
```

You can turn the AC charging state to off (or on) as follows:

```
power ac off
```

You can turn the Battery status to the following options: unknown, charging, discharging, not-charging, or full as follows:

```
power status full
```

You can turn the Battery Present state to true (or false) as follows:

```
power present true
```

You can turn the Battery health state to the following options: unknown, good, overheat, dead, overvoltage, or failure as follows:

```
power health good
```

You can show the current power settings by issuing the following command:

```
power display
```

Typical results from this request look something like this:

```
power display
AC: offline
status: Full
health: Good
present: true
capacity: 99
OK
```

Using Other Console Commands

There are also commands for simulating hardware events, port redirection, checking, starting, and stopping the virtual machine.

Quality assurance personnel will want to check out the event subcommands, which can be used to simulate key events for automation purposes. It's likely this is the same interface used by the ADB Exerciser Monkey, which presses random keys and tries to crash your application.

Enjoying the Emulator

Here are a few more tips for using the emulator, just for fun:

- On the Home screen, press and hold the desktop to change the wallpaper and add applications, shortcuts, and widgets to the desktop.
- If you press and hold an icon (usually an application icon) in the application tray, you can place a shortcut to it on your Home desktop for easy access.
- If you press and hold an icon on your Home desktop, you can move it around or dump it into the trash to get it off the desktop.
- Press and fling the phone's Home desktop to the left and right for more space. Depending on which version of Android you're running, you find a number of other pages, with app widgets such as Google search and lots of empty space where you can place other desktop items.
- Another way to change your wallpaper and add applications to your desktop is to press Menu on the desktop screen; then choose Add. Here you can also add shortcuts and picture frames widgets around your family photo, and so on, as shown in Figure A.14.

Understanding Emulator Limitations

The emulator is powerful, but it has several important limitations:

- It is not a device, so it does not reflect actual behavior, only simulated behavior.
- Simulation of phone calls, but you cannot place or receive true calls.
- Limited ability to determine device state (network state, battery charge).
- Limited ability to simulate peripherals (camera capture, headphones, SD Card insertion, location-based services).
- Limited API support (for example, no OpenGL ES 2 presently).
- Limited performance (modern devices often perform much better than the emulator at many tasks, such as video and animation).

Figure A.14   Customizing the emulator Home
screen with App widgets.

- Limited support for manufacturer or operator-specific device characteristics, themes, or user experiences. Some manufacturers, such as Motorola, have provided emulator add-ons to more closely mimic the behavior of specific devices.
- No USB or Bluetooth support.

The Android DDMS
Quick-Start Guide

The Dalvik Debug Monitor Service (DDMS) is a debugging tool provided with Android Software Development Kit (SDK). Developers use DDMS to provide a window into the emulator or the actual phone for debugging purposes as well as file and process management. It's a blend of several tools: a Task Manager, a File Explorer, an Emulator console, and a Logging console. This Quick–Start Guide is not complete documentation of the DDMS functionality. Instead, it is designed to get you up and running with common tasks. See the DDMS documentation provided with Android SDK for a complete list of features.

Using DDMS with Eclipse and as a Stand-Alone Application

If you use Eclipse with the Android Development Tools plug-in, the DDMS tool is tightly integrated with your development environment as a perspective. By using the DDMS Perspective (shown in Figure B.1, using the File Explorer to browse files on the emulator instance), you can explore any emulator instances running on the development machine and any Android devices connected via USB.

If you're not using Eclipse, the DDMS tool is also available within the /tools directory of Android SDK and you can launch it as a separate application, in which case it runs in its own process, as shown in Figure B.2 (sending an SMS message to the emulator).

Tip

There should be only one instance of the DDMS tool running at a given time. This includes the Eclipse perspective. Other DDMS launches are ignored; if you have Eclipse running and try to launch DDMS from the command line, you might see question marks instead of process names, and you see a debug output saying the instance of DDMS is being ignored.

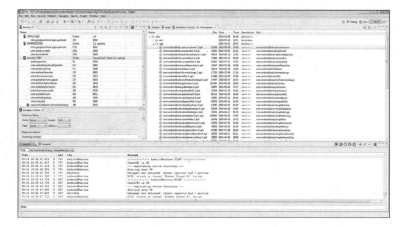

Figure B.1   The Eclipse DDMS Perspective with one emulator and two Android devices connected.

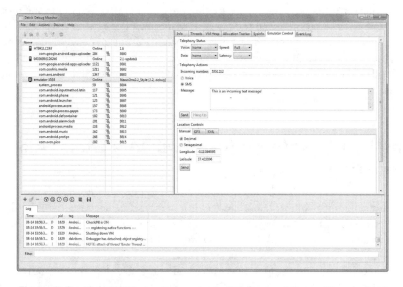

Figure B.2   The DDMS stand-alone tool with one emulator and two Android devices connected.

Getting Up to Speed Using Key Features of DDMS

Whether you use DDMS from Eclipse or as a stand-alone tool, be aware of a few key features:

- A list of running emulators and connected devices displays in the top-left corner.

- The File Explorer enables you to browse files on the emulator or device (including application files, directories, and databases) and pull and push files to the Android system.

- The LogCat window enables you to monitor the Android Logging console (`LogCat`). This is where calls to `Log.i()`, `Log.e()`, and other `Log` messages display.

- You can inspect individual processes (heap and thread updates). You can inspect individual threads. You can kill processes. You can prompt garbage collection on a process and then view the Heap for that application.

- You can track application memory allocation using the Allocation Tracker pane.

- You can take remote screenshots of the emulator or the device using the Screen Capture button.

- You have some helpful Emulator console functionality at your fingertips, such as the ability to send GPS information and to simulate incoming calls and SMS messages.

Some functionality applies only to the Eclipse DDMS Perspective; you can click on an individual process in an emulator or device and click the little green bug to attach a debugger to that process and debug using Eclipse, provided you have the source code open in the workspace. The process is similar if you're using another debugger, such as JSwat or jdebug.

Working with Processes

One of the most useful features of DDMS is the ability to interact with processes. As you might remember, each Android application runs in its own VM with its own user `id` on the operating system. Using the left pane of DDMS, you can browse all instances of the VM running on a device, each identified by its package name. You can

- Attach and debug applications in Eclipse
- Monitor threads
- Monitor the heap
- Stop processes
- Force Garbage Collection (GC)

For example, in Figure B.3, there is a package named `com.androidbook.myfirstandroidapp` running on the emulator. You can see the application's thread data in the right-hand pane.

Figure B.3   Using DDMS to display thread information about an application.

Attaching a Debugger to an Android Application

Although you'll use the Eclipse debug configurations to launch and debug your applications most of the time, you can also use DDMS to choose which application to debug and attach directly. To attach a debugger to a process, you need to have the package source code open in your Eclipse workspace. Now perform the following steps to debug:

1. On the emulator or device, verify that the application you want to debug is running.

2. In DDMS, find that application's package name and highlight it.

3. Click the little green bug button (![icon]) to debug that application.

4. Switch to the Debug Perspective of Eclipse as necessary; debug as you would normally.

Monitoring Thread Activity of an Android Application

You can use DDMS to monitor thread activity of an individual Android application. For an example of DDMS monitoring the threading activity of an application, refer to Figure B.3. Follow these steps:

1. On the emulator or device, verify that the application you want to monitor is running.

2. In DDMS, find that application's package name and highlight it.

3. Click the three black arrows button () to display the threads of that application. They appear in the right portion of the Threads tab. This data updates every four seconds by default.

4. On the Threads tab, you can choose a specific thread and press the Refresh button to drill down within that thread. The resulting Classes in use display below.

Note

You can also start thread profiling using the button with three black arrows and a red dot (▦).

Prompting Garbage Collection (GC)

You can use DDMS to force the Garbage Collector (GC) to run by following these steps:

1. On the emulator or device, verify that the application you want to run GC is running.

2. In DDMS, find that application's package name and highlight it.

3. Click the garbage can button (🗑) to cause garbage collection to run for the application. You can also do this from the Heap tab, as detailed next.

Monitoring Heap Activity

You can use DDMS to monitor heap statistics of an individual Android application. The heap statistics are updated after every GC. For an example of DDMS monitoring the heap status of an application, see Figure B.4. Follow these steps:

1. On the emulator or device, verify that the application you want to monitor is running.

2. In DDMS, find that application's package name and highlight it.

3. Click the green cylinder button (🛢) to display the heap information for that application. The statistics appear in the right portion of the Heap tab. This data updates after every GC. You can also cause GC operations from the Heap tab using the button Cause GC.

4. On the Heap tab, you can choose a specific type of object. The resulting graph in use displays at the bottom of the Heap tab, as shown in Figure B.4.

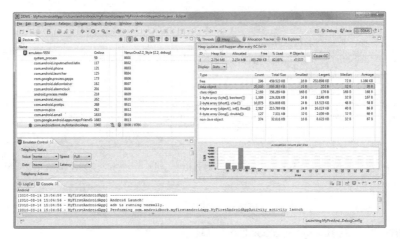

Figure B.4   Using DDMS to display heap information about an application.

Monitoring Memory Allocation

You can use DDMS to monitor memory allocated by a specific Android application. The memory allocation statistics are updated on demand by the developer. Follow these steps to track memory allocations:

1. On the emulator or device, verify that the application you want to monitor is running.

2. In DDMS, find that application's package name and highlight it.

3. Switch to the Allocation Tracker tab on the right pane.

4. Click the Start Tracking button to start tracking memory allocations and the Get Allocations to get the allocations at a given time.

5. To stop tracking allocations, click the Stop Tracking button.

The Android developer website has a write-up on how to track memory allocations at http://developer.android.com/resources/articles/track-mem.html.

Stopping a Process

You can use DDMS to kill an Android application by following these steps:

1. On the emulator or device, verify that the application you want to stop is running.

2. In DDMS, find that application's package name and highlight it.

3. Click the red stop sign button (🔳) to stop that process.

Working with the File Explorer

You can use DDMS to browse and interact with the Android file system on an emulator or device. Table B.1 shows some important areas of the Android file system.

Table B.1   **Important Directories in the Android File System**

Directory	Purpose
`/data/app/`	Where Android APK files are stored
`/data/data/<package name>/`	Application top-level directory; for example: `/data/data/com.androidbook.pettracker/`
`/data/data/<package name>/ shared_prefs/`	Application shared preferences directory Named preferences stored as XML files
`/data/data/<package name>/ files/`	Application file directory
`/data/data/<package name>/ cache/`	Application cache directory
`/data/data/<package name>/ databases/`	Application database directory; for example: `/data/data/com.androidbook.pettracker/ databases/test.db`
`/mnt/sdcard/`	External storage (SD Card)
`/mnt/sdcard/download/`	Where browser images are saved

Browsing the File System of an Emulator or Device

To browse the Android file system, follow these steps:

1. In DDMS, choose the emulator or device you want to browse.

2. Switch to the File Explorer tab. You see a directory hierarchy.

3. Browse to a directory or file location.

Keep in mind that directory listings in the File Explorer might take a moment to update when contents change.

> **Note**
>
> Some device directories, such as the /data directory, might not be accessible from the DDMS File Explorer.

Copying Files from the Emulator or Device

You can use File Explorer to copy files or directories from an emulator or a device file system to your computer by following these steps:

1. Using File Explorer, browse to the file or directory to copy and highlight it.

2. From the top-right corner of the File Explorer, click the Disk button with the ar-
    row ([🖼]) to pull the file from the device. Alternatively, you can pull down the drop-
    down menu next to the buttons and choose Pull File.

3. Type in the path where you want to save the file or directory on your computer
    and press Save.

Copying Files to the Emulator or Device

You can use File Explorer to copy files to an emulator or a device file system from your
computer by following these steps:

1. Using File Explorer, browse to the file or directory to copy and highlight it.

2. From the top-right corner of File Explorer, click the Phone button with the arrow
    ([📱]) to push a file to the device. Alternatively, you can pull down the drop-down
    menu next to the buttons and choose Push File.

3. Select the file or directory on your computer and press Open.

Tip

File Explorer also supports some drag-and-drop operations. This is the only way to push directories to the Android file system; however, copying directories to the Android file system
is not recommended because there's no delete option for them. You need to delete directories programmatically if you have the permissions to do so. That said, you can drag a file or
directory from your computer to File Explorer and drop it in the location you want.

Deleting Files on the Emulator or Device

You can use File Explorer to delete files (but not directories) on the emulator or device
file system. Follow these steps:

1. Using File Explorer, browse to the file you want to delete and highlight it.

2. In the top-right corner of File Explorer, click the red minus button ([➖]) to delete
    the file.

Warning

Be careful. There is no confirmation. The file is deleted immediately and is not recoverable.

Working with the Emulator Control

You can use DDMS to interact with instances of the emulator using the Emulator Control tab. You must select the emulator you want to interact with for the Emulator Control
tab to work. You can use the Emulator Control tab to

- Change telephony status
- Simulate incoming voice calls
- Simulate incoming SMS messages
- Send a location fix (GPS coordinates)

Simulating Incoming Voice Calls

To simulate an incoming voice call using the Emulator Control tab, use the following steps:

1. In DDMS, choose the emulator you want to call.

2. Switch to the Emulator tab. You work with the Telephony Actions.

3. Input the Incoming phone number. This might include only numbers, +, and #.

4. Select the Voice radio button.

5. Click the Call button.

6. In the emulator, your phone is ringing. Answer the call.

7. The emulator can end the call as normal, or you can end the call in DDMS using the Hang Up button.

Simulating Incoming SMS Messages

DDMS provides the most stable method to send incoming SMS messages to the emulator. You send an SMS much as you initiated the voice call. To simulate an incoming SMS message using the Emulator Control tab, use the following steps:

1. In DDMS, choose the emulator you want to send a message to.

2. Switch to the Emulator tab. You work with the Telephony Actions.

3. Input the Incoming phone number. This might include only numbers, +, and #.

4. Select the SMS radio button.

5. Type in your SMS message.

6. Click the Send button.

7. Over in the emulator, you receive an SMS notification.

Sending a Location Fix

The steps for sending GPS coordinates to the emulator are covered in Appendix A, "The Android Emulator Quick-Start Guide." Simply input the GPS information into the Emulator Control tab, click Send, and use the Maps application on the emulator to get the current position.

Working with Application Logging

The LogCat tool is integrated into DDMS. It is provided as a tab along the bottom of the DDMS user interface. You can control how much information displays by clicking on the little round circles with letters in them. The V stands for verbose (show everything) and is the default. The other options correspond to Debug (D), Information (I), Warning (W), and Error (E).

You can also create Filter tabs to display only the LogCat information associated with a Debug Tag. You can use the Plus (+) button to add a Filter tab and show only log entries matching a specific tag. It is helpful to create a unique debug tag string for your application logging. Then you can filter LogCat to show only your application logging activities. For example, if your application does this,

```
public static final String DEBUG_TAG = "MyFirstAppLogging";
Log.i(DEBUG_TAG, "This is info about MyFirstAndroidApp.");
```

you can create a LogCat filter using the plus sign. Name the filter and set the log tag to the string matching your debug tag:

```
MyFirstAppLogging
```

That's it. Now you have a LogCat tab called Logging My App, which displays only logging information with the tag unique to your application, as shown in Figure B.5.

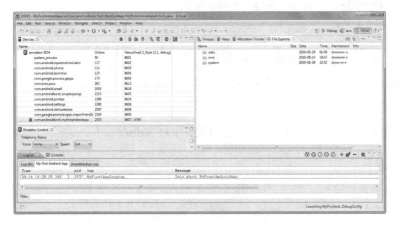

Figure B.5   Using a custom LogCat filter with DDMS.

Tip

If too many messages are collected by the LogCat logging tool, DDMS might not display log messages correctly. It's a good idea to clear the log from time to time.

Taking Screen Captures of Emulator and Device Screens

You can take screen captures of the emulator and the device from DDMS. The device captures are most useful for debugging, and this makes the DDMS tool appropriate for quality assurance personnel and developers. To capture a screenshot, take the following steps:

1. In DDMS, choose the emulator or device you want to take a capture of.

2. On the device or emulator, make sure you have the screen you want to take the screenshot of.

3. Click the multicolored square picture button ([■]) to take a screen capture. A capture window launches, as shown in Figure B.6.

Figure B.6   Using DDMS to take a screenshot.

4. Within the capture window, click the Save button to save the screen capture. Similarly, the Copy button stores the screenshot in your clipboard and the Refresh button updates the screenshot if the underlying device or emulator screen changed since you launched the capture window.

C

The Android Debug Bridge Quick-Start Guide

The Android Debug Bridge (ADB) is a client-server tool that interacts directly with Android devices and emulators using a command-line interface. You can use this tool, which is provided as part of the Android SDK, to manage and interact with emulator and device instances connected to a development machine and view logging and debugging information. ADB also provides the underpinnings for other tools, such as the Android Plug-In for Eclipse (ADT) and Dalvik Debug Monitor Service (DDMS). This Quick-Start Guide is not complete documentation of the ADB functionality. Instead, it is designed to get you up and running with common tasks. See the ADB documentation provided with the Android SDK for a complete list of features.

Much of the functionality provided by the ADB (such as the `LogCat` Android logging utility or pushing and pulling files using the File Explorer) is closely integrated into the development environment through DDMS and ADT. Developers might prefer to use these friendly methods to interact with devices and emulators; however, you can use ADB for automation and scripting purposes. You can also use ADB to customize functionality, instead of relying on the defaults exposed through secondary tools.

Listing Connected Devices and Emulators

You can use ADB to list all Android devices and emulator instances connected to a development machine. To do this, simply use the `devices` command of the `adb` command line. For example

```
adb devices
```

This command lists the emulators and devices attached to this machine by their serial number and state (`offline` or `device`). For emulator instances, the serial number is based on their unique port number. For example, in this case, we have one emulator instance (Port 5554) and one Android device:

```
C:\>adb devices
List of devices attached
emulator-5554   device
HT841LC1977     device
```

Directing ADB Commands to Specific Devices

When you know the serial number of the device you want to connect to, you can issue commands as follows:

```
adb —s <serial number> <command>
```

For example, to get the state of a specific device, type

```
adb -s emulator-5554 get-state
```

Instead of using the —s flag with a unique serial number, you can also use the —d flag to direct a command to the *only* device instance connected or the —e flag to direct a command to the *only* emulator instance, provided you have only one of each type connected. For example, if we have only one Android phone connected, we can query its serial number as follows:

```
adb -d get-serialno
```

Starting and Stopping the ADB Server

Sometimes you might need to manually restart the ADB Server process. We have, for example, needed to do this when we've had an emulator instance running for a long time and have repeatedly connected and disconnected the debugger, eventually resulting in a loss of LogCat logging. In this case, you might want to kill and restart the ADB server (and perhaps Eclipse).

Stopping the ADB Server Process

To terminate the ADB server process, use the `kill-server` command. For example, type

```
adb kill-server
```

Starting and Checking the ADB Server Process

You can start the ADB server using the `start-server` command.

```
adb start-server
```

You can also use the `start-server` command to check whether the server is running. If the server isn't running when other commands are issued, it is started automatically.

Issuing Shell Commands

ADB includes a shell interface (ash) where you can interact directly with the device and issue commands and run binaries. The ash shell has your typical file access commands, such as `pwd` and `ls`.

Tip

For more information on the ash shell, check out the Linux Blog Man at http://www.thelinuxblog.com/linux-man-pages/1/ash

Issuing a Single Shell Command

You can issue a single shell command without starting a shell session using the following command:

```
adb shell <command>
```

For example, to list all the files in the `/sdcard/download` directory on the emulator, type

```
adb -e shell ls /sdcard/download
```

Using a Shell Session

Often you might want to issue more than one command. In this case, you might want to start a shell session. To do so, simply type

```
adb shell
```

For example, to connect to a specific device instance by serial number and start a shell session, type

```
adb -s emulator-5554 shell
# <type commands here>
# exit
```

You can then issue commands. Ending your session is as easy as typing `exit`.

Tip

If you connect to a device instead of the emulator, you might see a $ as a prompt instead of a # prompt. This indicates user-level access, but the commands, such as `logcat` and `monkey`, work as described.

Using the Shell to Start and Stop the Emulator

Stopping the emulator makes it stop responding, although it still displays on your development machine. To stop the emulator, you can issue the `stop` command within the ADB shell.

```
adb -s emulator-5554 shell stop
```

You can then restart the emulator using the `start` command:

```
adb -s emulator-5554 shell start
```

You could also perform these commands from within a shell session, like this:

```
adb -s emulator-5554 shell
# stop
# start
```

Tip

You can also use the shell interface to run built-in command-line programs such as `sqlite3` to examine SQLite application databases and `monkey` to stress test an application. You can also install custom binaries on the emulator or device. We talk more about this later in the appendix.

Copying Files

You can use the ADB command line to copy files to and from your hard drive to an Android device. You need to know the full path information to the file you want to copy. File operations are subject to your user permissions (locally and remotely).

Sending Files to a Device or Emulator

You can copy files to the device using the `push` command, as follows:

```
adb push <local file path> <remote file path on device>
```

For example, to copy the file `Pic.jpg` from the local hard drive to a device's SD Card download directory, use the following command:

```
adb -s HT841LC1977 push c:\Pic.jpg /sdcard/download/Pic.jpg
```

Retrieving Files from a Device or Emulator

You can copy files from the device using the `pull` command, as follows:

```
adb pull <remote file path on device> <local file path>
```

For example, to copy the file `Lion.jpg` to your local hard drive from a device's SD Card download directory, use the following command:

```
adb -s HT841LC1977 pull /sdcard/download/Lion.jpg C:\Lion.jpg
```

Tip

If you put picture files onto your SD Card—virtual or otherwise—using this method, you might need to force the Android operating system to refresh using the Media Scanner (available in the Dev Tools application on the Emulator).

Installing and Uninstalling Applications

You can use ADB to install and uninstall packages (applications) on a given Android device or emulator. Although the Eclipse plug-in does this for developers automatically, this functionality is useful for developers not using the Eclipse and for those developers and testers who want to create automated build procedures and testing environments. ADB can also be used to install third-party application packages, including those that are self-distributed and not found on application stores such as the Android Market.

Note

All Android applications are installed as packages created with the Android Asset Packaging Tool (aapt). This is the tool used by the Eclipse plug-in as well.

Installing Applications

To install applications, first create an Android package (.apk) file, and then use the install command:

```
adb install <apk file path>
```

For example, to install the sample application `Snake` on the emulator, you could use the following command:

```
adb -e install C:\android-sdk\samples\Snake\bin\Snake.apk
821 KB/s (17656 bytes in 0.021s)
        pkg: /data/local/tmp/Snake.apk
Success
```

Reinstalling Applications

You can use the –r to reinstall the application package without overwriting its data. For example, you can now reinstall the `Snake` application without losing your data by using the following command:

```
adb -e install -r C:\Snake.apk
```

Uninstalling Applications

To uninstall an Android application, you need to know the name of its package:

```
adb uninstall <package>
```

For example, to uninstall the MyFirstAndroidApp application from the emulator, you can use the following command:

```
adb -e uninstall com.androidbook.myfirstandroidapp
```

Tip

You might use this command often if you switch between computers and, thus, switch signatures frequently. You can read more about signing applications in Chapter 29, "Selling Your Android Application."

Working with LogCat Logging

Android logging information is accessible through the LogCat utility. This utility is integrated into DDMS and Eclipse (using the ADT plug-in), but you can also access it directly from the ADB command line using the following command:

```
adb logcat <option> <filter>
```

This type of command is best done from within the adb shell.

Displaying All Log Information

For example, you can display all LogCat logging information from the emulator instance by opening the shell and typing the logcat command:

```
adb -e shell
# logcat
```

By default, the logging mode is set to brief. For example, the following is an Informational (I) log message (brief mode) from the debug tag called *AppLog* from process ID 20054:

```
I/AppLog(20054): An Informational Log message.
```

Including Date and Time with Log Data

Another useful mode is the time mode, which includes the date and time the log message was invoked. To change the logging mode, use the –v flag and specify the format. For example, to change to time mode, use the following adb shell command:

```
# logcat -v time
```

The resulting log messages are formatted with the date and time, followed by the event severity, tag, process ID, and log message:

```
01-05 21:52:22.465 I/AppLog(20054): Another Log Message.
```

Filtering Log Information

All the log information available through the LogCat tool can be overwhelmingly verbose. Most of the time, a filter or two is required to sift out only the messages you want to view. Filters are formatted tags and event priority pairs. The format for each filter is

```
<Tag Name>:<Lowest Event Priority to Print>
```

For example, a filter to display Informational log messages (and higher-priority messages including Warnings, Errors, and Fatal messages) from log messages tagged with the string AppLog would look like this:

```
AppLog:I
```

Tip

You can also use the asterisk (*), which means "all." So if you use an asterisk on the Tag side of the filter, it means "All tags." If you put it on the Event Priority side, it's much like using the V priority—the lowest priority, so all messages display.

Filtering by Event Severity

You can create filters to display only log events of a certain severity. The severity types (from lowest priority or most verbose to highest priority or least verbose) follow:

- Verbose (V)
- Debug (D)
- Info (I)
- Warning (W)
- Error (E)
- Fatal (F)
- Silent (S)

For example, the following shell command displays all Errors and Fatal errors but suppresses warnings, informational messages, debug messages, and verbose messages:

```
# logcat *:E
```

Filtering by Tag

You can use multiple filters, ending with a catch-all. Perhaps you want to see all messages from a specific application (a specific tag) and no others. In this case, you want to create a filter to show all messages for a given tag and another filter to suppress all other tags. We also change into time mode, so we get the date and time of the logged events messages. The following shell command displays all AppLog-tagged logging information and suppresses all other tags:

```
# logcat —v time AppLog:V *:S
```

This filter is roughly equivalent to this other command line:

```
# logcat —v time AppLog:* *:S
```

The resulting log messages are formatted with the date and time, followed by the event severity, tag, process ID, and message:

```
01-05 21:52:22.465 I/AppLog(20054): Another Log Message.
```

Clearing the Log

You can clear the emulator log using the −c flag:

```
adb −e logcat -c
```

or, from the ADB shell like this:

```
# logcat -c
```

Redirecting Log Output to a File

You can redirect log output to a file on the device using the −f flag. For example, to direct all informational logging messages (and those of higher priority) from the emulator to the file mylog.txt in the sdcard directory, you can use the following ADB shell command:

```
# logcat -f /sdcard/mylog.txt *:I
```

Note

This file is stored on the emulator or device. You need to pull it onto your desktop either using ADB or the DDMS File Explorer.

Accessing the Secondary Logs

Android has several different logs. By default, you look at the main log. However, an events log and a radio log also exist. You can connect to the other log buffers using the −b flag. For example, to connect to the event log to review events, type

```
# logcat -b events
```

The radio log is similarly accessed as follows:

```
# logcat −b radio
```

Controlling the Backup Service

Android 2.2 introduced a backup service that applications can use to archive important data in case of a factory reset or lost device. This service normally runs in the background, backing up data and restoring it on its own schedule. However, you can use the bmgr shell tool to prompt the backup service to do its thing, which is very helpful for testing backup functionality. You can check to see if the Backup Manager is enabled using the following ADB shell command:

```
# bmgr enabled
Backup Manager currently disabled
```

You can enable the Backup Manager from the ADB shell as follows:

```
# bmgr enable true
Backup Manager now enabled
```

Tip

The user can enable and disable the Backup Manager on a specific device by navigating to the backup settings, accessed via Settings, Privacy, Backup, and Restore.

Forcing Backup Operations

From the ADB shell, you can schedule a backup using the following command:

```
# bmgr backup <package>
```

For example, you could schedule a backup of the SimpleBackup application data as follows:

```
# bmgr backup com.androidbook.simplebackup
```

The previous commands only schedule the backup to occur at some point in the future. You can trigger all scheduled backup tasks with the following command:

```
# bmgr run
```

Forcing Restore Operations

From the ADB shell, you can force a restore using the following command:

```
# bmgr restore <package>
```

For example, you could force a restore of the SimpleBackup application data as follows:

```
# bmgr restore com.androidbook.simplebackup
```

Unlike the backup command, the restore command immediately causes a restore operation.

Wiping Archived Data

From the ADB shell, you can wipe archived data for a specific application using the following command:

```
# bmgr wipe <package>
```

For example, you wipe out all archived backup data from the SimpleBackup application as follows:

```
# bmgr wipe com.androidbook.simplebackup
```

Generating Bug Reports

You can create a rather verbose bug report to attach to application defects using the bugreport command. For example, to print the debug information for the sole emulator instance running on your development machine, use

```
adb -e bugreport
```

To print the debug information for the sole phone connected via USB, you issue this command instead:

```
adb –d bugreport
```

Using the Shell to Inspect SQLite Databases

You can use the standard `sqlite3` database tool from within the ADB shell. This tool enables you to inspect and interact directly with a SQLite database on the emulator. For a thorough explanation of the `sqlite3` tool, see Appendix E, "The SQLite Quick-Start Guide."

Using the Shell to Stress Test Applications

You can use the Exerciser/Monkey tool from within the ADB shell to send random user events to a specific application. Think of it as handing your phone (or emulator) to a monkey (or a baby, or a baby monkey) and letting it push random keys, causing random events on the phone—events that can crash your application if it doesn't handle them correctly. If your application crashes, the `monkey` application stops and reports the error, making this a useful tool for quality assurance.

Letting the Monkey Loose on Your Application

To launch the `monkey` tool, use the following ADB shell command:

```
# monkey –p <package> <options> <event count>
```

For example, to have the `monkey` tool generate five random events within the `GroceryList` application within the emulator, you would do the following:

```
adb -s emulator-5554 shell
# monkey -p com.androidbook.grocerylist 5
```

Listening to Your Monkey

You can watch each event generated by using the verbose flag –v. For example, to see which events you send to the preceding `GroceryList` application, you use this command:

```
adb -s emulator-5554 shell
# monkey -p com.androidbook.grocerylist -v 5
```

Here is the important output from this command:

```
:SendKey: 21    // KEYCODE_DPAD_LEFT
:Sending Trackball ACTION_MOVE x=-4.0 y=2.0
:Sending Trackball ACTION_UP x=0.0 y=0.0
:SendKey: 82    // KEYCODE_MENU
:SendKey: 22    // KEYCODE_DPAD_RIGHT
```

```
:SendKey: 23    // KEYCODE_DPAD_CENTER
:Dropped: keys=0 pointers=0 trackballs=0
// Monkey finished
```

You can tell from the verbose logging that the `monkey` application sent five events to the `GroceryList` application: a navigation event (left), two trackball events, the Menu button, and then two more navigation events (right, center).

Directing Your Monkey's Actions

You can specify the types of events generated by the `monkey` application. You basically give weights (percentages) to the different types of events. The event types available are shown in Table C.1.

Table C.1   **Monkey Event Types**

Event Type	Description	Default Percentage	Command-Line Flag	Event ID (As Shown in Verbose Mode)
Touch	Up/Down event on a single screen location	15%	—pct-touch	0
Motion	Down event on a single location, followed by some movement; then an Up event in a different screen location	10%	—pct-motion	1
Trackball	Trackball event, which are sometimes followed by a Click event	15%	—pct-track-ball	2
Basic Navigation	Up, Down, Left, Right	25%	—pct-nav	3
Major Navigation	Menu, Back, Center of DPAD, and such	15%	—pct-majornav	4
System Key	Home, Volume, Send, End, and such	2%	—pct-syskeys	5
Activity Switch	Randomly switch to other activities	2%	—pct-app-switch	6
Other Events	Key presses, other buttons	16%	—pct-anyevent	7

To use a different mix of events, you need to include the event type's command-line flag as listed in Table C.1, followed by the desired percentage:

```
# monkey [<command line flag> <percentage>...] <event count>
```

For example, to tell the Monkey to use only touch events, use the following command:

```
# monkey -p com.androidbook.grocerylist —pct-touch 100 -v 5
```

Or, let's say you want just Basic and Major navigation events (50%/50%):

```
# monkey -p com.androidbook.grocerylist —pct-nav 50 —pct-majornav 50
  -v 5
```

You get the picture.

Training Your Monkey to Repeat His Tricks

For random yet reproducible results, you can use the seed option. The seed feature enables you to modify the events that are produced as part of the event sequence, yet you can rerun sequence in the future (and verify bug fixes, for example). To set a seed, use the —s flag:

```
# monkey —p <package> -s <seed> —v <event count>
```

For example, in our command we used previously, we can change the five events by setting a different starting seed. In this case, we set a seed of 555:

```
# monkey -p com.androidbook.grocerylist -s 555 -v 5
```

Changing the seed changes the event sequence sent by the monkey, so as part of a stress test, you might want to consider generating random seeds, sending them to the monkey, and logging the results. When the application fails on a given seed, keep that seed (and any other command-line options, such as event type percentages) when you log the bug and rerun the test later to verify the bug fix.

Keeping the Monkey on a Leash

By default, the monkey generates events as rapidly as possible. However, you can slow down this behavior using the throttle option, as follows:

```
# monkey —throttle <milliseconds> <event count>
```

For example, to pause for 1 second (1000 milliseconds) between each of the five events issued to the GroceryList application, use the following command:

```
# monkey -p com.androidbook.grocerylist -v —throttle 1000 5
```

Learning More About Your Monkey

For more information about the `monkey` commands, see the Android SDK Reference website: http://developer.android.com/guide/developing/tools/monkey.html. You can also get a list of commands by typing `monkey` without any command options, like this:

```
adb -e shell monkey
```

Installing Custom Binaries via the Shell

You can install custom binaries on the emulator or device. For example, if you spend a lot of time working in the shell, you might want to install `BusyBox`, which is a free and useful set of command-line tools available under the GNU General Public License and has been called "The Swiss Army Knife of Embedded Linux" (thanks, Wikipedia for that little fact). `BusyBox` provides a number of helpful and familiar UNIX utilities, all packaged in a single binary—for example, utilities such as find and more. `BusyBox` provides many useful functions (although some might not apply or be permissible) on Android, such as the following:

[, [[, addgroup, adduser, adjtimex, ar, arp, arping, ash, awk, basename, bunzip2, bzcat, bzip2, cal, cat, catv, chattr, chgrp, chmod, chown, chpasswd, chpst, chroot, chrt, chvt, cksum, clear, cmp, comm, cp, cpio, crond, crontab, cryptpw, cut, date, dc, dd, deallocvt, delgroup, deluser, df, dhcprelay, diff, dirname, dmesg, dnsd, dos2unix, du, dumpkmap, dumpleases, echo, ed, egrep, eject, env, envdir, envuidgid, ether-wake, expand, expr, fakeidentd, false, fbset, fdflush, fdformat, fdisk, fgrep, find, fold, free, freeramdisk, fsck, fsck.minix, ftpget, ftpput, fuser, getopt, getty, grep, gunzip, gzip, halt, hdparm, head, hexdump, hostid, hostname, httpd, hwclock, id, ifconfig, ifdown, ifup, inetd, init, insmod, install, ip, ipaddr, ipcalc, ipcrm, ipcs, iplink, iproute, iprule, iptunnel, kbd_mode, kill, killall, killall5, klogd, last, length, less, linux32, linux64, linuxrc, ln, loadfont, loadkmap, logger, login, logname, logread, losetup, ls, lsattr, lsmod, lzmacat, makedevs, md5sum, mdev, mesg, microcom, mkdir, mkfifo, mkfs.minix, mknod, mkswap, mktemp, modprobe, more, mount, mountpoint, mt, mv, nameif, nc, netstat, nice, nmeter, nohup, nslookup, od, openvt, passwd, patch, pgrep, pidof, ping, ping6, pipe_progress, pivot_root, pkill, poweroff, printenv, printf, ps, pscan, pwd, raidautorun, rdate, readlink, readprofile, realpath, reboot, renice, reset, resize, rm, rmdir, rmmod, route, rpm, rpm2cpio, run-parts, runlevel, runsv, runsvdir, rx, sed, seq, setarch, setconsole, setkeycodes, setlogcons, setsid, setuidgid, sh, sha1sum, slattach, sleep, softlimit, sort, split, start-stop-daemon, stat, strings, stty, su, sulogin, sum, sv, svlogd, swapoff, swapon, switch_root, sync, sysctl, syslogd, tail, tar, taskset, tcpsvd, tee, telnet, telnetd, test, tftp, time, top, touch, tr, traceroute, true, tty, ttysize, udhcpc, udhcpd, udpsvd, umount, uname, uncompress, unexpand, uniq, unix2dos, unlzma, unzip, uptime, usleep, uudecode, uuencode, vconfig, vi, vlock, watch, watchdog, wc, wget, which, who, whoami, xargs, yes, zcat, zcip

All you need to do is install the binary (which is available online) using the following steps:

1. Download the `BusyBox` binary (at your own risk, or compile it for yourself). You can find the binary online at http://benno.id.au/blog/2007/11/14/android-busybox, where Benno has kindly hosted it for you. (Thanks, Benno!)

2. Make a directory called `/data/local/busybox/` on your emulator using the ADB shell; for example, `adb —e shell mkdir /data/local/busybox/`.

3. Copy the `BusyBox` binary to the directory you created; for example, `adb -e push C:\busybox /data/local/busybox/busybox`.

4. Launch the ADB shell; for example, `adb —e shell`.

5. Navigate to the `BusyBox` directory; for example, `#cd /data/local/busybox`.

6. Change the permissions on the `BusyBox` file; for example, `#chmod 777 busybox`.

7. Install `BusyBox`; for example, `#./busybox —install`.

8. Export the path for ease of use. Note: You need to reset the PATH for each session; for example, `#export PATH=/data/busybox:$PATH`.

You can find out more about `BusyBox` at http://www.busybox.net.

Exploring Other ADB Commands

There are also handy ADB networking commands for configuring port forwarding and running PPP over USB, among other things. You can use port forwarding to connect the Java debugger to a specific JDWP process by ID. To get a list of all ADB commands, type

```
adb help
```

D

Eclipse IDE Tips and Tricks

The Eclipse IDE is the most popular development environment for Android developers. In this appendix, we provide a number of helpful tips and tricks for using Eclipse to develop Android applications quickly and effectively.

Organizing Your Eclipse Workspace

In this section, we provide a number of tips and tricks to help you organize your Eclipse workspace for optimum Android development.

Integrating with Source Control Services

Eclipse has the ability to integrate with many source control packages using add-ons or plug-ins. This allows Eclipse to manage checking out a file—making it writable—when you first start to edit a file, checking a file in, updating a file, showing a file's status, and a number of other tasks, depending on the support of the add-on.

> **Tip**
>
> Common source control add-ons are available for CVS, Subversion, Perforce, git, Mercurial, and many other packages.

Generally speaking, not all files are suitable for source control. For Android projects, any file with the bin and gen directories shouldn't be in source control. To exclude these generically within Eclipse, go to Preferences, Team, Ignored Resources. You can add file suffixes such as *.apk, *.ap_, and *.dex by clicking the Add Pattern button and adding one at a time. Conveniently, this applies to all integrated source control systems.

Repositioning Tabs Within Perspectives

Eclipse provides some pretty decent layouts with the default perspectives. However, not every one works the same way. We feel that some of the perspectives have poor default layouts for Android development and could use some improvement.

Tip

Experiment to find a tab layout that works well for you. Each perspective has its own layout, too, and the perspectives can be task oriented.

For instance, the Properties tab is usually found on the bottom of a perspective. For code, this works fine because this tab is only a few lines high. But for resource editing in Android, this doesn't work so well. Luckily, in Eclipse, this is easy to fix: Simply drag the tab by left-clicking and holding on the tab (the title) itself and dragging it to a new location, such as the vertical section on the right side of the Eclipse window. This provides the much-needed vertical space to see the dozens of properties often found there.

Tip

If you mess up a perspective or just want to start fresh, you can reset it by choosing Window, Reset Perspective.

Maximizing Windows

Sometimes, you might find that the editor window is just too small, especially with all the extra little metadata windows and tabs surrounding it. Try this: Double-click the tab of the source file that you want to edit. Boom! It's now nearly the full Eclipse window size! Just double-click to return it to normal.

Minimizing Windows

You can minimize entire sections, too. For instance, if you don't need the section at the bottom that usually has the console or the one to the left that usually has the file explorer view, you can use the minimize button in each section's upper-right corner. Use the button that looks like two little windows to restore it.

Viewing Windows Side by Side

Ever wish you could see two source files at once? Well, you can! Simply grab the tab for a source file and drag it either to the edge of the editor area or to the bottom. You then see a dark outline, showing where the file will be docked—either side-by-side with another file or above or below another file. This creates a parallel editor area where you can drag other file tabs, as well. You can repeat this multiple times to show 3, 4, or more files at once.

Viewing Two Sections of the Same File

Ever wish you could see two places at once in the same source file? You can! Right-click the tab for the file in question and choose New Editor. A second editor tab for the same file comes up. With the previous tip, you can now have two different views of the same file.

Closing Unwanted Tabs

Ever feel like you get far too many tabs open for files you're no longer editing? I do! There are a number of solutions to this problem. First, you can right-click a file tab and choose Close Others to close all other open files. You can quickly close specific tabs by middle-clicking on each tab. (This even works on a Mac with a mouse that can middle click, such as one with a scroll wheel.)

Keeping Windows Under Control

Finally, you can use the Eclipse setting that limits the number of open file editors:

1. Open Eclipse's Preferences dialog.

2. Expand General, choose Editors, and check Close Editors Automatically.

3. Edit the value in Number of Opened Editors Before Closing.

Eight seems to be a good number to use for the Number of Opened Editors Before Closing option to keep the clutter down but to have enough editors open to still get work done and have reference code open. Note also that if you check Open New Editor under When All Editors Are Dirty or Pinned, more files will be open if you're actively editing more than the number chosen. Thus, this setting doesn't affect productivity when you're editing a large number of files all at once but can keep things clean during most normal tasks.

Creating Custom Log Filters

Every Android log statement includes a tag. You can use these tags with filters defined in LogCat. To add a new filter, click the green plus sign button in the LogCat pane. Name the filter—perhaps using the tag name—and fill in the tag you want to use. Now there is another tab in LogCat that shows messages that contain this tag. In addition, you can create filters that display items by severity level.

Android convention has largely settled on creating tags based on the name of the class. You see this frequently in the code provided with this book. Note that we create a constant in each class with the same variable name to simplify each logging call. Here's an example:

```
public static final String DEBUG_TAG = "MyClassName";
```

This convention isn't a requirement, though. You could organize tags around specific tasks that span many activities or could use any other logical organization that works for your needs.

Writing Code in Java

In this section, we provide a number of tips and tricks to help you implement the code for your Android applications.

Using Auto-Complete

Auto-complete is a great feature that speeds up code entry. If this feature hasn't appeared for you yet or has gone away, you can bring it up by pressing Ctrl+spacebar. Auto-complete not only saves time in typing but can be used to jog your memory about methods—or to help you find a new method. You can scroll through all the methods of a class and even see the Javadocs associated with them. You can easily find static methods by using the class name or the instance variable name. You follow the class or variable name with a dot (and maybe Ctrl+spacebar) and then scroll through all the names. Then you can start typing the first part of a name to filter the results.

Formatting Code

Eclipse has a built-in mechanism for formatting Java code. Formatting code with a tool is useful for keeping the style consistent, applying a new style to old code, or matching styles with a different client or target (such as a book or an article).

To quickly format a small block of code, select the code and press Ctrl+Shift+F in Windows (or Command+Shift+F on a Mac). The code is formatted to the current settings. If no code is selected, the entire file is formatted. Occasionally, you need to select more code—such as an entire method—to get the indentation levels and brace matching correct.

The Eclipse formatting settings are found in the Properties pane under Java Code Style, Formatter. You can configure these settings on a per-project or workspace-wide basis. You can apply and modify dozens of rules to suit your own style.

Creating New Classes

You can quickly create a new class and corresponding source file by right-clicking the package to create it and choosing New, Class. Then you enter the class name, pick a superclass and interfaces, and choose whether to create default comments and method stubs for the superclass for constructors or abstract methods.

Creating New Methods

Along the same lines as creating new classes, you can quickly create method stubs by right-clicking a class or within a class in the editor and choosing Source, Override/Implement Methods. Then you choose the methods for which you're creating stubs, where to create the stubs, and whether to generate default comment blocks.

Organizing Imports

When referencing a class in your code for the first time, you can hover over the newly used class name and choose Import "*Classname*" (*package name*) to have Eclipse quickly add the proper import statement.

In addition, the Organize Imports command (Ctrl+Shift+O in Windows or Cmd+Shift+O on a Mac) causes Eclipse to automatically organize your imports. Eclipse removes unused imports and adds new ones for packages used but not already imported.

If there is any ambiguity in the name of a class during automatic import, such as with the Android Log class, Eclipse prompts you with the package to import. Finally, you can configure Eclipse to automatically organize the imports each time you save a file. This can be set for the entire workspace or for an individual project.

Configuring this for an individual project gives you better flexibility when you're working on multiple projects and don't want to make changes to some code, even if the changes are an improvement. To configure this, perform the following steps:

1. Right-click the project and choose Properties.

2. Expand Java Editor and choose Save Actions.

3. Check Enable Project Specific Settings, Perform the Selected Actions on Save, and Organize Imports.

Renaming Almost Anything

Eclipse's Rename tool is quite powerful. You can use it to rename variables, methods, class names, and more. Most often, you can simply right-click the item you want to rename and then choose Refactor, Rename. Alternatively, after selecting the item, you can press Ctrl+Alt+R in Windows (or Cmd+Alt+R on a Mac) to begin the renaming process. If you are renaming a top-level class in a file, the filename has to be changed as well. Eclipse usually handles the source control changes required to do this, if the file is being tracked by source control. If Eclipse can determine that the item is in reference to the identically named item being renamed, all instances of the name are renamed as well. Occasionally, this even means comments are updated with the new name. Quite handy!

Refactoring Code

Do you find yourself writing a whole bunch of repeating sections of code that look, for instance, like the following?

```
TextView nameCol = new TextView(this);
nameCol.setTextColor(getResources().getColor(R.color.title_color));
nameCol.setTextSize(getResources().
getDimension(R.dimen.help_text_size));
nameCol.setText(scoreUserName);
table.addView(nameCol);
```

This code sets text color, text size, and text. If you've written two or more blocks that look like this, your code could benefit from refactoring. Eclipse provides two useful tools—Extract Local Variable and Extract Method—to speed this task and make it almost trivial.

Using the Extract Local Variable Tool

Follow these steps to use the Extract Local Variable tool:

1. Select the expression `getResources().getColor(R.color.title_color)`.

2. Right-click and choose Refactor, Extract Local Variable (or press Ctrl+Alt+L).

3. In the dialog that appears, enter a name for the variable and leave the Replace All Occurrences check box selected. Then click OK and watch the magic happen.

4. Repeat steps 1–3 for the text size.

The result should now look like this:

```
int textColor = getResources().getColor(R.color.title_color);
float textSize = getResources().getDimension(R.dimen.help_text_size);
TextView nameCol = new TextView(this);
nameCol.setTextColor(textColor);
nameCol.setTextSize(textSize);
nameCol.setText(scoreUserName);
table.addView(nameCol);
```

All repeated sections of the last five lines also have this change made. How convenient is that?

Using the Extract Method Tool

Now you're ready for the second tool. Follow these steps to use the Extract Method tool:

1. Select all five lines of the first block of code.

2. Right-click and choose Refactor, Extract Method (or choose Ctrl+Alt+M).

3. Name the method and edit the variable names anything you want. (Move them up or down, too, if desired.) Then click OK and watch the magic happen.

By default, the new method is below your current one. If the other blocks of code are actually identical, meaning the statements of the other blocks must be in the exact same order, the types are all the same, and so on, they will also be replaced with calls to this new method! You can see this in the count of additional occurrences shown in the dialog for the Extract Method tool. If that count doesn't match what you expect, check that the code follows exactly the same pattern. Now you have code that looks like the following:

```
addTextToRowWithValues(newRow, scoreUserName, textColor, textSize);
```

It is easier to work with this code than with the original code, and it was created with almost no typing! If you had ten instances before refactoring, you've saved a lot of time by using a useful Eclipse feature.

Reorganizing Code

Sometimes, formatting code isn't enough to make it clean and readable. Over the course of developing a complex activity, you might end up with a number of embedded classes and methods strewn about the file. A quick Eclipse trick comes to the rescue: With the file in question open, make sure the outline view is also visible.

Simply click and drag methods and classes around in the outline view to place them in a suitable logical order. Do you have a method that is only called from a certain class but available to all? Just drag it in to that class. This works with almost anything listed in the outline, including classes, methods, and variables.

Providing Javadoc-Style Documentation

Regular code comments are useful (when done right). Comments in Javadoc style appear in code completion dialogs and other places, thus making them even more useful. To quickly add a Javadoc comment to a method or class, simply press Ctrl+Shift+J in Windows (or Cmd+Alt+J on a Mac). Alternatively, you can choose Source, Generate Element Comment to prefill certain fields in the Javadoc, such as parameter names and author, thus speeding the creation of this style of comment.

Resolving Mysterious Build Errors

Occasionally, you might find that Eclipse is finding build errors where there were none just moments before. In such a situation, you can try a couple quick Eclipse tricks.

First, try refreshing the project: Simply right-click the project and choose Refresh or press F5. If this doesn't work, try deleting the R.java file, which you can find under the gen directory under the name of the particular package being compiled. (Don't worry: This file is created during every compile.) If the Compile Automatically option is enabled, the file is re-created. Otherwise, you need to compile the project again.

Finally, you can try cleaning the project. To do this, choose Project, Clean and choose the projects you want to clean. Eclipse removes all temporary files and then rebuilds the project(s). If the project was an NDK project, don't forget to recompile the native code.

Note

Send us your own tips or tricks for Android development in Eclipse! You can email them to androidwirelessdev+awad2e@gmail.com.

The SQLite Quick-Start Guide

The Android System allows individual applications to have private SQLite databases in which to store their application data. This Quick-Start Guide is not a complete documentation of the SQLite commands. Instead, it is designed to get you up and running with common tasks. The first part of this appendix introduces the features of the `sqlite3` command-line tool. We then provide an in-depth database example using many common SQLite commands. See the online SQLite documentation (www.sqlite.org) for a complete list of features, functionality, and limitations of SQLite.

Exploring Common Tasks with SQLite

SQLite is a lightweight and compact, yet powerful, embedded relational database engine available as public domain. It is fast and has a small footprint, making it perfect for phone system use. Instead of the heavyweight server-based databases such as Oracle and Microsoft SQL Server, each SQLite database is within a self-contained single file on disk.

Android applications store their private databases (SQLite or otherwise) under a special application directory:

```
/data/data/<application package name>/databases/<databasename>
```

For example, the database for the `PetTracker` application provided in this book is found at

```
/data/data/com.androidbook.PetTracker/databases/pet_tracker.db
```

The database file format is standard and can be moved across platforms. You can use the Dalvik Debug Monitor Service (DDMS) File Explorer to pull the database file and inspect it with third-party tools, if you like.

> **Tip**
>
> Application-specific SQLite databases are private files accessible only from within that application. To expose application data to other applications, the application must become a content provider. Content providers are covered in Chapter 11, "Sharing Data Between Applications with Content Providers."

Using the `sqlite3` Command-Line Interface

In addition to programmatic access to create and use SQLite databases from within your applications, which we discuss in Chapter 10, "Using Android Data and Storage APIs," you can also interact with the database using the familiar command-line `sqlite3` tool, which is accessible via the Android Debug Bridge (ADB) remote shell.

The command-line interface for SQLite, called `sqlite3`, is exposed using the ADB tool, which we cover in Appendix C, "The Android Debug Bridge Quick-Start Guide."

Launching the ADB Shell

You must launch the ADB shell interface on the emulator or device (if it is rooted) to use the `sqlite3` commands. If only one Android device (or emulator) is running, you can connect by simply typing

```
c:\>adb shell
```

If you want to connect to a specific instance of the emulator, you can connect by typing

```
adb —s <serialNumber> shell
```

For example, to connect to the emulator at port 5554, you would use the following command:

```
adb —s emulator-5554 shell
```

For more information on how to determine the serial number of an emulator or device instance, please see Appendix C.

Connecting to a SQLite Database

Now you can connect to the Android application database of your choice by name. For example, to connect to the database we created with the PetTracker application, we would connect like this:

```
c:\>adb -e shell
# sqlite3 /data/data/com.androidbook.PetTracker/databases/pet_tracker.db
SQLite version 3.6.22
Enter ".help" for instructions
sqlite>
```

Now we have the `sqlite3` command prompt, where we can issue commands. You can exit the interface at any time by typing

```
sqlite>.quit
```

or

```
sqlite>.exit
```

Commands for interacting with the `sqlite3` program start with a dot (.) to differentiate them from SQL commands you can execute directly from the command line. This syntax might be different from other programs you are familiar with (for example, `mysql` commands).

Warning

Most Android devices don't allow running the `sqlite3` command as emulators do. Rooted devices do allow this command.

Exploring Your Database

You can use the `sqlite3` commands to explore what your database looks like and interact with it. You can

- List available databases
- List available tables
- View all the indices on a given table
- Show the database schema

Listing Available Databases

You can list the names and file locations attached to this database instance. Generally, you have your main database and a temp database, which contains temp tables. You can list this information by typing

```
sqlite> .databases
seq name file
--- ---- -------------------------------------------------
0   main /data/data/com.androidbook.PetTracker/databases/...
1   temp
sqlite>
```

Listing Available Tables

You can list the tables in the database you connect to by typing

```
sqlite> .tables
android_metadata table_pets        table_pettypes
sqlite>
```

Listing Indices of a Table

You can list the indices of a given table by typing

```
sqlite>.indices table_pets
```

Listing the Database Schema of a Table

You can list the schema of a given table by typing

```
sqlite>.schema table_pets
CREATE TABLE table_pets (_id INTEGER PRIMARY KEY
AUTOINCREMENT,pet_name TEXT,pet_type_id INTEGER);
sqlite>
```

Listing the Database Schema of a Database

You can list the schemas for the entire database by typing

```
sqlite>.schema
CREATE TABLE android_metadata (locale TEXT);
CREATE TABLE table_pets (_id INTEGER PRIMARY KEY
AUTOINCREMENT,pet_name TEXT,pet_type_id INTEGER);
CREATE TABLE table_pettypes (_id INTEGER PRIMARY KEY
AUTOINCREMENT,pet_type TEXT);
sqlite>
```

Importing and Exporting the Database and Its Data

You can use the `sqlite3` commands to import and export database data and the schema and interact with it. You can

- Send command output to a file instead of to STDOUT (the screen)
- Dump the database contents as a SQL script (so you can re-create it later)
- Execute SQL scripts from files
- Import data into the database from a file

Note

The file paths are on the Android device, not your computer. You need to find a directory on the Android device in which you have permission to read and write files. For example, `/data/local/tmp/` is a shared directory.

Sending Output to a File

Often, you want the sqlite3 command results to pipe to a file instead of to the screen. To do this, you can just type the `output` command followed by the file path to which the results should be written on the Android system. For example

```
sqlite>.output /data/local/tmp/dump.sql
```

Dumping Database Contents

You can create a SQL script to create tables and their values by using the `dump` command. The `dump` command creates a transaction, which includes calls to CREATE TABLE and INSERT to populate the database with data. This command can take an optional table name or dump the whole database.

Tip

The dump command is a great way to do a full archival backup of your database.

For example, the following commands pipe the dump output for the `table_pets` table to a file, and then sets the output mode back to the console:

```
sqlite>.output /data/local/tmp/dump.sql
sqlite>.dump table_pets
sqlite>.output stdout
```

You can then use DDMS and the File Explorer to pull the SQL file off the Android file system. The resulting `dump.sql` file looks like this:

```
BEGIN TRANSACTION;
CREATE TABLE table_pets (
_id INTEGER PRIMARY KEY AUTOINCREMENT,
pet_name TEXT,
pet_type_id INTEGER);

INSERT INTO "table_pets" VALUES(1,'Rover',9);
INSERT INTO "table_pets" VALUES(2,'Garfield',8);
COMMIT;
```

Executing SQL Scripts from Files

You can create SQL script files and run them through the console. These scripts must be on the Android file system. For example, let's put a SQL script called `myselect.sql` in the `/data/local/tmp/` directory of the Android file system. The file has two lines:

```
SELECT * FROM table_pettypes;
SELECT * FROM table_pets;
```

We can then run this SQL script by typing

```
sqlite>.read /data/local/tmp/myselect.sql
```

You see the query results on the command line.

Importing Data

You can import formatted data using the import and separator commands. Files such as CSV use commas for delimiters, but other data formats might use spaces or tabs. You specify the delimiter using the separator command. You specify the file to import using the import command.

For example, put a CSV script called `some_data.csv` in the `/data/local/tmp/` directory of the Android file system. The file has four lines. It is a comma-delimited file of pet type IDs and pet type names:

```
18,frog
19,turkey
20,piglet
21,great white shark
```

You can then import this data into the `table_pettypes` table, which has two columns: an `_id` column and a pet type name. To import this data, type the following command:

```
sqlite>.separator ,
sqlite>.import /data/local/tmp/some_data.csv table_pettypes
```

Now, if you query the table, you see it has four new rows.

Executing SQL Commands on the Command Line

You can also execute raw SQL commands on the command line. Simply type the SQL command, making sure it ends with a semicolon (;). If you use queries, you might want to change the output mode to column so that query results are easier to read (in columns) and the headers (column names) are printed. For example

```
sqlite> .mode column
sqlite> .header on
sqlite> select * from table_pettypes WHERE _id < 11;
_id         pet_type
----------  ----------
8           bunny
9           fish
10          dog
sqlite>
```

You're not limited to queries, either. You can execute any SQL command you see in a SQL script on the command line if you like.

Tip

We've found it helpful to use the `sqlite3` command line to test SQL queries if our Android SQL queries with `QueryBuilder` are not behaving. This is especially true of more complicated queries.

You can also control the width of each column (so text fields don't truncate) using the `width` command. For example, the following command prints query results with the first column 5 characters wide (often an ID column), followed by a second column 50 characters wide (text column).

```
sqlite> .width 5 50
```

Warning

SQLite keeps the database schema in a special table called `sqlite_master`. You should consider this table read-only. SQLite stores temporary tables in a special table called `sqlite_temp_master`, which is also a temporary table.

Using Other `sqlite3` Commands

A complete list of `sqlite3` commands is available by typing

```
sqlite> .help
```

Understanding SQLite Limitations

SQLite is powerful, but it has several important limitations compared to traditional SQL Server implementations, such as the following:

- SQLite is not a substitute for a high-powered, server-driven database.
- Being file-based, the database is meant to be accessed in a serial, not a concurrent, manner. Think "single user"—the Android application. It has some concurrency features, but they are limited.
- Access control is maintained by file permissions, not database user permissions.
- Referential integrity is not maintained. For example, FOREIGN KEY constraints are parsed (for example, in CREATE TABLE) but not enforced automatically. However, using TRIGGER functions can enforce them.
- ALTER TABLE support is limited. You can use only RENAME TABLE and ADD COLUMN. You may not drop or alter columns or perform any other such operations. This can make database upgrades a bit tricky.
- TRIGGER support is limited. You cannot use `FOR EACH STATEMENT` or `INSTEAD OF`. You cannot create recursive triggers.
- You cannot nest TRANSACTION operations.
- VIEWs are read-only.
- You cannot use RIGHT OUTER JOINs or FULL OUTER JOINs.
- SQLite does not support STORED PROCEDUREs or auditing.
- The built-in FUNCTIONs of the SQL language are limited.
- See the SQLite documentation for limitations on the maximum database size, table size, and row size. The Omitted SQL page is very helpful (http://www.sqlite.org/omitted.html), as is the Unsupported SQL Wiki (http://www.sqlite.org/cvstrac/wiki?p=UnsupportedSql).

Learning by Example: A Student Grade Database

Let's work through a student "Grades" database to show standard SQL commands to create and work with a database. Although you can create this database using the `sqlite3` command line, we suggest using the Android application to create the empty Grades database, so that it is created in a standard "Android" way.

The setup: The purpose of the database is to keep track of each student's test results for a specific class. In this example, each student's grade is calculated from their performance on

- Four quizzes (each weighted as 10% of overall grade)
- One midterm (weighted as 25% of overall grade)
- One final (weighted as 35% of overall grade)

All tests are graded on a scale of 0–100.

Designing the Student Grade Database Schema

The Grades database has three tables: Students, Tests, and TestResults.

The Students table contains student information. The Tests table contains information about each test and how much it counts toward the student's overall grade. Finally, all students' test results are stored in the TestResults table.

Setting Column Datatypes

`sqlite3` has support for the following common datatypes for columns:

- INTEGER (signed integers)
- REAL (floating point values)
- TEXT (UTF-8 or UTF-16 string; encoded using database encoding)
- BLOB (data chunk)

Tip

Do not store files such as images in the database. Instead, store images as files in the application file directory and store the filename or URI path in the database.

Creating Simple Tables with AUTOINCREMENT

First, let's create the Students table. We want a student id to reference each student. We can make this the primary key and set its AUTOINCREMENT attribute. We also want the first and last name of each student, and we require these fields (no nulls). Here's our SQL statement:

```
CREATE TABLE Students (
id INTEGER PRIMARY KEY AUTOINCREMENT,
fname TEXT NOT NULL,
lname TEXT NOT NULL );
```

For the Tests table, we want a test id to reference each test or quiz, much like the Students table. We also want a friendly name for each test and a weight value for how much each test counts for the student's final grade (as a percentage). Here's our SQL statement:

```
CREATE TABLE Tests (
id INTEGER PRIMARY KEY AUTOINCREMENT,
testname TEXT,
weight REAL DEFAULT .10 CHECK (weight<=1));
```

Inserting Data into Tables

Before we move on, let's look at several examples of how to add data to these tables. To add a record to the Students table, you need to specify the column names and the values in order. For example

```
INSERT into Students
(fname, lname)
VALUES
('Harry', 'Potter');
```

Now, we're going to add a few more records to this table for Ron and Hermione. At the same time, we need to add a bunch of records to the Tests table. First, we add the Midterm, which counts for 25 percent of the grade:

```
INSERT into Tests
(testname, weight)
VALUES
('Midterm', .25);
```

Then we add a couple quizzes, which use the default weight of 10 percent:

```
INSERT into Tests (testname) VALUES ('Quiz 1');
```

Finally, we add a Final test worth 35 percent of the total grade.

Querying Tables for Results with SELECT

How do we know the data we've added is in the table? Well, that's easy. We simply query for all rows in a table using a SELECT:

```
SELECT * FROM Tests;
```

This returns all records in the Tests table:

```
id      testname          weight
-----   ---------------   ------
1       Midterm           0.25
2       Quiz 1            0.1
3       Quiz 2            0.1
4       Quiz 3            0.1
5       Quiz 4            0.1
6       Final             0.35
```

Now, ideally, we want the weights to add up to 1.0. Let's check using the SUM aggregate function to sum all the weight values in the table:

```
SELECT SUM(weight) FROM Tests;
```

This returns the sum of all weight values in the Tests table:

```
SUM(weight)
-----------
1.0
```

We can also create our own columns and alias them. For example, we can create a column alias called `fullname` that is a calculated column: It's the student's first and last names concatenated using the || concatenation.

```
SELECT fname||' '|| lname AS fullname, id FROM Students;
```

This gives us the following results:

```
fullname        id
-----------     --
Harry Potter    1
Ron Weasley     2
Hermione Granger 3
```

Using Foreign Keys and Composite Primary Keys

Now that we have our students and tests all set up, let's create the TestResults table. This is a more complicated table. It's a list of student-test pairings, along with the score.

The TestResults table pairs up student IDs from the Students table with test IDs from the Tests table. Columns, which link to other tables in this way, are often called foreign keys. We want unique student-test pairings, so we create a composite primary key from the student and test foreign keys. Finally, we enforce that the scores are whole numbers between 0 and 100. No extra credit or retaking tests in this class!

```
CREATE TABLE TestResults (
studentid INTEGER REFERENCES Students(id),
testid INTEGER REFERENCES Tests(id),
score INTEGER CHECK (score<=100 AND score>=0),
PRIMARY KEY (studentid, testid));
```

Tip

SQLite does not enforce foreign key constraints, but you can set them up anyway and enforce the constraints by creating triggers. For an example of using triggers to enforce foreign key constraints in SQL, check out the FullDatabase project provided on the book website for Chapter 10.

Now it's time to insert some data into this table. Let's say Harry Potter received an 82 percent on the Midterm:

```
INSERT into TestResults
(studentid, testid, score)
VALUES
(1,1,82);
```

Now let's input the rest of the student's scores. Harry is a good student. Ron is not a good student, and Hermione aces every test (of course). When they're all added, we can list them. We can do a SELECT ★ to get all columns, or we can specify the columns we want explicitly like this:

```
SELECT studentid, testid, score FROM TestResults;
```

Here are the results from this query:

```
studentid  testid    score
---------- ---------- -----
1          1          82
1          2          88
1          3          78
1          4          90
1          5          85
1          6          94
2          1          10
2          2          90
2          3          50
2          4          55
2          5          45
2          6          65
3          6          100
3          5          100
3          4          100
3          3          100
3          2          100
3          1          100
```

Altering and Updating Data in Tables

Ron's not a good student, and yet he received a 90 percent on Quiz #1. This is suspicious, so as the teacher, we check the actual paper test to see if we made a recording mistake. He actually earned 60 percent. Now we need to update the table to reflect the correct score:

```
UPDATE TestResults
SET score=60
WHERE studentid=2 AND testid=2;
```

You can delete rows from a table using the DELETE function. For example, to delete the record we just updated:

```
DELETE FROM TestResults WHERE studentid=2 AND testid=2;
```

You can delete all rows in a table by not specifying the WHERE clause:

```
DELETE FROM TestResults;
```

Querying Multiple Tables Using JOIN

Now that we have all our data in our database, it is time to use it. The preceding listing was not easy for a human to read. It would be much nicer to see a listing with the names of the students and names of the tests instead of their IDs.

Combining data is often handled by performing a JOIN with multiple table sources; there are different kinds of JOINS. When you work with multiple tables, you need to specify which table a column belongs to (especially with all these different id columns). You can refer to columns by their column name or by their table name, then a dot (.), and then the column name.

Let's relist the grades again, only this time, include the name of the test and the name of the student. Also, we limit our results only to the score for the Final (`test id 6`):

```
SELECT
Students.fname||' '|| Students.lname AS StudentName,
Tests.testname,
TestResults.score
FROM TestResults
JOIN Students
     ON (TestResults.studentid=Students.id)
JOIN Tests
     ON (TestResults.testid=Tests.id)
WHERE testid=6;
```

which gives us the following results (you could leave off the WHERE to get all tests):

```
StudentName          testname        score
------------------   --------------  -----
Harry Potter         Final           94
Ron Weasley          Final           65
Hermione Granger     Final           100
```

Using Calculated Columns

Hermione always likes to know where she stands. When she comes to ask what her final grade is likely to be, we can perform a single query to show all her results and calculate the weighted scores of all her results:

```
SELECT
Students.fname||' '|| Students.lname AS StudentName,
Tests.testname,
Tests.weight,
TestResults.score,
(Tests.weight*TestResults.score) AS WeightedScore
FROM TestResults
JOIN Students
     ON (TestResults.studentid=Students.id)
```

```
JOIN Tests
      ON (TestResults.testid=Tests.id)
WHERE studentid=3;
```

This gives us predictable results:

```
StudentName         testname weight score WeightedScore
----------------    -------- ------ ----- -------------
Hermione Granger    Midterm  0.25   100       25.0
Hermione Granger    Quiz 1   0.1    100       10.0
Hermione Granger    Quiz 2   0.1    100       10.0
Hermione Granger    Quiz 3   0.1    100       10.0
Hermione Granger    Quiz 4   0.1    100       10.0
Hermione Granger    Final    0.35   100       35.0
```

We can just add up the Weighted Scores and be done, but we can also do it via the query:

```
SELECT
Students.fname||' '|| Students.lname AS StudentName,
SUM((Tests.weight*TestResults.score)) AS TotalWeightedScore
FROM TestResults
JOIN Students
      ON (TestResults.studentid=Students.id)
JOIN Tests
      ON (TestResults.testid=Tests.id)
WHERE studentid=3;
```

Here we get a nice consolidated listing:

```
StudentName        TotalWeightedScore
---------------    ------------------
Hermione Granger 100.0
```

If we wanted to get all our students' grades, we need to use the GROUP BY clause. Also, let's order them so the best students are at the top of the list:

```
SELECT
Students.fname||' '|| Students.lname AS StudentName,
SUM((Tests.weight*TestResults.score)) AS TotalWeightedScore
FROM TestResults
JOIN Students
      ON (TestResults.studentid=Students.id)
JOIN Tests
      ON (TestResults.testid=Tests.id)
GROUP BY TestResults.studentid
ORDER BY TotalWeightedScore DESC;
```

This makes our job as teacher almost too easy, but at least we're saving trees by using a digital grade book.

```
StudentName              TotalWeightedScore
------------------------ ------------------
Hermione Granger         100.0
Harry Potter             87.5
Ron Weasley              46.25
```

Using Subqueries for Calculated Columns

You can also include queries within other queries. For example, you can list each Student and a count of how many tests they "passed," in which passing is getting a score higher than 60, as in the following:

```
SELECT
Students.fname||' '|| Students.lname AS StudentName,
Students.id AS StudentID,
(SELECT COUNT(*)
FROM TestResults
WHERE TestResults.studentid=Students.id
AND TestResults.score>60)
AS TestsPassed
FROM Students;
```

Again, we see that Ron needs a tutor:

```
StudentName      StudentID TestsPassed
-----------      --------- -----------
Harry Potter     1         6
Ron Weasley      2         1
Hermione Granger 3         6
```

Deleting Tables

You can always delete tables using the DROP TABLE command. For example, to delete the TestResults table, use the following SQL command:

```
DROP TABLE TestResults;
```

The Android Quick-Start Guide for Beginners

This appendix contains a number of quick tips for beginners getting started developing Android applications. It discusses how to install the Android SDK and tools and how to get up to speed with the essential development tools and writing applications, including the Top Ten Guidelines for Writing Successful Android Applications.

Configuring Your Development Environment

To write Android applications, you must configure your programming environment for development. The Java Development Kit (JDK), the Eclipse development environment, and the Android SDK are available for download on the web at no cost.

To configure your development environment, you must

1. Verify that your computer meets the system requirements for Android development.

2. Install a supported version of the Java Development Kit (JDK).

3. Install a supported development environment, such as Eclipse.

4. Review the Android License Agreement and install the Android SDK Starter Package on your development machine. You can download this package at http://developer.android.com/sdk/.

5. Install the Android Development Tools (ADT) plug-in for Eclipse. This step is completed from within Eclipse as a software update.

6. Use the Android SDK and AVD Manager (accessible from within Eclipse using the ADT plug-in) to download and install the appropriate Android platform versions and other components.

7. Configure your development computer for USB debugging. In some cases, you may need to install a USB driver in order to properly connect your computer to your Android device.

8. Configure your Android device for development purposes.

Tip

You can find the most recent and accurate list of system requirements for Android development at http://developer.android.com/sdk/requirements.html.

You can also find more information about configuring your development environment and using the tools in Chapter 2, "Setting Up Your Android Development Environment."

Verifying System Requirements

You can develop Android applications on the following operating systems:

- Windows XP (32-bit) or Vista (32-bit or 64-bit)
- Mac OS X 10.5.8 or later (x86 only)
- Linux (tested on Linux Ubuntu 8.04 LTS, Hardy Heron)

You will need several gigabytes of space to install all the tools necessary to develop Android applications.

Installing the Java Development Kit

You can develop Android applications using JDK 5 or 6. You can download the latest version of the Java Standard Edition JDK at Oracle's website (http://www.oracle.com/technetwork/java/javase/downloads/index.html).

Warning

The Java Runtime Environment (JRE) alone is not sufficient to develop Android applications. You need the full JDK.

Installing the Eclipse Development Environment for Java

Many developers use the popular Eclipse Integrated Development Environment (IDE) for Android development. The following Eclipse versions work well for Android development:

- Eclipse IDE for Java EE Developers
- Eclipse IDE for Java Developers
- Eclipse Classic (version 3.5 or higher)

You can download Eclipse at http://www.eclipse.org/downloads/.

Note

If you decide not to use Eclipse, you can find more information about other development tools for Android development at http://developer.android.com/guide/developing/other-ide.html.

Installing the Android SDK

Next, you need to install the SDK to develop Android applications. The Android SDK includes the Android JAR file (Android application framework classes) and Android documentation, tools, and sample code. The steps to install the Android SDK vary substantially depending upon factors such as which operating system you install to, which version of the SDK you install, and which IDE you use.

We highly recommend you follow the steps provided in the detailed instructions available online at the Android developer website: http://developer.android.com/sdk/installing.html. This website includes information on troubleshooting your installation on various platforms and is updated whenever a new version of the Android SDK is released.

Installing the Android Plug-In for Eclipse (ADT)

The Android plug-in for Eclipse (ADT) enables seamless integration with many of the Android development tools. To install the ADT, you must launch Eclipse and install a custom software update. Software updates are handled in different ways depending upon which version of Eclipse you are using. After installing the plug-in, configure the Android settings within the Eclipse preferences. For step-by-step instructions, see http://developer.android.com/sdk/eclipse-adt.html.

Downloading Android SDK Components

The Android SDK is componentized. This means that you can download each version of Android separately and target specific versions, such as 1.6 or 2.2. It also means that when a new version of Android is released (which happens pretty frequently), you can easily add the new version to your target platforms.

The Android SDK components installed on your development machine are managed using a tool called the Android SDK and AVD Manager. The simplest way to access this tool is by using the Android plug-in for Eclipse (ADT) that you installed in the previous step. You can launch this tool from within Eclipse. You can find detailed instructions on how to add components using the Android SDK and AVD Manager at http://developer.android.com/sdk/adding-components.html.

For this book, we recommend installing most, if not all, of the components available for download, including

- The SDK Tools and updates (if available, most are installed as part of the Starter package)
- All Android platforms, especially those used by your Android devices
- SDK add-ons, including Google API add-ons (in order to use Google Maps)

- The sample applications
- The platform documentation
- The USB Driver (needed for Windows installations only)

You're better off installing too much than struggling later on to determine out why something isn't working, only to find that you forgot to install a necessary component.

Upgrading the Android Software Development Kit

The Android SDK is always under development; inevitably, a new version of the Android SDK will be released. Use the Android SDK and AVD Manager to download the latest and greatest the platform has to offer. A new version of the Android SDK may involve additions, updates, and removals of libraries; package, class or method name changes; and updated tools. Each new version of the SDK receives a new API level. However, sometimes there are revisions that do not change the API level.
For each new version of the Android SDK, the following documentation is provided:

- **Platform Highlights:** A brief description of major changes to the SDK for users and developers
- **An API Differences Report:** A complete list of specific changes to the SDK
- **Release Notes:** A list of known issues with the SDK (usually found in the /docs directory on your Android SDK installation on your development machine)

These documents are essential reading for the Android developer. In theory, updated SDKs are backwards compatible, though this is not always the case. These documents can provide an important head's up on new features and help you identify application problems before users' devices receive the upgrade.

Tip

Looking for an old or unsupported version of the Android SDK? Check the Android SDK Archives available at http://developer.android.com/sdk/older_releases.html or expand the "Older Platforms" section in the navigation bar on the left at http://developer.android.com/sdk/index.html.

Problems with the Android Software Development Kit

You might occasionally come across problems with the SDK. If you think you've found a problem, you can find a list of open issues and their status at the Android project Issue Tracker website at http://code.google.com/p/android/issues/list.

You can report bugs for review by the Android team at http://source.android.com/source/report-bugs.html. Always check if there is an existing open bug before creating a new one. If there is, add your information to that defect. When creating a new defect, include as much information as possible when reporting a potential bug. (Sample code often helps.)

Configuring Your Android Hardware for Debugging

Your Android device must be configured for development purposes. These settings are configured on the device. From the Home screen of the device, select Menu, Settings, Applications to find the development settings. You should make the following changes to your device settings for debugging purposes:

- Enable Unknown Sources: This option allows your device to accept application packages from your development machine, as opposed to just those published through the Android Market. Not all handsets have this option.
- Under the Development menu, enable your device for debugging via a USB connection.
- Under the Development menu, consider checking the Stay Awake option to keep your device screen active while charging. This keeps your device from sleeping while you're working.
- Under the Development menu, consider checking the Allow Mock Locations option if you are developing any applications that use location-based services.

Configuring Your Operating System for Device Debugging

Finally, you might need to configure your development machine so that it can connect to your Android device via USB. If you're developing on a Windows operating system, you need to install a USB driver to connect to your device. The driver is available at http://dl. google.com/android/android_usb_windows.zip.

The Android Tools at a Glance

Let's take a quick tour of the tools you will use on a regular basis when developing Android applications. These are the core utilities you need regularly and those you should focus on when you're just getting started:

- **Eclipse:** The IDE is where you spend most of your time creating Android projects, writing Java code, designing XML resource files, and compiling and deploying your applications to emulators and devices.
- **The emulator:** The emulator is a software representation of an Android device that runs on your development machine. You can deploy, run, and test your applications on the emulator, which can be configured to mimic different types of devices.
- **Android devices:** The emulator just pretends to be a real device. You need to test your apps on real hardware from time to time to make sure all is well. Use a USB cable to debug application code right from the device, just like you do with the emulator.

- **The Android SDK and AVD Manager:** Accessed from within Eclipse (provided you installed the ADT plug-in) or from the command line, this utility keeps track of which Android versions you have installed on your development machine, but it also keeps track of your Android Virtual Devices (AVDs). AVDs dictate what type of device your emulator is pretending to be.

- **The Android SDK documentation:** We always have a web browser open to http:// developer.android.com/reference. Here you can search for and learn about specific classes, interfaces, methods, and more. The Dev Guide and Resources tabs are also very helpful. Offline documentation can be downloaded through the Android SDK and AVD Manager and usually starts with the name, "Documentation for Android SDK," and finishes with the specific level and revision.

As with any new tool, expect to spend a couple of days becoming comfortable before things run really smoothly. Take heart that the Android tools are, in our rather informed opinion, some of the best available on any mobile platform. Unfortunately, sometimes that's not saying much. If you're from a desktop or web development background, you might find some tools rather utilitarian and clunky, but look on the bright side: With each new release, the tools tend to improve.

Tip

When you're about to pull out your hair due to frustration, remind yourself that all the tools you're using are free. We think it helps...at least a little.

Android Terms: A Whimsical Glossary

When you're first getting started with Android development, it's easy to get swamped in the terminology. Here we provide a greatly simplified definition of some key terminology, which might help you get through the initially steep learning curve:

- **Mobile application development:** Writing apps for mobile platforms such as Android, iPhone, BlackBerry, and so on. This book covers Android topics.

- **Android hardware, device, handset, phone:** A device running the Android operating system; for example, a mobile phone or Internet tablet. Many developers use these terms interchangeably. It's worthwhile to remember that not all Android devices are phones.

- **Carrier, operator:** Companies that provide wireless service to consumers, and often sell them the devices to use that service; for example, Verizon, Orange, AT&T, China Mobile, and other telecoms.

- **Manufacturer, OEM:** Companies that design and manufacture the devices themselves; for example, Motorola, Samsung, LG, and so on.

- **Third parties, developers, content developers:** You and I, those wild and crazy guys and girls who want to develop apps for the world.
- **Wireless, service:** A connection without being plugged into a wall. The service usually provided by an operator or carrier, sometimes using tall metal towers that resemble trees.
- **The cloud, cloud-based services:** The Internet. Services that use the network, often relying on specific protocols.
- **Application servers:** Machines on the 'net that store and manipulate app data, as well as provide services to applications. Frequently used by social applications, applications with broad multi-platform support, and applications that require heavy processing power not available on mobile (the mobile app offloads hard work to the server; the server does it and sends results back to the mobile device; the user doesn't know the difference).

And now for some terminology from the Android SDK:

- **Java:** OK, if you don't know what Java is, you're probably moving too fast. Find yourself a good book on Java and learn about object-oriented programming and Java syntax before you embark on a career in Android mobile software development.
- **SDK, library, application framework:** A bunch of classes (in this case, for Android, in Java) and tools that enable third-party developers to develop apps for a platform.
- **Emulator:** Software that pretends to be a device; helpful for debugging.
- **Resource:** Some application data, such as a picture, a sound file, or a string of text, used by your application.
- **Android manifest file:** An XML file that defines the identity of an application, including its name, description, what activities it has, what permissions it uses, and so on.
- **Application package:** Application code and resources, packaged into a format called an .apk file, which the Android operating system understands and can install on a device.
- **Activity:** The class within the Android SDK that is the building block upon which all apps are written. An Activity generally controls a single screen or feature of an app. An app transitions from one activity to the next, each with a specific purpose.
- **Intent:** The class within the Android SDK that provides glue in order to transition between activities. Use intents to launch other activities within your application, or within other applications entirely!
- **Content provider:** An application can expose some of its data for use by other applications. Apps can be content providers (share their data) or use content providers (access other apps' data)

Ten Steps to Successful Android Applications

Now that you have your development environment up and running, and you have some idea of what you've signed yourself up for (fame and riches!), here are some important considerations to keep in mind as you begin to develop Android applications for the first time:

1. **Master the tools:** Brush up on your Java knowledge. Familiarize yourself with Eclipse and the Android SDK tools. For now, this is the best programming environment available for Android development, especially for beginners.

2. **Design for Android:** Android users expect the Android user experience. Don't try to mimic the behavior or look-and-feel of another mobile platform (such as the iPhone). Familiarize yourself with common Android user interface guidelines (for example, how the Back, Menu, and Search keys function).

3. **Develop for Android:** Use standard and well-accepted Android development paradigms. Understand how the Android platform works and take advantage of its benefits. Leverage common technologies that are widely available across many platforms, such as OpenGL ES, SQLite, XML, cloud-based data services, and so on.

4. **Ensure application interoperability:** Applications should use common intents to ensure tight integration with the underlying operating system. Create home screen app widgets and expose application data using content providers, live folders, and live wallpapers as appropriate to extend applications beyond traditional boundaries.

5. **Pay attention to the application lifecycle:** Android applications must be responsive, or you risk having the Android operating system kill your application. Spend the time to understand the application lifecycle, especially in terms of starting activities, pausing and resuming, and exiting. Avoid time-intensive processing on the UI thread; instead, perform these tasks asynchronously.

6. **Don't abuse device resources:** Mobile devices rely on resources such as the battery. Don't waste these resources or use them too aggressively. Enable users to adjust settings, such as network polling frequencies, to suit their needs and their device limitations.

7. **Don't violate the users' trust:** Treat users' personal data with respect. Use tried-and-true encryption technologies to secure the data and the communication channels to protect users' identity and personal information that your application accesses, uses, stores, or transmits.

8. **Use alternate resources:** Alternate resources can be used to support devices with different hardware and software configurations. Use them to support different screens and orientations, foreign languages, and more.

9. **Test on the device early and often:** There's nothing worse that developing an application on the emulator only to find that it doesn't work properly on actual

devices. Get your hands on real hardware early and make sure your application works as expected with all modes of operation on the hardware. (For example, when testing network applications, try with Wi-Fi, with slow wireless service, in airplane mode, and on battery power only.)

10. **Plan to maintain your app:** To be successful in Android development, you need to be in this for the long haul. Make a plan on how you're going to support and maintain your application after publication. You need to monitor how your application is performing on app stores such as the Android Market and update your application as needed. Users demand that the application functions properly for the long term; there is no "set and forget it" in Android.

Help! I'm Stuck!

We hope this overview will help you iron out the kinks when you're just getting started with Android application development. If you find yourself struggling, check out the following resources:

- http://groups.google.com/group/android-developers
- http://stackoverflow.com/questions/tagged/android

And, as always, feel free to drop us a line and ask us a question. Email us at androidwirelessdev+bn2e@gmail.com or visit our book blog at http://androidbook. blogspot.com, where you can find answers to frequently asked questions, responses to reader feedback, and more.

A Brief Walkthrough of an Android Application from Start to Finish

Sometimes the easiest way to learn something new is to take it apart and then put it back together again. In this appendix, we do just that—we provide a complete implementation of an Android application called PeakBagger 1.0 and deconstruct it, explaining each component in terms of features, user interface, and what's going on "under the hood." This appendix may make a lot more sense after you've mastered some of the concepts of this book, but feel free to peruse it even when you're just getting started.

Peak Bagging Explained

For those unfamiliar with the term, peak bagging is a sport in which you systematically hike to the summit of a set of mountains, usually defined by some sort of criteria, such as elevation or region. Additional criteria, such as what season you climb, or whether or not you had assistance (oxygen, a Sherpa guide, and so on) might also apply. The sport of peak bagging is very popular in New England; there are clubs devoted to summiting the highest 100 peaks in New England, as well as the White Mountains Four-Thousand-Footers list maintained by the Appalachian Mountain Club. For more information on peak bagging as a sport, see the Wikipedia site: http://en.wikipedia.org/wiki/Peak-bagging.

The PeakBagger Application Design

PeakBagger 1.0 is an Android application that enables users to log the mountains that they've climbed and compete with friends for the title of best mountaineer (based on the number of mountains summited). Users create an account and log the summits they have "bagged."

The application design is fairly straightforward. The Android application acts as a client that communicates with a remote application server (in this case, run using Google App

Engine). The server stores summit information, user data, user scores, and user friend relationships. This enables the server to generate high score charts, friends' score charts, and add new mountain information for users. The application also includes an App Widget, which is a simple control that can be added to the user's Home Screen in order to display the current number of peaks bagged.

> **Tip**
>
> The source code for the complete Android app client (PeakBagger 1.0) is available on the companion CD. The source code for the application server implementation is available as an open source project online at http://j.mp/b1xcFF, should you be interested in the details. Designing and implementing application servers is, unfortunately, beyond the scope of this book.

The PeakBagger Components Explained

The PeakBagger application has a number of different screens, each of which has its own activity class. These activities are all derived from a custom `Activity` base class called `BaseActivity`. We use the `BaseActivity` class to supply data and behavior we want available in all other activities of the application, such as

- A global LogCat debug tag (used for logging)
- The application server information (used for connecting)
- The XML tag names (used for XML parsing)
- The shared preference key names (used for storing user/app data)

Each screen of the PeakBagger application has an activity class to control its behavior and a related XML layout file to dictate its user interface (see Figure G.1). The important screens of the PeakBagger application are

- **The Splash screen:** This screen acts as the startup screen for the application. It displays the app name and some other information in a fancy way.
- **The Main Menu screen:** This screen acts as the main navigational screen for the application. It displays a list of options to jump to other screens, such as the Settings, Help, Scores, or Peak Bagging screens.
- **The Settings screen:** This screen enables the user to input her information.
- **The Help screen:** This screen provides some information about how to use the application.
- **The Scores screen:** This screen provides two views: top scores of all users, and scores of this particular user's friends, if any. Scores are calculated based on the number of peaks bagged by a specific user.
- **The Peak Bagging screen:** This screen, the Game screen in Figure G.1, enables the user to log which peaks he has summited.

Now let's look at each feature of the PeakBagger application in more detail.

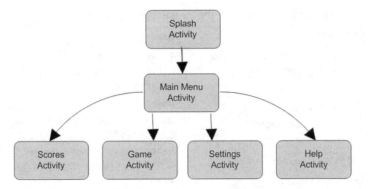

Figure G.1   The Activities in the PeakBagger application.

The Splash Screen

The Splash screen serves as the initial entry point for the application (see Figure G.2).

Figure G.2   The PeakBagger Splash screen.

This screen

- Displays the name and version of the application
- Animates the application logo (four mountains)
- Transitions automatically to the Main Menu screen after a period of time

The implementation details of the Splash screen are broken down in Table G.1.

Table G.1   **Implementation Details of the PeakBagger Splash Screen**

"Under the Hood"	User Interface
The features of this screen are implemented within the `SplashActivity` class. This class • Displays the layout using the `setContentView()` method • Loads some custom animations (as defined in the `/res/anim` directory) • Starts the animations, applying them to specific views including the `TextView` controls for the logos and the `ImageView` controls for each of the four mountain pictures • Starts the Main Menu activity using an explicit intent with the `startActivity()` method once the animation completes • Calls the `finish()` method so the Splash screen isn't shown when the Back key is pressed	The user interface of this screen is defined in the `/res/layout/splash.xml` layout resource file. **Notes:** The user interface is organized within a `LinearLayout` control. Inside the `LinearLayout` control, we use `TextView` controls to display the logo text and `ImageView` controls to display the pictures of the mountains. A `TableLayout` control is used to organize the `ImageView` controls into a grid.

Notes:

Animations must be handled as part of the activity lifecycle. Therefore, if the app is paused, the animations are cleared in the `onPause()` method of the activity; when the app resumes, the animations are restarted in the `onResume()` method.

The Main Menu Screen

The Main Menu screen serves as the main navigational screen in the game (see Figure G.3). This screen displays after the Splash screen and requires the user to choose where to go next.

This screen

- Automatically displays after the Splash screen
- Enables the user to choose "Bag a Peak!," "Settings," "View Scores," or "Help"

The implementation details of the Main Menu screen are broken down in Table G.2.

Figure G.3   The PeakBagger Main Menu screen.

Table G.2   **Implementation Details of the PeakBagger Main Menu Screen**

"Under the Hood"	User Interface
The features of this screen are implemented within the `MenuActivity` class. This class <ul><li>Displays the layout using the `setContentView()` method.</li><li>Loads some string resources into an array adapter and attaches it to the `ListView` in the layout.</li><li>Handles clicks on specific `ListView` items. Clicking on an item causes the associated screen activity to start using an explicit intent. For example, clicking on the item labeled "Help" launches the `HelpActivity` and so on.</li></ul>	The user interface of this screen is defined in the `/res/layout/menu.xml` layout resource file. The look and feel of each item in the `ListView` control is defined in the `menu_item.xml` layout resource file. **Notes:** The user interface is organized within a `RelativeLayout` control; this enables us to anchor views to the top, middle, and bottom of the screen. Within this layout, we display another `RelativeLayout` control with an `ImageView`, `TextView` and `ImageView`—this represents the title area at the top of the screen. Next, we anchor an `ImageView` of some mountain climbers to the bottom of the screen. Finally, we display a `ListView` control for the menu options, with a custom divider and selector.

The Help Screen

The Help screen instructs the user on how to use the application (see Figure G.4).

Figure G.4   The PeakBagger Help screen.

This screen

- Displays help text to the user, with scrolling ability
- Provides a method for the user to suggest new mountains

The implementation details of the Help screen are broken down in Table G.3.

Table G.3   **Implementation Details of the PeakBagger Help Screen**

"Under the Hood"	User Interface
The features of this screen are implemented within the `HelpActivity` class. This class	The user interface of this screen is defined in the `/res/layout/help.xml` layout resource file.
<ul><li>Displays the layout using the `setContentView()` method</li><li>Reads the contents of the text file called `/res/raw/help.txt` into a `String` variable</li><li>Sets the help text in a `TextView` control using the `setText()` method</li></ul>	**Notes:** The user interface is organized within a vertical `LinearLayout` control. Within this layout, we display another `RelativeLayout` control with an `ImageView`, `TextView`, and `ImageView`—this represents the title area at the top of the screen. The contents of the help are displayed with a `TextView` control with several special attributes enabled. The `autoLink` attribute makes all content such as addresses, phone numbers, and websites "linkable" so that the user can click on them to launch the Maps, Phone, or Browser app. Several other attributes make the `TextView` scrollable, in case the help content is long.
Notes: You can include files as your project resources in the `/res/raw` directory. You can open a data stream to a raw file using the `openRawResource()` method of the `Resources` class.	

The Scores Screen

The Scores screen enables the user to view users' scores (see Figure G.5).

This screen

- Displays top scores
- Displays the users' friends' scores (if any)

The implementation details of the Scores screen are broken down in Table G.4.

Figure G.5   The PeakBagger
Scores screen.

Table G.4   **Implementation Details of the PeakBagger Scores Screen**

"Under the Hood"

The features of this screen are implemented within the
ScoresActivity class.

This class

- Displays the layout using the setContentView()
  method

- Configures the TabHost control and adds its tabs

- Populates the bold header text for each
  TableLayout control used to display scores on both
  tabs (all or friends only)

- Spawns two asynchronous tasks (threads): one to
  download top scores from the application server and
  the other to download friends' scores.

- Indicates download progress using an indeterminate
  progress bar (swirling circle) in the top-right corner of
  the screen

- Downloads, parses, and displays scores on the appropriate tab as XML as they come in

Notes:

The AsyncTask class is used to keep time-intensive
operations from blocking the main UI thread, keeping the
app responsive even when downloading and parsing operations are occurring in the background.

User Interface

The user interface of this screen
is defined in the /res/layout/
scores.xml layout resource file.

Notes:

The user interface is organized
within a vertical LinearLayout
control. Within this layout, we display another RelativeLayout
control with an ImageView,
TextView, and ImageView—this
represents the title area at the
top of the screen. The contents of
the scores are displayed with two
tabs within a scrollable TabHost
control. A TableLayout control is
used to display scores in a grid-
like fashion. The TabHost control
has specific requirements for its
layout contents—see Chapter 8,
"Designing User Interfaces with
Layouts," for details.

The Settings Screen

The Settings screen enables users to edit and save game settings, including username and other important features (see Figure G.6).

This screen

- Enables users to input user information
- Enables users to add friends by email

Figure G.6   The PeakBagger Settings screen.

The implementation details of the Settings screen are broken down in Table G.5.

Table G.5   **Implementation Details of the PeakBagger Settings Screen**

"Under the Hood"	User Interface
The features of this screen are implemented within the `SettingsActivity` class. This class	The user interface of this screen is defined in the `/res/layout/splash.xml` layout resource file.
• Displays the layout using the `setContentView()` method	The user interface for the user's favorite summit dialog is defined in the `fav_summit_dialog.xml` layout file.
• Manages numerous views that collect input from the user, including `EditText` and `Spinner` controls	The `friend_entry.xml` layout resource defines the dialog for entering friends' email addresses.
• Manages `Button` controls that launch dialogs or intents (choose a picture from the Gallery or take a photo for your avatar) to collect more sophisticated input from the user	The `password_dialog.xml` layout resource defines the dialog for entering and confirming a password for the user.
• Manages custom dialogs to collect date, password, and location information from the user	The `settingsoptions.xml` menu resource defines the option menu elements displayed when the Menu button is pressed.
• Spawns asynchronous tasks (threads) to upload content to the application server in the following conditions: the user creates or updates account settings, adds, or changes his avatar image, or adds a friend by her email address	**Notes:** The user interface is organized within a vertical `LinearLayout` control. Within this layout, we display another `RelativeLayout` control with an `ImageView`, `TextView` and `ImageView`—this represents the title area at the top of the screen. The rest of the settings controls are encapsulated within a `ScrollView` so that users can scroll through the settings, which take up more room than the screen allows. Controls can be displayed side-by-side using horizontally oriented `LinearLayout` controls.
Notes: This application only uploads user settings to the application server (one-way sync). The only information transferred back is the user ID, which is uniquely assigned based upon information such as the handset ID.	

The Peak Bagging Screen

The Peak Bagging screen displays the mountain listing (see Figure G.7). This screen

- Displays a series of mountains
- Handles yes/no input and keeps track of the number of summits

The implementation details of the Peak Bagging screen are broken down in Table G.6.

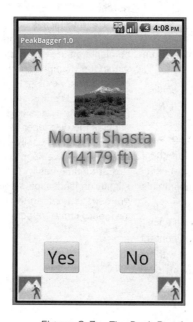

Figure G.7   The Peak Bagging screen.

Table G.6   **Implementation Details of the Peak Bagging Screen**

"Under the Hood"	User Interface
The features of this screen are implemented within the `GameActivity` class. This class	The user interface of this screen is defined in the `/res/layout/game.xml` layout resource file.
• Displays the layout using the `setContentView()` method.	The `gameoptions.xml` menu resource defines the options menu elements that display when the Menu button is pressed.
• Uses the SharedPreferences class to keep application state.	**Notes:**
• Spawns an asynchronous task (thread) to download a new batch of mountains from the application server.	The user interface is organized within `RelativeLayout` controls, allowing icons to be displayed in each corner of the screen. Within the visual boundaries defined by the corner icons, we display one `ImageSwitcher`, one `TextSwitcher`, and two `Button` controls (Yes/No). The `ImageSwitcher` control enables the developer to change the source image at runtime easily. The `TextSwitcher` enables the developer to change the source text at runtime easily. The layout is altered slightly on landscape screens: The `TextSwitcher` is to the right of the `ImageSwitcher` rather than below it.
• Collects information about which peaks the user has bagged by asking Yes/No questions about specific mountains. Two `Button` controls are used: A yes answer increments the user's score; with either answer, the screen updates after a user's answer and displays the next mountain's information.	
• A fade animation is used between each mountain shown to the user. The content of the image and text associated with the mountain is changed after each `Button` control click.	
Notes:	
Mountain data (XML) is downloaded from the application server in small batches and parsed. Each mountain is displayed in sequence, with special case handling when no more mountain data is available.	

The PeakBagger App Widget

The Home screen App Widget associated with the PeakBagger application displays the user's current number of bagged peaks (see Figure G.8).

The implementation details of the App Widget are broken down in Table G.7. App Widgets are discussed in detail in Chapter 22, "Extending Android Application Reach."

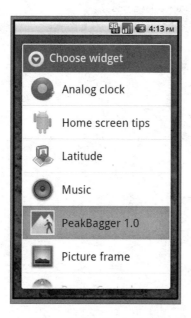

Figure G.8   The PeakBagger App Widget.

Table G.7   **Implementation Details of the PeakBagger App Widget**

"Under the Hood"	User Interface
The features of the App Widget are implemented within the `PeakBaggerWidgetProvider` class. This class	The user interface of the App Widget is defined in the `/res/layout/widget.xml` layout resource file.
<ul><li>Manages a special service that controls the App Widget updates</li><li>Provides a `Server` implementation that supplies data to the App Widget using the `RemoteViews` class; uses a thread to asynchronously retrieve the latest user data from the application server</li><li>Handles clicks by launching the Main Menu screen of the PeakBagger application</li></ul>	**Notes:** The user interface is organized within a `RelativeLayout` control. Within this layout, we display an `ImageView` (the user's avatar) and two `TextView` controls (the user's nickname and current score). These controls are compatible with `RemoteViews`, and therefore allowed within App Widgets.

Table G.7   **Continued**

Notes:

App Widgets must be registered within the
Android Manifest file. They also require their
own definition file—in this case,
`/res/xml/widget_info.xml` provides this
information. See the `<receiver>` and
`<server>` sections of the Android Manifest
file for details.

Index

B

E

F

N

Q

R

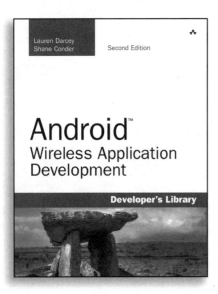

FREE Online Edition

Your purchase of **Android Wireless Application Development** includes access to a free online edition for 45 days through the Safari Books Online subscription service. Nearly every Addison-Wesley Professional book is available online through Safari Books Online, along with more than 5,000 other technical books and videos from publishers such as, Cisco Press, Exam Cram, IBM Press, O'Reilly, Prentice Hall, Que, and Sams.

SAFARI BOOKS ONLINE allows you to search for a specific answer, cut and paste code, download chapters, and stay current with emerging technologies.

Activate your FREE Online Edition at
www.informit.com/safarifree

> **STEP 1:** Enter the coupon code: IYWUQGA.

> **STEP 2:** New Safari users, complete the brief registration form.
> Safari subscribers, just log in.

If you have difficulty registering on Safari or accessing the online edition,
please e-mail customer-service@safaribooksonline.com

Addison Wesley   Adobe Press   ALPHA   Cisco Press   FT Press   IBM Press   lynda.com   Microsoft Press   New Riders

O'REILLY   Peachpit Press   PRENTICE HALL   que   Redbooks   SAMS   SAS Publishing   Sun microsystems   WILEY